Lecture Notes in Computer Science 15887

Founding Editors

Gerhard Goos
Juris Hartmanis

The series Lecture Notes in Computer Science (LNCS), including its subseries Lecture Notes in Artificial Intelligence (LNAI) and Lecture Notes in Bioinformatics (LNBI), has established itself as a medium for the publication of new developments in computer science and information technology research, teaching, and education.

LNCS enjoys close cooperation with the computer science R & D community, the series counts many renowned academics among its volume editors and paper authors, and collaborates with prestigious societies. Its mission is to serve this international community by providing an invaluable service, mainly focused on the publication of conference and workshop proceedings and postproceedings. LNCS commenced publication in 1973.

Osvaldo Gervasi · Beniamino Murgante ·
Chiara Garau · Yeliz Karaca ·
Maria Noelia Faginas Lago · Francesco Scorza ·
Ana Cristina Braga
Editors

Computational Science and Its Applications – ICCSA 2025 Workshops

Istanbul, Turkey, June 30 – July 3, 2025
Proceedings, Part II

 Springer

Editors
Osvaldo Gervasi ⓘ
University of Perugia
Perugia, Italy

Beniamino Murgante ⓘ
University of Basilicata
Potenza, Italy

Chiara Garau ⓘ
University of Cagliari
Cagliari, Italy

Yeliz Karaca ⓘ
University of Massachusetts
Worcester, MA, USA

Maria Noelia Faginas Lago ⓘ
University of Perugia
Perugia, Italy

Francesco Scorza ⓘ
University of Basilicata
Potenza, Italy

Ana Cristina Braga ⓘ
University of Minho
Braga, Portugal

ISSN 0302-9743   ISSN 1611-3349 (electronic)
Lecture Notes in Computer Science
ISBN 978-3-031-97588-2   ISBN 978-3-031-97589-9 (eBook)
https://doi.org/10.1007/978-3-031-97589-9

Preface

The compiled 14 volumes (LNCS volumes 15886–15899) consist of the peer-reviewed papers from the 68 Workshops of the 2025 International Conference on Computational Science and Its Applications (ICCSA 2025), which was held between June 30 – July 3, 2025 in Istanbul (Türkiye). The peer-reviewed papers of the main conference tracks are published in a separate set made up of three volumes (LNCS 15648–15650).

The conference was held in a hybrid form, with the large majority of participants in presence, hosted by Galatasaray University, Istanbul, Türkiye. We enabled virtual participation for those who did not attend the event in person due to logistical, political and economic problems, by adopting a technological infrastructure via open-source software (jitsi + riot) and a commercial Cloud infrastructure.

With the 2025 edition, ICCSA celebrated its 25th anniversary, a quarter of a century as a memorable moment that is harmoniously aligned with Istanbul, an extraordinary city located at the crossroads and acting as a bridge connecting Asia and Europe, representing different cultures, beliefs as well as lifestyles, which highlights its intercultural fabric.

ICCSA 2025 marked another fruitful and thought-provoking academic event in the International Conferences on Computational Science and Its Applications (ICCSA) conference series, previously held in Hanoi, Vietnam (2024), Athens, Greece (2023), Málaga, Spain (2022), Cagliari, Italy (hybrid with a few participants in presence in 2021 and completely online in 2020), whilst earlier editions took place in Saint Petersburg, Russia (2019), Melbourne, Australia (2018), Trieste, Italy (2017), Beijing, China (2016), Banff, Canada (2015), Guimaraes, Portugal (2014), Ho Chi Minh City, Vietnam (2013), Salvador, Brazil (2012), Santander, Spain (2011), Fukuoka, Japan (2010), Suwon, South Korea (2009), Perugia, Italy (2008), Kuala Lumpur, Malaysia (2007), Glasgow, UK (2006), Singapore (2005), Assisi, Italy (2004), Montreal, Canada (2003), and (as ICCS) Amsterdam, the Netherlands (2002) and San Francisco, USA (2001).

Computational Science constitutes the main pillar of most present research, industrial and commercial applications, and plays a unique role in exploiting ICT innovative technologies, and the ICCSA conference series has, accordingly, provided ample opportunities to researchers and industry practitioners to discuss new ideas, to share complex problems and their solutions, and to shape new trends in Computational Science. As the conference mirrors society from a scientific point of view, this year's undoubtedly dominant theme was large language models, machine learning and Artificial Intelligence (AI) and their applications in the most diverse technological, economic and industrial fields, amongst the others.

The ICCSA 2025 conference was structured in six general tracks covering the fields of computational science and its applications: Computational Methods, Algorithms and Scientific Applications – High Performance Computing and Networks – Geometric Modeling, Graphics and Visualization – Advanced and Emerging Applications – Information Systems and Technologies – Urban and Regional Planning. In addition, the conference consisted of 68 workshops, focusing on topical issues of utmost importance to science, technology and society: from new computational approaches for earth science, to mathematical methods for image processing, new statistical and optimization methods, several Artificial Intelligence approaches, sustainability issues, smart cities and related technologies, to name some.

In the Workshops' proceedings, we accepted 362 full papers, 37 short papers and 2 Ph.D. Showcase papers from total of 1043 submissions (Acceptance rate 38.4%). In the Main Conference Proceedings, we accepted 71 full papers, 6 short papers and 1 Ph.D. Showcase paper from 269 submissions to the General Tracks of the Conference (with an acceptance rate of 29.9%). We would like to convey our sincere appreciation to the workshops' chairs and co-chairs and program committee members for their diligent work, commitment and dedication.

The success and consistent maintenance of the ICCSA conference series in general, and of ICCSA 2025 in particular, rely upon the support of many people: authors, presenters, participants, keynote speakers, workshop chairs, session chairs, organizing committee members, student volunteers, Program Committee members, Advisory Committee members, International Liaison chairs, reviewers and other individuals in various roles. Thus, we take this opportunity to wholehartedly thank each and everyone.

We additionally wish to thank publisher Springer for their agreement to publish the proceedings, besides sponsoring part of the best papers awards and for their kind assistance and cooperation during the editing process.

We would cordially like to invite you to refer to the ICCSA website https://iccsa.org, where you can find the relevant details regarding this academic endeavor and event of ours.

June 2025

Osvaldo Gervasi
Yeliz Karaca
Beniamino Murgante
Chiara Garau

A Welcome Message from the Organizers

The International Conference on Computational Science and Its Applications (ICCSA) reflects a culmination of meticulous and dedicated efforts and academic endeavors toward the progress of science and technology.

One of the most noteworthy aspects of ICCSA is its fostering of a collective spirit, bringing together a plethora of participants from all over the world. Correspondingly, this merging power manifests itself in the 25th anniversary of ICCSA, which is a quarter of a century, in Istanbul, Türkiye, which connects and acts as a bridge between two continents, namely Asia and Europe. This unique location in the world hosts the 25th year of ICCSA at Galatasaray University, located on Çırağan Avenue by Istanbul's Bosphorus, which is an established international university bestowed with a distinctive past of teaching tradition, research and education exceeding five centuries.

Istanbul, having served as the capital city of four empires, namely the Roman Empire (330–395), the Byzantine Empire (395–1204 and 1261–1453), the Latin Empire (1204–1261) and the Ottoman Empire (1453–1922), is an exceptional city of the Republic of Türkiye founded by Mustafa Kemal Atatürk.

Situated at a strategic location along the historic Silk Road, Istanbul is at the core of extending rail networks which span across Europe and West Asia along with the only sea route between the Black Sea and the Mediterranean.

The cultural, historical and economic pulses of the country are evident in Istanbul whose rooted origins have embraced varying beliefs, lifestyles and populace, which highlights the city's mosaic quality with blended fabric in a constant harmonious flow. This has enabled cultures to grow and be nurtured, which is profoundly rooted in its urban culture.

Computational Science constitutes the main pillar of most present research, industrial and commercial activities besides manifesting a unique role in exploiting and addressing innovative Information and Communication Technologies. Thus, the 25-year-old ICCSA conference series provides remarkable opportunities to get acquainted with leading researchers, scientists, scholars, practitioners and many more while exchanging innovative ideas and initiating new partnerships, associations and bonds.

With the hosting of Galatasaray University, I would personally and on behalf of the Local Organizing Committee, with the members Emre Alptekin, Gülfem Işıklar Alptekin, Cengiz Kahraman, Abdullah Çağrı Tolga and Ayberk Zeytin, like to convey our sincere gratitude and thanks to everyone who exerted their efforts in and contributed to the realization of ICCSA 2025. With these notes and remarks, welcome to Istanbul!

Cordially yours,

On behalf of the Local Organizing Committee.

June 2025   Yeliz Karaca

Organization

Honorary General Chairs

Bernady O. Apduhan   Kyushu Sangyo University, Japan
Kenneth C. J. Tan   Sardina Systems, UK

General Chairs

Yeliz Karaca   University of Massachusetts, USA
Osvaldo Gervasi   University of Perugia, Italy
David Taniar   Monash University, Australia

Program Committee Chairs

Beniamino Murgante   University of Basilicata, Italy
Chiara Garau   University of Cagliari, Italy
Ana Maria A. C. Rocha   University of Minho, Portugal
A. Çağrı Tolga   Galatasaray University, Turkey

International Advisory Committee

Jemal Abawajy   Deakin University, Australia
Dharma P. Agarwal   University of Cincinnati, USA
Rajkumar Buyya   Melbourne University, Australia
Claudia Bauzer Medeiros   University of Campinas, Brazil
Manfred M. Fisher   Vienna University of Economics and Business,
     Austria
Pierre Frankhauser   University of Franche-Comté/CNRS, France
Marina L. Gavrilova   University of Calgary, Canada
Sumi Helal   University of Florida, USA & Lancaster
     University, UK
Bin Jiang   University of Gävle, Sweden
Yee Leung   Chinese University of Hong Kong, China

International Liaison Chairs

Ivan Blečić	University of Cagliari, Italy
Giuseppe Borruso	University of Trieste, Italy
Elise De Donker	Western Michigan University, USA
Maria Noelia Faginas Lago	University of Perugia, Italy
Maria Irene Falcão	University of Minho, Portugal
Robert C. H. Hsu	Chung Hua University, Taiwan
Yeliz Karaca	University of Massachusetts Chan Medical School, USA
Tae-Hoon Kim	Zhejiang University of Science and Technology, China
Vladimir Korkhov	Saint Petersburg University, Russia
Takashi Naka	Kyushu Sangyo University, Japan
Rafael D. C. Santos	National Institute for Space Research, Brazil
Maribel Yasmina Santos	University of Minho, Portugal
Anastasia Stratigea	National Technical University of Athens, Greece

Workshop and Session Organizing Chairs

Beniamino Murgante	University of Basilicata, Italy
Chiara Garau	University of Cagliari, Italy

Award Chair

Wenny Rahayu	La Trobe University, Australia

Publicity Committee Chairs

Elmer Dadios	De La Salle University, Philippines
Nataliia Kulabukhova	Saint Petersburg University, Russia
Daisuke Takahashi	Tsukuba University, Japan
Shangwang Wang	Beijing University of Posts and Telecommunications, China

Local Organizing Committee Chairs

Emre Alptekin	Galatasaray University, Turkey
Gülfem Işıklar Alptekin	Galatasaray University, Turkey
Cengiz Kahraman	İstanbul Technical University, Turkey
A. Çağrı Tolga	Galatasaray University, Turkey
Ayberk Zeytin	Galatasaray University, Turkey

Technology Chair

Damiano Perri	University of Perugia, Italy

Program Committee

Vera Afreixo	University of Aveiro, Portugal
Vladimir Alarcon	Northern Gulf Institute, USA
Filipe Alvelos	University of Minho, Portugal
Debora Anelli	Polytechnic University of Bari, Italy
Hartmut Asche	Hasso-Plattner-Institut für Digital Engineering Ggmbh, Germany
Nizamettin Aydın	İstanbul Technical University, Turkey
Ginevra Balletto	University of Cagliari, Italy
Nadia Balucani	University of Perugia, Italy
Socrates Basbas	Aristotle University of Thessaloniki, Greece
David Berti	ART SpA, Italy
Michela Bertolotto	University College Dublin, Ireland
Sandro Bimonte	CEMAGREF, TSCF, France
Ana Cristina Braga	University of Minho, Portugal
Tiziana Campisi	Kore University of Enna, Italy
Yves Caniou	Université Claude Bernard Lyon 1, France
Alessandra Capolupo	Polytechnic University of Bari, Italy
José A. Cardoso e Cunha	Universidade Nova de Lisboa, Portugal
Rui Cardoso	University of Beira Interior, Portugal
Leocadio G. Casado	University of Almería, Spain
Mete Celik	Erciyes University, Turkey
Maria Cerreta	University of Naples Federico II, Italy
Ta Quang Chieu	Thuyloi University, Vietnam
Rachel Chien-Sing Lee	Sunway University, Malaysia
Birol Ciloglugil	Ege University, Turkey
Mauro Coni	University of Cagliari, Italy

Workshops

Workshop on Advancements in Applied Machine-Learning and Data Analytics (AAMDA 2025)

Workshop Organizers

Alessandro Costantini	INFN, Italy
Daniele Cesini	INFN, Italy
Elisabetta Ronchieri	INFN, Italy
Barbara Martelli	INFN, Italy

Workshop Program Committee Members

Alessandro Costantini	Istituto Nazionale di Fisica Nucleare (INFN), Italy
Daniele Cesini	Istituto Nazionale di Fisica Nucleare (INFN), Italy
Elisabetta Ronchieri	Istituto Nazionale di Fisica Nucleare (INFN), Italy
Barbara Martelli	Istituto Nazionale di Fisica Nucleare (INFN), Italy
Luca Dell'Agnello	Istituto Nazionale di Fisica Nucleare (INFN), Italy

Advanced and Innovative Web Apps 2025 (AIWA 2025)

Workshop Organizers

Damiano Perri	University of Perugia, Italy
Osvaldo Gervasi	University of Perugia, Italy
Stelios Kouzeleas	International Hellenic University, Greece
Sergio Tasso	University of Perugia, Italy

Workshop Program Committee Members

David Berti	ART SpA, Italy
JungYoon Kim	Gachon University, South Korea
TaiHoon Kim	Zhejiang University of Science and Technology, China

Advanced Processes of Mathematics and Computing Models in Complex Data-Intensive Computational Systems (AMCM 2025)

Workshop Organizers

Yeliz Karaca	University of Massachusetts Chan Medical School and Massachusetts Institute of Technology, USA
Dumitru Baleanu	Lebanese American University, Lebanon
Osvaldo Gervasi	University of Perugia, Italy
Yudong Zhang	University of Leicester, UK
Majaz Moonis	University of Massachusetts Chan Medical School and Massachusetts Institute of Technology, USA

Workshop Program Committee Members

TaeHoon Kim	Zhejiang University of Science and Technology, China
Martin Bohner	Missouri University of Science and Technology, USA
Shuihua Wang	University of Leicester, UK
Khan Muhammad	Sungkyunkwan University, South Korea
Mahmoud Abdel-Aty	Sohag University, Egypt
Aziz Dursun	Virginia Polytechnic Institute and State University, USA
Kemal Güven Gülen	Namık Kemal University, Turkey
Akif Akgül	Hitit Üniversitesi, Turkey

Advanced Numerical Approaches for Assessment and Design of No-Tension Masonry Structures (ANAMS 2025)

Workshop Organizers

Antonino Iannuzzo	Universitá degli studi del Sannio, Italy
Carlo Olivieri	Universitá Telematica Pegaso, Italy
Andrea Montanino	CIMNE, Spain
Elham Mousavian	University of Edinburgh, UK

Workshop Program Committee Members

Pietro Meriggi	Roma Tre University, Italy
Francesca Perelli	University of Naples Federico II, Italy
Marialuigia Sangirardi	University of Oxford, UK
Sam Cocking	University of Cambridge, UK

Matteo Salvalaggio	University of Minho, Portugal
Vittorio Paris	University of Bergamo, Italy
Luigi Sibille	Norwegian University of Science and Technology, Norway
Natalia Pingaro	Politecnico di Milano, Italy
Martina Buzzetti	Politecnico di Milano, Italy
Generoso Vaiano	Pegaso Telematic University, Italy
Alessandra Capolupo	Politecnico di Bari, Italy
Amal Gerges	Università degli Studi di Cagliari, Italy
Fabian Orozco	National Autonomous University of Mexico, Mexico
Nathanael Savalle	Polytech Clermont and Université Clermont Auvergne, France
Luca Umberto Argiento	University of Naples Federico II, Italy
Bartolomeo Pantó	Durham University, UK

Unveiling the Synergies Between Air Quality and Climate PlAnning (AQCliPA 2025)

Workshop Organizers

Angela Pilogallo	University of L'Aquila, Italy
Luigi Santopietro	University of Basilicata, Italy
Filomena Pietrapertosa	IMAA CNR, Italy
Monica Salvia	IMAA CNR, Italy
Carlo Trozzi	IMAA CNR, Italy
Valeria Scapini	Central University of Chile, Chile

Workshop Program Committee Members

Lucia Saganeiti	IMAA-CNR, Italy
Lorena Fiorini	University of L'Aquila, Italy
Antonio Mazza	IMAA-CNR, Italy
Gabriele Nolè	IMAA-CNR, Italy
Carmen Guida	University of Naples "Federico II", Italy
Floriana Zucaro	University of Naples "Federico II", Italy
Sabrina Lai	University of Cagliari, Italy
Chiara Garau	University of Cagliari, Italy

Advancements in Spatial assessment of Socio-Ecological SystemS (ASSESS 2025)

Workshop Organizers

Daniele Cannatella	TU Delft, The Netherlands
Giuliano Poli	University of Naples Federico II, Italy
Eugenio Muccio	TU Delft, The Netherlands
Claudiu Forgaci	TU Delft, The Netherlands

Workshop Program Committee Members

Daniele Cannatella	TU Delft, The Netherlands
Giuliano Poli	University of Naples Federico II, Italy
Eugenio Muccio	University of Naples Federico II, Italy
Claudiu Forgaci	TU Delft, The Netherlands
Maria Cerreta	University of Naples Federico II, Italy
Maria Somma	University of Naples Federico II, Italy
Laura Di Tommaso	University of Naples Federico II, Italy
Sabrina Sacco	Politecnico di Milano, Italy
Piero Zizzania	University of Naples Federico II, Italy
Gaia Daldanise	CNR IRISS, Italy
Benedetta Grieco	University of Naples Federico II, Italy
Giuseppe Ciciriello	University of Naples Federico II, Italy
Marta Dell'Ovo	Politecnico di Milano, Italy
Francesco Piras	University of Cagliari, Italy
Diana Rolando	Politecnico di Torino, Italy
Stefano Cuntò	University of Naples Federico II, Italy
Ludovica La Rocca	University of Naples Federico II, Italy

Blockchain and Distributed Ledgers: Technologies and Applications (BDLTA 2025)

Workshop Organizers

Vladimir Korkhov	Saint Petersburg State University, Russia
Elena Stankova	Saint Petersburg State University, Russia
Nataliia Kulabukhova	Saint Petersburg State University, Russia

Workshop Program Committee Members

Adam Belloum	University of Amsterdam, the Netherlands
Dmitrii Vasiunin	Deutsche Telekom Cloud Services E.P.E., Greece
Serob Balyan	Osensus Arm LLC, Armenia
Suren Abrahamyan	Osensus Arm LLC, Armenia
Ashot Sergey Gevorkyan	NAS of Armenia, Armenia

Michal Hnatic	Univerzita Pavla Jozefa Šafárika v Košiciach, Slovakia
Michail Panteleyev	Saint Petersburg Electrotecnical University, Russia
Martin Vala	Univerzita Pavla Jozefa Šafárika v Košiciach, Slovakia
Nodir Zaynalov	Tashkent University of Information Technologies named after Muhammad al Khwarizmi, Uzbekistan
Michail Panteleyev	Saint Petersburg Electrotecnical University, Russia
Alexander Degtyarev	Saint Petersburg University, Russia
Alexander Bogdanov	St. Petersburg State University, Russia

Bio and Neuro Inspired Computing and Applications (BIONCA 2025)

Workshop Organizers

Nadia Nedjah	State University of Rio de Janeiro, Brazil
Luiza de Macedo Mourelle	State University of Rio de Janeiro, Brazil

Workshop Program Committee Members

Nadia Nedjha	State University of Rio de Janeiro, Brazil
Luiza de Macedo Mourelle	State University of Rio de Janeiro, Brazil
Luigi Maciel Ribeiro	State University of Rio de Janeiro, Brazil
Joelmir Ramos	Federal University of Rio de Janeiro, Brazil
Rogério Moraes	Brazilian Navy, Brazil
Marcos Santana Farias	Institute of Nuclear Energy, Brazil
Luneque Silva Jr.	Federal University of ABC, Brazil
Alan Oliveira	University of Lisboa, Portugal
Brij Bhooshan Gupta	Asia University, Taiwan

Computational and Applied Mathematics (CAM 2025)

Workshop Organizers

Maria Irene Falcão	University of Minho, Portugal
Fernando Miranda	University of Minho, Portugal

Workshop Program Committee Members

Fernando Miranda	University of Minho, Portugal
Graça Tomaz	Polytechnic of Guarda, Portugal
Helmuth Malonek	University of Aveiro, Portugal

Isabel Cacao	University of Aveiro, Portugal
João Morais	Autonomous Technological Institute of Mexico, Mexico
Lidia Aceto	University of Eastern Piedmont, Italy
Luís Ferrás	University of Porto, Portugal
M. Irene Falcão	University of Minho, Portugal
Patrícia Beites	University of Beira Interior, Portugal
Paulo Amorim	FGV EMAp, Brazil
Regina de Almeida	University of Trás-os-Montes e Alto Douro, Portugal
Ricardo Severino	University of Minho, Portugal

Computational and Applied Statistics (CAS 2025)

Workshop Organizer

Ana Cristina Braga	ALGORITMI Research Centre, LASI, University of Minho, Portugal

Workshop Program Committee Members

Adelaide Freitas	University of Aveiro, Portugal
Andreas Futschik	Johannes Kepler University Linz, Austria
Ana Cristina Braga	University of Minho, Portugal
Ângela Silva	University of Minho, Portugal
Arminda Manuela Gonçalves	University of Minho, Portugal
Carina Silva	Polytechnic Intitute of Lisbon, Portugal
Elisete Correia	University of Trás-os-Montes e Alto Douro, Portugal
Frank Westad	Norwegian University of Science and Technology, Norway
Isabel Natario	New University of Lisbon, Portugal
Irene Oliveira	University of Trás-os-Montes e Alto Douro, Portugal
Ivan Rodriguez Conde	University of Vigo, Spain
Joaquim Gonçalves	Instituto Politécnico do Cávado e do Ave, Portugal
Lino Costa	University of Minho, Portugal
Marco Reis	University of Coimbra, Portugal
Maria Filipa Mourão	Polytechnic Institute of Viana do Castelo, Portugal
Maria João Polidoro	Polytechnic Institute of Porto, Portugal
Martin Perez Perez	University of Vigo, Spain
Michal Abrahamowicz	McGill University, Canada
Vera Afreixo	University of Aveiro, Portugal

Werner G. Müller	Johannes Kepler University Linz, Austria
Bruna Silva Ramos	University Lusiada de Famalicão, Portugal
Inês Sousa	University of Minho, Portugal
Luís Miguel Rocha Matos	University of Minho, Portugal
Manuel Carlos Figueiredo	University of Minho, Portugal

Cyber Intelligence and Applications (CIA 2025)

Workshop Organizer
Gianni D'Angelo	University of Salerno, Italy

Workshop Program Committee Members
Gianni D'Angelo	University of Salerno, Italy
Francesco Palmieri	University of Salerno, Italy
Massimo Ficco	University of Salerno, Italy
Arcangelo Castiglione	University of Salerno, Italy

Computational Methods for Business Analytics (CMBA 2025)

Workshop Organizers
Cláudio Alves	Universidade do Minho, Portugal
Telmo Pinto	Universidade do Minho, Portugal

Workshop Program Committee Members
Abdulrahim Shamayleh	American University of Sharjah, United Arab Emirates
Ana Rocha	University of Minho, Portugal
Angelo Sifaleras	University of Macedonia, Greece
Cristóvão Silva	University of Coimbra, Portugal
José Valério de Carvalho	University of Minho, Portugal
Miguel Vieira	Universidade Lusófona, Portugal
Rita Macedo	Université de Lille, France
Ana Moura	Universidade de Aveiro, Portugal
Cristina Lopes	ISCAP, Portugal
Eliana Costa e Silva	Instituto Politécnico do Porto, Portugal

Computational Methods, Statistics and Industrial Mathematics (CMSIM 2025)

Workshop Organizers

Maria Filomena Teodoro	IST ID, Instituto Superior Técnico, Portugal
Marina Alexandra Pedro Andrade	ISCTE – Lisbon University Institute, Portugal
Paula Simões	University of Lisbon, Portugal
Teresa A. Oliveira	IST ID, Instituto Superior Técnico, Portugal

Workshop Program Committee Members

Amilcar Oliveira	Universidade Aberta and Universidade de Lisboa, Portugal
Victor Lobo	Escola Naval and NOVA IMS Almada, Portugal
António Pacheco	IST Universidade de Lisboa, Portugal
Eliana Costa	Escola Superior de Tecnologia e Gestão IPPorto, Portugal
Aldina Correia	Escola Superior de Tecnologia e Gestão IPPorto, Portugal
Fernando Carapau	University of Évora, Portugal
Ricardo Moura	Portuguese Naval Academy, Portugal
Ana Borges	Escola Superior de Tecnologia e Gestão IPPorto, Portugal
Cristina Lopes	ISCAP IPPorto, Portugal
Fernanda Costa	University of Minho, Portugal
Cabrita Carlos	IPBeja, Portugal
Maria Luísa Morgado	University of Trás os Montes e Alto Douro and University of Lisboa, Portugal
Rosário Ramos	Universidade Aberta, Portugal
Sofia Rézio	Iscal, Instituto Politécnico de Lisboa, Portugal
Matteo Sacchet	University of Turin, Italy
Marina Marchisio Conte	University of Turin, Italy
António Seijas-Macias	University of Coruña, Spain
Luís F. A. Teodoro	University of Glasgow, UK and University of Oslo, Norway
Christos Kitsos	University of West Attica, Greece
M. Filomena Teodoro	Universidade de Lisboa, Portugal
Marina A. P. Andrade	Instituto Universitário de Lisboa, Portugal
Paula Simões	Military Academy and Universidade Nova de Lisboa, Portugal
Teresa Oliveira	Universidade Aberta and Universidade de Lisboa, Portugal

Computational Optimization and Applications (COA 2025)

Workshop Organizers

Ana Rocha	ALGORITMI Research Centre, LASI, University of Minho, Portugal, Portugal
Humberto Rocha	ALGORITMI Research Centre, LASI, University of Minho, Portugal, Portugal

Workshop Program Committee Members

Florbela Fernandes	Polytechnic Institute of Bragança, Portugal
Clara Vaz	Polytechnic Institute of Bragança, Portugal
Ana Pereira	Polytechnic Institute of Bragança, Portugal
Filipe Alvelos	University of Minho, Portugal
Joana Dias	University of Coimbra, Portugal
Eligius M. T. Hendrix	University of Málaga, Spain
Emerson José de Paiva	Federal University of Itajubá, Brazil
Ana Paula Teixeira	University of Trás-os-Montes and Alto Douro, Portugal
Lino Costa	Universidade do Minho, Portugal

Coastal Cities Versus Inland Areas. Hypotheses for Sustainable Regeneration Through Ecosystem Services of 'Hooking' and Rehabilitation of Brownfield Sites (CoastalCities_VS_InlandAreas 2025)

Workshop Organizers

Celestina Fazia	Università di Enna Kore, Italy
Angrilli Massimo	University of Chieti-Pescara, Italy
Valentina Ciuffreda	University of Chieti-Pescara, Italy
Maurizio Oddo	Università di Enna Kore, Italy
Marcello Sestito	Università di Enna Kore, Italy
Clara Stella Vicari Aversa	University of Reggio Calabria, Italy

Workshop Program Committee Members

Alessandro Camiz	Università d'Annunzio, Italy
Thowayeb Hassan	King Faisal University, Saudi Arabia
Alessandro Barracco	Università Kore di Enna, Italy
Mario Morrica	University of Urbino, Italy
Mariana Ratiu	University of Oradea, Romania
Alanda Akamana	Mohammed VI Polytechnic University, Morocco
Kaoutare Amini Alaoui	Mohammed VI Polytechnic University, Morocco

Computational Astrochemistry 2025 (CompAstro 2025)

Workshop Organizers

Marzio Rosi	University of Perugia, Italy
Daniela Ascenzi	University of Trento, Italy
Nadia Balucani	University of Perugia, Italy
Stefano Falcinelli	University of Perugia, Italy

Workshop Program Committee Members

Dario Campisi	Università degli Studi di Perugia, Italy
Giacomo Giorgi	Università degli Studi di Perugia, Italy
Andrea Giustini	Università degli Studi di Perugia, Italy
Luca Mancini	Università degli Studi di Perugia, Italy
Albert Rimola	Universitat Autònoma de Barcelona, Spain
Gianmarco Vanuzzo	Università degli Studi di Perugia, Italy
Dimitrios Skouteris	Master-Tec, Italy
Piero Ugliengo	Università degli Studi di Torino, Italy
Franco Vecchiocattivi	Università degli Sudi di Perugia, Italy
Giacomo Pannacci	Università degli Studi di Perugia, Italy
Costanza Borghesi	Università degli Studi di Perugia, Italy
Marco Parriani	Università degli Studi di Perugia, Italy
Marta Loletti	Università degli Studi di Perugia, Italy
Fernando Pirani	Università degli Studi di Perugia, Italy
Andrea Lombardi	Università degli Studi di Perugia, Italy
Noelia Faginas Lago	Università degli Studi di Perugia, Italy
Paolo Tosi	Università di Trento, Italy
Cecilia Coletti	Università degli Studi Chieti-Pescara, Italy
Nazzareno Re	Università degli Studi Chieti-Pescara, Italy
Linda Podio	Osservatorio Astrofisico di Arcetri INAF, Italy
Claudio Codella	Osservatorio Astrofisico di Arcetri INAF, Italy
Gabriella Di Genova	Università degli Studi di Perugia, Italy

Computational Methods for Porous Geomaterials (CompPor 2025)

Workshop Organizers

Vadim Lisitsa	IPGG SB RAS, Russia
Evgeniy Romenski	IPGG SB RAS, Russia

Workshop Program Committee Members

Vadim Lisitsa	Institute of Petroleum Geology and Geophysics SB RAS, Russia
Evgeniy Romenski	Sobolev Institute of Mathematics SB RAS, Russia
Vladimir Cheverda	Sobolev Institute of Mathematics SB RAS, Russia
Tatyana Khachkova	IPGG SB RAS, Russia
Dmitry Prokhorov	IPGG SB RAS, Russia
Mikhail Novikov	Sobolev Institute of Mathematics SB RAS, Russia
Sergey Solovyev	Sobolev Institute of Mathematics SB RAS, Russia
Kirill Gadylshin	LLC RNBashNIPIneft, Russia
Olga Stoyanovskaya	Lavrentev Institute of Hydrodynamics SB RAS, Russia
Yerlan Amanbek	Nazarbaev University, Kazakstan

Workshop on Computational Science and HPC (CSHPC 2025)

Workshop Organizers

Elise de Doncker	Western Michigan University, USA
Hideo Matsufuru	High Energy Accelerator Research Organization, Japan

Workshop Program Committee Members

Elise de Doncker	Western Michigan University, USA
Hideo Matsufuru	High Energy Accelerator Research Organization (KEK), Japan
Fukuko Yuasa	KEK, Japan
Issaku Kanamori	RIKEN, Japan
Hiroshi Daisaka	Hitotsubashi University, Japan
Norikazu Yamada	KEK, Japan
Naohito Nakasato	University of Aizu, Japan
Robert Makin	Western Michigan University, USA

Cities, Technologies and Planning 2025 (CTP 2025)

Workshop Organizers

Giuseppe Borruso	University of Trieste, Italy
Beniamino Murgante	University of Basilicata, Italy
Malgorzata Hanzl	Lodz University of Technology, Poland
Anastasia Stratigea	National Technical University of Athens, Greece
Ljiljana Zivkovic	Republic Geodetic Authority, Serbia
Ginevra Balletto	University of Trieste, Italy

Workshop Program Committee Members

Giuseppe Borruso	University of Trieste, Italy
Beniamino Murgante	University of Basilicata, Italy
Malgorzata Hanzl	Lodz University of Technology, Poland
Anastasia Stratigea	National Technical University of Athens, Greece
Ljiljiana Zivkovic	Republic Geodetic Authority of Serbia, Serbia
Ginevra Balletto	University of Cagliari, Italy
Silvia Battino	University of Sassari, Italy
Mara Ladu	University of Cagliari, Italy
Maria del Mar Munoz Leonisio	University of Cádiz, Spain
Ahinoa Amaro Garcia	University of Las Palmas of Gran Canaria, Spain
Maria Attard	University of Malta, Malta
Enrico D'agostini	World Maritime University, Sweden
Francesca Krasna	University of Trieste, Italy
Brisol Garcia Garcia	Polytechnic University of Quintana Roo, Mexico
Tu Anh Trinh	UEH University, Vietnam
Giovanni Mauro	Università degli Studi della Campania, Italy
Maria Ronza	University of Naples Federico II, Italy
Massimiliano Bencardino	University of Salerno, Italy
Tomasz Bradecki	Silesian University of Technology, Poland
Dorota Kamrowska-Załuska	Gdańsk University of Technology, Poland
Iwona Jażdżewska	University of Lodz, Poland
Yiota Theodora	National Technical University of Athens, Greece
Apostolos Lagarias	University of Thessaly, Greece
George Tsilimigkas	University of the Aegean, Greece
Akrivi Leka	National Technical University of Athens, Greece
Maria Panagiotopoulou	National Technical University of Athens, Greece
Andrea Gallo	Ca' Foscari University of Venice, Italy
Francesca Sinatra	University of Trieste, Italy

Digital Transition: Effects on Housing Mobility, Market, Land Governance (DIGITRANS 2025)

Workshop Organizers

Fabrizio Battisti	University of Florence, Italy
Fabiana Forte	University of Campania, Italy
Orazio Campo	Sapienza University of Rome, Italy
Alessio Pino	Kore University of Enna, Italy
Carlo Pisano	University of Florence, Italy
Mariolina Grasso	Kore University of Enna, Italy

Workshop Program Committee Members

Fabrizio Battisti	University of Florence, Italy
Fabiana Forte	Università della Campania Luigi Vanvitelli, Italy
Orazio Campo	University of Rome "La Sapienza", Italy
Alessio Pino	Kore University of Enna, Italy
Carlo Pisano	University of Florence, Italy
Mariolina Grasso	Università Kore di Enna, Italy

Evaluating Inner Areas Potentials (EIAP 2025)

Workshop Organizers

Diana Rolando	Politecnico di Torino, Italy
Alice Barreca	Politecnico di Torino, Italy
Manuela Rebaudengo	Politecnico di Torino, Italy
Giorgia Malavasi	Politecnico di Torino, Italy

Workshop Program Committee Members

John Accordino	Virginia Commonwealth University, USA
Francesco Bruzzone	Università Iuav di Venezia, Italy
Maria Cerreta	Università degli Studi di Napoli Federico II, Italy
Maddalena Chimisso	Università degli Studi del Molise, Italy
Chiara Chioni	Università degli Studi di Trento, Italy
Annalisa Contato	Università degli Studi di Palermo, Italy
Cristina Coscia	Politecnico di Torino, Italy
Marta Dell'Ovo	Politecnico di Milano, Italy
Benedetta Di Leo	Università Politecnica delle Marche, Italy
Sara Favargiotti	Università degli Studi di Trento, Italy
Maddalena Ferretti	Università Politecnica delle Marche, Italy
Salvo Giuffrida	Università degli Studi di Palermo, Italy
Barbara Lino	Università degli Studi di Palermo, Italy
Umberto Mecca	Politecnico di Torino, Italy
Beatrice Mecca	Politecnico di Torino, Italy
Giuliano Poli	Università degli Studi di Napoli Federico II, Italy
Marco Rossitti	Politecnico di Milano, Italy
Alexandra Stankulova	Politecnico di Torino, Italy
Elena Todella	Politecnico di Torino, Italy
Asja Aulisio	Politecnico di Torino, Italy
Giulia Datola	Politecnico di Milano, Italy

Francesco Calabrò   Università degli Studi Mediterranea di Reggio
                                     Calabria, Italy
Valeria Saiu   Università degli Studi di Cagliari, Italy
Maria Rosa Trovato   Università di Catania, Italy

Econometric and Multidimensional Evaluation in Urban Environment (EMEUE 2025)

Workshop Organizers

Maria Cerreta   University of Naples Federico II, Italy
Carmelo Maria Torre   Polytechnic University of Bari, Italy
Pierluigi Morano   Polytechnic University of Bari, Italy
Simona Panaro   University of Naples Federico II, Italy
Felicia Di Liddo   University of Naples Federico II, Italy
Debora Anelli   University of Naples Federico II, Italy

Workshop Program Committee Members

Carmelo Maria Torre   Polytechnic University of Bari, Italy
Maria Cerreta   University of Naples Federico II, Italy
Pierluigi Morano   Polytechnic University of Bari, Italy
Francesco Tajani   Sapienza University of Rome, Italy
Simona Panaro   University of Naples Federico II, Italy
Felicia di Liddo   Polytechnic University of Bari, Italy
Debora Anelli   Sapienza University of Rome, Italy
Giuliano Poli   University of Naples Federico II, Italy
Maria Somma   University of Naples Federico II, Italy
Simona Panaro   University of Campania Luigi Vanvitelli, Italy
Laura Di Tommaso   University of Naples Federico II, Italy
Caterina Loffredo   University of Naples Federico II, Italy
Ludovica La Rocca   University of Naples Federico II, Italy
Sabrina Sacco   Politecnico di Milano, Italy
Piero Zizzania   University of Naples Federico II, Italy
Gaia Daldanise   CNR IRISS, Italy
Benedetta Grieco   University of Naples Federico II, Italy
Giuseppe Ciciriello   University of Naples Federico II, Italy
Marta Dell'Ovo   Politecnico di Milano, Italy
Daniele Cannatella   TU Delft University, The Netherlands
Eugenio Muccio   University of Naples Federico II, Italy
Sveva Ventre   University of Naples Federico II, Italy

Governance of Energy Transition: Environmental, Landscape, Social and Spatial Planning (ENERGY_PLANNING 2025)

Workshop Organizers

Mara Ladu	University of Cagliari, Italy
Ginevra Balletto	University of Cagliari, Italy
Emilio Ghiani	University of Cagliari, Italy
Alessandra Marra	University of Salerno, Italy
Roberto De Lotto	University of Pavia, Italy
Balázs Kulcsár	Chalmers University of Technology, Sweden

Workshop Program Committee Members

Riccardo Trevisan	University of Cagliari, Italy
Marco Naseddu	University of Cagliari, Italy
Giuseppe Borruso	University of Trieste, Italy
Andrea Gallo	University of Trieste, Italy
Francesca Sinatra	University of Trieste, Italy
Maria Attard	University of Malta, Malta
Tu Anh Trinh	UEH University Ho Chi Minh City, Vietnam
Marcello Tadini	University of Eastern Piedmont, Italy
Luigi Mundula	University for Foreigners of Perugia, Italy
Silvia Battino	University of Sassari, Italy
Maria del Mar Munoz Leonisio	University of Cádiz, Spain
Anna Richiedei	University of Brescia, Italy
Michele Pezzagno	University of Brescia, Italy
Federico Mertellozzo	University of Firenze, Italy
Marco Mazzarino	IUAV University Venice, Italy

Ecosystem Services in Spatial Planning for Climate Neutral Urban and Rural Areas (ESSP 2025)

Workshop Organizers

Sabrina Lai	University of Cagliari, Italy
Francesco Scorza	University of Basilicata, Italy
Corrado Zoppi	University of Cagliari, Italy
Beniamino Murgante	University of Basilicata, Italy
Carmela Gargiulo	University of Naples Federico II, Italy
Floriana Zucaro	University of Naples Federico II, Italy

Workshop Program Committee Members

Alfonso Annunziata	University of Basilicata, Italy
Ginevra Balletto	University of Cagliari, Italy
Ivan Blečić	University of Cagliari, Italy
Giuseppe Borruso	University of Trieste, Italy
Barbara Caselli	University of Parma, Italy
Maria Cerreta	University of Naples Federico II, Italy
Chiara Garau	University of Cagliari, Italy
Carmen Guida	University of Naples Federico II, Italy
Federica Isola	University of Cagliari, Italy
Francesca Leccis	University of Cagliari, Italy
Federica Leone	University of Cagliari, Italy
Silvia Rossetti	University of Parma, Italy
Luigi Santopietro	University of Basilicata, Italy
Carmelo Torre	Polytechnic of Bari, Italy

The 15th International Workshop on Future Information System Technologies and Applications (FiSTA 2025)

Workshop Organizers

Bernady O. Apduhan	Kyushu Sangyo University, Japan
Rafael Santos	Brazilian National Institute for Space Research, Brazil

Workshop Program Committee Members

Agustinus Borgy Waluyo	Monash University, Australia
Andre Ricardo Abed Grégio	Federal University of Paraná, Brazil
Eric Pardede	La Trobe University, Australia
Kai Cheng	Kyushu Sangyo University, Japan
Ching-Hsien Hsu	Asia University, Taiwan
Fenghui Yao	Tennessee State University, USA
Yusuke Gotoh	Okayama University, Japan
Alvaro Fazenda	Federal University of São Paulo, Brazil
Kazuaki Tanaka	Kyushu Institute of Technology, Japan
Tengku Adil	MARA Technological University, Malaysia
Toshihiro Yamauchi	Okayama University, Japan
Yasuaki Sumida	Kyushu Sangyo University, Japan
Earl Ryan Aleluya	MSU-Iligan Institute of Technology, Philippines
Cherry Mae G. Villame	MSU-Iligan Institute of Technology, Philippines
Anton Louise De Ocampo	Batangas State University, Philippines
Krishnamoorthy Ranganthan	Chennai Institute of Technology, India

Flow Management in Urban Contexts (FMUC 2025)

Workshop Organizers

Alessio Pino	Kore University of Enna, Italy
Giovanna Acampa	Kore University of Enna, Italy

Workshop Program Committee Members

Giovanna Acampa	University of Florence, Italy
Alessio Pino	Kore University of Enna, Italy
Mariolina Grasso	Università Kore di Enna, Italy
Fabrizio Battisti	University of Florence, Italy
Fabrizio Finucci	Roma Tre University, Italy
Antonella G. Masanotti	Roma Tre University, Italy
Daniele Mazzoni	Roma Tre University, Italy

Geographical Analysis, Urban Modeling, Spatial Statistics 2025 (Geog-And-Mod 2025)

Workshop Organizers

Beniamino Murgante	University of Basilicata, Italy
Giuseppe Borruso	University of Trieste, Italy
Hartmut Asche	University of Potsdam, Germany
Rodrigo Tapia McClung	CentroGeo, Mexico
Andreas Fricke	University of Potsdam, Germany

Workshop Program Committee Members

Giuseppe Borruso	University of Trieste, Italy
Beniamino Murgante	University of Basilicata, Italy
Hartmut Asche	University of Potsdam, Germany
Rodrigo Tapia-McClung	Centro de Investigación en Ciencias de Información Geoespacial (CentroGeo), Mexico
Andreas Fricke	University of Potsdam, Germany
Malgorzata Hanzl	Lodz University of Technology, Poland
Anastasia Stratigea	National Technical University of Athens, Greece
Ljiljiana Zivkovic	Republic Geodetic Authority of Serbia, Serbia
Ginevra Balletto	University of Cagliari, Italy
Silvia Battino	University of Sassari, Italy
Mara Ladu	University of Cagliari, Italy
Maria del Mar Munoz Leonisio	University of Cádiz, Spain
Ahinoa Amaro Garcia	University of Las Palmas of Gran Canaria, Spain
Maria Attard	University of Malta, Malta

Enrico D'agostini	World Maritime University, Sweden
Francesca Krasna	University of Trieste, Italy
Brisol García García	Polytechnic University of Quintana Roo, Mexico
Tu Anh Trinh	UEH University, Vietnam
Giovanni Mauro	Università degli Studi della Campania, Italy
Maria Ronza	University of Naples Federico II, Italy
Massimiliano Bencardino	University of Salerno, Italy
Andrea Gallo	Ca' Foscari University of Venice, Italy
Francesca Sinatra	University of Trieste, Italy
Salvatore Dore	University of Trieste, Italy

Geogames for Sustainable Development (Geogames 2025)

Workshop Organizer
| Alenka Poplin | Iowa State University, USA |

Workshop Program Committee Members
Alenka Poplin	Iowa State University, USA
Bruno Amaral de Andrade	Portucalense University, Portugal
Brian Tomaszewski	Rochester Institute of Technology, USA
Deepak Marhatta	Tribhuvan University, Nepal
Alessandro Plaisant	University of Sassari, Italy
David Schwartz	Rochester Institute of Technology, USA
Silvia Rossetti	University of Parma, Italy
Floriana Zucaro	University of Naples Federico II, Italy
Alfonso Annunziata	University of Basilicata, Italy
Reza Askarizad	University of Cagliari, Italy
Chiara Garau	University of Cagliari, Italy
Tanja Congiu	University of Sassari, Italy

Geomatics for Resource Monitoring and Management (GRMM 2025)

Workshop Organizers
Alberico Sonnessa	Politecnico di Bari, Italy
Eufemia Tarantino	Politecnico di Bari, Italy
Alessandra Capolupo	Politecnico di Bari, Italy

Workshop Program Committee Members
| Umberto Fratino | Politecnico di Bari, Italy |
| Valeria Monno | Politecnico di Bari, Italy |

Antonino Maltese	Università degli studi di Palermo, Italy
Athos Agapiou	Cyprus University of Technology, Cyprus
Michele Mangiameli	Università di Catania, Italy
Angela Gorgoglione	Universidad de la República de Uruguay, Uruguay
Roberta Ravanelli	University of Liège, Belgium
Ester Scotto di Perta	Università degli studi di Napoli Federico II, Italy
Giacomo Caporusso	CNR, Italy
Andrea Montanino	International Centre for Numerical Methods in Engineering of Barcelona, Spain
Antonino Iannuzzo	Università degli studi del Sannio, Italy
Alessandro Pagano	Politecnico di Bari, Italy
Francesco Di Capua	Università degli Studi della Basilicata, Italy
Albertini Cinzia	CNR-IREA, Italy
Alessandra Saponieri	Università degli studi del Salento, Italy
PierFrancesco Recchi	Università degli studi di Napoli Federico II, Italy
Vincenzo Totaro	Politecnico di Bari, Italy
Stefania Santoro	CNR Water Research Institute, Italy
Francesco Bimbo	University of Foggia, Italy
Cristina Proietti	Istituto Nazionale di Geofisica e Vulcanologia, Italy
Carla Cavallo	University of Salerno, Italy
Gaetano Falcone	Università degli Studi di Napoli Federico II, Italy
Valeria Belloni	Sapienza University of Rome, Italy
Alessandra Mascitelli	University of Chieti-Pescara, Italy

HERitage and CLIMAte neutrality. Resilient approach for nature centered/based sustainable cities (HERCLIMA 2025)

Workshop Organizers

Celestina Fazia	Università di Enna Kore, Italy
Angrilli Massimo	University of Chieti-Pescara, Italy
Clara Stella Vicari Aversa	University of Reggio Calabria, Italy
Dorina Camelia Ilies	University of Oradea, Romania
Mariana Ratiu	University of Oradea, Romania

Workshop Program Committee Members

Alessandro Camiz	Università d'Annunzio, Italy
Mario Morrica	University of Urbino, Italy
Thowayeb Hassan	King Faisal University, Saudi Arabia
Alessandro Barracco	Università Kore di Enna, Italy
Kaoutare Amini Alaoui	Mohammed VI Polytechnic University (UM6P), Morocco

Mariana Ratiu	University of Oradea, Romania
Valentina Ciuffreda	Università Chieti-Pescara, Italy

International Workshop on Information and Knowledge in the Internet of Things (IKIT 2025)

Workshop Organizers

Teresa Guarda	Universidad Estatal Península de Santa Elena, Ecuador
Luis Enrique Chuquimarca Jimenez	Universidad Estatal Península de Santa Elena, Ecuador
Gustavo Gatica	Universidad Andrés Bello, Chile
Filipe Mota Pinto	Polytechnic Institute of Leiria, Portugal
Arnulfo Alanis	Instituto Tecnológico de Tijuana, Mexico
Luis Mazon	Universidad Estatal Península de Santa Elena, Spain

Workshop Program Committee Members

Arnulfo Alanis	Instituto Tecnológico de Tijuana, Mexico
Bruno Sousa	University of Coimbra, Portugal
Carlos Balsa	Instituto Politécnico de Bragança, Portugal
Filipe Mota Pinto	Instituto Politécnico de Leiria, Portugal
Gustavo Gatica	Universidad Andrés Bello, Chile
Isabel Lopes	Instituto Politécnico de Bragança, Portugal
José-María Díaz-Nafría	Universidad a Distancia, Spain
Maria Fernanda Augusto	BiTrum Research Group, Spain
Maria Isabel Ribeiro	Instituto Politécnico Bragança, Portugal
Modestos Stavrakis	University of the Aegean, Greece
Simone Belli	Universidad Complutense de Madrid, Spain
Walter Lopes Neto	Instituto Federal de Educação, Brazil

International Workshop on territorial Planning to integrate Risk prevention and urban Ontologies (IWPRO 2025)

Workshop Organizers

Beniamino Murgante	University of Basilicata, Italy
Roberto De Lotto	University of Pavia, Italy
Elisabetta Maria Venco	University of Pavia, Italy
Caterina Pietra	University of Pavia, Italy

Workshop Program Committee Members

Stefano Borgo	Consiglio Nazionale delle Ricerche ISTC, Italy
Valentina Costa	Università di Genova, Italy
Hamid Danesh Pajouh	Middle East Technical University, Turkey
Ilaria Delponte	Università di Genova, Italy
Lorena Fiorini	Università de L'Aquila, Italy
Veronica Gazzola	Politecnico di Milano, Italy
Ghazaleh Goodarzi	Islamic Azad University, Iran
Michele Grimaldi	Università degli Studi di Salerno, Italy
Alessandra Marra	Università degli Studi di Salerno, Italy
Naghmeh Mohammadpourlima	Åbo Akademi University, Finland
Francesca Pirlone	Università di Genova, Italy
Silvia Rossetti	Università di Parma, Italy
Bahareh Shahsavari	University of Minnesota, USA
Ilenia Spadaro	Università di Genova, Italy
Maria Rosaria Stufano Melone	Politecnico di Bari, Italy

Regional Connectivity, Spatial Accessibility and MaaS for Social Inclusion (MaaS 2025)

Workshop Organizers

Mara Ladu	University of Cagliari, Italy
Ginevra Balletto	University of Cagliari, Italy
Gianfranco Fancello	University of Cagliari, Italy
Tanja Congiu	University of Sassari, Italy
Patrizia Serra	University of Cagliari, Italy
Francesco Piras	University of Cagliari, Italy

Workshop Program Committee Members

Marco Naseddu	University of Cagliari, Italy
Italo Meloni	University of Cagliari, Italy
Giuseppe Borruso	University of Trieste, Italy
Andrea Gallo	University of Trieste, Italy
Francesca Sinatra	University of Trieste, Italy
Maria Attard	University of Malta, Malta
Tu Anh Trinh	UEH University, Vietnam
Marcello Tadini	University of Eastern Piedmont, Italy
Luigi Mundula	University for Foreigners of Perugia, Italy
Silvia Battino	University of Sassari, Italy
Brunella Brundu	University of Sassari, Italy
Veronica Camerada	University of Sassari, Italy

Maria del Mar Munoz Leonisio   University of Cádiz, Spain
Anna Richiedei   University of Brescia, Italy
Michele Pezzagno   University of Brescia, Italy
Marco Mazzarino   IUAV University Venice, Italy

The Development of Urban Mobility Management, Road Safety and Risk Assessment (MANTAIN 2025)

Workshop Organizers
Antonio Russo   Università degli Studi di Enna, Italy
Corrado Rindone   University of Reggio Calabria, Italy
Antonio Polimeni   University of Messina, Italy
Florin Rusca   Politehnica University of Bucharest, Romania
Grigorios Fountas   Aristotle University of Thessaloniki, Greece
Antonio Comi   University of Rome Tor Vergata, Italy

Workshop Program Committee Members
Massimo Di Gangi   University of Messina, Italy
Orlando Marco Belcore   University of Messina, Italy
Antonio Polimeni   University of Messina, Italy
Socrates Basbas   Aristotle University of Thessaloniki, Greece
Claudia Caballini   Polytechnic of Torino, Italy
Efstathios Bouhouras   Aristotle University of Thessaloniki, Greece
Stefano Ricci   Sapienza University of Rome, Italy
Marina Zanne   University of Lubljana, Slovenia
Kh Md Nahiduzzaman   Mohammed VI Polytechnic University, Morocco
Alexsandra Deluka Tibljaš   University of Rijeka, Croatia
Guilhermina Torrao   Aston University, UK

Multidimensional Evolutionary Evaluations for Transformative Approaches (MEETA 2025)

Workshop Organizers
Maria Cerreta   University of Naples Federico II, Italy
Giuliano Poli   University of Naples Federico II, Italy
Maria Somma   University of Naples Federico II, Italy
Gaia Daldanise   CNR IRISS, Italy
Ludovica La Rocca   University of Naples Federico II, Italy

Workshop Program Committee Members

Maria Cerreta	University of Naples Federico II, Italy
Giuliano Poli	University of Naples Federico II, Italy
Maria Somma	University of Naples Federico II, Italy
Laura Di Tommaso	University of Naples Federico II, Italy
Sabrina Sacco	Politecnico di Milano, Italy
Piero Zizzania	University of Naples Federico II, Italy
Gaia Daldanise	CNR IRISS, Italy
Benedetta Grieco	University of Naples Federico II, Italy
Giuseppe Ciciriello	University of Naples Federico II, Italy
Marta Dell'Ovo	Politecnico di Milano, Italy
Daniele Cannatella	TU Delft, The Netherlands
Eugenio Muccio	University of Naples Federico II, Italy
Francesco Piras	University of Cagliari, Italy
Diana Rolando	Politecnico di Torino, Italy
Sveva Ventre	University of Naples Federico II, Italy
Caterina Loffredo	University of Naples Federico II, Italy
Ludovica La Rocca	University of Naples Federico II, Italy
Simona Panaro	University of Campania Luigi Vanvitelli, Italy

Building Multi-dimensional Models for Assessing Complex Environmental Systems (MES 2025)

Workshop Organizers

Vanessa Assumma	University of Bologna, Italy
Caterina Caprioli	Politecnico di Torino, Italy
Giulia Datola	Politecnico di Milano, Italy
Federico Dell'Anna	University of Bologna, Italy
Marta Dell'Ovo	Politecnico di Milano, Italy
Marco Rossitti	Politecnico di Milano, Italy

Workshop Program Committee Members

Vanessa Assumma	Università di Bologna, Bologna
Caterina Caprioli	Politecnico di Torino, Italy
Giulia Datola	DAStU Politecnico di Milano, Italy
Federico Dell'Anna	Politecnico di Torino, Italy
Marta Dell'Ovo	Politecnico di Milano, Italy
Marco Rossitti	Politecnico di Milano, Italy
Francesca Torrieri	Politecnico di Milano, Italy
Mariarosaria Angrisano	Università Telematica Pegaso, Italy
Maksims Feofilovs	Riga Technical University, Latvia

Danny Caprini	Politecnico di Milano, Italy
Giulio Cavana	Politecnico di Torino, Italy
Sebastiano Barbieri	Politecnico di Torino, Italy
Marta Bottero	Politecnico di Torino, Italy
Francesco Cosentino	Politecnico di Milano, Italy
Silvia Ronchi	Politecnico di Milano, Italy
Chiara Mazzarella	TU Delft, Netherlands
Marco Volpatti	Politecnico di Torino, Italy
Chiara D'Alpaos	Università degli Studi di Padova, Italy
Alessandra Oppio	Politecnico di Milano, Italy
Alessia Crisopulli	Politecnico di Milano, Italy
Domenico D'Uva	Politecnico di Milano, Italy
Giorgia Malavasi	Politecnico di Torino, Italy
Rubina Canesi	Università degli Studi di Padova, Italy
Elena Todella	Politecnico di Torino, Italy
Beatrice Mecca	Politecnico di Torino, Italy
Giulia Marzani	University of Bologna, Italy
Isabella Giovanetti	University of Bologna, Italy
Lucia Petronio	University of Bologna, Italy
Franco Corti	University of Padova, Italy
Salvatore De Pascalis	Politecnico di Milano, Italy
Valeria Vitulano	Politecnico di Torino, Italy
Lorenzo Diana	Università degli studi di Napoli Federico II, Italy
Maksims Feofilovs	Riga Technical University, Latvia
Marco De Luca	Politecnico di Torino, Italy
Ilaria Cazzola	Politecnico di Torino, Italy
Andrea De Toni	Politecnico di Milano, Italy
Eugenio Muccio	University of Naples Federico II, Italy
Giuliano Poli	University of Naples Federico II, Italy
Francesco Sica	University "La Sapienza" of Rome, Italy
Elena Di Pirro	Università degli Studi del Molise, Italy
Riccardo Alba	Università di Torino, Italy
Irene Regaiolo	Università di Torino, Italy
Francesca Cochis	Università di Torino, Italy

Modelling Liveable Cities: Techniques, Methods, Challenges, and Perspectives Behind the 'X-Minute' City (MLC 2025)

Workshop Organizers

Federico Mara	University of Pisa, Italy
Valerio Cutini	University of Pisa, Italy
Alessandro Araldi	Université Côte d'Azur, France

| Flávia Lopes | Chalmers University of Technology, Sweden |
| Giovanni Fusco | Université Côte d'Azur, France |

Workshop Program Committee Members

Simone Rusci	University of Pisa, Italy
Lorena Fiorini	University of L'Aquila, Italy
Chiara Di Dato	University of L'Aquila, Italy
Francesco Zullo	University of L'Aquila, Italy
Alfonso Annunziata	University of Basilicata, Italy
Beniamino Murgante	University of Basilicata, Italy
Alessandro Araldi	Universitè Côte d'Azur, France
Chiara Garau	University of Cagliari, Italy
Giampiero Lombardini	Università di Genova, Italy
Flavia Lopes	Chalmers University of Technology, Sweden
Giovanni Fusco	Universitè Côte d'Azur, France

Mathematical Methods for Image Processing and Understanding 2025 (MMIPU 2025)

Workshop Organizers

Ivan Gerace	Università degli Studi di Perugia, Italy
Gianluca Vinti	Università degli Studi di Perugia, Italy
Arianna Travaglini	Università degli Studi della Basilicata, Italy

Workshop Program Committee Members

Ivan Gerace	University of Perugia, Italy
Gianluca Vinti	University of Perugia, Italy
Arianna Travaglini	University of Basilicata, Italy
Marco Baioletti	University of Perugia, Italy
Marco Donatelli	University of Insubria, Italy
Anna Tonazzini	C.N.R. Pisa, Italy
Muhammad Hanif	Ghulam Ishaq Khan Institute of Engineering Sciences and Technology, Pakistan
Francesco Marchetti	University of Padua, Italy
Wolfgang Erb	University of Padua, Italy
Danilo Costarelli	University of Perugia, Italy
Francesco Santini	University of Perugia, Italy
Valentina Giorgetti	University of Perugia, Italy

Mobility Opportunities Bridging Inequalities: Social Inclusion and Gender Equity Initiatives Strategies Against Fragmentation and Complexity of Mobility (MOBIL-EGI 2025)

Workshop Organizers

Tiziana Campisi	University of Enna Kore, Italy
Guilhermina Torrao	Aston University, UK
Socrates Basbas	Aristotle University of Thessaloniki, Greece
Tanja Congiu	University of Sassari, Italy
Stefanos Tsigdinos	National Technical University of Athens, Greece
Florin Nemtanu	Politehnica University of Bucharest, Romania

Workshop Program Committee Members

Massimo Di Gangi	University of Messina, Italy
Orlando Marco Belcore	University of Messina, Italy
Francesco Russo	Mediterranean University of Reggio Calabria, Italy
Alexandros Nikitas	University of Huddersfield, UK
Marilisa Nigro	Rome Tre University, Italy
Kh Md Nahiduzzaman	Mohammed VI Polytechnic University, Morocco
Efstathios Bouhouras	Aristotle University of Thessaloniki, Greece
Antonio Comi	University of Rome Tor Vergata, Italy
Edouard Ivanjko	University of Zagreb, Slovenia
Osvaldo Gervasi	University of Perugia, Italy
Beniamino Murgante	University of Basilicata, Italy
Chiara Garau	University of Cagliari, Italy

MOdels and indicators for assessing and measuring the urban settlement deVElopment in the view of NET ZERO by 2050 (MOVEto0 2025)

Workshop Organizers

Lorena Fiorini	University of L'Aquila, Italy
Lucia Saganeiti	CNR-IMAA, Italy
Angela Pilogallo	CNR-IMAA, Italy
Alessandro Marucci	University of L'Aquila, Italy
Francesco Zullo	University of L'Aquila, Italy

Workshop Program Committee Members

Ginevra Balletto	University of Cagliari, Italy
Giuseppe Borruso	University of Trieste, Italy
Chiara Garau	University of Cagliari, Italy

Beniamino Murgante	University of Basilicata, Italy
Giulia Desogus	University of Cagliari, Italy
Ljiljana Zivkovic	Republic Geodetic Authority, Serbia
Luigi Santopietro	University of Basilicata, Italy
Ilaria Delponte	University of Genoa, Italy
Carmen Guida	University of Naples Federico II, Italy
Chiara Di Dato	University of L'Aquila, Italy

5th Workshop on Privacy in the Cloud/Edge/IoT World (PCEIoT 2025)

Workshop Organizers

Lelio Campanile	Università degli Studi della Campania Luigi Vanvitelli, Italy
Mauro Iacono	Università degli Studi della Campania Luigi Vanvitelli, Italy
Michele Mastroianni	Università degli Studi di Foggia, Italy

Workshop Program Committee Members

Arcangelo Castiglione	Università degli Studi di Salerno, Italy
Maria Ganzha	Warsaw University of Technology, Poland
Daniel Grzonka	Cracow University of Technology, Poland
Antonio Iannuzzi	Università degli Studi Roma Tre, Italy
Armando Tacchella	Università degli Studi di Genova, Italy
Biagio Boi	University of Salerno, Italy
Marco De Santis	University of Salerno, Italy
Fiammetta Marulli	Università degli Studi della Campania "L. Vanvitelli", Italy
Christian Riccio	Università degli Studi della Campania "L. Vanvitelli", Italy
Luigi Piero Di Bonito	Università degli Studi di Napoli Federico II, Italy

Preserving Our Past: Spatial and Remote Sensing Technologies for Cultural Heritage in a Changing Climate (POP 2025)

Workshop Organizers

Maria Danese	CNR-ISPC, Italy
Nicola Masini	CNR-ISPC, Italy
Rosa Lasaponara	CNR-IMAA, Italy

Workshop Program Committee Members

Maria Danese	CNR-ISPC, Italy
Nicola Masini	CNR-ISPC, Italy
Rosa Lasaponara	CNR-IMAA, Italy
Dario Gioia	CNR-ISPC, Italy
Giuseppe Corrado	Università degli Studi della Basilicata, Italy
Canio Sabia	CNR-ISPC, Italy

Processes, methods and tools towards RESilient cities and cultural and historic sites prone to SOD and ROD disasters (RES 2025)

Workshop Organizers

Elena Cantatore	Polytechnic University of Bari, Italy
Dario Esposito	Polytechnic University of Bari, Italy
Alberico Sonnessa	Polytechnic University of Bari, Italy

Workshop Program Committee Members

Elena Cantatore	Politecnico di Bari, Italy
Dario Esposito	Politecnico di Bari, Italy
Alberico Sonnessa	Politecnico di Bari, Italy
Valeria Belloni	Sapienza University of Rome, Italy
Michela Ravanelli	Sapienza University of Rome, Italy
Silvano Dal Sasso	University of Basilicata, Italy
Francesco Chiaravalloti	CNR - IRPI, Italy
Roberta Ravanelli	University of Liège, Belgium
Alessandra Mascitelli	University of Chieti-Pescara, Italy
Francesco Di Capua	University of Basilicata, Italy
Gabriele Bernardini	Università Politecnica delle Marche, Italy
Vito Domenico Porcari	University of Basilicata, Italy
Carmen Rosa Fattore	University of Basilicata, Italy
Stefania Santoro	Water Research Institute, Italy

Scientific Computing Infrastructure (SCI 2025)

Workshop Organizers

Vladimir Korkhov	Saint Petersburg State University, Russia
Elena Stankova	Saint Petersburg State University, Russia
Nataliia Kulabukhova	Saint Petersburg State University, Russia

Workshop Program Committee Members

Adam Belloum	University of Amsterdam, the Netherlands
Dmitrii Vasiunin	Deutsche Telekom Cloud Services E.P.E., Greece
Serob Balyan	Osensus Arm LLC, Armenia
Suren Abrahamyan	Osensus Arm LLC, Armenia
Ashot Sergey Gevorkyan	NAS of Armenia, Armenia
Michal Hnatic	Univerzita Pavla Jozefa Šafárika v Košiciach, Slovakia
Michail Panteleyev	Saint Petersburg Electrotecnical University, Russia
Martin Vala	Univerzita Pavla Jozefa Šafárika v Košiciach, Slovakia
Nodir Zaynalov	Tashkent University of Information Technologies named after Muhammad al Khwarizmi, Uzbekistan
Michail Panteleyev	Saint Petersburg Electrotecnical University, Russia
Alexander Degtyarev	Saint Petersburg University, Russia
Alexander Bogdanov	St. Petersburg State University, Russia

Ports and Logistics of the Future - Smartness and Sustainability (SmartPorts 2025)

Workshop Organizers

Andrea Gallo	Università degli Studi di Trieste, Italy
Gianfranco Fancello	University of Cagliari, Italy
Giuseppe Borruso	Università degli Studi di Trieste, Italy
Enrico D'agostini	World Maritime University, Sweden
Silvia Battino	Università degli Studi di Sassari, Italy
Veronica Camerada	Università degli Studi di Sassari, Italy

Workshop Program Committee Members

Giuseppe Borruso	University of Trieste, Italy
Beniamino Murgante	University of Basilicata, Italy
Ginevra Balletto	University of Cagliari, Italy
Silvia Battino	University of Sassari, Italy
Mara Ladu	University of Cagliari, Italy
Maria del Mar Munoz Leonisio	University of Cádiz, Spain
Ahinoa Amaro Garcia	University of Las Palmas of Gran Canaria, Spain
Maria Attard	University of Malta, Malta
Enrico D'agostini	World Maritime University, Sweden
Francesca Krasna	University of Trieste, Italy

Tu Anh Trinh	UEH University - Ho Chi Minh City, Vietnam
Giovanni Mauro	Università degli Studi della Campania, Italy
Maria Ronza	University of Naples Federico II, Italy
Massimiliano Bencardino	University of Salerno, Italy
Andrea Gallo	Ca' Foscari University of Venice, Italy
Francesca Sinatra	University of Trieste, Italy
Salvatore Dore	University of Trieste, Italy
Veronica Camerada	University of Sassari, Italy
Brunella Brundu	University of Sassari, Italy
Gianfranco Fancello	University of Cagliari, Italy
Marcello Tadini	University of Eastern Piedmont, Italy
Marco Mazzarino	IUAV University Venice
José Ángel Hernández Luis	University of Las Palmas de Gran Canaria, Spain
Marco Naseddu	University of Cagliari, Italy
Maurizio Cociancich	Adriafer, Italy
Giovanni Longo	University of Trieste, Italy
Luca Toneatti	University of Trieste, Italy
Martina Sinatra	University of Cagliari, Italy
Enrico Vanino	University of Sheffield, UK
Patrizia Serra	University of Cagliari, Italy
Agostino Bruzzone	University of Genoa, Italy
Marco Petrelli	University of Roma 3, Italy

Smart Transport and Logistics - Smart Supply Chains (SmarTransLog 2025)

Workshop Organizers

Francesca Sinatra	University of Trieste, Italy
Maria del Mar Munoz	Universidad de Cádiz, Spain
Brunella Brundu	University of Sassari, Italy
Patrizia Serra	University of Cagliari, Italy
Salvatore Dore	University of Trieste, Italy
Marco Naseddu	University of Cagliari, Italy

Workshop Program Committee Members

Giuseppe Borruso	University of Trieste, Italy
Beniamino Murgante	University of Basilicata, Italy
Ginevra Balletto	University of Cagliari, Italy
Silvia Battino	University of Sassari, Italy
Mara Ladu	University of Cagliari, Italy
Maria del Mar Munoz Leonisio	University of Cádiz, Spain
Ahinoa Amaro Garcia	University of Las Palmas of Gran Canaria, Spain

Maria Attard	University of Malta, Malta
Enrico D'agostini	World Maritime University, Sweden
Francesca Krasna	University of Trieste, Italy
Tu Anh Trinh	UEH University, Vietnam
Giovanni Mauro	Università degli Studi della Campania, Italy
Maria Ronza	University of Naples Federico II, Italy
Massimiliano Bencardino	University of Salerno, Italy
Andrea Gallo	Ca' Foscari University of Venice, Italy
Francesca Sinatra	University of Trieste, Italy
Salvatore Dore	University of Trieste, Italy
Veronica Camerada	University of Sassari, Italy
Brunella Brundu	University of Sassari, Italy
Gianfranco Fancello	University of Cagliari, Italy
Marcello Tadini	University of Eastern Piedmont, Italy
Marco Mazzarino	IUAV University Venice
José Ángel Hernández Luis	University of Las Palmas de Gran Canaria, Spain
Marco Naseddu	University of Cagliari, Italy
Maurizio Cociancich	Adriafer, Italy
Giovanni Longo	University of Trieste, Italy
Luca Toneatti	University of Trieste, Italy
Martina Sinatra	University of Cagliari, Italy
Enrico Vanino	University of Sheffield, UK
Patrizia Serra	University of Cagliari, Italy
Agostino Bruzzone	University of Genoa, Italy
Marco Petrelli	University of Roma 3, Italy

Smart Tourism (SmartTourism 2025)

Workshop Organizers

Silvia Battino	University of Sassari, Italy
Francesca Krasna	University of Trieste, Italy
Ainhoa Amaro	University of Las Palmas de Gran Canaria, Spain
Maria del Mar Munoz	University of Cádiz, Spain
Brisol García García	Polytechnic University of Quintana Roo, Mexico
Marta Meleddu	University of Sassari, Italy

Workshop Program Committee Members

Giuseppe Borruso	University of Trieste, Italy
Beniamino Murgante	University of Basilicata, Italy
Gianfranco Fancello	University of Cagliari, Italy
Mara Ladu	University of Cagliari, Italy

Martina Sinatra	University of Cagliari, Italy
Salvatore Dore	University of Trieste, Italy
Marco Mazzarino	IUAV University Venice, Italy
Veronica Camerada	University of Sassari, Italy
Brunella Brundu	University of Sassari, Italy
Maria Attard	University of Malta, Malta
Ginevra Balletto	University of Cagliari, Italy
Giovanni Mauro	University degli Studi della Campania, Italy
Salvatore Lampreu	University of Sassari, Italy
Maria Ronza	University of Naples, Italy
Massimiliano Bencardino	University of Salerno, Italy

Sustainable evolution of long-Distance frEight and paSsenger Transport (SOLIDEST 2025)

Workshop Organizers

Francesco Russo	University of Reggio Calabria, Italy
Andreas Nikiforiadis	Democritus University of Thrace, Greece
Orlando Marco Belcore	University of Messina, Italy
Antonio Comi	University of Rome Tor Vergata, Italy
Tiziana Campisi	Kore University of Enna, Italy
Aura Rusca	Politehnica University of Bucharest, Romania

Workshop Program Committee Members

Massimo Di Gangi	University of Messina, Italy
Orlando Marco Belcore	University of Messina, Italy
Antonio Polimeni	University of Messina, Italy
Socrates Basbas	Aristotle University of Thessaloniki, Greece
Efstathios Bouhouras	Aristotle University of Thessaloniki, Greece
Marina Zanne	University of Lubljana, Slovenia
Marilisa Nigro	Rome Tre University, Italy
Edoardo Marcucci	Molde University College, Norway
Eugen Rosca	Polytechnic University of Bucharest, Romania
Kh Md Nahiduzzaman	Mohammed VI Polytechnic University, Morocco
Beniamino Murgante	University of Basilicata, Italy
Chiara Garau	University of Cagliari, Italy

Sustainability Performance Assessment: Models, Approaches, and Applications Toward Interdisciplinary and Integrated Solutions (SPA 2025)

Workshop Organizers

Francesco Scorza	University of Basilicata, Italy
Sabrina Lai	University of Cagliari, Italy
Francesco Rotondo	Università Politecnica delle Marche, Italy
Jolanta Dvarioniene	Kaunas University of Technology, Lithuania
Michele Campagna	University of Cagliari, Italy
Corrado Zoppi	University of Cagliari, Italy

Workshop Program Committee Members

Federico Amato	University of Lausanne, Switzerland
Ferdinando Di Carlo	University of Basilicata, Italy
Maddalena Floris	University of Cagliari, Italy
Federica Isola	University of Cagliari, Italy
Giuseppe Las Casas	University of Basilicata, Italy
Federica Leone	University of Cagliari, Italy
Giampiero Lombardini	University of Genoa, Italy
Federico Martellozzo	University of Florence, Italy
Alessandro Marucci	University of L'Aquila, Italy
Ana Clara Moura	Universidade Federal de Minas Gerais, Brazil
Beniamino Murgante	University of Basilicata, Italy
Silviu Nate	Lucian Blaga University of Sibiu, Romania
Anastasia Stratigea	National Technical University of Athens, Greece
Francesco Zullo	University of L'Aquila, Italy
Luigi Santopietro	University of Basilicata, Italy
Benedetto Manganelli	University of Basilicata, Italy

Specifics of Smart Cities Development in Europe (SPEED 2025)

Workshop Organizers

Chiara Garau	University of Cagliari, Italy
Katarína Vitálišová	Matej Bel University, Slovak Republic
Marco Fanfani	University of Florence, Italy
Anna Vaňová	Matej Bel University, Slovak Republic
Kamila Borsekova	Matej Bel University, Slovak Republic
Paola Zamperlin	University of Florence, Italy

Workshop Program Committee Members

Claudia Loggia	University of KwaZulu-Natal, South Africa
Francesca Maltinti	University of Cagliari, Italy
Alessandro Plaisant	University of Sassari, Italy
Alenka Poplin	Iowa State University, USA
Silvia Rossetti	University of Parma, Italy
Gerardo Carpentieri	University of Naples Federico II, Italy
Carmen Guida	University of Naples Federico II, Italy
Floriana Zucaro	University of Naples Federico II, Italy
Anastasia Stratigea	National Technical University of Athens, Greece
Yiota Theodora	National Technical University of Athens, Greece
Giovanna Concu	University of Cagliari, Italy
Paolo Nesi	University of Florence, Italy
Emanuele Bellini	University of Roma Tre, Italy
Mana Dastoum	Polytechnic University of Madrid, Spain
Barbara Caselli	University of Parma, Italy
Martina Carra	University of Brescia, Italy
Alfonso Annunziata	University of Basilicata, Italy
Elisabetta Venco	University of Pavia, Italy
Caterina Pietra	University of Pavia, Italy
Enrico Collini	University of Florence, Italy
Luciano Alessandro Ipsaro Palesi	University of Florence, Italy

Smart, Safe, and Healthy Cities (SSHC 2025)

Workshop Organizers

Chiara Garau	University of Cagliari, Italy
Gerardo Carpentieri	University of Naples Federico II, Italy
Carmen Guida	University of Naples Federico II, Italy
Tanja Congiu	University of Sassari, Italy
Martina Carra	University of Brescia, Italy
Alenka Poplin	Iowa State University, USA

Workshop Program Committee Members

Rosaria Battarra	Istituto di Studi sul Mediterraneo, Italy
Barbara Caselli	University of Parma, Italy
Francesca Maltinti	University of Cagliari, Italy
Romano Fistola	Università degli Studi di Napoli Federico II, Italy
Alessandro Plaisant	University of Sassari, Italy
Silvia Rossetti	University of Parma, Italy
Marco Fanfani	University of Florence, Italy
Reza Askarizad	University of Cagliari, Italy

Floriana Zucaro	University of Naples Federico II, Italy
Anastasia Stratigea	National Technical University of Athens, Greece
Yiota Theodora	National Technical University of Athens, Greece
Giovanna Concu	University of Cagliari, Italy
Francesco Zullo	University of L'Aquila, Italy
Paola Zamperlin	University of Florence, Italy
Vincenza Torrisi	University of Catania, Italy
Tiziana Campisi	University of Enna Kore, Italy
Katarína Vitálišová	Matej Bel University, Slovakia
Tazyeen Alam	University of Cagliari, Italy
Mana Dastoum	Polytechnic University of Madrid, Spain
Martina Carra	University of Brescia, Italy
Alfonso Annunziata	University of Basilicata, Italy
Elisabetta Venco	University of Pavia, Italy
Caterina Pietra	University of Pavia, Italy

Smart and Sustainable Island Communities (SSIC 2025)

Workshop Organizers

Chiara Garau	University of Cagliari, Italy
Anastasia Stratigea	National Technical University of Athens, Greece
Yiota Theodora	National Technical University of Athens, Greece
Giovanna Concu	University of Cagliari, Italy

Workshop Program Committee Members

Milena Metalkova-Markova	University of Portsmouth, UK
Tarek Teba	University of Portsmouth, UK
Alenka Poplin	Iowa State University, USA
Gerardo Carpentieri	University of Naples Federico II, Italy
Carmen Guida	University of Naples Federico II, Italy
Floriana Zucaro	University of Naples Federico II, Italy
Silvia Rossetti	University of Parma, Italy
Barbara Caselli	University of Parma, Italy
Martina Carra	University of Brescia, Italy
Alfonso Annunziata	University of Basilicata, Italy
Maria Panagiotopoulou	National Technical University of Athens, Greece
Apostolos Lagarias	University of Thessaly, Greece
Paola Zamperlin	University of Florence, Italy
Vincenza Torrisi	University of Catania, Italy
Giuseppina Vacca	University of Cagliari, Italy
Roberto Minunno	Curtin University, Australia
Marco Zucca	University of Cagliari, Italy

Elisabetta Venco	University of Pavia, Italy
Caterina Pietra	University of Pavia, Italy
Pietro Crespi	Politecnico di Milano, Italy

From STreet Experiments to Planned Solutions (STEPS 2025)

Workshop Organizers

Silvia Rossetti	Università degli Studi di Parma, Italy
Angela Ricciardello	Kore University of Enna, Italy
Francesco Pinna	Università degli Studi di Cagliari, Italy
Chiara Garau	Università degli Studi di Cagliari, Italy
Tiziana Campisi	Kore University of Enna, Italy
Vincenza Torrisi	University of Catania, Italy

Workshop Program Committee Members

Martina Carra	University of Brescia, Italy
Barbara Caselli	University of Parma, Italy
Tanja Congiu	University of Sassari, Italy
Gabriele D'Orso	University of Palermo, Italy
Matteo Ignaccolo	University of Catania, Italy
Md Kh Nahiduzzaman	Mohammed VI Polytechnic University, Morocco
Muhammad Ahmad Al-Rashid	University of Malaya, Malaysia
Alessandro Plaisant	University of Sassari, Italy
Marianna Ruggieri	University of Enna Kore, Italy
Michele Zazzi	University of Parma, Italy

Sustainable Tourism Evaluations: approaches, methods and indicators (STEva 2025)

Workshop Organizers

Mariolina Grasso	Università Kore di Enna, Italy
Fabrizio Finucci	Roma Tre University, Italy
Daniele Mazzoni	Roma Tre University, Italy
Antonella G. Masanotti	Roma Tre University, Italy
Giovanna Acampa	University of Florence, Italy

Workshop Program Committee Members

Giovanna Acampa	University of Florence, Italy
Fabrizio Finucci	Roma Tre University, Italy
Mariolina Grasso	"Kore" University of Enna, Italy

Alberto Marzo	Ministero della Cultura, Italy
Antonella G. Masanotti	Roma Tre University, Italy
Daniele Mazzoni	Roma Tre University, Italy
Rocco Murro	Sapienza University of Rome, Italy
Claudio Piferi	University of Florence, Italy
Alessio Pino	"Kore" University of Enna, Italy
Nicoletta Setola	University of Florence, Italy
Laura Calcagnini	Roma Tre University, Italy
Antonio Magarò	Roma Tre University, Italy
Janos Ghyerghyak	University of Pécs, Hungary
Ágnes Borsos	University of Pécs, Hungary
Fabrizio Battisti	University of Florence, Italy

Sustainable Development of Ports (SUSTAINABLEPORTS 2025)

Workshop Organizers

Tiziana Campisi	University of Enna KORE, Italy
Giuseppe Musolino	University of Reggio Calabria, Italy
Efstathios Bouhouras	Aristotle University of Thessaloniki, Greece
Elen Twrdy	University of Ljubljana, Slovenia
Elena Cocuzza	University of Catania, Italy
Aura Rusca	Politehnica University of Bucharest, Romania

Workshop Program Committee Members

Massimo Di Gangi	University of Messina, Italy
Orlando Marco Belcore	University of Messina, Italy
Antonio Polimeni	University of Messina, Italy
Claudia Caballini	Polytechnic of Torino, Italy
Gianfranco Fancello	University of Cagliari, Italy
Marina Zanne	University of Lubljana, Slovenia
Stefano Ricci	Sapienza University of Rome, Italy
Beniamino Murgante	University of Basilicata, Italy
Chiara Garau	University of Cagliari, Italy

Theoretical and Computational Chemistry and Its Applications (TCCMA 2025)

Workshop Organizers

Noelia Faginas Lago	Università di Perugia, Italy
Andrea Lombardi	Università di Perugia, Italy
Marcos Mandado Alonso	University of Vigo, Spain

Workshop Program Committee Members

Noelia Faginas-Lago	University of Perugia, Italy
Andrea Lombardi	University of Perugia, Italy
Marcos Mandado	University of Vigo, Spain
Angeles Peña	University of Vigo, Spain
Luca Mancini	Universiy of Perugia, Italy
Massimiliano Bartolomei	CSIC, Spain
Cecilia Coletti	University of Chieti-Pescara, Italy
Iñaki Tuñón	Universidad de Valencia, Spain
Albert Rimola Gilbert	Universitat Autònoma de Barcelona, Spain
Stefano Falcinelli	University of Perugia, Italy
Dario Campisi	University of Perugia, Italy
Ernesto García Para	University of the Basque Country, Spain
Giacomo Giorgi	University of Perugia, Italy
Tomás González Lezana	IFF CSIC, Spain
Enrique M. Cabaleiro Lago	Universidade de Santiago de Compostela, Spain
Aurora Costales	Universidad de Oviedo, Spain
Angel Martin	Universidad de Oviedo, Spain
Jose Manuel	University of Vigo, Spain
Annarita Laricchiuta	CNR ISTP Bari, Italy
Fernando Pirani	University of Perugia, Italy

Transport Infrastructures for Smart Cities (TISC 2025)

Workshop Organizers

Francesca Maltinti	University of Cagliari, Italy
Mauro Coni	University of Cagliari, Italy
Benedetto Barabino	University of Brescia, Italy
Nicoletta Rassu	University of Cagliari, Italy
James Rombi	University of Cagliari, Italy

Workshop Program Committee Members

Francesco Pinna	University of Cagliari, Italy
Chiara Garau	University of Cagliari, Italy
Mauro D'Apuzzo	University of Cassino, Italy
Roberto Minunno	Curtin University, Australia
Tiziana Campisi	University of Enna Kore, Italy
Roberto Ventura	University of Brescia, Italy
Alessandro Plaisant	University of Sassari, Italy
Massimo Di Francesco	University of Cagliari, Italy

| Vincenza Torrisi | University of Catania, Italy |
| Paola Zamperlin | University of Florence, Italy |

Transforming Urban Analytics: The Impact of Crowdsourced Mapping and Advanced AI Techniques on Future Cities (Tr-UrbAna 2025)

Workshop Organizers

Ayse Giz Gulnerman Gengec	Ankara Hacı Bayram Veli University, Turkey
Müslüm Hacar	Tildiz Technical University, Turkey
Himmet Karaman	Istanbul Technical University, Turkey

Workshop Program Committee Members

Beniamino Murgante	University of Basilicata, Italy
Abdulkadir Memduhoğlu	Harran University, Turkey
Zeynel Abidin Polat	İzmir Katip Çelebi University, Turkey
Güzide Miray Perihanoğlu	Van Yüzüncü Yıl University, Turkey
Tugba Memisoglu Baykal	Ankara Hacı Bayram Veli University, Turkey

From structural to TRAnsformative-change of City Environment: challenges and solutions and perspectives (TRACE 2025)

Workshop Organizers

Pierluigi Morano	Polytechnic University of Bari, Italy
Maria Rosaria Guarini	Sapienza University of Rome, Italy
Francesco Sica	Sapienza University of Rome, Italy
Francesco Tajani	Sapienza University of Rome, Italy
Marco Locurcio	Polytechnic University of Bari, Italy
Debora Anelli	Polytechnic University of Bari, Italy

Workshop Program Committee Members

Felicia di Liddo	Politecnico di Bari, Italia
Valeria Saiu	Università di Cagliari, Italia
Emma Sabatelli	Sapienza Università di Roma, Italia
Antonella Roma	Sapienza Università di Roma, Italia
Giuseppe Cerullo	Sapienza Università di Roma, Italia
Lucia della Spina	Università di Reggio Calabria, Italia
Alejandro Segura de la Cal	Politecnico di Madrid, Spain
Yilsy Nuñez	Politecnico di Madrid, Spain
Gabriella Maselli	Università di Salerno, Italy
Maria Rosa Trovato	Università di Catania, Italy

Manuela Rebaudengo	Politecnico di Torino, Italy
Pierfrancesco De Paola	Università di Napoli Federico II, Italy
Daniela Tavano	Università della Calabria, Italy
Maria Saez	University of Granada, Spain
Paola Amoruso	LUM "Giuseppe Degennaro" University, Italy

Temporary Real Estate management: Approaches and methods for Time-integrated impact assessments and evaluations (TREAT 2025)

Workshop Organizers

Chiara Mazzarella	TUDelft, The Netherlands
Hilde Remoy	TUDelft, The Netherlands
Maria Cerreta	University of Naples Federico II, Italy

Workshop Program Committee Members

Chiara Mazzarella	TU Delft, The Netherlands
Hilde Remoy	TU Delft, The Netherlands
Maria Cerreta	University of Naples Federico II, Italy
Maria Somma	University of Naples Federico II, Italy
Simona Panaro	University of Campania Luigi Vanvitelli, Italy
Laura Di Tommaso	University of Naples Federico II, Italy
Caterina Loffredo	University of Naples Federico II, Italy
Ludovica La Rocca	University of Naples Federico II, Italy
Sabrina Sacco	Politecnico di Milano, Italy
Piero Zizzania	University of Naples Federico II, Italy
Gaia Daldanise	CNR IRISS, Italy
Benedetta Grieco	University of Naples Federico II, Italy
Giuseppe Ciciriello	University of Naples Federico II, Italy
Marta Dell'Ovo	Politecnico di Milano, Italy
Daniele Cannatella	TU Delft, The Netherlands
Eugenio Muccio	University of Naples Federico II, Italy
Sveva Ventre	University of Naples Federico II, Italy

Supporting the Transition to Ecological Economy in Cities Regeneration: Circular Model Tools for Reusing Architecture and Infrastructures (TReE 2025)

Workshop Organizers

Mariarosaria Angrisano	Pegaso University, Italy
Giulio Cavana	Politecnico di Torino, Italy
Francesca Buglione	CNR-ISPC, Italy

| Antonia Gravagnuolo | CNR-ISPC, Italy |
| Piera Della Morte | Pegaso University, Italy |

Workshop Program Committee Members

Giulia Datola	Politecnico di Milano, Italy
Vanessa Assumma	University of Bologna, Italy
Marco Volpatti	Politecnico di Torino, Italy
Sebastiano Barbieri	Politecnico di Torino, Italy
Caterina Caprioli	Politecnico di Torino, Italy
Marta Dell'Ovo	Politecnico di Milano, Italy
Federico Dell'Anna	Politecnico di Torino, Italy
Elena Todella	Politecnico di Torino, Italy
Danny Casprini	Politecnico di Milano, Italy
Grazia Neglia	Università Telematica Pegaso, Italy
Francesca Nocca	Università degli Studi di Napoli Federico II, Italy
Giulio Cavana	Politecnico di Torino, Italy
Francesca Buglione	CNR-IPSC, Italy
Marco Rossitti	Politecnico di Milano, Italy
Jhon Escorcia	Politecnico di Torino, Italy
Beatrice Mecca	Politecnico di Torino, Italy
Sara Biancifiori	Politecnico di Torino, Italy

Urban Digital Twins and Data Spaces: Shaping the Future of Sustainable Cities (TwinAbleCities 2025)

Workshop Organizers

Dessislava Petrova Antonova	Sofia University, GATE Institute, Bulgaria
Beniamino Murgante	University of Basilicata, Italy
Senthil Rajendran	RMSI, Bahrain
Tiziana Campisi	Kore University of Enna, Italy
Mila Koeva	University of Twente, The Netherlands

Workshop Program Committee Members

Dessislava Petrova-Antonova	Sofia University, Bulgaria
Mila Koeva	The University of Twente, The Netherlands
Beniamino Murgante	University of Basilicata, Italy
Senthil Rajendran	RMSI, Bahrain
Tiziana Campisi	Kore University of Enna, Italy

Urban Regeneration: Innovative Tools and Evaluation Model (URITEM 2025)

Workshop Organizers

Fabrizio Battisti	University of Florence, Italy
Giovanna Acampa	University of Florence, Italy
Orazio Campo	Sapienza University of Rome, Italy
Melania Perdonò	University of Florence, Italy

Workshop Program Committee Members

Fabrizio Battisti	University of Florence, Italy
Giovanna Acampa	University of Florence, Italy
Orazio Campo	University of Rome "La Sapienza", Italy
Melania Perdonò	Università degli Studi di Firenze, Italy

Urban Space Accessibility and Mobilities (USAM 2025)

Workshop Organizers

Chiara Garau	DICAAR, University of Cagliari, Italy
Alessandro Plaisant	University of Sassari, Italy
Barbara Caselli	University of Parma, Italy
Mauro D'Apuzzo	University of Cassino and Southern Lazio, Italy
Gabriele D'Orso	University of Palermo, Italy
Matteo Ignaccolo	University of Catania, Italy

Workshop Program Committee Members

Mauro Coni	University of Cagliari, Italy
Martina Carra	University of Brescia, Italy
Tiziana Campisi	University of Enna Kore, Italy
Tanja Congiu	University of Sassari, Italy
Francesca Maltinti	University of Cagliari, Italy
Silvia Rossetti	University of Parma, Italy
Barbara Caselli	University of Parma, Italy
Angela Pilogallo	University of L'Aquila, Italy
Lorena Fiorini	University of L'Aquila, Italy
Reza Askarizad	University of Cagliari, Italy
Francesco Pinna	University of Cagliari, Italy
Aime Tsinda	University of Rwanda, Rwanda
Youssef El Ganadi	International University of Rabat, Morocco
Marco Migliore	University of Palermo, Italy
Alessio Salvatore	Italian National Research Council, Italy
Giuseppe Stecca	Italian National Research Council, Italy

Paola Zamperlin	University of Florence, Italy
Vincenza Torrisi	University of Catania, Italy
Gerardo Carpentieri	University of Naples Federico II, Italy
Carmen Guida	University of Naples Federico II, Italy
Floriana Zucaro	University of Naples Federico II, Italy
Alfonso Annunziata	University of Basilicata, Italy
Elisabetta Venco	University of Pavia, Italy
Caterina Pietra	University of Pavia, Italy
Tazyeen Alam	University of Cagliari, Italy
Valerio Cutini	University of Pisa, Italy

UX Mobility 2025: Placing User Experience at the Center of Urban Mobility: Methods and Frameworks (UXM 2025)

Workshop Organizers

Carmen Guida	Università degli Studi di Napoli Federico II, Italy
Gerardo Carpentieri	Università degli Studi di Napoli Federico II, Italy
Federico Messa	Systematica srl, Italy
Lamia Abdelfattah	Systematica srl, Italy

Workshop Program Committee Members

Rosaria Battarra	Istituto di Studi sul Mediterraneo CNR, Italy
Romano Fistola	Università degli Studi di Napoli Federico II, Italy
Lucia Saganeiti	IMAA-CNR, Italy

Virtual Reality and Augmented reality and applications (VRA 2025)

Workshop Organizers

Damiano Perri	University of Perugia, Italy
Osvaldo Gervasi	University of Perugia, Italy
Chau Ma Thi	University of Engineering and Technology, Vietnam National University, Hanoi, Vietnam
Paolo Nesi	University of Florence, Italy
Pierfrancesco Bellini	University of Florence, Italy

Workshop Program Committee Members

| David Berti | ART SpA, Italy |
| JungYoon Kim | Gachon University, South Korea |

TaiHoon Kim	Zhejiang University of Science and Technology, China
Marcelo de Paiva Guimares	Federal University of São Paulo, Brazil
Sergio Tasso	University of Perugia, Italy

Workshop on Advanced and Computational Methods for Earth Science Applications (WACM4ES 2025)

Workshop Organizers

Luca Piroddi	University of Cagliari, Italy
Patrizia Capizzi	University of Palermo, Italy
Marilena Cozzolino	University of Molise, Italy
Sebastiano D'Amico	University of Malta, Malta
Chiara Garau	University of Cagliari, Italy
Giuseppina Vacca	University of Cagliari, Italy

Workshop Program Committee Members

Andrea Angelini	CNR ISPC, Italy
Ilaria Barone	Università degli Studi di Padova, Italy
Patrizia Capizzi	University of Palermo, Italy
Luigi Capozzoli	CNR, Italy
Alberto Carletti	University of Cagliari, Italy
Emanuele Colica	University of Malta, Malta
Marilena Cozzolino	Università del Molise, Italy
Sebastiano D'Amico	University of Malta, Malta
Chiara Garau	University of Cagliari, Italy
Luciano Galone	University of Malta, Malta
Peter Iregbeyen	University of Malta, Malta
Mariano Lisi	Basilicata Aerospace Cluster CLAS, Italy
Raffaele Martorana	Università di Palermo, Italy
Paolo Mauriello	Università del Molise, Italy
Veronica Pazzi	University of Florence, Italy
Raffaele Persico	Università della Calabria, Italy
Luca Piroddi	University of Cagliari, Italy
Sina Saneiyan	Binghamton University, USA
Mercedes Solla	Universidade de Vigo, Spain
Deodato Tapete	ASI, Italy
Giuseppina Vacca	University of Cagliari, Italy
Enrica Vecchi	University of Cagliari, Italy

Sponsoring Organizations

ICCSA 2025 would not have been possible without the tremendous support of many organizations and institutions, for which all organizers and participants of ICCSA 2025 express their sincere gratitude:

Galatasaray University, Istanbul, Türkiye
(https://gsu.edu.tr/en)

African Mathematical Union
(https://www.africanmathunion.org/)

Springer Nature Switzerland AG, Switzerland
(https://www.springer.com)

The University of Massachusetts, USA
(https://www.umass.edu/)

University of Perugia, Italy
(https://www.unipg.it)

University of Basilicata, Italy
(http://www.unibas.it)

Monash University, Australia
(https://www.monash.edu/)

Kyushu Sangyo University, Japan
(https://www.kyusan-u.ac.jp/)

Universidade do Minho
Escola de Engenharia

University of Minho, Portugal
(https://www.uminho.pt/)
Venue
ICCSA 2025 took place in: **Galatasaray University, Istanbul, Türkiye**

Additional Reviewers

Reviewers
The review tasks for each workshop have been carried out by the workshop Organizers
and the members of the workshop Program Committee.

Plenary Lectures

Sky Safe with GAI and Post-quantum Computing

Elizabeth Chang

Professor of Cyber Security and Head of Discipline, University of the Sunshine Coast, Australia

Abstract. Professor Chang's talk in this presentation has two distinct parts. To start, she will introduce the landscape of cybersecurity development, attacks, threats, and vulnerabilities, as well as state-of-the-art cyber protection, cyber defence, and cyber incident prevention. This is followed by a discussion of the impact of Generative AI (GAI) and quantum-safe cryptographic computing, highlighting the major issues and challenges in research, education, and training. In conclusion, she will present a vision for Sky Safe solutions, aiming to achieve cyber resilience that supports business and economic stability, enhances human capabilities, and promotes environmental sustainability.

Disaster Preparedness and Risk Profiling in the Digital Era from Earth Observation Lens

Jagannath Aryal

Department of Infrastructure Engineering, University of Melbourne, Australia

Abstract. Natural hazards which turn into disasters result in severe losses of lives, infrastructure, and property. Disasters such as earthquakes and landslides and their impacts on transportation safety, infrastructure resilience, and displacement of people to new places are challenges. To address such challenges, earth observation data and intelligent methods can provide potential solutions in developing decision support systems. This talk will present the state of the art in Earth observation for disaster resilience using intelligent methods. In the Earth observation space, digitalisation has revolutionised the way we map, monitor, and develop decision support systems. Global case study examples covering earthquake-induced landslides from the Himalayan region will cover the digital capabilities. The digital capabilities will embrace object recognition, interpretation, and their accurate and precise capture to integrate into digital models. The developed digital models from representative case studies can be leveraged in other jurisdictions in profiling risks to protect lives and infrastructure and creating disaster preparedness in the era of digital age and digital economy.

Intelligent Image Enhancement for Real-World Applications in Adverse Atmospheric Conditions

Khan Muhammad

Department of Global Convergence, Sungkyunkwan University, South Korea

Abstract. The adverse impacts of atmospheric conditions such as haze, fog, and low-light environments pose significant challenges for real-world applications reliant on computer vision, including autonomous driving, surveillance, and remote sensing. This keynote explores cutting-edge advancements in intelligent image enhancement, drawing insights from two pivotal studies. The first introduces HazeSpace2M, a comprehensive dataset and novel classification-guided dehazing framework that improves image clarity across diverse atmospheric conditions, addressing the gap between synthetic and real-world dehazing performance. The second focuses on LoLI-Street, a benchmark for low-light image enhancement tailored to urban environments, extending beyond enhancement to enable robust object detection and scene understanding. Taken together, these contributions demonstrate how integrating domain-specific datasets, advanced algorithms, and performance benchmarks can significantly elevate the reliability of computer vision systems under challenging weather and lighting conditions. Attendees will gain valuable insights into the methodologies, datasets, and practical applications driving innovation in this field, with implications for research and industry alike.

In Memory of Carmelo Torre

Unfortunately, Professor Carmelo Torre, one of the cornerstones of the ICCSA Conference, passed away last December, leaving everyone stunned and deeply saddened. His loss has created a profound void within our academic community. Carmelo was not only a respected scholar and dedicated contributor to the success and growth of ICCSA, but also a generous colleague, mentor, and friend to many. His intellectual rigor, warm personality, and unwavering commitment to advancing research will be remembered with great admiration. As we continue the work he helped shape, we honor his legacy and the indelible mark he left on all of us. Carmelo Torre graduated in engineering at the Polytechnic of Bari with a thesis on urban planning under Dino Borri's guidance. He began his research career by collaborating with Franco Selicato. During his PhD at the University of Naples Federico II under Luigi Fusco Girard, he specialized in real estate market analysis and multi-criteria evaluation methods. He explored the social impacts of urban transformations with his lifelong friend Maria Cerreta. His first ICCSA participation was in Perugia in 2008, in the session Geographical Analysis, Urban Modeling, Spatial Statistics. Instantly captivated by the conference, his charisma enabled him to involve various Italian scientific communities, including those in real estate and statistics. ICCSA became a yearly commitment for him, where he valued the high editorial quality of the proceedings and the dynamic post-presentation discussions and debates he passionately and expertly enriched. In 2012, alongside Maria Cerreta and Paola Perchinunno, he organized the workshop Econometrics and Multidimensional Evaluation in the Urban Environment (EMEUE), fostering dialogue on critical topics. His influence steadily grew, drawing numerous research groups to ICCSA and establishing real estate and assessment as one of the conference's leading fields. A pillar of ICCSA, he was involved across all facets of the event. Torre's contributions to academic discourse were marked by intellectual rigor and innovative thinking. His conference interventions consistently challenged conventional wisdom, offering insights transcending disciplinary boundaries. Beyond the conference, he passionately advocated for equity and social justice. His left-leaning ideology, though firm, earned respect from those with differing views, thanks to his sincerity and loyalty. He was creative, generous, and always willing to help, even at a personal cost. Despite battling illness, he maintained his characteristic optimism, warmth, cheerfulness, and commitment, supported by his partner, Caterina Rinaldo. His legacy lives on in his ideas, dedication, and unmatched generosity.

Contents – Part II

Unveiling the Synergies Between Air Quality and Climate PlAnning (AQCliPA 2025)

Indoor and Outdoor Air Pollution and Its Health Impact in Chile   3
    Valeria Scapini, Gabriela Zapata-Román, and Jean Paul Quinteros

"Sherry Triangle", Investigating Tourism Ecosystem in Andalusia (ES)   16
    *Imane Elhabchi, Angelica Piliero, Rachele Vanessa Gatto,
    and Francesco Scorza*

Performance Analysis and Science Mapping on High Performance
Computing in the Era of Artificial Intelligence   27
    Haruna Chiroma

A Dismissed Train Line as a New Pillar for Sustainable Tourism
Development in Corsica: "The Maquis Way" Strategy   40
    *Vincenza Pappalardi, Rafaele Nolè, Rachele Vanessa Gatto,
    and Francesco Scorza*

Advancements in Spatial Assessment of Socio-Ecological SystemS (AS-SESS 2025)

Planning for Environmental Justice. A Multi-methodological Approach   53
    *Marta Dell'Ovo, Silvia Ronchi, Irene Regaiolo, Andrea De Toni,
    Riccardo Alba, Enrico Caprio, Francesca Cochis,
    and Daniel Edward Chamberlain*

Spatial Analysis in Multi-Value Assessment for Rural Landscapes:
A Comparative Study of ES, LS, and LCA Frameworks   67
    Benedetta Grieco, Sabrina Sacco, Daniele Cannatella, and Maria Cerreta

High-Resolution Coastal Vulnerability Assessment: Integrating Ecosystem
Services Mapping for Sustainable Urban Management in the Naples
Coastline   84
    Ivan Murano, Giuliano Poli, Maria Somma, and Mattia Federico Leone

Blockchain and Distributed Ledgers: Technologies and Applications (BDLTA 2025)

Efficient Application of Multi-Layer Data Processing with PBFT and RAFT for Transaction Forecasting Using LSTM 103
Alexander Bogdanov, Jasur Kiyamov, Valery Khvatov, Gennady Dik, Aleksandr Dik, Egor Savkov, and Aleksandr Shchegolev

Towards Secure Cross-Organizational Data Transfer: A Blockchain-Enabled Message Broker Approach 115
Gleb Slepenkov and Vladimir Korkhov

Computational and Applied Mathematics (CAM 2025)

Two Families of W-Methods: Analysis and Application on Battery Models 133
Dajana Conte and Giovanni Pagano

The Mandelbrot Set for a Coquaternionic Family of Quadratics 150
Maria Irene Falcão, Fernando Miranda, and Ricardo Severino

Mixed Integer Linear Formulation for the Multiple Trip Aircraft Refueling Problem of a Brazilian Company 163
Karyne Alves Zampirolli and André Renato Sales Amaral

Symbolic and Numerical Computation of Coquaternionic Functions in *Mathematica* 181
Maria Irene Falcão, Fernando Miranda, and Ricardo Severino

Pascal Trapezoids as Wigner Numbers and Some Combinatorial Properties 195
Isabel Cação, M. Irene Falcão, Helmuth R. Malonek, and Graça Tomaz

Predicting Information Diffusion on Social Media Using an Epidemiological Approach 208
Dajana Conte, Samira Iscaro, and Beatrice Paternoster

Discrete Gradient θ-Methods for Port-Hamiltonian Systems 225
Raffaele D'Ambrosio and Simone Di Donato

Mean-Square Monotonicity Analysis of θ-Maruyama Methods 237
Helena Bišćević and Raffaele D'Ambrosio

Solution of Quaternion Equations with Imprecisely Defined Coefficients 249
Rogério Serôdio and José Vitória

Computational and Applied Statistics (CAS 2025)

Predicting Obstetric Outcome Through a Web Application Using
a Multinomial Logistic Regression Model 269
    Márcia Oliveira, Ana Cristina Braga, and Rosete Nogueira

The Mediating Role of Occupational Self-efficacy in the Relationship
Between Employees' Perceived Trust and Work Engagement 287
    Karma Lhaden and Isabel Dórdio Dimas

RidGME Estimation and Inference in Ill-Conditioned Models 300
    Pedro Macedo, Jorge Cabral, Vera Afreixo, Francisco Macedo,
    and Mario Angelelli

Development of Reference Percentile Growth Curves for Placental
Parameters Using Advanced Statistical Models 314
    Daniela Lemos, Ana Cristina Braga, and Rosete Nogueira

Comparison of Different Estimators for the Rayleigh Gamma Gompertz's
Parameters and Reliability Function 332
    Nadia Hashim Al-Noor, Rafida M. Elobaid, and Suzan J. Obaiys

Pricing Models in Individual Health Insurance 347
    Ângelo Cunha and A. Manuela Gonçalves

Revisiting the Fail-Safe Number in Meta-analysis: Insights
from a Simulation Study 365
    Vera Afreixo, Vanusa Rocha, Filipa Rocha, and Miguel Felgueiras

Investigating Student Retention in an Economics Degree Programme 377
    Francesca Pierri and Chrys Caroni

Time-Dependent and Non-linear Predictor Effects in Survival Analyses:
A Case Study Comparing Alternative Models for Cancer Mortality 393
    Michal Abrahamowicz, Marie-Eve Beauchamp, Richard J. Cook,
    Malka Gorfine, Jason Agulnik, Bruno Gagnon, and Steve Ferreira Guerra

Factors Influencing Trust in Human-Robot Interaction: A Case Study 411
    Letícia Cocato, Wolfram Erlhagen, Estela Bicho, Paulo Vicente,
    and Flora Ferreira

Author Index 425

Unveiling the Synergies Between Air Quality and Climate PlAnning (AQCliPA 2025)

Indoor and Outdoor Air Pollution and Its Health Impact in Chile

Valeria Scapini[1,2(✉)], Gabriela Zapata-Román[1,3], and Jean Paul Quinteros[1]

[1] Universidad Central de Chile, Santiago, Chile
valeria.scapini@ucentral.cl
[2] Universidad de Valparaíso, Valparaíso, Chile
[3] University of Manchester, Manchester, UK

Abstract. Air pollution poses a significant global health threat, with nearly 99% of the population exposed to levels exceeding WHO recommendations. In Chile, where several cities rank among the most polluted in Latin America, both outdoor air pollution (PM10) and indoor pollution from solid fuel use are major contributors to adverse health outcomes. This study examines the impact of indoor and outdoor air pollution on emergency care visits for respiratory and circulatory diseases using weekly panel data at the municipality level in Chile's most polluted regions. Indoor pollution is proxied by the share of households using solid fuels, while PM10 concentrations represent outdoor exposure. We employ Ordinary Least Squares (OLS) models with fixed effects for year, week, and municipality to control for unobserved heterogeneity and shared shocks. To address potential endogeneity—particularly the link between pollution exposure and socioeconomic disadvantage—we implement a two-stage least squares (2SLS) approach with an instrumental variable. Results indicate that both solid fuel use and PM10 levels are significantly associated with increased emergency visits, especially for respiratory diseases. The study draws on data from national meteorological, air quality, health, and socioeconomic sources. Our findings emphasize the compounded health risks of environmental pollution and underscore the need for targeted interventions in energy policy and public health. By integrating indoor and outdoor pollution sources, this research contributes to a more comprehensive understanding of environmental health burdens and supports progress toward Sustainable Development Goals related to health, clean energy, and inequality reduction.

Keywords: Indoor air pollution · health outcomes · solid fuels · outdoor pollution · household energy sources Chile

1 Introduction

Globally, 99% of the population is exposed to air pollution levels that exceed World Health Organization (WHO) recommendations, contributing to respiratory diseases, cardiovascular conditions, strokes, and lung cancer. A large percentage of people (2.6 billion), also live with high levels of household indoor air pollution. When combined, these indoor and outdoor pollution effects equate to approximately seven million premature deaths annually (WHO, 2021).

© The Author(s), under exclusive license to Springer Nature Switzerland AG 2026
O. Gervasi et al. (Eds.): ICCSA 2025 Workshops, LNCS 15887, pp. 3–15, 2026.
https://doi.org/10.1007/978-3-031-97589-9_1

Air contamination—in particular our exposure to the invisible threat of particulate matter (PM10)—is now recognized as a major threat to human health. When we breathe, such invisible contaminates can penetrate deep into our lungs, reaching the alveoli and absorbing into the blood. Exposure to PM10 contamination can cause multiple dangerous conditions, including inflammation of the lungs, system stress and serious chronic diseases (Kumar et al., 2023; Singh & Rastogi, 2022). Long-term exposure is now closely linked with serious respiratory and cardivascular conditions, as well as incidence of Covid- 19 (Scapini et al., 2023) and neurological dangers such as cognitive decline (Goel & Sen, 2024). As a result, particulate matter has been classified as a carcinogen, and placed within the brackets of other harmful chemicals and emissions such as cigarette smoke (Cui et al., 2015; Raaschou-Nielsen et al., 2016).

Sources of such pollution indoors, for example indoor cooking and heating fuels such as firewood and coal, are also now well documented to have negative effects on health, including higher risks of serious, long term respiratory illness. Vulnerable groups such as the elderly, and children, are particularly at risk to this contamination due to various factors (Guercio et al., 2021; Karottki et al., 2015). Research from various countries, such as Peru and Turkey, confirm the risk and impact of household air pollution on individual and family health, even when socioeconomic and demographic variables are considered (Gajate-Garrido, 2013; Ipek & Ipek, 2021).

In Chile, air pollution remains a critical public health issue. According to IQAir (2022), eight of the fifteen most polluted cities in Latin America are located in Chile, with fine particulate matter levels far exceeding WHO guidelines. These levels are driven by both industrial and transportation emissions, as well as household use of solid fuels. The Chilean National Environmental Survey reports that 32.8% of the population perceives air pollution as the country's most pressing environmental problem, and nearly half live in municipalities with regular or poor air quality. In southern Chile—especially in regions like Maule, Biobío, Ñuble, La Araucanía, Los Ríos, Los Lagos, and Aysén—firewood remains the primary source of energy for heating and, in some cases, for cooking. Firewood combustion accounts for up to 94% of fine particulate matter emissions in cities in these regions (MMA, 2020).

Notably, the health effects of particulate pollution are not uniform across the population. Socioeconomic disparities play a critical role in mediating both exposure and vulnerability. Research from China and the United States has shown that low-income populations experience more severe health consequences from pollution exposure due to factors like neighborhood disadvantage and limited access to health care or cleaner energy alternatives (Lee et al., 2023; Yang et al., 2022). During the COVID-19 pandemic, studies further demonstrated that particulate pollution exacerbated the virus's spread (Scapini et al., 2023), with disproportionate effects on disadvantaged groups (Allen et al., 2021).

This study investigates the health effects of both indoor and outdoor air pollution in Chile, with a focus on respiratory and circulatory diseases. While most existing research tends to focus exclusively on either outdoor pollution or localized case studies of indoor air quality, our analysis integrates both sources of exposure using a panel data approach. We use weekly data at the municipality level, concentrating on some of the most polluted urban areas in the country, to better understand the acute health impacts of environmental pollution.

Indoor air pollution is proxied by the percentage of households using solid fuels for domestic purposes, while outdoor air pollution is measured by weekly average PM10 concentrations. We estimate the association between these exposures and emergency care visits using linear fixed-effects models that account for unobserved heterogeneity across municipalities and over time. The analysis includes city (municipality), year, and epidemiological week fixed effects to control for time-invariant characteristics and common shocks. To strengthen causal identification and address potential endogeneity—particularly concerns that pollution exposure may be correlated with unobserved determinants of health outcomes—we implement a two-stage least squares (2SLS) approach using accumulated precipitation as an instrument for PM10. This strategy provides robustness to our main findings by offering more credible estimates of the health impacts of air pollution.

This research uses data from the Chilean Meteorological Directorate, the National Air Quality Information System, the Department of Health Statistics of the Ministry of Health, and the CASEN National Income Survey. By highlighting the intersection of environmental conditions, energy access, and health equity in Chile, the study contributes to Sustainable Development Goals (SDGs) 3 (Good Health and Well-Being), 7 (Affordable and Clean Energy), and 10 (Reduced Inequalities).

2 Data Sources

This study examines the effects of meteorological variables, atmospheric pollution, and indoor firewood use on health outcomes by utilizing multiple data sources at the municipal level and by statistical week. The analysis focuses on municipalities with the highest frequency of critical air quality episodes (alerts, pre-emergencies, and environmental emergencies) in 2023, as reported by the Ministry of the Environment. The selected cities include Coyhaique, Temuco, Chillan, Osorno, Talca, Los Angeles, Curico, Rancagua, and Concepcion. Santiago, the capital, is excluded due to its size (it concentrates more than 40% of the country's population) and specific urban characteristics.

The dataset includes weekly information from 2015 to 2022, obtained from publicly available sources, including the Chilean Meteorological Directorate, the National Air Quality Information System, and the Department of Health Statistics of the Ministry of Health. Meteorological data, specifically average temperature and precipitation are retrieved from records maintained by the Chilean Meteorological Directorate (DMC), which operates under the Directorate General of Civil Aeronautics. These records originate from meteorological stations in major cities.

Air pollution data are sourced from monitoring stations of the National Air Quality Information System of the Ministry of the Environment, which measure particulate matter (PM10) concentrations, reported in $\mu g/m^3$.

Health outcome data include emergency care visits, categorized by statistical week and cause. The causes considered are respiratory diseases, circulatory diseases, trauma and poisoning, mental disorders, acute diarrhea, and other conditions. we will focus on respiratory diseases such as such as acute respiratory infections, influenza, pneumonia, bronchitis, bronchial obstructive crisis, covid-19, among others and circulatory diseases like acute myocardial infarction, stroke, hypertensive crisis and severe arrhythmia. This information is obtained from the Department of Health Statistics and Information (DEIS) of the Ministry of Health.

Energy use data are drawn from the Chilean National Socioeconomic Characterization Survey (CASEN), conducted by the Ministry of Social Development and Family. This analysis uses CASEN survey waves from 2015, 2017, and 2022, which are nationally and regionally representative, and also representative for the major cities included in this study. The survey samples comprise 83,887 households (266,968 individuals) in 2015, 70,948 households (216,439 individuals) in 2017, and 72,056 households (202,231 individuals) in 2022. Starting in 2015, CASEN includes detailed information on the energy sources used for cooking and heating, allowing for the assessment of indoor air pollution exposure. Using this household-level data, we estimate the average use of solid fuels by municipality—the statistical unit of analysis in this study.

The integration of these datasets enables a structured analysis of the relationship between air pollution, meteorological factors, and health outcomes. Descriptive statistics of the sample are in Table 1.

Table 1. Descriptive Statistics

City	Variable	2015	2016	2017	2018	2019	2020	2021	2022
Rancagua	Average solid fuel use %	0.22	0.20	0.19	0.18	0.17	0.16	0.15	0.15
	Respiratory diseases	1,261	1,161	1,156	1,072	1,168	344	440	1,237
	Circulatory diseases	147	116	90	111	131	119	120	126
Curico	Average solid fuel use %	0.60	0.58	0.56	0.55	0.54	0.53	0.51	0.50
	Respiratory diseases	1,372	1,304	1,493	1,492	1,464	278	392	1,460
	Circulatory diseases	79	80	85	88	77	62	66	70
Talca	Average solid fuel use %	0.45	0.42	0.39	0.37	0.35	0.33	0.31	0.29
	Respiratory diseases	2,116	1,850	1,825	1,702	1,655	437	849	2,206
	Circulatory diseases	123	114	122	133	134	109	137	137
Chillan	Average solid fuel use %	0.65	0.65	0.66	0.63	0.61	0.58	0.56	0.54

(continued)

Table 1. (*continued*)

City	Variable	2015	2016	2017	2018	2019	2020	2021	2022
	Respiratory diseases	1,162	1,038	1,124	1,156	1,145	243	219	816
	Circulatory diseases	103	97	98	106	127	97	84	93
Concepción	Average solid fuel use %	0.43	0.42	0.41	0.41	0.40	0.40	0.39	0.39
	Respiratory diseases	1,621	1,475	1,543	1,553	1,624	326	353	1,339
	Circulatory diseases	107	94	74	105	138	108	114	125
Los Angeles	Average solid fuel use %	0.82	0.81	0.81	0.79	0.78	0.77	0.76	0.74
	Respiratory diseases	2,060	2,014	2,051	1,891	1,633	400	263	1,193
	Circulatory diseases	176	163	169	193	203	163	151	142
Temuco	Average solid fuel use %	0.75	0.74	0.74	0.73	0.71	0.70	0.69	0.68
	Respiratory diseases	1,027	937	914	927	887	222	510	1,497
	Circulatory diseases	116	109	110	111	91	75	114	105
Osorno	Average solid fuel use %	0.91	0.89	0.87	0.85	0.83	0.81	0.78	0.76
	Respiratory diseases	1,429	1,378	1,345	1,312	1,249	274	254	969
	Circulatory diseases	76	73	72	79	90	82	76	80
Coyhaique	Average solid fuel use %	0.93	0.90	0.86	0.84	0.83	0.82	0.80	0.79
	Respiratory diseases	458	425	443	417	395	85	90	329
	Circulatory diseases	28	33	27	26	27	23	25	31

Note: Respiratory and circulatory diseases refer to the weekly average number of emergency care visits related to these conditions.

3 Methodology

Our hypothesis is that higher use of solid fuels at the household level contributes to increased indoor air pollution, which in turn may be associated with a greater burden of respiratory and circulatory diseases. To assess this relationship, we estimate panel data models using weekly information at the municipality level. The dependent variables are emergency care visits for (1) respiratory diseases and (2) circulatory diseases. Explanatory variables include: (a) the percentage of households in the municipality using solid fuels for domestic purposes as a proxy for indoor air pollution; (b) outdoor air pollution indicator (PM10); and (c) average weekly temperature. This approach allows us to capture both indoor and outdoor environmental influences on acute health outcomes across time and space.

The stochastic model to be estimated is specified to examine the relationship between geographical variables and health indicators by cause and age group. The econometric model is formulated as follows:

$$y_{it} = f(MP10_{it}, CS_{it}, T_{it}) \tag{1}$$

where:

y_{it}: Number of emergency care services, worked in logarithmic scale, at municipality i at week t

CS_{it}: Is an indicator showing the proportion of dwellings that use solid fuels inside the home, at municipality i at week t

$MP10_{it}$: Atmospheric pollution, average concentration level of particulate matter PM10, at municipality i at week t

T_{it}: : Average ambient temperature (°C), at municipality i at week t

The first preliminary stochastic model corresponds to a fixed effects specification (2), estimated under the assumption that error variances may be heteroscedastic. To account for this, we employ robust standard errors, which allow consistent estimation of standard errors even in the presence of unknown heteroscedasticity.

$$y_{it} = \beta_0 + \beta_1 CS_{it} + \beta_2 MP10_{it} + \beta_3 T_{it} + v_{it} + \varepsilon_{it}, \tag{2}$$

$$\varepsilon_{it} \sim N\left(0, \sigma_{it}^2\right); \ Cov\left(\varepsilon_{it}, \varepsilon_{jt}\right) = 0; \ i \neq j; t \neq s \tag{3}$$

We include fixed effects in the model to improve identification and control for unobserved heterogeneity across municipalities and over time. Specifically, the estimation incorporates city fixed effects to capture time-invariant characteristics such as baseline infrastructure, geographic conditions, or long-term socioeconomic factors that could influence both pollution levels and health outcomes. Additionally, we include week fixed effects to account for national shocks, seasonal variation, and trends affecting all municipalities simultaneously, such as influenza outbreaks or national policy changes. The fixed effects specification allows us to isolate within-city variation over time, thus strengthening the causal interpretation of the estimated parameters.

To address potential endogeneity in the pollution variable—particularly the concern that more polluted areas may be systematically associated with lower-income populations and worse baseline health outcomes—we implement a two-stage least squares

(2SLS) estimation strategy. Accumulated precipitation is used as an instrumental variable (IV) for PM10 concentrations, based on its strong negative correlation with pollution levels and its assumed exogeneity with respect to health outcomes. In the first stage, predicted values of PM10 are obtained from a regression on the instrument and control variables. These fitted values are then used in the second stage as regressors in the main equation, estimating the impact of pollution on emergency care visits. This approach improves causal identification and provides more reliable estimates of the health effects of air pollution.

4   Results

The baseline specification is a fixed-effects model estimated using robust standard errors to account for potential violations of the homoscedasticity assumption. This model includes fixed effects for city, year, and epidemiological month, which control for time-invariant differences across municipalities as well as shared temporal shocks. Given the structure of the data and the rejection of the random effects specification based on the Hausman test, fixed effects were preferred to ensure more reliable estimates.

Table 2 presents the results from two fixed-effects specifications for weekly emergency visits due to respiratory and circulatory diseases. The first pair of columns examines the association between total household solid fuel use (across cooking, heating, and water heating) and emergency visits. The second pair of columns isolates the effect of solid fuel use specifically for heating purposes.

In both sets of models, solid fuel use is positively and significantly associated with emergency visits. A 10-percentage-point increase in the share of households using solid fuels for any purpose is associated with a 16.38% increase in respiratory emergency visits and an 8.69% increase in circulatory visits per week. When the analysis focuses solely on solid fuel use for heating, the estimated effects are even larger: a 10-percentage-point increase is associated with a 21.15% increase in respiratory visits and an 11.76% increase in circulatory visits. These findings confirm that indoor air pollution—particularly from heating with solid fuels—is a strong contributor to acute health outcomes, with respiratory conditions being more sensitive than circulatory ones.

The R-squared values (0.783 for respiratory and 0.85 for circulatory conditions) indicate a strong model fit in both cases, particularly for circulatory diseases. These results suggest that the included covariates—such as solid fuel use, PM10 levels, and temperature—explain a large proportion of the variation in weekly emergency visits.

Additional covariates yield meaningful effects. PM10 levels are positively and significantly associated with both respiratory and circulatory conditions, reinforcing the importance of outdoor air pollution as a driver of acute illness. In contrast, temperature is positively associated only with respiratory visits, suggesting that environmental stress—likely from extreme heat or cold—may trigger respiratory issues. At the same time, no significant association is found with circulatory emergencies.

Overall, the results show that indoor and outdoor air pollution substantially affects population health. The stronger effects observed for respiratory conditions are consistent with biological mechanisms, as particulate matter more directly and immediately impacts respiratory tissues.

Table 2. Linear fixed effects regression results - air pollution and weekly emergency visits by type of disease

	Respiratory diseases (log) Model (1)	Circulatory diseases (log) Model (2)	Respiratory diseases (log) Model (3)	Circulatory diseases (log) Model (4)
MP10	0.00160***	0.000433***	0.00160***	0.000434***
	(0.00031)	(0.00017)	(0.00031)	(0.00017)
% of solid fuel consumption	1.638***	0.869***		
	(0.42700)	(0.25100)		
% of solid fuel consumption for heating			2.072***	1.176***
			(0.41300)	(0.24600)
Average atmospheric temperature	0.0114**	-0.00257	0.0115**	-0.00254
	(0.00463)	(0.00202)	(0.00462)	(0.00202)
Constant	6.212***	4.660***	6.119***	4.593***
	(0.15100)	(0.07950)	(0.14800)	(0.07820)
City/year/month fixed effects	Yes	Yes	Yes	Yes
Observations	3,744	3,744	3,744	3,744
R-squared	0.783	0.850	0.783	0.850

Note: Respiratory and circulatory diseases refer to the weekly average number of emergency care visits related to these conditions. Robust standard errors in parentheses. Significance level: *** $p < 0.01$, ** $p < 0.05$, * $p < 0.1$
Source: Own elaboration

To address potential endogeneity in air pollution exposure—particularly the possibility that more polluted areas tend to coincide with lower-income populations and worse baseline health outcomes—we estimate a two-stage least squares (2SLS) model. Accumulated precipitation is used as an instrumental variable for PM10 concentrations, based on its strong negative correlation with pollution levels and its assumed exogeneity with respect to emergency health outcomes. The first stage of the model, along with tests of instrument strength and endogeneity, are reported in the appendix (Tables A1 and A2). These tests confirm the relevance of the instrument and suggest that endogeneity is present and statistically significant in the models using solid fuel for heating. At the same time, evidence is suggestive but inconclusive for models using total solid fuel consumption.

Table 2 presents the results of the second stage of the 2SLS estimation. All models include fixed effects for city, year, and epidemiological month, and are estimated using robust standard errors to account for heteroscedasticity. Model (IV1) and (IV2) report estimates using total household solid fuel consumption, while Model (IV3) and (IV4) focus on solid fuel use specifically for heating purposes.

Table 3. 2SLS Fixed effects estimates - Impact of PM10 and household solid fuel use on emergency visits for respiratory and circulatory diseases

	Respiratory diseases (log) Model (IV1)	Circulatory diseases (log) Model (IV2)	Respiratory diseases (log) Model (IV3)	Circulatory diseases (log) Model (IV4)
MP10	0.00334***	0.00123**	0.00338***	0.00126**
	(0.00109)	(0.00053)	(0.00108)	(0.00053)
% of solid fuel consumption	1.617***	0.859***		
	(0.42800)	(0.24900)		
% of solid fuel consumption for heating			2.062***	1.171***
			(0.41300)	(0.24500)
Average atmospheric temperature	0.0145***	−0.00115	0.0147***	−0.00107
	(0.00493)	(0.00222)	(0.00492)	(0.00222)
Constant	6.079***	4.599***	5.981***	4.529***
	(0.16700)	(0.08950)	(0.16500)	(0.08880)
City/year/month fixed effects	Yes	Yes	Yes	Yes
Observations	3,744	3,744	3,744	3,744
R-squared	0.781	0.849	0.781	0.849

Note: Respiratory and circulatory diseases refer to the weekly average number of emergency care visits related to these conditions. Robust standard errors in parentheses. Significance level: *** $p < 0.01$, ** $p < 0.05$, * $p < 0.1$.
Source: Own elaboration.

The results confirm a strong and statistically significant association between PM10 concentrations and emergency visits for both respiratory and circulatory conditions. A one-unit increase in PM10 is associated with a 0.33% increase in respiratory visits ($p < 0.01$) and a 0.12% increase in circulatory visits ($p < 0.05$). These effects are larger than those obtained under OLS, suggesting that models not accounting for endogeneity may underestimate the true health impacts of air pollution.

Regarding indoor pollution, a 10-percentage-point increase in the share of households using solid fuels for any domestic purpose is associated with a 16.17% increase in emergency visits for respiratory conditions and an 8.59% increase for circulatory conditions. When restricting the analysis to solid fuel use for heating only, the estimated effects are stronger: 20.62% and 11.71% increases in respiratory and circulatory emergencies, respectively. These findings highlight the health burden imposed by indoor heating practices involving solid fuels.

The average atmospheric temperature is also positively associated with respiratory emergencies across all specifications, possibly reflecting the role of extreme temperatures in exacerbating respiratory conditions. No statistically significant association is found between temperature and circulatory visits.

Overall, these results reinforce the conclusion that both outdoor and indoor sources of air pollution significantly affect acute health outcomes, especially for respiratory diseases. The use of an instrumental variable strengthens the causal interpretation of these relationships, particularly in the models focused on indoor heating.

5 Discussion

Our findings confirm that both air pollution and indoor pollution resulting from the use of fossil fuels for heating and cooking, as well as temperature, have a strong and statistically significant impact on city-level health outcomes. These results are consistent with previous studies that have linked outdoor pollution and cardiovascular and respiratory diseases on the one hand (Kumar et al., 2023; Singh & Rastogi, 2022; Scapini et al., 2023; Goel & Sen, 2024), and on the other hand, previous studies that have linked solid fuel use to higher risks of cardiovascular and respiratory diseases (Gajate-Garrido, 2013; Goel & Sen, 2024; Kumar et al., 2023; Lee et al., 2023; Ipek & Ipek, 2021; Singh & Rastogi, 2022). For example, studies by Guercio et al. (2021) and Karottki et al. (2015), demonstrate an increased risk of chronic respiratory diseases associated with the use of solid fuels for heating, particularly among vulnerable groups.

Our results provide evidence of the need to design public health interventions that specifically address both indoor air quality—particularly that associated with the use of solid fuels for heating—and outdoor air pollution. In this regard, the findings underscore the importance of promoting policies aimed at mitigating these risks, especially in the areas most affected by pollution in Chile, as documented in air quality studies of cities such as Coyhaique and Temuco (MMA, 2020).

Furthermore, this study aligns with existing evidence that highlights the role socioeconomic conditions play in determining levels of exposure to air pollution. Previous research indicates that lower-income populations are more exposed due to limited access to cleaner energy sources and the widespread use of solid fuels for home heating (Yang et al., 2022).

To account for spatially varying but time-invariant factors such as socioeconomic conditions, we include city-level fixed effects in our models. In addition, to address potential endogeneity in outdoor air pollution—arising, for example, from reverse causality or omitted variables—we implement an instrumental variable approach. This strategy strengthens the causal interpretation of our estimates and confirms that both indoor and outdoor pollution are significantly associated with adverse population health outcomes.

A key limitation of this study is the absence of direct measurements of indoor air pollution. Instead, we use the proportion of households relying on solid fuels as a proxy, extrapolating this variable for years in which direct data were unavailable. While this approach enables a partial estimation of exposure to indoor pollution, it may not fully capture the actual magnitude of the problem.

6   Conclusion

This study provides robust empirical evidence that both indoor and outdoor air pollution significantly affect health outcomes in Chile's most polluted cities. Exposure to particulate matter is strongly associated with increased emergency care visits for respiratory and cardiovascular conditions. The use of solid fuels for indoor heating, in particular, emerges as a key driver of these adverse effects, underscoring the importance of monitoring and addressing indoor air quality alongside ambient pollution levels.

The findings point to the need for public health responses considering environmental exposures occurring within households, not just in urban outdoor environments. The analysis strengthens causal inference by employing an instrumental variable strategy and municipality-level fixed effects and confirms that air pollution, regardless of its source, contributes to acute health burdens.

Rather than reiterating broad calls for clean energy transitions, the results support the implementation of targeted, evidence-based interventions to reduce reliance on solid fuels and improve energy efficiency at the household level. The positive and statistically significant association between indoor air pollution and emergency room visits for respiratory and circulatory conditions reinforces this need. As emphasized in international literature (Kumar et al., 2023; Singh & Rastogi, 2022), replacing solid fuels with cleaner alternatives improves air quality, reduces harmful emissions, contributes to climate change mitigation, and enhances public health.

Finally, addressing the health impacts of air pollution requires intersectoral coordination across energy, health, and economic development policies, along with implementation across multiple levels of governance—national, regional, and municipal. Future research should expand geographic coverage and incorporate variables such as housing materials, certified fuel use, and policy instruments like energy subsidies to better inform these multisectoral strategies.

Appendix

Table A1. First-Stage Regression Results - Dependent variable: PromMP10 (mean particulate matter 10μm)

	MP10	MP10
Total precipitation	−0.295***	−0.295***
	(0.0180)	(0.0180)
% of solid fuel consumption	35.35	
	(28.3800)	
% of solid fuel consumption for heating		27.25
		(27.4000)

(continued)

Table A1. (*continued*)

	MP10	MP10
Average atmospheric temperature	−1.469***	−1.468***
	(0.2660)	(0.2660)
Constant	65.78***	67.75***
	(9.0680)	(8.7870)
City/year/month fixed effects	Yes	Yes
Observations	3,744	3,744
R-squared	0.52	0.52

Note: Instrument Total precipitation. Robust standard errors in parentheses. Significance level: *** $p < 0.01$, ** $p < 0.05$, * $p < 0.1$
Source: Own elaboration

Table A2. Tests for Endogeneity of PromMP10

	Test	Statistic	p-value
Model (1)	Durbin (χ^2)	2.8916	0.0890
	Wu-Hausman (F)	2.8198	0.0932
Model (2)	Durbin (χ^2)	2.4592	0.1168
	Wu-Hausman (F)	2.3622	0.1244
Model (3)	Durbin (χ^2)	3.0125	0.0826
	Wu-Hausman (F)	2.9377	0.0866
Model (4)	Durbin (χ^2)	2.6255	0.1052
	Wu-Hausman (F)	2.5206	0.1125

Note: Endogeneity tests for *PromMP10* using the Durbin and Wu–Hausman statistics. The null hypothesis is that *PromMP10* is exogenous. Although none of the tests reject the null at the 1% level, some models (e.g., Model 3) show p-values below 10%, suggesting potential endogeneity concerns. The instrumental variable approach is therefore used as a robustness check to account for possible bias from omitted variables or reverse causality.Source: Own elaboration

References

Allen, O., Brown, A., Wang, E.: Socioeconomic disparities in the effects of pollution on spread of Covid-19: evidence from US counties, p. 21249303. medRxiv (2021). https://doi.org/10.1101/2021.01.06.21249303

Cui, P., Huang, Y., Han, J., Song, F., Chen, K.: Ambient particulate matter and lung cancer incidence and mortality: a meta-analysis of prospective studies. Eur. J. Pub. Health **25**(2), 324–329 (2015). https://doi.org/10.1093/eurpub/cku145

Gajate-Garrido, G.: The impact of indoor air pollution on the incidence of life threatening respiratory illnesses: evidence from young children in Peru. J. Dev. Stud. **49**(4), 500–515 (2013). https://doi.org/10.1080/00220388.2012.709617

Goel, K., Sen, A.: Epidemiology of fine particulate air pollution and human health impacts. In: Air Quality and Human Health, pp. 111–119. Springer (2024). https://doi.org/10.1007/978-981-97-1363-9_8

Guercio, V., et al.: Exposure to indoor and outdoor air pollution from solid fuel combustion and respiratory outcomes in children in developed countries: a systematic review and meta-analysis. Sci. Total Environ. *755*(Pt 1), 142187 (2021). https://doi.org/10.1016/j.scitotenv.2020.142187

İPEK, Ö., İPEK, E.: Effects of indoor air pollution on household health: evidence from Turkey. Environ. Sci. Pollut. Res. **28**(47), 67519–67527 (2021). https://doi.org/10.1007/s11356-021-15175-9

IQAir: 2022 World air quality report (2022). https://www.iqair.com/world-air-quality-report

Karottki, D.G., et al.: Indoor and outdoor exposure to ultrafine, fine and microbiologically derived particulate matter related to cardiovascular and respiratory effects in a panel of elderly urban citizens. Int. J. Environ. Res. Public Health **12**(2), 1667–1686 (2015). https://doi.org/10.3390/ijerph120201667

Kumar, P., Singh, A.B., Arora, T., Singh, S., Singh, R.: Critical review on emerging health effects associated with the indoor air quality and its sustainable management. Sci. Total. Environ. **872**, 162163 (2023). https://doi.org/10.1016/j.scitotenv.2023.162163

Lee, H., Kravitz-Wirtz, N., Rao, S., Crowder, K.: Effects of prolonged exposure to air pollution and neighborhood disadvantage on self-rated health among adults in the United States: evidence from the panel study of income dynamics. Environ. Health Perspect. **131**(8), 87001–87010 (2023). https://doi.org/10.1289/EHP11268

MMA: Encuesta nacional de medio ambiente 2020. Ministerio del Medio Ambiente, Gobierno de Chile (2020). https://mma.gob.cl/encuestas-nacionales-del-medio-ambiente/

Raaschou-Nielsen, O., et al.: Particulate matter air pollution components and risk for lung cancer. Environ. Int. **87**, 66–73 (2016). https://doi.org/10.1016/j.envint.2015.11.007

Scapini, V., Torres, S., Rubilar-Torrealba, R.: Meteorological, PM2. 5 and PM10 factors on SARS-CoV-2 transmission: the case of southern regions in Chile. Environ. Pollut. **322** (2023). https://doi.org/10.1016/j.envpol.2022.120961

Singh, A., Rastogi, N.: Airborne particles in indoor and outdoor environments. In: Airborne Particulate Matter, pp. 47–73. Springer (2022). https://doi.org/10.1007/978-981-16-5387-2_4

WHO: WHO global air quality guidelines. Particulate matter (PM2.5 and PM10), ozone, nitrogen dioxide, sulfur dioxide and carbon monoxide, p. 290. World Health Organization (2021). https://www.who.int/publications/i/item/9789240034228

Yang, Z., et al.: Does income inequality aggravate the impacts of air pollution on physical health? Evidence from China. Environ. Dev. Sustain. **24**(2), 2120–2144 (2022). https://doi.org/10.1007/s10668-021-01522-w

"Sherry Triangle", Investigating Tourism Ecosystem in Andalusia (ES)

Imane Elhabchi[1], Angelica Piliero[1], Rachele Vanessa Gatto[2] (iD),
and Francesco Scorza[2](✉) (iD)

[1] DIUSS, University of Basilicata, Via Lanera, Matera, Italy
{imane.elhabchi,angelica.piliero,
jaime.delpino}@studenti.unibas.it
[2] School of Engineering, University of Basilicata, Viale dell'Ateneo Lucano, Potenza, Italy
{rachelevanessa.gatto,francesco.scorza}@unibas.it

Abstract. Sustainable development strategies at urban and regional levels encompass a multidisciplinary discourse integrating global perspectives with practical insights into sustainable urban planning, land use, transportation, and ecological design. Addressing the tensions between economic growth, social equity, and environmental preservation, current trends in policy recommendations draw from international institutions and academic research. Tourism emerges as a pivotal sector in urban sustainability discourse, shaping policy and design across multiple scales and stakeholders. This paper presents a case study applying the STESY model to in Andalusia (Spain) a region witnessing substantial growth in its tourism industry. With eno-gastronomic and cultural tourism as its focus, the study employs open data and cluster analysis to identify local tourism Destination Areas, guided by a strategic framework developed through collaborative efforts with architectural students from the University of Basilicata. Focusing on tourism as a critical component of territorial planning, the paper advocates for a decision support system aligned with the New Urban Agenda, emphasizing context-based design and sustainable development principles. The methodology outlines the STESY model application, culminating in a proposed development strategy titled "Sherry Triangle" aimed at enhancing Andalusia's tourism ecosystem while preserving its local identity and sustainability. Discussions and conclusions highlight research insights, limitations, and future directions for sustainable tourism development.

Keywords: New Urban Agenda · Sustainable development · Sustainable tourism ecosystem · STESY

1 Introduction

Different regions face sustainable development strategies for sustainable tourism enhancement under the umbrella concept of regional development from the global perspective[1–3] to the operational level of key essays discussing various aspects of sustainable urban planning, land use, transportation, and ecological design [4]. Challenges and opportunities of sustainable urban development [5, 6] generally are positioned in

O. Gervasi et al. (Eds.): ICCSA 2025 Workshops, LNCS 15887, pp. 16–26, 2026.
https://doi.org/10.1007/978-3-031-97589-9_2

the conflicts between economic growth, social equity, and environmental preservation in urban planning [7].

Current trends, more than standard rules, in policy recommendations are at the basis of key international institutional references [8, 9] and academic applications [10–13].

Tourism is a key sector for current debate in urban sustainability [14–16] and it represents and horizontal domain of policy making and design implementation in a multiscale[17] and multistakeholder perspective [18]. In this research paper we refer to an application of the STESY model [19] in a specific case study: the "Sherry Triangle" in Spain. The Sherry Triangle in southern Spain is a destination for wine lovers and culture seekers. This sun-drenched region in Andalusia offers a perfect blend of history, gastronomy, and traditions representing a relevant case study of tourism phenomena investigation. Local tourism offer includes visits to world-famous sherry bodegas (wineries), attending flamenco performances, and local food tasting. Wine tourism plays a significant role in the local economy, generating approximately €75.5 million in 2022. This figure represents a 39% increase compared to 2021, highlighting the sector's robust recovery post-pandemic. Notably, around 80% of these tourists were domestic travelers, with the remaining 20% comprising international visitors.

Whether strolling through the charming old towns or experiencing the coastal beauty, the Sherry Triangle provides an authentic taste of Southern Spain but also structural imbalances that will be addressed by the design phase.

The objective of the application is to design a strategic framework for developing local tourism system on the ground of a robust analytical process oriented to identify local tourism Destination Areas according to STESY methodological framework. Open data and cluster analysis are applied in order to combine interpretative approach to quantitative design during studio lab developed with architectural university students at the University of Basilicata.

"Tourism as a territorial planning component" represents the disciplinary position of this paper, we aim at provide qualified decision support system in defining and support policy making territorial development process referring to the New Urban Agenda as a toolkit for better decision and better "context based" design [20–22].

The first section of the paper presents the research methodological framework and process. Then the case study area is described and the analytical approach is detailed. The proposed development strategy "The Sherry Route" integrating local slow mobility options to improve the link among the three corners of the "Sherry Triangle" is discussed in terms of tourism eco-system. Discussions and conclusions section proposes main highlights of the research, limitations and future perspectives.

2 Background and Scope of the Research

The STESY model represents the conceptual framework for analyzing and organizing knowledge related to specialized tourism phenomena in the case study area, with a particular focus on spatial and territorial aspects and the relation among elements of the local tourism chain. This taxonomy provides a structured system for classifying and managing information, supporting the analytical process from the initial phase of territorial classification to the development of strategic decision-making frameworks.

The hierarchical approach of the model enables the classification of specialized tourism into three distinct levels: Specialized Tourism Ecosystem, Specialized Tourism System, and Specialized Destination Area (DAj). The latter represents the primary unit of analysis for describing the territorial tourism supply. A DAj d[19]oes not necessarily correspond to traditional administrative boundaries but is instead defined by the spatial and functional organization of the local tourism system. Consequently, a DAj may encompass multiple municipalities or, conversely, multiple DAj may exist within a single municipal boundary. The conceptualization of DAj is formalized as follows:

$$DA_j = f(a_j, s_j, r)$$

where:

- a_j (Attractors) refers to physical points of interest (POIs), including officially recognized national and international tourist attractions (e.g., UNESCO sites, certified historic villages, Blue Flag locations, etc.).
- s_j (Services) includes facilities within the tourism supply chain, such as accommodations and restaurants, each defined by specific locations and attributes.
- r (Reachability) represents the accessibility of the destination, encompassing the infrastructural and organizational system that allows visitors to reach the area via different modes of transportation (e.g., train stations, bus terminals, parking facilities).

A key aspect of the STESY model is the concept of tourism specialization (j), which categorizes a destination on the basis of its predominant tourism type (e.g., cultural, gastronomic, nature-based tourism). This approach enables a detailed understanding of the relationships between functional sub-regions within a territory, facilitating the formulation of data-driven tourism development strategies. By applying this methodology to selected case studies, it is possible to construct a territorial network, enhancing the comprehension of spatial interconnections within the tourism system.

The research approach is based on the following phases (Fig. 1):

1. Analysis: Case study description through main tourism statistics, policies and analytics.
2. Application of STESY model: spatial data selection and classification, stakeholder identification, DA identification and benchmarking
3. Design: objectives identification, territorial scenario and design solutions, NUA compliance assessment.

2.1 Case Study Analysis: Sherry Triangle

The study focusses on the cities of Jerez de la Frontera, El Puerto de Santa María, and Sanlúcar de Barrameda in the South of Spain. This area, known as the "Sherry Triangle" is characterized by a strong winemaking tradition, which represents a significant part of the local economic income. The three cities contribute 0.70% of Spanish tourism system, which is part of the 3% represented by the province of Cadiz and 13% of Andalusia.

Jerez Airport recorded around 200,000 passengers, marking an increase compared to previous years (www.turismojerez.com, visited 20/03/2024).

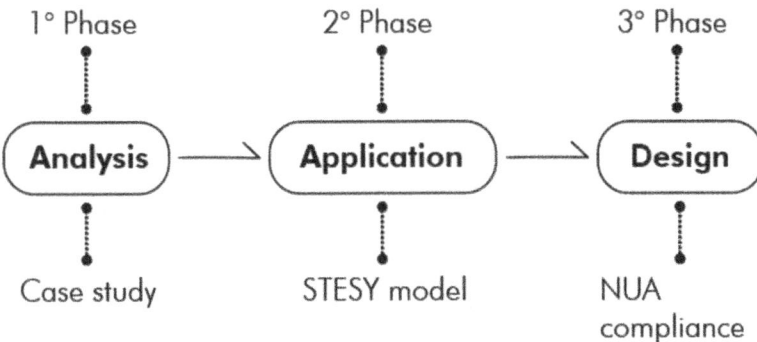

Fig. 1. Description of the methodological framework.

However, Jerez Airportdoes not account for the highest tourist flow in the Andalusian province, as cars remain the most commonly used means of transport, with about 87% of tourists choosing this option to reach the area (www.turismojerez.com visited 20/03/2024). Over the years, accommodation facilities have experienced significant growth, with Jerez leading the way, offering nearly 40,000 beds (Fig. 2). This has resulted in an increase in occupied overnight stays, with the three cities collectively reaching approximately 115,000 overnight stays for all tourists (Fig. 2).

Wine tourism saw a peak in visitors to Jerez in 2018–2019, surpassing 400,000. This trend began to rise again after the COVID pandemic crises, affecting and all three cities contributed similarly. However, Sanlúcar is now the city receiving the highest number of winery-related tourists, with 320,000 visitors in 2022 (Fig. 2).

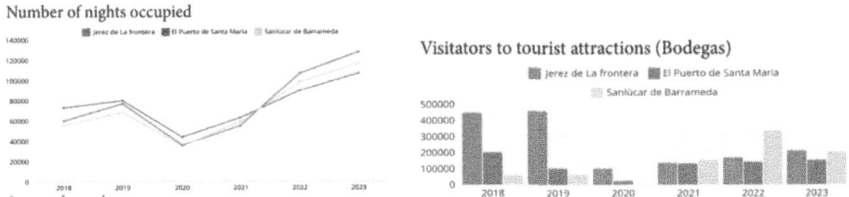

Fig. 2. Personal elaboration of municipal data. Sources: www.turismojerez.com, www.elpuertod esantamaria.es, https://sanlucarinformacion.es/.

2.2 Application of STESY Model

The analysis of the territorial system and tourism offer of "Cherry triangle" was conducted by dividing the territorial elements (represented as POIs) into three main categories according to STESY model: Attractors, Services, Reachability.

The study area highlights the significant presence of services, cultural, and religious attractions. Services account for 73% of the identified points, with 79% consisting of traditional bars and restaurants, confirming the importance of gastronomic tourism.

Additionally, 46% of the main attractions are related to wineries, emphasizing the value of the region's winemaking heritage for local tourism [23–26].

To identify the DAj and then to analyze the distribution of the services, the tourist attractions, and the reachability of the three cities per each DAj, the GeoDa analysis software was used [27, 28].

The results (Fig. 3) showed 3 distinct DAs located in the three administrative boundaries of the Sherry triangle. DA in Jerez de la Frontera and DA in El Puerto de Santa María have a higher concentration of services and attractions, along with good accessibility due to key infrastructure such as the airport (for Jerez) and the port and railway network (for El Puerto). In contrast, DA in Sanlúcar de Barrameda displayed significant challenges:

- Limited Accessibility: The city is less connected, relying mainly on private vehicles or regional buses.
- Fewer Attractions: The analysis highlighted a lower presence of cultural and tourist attractions, which could weaken the overall tourism offering.

The figure below describes the spatial distribution of main POIs categories included in the analytical process.

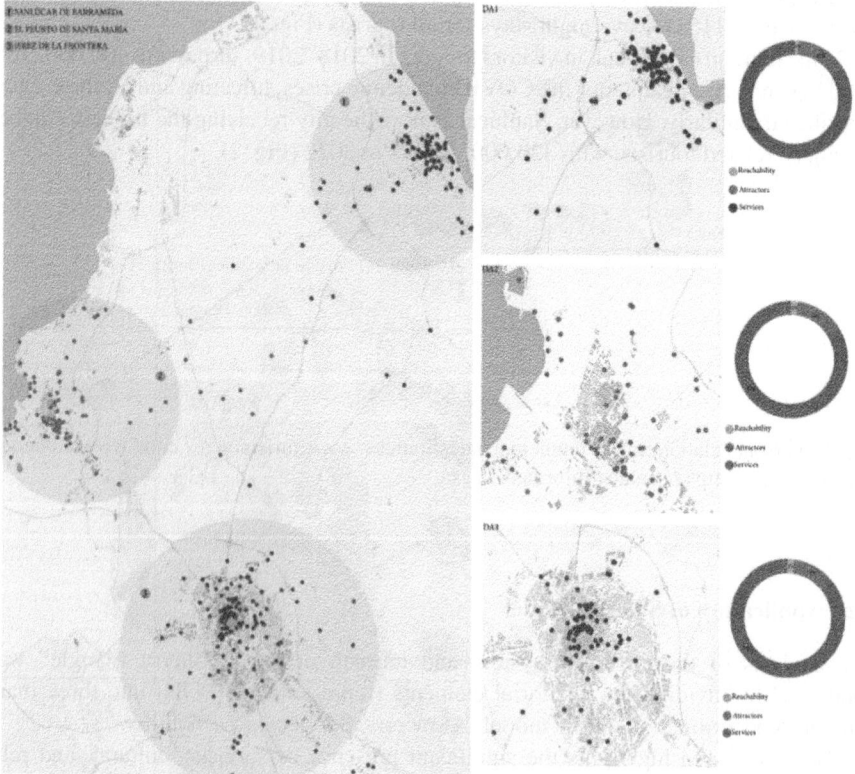

Fig. 3. Study area with Destination areas identification and evaluation.

2.3   Design: The Sherry Route

To enhance wine tourism and improve connectivity between DA Jerez de la Frontera, DA El Puerto de Santa María, and DA Sanlúcar de Barrameda, several actions proposals have been developed in line with the objectives of the New Urban Agenda on the basis of the methodological approach oriented to the downscaling of NUA principles [29–33].

One of the main initiatives focuses on improving transportation, with particular attention to Sanlúcar, which currently faces disadvantages due to limited access infrastructure. Strengthening the connections between the three cities would help reduce territorial inequalities and ensure a more efficient and inclusive transport system, aligning with New Urban Agenda [34] which aims to provide safe, sustainable, and accessible transport for all[35–37].

Another initiative is oriented to define a pedestrian route that passes through the region's vineyards, offering visitors an immersive and direct experience of the territory.

This itinerary would not only promote slow tourism but also contributes to the enhancement of the natural heritage by ensuring accessible and sustainable spaces, encouraging access to inclusive and safe green spaces.

To support this project, the construction of three tasting facilities along the route has been proposed, where visitors can explore local wine varieties and learn about the production processes. This initiative would not only foster economic growth and employment but would also contribute to the protection and promotion of the region's food and wine heritage, reinforcing the link between culture and sustainable development.

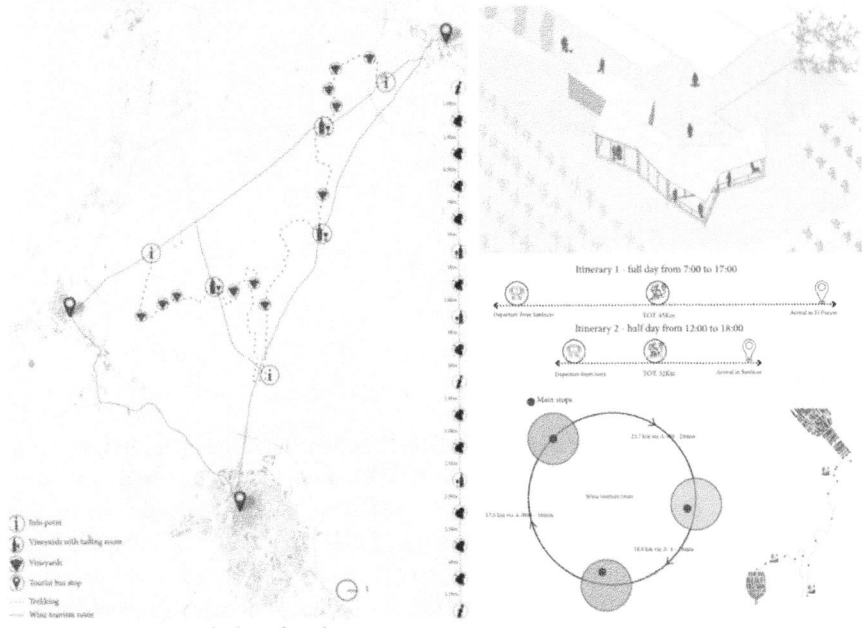

Fig. 4. Design: Strada dello Sherry

Finally, a key aspect of the project is the promotion of slow and sustainable tourism, offering authentic experiences that respect the environmental features and local traditions. This strategy aims to reduce environmental impact while enhancing cultural identity by involving local actors in the tourism process.

Overall, these proposals represent an integrated approach to enhance the appeal of the "Sherry Triangle," strengthening its infrastructures, and promoting its rich food and wine heritage.

Through the identification of DAs and Components, the primary stakeholders detected. The Wine producers are the main actors involved in the supply of eno-gastronomic attractors. Tourism operators manage the facilities and services related to the value chain while local authorities are responsible for infrastructure and development strategies (Figs. 4 and 5).

Fig. 5. Design: Project view.

3   Discussion e Conclusions

This paper reports the results of a specific studio experience developed with architectural students handling the implementation of the STESY model as a structured approach in tourism strategic design in a target area [33, 38]. The "Sherry Triangle" in southern Spain represents a significant study case as it includes strong identity value connected with a well-known tourism identity (the Sherry production) combined with inland and rural characters defining infrastructural and organizational challenges for the sustainable management of tourism phenomena. Such elements refer to a specific tourism category: eno-gastronomic tourism. Those main features are common in many European territories where the presence of quality food traditions is currently driven towards economic development processes based on tourism exploitation. From the early stages of context analysis and data collection the methodological framework driven a territorial design process toward specific place-based proposal including architectural and organizational elements under the umbrella of NUA downscaling [39–42].

The applied research process delivered an effective collective learning both for students, tutors and involved technicians demonstrating the advantages of applying a structured methodology in strategic design focusing on tourism development as a component of territorial planning connected with real estate values and the complex framework of other territorial resources [43–47].

The limitations regard the need to extend this approach to additional case studies comparing results and connecting the analytical approach to real territorial development applications.

References

1. Verma, P., Raghubanshi, A.S.: Urban sustainability indicators: challenges and opportunities. Ecol. Indic. **93**, 282–291 (2018). https://doi.org/10.1016/J.ECOLIND.2018.05.007
2. Wakil, M.A.: Bibliometric and visualised review of the knowledge domain of coastal tourism research. Sustain. Communit. **1**, 2360221 (2024). https://doi.org/10.1080/29931282.2024.236 0221
3. Song, J., Chen, Y.: Optimizing cultural heritage tourism routes using Q-learning: a case study of Macau. Sustain. Communit. **2**, 2475794 (2025). https://doi.org/10.1080/29931282.2025. 2475794
4. Wheeler, S.M., Beatley, T.: The sustainable urban development reader, 3rd edn., pp. 1–631 (2014)
5. Scorza, F., Grecu, V.: Assessing Sustainability: research Directions and Relevant Issues. In: Gervasi, O., et al. (eds.) Computational Science and its Applications -- ICCSA 2016: 16th International Conference, Beijing, China, 4–7 July 2016, Proceedings, Part I, pp. 642–647. Springer International Publishing, Cham (2016). https://doi.org/10.1007/978-3-319-42085-1_55
6. Dvarioniene, J., Grecu, V., Lai, S., Scorza, F.: Four perspectives of applied sustainability: Research implications and possible integrations. LNCS, vol. 10409, pp. 554–563 (2017). https://doi.org/10.1007/978-3-319-62407-5_39
7. Campbell, S.: Green Cities, Growing Cities, just Cities? Urban planning and the contradictions of sustainable development. Classic Read. Urban Plann., 308–326 (2018). https://doi.org/10. 4324/9781351179522-25
8. Inforegio - The Urban Agenda for the EU, https://ec.europa.eu/regional_policy/policy/the mes/urban-development/agenda_en. Accessed 17 Mar 2025
9. World cities report (2024). https://unhabitat.org/wcr/. Accessed 17 Mar 2025
10. UN HABITAT: New Urban Agenda. United Nations (2016)
11. Caprotti, F., et al.: The new urban agenda: key opportunities and challenges for policy and practice. Urban Res Pract. **10**, 367–378 (2017). https://doi.org/10.1080/17535069.2016.127 5618
12. Las Casas, G., Scorza, F., Murgante, B.: New urban agenda and open challenges for urban and regional planning. In: Calabrò, F., Della Spina, L., and Bevilacqua, C. (eds.) New Metropolitan Perspectives. ISHT 2018, pp. 282–288. Springer, Cham (2019). https://doi.org/10.1007/978-3-319-92099-3_33

13. Scorza, F.: Training decision-makers. In: GEODESIGN Workshop Paving the Way for New Urban Agenda (2020).https://doi.org/10.1007/978-3-030-58811-3_22
14. Sharpley, R.: Host perceptions of tourism: a review of the research. Tour. Manag. **42**, 37–49 (2014). https://doi.org/10.1016/j.tourman.2013.10.007
15. Gatto, R.V., Scorza, F.: Tourism ecosystem domains. In: Gervasi, O. (ed.) Computational Science and its Applications - ICCSA 2023. Springer (2023). https://doi.org/10.1007/978-3-031-37123-3_7
16. Arslan, E.N., Dişli, G.: Architectural heritage and traditional knowledge systems: insights from the ancient settlement of Kilistra, Türkiye#. Sustain. Communit. **2**, 2477145 (2025). https://doi.org/10.1080/29931282.2025.2477145
17. Batty, M., Milton, R.: A new framework for very large-scale urban modelling. Urban Stud. J. Limit. **58**, 2021 (2021). https://doi.org/10.1177/0042098020982252
18. Bäckstrand, K.: Multi-stakeholder partnerships for sustainable development: Rethinking legitimacy, accountability and effectiveness. Eur. Environ. **16**, 290–306 (2006). https://doi.org/10.1002/eet.425
19. Gatto, R.V., Corrado, S., Scorza, F.: Taxonomy for specialized tourism Ecosystems : new geographies for sustainable territorial planning. Habitat Int. (2025)
20. Las Casas, G., Scorza, F., Murgante, B.: Conflicts and sustainable planning: peculiar instances coming from Val D'agri structural inter-municipal plan. In: Papa, R., Fistola, R., and Gargiulo, C. (eds.) Smart Planning: Sustainability and Mobility in the Age of Change, pp. 163–177. Springer (2018). https://doi.org/10.1007/978-3-319-77682-8_10
21. Scorza, F., Las Casas, G.B., Murgante, B., Francesco, S., Las Casas, G.B., Beniamino, M.: That's ReDO: ontologies and regional development planning. In: Computational Science and Its Applications – ICCSA 2012, pp. 640–652. Springer, Heidelberg (2012). https://doi.org/10.1007/978-3-642-31075-1_48
22. Scorza, F.: Towards self energy-management and sustainable citizens' engagement in local energy efficiency agenda. Int. J. Agric. Environ. Inf. Syst. (IJAEIS). **7**, 44–53 (2016). https://doi.org/10.4018/ijaeis.2016010103
23. Gatto, R.V., Scorza, F.: Sustainable tourism ecosystem balancing territorial values: a place-based perspective. In: Gervasi, O. (ed.) Computational Science and its Applications - ICCSA 2023. Springer, Cham (2023). https://doi.org/10.1007/978-3-031-37123-3_8
24. Gatto, R., Santopietro, L., Scorza, F.: Roghudi: developing knowledge of the places in an abandoned inland municipality. LNCS, vol. 13382, pp. 48–53 (2022). https://doi.org/10.1007/978-3-031-10592-0_5/COVER
25. Gatto, R., Santopietro, L., Scorza, F.: Tourism and abandoned inland areas development demand: a critical appraisal. LNCS, vol. 13382, pp. 40–47 (2022). https://doi.org/10.1007/978-3-031-10592-0_4/COVER
26. Gatto, R.V., Corrado, S., Scorza, F.: Towards a definition of tourism ecosystem. In: 18th International Forum on Knowledge Asset Dynamics (IFKAD) - Managing Knowledge for Sustainability (2023)
27. Anselin, L., Syabri, I., Kyo, Y.: GeoDa: An introduction to spatial data analysis. In: Fischer Manfred M. and Getis, A. (ed.) Handbook of Applied Spatial Analysis: Software Tools, Methods and Applications, pp. 73–89. Springer, Heidelberg (2010). https://doi.org/10.1007/978-3-642-03647-7_5
28. Anselin, L., Li, X., Koschinsky, J.: GeoDa, from the desktop to an ecosystem for exploring spatial data. Geogr. Anal. **54**, 439–466 (2022). https://doi.org/10.1111/gean.12311
29. Santopietro, L., Solimene, S., Lucchese, M., Di Carlo, F., Scorza, F.: An economic appraisal of the SE(C)AP public interventions towards the EU 2050 target: the case study of Basilicata region. Cities **149** (2024). https://doi.org/10.1016/j.cities.2024.104957

30. Scorza, F., Pilogallo, A., Las Casas, G.: Investigating tourism attractiveness in inland areas: ecosystem services, open data and smart specializations. In: Calabrò, F., Della Spina, L., and Bevilacqua, C. (eds.) New Metropolitan Perspectives, pp. 30–38. Springer International Publishing, Cham (2018). https://doi.org/10.1007/978-3-319-92099-3_4

31. Scorza, F., Fortunato, G.: Active mobility-oriented urban development: a morpho-syntactic scenario for a mid-sized town. Eur. Plann. Stud., 1–25 (2022). https://doi.org/10.1080/096 54313.2022.2077094

32. Scorza, F., Fortunato, G.: Cyclable cities: building feasible scenario through urban space morphology assessment. J. Urban Plan. Dev. **147**, 05021039 (2021). https://doi.org/10.1061/(ASCE)UP.1943-5444.0000713

33. Santopietro, L., Scorza, F.: Voluntary planning and city networks: a systematic bibliometric review addressing current issues for sustainable and climate-responsive planning. sustainability. 16 (2024). https://doi.org/10.3390/su16198655

34. Scorza, F., et al.: Overcoming interoperability weaknesses in e-government processes: organizing and sharing knowledge in regional development programs using ontologies. In: Organizational, Business, and Technological Aspects of the Knowledge Society, pp. 243–253. Springer (2010). https://doi.org/10.1007/978-3-642-16324-1_26

35. Fortunato, G., Scorza, F., Murgante, B.: Cyclable City: a territorial assessment procedure for disruptive policy-making on urban mobility. In: Misra, S., et al. (eds.) Computational Science and Its Applications – ICCSA 2019, pp. 291–307. Springer, Cham (2019). https://doi.org/10.1007/978-3-030-24311-1_21

36. Scorza, F., Fortunato, G., Carbone, R., Murgante, B., Pontrandolfi, P.: Increasing urban walkability through citizens' participation processes. Sustainability. **13**, 5835 (2021). https://doi.org/10.3390/su13115835

37. Carbone, R., et al.: Using open data and open tools in defining strategies for the enhancement of Basilicata region. In: LNCS (including subseries LNAI and LNB), pp. 725–733. Springer Verlag (2018). https://doi.org/10.1007/978-3-319-95174-4_55

38. Scorza, F., Gatto, R.V.: Identifying territorial values for tourism development: the case study of Calabrian Greek area. Sustainability **15**, 5501 (2023). https://doi.org/10.3390/SU15065501

39. Fortunato, G., Scorza, F., Murgante, B.: Hybrid Oriented Sustainable Urban Development: A Pattern of Low-Carbon Access to Schools in the City of Potenza. In: Gervasi, O., et al. (eds.) Springer, Cham (2020). https://doi.org/10.1007/978-3-030-58820-5_15

40. Scorza, F., Santopietro, L.: A systemic perspective for the Sustainable Energy and Climate Action Plan (SECAP). Eur. Plann. Stud., 1–21 (2021). https://doi.org/10.1080/09654313.2021.1954603

41. Santopietro, L., Scorza, F.: The Italian experience of the covenant of mayors: a territorial evaluation. Sustainability **13**, 1289 (2021). https://doi.org/10.3390/su13031289

42. Santopietro, L., Scorza, F., Murgante, B.: Multiple components in GHG stock of transport sector: technical improvements for SECAP baseline emissions inventory assessment. TeMA – J. Land Use, Mob. Environ. **15**, 5–24 (2022). https://doi.org/10.6092/1970-9870/8391

43. Manganelli, B., Morano, P., Tajani, F.: House prices and rents. the Italian experience. WSEAS Trans. Bus. Econ. **11**, 219–226 (2014)

44. Tajani, F., Morano, P.: Concession and lease or sale? A model for the enhancement of public properties in disuse or underutilized. WSEAS Trans. Bus. Econ. **11**, 787–800 (2014)

45. Tajani, F., Morano, P., Torre, C.M., Di Liddo, F.: An analysis of the influence of property tax on housing prices in the Apulia region (Italy). Buildings **7**, 1–15 (2017). https://doi.org/10.3390/buildings7030067
46. Manganelli, B., Morano, P., Tajani, F.: Risk assessment in estimating the capitalization rate. WSEAS Trans. Bus. Econ. **11**, 199–208 (2014)
47. Locurcio, M., Tajani, F., Morano, P., Anelli, D., Manganelli, B.: Credit risk management of property investments through multi-criteria indicators. Risks. **9**, 1–23 (2021). https://doi.org/10.3390/risks9060106

Performance Analysis and Science Mapping on High Performance Computing in the Era of Artificial Intelligence

Haruna Chiroma$^{(\boxtimes)}$

College of Computer Science and Engineering, University of Hafr Batin, Hafr Batin, Saudi Arabia
charuna@uhb.edu.sa

Abstract. The demand for high-performance computing (HPC) systems is increasing due to the growing need for large-scale computation and the rapid evolution of artificial intelligence. Previous bibliometric analyses on HPC are outdated, leaving the research community without an up-to-date investigation of the field. To bridge this gap and support the development of HPC while informing policymakers, this paper conducts a performance analysis and science mapping of HPC research. The study examines different aspects, including publication characteristics, research disciplines, trends, keyword co-occurrence, prolific authors, contributing countries, funding agencies, and document types. Findings indicate that researchers from the United States of America lead in HPC research. The Oak Ridge National Laboratory contributed the highest number of articles in the field of HPC. It is found that HPC research results are predominantly published in conferences. The top two leading funders of HPC research are from the United States of America. The United States of America play a pivotal role in linking different regions, facilitating cross-border research and innovation in HPC research. Mapping analysis shows that High-Performance Computing, Cloud Computing, Scientific Computing and Sparse Matrix-Vector Multiplication as frequent keywords highlights the core focus areas in HPC research. The article serves as a valuable resource for the research community, policymakers, funding agencies, industry professionals, and students seeking insights into the landscape of HPC research in this era of AI.

Keyword: Bibliometric Analysis · Co-Authorship · Collaborating Countries · High Performance Computing

1 Introduction

The world is currently experiencing an artificial intelligence (AI) boom, where AI technologies are penetrating almost every aspect of the society. Businesses and organizations are increasingly adopting AI to keep pace with current trends and remain competitive in the market.

AI technology requires high-cost computational power to achieve its target efficiency [1, 2]. Because of the AI highly ambitious nature, it relies on the support of

O. Gervasi et al. (Eds.): ICCSA 2025 Workshops, LNCS 15887, pp. 27–39, 2026.
https://doi.org/10.1007/978-3-031-97589-9_3

high-performance computing (HPC) paradigms [3]. The HPC capabilities go beyond conventional computers, which typically have a single or a few processors (fewer than 10) [4, 5]. HPC systems consist of hundreds of thousands or even millions of cores (e.g., CPUs and accelerators such as GPUs) designed for complex modeling, scientific computations, and climate simulations. More recently, HPC has been increasingly deployed for pre-training and inference of advanced AI models [6], such as ChatGPT. The demand for the HPC infrastructure is increasing as a result of fast evolution in AI technology. This development has led to the intersection of AI with HPC [7–9].

Bibliometric analysis, also known as Scientometric analysis, is conducted to gain insights into the landscape and structure of a research field [10, 11]. It has been applied in different areas of computing, such as modeling the built environment on HPC [12], Apache Hadoop research trends [13], HPC scalability and deep learning architecture [14], AI in the Internet of Medical Things [15], and metaheuristic algorithms [16]. These studies help track developments, identify key contributors, and reveal emerging trends in computing research.

A bibliometric analysis was conducted on the research progress in HPC, incorporating both performance analysis and science mapping to provide insights into the field [17]. However, this bibliometric analysis is now outdated, leaving the research community without an up-to-date investigation of HPC for over a decade. Recently, a bibliometric analysis on the intersection of quantum computing and HPC was conducted to provide an overview of current developments in this area and the correlation between the HPC and the quantum computing [18]. However, that study specifically focuses on the intersection between quantum computing and HPC, whereas the current study primarily focuses on the bibliometric analysis of HPC as a whole to provide an updated landscape of bibliometric analysis of HPC research to close the over 10 years gap.

The paper compares the publication trends of the top five sources of HPC research documents over a period of more than 10 years to understand the evolution of publication patterns in the era of AI. Secondly, it examines the publication behavior and collaboration patterns among countries and authors, as well as word co-occurrence to identify the core focus areas in HPC research. Thirdly, it investigates funding agencies, subject areas, and types of publications to understand HPC community priorities. Achieving these objectives provides valuable insights into publication trends and the overall landscape of HPC research.

The article is structured as follows: Sect. 2 presents the methodology, followed by the results and discussion in Sect. 3. Finally, Sect. 4 provides the concluding remarks.

The contributions to knowledge in summary are provided as follows:

- The study provides an updated bibliometric analysis of HPC research, addressing a 10-year gap in the field making it a valuable resource for researchers and policymakers.
- The study analyzes publication trends, keyword co-occurrence, and subject areas to identify core focus areas in HPC research.
- The study reveal that High-Performance Computing, Cloud Computing, Scientific Computing, and Sparse Matrix-Vector Multiplication are dominant themes, providing insights into the evolving landscape of HPC research.
- The study ranks the most prolific countries, institutions, and authors in HPC research.

- The study identifies four major co-authorship clusters, emphasizing international collaboration trends.
- The study finds that HPC research prioritizes rapid dissemination, favoring conferences for quick knowledge sharing and networking.

2 Methodology

This section present the bibliometric analysis procedure comprising of different stages including aim and scope, selection of technique, search term and data; lastly, data analysis and visualization (Fig. 1). The bibliometric procedure is adopted from Donthu et al. [19]. The detailed activities in each of the stage is discussed as follows:

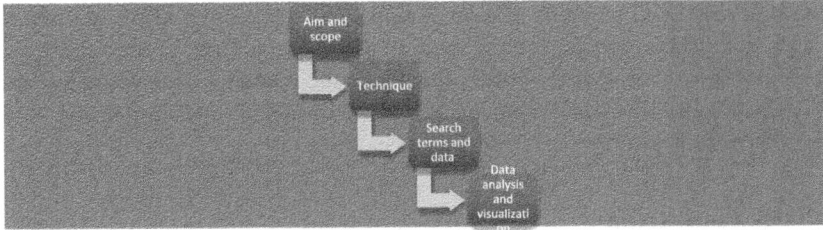

Fig. 1. Procedure for conducting bibliometric analysis

The aim of this study is to identify prolific authors, funders, institutions, countries, conferences, and journals in HPC research from the perspective of performance analysis. From a science mapping perspective, the study seeks to uncover the structural network of author-country collaborations, co-authorship relationships, and co-word occurrences, which contribute to the intellectual structure of HPC research. The scope of HPC research is extensive enough to justify both performance analysis and science mapping. The study aims to identify general themes, influential collaborating countries, and authorship collaborations within the period under study. To achieve this, co-word analysis, co-authorship analysis between countries, and co-authorship analysis between authors were adopted. Additionally, performance analysis was conducted by examining the total number of publications.

Keywords were formulated within the scope of the study defined at the first stage. Querying database requires keywords for effective retrieval of information about the HPC research publications. The curated search terms are as follows: *"SUPERCOMPUTERS" OR "HIGH AND PERFORMANCE AND COMPUTING" OR "PARALLEL AND COMPUTING" OR "CLUSTER AND SYSTEMS" OR "EXASCALE AND COMPUTING"*. The search terms were obtained from the literature. The academic database chosen for the data collection is Scopus database alone instead of multiple databases because of different data format and combining them can introduce error. Therefore, focusing on only Scopus eliminate the possibility of introducing error in the data. The data were collected from 2013 to 2024 limiting to English language. The results returned is 8,337 documents. The number of articles published within the study period exceeds

8,000, well above the 500-article benchmark considered sufficient for bibliometric analysis. The data was pre-processed by removing duplicates and unwanted field (e.g., DOI), reconciling discrepancies, ensure only valid affiliations were allowed and merged multiple entries. The data retrieved from the Scopus database was analysed using the analysis module of the Scopus. The analysed data based on the Scopus analysis module produce the performance analysis visualization for different components such as institutions, funders, subject area, authors, publication types, countries. On the other hand, the data was run to produce the intellectual structural networks.

3 Results and Discussion

This section presents the results obtained from the bibliometric analysis, including performance analysis and mapping. The analysis covers the sources of documents, subject areas, publication trends, prolific authors, prolific countries, prolific institutions, sponsors, and document types. On the other hand, the it includes co-authorship analysis between countries, co-authorship analysis between authors and word co-occurrence analysis between keywords.

3.1 Publications Trend

Figure 2 presents the publication trends in HPC from 2023 to 2024 for the top five sources with the highest document counts. From 2013 the publications trend start increasing for all the top five sources. While publication numbers have fluctuated over time, there was generally an increase followed by a decline, particularly starting in 2019 when all the top five sources experienced a sharp drop in output. The sharp drop in output from 2019 suggests that the field may be experiencing changes in research priorities, funding, or publication strategies.

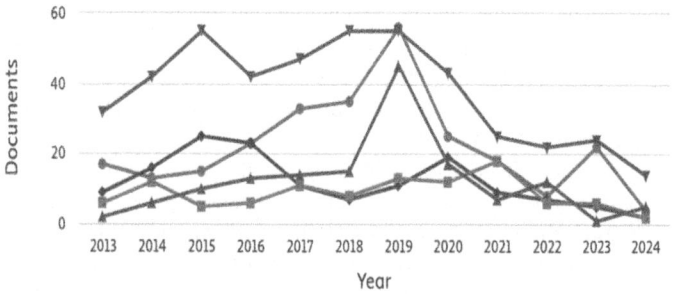

Fig. 2. Publications trend by source per year

This could reflect shifts in the HPC community or broader challenges in sustaining high publication volume. Lecture Notes in Computer Science (LNCS) and the ACM International Conference Proceedings (ACMICP) series occupied the first and second positions, respectively, in terms of publication output. The prominence of LNCS and ACMICP highlights their critical role as primary channels for disseminating HPC research.

3.2 Productivity by Country

Figure 3 depicts the ten most prolific countries publishing research on HPC. Researchers from the United States of America lead in HPC publications, contributing articles more than other countries. They are followed by China, which occupies a distant second position, emphasizing the significant role of the United States of America in HPC research.

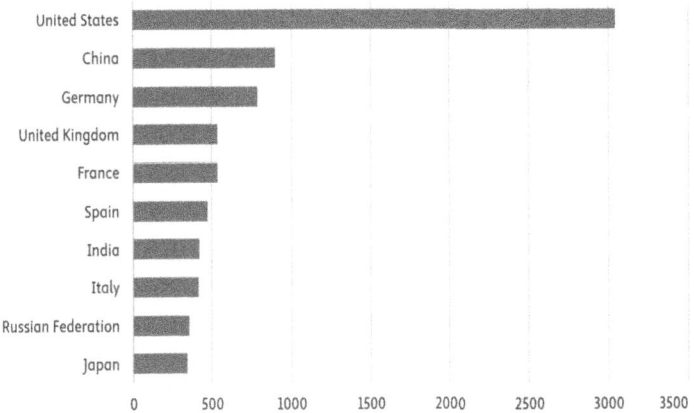

Fig. 3. High performance computing publication productivity by country

The United States of America leads HPC publications by a significant margin, indicating robust funding, research infrastructure, and strong international collaborations that position it as a global leader in HPC research. Although China ranks second, the large gap between its output and that of the United States of America suggests that while China is rapidly advancing, the United States of America maintains a substantial lead in HPC research activity. Figure 3 emphasizes that the United States of America plays a pivotal role in advancing HPC research worldwide, with China emerging as a key contributor, albeit with room to grow relative to the United States of America. A closer observation indicate that most of the countries on the chart are from Europe, emphasizing the strong presence of HPC researchers in that region.

3.3 Prolific Institutions

Figure 4 illustrate the 10 prolific institutions contributing research in the field of HPC. The illustration shows that the researchers from *Oak Ridge National Laboratory* contributed the highest number of articles followed by authors from *Argonne National Laboratory* and those from *Lawrence Berkeley National Laboratory* occupying the third position. Close observations indicate that most of the institutions are from United Sates of America.

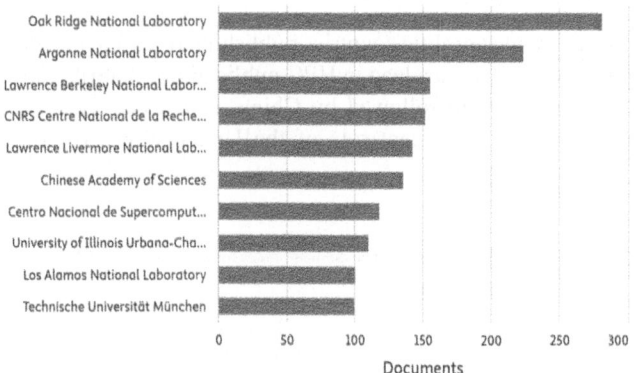

Fig. 4. Prolific institutions in high performance computing research

The trend illustrate the significant contributions of the authors from those institution in the field of HPC. This insight corroborate with the findings that indicate United States of America is the most prolific country in the area of HPC (Fig. 3). In the November 2024 TOP500 where the top-performing HPC system is El Capitan at *Lawrence Livermore National Laboratory*, United Sates of America. Other leading HPC systems include Frontier at *Oak Ridge National Laboratory*, United Sates of America; Aurora at *Argonne National Laboratory*, United Sates of America; and Jean Zay H100 at *CNRS Centre National de la Recherche Scientifique*, France.

3.4 Documents Type and Subject Area

Figure 5 presents HPC research output by document type. It highlights that HPC research results are predominantly published in conferences, followed by journals, with these two sources accounting for over 94% of all documents on HPC. This suggests that the HPC community prioritizes rapid communication and discussion of emerging findings, as conferences offer faster publication cycles and direct networking opportunities. It also implies that while journals remain important for in-depth research, other publication types play a minimal role in this fast-evolving field.

Figure 6 shows that HPC is a multidisciplinary research area that integrates different subject fields. However, a large portion of the research is dominated by Computer Science (41.3%) and Mathematics (16.7%), which occupy the first and second positions, respectively, followed by a third position in Engineering (16.3%). This distribution clearly confirms the multidisciplinary nature of HPC. HPC research spans different

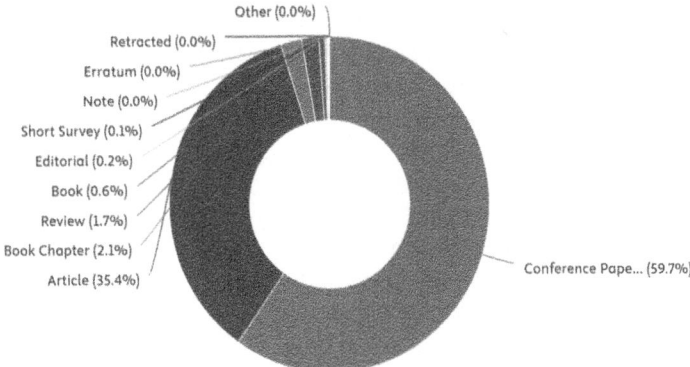

Fig. 5. High performance computing publications of documents by type

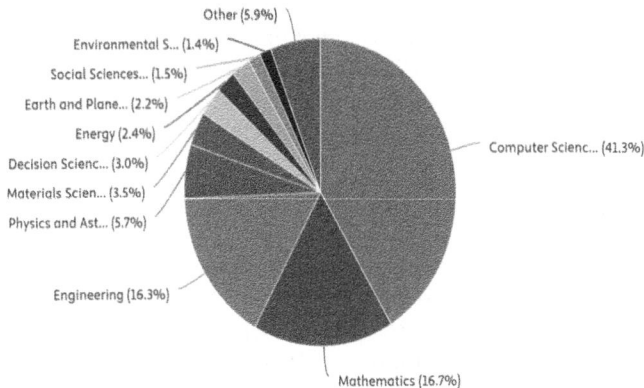

Fig. 6. High performance computing documents by subject area

fields, confirming that its development depends on the integration of multiple disciplines. With 41.3% of the research focused on computer science, it's clear that software development, algorithms, and computational methods are the primary drivers behind HPC systems. This emphasises the fact that regardless of hardware sophistication, effective HPC solutions fundamentally rely on robust computational frameworks. Mathematics, accounting for 16.7% of the research, highlights the essential role of quantitative analysis and theoretical foundations in advancing HPC capabilities. Engineering, making up 16.3%, plays a critical role in the design, implementation, and practical application of HPC systems, bridging the gap between theoretical research and real-world use.

3.5 Prolific Authors

Figure 7 highlights the top 10 prolific authors contributing the highest number of publications in the area of HPC. Chen, Y. is the researcher with the most publications, as indicated by the longest bar, followed by Dongarra, J. and Quintana-Orti, E.S. occupying the second and third positions respectively.

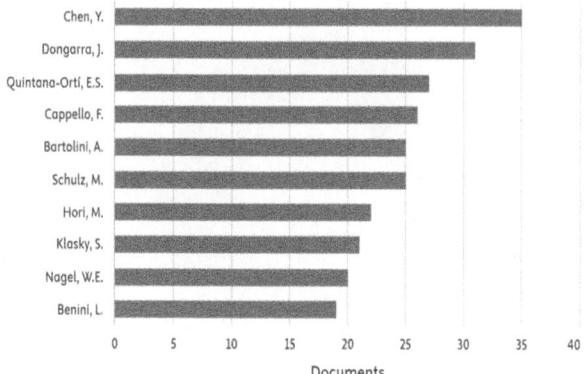

Fig. 7. High performance computing prolific authors by productivity

This suggests that these individuals are not only highly active in HPC research but may also be key influencers driving innovation and setting research trends in the field. Their substantial output indicates a deep engagement with HPC topics, which likely translates into significant impact on advancing HPC technologies and methodologies.

3.6 Funders

Figure 8 presents the top 10 funders of research in the field of HPC, ranked by the number of published documents. Notably, the National Science Foundation and the U.S. Department of Energy occupy the first and second positions, respectively. The leading funders are from the United States, Europe, and China, with the top two agencies located in the United States of America.

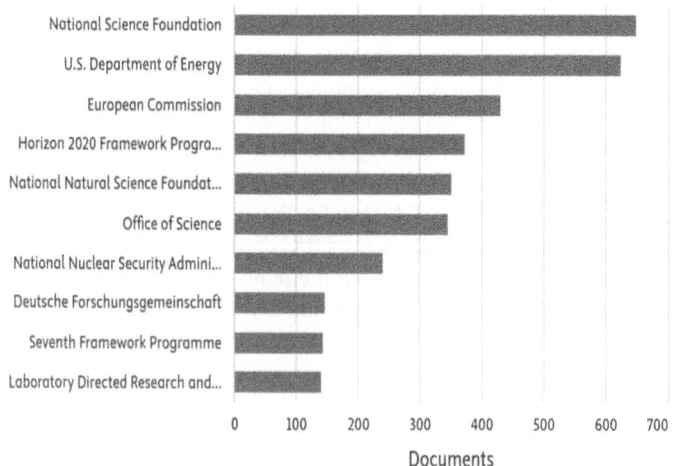

Fig. 8. Sponsors of high performance computing research

This indicates that the United States of America is a major driver of HPC research, benefiting from substantial governmental support that likely contributes to its leadership in the field. Additionally, the presence of top funders from Europe and China reflects a global commitment to HPC, although the U.S. funding agencies have a clear edge. This concentrated funding landscape highlights the strategic importance placed on HPC research, as robust financial support is essential for advancing HPC technologies and maintaining competitive research outputs on a global scale.

3.7 Country Co-authorship Analysis

Figure 9 presents the co-authorship network of HPC publications among authors from different countries. Each node represents a country, while the edges between nodes indicate co-authorship relationships. Thicker edges signify stronger collaboration between countries, and larger nodes represent a higher volume of authorship from that country. The network formed four major clusters: Cluster 1 is led by the United States of America; Cluster 2, by the United Kingdom; Cluster 3, by China; and Cluster 4, by Germany. There is strong collaboration between authors from the United States and China, between the United States and the United Kingdom, and between Germany and the United Kingdom, as indicated by the thick edges connecting these countries. Four major clusters have formed, led by the United States of America, UK, China, and Germany, indicating that while there are strong regional research bases, these countries serve as central hubs driving HPC research. The thick edges between the USA and China, as well as between the USA and the UK, suggest robust collaborative relationships.

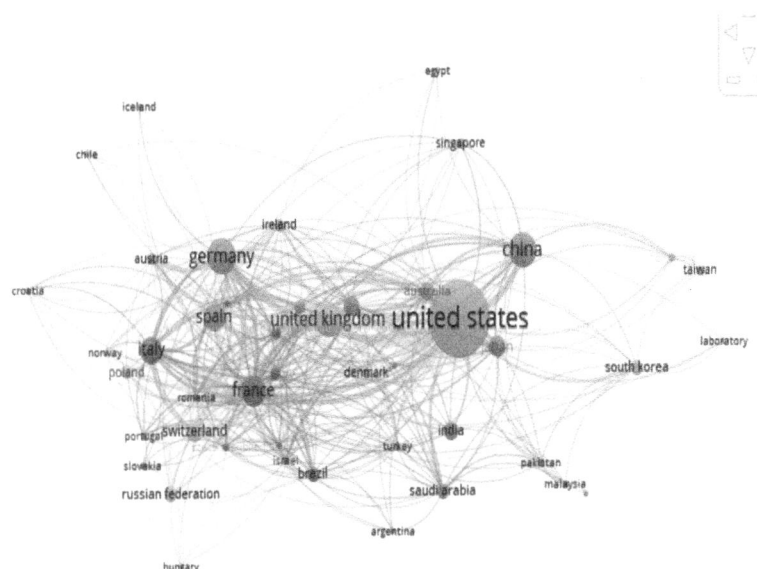

Fig. 9. Co-authorship analysis between countries

These connections highlight the pivotal role the USA plays in linking different regions, facilitating cross-border research and innovation in HPC research. The noticeable connection between Germany and the UK highlights active collaboration within Europe, contributing significantly to the HPC research landscape. Despite geopolitical differences, the strong collaborations especially between the USA and China indicate that scientific research in HPC transcends borders. This international cooperation is essential for pooling resources, sharing expertise, and advancing the field of HPC. In the November 2024 TOP500 list, out of the top 10 performing HPC systems globally, five are from the United States of America.

3.8   Author Co-authorship Analysis

Figure 10 presents the co-authorship collaborative network, illustrating the relationships among authors who publish research articles in the field of HPC. In this network, each node represents an author, and the connecting links indicate collaborations between authors. Thicker links denote stronger collaborative relationships, while larger nodes indicate a higher volume of publications by that author. The network forms five major clusters, each led by key authors: Cluster 1: Led by Dongarra, J.; Cluster 2: Led by Chen, Y., Cluster 3: Led by Wang, Y.; Cluster 4: Led by Yang, C.; Cluster 5: Led by Capello, F. and Liu, Y. These clusters highlight the emergence of central figures who play a pivotal role in fostering research collaboration in HPC.

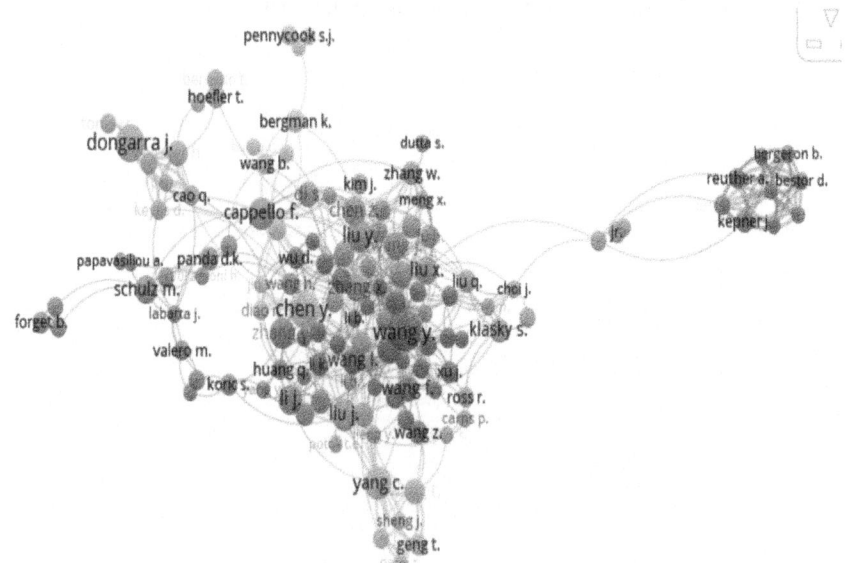

Fig. 10. Co-Authorship Analysis between authors

The thickness of the links indicates the intensity of collaboration among the authors. The network shows that these key authors not only publish frequently but also maintain strong, influential partnerships with their peers. The larger nodes for these key authors suggest a high publication output, which coupled with their extensive collaborative ties, highlights their significant impact on advancing HPC research. Their centrality in the network indicates that they are likely to influence research directions and innovation within the field of HPC.

3.9 Keywords Co-occurrence

Figure 11 depicts the co-occurrence network of keywords frequently appearing in HPC research articles published by multiple authors. In this network: Node represent keywords, with larger nodes indicating a higher frequency of keyword appearances across multiple publications. Links between nodes represent the co-occurrence of keywords, with thicker links signifying that the connected keywords frequently appear together in research articles.

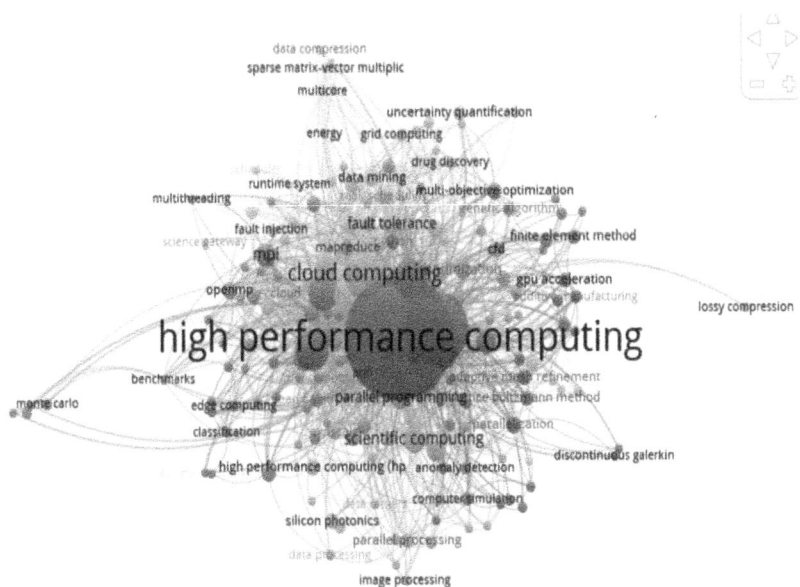

Fig. 11. Co-occurrence between authors keywords

The keywords identified from different clusters in the network include High-Performance Computing, Cloud Computing, Scientific Computing, and Sparse Matrix-Vector Multiplication. The presence of High-Performance Computing, Cloud Computing, and Scientific Computing as frequent keywords highlights the core focus areas in HPC research. The inclusion of Sparse Matrix-Vector Multiplication suggests a strong connection to numerical methods and computational efficiency, which are critical for optimizing HPC applications. The clustering of these keywords suggests interdisciplinary research, where HPC is frequently integrated with cloud computing and scientific computing methods. The larger nodes suggest that these keywords are dominant themes in HPC research, making them potential research hotspots.

4   Conclusions, Limitations and Future Research

The study present performance analysis and science mapping of HPC research for over 10 years period to uncover new pattern within the HPC research landscape. The study investigates funding agencies, subject areas, prolific countries, authors, institutions, publication behavior and collaborations. The study provides a comprehensive, data-driven assessment of the current state of HPC research in the era of AI. The area of HPC is dominated by USA. The study highlight the pivotal role of USA in linking different regions to facilitate cross-border research and innovation in HPC research. High-Performance Computing, Cloud Computing, Scientific Computing and Sparse Matrix-Vector Multiplication are found to be the core focus areas in HPC research. It is believed that this bibliometric study can offer valuable insights for researchers, funding agencies, and policymakers in HPC research decision-making process in this era of AI. These dimensions offer a holistic view of the field's dynamics, demonstrating how collaboration networks, funding mechanisms, and research agendas have evolved in response to the rapid evolving field of AI. However, the study is limited to data from the Scopus database, and the PRISMA guideline was not adopted, as the study primarily focuses on bibliometric analysis. Analyses such as h-index, m-index, g-index, i-index (e.g., i-10, i-100), single authorship analysis, proportion of cited publications, citations per cited publication, Bradford's law, academia–industry collaboration, and institutional collaborations were not included. It would be interesting for future studies to explore these comprehensive aspects in conjunction with in-depth state-of-the-art advances by adopting the PRISMA guideline using data from sources such as Web of Science, Scopus and the DBLP Computer Science Bibliography.

Disclosure of Interests.   "The author declare that there is no any conflict of interest".

References

1. Swain, S.R., Parashar, A., Singh, A.K., Lee, C.N.: An intelligent virtual machine allocation optimization model for energy-efficient and reliable cloud environment. J. Supercomput. **81**(1), 1–26 (2025)
2. Rrapaj, E., Bhalachandra, S., Zhao, Z., Austin, B., Nam, H.A., Wright, N.J.: Power consumption trends in supercomputers: a study of NERSC's Cori and Perlmutter Machines. In: ISC High Performance 2024 Research Paper Proceedings (39th International Conference), pp. 1–10. Prometeus GmbH (2024)
3. Ettifouri, I., Zbakh, M., Tadonki, C.: The need for HPC in AI solutions. In: International Conference of Cloud Computing Technologies and Applications, pp. 137–159. Springer, Cham (2024). https://doi.org/10.1007/978-3-031-78698-3_8
4. Shankar, S., Reuther, A.: Trends in energy estimates for computing in ai/machine learning accelerators, supercomputers, and compute-intensive applications. In: 2022 IEEE High Performance Extreme Computing Conference (HPEC), pp. 1–8. IEEE (2022)
5. Sterling, T., Brodowicz, M., Anderson, M.: High Performance Computing: Modern Systems and Practices. Morgan Kaufmann (2017)

6. Li, B., Basu Roy, R., Wang, D., Samsi, S., Gadepally, V., Tiwari, D.: Toward sustainable hpc: Carbon footprint estimation and environmental implications of hpc systems. In: Proceedings of the International Conference for High Performance Computing, Networking, Storage and Analysis, pp. 1–15 (2023)
7. Sarma, R., Inanc, E., Aach, M., Lintermann, A.: Parallel and scalable AI in HPC systems for CFD applications and beyond. Front. High Perform. Comput. **2**, 1444337 (2024)
8. An, W., et al.: Fire-Flyer AI-HPC: a cost-effective software-hardware co-design for deep learning. In: SC24: International Conference for High Performance Computing, Networking, Storage and Analysis, pp. 1–23. IEEE (2024)
9. Wulff, E., Girone, M., Pata, J.: Hyperparameter optimization of data-driven AI models on HPC systems. J. Phys. Conf. Ser. **2438**(1), 012092. IOP Publishing (2023)
10. Broadus, R.: Toward a definition of "bibliometrics." Scientometrics **12**(5–6), 373–379 (1987)
11. Pritchard, A.: Statistical bibliography or bibliometrics. J. Documen. **25**, 348 (1969)
12. Aghimien, E.I., Aghimien, L.M., Petinrin, O.O., Aghimien, D.O.: High-performance computing for computational modelling in built environment-related studies–a scientometric review. J. Eng. Des. Technol. **19**(5), 1138–1157 (2021)
13. Zhang, J., Lin, M.: A comprehensive bibliometric analysis of Apache Hadoop from 2008 to 2020. Int. J. Intell. Comput. Cybern. **16**(1), 99–120 (2023)
14. Gbedawo, W.V., Dzikunu, A., Nyamadi, M.: Scalability and efficiency of deep learning models on high-performance computing clusters: bibliometric analysis. African J. Appl. Res. **10**(2), 283–305 (2024)
15. Chiroma, H., Hashem, I.A.T., Maray, M.: Bibliometric analysis for artificial intelligence in the internet of medical things: mapping and performance analysis. Front. Artif. Intell. **7**, 1347815 (2024)
16. Ezugwu, A.E., et al.: Metaheuristics: a comprehensive overview and classification along with bibliometric analysis. Artif. Intell. Rev. **54**, 4237–4316 (2021)
17. Liu, Z., Liu, Y., Guo, Y., Wang, H.: Progress in global parallel computing research: a bibliometric approach. Scientometrics **95**, 967–983 (2013)
18. Garcia-Buendia, N., Muñoz-Montoro, A.J., Cortina, R., Maqueira-Marín, J.M., Moyano-Fuentes, J.: Mapping the landscape of quantum computing and high performance computing research over the last decade. IEEE Access (2024). https://doi.org/10.1109/ACCESS.2024.3411307
19. Donthu, N., Kumar, S., Mukherjee, D., Pandey, N., Lim, W.M.: How to conduct a bibliometric analysis: an overview and guidelines. J. Bus. Res. **133**, 285–296 (2021)

A Dismissed Train Line as a New Pillar for Sustainable Tourism Development in Corsica: "The Maquis Way" Strategy

Vincenza Pappalardi[1], Rafaele Nolè[1], Rachele Vanessa Gatto[2] (iD),
and Francesco Scorza[2](✉) (iD)

[1] DIUSS, University of Basilicata, Via Lanera, Matera, Italy
{vincenza.pappalardi,martina.dalessandro,francesca.lamico,
raffaele.nole}@studenti.unibas.it
[2] School of Engineering, University of Basilicata, Viale dell'Ateneo Lucano, Potenza, Italy
{rachelevanessa.gatto,francesco.scorza}@unibas.it

Abstract. Tourism represents an opportunity for boosting the development of marginalized, less populated areas. However, poor management of the tourism supply can lead to unbalanced territorial development. In recent years, Mediterranean islands have experienced an increase in tourist presence, due to global tourism trends and low-cost international travel. The case study of Corsica offers an opportunity to discuss the challenges faced by islands experiencing growing tourism pressure. Through the lens of the STESY model this research describe and analyze the island's tourism phenomena. The aim is to provide a comprehensive overview of tourism distribution across the territory, identify both critical issues and strengths, and support the design of context-specific, targeted strategies. The methodological framework combining open data and cluster analysis to identify local tourism Destination Areas. The design proposal "The Maquis Way", envisions the reuse of a dismissed railway as a cycling route to connect Corsica's eastern coast with inland areas, enhancing spatial and tourism connectivity. By positioning tourism as a core component of territorial planning, the study contributes to the debate on sustainable urban development and offers a decision-support framework aligned with the principles of the New Urban Agenda.

Keywords: New Urban Agenda · Sustainable development · Sustainable tourism ecosystem · STESY

1 Introduction

Mediterranean Islands represent major destinations for worldwide tourism due to a number unique values: landscape, nature, history and culture. To benefit of such generalized world tourism reputation becomes an extraordinary opportunity for socio-economic development but raising awareness on spatial sustainability suggests to compare such positive benefits with other the territorial issues, that in island areas are characterized by peculiar features [1–3].

© The Author(s), under exclusive license to Springer Nature Switzerland AG 2026
O. Gervasi et al. (Eds.): ICCSA 2025 Workshops, LNCS 15887, pp. 40–49, 2026.
https://doi.org/10.1007/978-3-031-97589-9_4

The debate on sustainable development strategies for sustainable tourism enhancement under the umbrella concept of regional development become more and more pressing due to the tourism boom in the post covid era. From the global perspective [4] to the operational level of key essays discussing various aspects of sustainable urban planning, land use, transportation, and ecological design [5]. Challenges and opportunities of sustainable urban development generally are positioned in the conflicts between economic growth, social equity, and environmental preservation in urban planning [6].

Current trends, more than standard rules, in policy recommendations are at the basis of key international institutional references and academic applications [7–10].

Tourism becomes a key sector for current debate in regional sustainability [11, 12] and it represents and horizontal domain of policy making and design implementation in a multiscale [13, 14] and multistakeholder perspective [15].

In the basis of those mainstream issues, in this research paper we refer to an application of the STESY model [16] in a specific case study: the Corsica. The island, famed for its rugged coastline and pristine beaches, draws tourists seeking natural beauty and beach tourism. Corsica attracts huge tourists flows annually even presenting a pure seasonality in trends. Overall, Corsica's tourism sector has demonstrated resilience, with a notable recovery in 2024 following the challenges posed by the pandemic and subsequent economic factors. In facts, Corsica's tourism industry has experienced significant fluctuations from the COVID-19 pandemic through 2024. In 2020, the COVID led to a sharp decline in tourism, with international visitors dropping from 30% to just 10% of total arrivals, while in 2022 Corsica saw a significant rebound, recording 3.4 million travelers distinguished in domestic and international tourists. In 2024 official data reported 9.9 million nights a relevant number posing sustainability issue of tourism phenomena in a region counting for 355.528 inhabitants (2024. The territorial tourism promotion is focused on the opportunities for relaxation and adventure that tourist can enjoy in the island enhanced by the unique stunning Mediterranean landscapes.

Beyond focusing on peculiar features of the case study area this work provide an experimentation of the STESY methodology in order to design a strategic framework for developing local tourism system on the ground of a robust analytical process oriented to identify local tourism Destination Areas. Open data and cluster analysis are applied in order to combine interpretative approach to quantitative design during studio lab developed with architectural university students at the University of Basilicata.

"Tourism as a territorial planning component" represents the disciplinary position of this paper, we aim at provide qualified decision support system in defining and support policy making territorial development process referring to the New Urban Agenda as a toolkit for better decision and better "context based" design [17–19].

The first section of the paper presents the research methodological framework and process. Then the case study area is described and the analytical approach is detailed. The proposed development strategy "The Maquis Way" integrating reuse of a dismissed train line for cycling as a new pillar for sustainable tourism development in Corsica, represents an option to improve the link among the Est-Cost of the island connecting coastal area with inner ones and promoting diagonalization in tourism supply. Discussions and conclusions section proposes main highlights of the research, limitations and future perspectives.

2 Background and Scope of the Research

The STESY model [16, 20] serves as a conceptual framework for analyzing and organizing knowledge related to specialized tourism phenomena, with a particular focus on spatial and territorial aspects. This taxonomy provides a structured system for classifying and managing information, supporting the analytical process from the initial phase of territorial classification to the development of strategic decision-making frameworks. The hierarchical approach of the model enables the classification of specialized tourism into three distinct levels: Specialized Tourism Ecosystem, Specialized Tourism System, and Specialized Destination Area (DAj). The latter represents the primary unit of analysis for describing the territorial tourism supply. A DAj does not necessarily correspond to traditional administrative boundaries but is instead defined by the spatial and functional organization of the local tourism system. Consequently, a DAj may encompass multiple municipalities or, conversely, multiple DAj may exist within a single municipal boundary. The conceptualization of DAj is formalized as follows:

Where:

- aj (Attractors) refers to physical points of interest (POIs), including officially recognized national and international tourist attractions (e.g., UNESCO sites, certified historic villages, Blue Flag locations, etc.).
- sj (Services) includes facilities within the tourism supply chain, such as accommodations and restaurants, each defined by specific locations and attributes.
- r (Reachability) represents the accessibility of the destination, encompassing the infrastructural and organizational system that allows visitors to reach the area via different modes of transportation (e.g., train stations, bus terminals, parking facilities).

A key aspect of the STESY model is the concept of tourism specialization (j), which categorizes a destination based on its predominant tourism type (e.g., cultural, gastronomic, nature-based tourism). This approach enables a detailed understanding of the relationships between functional sub-regions within a territory, facilitating the formulation of data-driven tourism development strategies. By applying this methodology to selected case studies, it is possible to construct a territorial network, enhancing the comprehension of spatial interconnections within the tourism system.

The research approach is based on the following phases (Fig. 1):

1. Analysis: Case study description through main tourism statistics, policies and analytics.
2. Application of STESY model: spatial data selection and classification, stakeholder identification, DA identification and benchmarking
3. Design: objectives identification, territorial scenario and design solutions, NUA compliance assessment.

The methodological framework is applied in Corsica case study highlighting issues and opportunities in tourism development strategy. The framework is structured in three different phases that start from the evaluation of tourism supply in given territories to support the design proposal in order to consider specific identity values of territories.

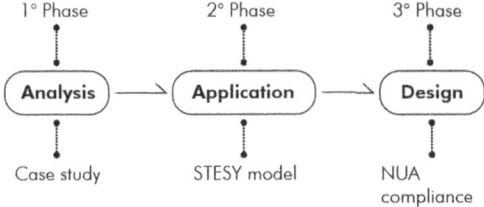

Fig. 1. Description of the methodological framework.

2.1 "Corsica": The Mediterranean Island

Tourism represents one of the main economic drivers of Corsica, a French island located in the Mediterranean Sea. Known for its natural beauty, beaches, mountainous landscapes, and rich cultural heritage, Corsica has developed a dynamic tourism sector that significantly contributes to the local GDP.

The annual occupancy of accommodation facilities highlights a preference for campsites, which record 4,457,055 presences, compared to 3,308,954 in hotels and 3,130,457 in other collective accommodation facilities (AHTC). This study suggests that tourists tend to favor camping over hotels (Fig. 2).

Regarding annual passenger traffic, both air and maritime traffic have shown a steady increase over time, correlating with the rise in tourist influx. Particularly, maritime transport has played a significant role in facilitating this growth.

An analysis of tourist activities reveals that the beach is the most popular choice (54.3%), followed by heritage-related activities (20.6%), cultural experiences (16.7%), and gastronomy (12.7%). This data confirms that Corsica is primarily a seaside destination, although cultural tourism remains significant.

The study also examines the preferred means of transport among tourists, with Uber being the most widely used (60.6%), followed by buses (17.4%), trains (4.3%), and other modes of transport (8.7%). This suggests that Corsica's public transport network is insufficient to meet demand.

Examining the monthly occupancy rates of accommodation facilities, there is a notable surge in demand during the summer months, peaking between June and August. This clearly indicates that tourism in Corsica is highly seasonal.

2.2 Application of STESY Model

The analysis of the territorial system and tourism offer of the Corsica island was conducted by dividing the elements into three main categories according to STESY model: Attractors, Services, Reachability.

From an initial survey of the elements identified within the study area, it emerges that the majority of attractors (54%) correspond to beaches. This indicates a predominance of seaside tourism over nature-based tourism attractions. The spatial distribution of the elements identified through the STESY taxonomy also reveals a continuous line of POIs along the waterfront near the beaches, while in the island's interior, they appear sparsely and unevenly distributed.

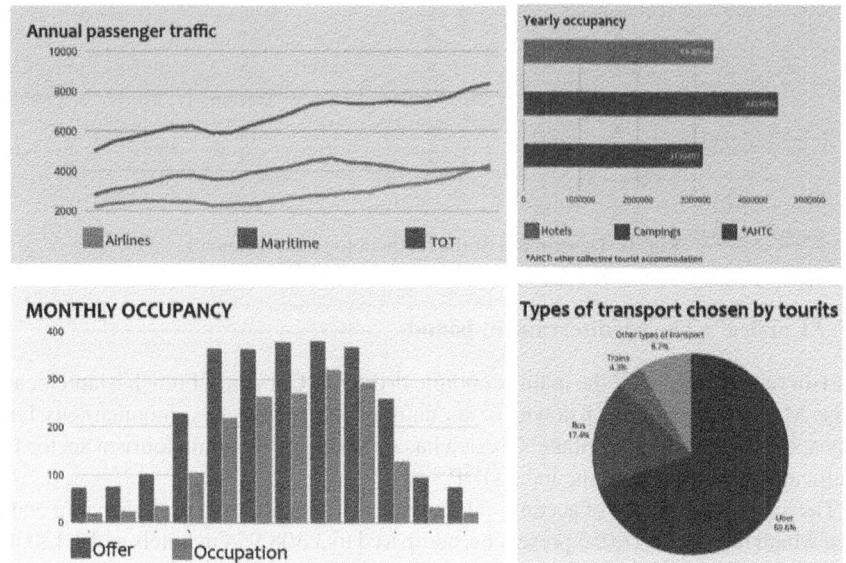

Fig. 2. Personal elaboration of data INSEE (Institut national de la statistique et des études économiques).

Using the GEODA software [21–23], a cluster analysis was conducted to identify the Destination Areas. The selected Destination Areas have a lower incidence of Reachability Points. These destinations, identified as "DA Aleira" and "DA Porto Vecchio," are subject to further thematic analytical study concerning coastal mobility.

As shown in the Fig. 3, investigations highlight a predominant use of cars as the main mode of transport. During the study on alternative mobility, it was found that along DA Aleira and DA Porto Vecchio, there is an abandoned railway line (Bastia-Porto Vecchio railway line) that was decommissioned during World War II after sustaining damage from bombings.

2.3 Design: The Maquis Way

The Maquis Way project was conceived to address the connectivity issues along Corsica's east coast. By transforming the decommissioning of the Bastia-Porto Vecchio railway line into a greenway, the project promotes sustainable mobility, encouraging the use of bicycles and pedestrian paths over traditional motor vehicles.

This initiative aligns with a broader vision of slow tourism, offering an alternative to beach tourism while fostering a deeper connection with the island's natural and cultural heritage.

Inspired by the principles of the New Urban Agenda (NUA), Maquis Way focuses on sustainable urban mobility, environmental resilience, and inclusive economic growth. The project includes various nature-based solutions (NBSs) to minimize its environmental impact and integrates eco-friendly transport solutions to reduce dependency on

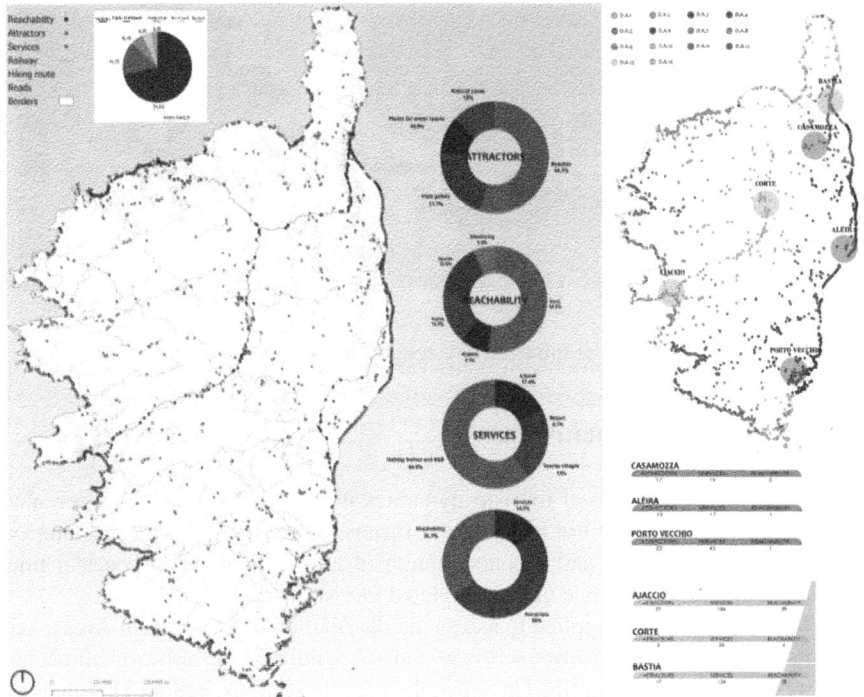

Fig. 3. Study area with Destination areas identification and evaluation.

cars. Along the route, travellers will find camping areas, picnic spots, and e-bike rental stations, strategically placed to enhance the overall experience.

The greenway is designed with different difficulty levels—ranging from flat and accessible sections to more challenging hilly and mountainous terrain—allowing visitors to choose routes based on their preferences and physical abilities. Travel time estimates vary depending on the means of transport: 32–34 h on foot, 6–7 h by bike, and 3 h by car.

Beyond its ecological and mobility benefits, the project is expected to have a significant economic impact, particularly in addressing the seasonality of tourism. Currently, Corsica experiences an influx of visitors during the summer, while winter tourism remains underdeveloped [24]. By creating an all-season attraction, Maquis Way is projected to increase local revenues, particularly benefiting businesses and communities along the route.

The name Maquis Way carries a dual significance. The term Maquis refers to Corsica's characteristic dense shrubland, but it also recalls the Maquisards, members of the French Resistance who sought refuge in the island's rugged landscapes during World War II. This historical connection is particularly relevant, as the railway itself was damaged by bombings and never restored. By repurposing it into a greenway, the project pays tribute to both Corsica's natural heritage and its legacy of resilience and independence (Figs. 4 and 5).

Fig. 4. Rail-infrastructure system and Project view.

3   Discussion and Conclusions

The study explores place-based tourism dynamics in Corsica. The analysis revealed a significant reliance on car use as the main means of transportation, a pronounced seasonality in tourist flows, and a concentration of attractors along the coastal line, largely linked to the prominence of beach-related tourism.

The STESY model was applied to assess the distribution of Destination Areas, and through its components—attractors, services, and accessibility—the territorial impact of tourism was quantitatively described in a spatially organized configuration. This analysis lays the groundwork for the formalization of targeted hard and soft measures structuring a sustainable development strategy [25, 26].

The results demonstrate that the proposed strategy positively contributes to a project vision aimed at enhancing the territory by requalify the disused railway line. Slow mobility is introduced as an alternative transportation system, alongside the promotion of nature-based experiential tourism as a form of supply diversification.

The proposal is inspired by the principles of the New Urban Agenda, fostering environmental identity and responsible tourism practices. The requalification of the abandoned railway track—equipped with camping areas, picnic spots, and bike rental services—caters to a model of tourism that balances the needs of both locals and visitors [27–31].

Furthermore, it strengthens DAj with lower accessibility Point of Interest (POI) density by introducing bicycle stations, and rebalances the regional tourism offer by enhancing hiking trails in response to the current dominance of beach-related attractors.

Limitation relies on data sources (mainly based on open data - Open Street Map - implemented in the STESY model [32–35]) and lack of local stakeholders' participation [10, 36] in the design phases in order to enhance the local validations of the proposal.

This study is part of the output developed within a university studio course during the academic semester program of architecture students at the University of Basilicata. Therefore, the character of the application is an academic proposal more than a real case study test. It reinforces a teaching objective oriented to test downscaling of the New Urban Agenda Principles on different topics and thematic area.

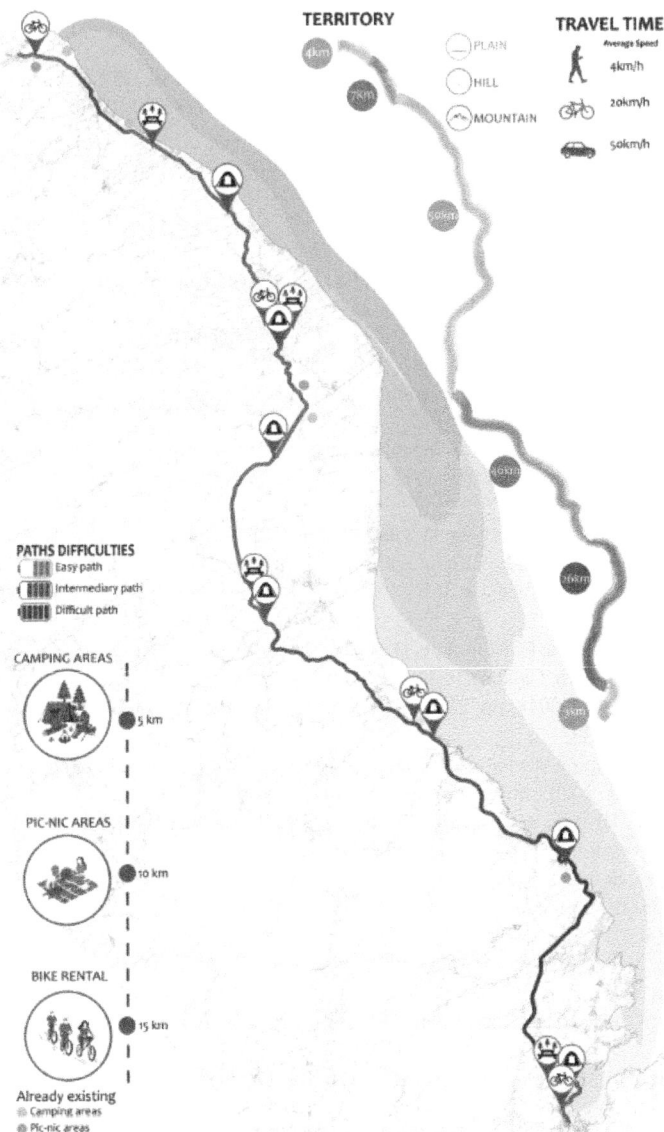

Fig. 5. Design: The Maquis Way.

Future research should explore advanced spatial analysis techniques and participatory approaches to refine the STESY model implementation [37] placing results in the framework of real decisions making processes for tourism policymaking in Corsica.

References

1. Wakil, M.A.: Bibliometric and visualised review of the knowledge domain of coastal tourism research. Sustain. Communit. **1**, 2360221 (2024). https://doi.org/10.1080/29931282.2024.2360221

2. Song, J., Chen, Y.: Optimizing cultural heritage tourism routes using Q-learning: a case study of Macau. Sustain. Communit. **2**, 2475794 (2025). https://doi.org/10.1080/29931282.2025.2475794

3. Arslan, E.N., Dişli, G.: Architectural heritage and traditional knowledge systems: insights from the ancient settlement of Kilistra, Türkiye#. Sustain. Communit. **2**, 2477145 (2025). https://doi.org/10.1080/29931282.2025.2477145

4. Verma, P., Raghubanshi, A.S.: Urban sustainability indicators: challenges and opportunities. Ecol. Indic. **93**, 282–291 (2018). https://doi.org/10.1016/J.ECOLIND.2018.05.007

5. Wheeler, S.M., Beatley, T.: The Sustainable Urban Development Reader, 3rd edn., pp. 1–631 (2014).

6. Campbell, S.: Green cities, growing cities, just cities? Urban planning and the contradictions of sustainable development. classic readings in urban planning, pp. 308–326 (2018). https://doi.org/10.4324/9781351179522-25

7. UN HABITAT: New urban agenda. United Nations (2016)

8. Caprotti, F., et al.: The new urban agenda: key opportunities and challenges for policy and practice. Urban Res. Pract. **10**, 367–378 (2017). https://doi.org/10.1080/17535069.2016.1275618

9. Las Casas, G., Scorza, F., Murgante, B.: New urban agenda and open challenges for urban and regional planning. In: Calabrò, F., Della Spina, L., and Bevilacqua, C. (eds.) New Metropolitan Perspectives. ISHT 2018, pp. 282–288. Springer, Cham (2019). https://doi.org/10.1007/978-3-319-92099-3_33

10. Scorza, F.: Training decision-makers: GEODESIGN Workshop Paving the Way for New Urban Agenda (2020). https://doi.org/10.1007/978-3-030-58811-3_22

11. Sharpley, R.: Host perceptions of tourism: a review of the research. Tour. Manag. **42**, 37–49 (2014). https://doi.org/10.1016/j.tourman.2013.10.007

12. Gatto, R.V., Scorza, F.: Tourism ecosystem domains. In: Gervasi, O. (ed.) Computational Science and Its Applications - ICCSA 2023. Springer (2023). https://doi.org/10.1007/978-3-031-37123-3_7

13. Batty, M., Milton, R.: A new framework for very large-scale urban modelling. Urban Stud. J. Limited **58**, 2021 (2021). https://doi.org/10.1177/0042098020982252

14. Batty, M.: On scale and size. Environ. Plan. B Urban Anal. City Sci. **47**, 359–362 (2020). https://doi.org/10.1177/2399808320910839

15. Bäckstrand, K.: Multi-stakeholder partnerships for sustainable development: Rethinking legitimacy, accountability and effectiveness. Eur. Environ. **16**, 290–306 (2006). https://doi.org/10.1002/eet.425

16. Gatto, R.V., Corrado, S., Scorza, F.: Taxonomy for specialized Tourism ecosystems : new geographies for sustainable territorial planning. Habitat Int. (2025)

17. Scorza, F., Fortunato, G.: Active mobility-oriented urban development: a morpho-syntactic scenario for a mid-sized town. Eur. Plann. Stud., 1–25 (2022). https://doi.org/10.1080/09654313.2022.2077094

18. Santopietro, L., Scorza, F.: Voluntary planning and city networks: a systematic bibliometric review addressing current issues for sustainable and climate-responsive planning. Sustainability **16** (2024). https://doi.org/10.3390/su16198655

19. Garau, C., Annunziata, A., Yamu, C.: A walkability assessment tool coupling multi-criteria analysis and space syntax: the case study of Iglesias, Italy. Eur. Plann. Stud., 1–23 (2020). https://doi.org/10.1080/09654313.2020.1761947

20. Scorza, F., Gatto, R.V.: Identifying territorial values for tourism development: the case study of Calabrian Greek area. Sustainability **15**, 5501 (2023). https://doi.org/10.3390/SU15065501
21. Anselin, L., Syabri, I., Kho, Y.: GeoDa: an introduction to spatial data analysis. Geogr. Anal. **38**, 5–22 (2006). https://doi.org/10.1111/j.0016-7363.2005.00671.x
22. Anselin, L., Syabri, I., Kho, Y.: GeoDa: an introduction to spatial data analysis. In: Fischer, M., Getis, A. (eds.) Handbook of Applied Spatial Analysis: Software Tools, Methods and Applications, pp. 73–89. Springer, Heidelberg (2010). https://doi.org/10.1007/978-3-642-036 47-7_5
23. Anselin, L., Li, X., Koschinsky, J.: GeoDa, from the desktop to an ecosystem for exploring spatial data. Geogr Anal. **54**, 439–466 (2022). https://doi.org/10.1111/gean.12311
24. Huda, S.S.M.S.: Potential of neighborhood tourism in new normal: a research agenda. Sustain. Communit. **1**, 2371578 (2024). https://doi.org/10.1080/29931282.2024.2371578
25. Te Brömmelstroet, M., et al.: Have a good trip! expanding our concepts of the quality of everyday travelling with flow theory. Appl. Mobilities **7**, 352–373 (2022). https://doi.org/10.1080/23800127.2021.1912947
26. Papa, E., Bertolini, L.: Accessibility and transit-oriented development in European metropolitan areas. J. Transp. Geogr. **47**, 70–83 (2015). https://doi.org/10.1016/j.jtrangeo.2015.07.003
27. Manganelli, B., Morano, P., Tajani, F.: House prices and rents. The Italian experience. WSEAS Trans. Bus. Econ. **11**, 219–226 (2014)
28. Tajani, F., Morano, P.: Concession and lease or sale? A model for the enhancement of public properties in disuse or underutilized. WSEAS Trans. Bus. Econ. **11**, 787–800 (2014)
29. Tajani, F., Morano, P., Torre, C.M., Di Liddo, F.: An analysis of the influence of property tax on housing prices in the Apulia region (Italy). Buildings **7**, 1–15 (2017). https://doi.org/10.3390/buildings7030067
30. Manganelli, B., Morano, P., Tajani, F.: Risk assessment in estimating the capitalization rate. WSEAS Trans. Bus. Econ. **11**, 199–208 (2014)
31. Locurcio, M., Tajani, F., Morano, P., Anelli, D., Manganelli, B.: Credit risk management of property investments through multi-criteria indicators. Risks. **9**, 1–23 (2021). https://doi.org/10.3390/risks9060106
32. Corrado, S., Scorza, F.: Machine learning based approach to assess territorial marginality. In: Gervasi, O., Murgante, B., Hendrix, E.M.T., Taniar, D., Apduhan, B.O. (eds.) (including subseries Lecture Notes in Artificial Intelligence and Lecture Notes in Bioinformatics), vol. 13376, pp. 292–302 (2022). https://doi.org/10.1007/978-3-031-10450-3_25/COVER
33. Zoppi, C., Lai, S.: Assessment of the regional Landscape Plan of Sardinia (Italy): a participatory-action-research case study type. Land Use Policy **27**, 690–705 (2010)
34. Isola, F., Leone, F., Zoppi, C.: Mapping of ecological corridors as connections between protected areas: a study concerning Sardinia, Italy. Sustainability **14**, 6588 (2022). https://doi.org/10.3390/SU14116588
35. Scorza, F., Santopietro, L., Corrado, S., Dastoli, P.S., Santarsiero, V., Gatto, R., Murgante, B.: Training for Territorial Sustainable Development Design in Basilicata Remote Areas: GEODESIGN Workshop. In: Gervasi, O., Murgante, B., Misra, S., Rocha, A.M.A.C., Garau, C. (eds.) LNCS (including subseries Lecture Notes in Artificial Intelligence and Lecture Notes in Bioinformatics), vol. 13379, pp. 242–252 (2022). https://doi.org/10.1007/978-3-031-10545-6_17/COVER
36. Steinitz, C., Orland, B., Fisher, T., Campagna, M.: Geodesign to address global change. Intell. Environ., 193–242 (2023). https://doi.org/10.1016/B978-0-12-820247-0.00016-3
37. Gatto, R.V., Corrado, S., Scorza, F.: Towards a definition of tourism ecosystem. In: 18th International Forum on Knowledge Asset Dynamics (IFKAD) - MANAGING KNOWLEDGE FOR SUSTAINABILITY (2023)

Advancements in Spatial Assessment of Socio-Ecological SystemS (AS- SESS 2025)

Planning for Environmental Justice.
A Multi-methodological Approach

Marta Dell'Ovo[1,3] , Silvia Ronchi[1,3(✉)] , Irene Regaiolo[2,3] ,
Andrea De Toni[1,3] , Riccardo Alba[2,3] , Enrico Caprio[2,3] , Francesca Cochis[2,3] ,
and Daniel Edward Chamberlain[2,3]

[1] Department of Architecture and Urban Studies (DAStU), Politecnico di Milano,
20133 Milan, Italy
silvia.ronchi@polimi.it
[2] Department of Life Sciences and Systems Biology, Università di Torino, 10123 Turin, Italy
[3] NBFC—National Biodiversity Future Center, 90133 Palermo, Italy

Abstract. Urbanization is rapidly transforming natural landscapes, intensifying socio-environmental inequalities, and creating disparities in both the provision of ecosystem services (ES) and urban biodiversity. This paper suggests a multidisciplinary and multi-methodological approach to evaluate urban biodiversity, ES supply, and socioeconomic vulnerability to examine environmental justice. Based on the "Luxury Effect" hypothesis, which supposes a positive association between wealth and biodiversity in urban environments, the paper investigates the relationship between differences in urban nature and more general trends in social inequality. Biodiversity and green infrastructure may significantly improve urban quality of life, but the benefits are often unequally distributed, being wealthy communities usually favored more than others.

To bridge the gap between theory and practice, the study suggests a new framework integrating quantitative and qualitative data, like biodiversity surveys with geographical and multicriteria decision analysis (MCDA). The methodology will be tested and validated in four Italian cities - Milan, Rome, Turin, and Naples - each reflecting distinct ecological, social, and economic situations. Our technique identifies regional patterns of inequality and prioritizes areas for policy intervention by overlaying biodiversity and ES data over socioeconomic characteristics. This integrated paradigm advances theoretical discussions on environmental justice and encourages the development of more inclusive, data-driven urban planning methods. The approach is still in the validation phase but shows strong potential for scalability and adaptability across diverse urban contexts. Ultimately, the study aims to inform sustainable planning practices that ensure a fairer distribution of environmental benefits, enhancing cities' ecological resilience and social well-being.

Keywords: Ecosystem Services · Socio-economic analysis · Biodiversity

O. Gervasi et al. (Eds.): ICCSA 2025 Workshops, LNCS 15887, pp. 53–66, 2026.
https://doi.org/10.1007/978-3-031-97589-9_5

1 Introduction

The urbanization rate is drastically increasing worldwide, and its impacts are driving many environmental changes at multiple scales, leading to land cover modifications, climate change, pollution levels and biogeochemical cycle alterations, and loss of bio-diversity [1, 2]. In the last decades, people worldwide have increasingly concentrated in urban areas, with European cities well above the global rate of urbanization, making the equitable distribution of urban nature an urgent issue. Indeed, 68% of the world's population is projected to live in urban areas by 2050, and Europe's urbanization rate is expected to rise to 84% [3]. Expanding the built-up coverage to host urban dwellers and their activities is thus inevitable. The significant implications of people's overconcen-tration in cities are widely known undesirable side-effects such as congestion, pollution, and deterioration of people's quality of life [4, 5] since people in urban areas with low experiences of nature tend to have worse mental and physical health [6, 7]. Exposure to nature and related ecosystem services reduces the risk of poor mental health, car-diovascular disease mortality [8], healing times [9], respiratory illness, and allergies if green spaces in urban environments are properly planned [10], among others. Although people are persuaded to increase their health and well-being, they face environmental injustices in most of the largest cities, particularly concerning the inequality in urban green provision and related benefits [11]. Environmental injustice is described as the unfair distribution of environmental benefits across different social groups. The term originally related to the condition of unequal exposure of marginalized communities to environmental hazards [12, 13]; the concept has since evolved to encompass access to environmental goods, such as green spaces and related services, in contemporary urban contexts [14]. Environmental injustice has clear repercussions on contemporary urban planning patterns, with consequences such as environmental gentrification and social exclusion [15]. In most of the largest cities, the environmental injustice is strictly related to the socio-economic status [16, 17], giving rise to what is known as the Luxury Effect. The term Luxury Effect has been coined to describe a specific inequality in the urban green provision, thus an environmental injustice, hypothesizing a positive relationship between wealth and biodiversity in urban areas [18, 19].

On the one hand, socio-economic factors can influence the presence of urban biodi-versity, affecting a wide range of taxonomic groups (e.g. plants, birds, insects) [18–21]. Indeed, recent research has found a positive association between household income and plant diversity in various U.S. cities [18], and similarly, a study in the mid-sized European city of Vitoria-Gasteiz showed that neighborhoods with higher educational attainment, a proxy for socio-economic status, also had greater tree and bird species richness, thus empirically confirming the Luxury Effect [17]. On the other hand, the Luxury Effect needs to be further investigated since there is currently no consensus on the issue; it may depend on specific contexts rather than being a universal concept [22]. Indeed, the Luxury Effect is present in multiple geographies and for multiple taxa, including birds [18, 19, 21, 23]. For example, there is evidence that socio-economic factors, such as income level, are significantly positively correlated with birds' species richness [19] and abundance [24]. Birds can deliver different Ecosystem Services (ES); however, there is a paucity of literature explicitly measuring ES about the presence of species in the heterogeneous urban landscape [25].

Cities are crucial places to understand these fundamental changing processes, and where ecologists and urban planners should work together to develop policies and strategies to ensure a better urban life while maximizing biodiversity and urban ecosystem functions [1, 26]. Guaranteeing urban sustainable development is key to addressing Goal 11 of the Sustainable Development Agenda [27] and can contribute to tackling the global environmental crisis we face.

To bridge this knowledge gap, our study investigates how socio-economic disparities affect urban biodiversity, particularly birds, and access to ES where wealthy neighborhoods experience greater biodiversity and green space benefits, ultimately informing sustainable planning practices and ensuring environmental justice.

2   State of the Art

The introduction clearly shows the crucial role of green spaces in impacting life quality and environmental equity. However, their unequal distribution negatively affects the most disadvantaged segments of the population and exacerbates the existing gap. Considering the main important concepts previously stated, such as biodiversity, Ecosystem Services (ES), and socio-economic assessment, within this section, the most used methodologies for their analysis will be explored by considering the focus of the research and the spatial analysis. Within this context, urban green spaces refer to public or semi-public accessible vegetated areas in an urban context that provide a range of ES, combating many urban ills. These areas - i.e., parks, forests, tree-lined streets, green corridors, riverbanks, urban agriculture, community gardens - are diverse, varying in size, vegetation cover, species richness, and environmental quality [28, 29].

2.1   Assessing Biodiversity

Biodiversity is essential to promote ecosystem functioning [30] in urban areas, and its monitoring allows us to understand how ecological communities react to anthropogenic pressures [31]. In a world that is experiencing a progressive loss of human-nature interactions ('extinction of experience,' [32]), cities can offer opportunities for urban dwellers to stay connected with nature, and the numerous interactions occurring in urban areas, even if with nonnative or pest species, can be crucial for biodiversity conservation worldwide [33]. Understanding how to manage urban biodiversity is relevant to ensure positive cascade effects on the ecosystem functioning and maximizing associated ES [31].

Sampling methods used to assess biodiversity can vary depending on the objectives of the assessment, the target taxa, and the study area. Biodiversity experts perform surveys to collect data on species, communities, or habitats in a defined amount of space and time. Surveys can provide a snapshot of environmental and biological features occurring in the study area. Importantly, they can allow the investigation of species diversity and abundance – i.e., the presence/absence of a species, how many species (and individuals per species) are present – and their spatial distribution [34]. Direct observation or passive sampling methods can be used to collect data on biodiversity. Standard animal sampling designs, primarily employed also in urban contexts [31], can involve the collection of data through, for example, point counts (e.g., very common in bird studies [35]) and Pollard's transects (e.g., defined for butterfly studies, [36, 37] whereas circular or round plots can be used to survey vegetation. Standard methods can include, but are not limited to, (i) physical traps (e.g., pan traps, pitfall traps) and nets (to capture the specimen directly, e.g., amphibians, mammals, reptiles, invertebrates like bees, butterflies, ants, or spiders), (ii) passive acoustic recorders (e.g., for bats, birds, amphibians) and camera traps (e.g., for mammals), (iii) opportunistic data collection through Citizen Science programs [31]. The precise area to conduct the survey (e.g., point count, plot) or to locate the trap (e.g., camera trap) can be selected randomly or by following a grid/transect disposition. The development of citizen science programs is increasing worldwide, especially for taxa like birds and butterflies, and they are also known to improve public engagement with nature and increase the availability of data valuable to understand the dynamics of urban biodiversity [38]. Furthermore, museum collections and atlas data can contribute to biodiversity assessment [31]. All these methodologies should be adapted to the objectives of the evaluation.

2.2   Assessing Ecosystem Services Provision

ES have garnered significant attention across various fields in recent years, being applied in stakeholder awareness decision-making processes for planning, policy design, and sustainable development [39]. ES are the subject of numerous steering documents and guidelines for international organizations (e.g., the United Nations Environment Programme (UNEP), the International Union for Conservation of Nature (IUCN), and the Intergovernmental Science-Policy Platform on Biodiversity and Ecosystem Services (IPBES). They also represent the topic of a growing number of scientific studies that have explored the possibilities of implementing an ES-based strategy, emphasizing their crucial role in supporting decision-makers (among the many: [40–42] ES are widely considered an effective tool for identifying and communicating the benefits and values of nature related to human health and well-being, particularly in urban areas [43]. Climate change is a major contributor to global greenhouse gas (GHG) atmospheric emissions and disproportionately affects metropolitan areas. [44, 45]. Cities are particularly vulnerable to climate change, including urban heat islands, floods, and biodiversity loss, which endanger people's health and well-being, highlighting the need for more progressive urban planning. Within this context, urban green spaces play a critical role in enhancing the provision of ES and climate change adaptation, including urban stormwater regulation, carbon sequestration, urban cooling capacity, air purification, and habitat preservation. These ES are all strictly connected to several human benefits, such as recreational opportunities and social cohesion.

Ensuring the availability and accessibility of nature in cities is a matter of environmental sustainability and a priority of public health and social equity, especially in the climate change era.

Generally, citizens who are vulnerable to socio-economic aspects are often the most at risk from environmental hazards [46] and receive the least amount of assistance from ES providers and Green and Blue Infrastructure (GBI) [47]. The unequal distribution of ES in cities worsens social inequality by making it harder for marginalized groups to adapt to environmental stresses. ES assessment is a valuable tool for advancing environmental equality as it has the potential to shed light on the distribution of these advantages, supporting strategies that aim to equal and inclusive ES provision and access for all socioeconomic groups. Thus, one of the most essential methodological strategies for closing the gap between ecological information, planning, and policy is mapping and evaluating ES [48, 49].

Understanding the spatial distribution of ES is critical for assessing the multifunctional roles that natural and semi-natural areas play within cities, as well as analyzing how various segments of the urban population have access to environmental benefits. Some discrepancies, such as those in the quantity and quality of green areas in urban neighborhoods and the recreational and social possibilities available, can be identified by comparing variations in the ES distribution. Patterns of disparity in the benefit of areas with high ES capacity are revealed using ES spatial modelling.

2.3   Assessing the Socio-Economic Dimension

Socio-economic studies play a key role in analyzing urban inequalities and supporting research on the distribution of green spaces, accessibility to services, and environmental impacts on the population. By integrating geospatial methodologies with statistical and economic approaches, these studies make it possible to identify the most vulnerable areas and develop more inclusive urban planning strategies. In detail, this analysis could be created by applying the quantitative and qualitative methodology to reveal whether low-income neighborhoods have fewer green spaces or whether these are of lower quality, whether there are barriers to access for specific categories of users, and whether urban sprawl is occurring sustainably or exacerbating inequalities [50].

Assessing how urban green space affects health, well-being, and economic development is relevant, and it is evident that there is a correlation between high levels of pollution, the heat island effect, and worsening mental health. From an economic perspective, green areas affect property's market value by generating phenomena such as gentrification [51]. Given the complexity of the problem and the territorial distribution of the criteria, a spatial multicriteria analysis is suggested to consider conflictual values and visually represent the analysis. Geographic Information System software allows us to map inequalities, identifying areas with less green space or more pollution [52]. At the same time, statistical analysis and econometric models, such as multiple regressions and spatial models, are used to correlate socio-economic variables with environmental factors [53, 54].

In contrast, logistic regression models predict the probability that a given population uses green spaces (or does not) [55]. An interesting aspect of [56] is the gap between the perception of environmental benefits and their usability. In addition, some studies adopt economic valuation models to estimate the value of green spaces [57] by combining financial and environmental data to measure the value of urban green space by applying Willingness to Pay (WTP) as a methodology to measure how much people would be willing to pay for environmental improvements [58]. Other approaches, which could be more qualitative and participatory, use interviews, surveys, and focus groups to collect data on perceptions of green spaces and the experiences of different communities [56]. Among the criteria to analyze for socio-economic studies, it is possible to mention the average income of the population [59, 60], gender inequality [60], education level, and environmental awareness [56].

2.4 Gaps in the Studies Analyzed

Despite the existing studies and the high interest in this topic, the integration between different disciplines and fields of research described above deserves to be explored in more depth. A limited combination of qualitative and quantitative data emerges from the literature analyzed. [61] apply a technical approach that does not consider the social value provided by green spaces and does not measure the perception of users. [57] is intensely focused on economic evaluation but lacks a strong socio-spatial component. Another criticality is the selection of case studies, mainly big cities, where the problem of green distribution is most apparent. Still, they neglect suburbs and small towns, where green might be there but poorly managed or inaccessible [56].

To overcome these gaps, developing more integrated studies with an approach that combines spatial, economic, and social analyses is essential, as well as adopting participatory methodologies and long-term studies. This can guide decision-makers in making more conscious and sustainable decisions, which can help mitigate the Luxury Effect and foster environmental justice.

3 Methodological Approach Proposal

Considering the critical issues raised in the previous section, an integrated approach involving public agencies, academics, and civil society is essential. This will ensure that urban planning considers economic efficiency, social inclusion, and environmental sustainability. Given this premise, the paper proposes a multi-methodological approach based on the main features of biodiversity, ES, and socio-economic assessment, combining their strengths to obtain an interdisciplinary approach (Fig. 1). Within this context, the theoretical part will be presented, while the future development of the research will consider its application.

Spatial visualization and analysis are the starting point of the methodological proposal since they are fundamental in identifying urban disparities and developing more sustainable and inclusive urban planning strategies. Given the complexity of the problem to be addressed and the sometimes-conflictual values to be considered [62, 63], a Multi-criteria Decision Analysis (MCDA) is the most consistent approach to be applied. It can collect both qualitative and quantitative data to manage different needs and expectations elicited by various stakeholders, and to provide guidelines and suggestions to aid the decision [64]. Each discipline involved deserves to be investigated with coherent criteria and spatially visualized to understand the correlation with the Luxury Effect. Regarding the socio-economic dimension, given the objective of replicating the methodology in different Italian cities, indicators have been selected considering their availability at the national scale since the project is part of the National Biodiversity Future Center. Considering studies already developed on this topic [17, 20, 65, 66], it has been selected a consistent set of criteria consisting of the evaluation of i) the market value of residential buildings, ii) the income of the population, iii) the age, and precisely the percentage of elderly people (>65 years old), and iv) the level of education. The aggregation of that data allows us to obtain a representative index of the socio-economic condition of citizens. At the same time, for the analysis of the ES provision, it is strategic to analyze aspects that support the comprehension of the quality of the green spaces, not only given by their presence [67]. Crucial and robust indicators are: i) carbon storage, estimating the current amount of carbon stored; ii) habitat quality, estimating the distribution of habitat and vegetation types across a landscape and assessing their level of degradation; iii) urban cooling, estimating the index of heat mitigation, and iv) urban stormwater retention, estimating the runoff retention, and groundwater recharge. Given the high synergies among those criteria, performing a principal component analysis to reduce strongly correlated data could be strategic before the aggregation in a final quality index [68].

This preliminary analysis and its spatial visualization, supported by bivariate analysis, allow the combination of these two disciplines, Social and Economic studies, and Urban planning, to understand where policies for green area improvement should be concentrated to distribute the natural capital and its benefits equally. Within this context, the contribution of biodiversity is missing, which is essential to analyze the Luxury Effect. The approach proposes the integration of a third layer consisting of data on bird species richness collected through point counts. Overlapping this additional information will allow us to understand if the wealthiest areas, and with a more significant provision of ES, are related to higher biodiversity. In this context, evidence and research are as strategic as urgent to support policies, better management practices, and strategies towards environmental justice. This objective can be achieved only by considering the perception of residents and policymakers about the benefits provided by natural capital. In addition to collecting quantitative data, the methodology proposes the support of surveys to assess a more qualitative dimension, eliciting the intangible values of users to understand whether there is adequate equity in the use of green areas.

Spatial mapping of ES through MCDA approaches represents a strategic methodological innovation to address the complexity and multidimensionality of urban planning challenges. This combination allows for the spatial prioritization of interventions by balancing ecological, social, and economic criteria, and can support deliberative processes by defining trade-offs and synergies. The contribution raises attention on how to operationalize environmental justice and equity through data-informed, spatially explicit planning strategies.

By integrating these elements, the methodology can provide a comprehensive, multidimensional analysis of cities and urban areas from the perspective of green gentrification and the Luxury Effect to inform practical policy recommendations. The method proposed is still under review and needs additional tests to be validated, especially the analysis and integration of tangible and intangible values. Still, it is promising, given the support of robust methodologies applied in different disciplines and combined comprehensively.

4   How to Validate and Test the Methodological Approach

Although the concept of ES has improved our knowledge of the connections between ecological processes and human well-being, its use in assessments focused on environmental justice is still in its infancy [69–71]. By combining biodiversity, ES, and socioeconomic data, this approach has the potential to go beyond traditional environmental justice analyses, which are frequently only concerned with the distribution of environmental harms. This triple articulation makes it possible to comprehend how patterns of environmental

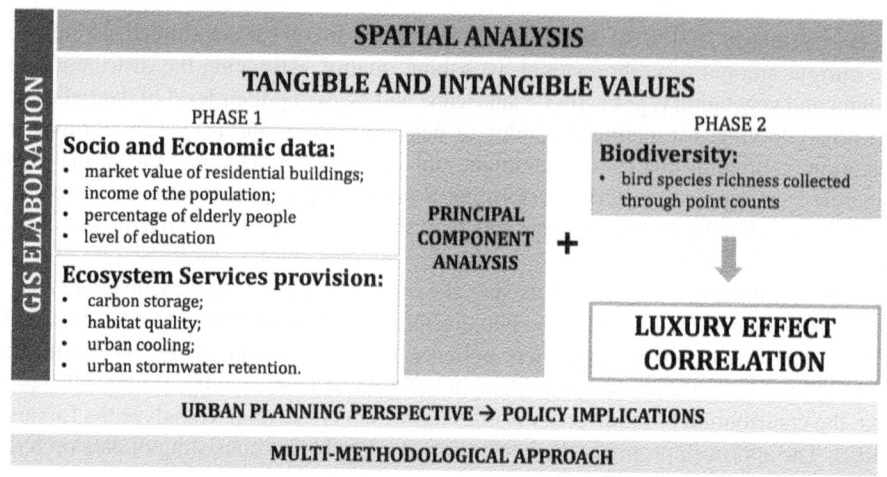

Fig. 1. Scheme of the approach proposed.

injustice are created or perpetuated by the interaction of ecological degradation, service delivery, and socio-economic vulnerability. In addition to strengthening our conceptual understanding of environmental inequality, this method offers a stronger foundation for creating just and long-lasting policy solutions.

Nevertheless, empirical research that methodically incorporates these three dimensions is still scarce despite its conceptual promise. Current research frequently ignores them or uses disjointed approaches, missing the chance to develop a truly transformative and interdisciplinary framework for evaluating and addressing environmental justice. Bridging this gap represents a critical frontier for both research and practice about different disciplines (social, environmental, economic, and planning), emphasizing the inherently multidisciplinary nature of the approach proposed in the article.

As a future perspective, to validate the theoretical framework and evaluate its applicability across various urban contexts, our methodological approach will be operationally tested in four Italian cities: Rome, Milan, Naples, and Turin. These metropolitan areas, while all situated within the same national context, represent diverse geographic, climatic, socio-economic, and ecological profiles, offering a range of urban scales and governance structures. This diversity provides a significant opportunity to test the flexibility and robustness of the framework across different urban realities.

This comparative analysis will allow for investigating the contribution of biodiversity, ES, and socio-economic variables in distributing environmental justice patterns. It can contribute to identifying the presence of mechanisms related to the Luxury effect and reflect on how structural inequalities in planning decisions have created the conditions for these dynamics to develop. Urban planning plays a fundamental role in attenuating or reinforcing these patterns: for example, planning policies, land use regulations and investments (real estate or infrastructure) have the capacity, directly or indirectly, to shape and influence the distribution of resources, often embedding structural advantages or disadvantages in the urban fabric [72]. The application of this method in several case studies enables the identification of context-specific dynamics by applying the framework to several case studies while recognizing similarities and differences that can guide more comprehensive, scalable approaches to equitable and sustainable urban planning.

Through this comparative application, the research aims to identify which variable exerts the most significant influence on the distribution of environmental injustices in each urban area considered. By discerning the most salient drivers in each case study, the project can generate both locally specific insights and broader, generalizable knowledge. Finally, this process supports the development of scalable and adaptable planning and policy strategies sensitive to place-based complexities while aligning with the overarching goals of equity and sustainability.

5   Conclusions and Future Perspectives

The current contribution proposes an overview of the current state of the art of multidisciplinary studies to investigate the distribution and accessibility of green spaces in urban areas often characterized by substantial socio-spatial inequalities, with particularly significant effects on vulnerable communities. Phenomena such as the Luxury Effect are recurrent in cities worldwide, primarily where land-use planning promotes real estate development and aesthetic improvement rather than social equity. At the same time, green gentrification emerges as a critical problem: interventions aimed at improving environmental quality by creating or enhancing green areas often result in higher property prices and the displacement of poorer populations. This contradicts the principles of environmental and social justice on which such interventions should be based, helping to perpetuate or even exacerbate pre-existing inequalities.

The studies analyzed also highlight the lack of integrated approaches capable of combining spatial, economic, and social analyses and adopting a longitudinal perspective to monitor the effects of urban greening projects over time. In addition, the limited involvement of local communities and social actors in the decision-making process is a further obstacle to creating more inclusive and sustainable cities. Furthermore, planning strategies that actively address equity, affordability, social inclusion, and ecological and aesthetic goals must direct urban regeneration processes, ensuring that the transformation of urban space benefits all inhabitants.

Given these premises, it seems crucial to direct future research and urban policies toward a more inclusive, integrated, and participatory approach. There is a need to develop analysis models capable of considering the spatial distribution of urban green space and its actual and perceived accessibility by different social groups, including older people, children, migrants, women, and people with disabilities. Public policies must overcome the Luxury Effect by ensuring an equitable distribution of green spaces, even in less affluent neighborhoods. At the same time, they must address the risk of green gentrification through tools such as accessible housing, resident community protection, and urban design criteria that consider the socio-economic diversity of territories. In addition, it is essential to promote continuous and participatory monitoring, involving citizens and local actors in decisions and assessing the long-term impact of policies. Through a more coherent integration of quantitative (GIS, statistical models) and qualitative (surveys, interviews, focus groups) analyses, it will be possible to build more just and resilient cities where urban greening is not a privilege of the few but a right for all.

Funding. This research was funded by the Italian National Recovery and Resilience Plan (NRRP), Mission 4 Component 2 Investment 1.4—Call for tender No. 3138 of 16 December 2021, rectified by Decree n.3175 of 18 December 2021 of the Italian Ministry of University and Research funded by the European Union—NextGenerationEU. Award Number: Project code CN_00000033, Concession Decree No. 1034 of 17 June 2022 adopted by the Italian Ministry of University and Research, CUP,H43C22000530001 Project title "National Biodiversity Future Center—NBFC".

Credit Author Statement. Conceptualization: M.D.O., S.R., I.R., E.C., D.C.; Data curation: M.D.O., S.R., I.R., F.C.; Formal analysis: M.D.O., S.R., I.R.; Methodology: M.D.O., S.R., I.R.; Project administration: D.C.; Software: M.D.O., S.R., I.R., R.A., E.C., Supervision: E.C., D.C.; Validation: M.D.O., S.R., I.R., A.D.T., R.A., E.C., F.C., D.C.; Visualization: M.D.O., S.R.; Writing – original draft: M.D.O., S.R., I.R., A.D.T; Writing - Review & Editing: M.D.O., S.R., I.R., A.D.T.

Disclosure of Interests. The authors have no competing interests to declare that are relevant to the content of this article.

References

1. Grimm, N.B., et al.: Global change and the ecology of cities. Science **1979**(319), 756–760 (2008). https://doi.org/10.1126/SCIENCE.1150195/SUPPL_FILE/GRIMM.SOM.REV.PDF
2. Aronson, M.F.J., et al.: A global analysis of the impacts of urbanization on bird and plant diversity reveals key anthropogenic drivers. Proc. Royal Soc. B Biol. Sci. **281** (2014). https://doi.org/10.1098/RSPB.2013.3330
3. The world population prospects: 2015 Revision | Latest major publications - united nations department of economic and social affairs. https://www.un.org/en/development/desa/public ations/world-population-prospects-2015-revision.html. Accessed 27 Mar 2025
4. Kuddus, M.A., Tynan, E., McBryde, E.: Urbanization: a problem for the rich and the poor? Public Health Rev. **41** (2020). https://doi.org/10.1186/S40985-019-0116-0
5. De Toni, A., Colaninno, N., Morello, E.: Aree Produttive – Aree Pro-Adattive: il contributo delle aree produttive alla resilienza urbana e allo sviluppo sostenibile. In: La declinazionedella sostenibilità ambientalenella disciplina urbanistica, pp. 161–166. Planum Publisher (2023)
6. Cox, D.T.C., Shanahan, D.F., Hudson, H.L., Fuller, R.A., Gaston, K.J.: The impact of urbanisation on nature dose and the implications for human health. Landsc. Urban Plan. **179**, 72–80 (2018). https://doi.org/10.1016/J.LANDURBPLAN.2018.07.013
7. Feng, J., Li, Q.: Investigate physiological and psychological responses to environment scenes, elements and components in different urban settings. Sci. Rep. **15**, 1–12 (2025). https://doi.org/10.1038/s41598-025-86448-3
8. Donovan, G.H., et al.: The relationship between trees and human health: evidence from the spread of the emerald ash borer. Am. J. Prev. Med. **44**, 139–145 (2013). https://doi.org/10.1016/J.AMEPRE.2012.09.066
9. Ulrich, R.S.: View through a window may influence recovery from surgery. Science **224**, 420–421 (1984). https://doi.org/10.1126/SCIENCE.6143402
10. Zhao, T., et al.: Urban greenspace under a changing climate: benefit or harm for allergies and respiratory health? Environ Epidemiol. **9**, e372 (2025). https://doi.org/10.1097/EE9.0000000000000372

11. Han, Y., He, J., Liu, D., Zhao, H., Huang, J.: Inequality in urban green provision: a comparative study of large cities throughout the world. Sustain. Cities Soc. **89**, 104229 (2023). https://doi.org/10.1016/J.SCS.2022.104229

12. Bullard, R.D.: Confronting Environmental Racism: Voices from the Grassroots. South End Press (1993)

13. Bullard, R.D.: Dumping in Dixie: Race, class, and Environmental Quality. Routledge (2018)

14. Jennings, V., Johnson Gaither, C., Gragg, R.S.: Promoting environmental justice through urban green space access: a synopsis. Environ. Justice **5**, 1–7 (2012). https://doi.org/10.1089/env.2011.0007

15. Anguelovski, I.: From toxic sites to parks as (green) LULUs? New challenges of inequity, privilege, gentrification, and exclusion for urban environmental justice. J. Plan. Lit. **31**, 23–36 (2016)

16. Hope, D., et al.: Socioeconomics drive urban plant diversity. Proc. Natl. Acad. Sci. **100**, 8788–8792 (2003)

17. Aznarez, C., Svenning, J.C., Pacheco, J.P., Have Kallesøe, F., Baró, F., Pascual, U.: Luxury and legacy effects on urban biodiversity, vegetation cover and ecosystem services. NPJ Urban Sustain. **3**, 1–11 (2023). https://doi.org/10.1038/s42949-023-00128-7

18. Hope, D., et al.: Socioeconomics drive urban plant diversity. Proc. Natl. Acad. Sci. U.S.A. **100**, 8788–8792 (2003). https://doi.org/10.1073/PNAS.1537557100/ASSET/9F5 B8293-C983-4B01-B5B3-90DE21ECFEE5/ASSETS/GRAPHIC/PQ1537557002.JPEG

19. Chamberlain, D.E., Henry, D.A.W., Reynolds, C., Caprio, E., Amar, A.: The relationship between wealth and biodiversity: a test of the Luxury Effect on bird species richness in the developing world. Glob. Chang. Biol. **25**, 3045–3055 (2019). https://doi.org/10.1111/GCB.14682

20. Leong, M., Dunn, R.R., Trautwein, M.D.: Biodiversity and socioeconomics in the city: a review of the luxury effect. Biol. Lett. **14** (2018). https://doi.org/10.1098/RSBL.2018.0082

21. Reynolds, C., Henry, D.A.W., Kalyan, B., Pencharz, P., Shilubane, N.: Citizen science reveals socio-economic influences on solitary bee abundance across multiple scales in a Global South city. Landsc. Ecol. **40**, 1–16 (2025). https://doi.org/10.1007/S10980-025-02047-7/FIG URES/2

22. Su, L., Tang, H., He, G., Nizamani, M.M., Wang, H.: Wealth and altitude explain urban plant diversity in residential areas of Hainan, China. Land (Basel). **14**, 328 (2025). https://doi.org/10.3390/LAND14020328/S1

23. Lopez, B., Minor, E., Crooks, A.: Insights into human-wildlife interactions in cities from bird sightings recorded online. Landsc. Urban Plan. **196**, 103742 (2020). https://doi.org/10.1016/J.LANDURBPLAN.2019.103742

24. Wood, E.M., Esaian, S., Benitez, C., Ethington, P.J., Longcore, T., Pomara, L.Y.: Historical racial redlining and contemporary patterns of income inequality negatively affect birds, their habitat, and people in Los Angeles, California. Ornithological Appl. **126** (2024). https://doi.org/10.1093/ORNITHAPP/DUAD044

25. Pejchar, L., Rega-Brodsky, C.C., Vázquez, L.B., MacGregor-Fors, I.: Bird-mediated ecosystem services and disservices in cities and towns. Front. Ecol. Environ., e2835 (2025). https://doi.org/10.1002/FEE.2835

26. Rossitti, M., Oppio, A., Torrieri, F., Dell'Ovo, M.: Tactical Urbanism Interventions for the Urban Environment: Which Economic Impacts? (2023). https://doi.org/10.3390/land12071457

27. The sustainable development goals report (2018)

28. Fuller, R.A., Gaston, K.J.: The scaling of green space coverage in European cities. Biol. Lett. **5**, 352–355 (2009). https://doi.org/10.1098/RSBL.2009.0010

29. Gobster, P.H.: Urban parks as green walls or green magnets? Interracial relations in neighborhood boundary parks. Landsc. Urban Plan. **41**, 43–55 (1998). https://doi.org/10.1016/S0169-2046(98)00045-0

30. Weiskopf, S.R., Lerman, S.B., Isbell, F., Lyn Morelli, T.: Biodiversity promotes urban ecosystem functioning. Ecography **2024** (2024). https://doi.org/10.1111/ECOG.07366

31. Rega-Brodsky, C.C., et al.: Urban biodiversity: state of the science and future directions. Urban Ecosyst. **25**, 1083–1096 (2022). https://doi.org/10.1007/S11252-022-01207-W/FIGURES/5

32. Gaston, K.J., Soga, M.: Extinction of experience: the need to be more specific. People Nat. **2**, 575–581 (2020). https://doi.org/10.1002/PAN3.10118/SUPPINFO

33. Dunn, R.R., Gavin, M.C., Sanchez, M.C., Solomon, J.N.: The pigeon paradox: dependence of global conservation on urban nature. Conserv. Biol. **20**, 1814–1816 (2006). https://doi.org/10.1111/J.1523-1739.2006.00533.X

34. Hill, D., Fasham, M., Tucker Graham, Shewry, M., Shaw, P.: Handbook of Biodiversity Methods: Survey, Evaluation and Monitoring. Handbook of Biodiversity Methods (2005). https://doi.org/10.1017/CBO9780511542084

35. Bibby, C., Burgess, N., Hill, D.: Bird Census Techniques. 2nd edn. Sandra Lambton, vol. 302 (2000)

36. Pollard, E.: A method for assessing changes in the abundance of butterflies. Biol. Conserv. **12**, 115–134 (1977). https://doi.org/10.1016/0006-3207(77)90065-9

37. Pollard, E.., Yates, T.J..: Monitoring Butterflies for Ecology and Conservation : The British Butterfly Monitoring Scheme. Chapman & Hall (1993)

38. Knapp, S., et al.: A research agenda for urban biodiversity in the global extinction crisis. Bioscience **71**, 268–279 (2021). https://doi.org/10.1093/BIOSCI/BIAA141

39. Cortinovis, C., Geneletti, D.: Ecosystem services in urban plans: What is there, and what is still needed for better decisions. Land Use Policy **70**, 298–312 (2018). https://doi.org/10.1016/j.landusepol.2017.10.017

40. Costanza, R., et al.: Twenty years of ecosystem services: how far have we come and how far do we still need to go? Ecosyst. Serv. **28**, 1–16 (2017). https://doi.org/10.1016/j.ecoser.2017.09.008

41. Tengö, M., et al.: Weaving knowledge systems in IPBES, CBD and beyond—lessons learned for sustainability (2017). https://doi.org/10.1016/j.cosust.2016.12.005

42. de Groot, R., Alkemade, R., Braat, L., Hein, L., Willemen, L.: Challenges in integrating the concept of ecosystem services and values in landscape planning, management and decision making. Ecol. Complex. **7**, 260–272 (2010). https://doi.org/10.1016/j.ecocom.2009.10.006

43. Grêt-Regamey, A., Altwegg, J., Sirén, E.A., van Strien, M.J., Weibel, B.: Integrating ecosystem services into spatial planning—A spatial decision support tool. Landsc. Urban Plan. **165**, 206–219 (2017). https://doi.org/10.1016/j.landurbplan.2016.05.003

44. Demuzere, M., et al.: Mitigating and adapting to climate change: multi-functional and multi-scale assessment of green urban infrastructure. J. Environ. Manage. **146**, 107–115 (2014). https://doi.org/10.1016/J.JENVMAN.2014.07.025

45. Caprioli, C., Dell'Anna, F., Fiermonte, F.: Renewable energy sources and ecosystem services: measuring the impacts of ground-mounted photovoltaic panels. In: Gervasi, O., et al. (eds.) LNCS (including subseries Lecture Notes in Artificial Intelligence and Lecture Notes in Bioinformatics), vol. 14108, pp. 429–443 (2023). https://doi.org/10.1007/978-3-031-37117-2_29/TABLES/2

46. Cutter, S.L., Boruff, B.J., Shirley, W.L.: Social vulnerability to environmental hazards*. Soc. Sci. Q. **84**, 242–261 (2003). https://doi.org/10.1111/1540-6237.8402002

47. European Commission - Directorate-general for environment: building a green infrastructure for Europe. Publications office of the European Union, Luxembourg (2013). https://doi.org/10.2779/54125

48. Maes, J., et al.: Mapping ecosystem services for policy support and decision making in the European Union. Ecosyst. Serv. **1**, 31–39 (2012). https://doi.org/10.1016/J.ECOSER.2012.06.004

49. Caprioli, C., Bottero, M., Mondini, G.: Urban ecosystem services: a review of definitions and classifications for the identification of future research perspectives. In: Gervasi, O., et al. (eds.) LNCS (including subseries Lecture Notes in Artificial Intelligence and Lecture Notes in Bioinformatics), vol. 12253, pp. 332–344 (2020). https://doi.org/10.1007/978-3-030-58814-4_23/TABLES/1

50. Yang, W., Yang, R., Zhou, S.: The spatial heterogeneity of urban green space inequity from a perspective of the vulnerable: a case study of Guangzhou. China. Cities. **130**, 103855 (2022). https://doi.org/10.1016/J.CITIES.2022.103855

51. Anguelovski, I., Connolly, J.J.T., Masip, L., Pearsall, H.: Assessing green gentrification in historically disenfranchised neighborhoods: a longitudinal and spatial analysis of Barcelona Assessing green gentrification in historically disenfranchised neighborhoods: a longitudinal and spatial analysis of Barcelona. Urban Geogr., pp. 458–491 (2017). https://doi.org/10.1080/02723638.2017.1349987

52. Macedo, J., Haddad, M.A.: Equitable distribution of open space: Using spatial analysis to evaluate urban parks in Curitiba. Brazil. Environ. Plann. B Plann. Des. **43**, 1096–1117 (2016). https://doi.org/10.1177/0265813515603369

53. Datola, G., Oppio, A.: NBS design and implementation in urban systems: dimensions, challenges and issues to construct a comprehensive evaluation framework. LNCS (including subseries Lecture Notes in Artificial Intelligence and Lecture Notes in Bioinformatics), vol. 14108, pp. 444–454 (2023). https://doi.org/10.1007/978-3-031-37117-2_30/TABLES/1

54. Sugoni, G., Assumma, V., Bottero, M.C., Mondini, G.: Development of a decision-making model to support the strategic environmental assessment for the revision of the municipal plan of Turin (Italy). In: Land 2023, vol. 12, pp. 609 (2023). https://doi.org/10.3390/LAND12030609

55. Valentini, I., Nurchis, M.C., Altamura, G., Cicchetti, A., Damiani, G., Arbia, G.: The impact of socio-economic conditions on individuals' health: development of an index and examination of its association with three of the most frequently registered diseases in Lazio region of Italy. Soc. Indic. Res. **173**, 691–708 (2024). https://doi.org/10.1007/S11205-024-03354-3/FIGURES/2

56. Schindler, M.: Nature orientation and opportunity: Who values and who has opportunity for satisfactory green spaces in proximity to their place of residence. Urban Urban Green. **84**, 127924 (2023). https://doi.org/10.1016/J.UFUG.2023.127924

57. Lang, S.: Urban green valuation integrating biophysical and qualitative aspects. Eur. J. Remote Sens. **51**, 116–131 (2018). https://doi.org/10.1080/22797254.2017.1409083

58. Borzino, N., Chng, S., Mughal, M.O., Schubert, R.: Willingness to pay for urban heat island mitigation: a case study of Singapore. In: Climate 2020, vol. 8, pp. 82 (2020). https://doi.org/10.3390/CLI8070082

59. Lockwood, T., Coffee, N.T., Rossini, P., Niyonsenga, T., McGreal, S.: Does where you live influence your socio-economic status? Land Use Policy **72**, 152–160 (2018). https://doi.org/10.1016/J.LANDUSEPOL.2017.12.045

60. Zhang, Z., Zhang, G., Su, B.: The spatial impacts of air pollution and socio-economic status on public health: empirical evidence from China. Socioecon. Plann. Sci. **83**, 101167 (2022). https://doi.org/10.1016/J.SEPS.2021.101167

61. Alavi, S.A., Esfandi, S., Tayebi, S., Shamsipour, A., Sharifi, A.: Assessing the connectivity of urban green spaces for enhanced environmental justice and ecosystem service flow: a study of Tehran using graph theory and least-cost analysis. SSRN Electron. J. (2024). https://doi.org/10.2139/SSRN.4817429

62. Bouyssou, D.: Building criteria: a prerequisite for MCDA. In: Readings in Multiple Criteria Decision Aid, pp. 58–80 (1990). https://doi.org/10.1007/978-3-642-75935-2_4

63. Dell'Ovo, M., Oppio, A., Capolongo, S.: Structuring the decision problem. a spatial multi-methodological approach. In: Decision Support System for the Location of Healthcare Facilities. Springer Briefs Applied Sciences and Technology, pp. 29–51 (2020). https://doi.org/10.1007/978-3-030-50173-0_2

64. Fancello, G., Tsoukiàs, A.: Learning urban capabilities from behaviours. a focus on visitors values for urban planning. Socioecon Plann. Sci. **76**, 100969 (2021). https://doi.org/10.1016/J.SEPS.2020.100969

65. Kim, J., Ewing, R., Rigolon, A.: Does green infrastructure affect housing prices via extreme heat and air pollution mitigation? A focus on green and climate gentrification in Los Angeles county, 2000–2021. Sustain. Cities Soc. **102**, 105225 (2024). https://doi.org/10.1016/J.SCS.2024.105225

66. Cao, Y., et al.: Mapping urban green equity and analysing its impacted mechanisms: a novel approach. Sustain. Cities Soc. **101**, 105071 (2024). https://doi.org/10.1016/J.SCS.2023.105071

67. Cardone, B., Cerreta, M., Di Martino, F., Miraglia, V., Sacco, S.: A fuzzy-based emotion detection method to classify the attractiveness of urban green spaces. Evol. Intell. **17**, 3921–3933 (2024). https://doi.org/10.1007/S12065-024-00964-1/FIGURES/11

68. Salata, S., Grillenzoni, C.: A spatial evaluation of multifunctional ecosystem service networks using principal component analysis: a case of study in Turin. Italy. Ecol Indic. **127**, 107758 (2021). https://doi.org/10.1016/J.ECOLIND.2021.107758

69. Boone, C.G., Cadenasso, M.L., Grove, J.M., Schwarz, K., Buckley, G.L.: Landscape, vegetation characteristics, and group identity in an urban and suburban watershed: Why the 60s matter. Urban Ecosyst. **13**, 255–271 (2010). https://doi.org/10.1007/S11252-009-0118-7/TABLES/4

70. Pham, T.T.H., Apparicio, P., Séguin, A.M., Landry, S., Gagnon, M.: Spatial distribution of vegetation in Montreal: an uneven distribution or environmental inequity? Landsc. Urban Plan. **107**, 214–224 (2012). https://doi.org/10.1016/J.LANDURBPLAN.2012.06.002

71. Ernstson, H.: The social production of ecosystem services: a framework for studying environmental justice and ecological complexity in urbanized landscapes. Landsc. Urban Plan. **109**, 7–17 (2013). https://doi.org/10.1016/J.LANDURBPLAN.2012.10.005

72. Kabisch, N., Haase, D.: Green justice or just green? Provision of urban green spaces in Berlin Germany. Landsc. Urban Plann. **122**, 129–139 (2014). https://doi.org/10.1016/J.LANDURBPLAN.2013.11.016

Spatial Analysis in Multi-Value Assessment for Rural Landscapes: A Comparative Study of ES, LS, and LCA Frameworks

Benedetta Grieco[1](✉) ⓘD, Sabrina Sacco[2] ⓘD, Daniele Cannatella[3] ⓘD, and Maria Cerreta[1] ⓘD

[1] Department of Architecture (DiARC), University of Naples Federico II, via Toledo 402, 80134 Naples, Italy
{benedetta.grieco,maria.cerreta}@unina.it
[2] Department of Design, Polytechnic University of Milan, Via Durando 10, 20158 Milan, Italy
sabrina.sacco@polimi.it
[3] TU Delft, Faculty of Architecture and the Built Environment, Julianalaan 134, 2628 BL Delft, The Netherlands
d.cannatella@tudelft.nl

Abstract. Rural landscapes, such as Italian Inner areas, hold rich cultural, ecological, and heritage values. Yet, these peculiar landscapes are characterised by isolation, demographic decline, and limited access to essential services. These conditions present a unique challenge for landscape valuation and traditional assessment methods based on their spatial characteristics. Spatial analysis provides both conceptual and operational tools to navigate the complexity of landscapes. However, current approaches still face significant methodological and theoretical challenges in effectively capturing and representing inner areas' tangible and intangible values. The heterogeneous nature of existing spatial approaches makes it difficult to directly compare results, while the integration of perceptual data remains difficult due to the limitations of current GIS tools and models. These challenges highlight the need for more comprehensive assessment frameworks capable of overcoming existing limitations and providing a holistic understanding of landscape values.

To address these gaps, this study conducts a comparative analysis of three key landscape valuation frameworks–Ecosystem Services (ES), Landscape Services (LS) and Landscape Character Assessment (LCA). Through a semi-structured literature review, this contribution explores how these frameworks assess landscape values, and examines their respective criteria. Results show that ES and LS frameworks primarily value landscapes based on the benefits they provide to people, while LCA emphasises qualitative aspects such as perception and identity, recognising the intrinsic value of landscapes beyond their functional use. The analysis highlights critical gaps in current approaches, including their predominantly anthropocentric perspective and limited integration of multiple values into decision-making processes. We need for a more inclusive and spatially explicit valuation framework that places landscapes, especially in marginalised areas, at the centre of valuation processes and recognises their multiple, interconnected values.

© The Author(s), under exclusive license to Springer Nature Switzerland AG 2026
O. Gervasi et al. (Eds.): ICCSA 2025 Workshops, LNCS 15887, pp. 67–83, 2026.
https://doi.org/10.1007/978-3-031-97589-9_6

Keywords: Ecosystem Services · Landscape Services · Landscape Character Assessment · Landscape Valuation · Spatial Analysis

1 Introduction

Over the past century, the concept of landscape has undergone a significant transformation. Once rooted in the idyllic notion of nature as a retreat, it has evolved into a more nuanced understanding of landscape as a dynamic, living system. This contemporary view recognises landscapes as complex, ever-evolving systems shaped by the continuous interplay between human activities and natural processes [1]. This evolutionary perspective highlights the ecological, social, and cultural dimensions of landscape as deeply intertwined. As living systems, landscapes are shaped by a range of interrelated factors: climatic conditions, geomorphology, the availability of natural resources, local knowledge, governance structures, and technological and economic capacities, [2]. From an ecological perspective, landscape value is often associated with ideals of natural integrity and approaches aiming at minimal human intervention [3]. In contrast, from an anthropocentric standpoint, landscape values are defined in terms of the tangible and intangible benefits they provide to society, such as ecosystem services, cultural identity, and aesthetic or recreational functions [4]. These diverse influences often give rise to competing interests and value systems that undermine landscape planning, management, and maintenance.

Emblematic is the case of Italian Inner Areas, where such tensions tend to be more pronounced.

The National Strategy for Inner Areas (SNAI), identifies inner areas as areas characterised by geographical remoteness and difficulties in accessing basic services, resulting in depopulation and economic decline [5].

On the other hand, they are reservoirs of valuable natural, economic and cultural resources [6, 7]. This strict national framing provides the conceptual foundation for the present study, guiding the identification and analysis of the rural landscapes addressed throughout the paper.

The SNAI represents a first institutional attempt to systematically define and classify these rural landscapes.

However, this approach has been the subject of debate in the literature, as it tends to highlight what these territories lack compared to urban standards, rather than highlighting their specificities and local potential.

As a result, different models for interpreting and intervening in these areas have emerged, viewing these landscapes not as something to be mapped indiscriminately and a priori, but as something to be interpreted and defined in response to emerging goals and objectives [8].

Despite the increasing momentum in theory and practice, even the most critical perspectives often remain urban-centric, falling short of grasping the unique specificities of rural landscapes. In response, a shift in perspective is required, moving beyond urban-based interpretative models toward tools that can better capture the complexity of such marginal landscapes and guide more effective planning, policymaking, and design.

In this panorama, the valorisation of rural landscapes requires integrated strategies and transdisciplinary approaches [10], capable of capturing the multidimensionality of territorial values [11, 12] and promoting actions aimed at preserving their identity and enhancing their attractiveness, while at the same time promoting sustainable development [9].

Landscape assessment plays a central role in this process: it not only identifies tangible and intangible values, but also contributes to understanding the importance of the landscape for local communities and the environment [13]. It thus becomes a strategic tool capable of mediating between perceptions, actions and policy choices, offering an articulated and participatory reading of the territory. Central to this process is the concept of "value", which demands thorough reflection on its nature and its implications for decision-making processes [14, 15].

Another key component of landscape assessment is its spatial dimension, which facilitates the translation of abstract concepts into concrete, spatially explicit representations. This spatialisation provides essential tools for informed territorial planning and management [16]. In particular, mapping techniques allow for the representation of both the supply and demand of specific landscape elements [17], enabling a comprehensive evaluation of the area that accounts for the spatial relationships—such as the distance between supply and benefiting areas—fundamental to landscape functionality and equity [18–20]. Nevertheless, despite advances in landscape planning and assessment practices, effectively capturing and spatialising the diversity of rural landscape values remains a persistent challenge. Current valuation frameworks, largely shaped by urban logics and sectoral approaches, struggle to capture the complex and multifaceted nature of these landscapes. They often neglect intangible cultural values, local ecological knowledge and multifunctional land uses, resulting in partial, fragmented and ultimately inadequate analyses. To overcome these limitations, new tools and methods are needed that can reveal the diverse landscape values of inner areas-values that are too often invisible in conventional planning processes-in order to move beyond urbanist paradigms and towards a post-anthropocentric understanding of territory.

The objective of this study is to conduct a comparative analysis of three landscape assessment frameworks—Ecosystem Services (ES), Landscape Services (LS), and Landscape Character Assessment (LCA)—to examine how each approach, through its specific criteria and methodologies, contributes to the representation, mapping, and assessment of the multiple values associated with the landscape. While not exhaustive, these frameworks are among the most widely used and show a methodological advancement from a mainly quantitative to a more qualitative assessment. Understanding how these conceptualised models translate tangible and intangible landscape values into spatial terms is essential to support informed and sustainable decision-making processes in spatial management and planning.

In the light of these considerations, this study poses the following research questions: *1) Which material and non-material aspects of the rural landscape are considered in the ES, LS and LCA frameworks? 2) What methods and tools are used to spatialise the landscape values (GIS, statistical models, perception maps, etc.) and what are the main differences in representation? 3) What are the strengths and weaknesses of each approach in supporting decision making in landscape planning?*

Through a semi-structured literature review, the study aims to highlight the conceptual and methodological specificities of these frameworks and to identify their potential and limitations in capturing landscape values complexity. It also aims to explore possible perspectives for a more integrated approach to landscape valuation, capable of taking into account different value dimensions and their spatial distribution. This perspective can contribute to the development of more effective strategies for landscape management and planning, promoting an interdisciplinary and sustainable vision of landscape.The structure of the present study is as follows. The next section provides a detailed description of three consolidated landscape valuation frameworks. Then, Sect. 3 presents the methodology used, distinguishing between the different frameworks examined and the specific ways in which the analysis was conducted. Section 4 presents the results obtained. Finally, Sect. 5 offers a critical reflection on the findings and outlines possible future research directions.

2 Landscape Assessment Framework: In Comparison

This contribution focuses on the analysis and comparison of three consolidated landscape valuation frameworks - Ecosystem Services ES, Landscape Services LS, Landscape Character Assessment LCA- which interpret the values expressed by rural landscapes in complementary - but different - ways. Each approach emphasises different dimensions of landscape. These three frameworks represent theoretical and operational models already established in the scientific literature, selected because they are particularly relevant to understanding the complexity and multidimensionality of the rural landscape. They provide a starting point for building a solid and shared knowledge base that is useful for reflecting on the different ways in which landscape can be assessed, represented and managed.

Ecosystem Services (ES): The concept of (ES) emerged in the 1980s and increased in importance with the contributions of [21] and [22]. The Millennium Ecosystem Assessment (MEA) [23], carried out to assess the consequences of ecosystem change for people, focusing on the interlinkages between nature and human well-being, and, in particular, on ES as benefits people get from ecosystems. MEA highlighted the need to value the benefits that ecosystems provide to humans, influencing follow-up initiatives such as The Economics of Ecosystems and Biodiversity [24] and the Common International Classification of Ecosystem Services [25]. Today, ES and their assessment are central to environmental policy and scientific research [19]. Spatial maps of ES support environmental governance, but diversity in mapping methods and terminologies generates in their application [26]. The MEA classified ES into four categories: supporting (core ecological processes), provisioning (material goods such as food and water), regulating (e.g. climate control) and cultural (intangible benefits). The TEEB framework took up this classification and emphasised the environmental, socio-cultural and economic value of ES to support policy decisions. CICES then refined this classification by distinguishing between provisioning, regulatory and cultural services, excluding support services, which are considered as underlying processes.

The Intergovernmental Science-Policy Platform on Biodiversity and Ecosystem Services (IPBES) introduced the concept of nature's contributions to people (PCNs), which broadens the view of ES and values indigenous and local knowledge [27]. NCPs are divided into material, regulatory and non-material contributions, emphasising the relationship between nature and society. IPBES, inspired by previous frameworks such as the MEA, promotes a pluralistic approach to nature values, recognising the diversity of perspectives and the need to integrate them into decision-making processes [28].

Landscape Services (LS): The approach integrates the logic of ES with landscape aspects, taking into account social and cultural perceptions. The services provided by the landscape result from the interaction between man and the territory. In recent years, LS have gained importance in landscape planning and have deepened the issue of spatialisation of landscape characteristics [29, 30]. In contrast to ES, LS provides a more contextual view and includes man-made areas, which is crucial for participatory planning [31]. Termorshuizen and Opdam [32] distinguish landscape from ecosystem and define LSs as 'spatial human ecosystems' that generate ecological, social and economic values. This approach promotes interdisciplinary integration in the assessment of LS [33]. However, LS still lacks a systematic classification, unlike ES, which are based on models such as MEA, TEEB, CICES and IPBES. Some studies have tried to integrate them into ES [34], developing categorisations based on CICES, but these are similar to ES, highlighting the need for a specific model for LS that takes into account the relationships between services, landscape characteristics and human values. When applied at the landscape scale, ES risks losing their functionality due to an overemphasis on biophysical aspects [35]. Understanding the dynamics of LS at different scales is crucial for the analysis of spatial heterogeneity [36].

Landscape Character Assessment (LCA): A qualitative approach to analysing the identity and perceptual aspects of landscape, used in spatial planning to describe its distinctive characteristics, with a focus on cultural and historical value rather than quantifying ecosystem benefits. Understanding landscape character is essential for preserving its uniqueness and diversity, especially in rural contexts [37–39]. Traditionally, landscape valuation has used quantitative approaches to estimate its ecological, economic and cultural values. In the 1990s, the trend was reversed towards an LCA approach that focuses on mapping and analysing landscape characteristics such as soil morphology, vegetation and settlements [40]. Supported by the European Landscape Convention, it has spread across Europe as a key tool for landscape management [41]. More recently, LCA has integrated functional ecological elements and intangible cultural aspects, enriching indicators of landscape perception [42, 43]. However, landscape perception varies between local communities, which modify and value different areas according to their own needs. In recent years, there has been an increasing demand to assess preferences for multiple services, including not only ecological and regulatory aspects, but also aesthetic and cultural ones [44, 45]. This highlights the importance of a contextualised approach to landscape management.

The preliminary analysis revealed an important gap in the existing literature: no study to date has systematically addressed the three landscape assessment frameworks simultaneously and in an integrated manner. In particular, the existing literature has mainly analysed the relationship between ecosystem services (ES) and landscape services (LS) [31] or between ecosystem services (ES) and landscape character assessment

(LCA) [46], leaving partly unexplored the possibility of a broader and more structured comparison between all three conceptual frameworks.

3 Methodology

The methodology aims to build a strong comparative knowledge base to understand how different assessment frameworks propose specific interpretations of landscape.

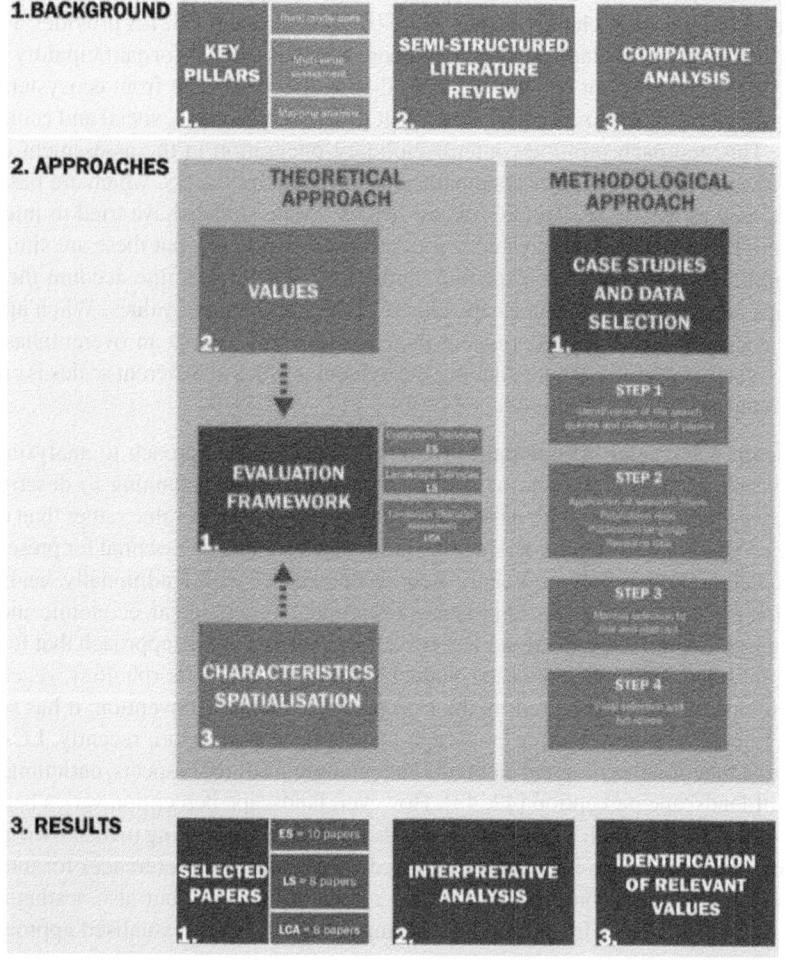

Fig. 1. Methodological framework of the research, divided into phases and operational steps.

By examining the most widely used approaches to landscape assessment, the study seeks to identify the underlying logics, values and spatial implications inherent in each framework. This analytical foundation allows for a critical examination of the landscape through multiple lenses, highlighting the different ways in which values are defined and mapped. To this end, the methodology is structured around three key pillars-rural landscapes, multi-value assessment and mapping analysis-which are explored through a systematic literature review, allowing for a comparative reading of methodologies and conceptual perspectives, while maintaining a constant attention to the role of values and their spatialisation. (see Fig. 1) .

The proposed methodology defines a common knowledge base, developed through an in-depth analysis of the issues of the three main pillars, conducted through a semi-structured review [47, 48], and a comparative analysis.

The methodological approach adopted therefore required a rigorous selection of documents, based on specific explicit inclusion and exclusion criteria, to ensure the relevance and relevance of the sources to the research objective. The analysis of the data extracted from the selected studies was carried out in a systematic way, focusing on the comparability of the results and the possibility of integration between the different methodological approaches studied. The collection of sources was carried out through the Scopus database (2025), chosen for its wide coverage of high quality scientific publications. This first stage (Step 1) was followed by a further selection of papers, identified through analysis of bibliographies of review articles and citations of the most relevant papers. In order to achieve greater coherence and focus in the analysis, the selection of case studies was limited to rural landscapes. In order to obtain a broader and more complete vision, the research was not limited to the Italian context alone, but also included studies carried out at European and international level, where relevant, in order to identify possible methodological and applicative relationships and links. It is important to emphasize that the European and international cases considered were selected based on the characteristics defined from the perspective proposed by the Italian panorama.

Due to the high number of results obtained, filtering criteria were introduced based on Date of publication, differentiated according to the frameworks analysed; language of publication, with a preference for articles in English; type of resource, selecting only peer-reviewed scientific articles (Step 2).

After applying the filters, the resulting number of articles was subjected to a manual selection based on the relevance of the title and the reading of the abstract (Step 3).

The final selected papers were collected, organised and analysed using the *Zotero* platform, which proved to be a fundamental support for the systematic management of sources (Step 4). Only through this rigorous procedure was it possible to carry out an interpretative analysis and identify the relevant related values.

This procedure allowed the final selection of 10 case studies for ES, 8 case studies for LS and finally 8 articles for LCA.

For the comparative analysis, a systematisation table has been developed in order to collect and analyse each paper in a structured and coherent way, paying particular attention to the ways in which values are identified, interpreted and spatialised within each framework (see Table 1). The table allows for a standardised comparison, highlighting both methodological convergences and divergences, as well as the peculiarities of each approach. Specifically, each article has been examined according to a set of criteria aimed at tracing the ways in which landscape values are conceptualised and translated into spatial representations. The structure of the table includes:

Reference framework (R.F.): the theoretical and methodological framework adopted.
Spatial Unit (S.U.): indicates the scale of application, which can vary from a local scale-focusing on smaller and more restricted areas, perhaps municipalities or hamlets, where a closer reading of the territory of the material and immaterial elements that define the identity of the place is favoured-to a territorial scale, including the set of ecological, infrastructural, cultural, economic relationships on a larger scale, often supra-municipal, where the landscape is read as a complex and interconnected system.
Highlighted Values: particular attention has been focused on the spatialization of the values considered in the various studies. The "Highlighted Value" underlines the values potentially detectable in the analysed documents. This interpretive approach allows for a nuanced understanding of how values are intertwined with spatial aspects across different research perspectives.
Spatialised Criteria: focuses on analysis of the criteria used for total landscape spatial valuation.
Evaluation Methods and Tools: identification of the methods and tools used for spatial analysis and data evaluation.
Authors.

The adoption of this approach made it possible to draw up a detailed profile of each contribution, almost like an "identikit" of the papers studied. This approach also facilitated the recognition of the potential and limitations of each framework, allowing a better understanding of the differences between approaches and the identification of the most effective strategies for evaluating spatial data.

4 Results

This paper provides a partial overview of the current approach to landscape assessment in rural areas, with reference to ES, LS, and LCA (see Table 1). Only nine of the papers selected during the literature review—three for each assessment framework—are included, as they are the most relevant and illustrative for the research under consideration.

Following the comparative study, it is interesting to note the different approaches to landscape analysis. The LCA case studies focus on a specific landscape value, such as aesthetics and perception, using innovative approaches such as social media analysis. The LS case studies highlight the importance of shared values and stakeholder conflicts in landscape management. However, their effectiveness is variable and often affected by methodological limitations, spatial scale issues and the quality of the data used. Ultimately, ES analyse the landscape in terms of services, and the main difficulty lies in the availability of the data associated with the study.

Specifically, the comparison produced the following results:

Landscape Character Assessment (LCA). Lieskovský et al. [49] attempt to assess the aesthetic value of landscapes based on the density of photos shared on Panoramio. Although the method is innovative in its ability to use user-generated big data, it introduces a clear bias: the aesthetic, intrinsic, identity, social and natural value of an area is not measured objectively, but rather based on the accessibility of the place and its popularity among photographers. Historic monuments, parks, museums, woodlands, lakes, castles, hills and places of natural interest are most often photographed, but the result is a biased analysis in which more remote or less accessible and documented landscapes

Table 1. The results of the comparative analysis.

R.F	S.U.	Highlighted Values	Spatialised criteria	Evaluation methods and tools	Authors
LCA	Territorial scale	Intrinsic value, identity value, aesthetic value, social value, local character value, naturalistic value	Urban areas Natural areas Agricultural zones Agroforesy areas	• GIS • Geolocated social media photos Google Panoramio • Land cover map CORINE Land Cover 2006 (CLC)	Lieskovský et. al. 2017
LCA	Local Scale	Intrinsic value, naturalistic value, value of local character, social value, identity value	Coherence Disturbance Historicity Visuality Complexity Naturalness	• GIS • Photos, Visual methods • Surveys of experts and the public • Multi criteria techniques for evaluation	Martín et. al. 2016
LCA	Territorial scale	Intrinsic value, local character value, identity value, social value, historical value, environmental value	Toponymic heritage Mill zones Traditional farming systems	• GIS • Interview • Strong community involvement • Historic Landscape Analysis (HLA) • Historic Landscape Characterization (HLC)	Hearn 2021

(continued)

Table 1. (*continued*)

R.F	S.U.	Highlighted Values	Spatialised criteria	Evaluation methods and tools	Authors
LS	Local scale	Environmental value, intrinsic value ecological value, social value	Water provision areas Water regulation areas Pollination Effectiveness of net primary production (NPPact) Socio-cultural connectivity	• GIS • Multi-Criteria Analysis • InVEST Model • LULC map and Data • Community involvement	Darvishi et. al. 2021
LS	Local scale	Environmental value, intrinsic value ecological value, social value, livability value, legacy value	Cultural identity Provisioning Regulation	• GIS • Interviews • Workshops • PCA Analysis • Community involvement	Baylan. and Karadeniz. 2017
LS	Local/regional scale	Environmental value, ecological value, economic value, social value, identity value	Carrier Regulation Information Provisioning	• GIS • Multi-Criteria Analysis • ANP, Spatial weighted overly • Kernel Density Estimation (KDE): Applied to point indicators	Cerreta et. al. 2021
ES	Local scale	Environmental value, ecological value, economic value, legacy value	Marginal croplands / Low-management fields Potentially low productivity croplands Density of marginal agricultural lands Wood BBES and food provision	• GIS • Analysis of satellite data • Remote sensing techniques	Longato et al. 2019

(*continued*)

Table 1. (*continued*)

R.F	S.U.	Highlighted Values	Spatialised criteria	Evaluation methods and tools	Authors
ES	National scale	Environmental value, ecological value, economic value, legacy value	Pollination; Regulation & maintenance	• GIS • Management analysis	Peciña et al. 2019
			Ethnobotanical areas		
			Nutrient cycling; Regulation & maintenance		
			Nutrient retention; Regulation & maintenance		
			Biomass production; Provisioning		
ES	Local scale	Environmental value, ecological value, economic value	Urbanization level (UL)	• GIS • Multi-Criteria Analysis • InVEST Model • Coupling Coordination Degree (CCD) • Hotspots analysis (Getis-Ord Gi* statistic) • GeoDetector model • Geographically Weighted Regression (GWR) model	Bi et al. 2023
			Water-related ecosystem services (WES)		
			Water provision		
			Soil conservation		
			Water purification		

may be undervalued online. Hearn [50] proposes an ethnographic approach to the characterisation of river landscapes, especially the Douro River, combining interviews, GIS and participatory mapping. These methods allow to capture the historical, cultural, ecological and social values of rural landscape. One of the limitations of this approach is that relying on collective memory carries the risk of distortions and arbitrary reconstructions, especially in contexts where the historical narrative is fragmented or politicised. Martin et al. [51] analyse the character and quality of rural landscape as seen from highways in Madrid. They use GIS, photography and multi-criteria methods to assess whether the highway conveys the character of the landscape to which it belongs. The natural, local character, social and identity values of the area are mapped. However, the methodology used suffers from the inherent difficulty of translating the visual experience into a quantitative assessment. The quality of a landscape cannot be reduced to the sum of measurable parameters and any attempt at objectification runs the risk of being artificial.

Landscape Services (LS). Cerreta et al. [52] adopt a more structured approach, combining GIS, multi-criteria methods and public participation to assess the resilience of rural landscape services in the Partenio Regional Park (PRP). Tourist facilities, housing, transport, cultivation functions and environmental, cultural and artistic regulation are spatialised to express environmental, ecological, cultural and economic values. Although the integration of local perceptions is a positive aspect, there is a risk that the decision-making process will be influenced by strong subjectivity. The use of the Analytic Network Process (ANP) allows the weighting of different components, but the complexity of the model can make it difficult to apply in broader contexts without a wide availability of data. Baylan and Karadeniz [53] use a combination of GIS, interviews and statistical analysis to explore stakeholder conflicts in wetland management in Ekşisu, Turkey. While the interdisciplinary approach helps to capture different landscape's values-aesthetic, receptive, spiritual, intrinsic, economic, biodiversity-,it is weak in its ability to quantify and standardise the results. The difficulty of capturing intangible values, such as spirituality or cultural identity, limits the effectiveness of the method and leaves unresolved the problem of translating perceptions into concrete management actions. Darvishi et al. [54] attempt to address the issue of trade-offs between landscape services for socio-cultural functional area-based assessment through GIS analysis in the city of Qazvin, Iran. The lack of a truly interdisciplinary framework leads to a reductive vision in which the integration between environmental, social and economic dimensions remains superficial. Furthermore, the lack of active stakeholder involvement leaves open the question of the practical applicability of the results, which risk remaining at a theoretical level.

Ecosystem Services (ES). Bi et al. [55] develop a national mapping of ecosystem services in Estonian semi-natural grasslands using GIS and remote sensing. The work maps the geographical distribution of WES levels, the identification of UL and WES spatial hot and cold spots, and the spatial distribution of CCD between UL and WES. Despite the large spatial scale of the analysis, the work is weakened by the use of proxy indicators that do not always accurately reflect the complexity of ecosystem services. The over-reliance on satellite data, while making the method replicable, risks providing a distorted view that ignores local dynamics and more subtle ecological variables that cannot be captured by low resolution imagery. Longato et al. [56] address the relationship between bioenergy and ecosystem services in the municipality of Rovigo, Italy, using GIS and satellite data to classify marginal lands. Ecological, economic and environmental values are mapped. Problems encountered include the quality of satellite data - vegetation indices - which can vary significantly, and the ability to distinguish between truly marginal land and simply underutilised land. Finally, Peciña et al. [57] use the InVEST model and advanced GIS analysis to explore the links between urbanisation and water ecosystem services in China. The characteristics of living systems that enable health-promoting activities are mapped. Although the InVEST model is widely used, it is not always able to capture the complex dynamics of water services, especially in rapidly changing urban environments. Furthermore, the analysis focuses almost exclusively on biophysical aspects, neglecting the role of socio-economic dynamics in water resource management.

5 Discussions and Conclusions

The analysis of different landscape valuation frameworks reveals a considerable diversity of methodological and theoretical approaches, each with specific strengths and limitations. One of the main observations that emerged concerns the overlap between ES and LS frameworks. Although different in their premises, these two approaches are often intertwined, making a clear conceptual separation difficult. However, LS introduce some distinctive elements, including the concept of CES and multifunctional landscapes. These aspects broaden the perspective to include not only the biophysical and economic dimensions of landscape, but also the cultural, social and identity dimensions. One element that clearly distinguishes the ES and LS frameworks from LCA is the level of theoretical structuring. While the first two refer to consolidated theoretical frameworks and relatively codified categories, the LCA appears less formalised and more difficult to fit into precise theoretical schemes. While this aspect makes it flexible and adaptable to different contexts, it also makes the standardisation of analyses and their replicability more difficult. In addition, LCA is characterised by a strong emphasis on the involvement of local communities, an element that seems almost a methodological prerequisite for understanding the specificities of the landscape. This participatory approach makes it a more democratic methodology, capable of capturing the perceptual dimension of the landscape, but at the same time introduces interpretative variability that limits its applicability on a large scale.

A key issue concerns the different values considered and mapped within the frameworks analysed.

ES, while including the ecological dimension, tend to privilege a reading of the landscape in terms of human benefits. They often focus on economic aspects, both in terms of use and non-use values, and seek to quantify the contribution of natural systems to human well-being in terms of services provided. However, this approach falls short in its ability to represent the intrinsic value of the landscape and its cultural identity. LS represent a step in this direction, attempting to capture the multidimensionality of landscape in a more articulate way. While not completely excluding an economic perspective, they also seek to integrate elements of place identity and social perception into the valuation framework. This makes their approach more comprehensive than that of ES, while maintaining some critical issues of measurement and standardisation of qualitative data. LCA, introduces a radical change in perspective, placing the perceptual and symbolic dimension of landscape at the centre, shifting the focus to characterising the landscape as perceived by people, with a strong emphasis on intrinsic values, whether anthropocentric or not. The methods used, such as social media image analysis or visual surveys, attempt to capture the collective sensibility towards landscape, without claiming to translate these values into economic terms. However, the risk of interpretation bias is high, and the reliance on data sources that are not always stable (such as digital platforms) makes this approach less reliable in the long term.

The analysis carried out shows that there is currently no landscape valuation framework capable of fully and satisfactorily capturing the multiplicity of value dimensions associated with rural landscapes. This suggests the need for a more holistic and pluralistic approach. Although some attempts to construct new, more inclusive models of environmental valuation have been explored in the literature [58], methodological and operational difficulties remain. The increasing availability of big data and the use of artificial intelligence may offer new opportunities to overcome current limitations in data collection and interpretation. However, the main challenge remains to place the landscape at the centre of decision-making processes, especially in marginal territorial contexts.

In this scenario, this paper proposes itself as a possible methodological way forward, based on the multidimensionality of landscape values. The approach does not start from what is missing, but from what exists and can be recognised as having value - be it intrinsic, utilitarian, existential, social or symbolic. The aim is to define guidelines for building a framework that can not only overcome the urban-centric paradigm, but also pave the way for a more than human vision. In this perspective, landscape should be considered as a complex relational space that includes humans and non-humans, ecological and cultural systems, temporal pluralities and alternative forms of habitability, recognising marginal landscapes as true territories of the possible.

Acknowledgments. The authors jointly conceived and developed the approach and decided on the overall purpose and structure of the paper: conceptualization and methodology, B.G., S.S., D.C., and M.C.; case study review, B.G.; validation, B.G., S.S., D.C, and M.C; data curation, B.G.; writing-preparation of original draft, B.G.; writing-review and editing, B.G., S.S., D.C, and M.C; visualization, B.G.; supervision, S.S, D.C, and M.C. All authors read and accepted the published version of the manuscript. This contribution forms part of the research activities developed within the 'GRINS – Growing Resilient, Inclusive and Sustainable' project. This project is financed by the National Recovery and Resilience Plan (NRRP), Mission 4 (Infrastructure and Research), Component 2 (From Research to Enterprise), Investment 1.3 (Extended Partnerships), Theme 9 (Economic and Financial Sustainability of Systems and Territories) (https://www.grins.it/progetto).

Disclosure of Interests The authors have no competing interests to declare relevant to this article's content.

References

1. De L'europe, C.: European Landscape Convention and reference documents EUROPEAN LANDSCAPE CONVENTION CONVENTION EUROPÉNNE DU PAYSAGE EUROPEAN LANDSCAPE CONVENTION CONVENTION EUROPÉNNE DU PAYSAGE. www.coe.int/Conventioneuropeennedupaysage
2. Bartel, A.: Analysis of landscape pattern: towards a 'top down' indicator for evaluation of landuse (2000). www.elsevier.com/locate/ecolmodel
3. Integrating Landscape Ecology into Natural Resource Management: Cambridge University Press (2002). https://doi.org/10.1017/cbo9780511613654
4. Tempesta, T., Thiene, M.: Percezione e valore del paesaggio (2006)

5. Strategia nazionale per le Aree interne: definizione, obiettivi, strumenti e governance* *Documento tecnico collegato alla bozza di Accordo di Partenariato trasmessa alla CE il 9 dicembre 2013

6. De Toni, A., et al.: Inner peripheries: dealing with peripherality and marginality issues within the European policy framework. TERRA: Revista de Desarrollo Local **7**, 24–47 (2020). https://doi.org/10.7203/terra.7.17239

7. Wu, Y., Wang, H., Wang, Z., Zhang, B., Meyer, B.C.: Knowledge mapping analysis of rural landscape using CiteSpace MDPI (2020). https://doi.org/10.3390/SU12010066

8. Cerreta, M., D'Agostino, A., Vannelli, G., Zizzania, P.: Internet areas. A culture-led strategy of widespread projects for montagna materana (Italy). In: Smart Innovation, Systems and Technologies, Springer Science and Business Media Deutschland GmbH, pp. 188–197 (2021). https://doi.org/10.1007/978-3-030-48279-4_18

9. Cerreta, M., Poli, G.: A complex values map of marginal urban landscapes: an experiment in Naples (Italy). Int. J. Agric. Environ. Inf. Syst. **4**(3), 41–62 (2013). https://doi.org/10.4018/ijaeis.2013070103

10. Liew, A., Sundaram, D.: Flexible modelling and support of interrelated decisions. Decis. Support. Syst. **46**(4), 786–802 (2009). https://doi.org/10.1016/j.dss.2008.11.016

11. Cerreta, M.: Thinking through complex values. In: Making Strategies in Spatial Planning, Springer Netherlands, pp. 381–404 (2010). https://doi.org/10.1007/978-90-481-3106-8_21

12. Montuori, A.: Edgar Morin and Complex Thought (2013). https://www.researchgate.net/publication/260603130

13. Solecka, I.: The use of landscape value assessment in spatial planning and sustainable land management — a review. Landsc. Res. **44**(8), 966–981 (2019). https://doi.org/10.1080/01426397.2018.1520206

14. O'Brien, K.L., Wolf, J.: A values-based approach to vulnerability and adaptation to climate change. Wiley Interdiscip. Rev. Clim. Change **1**(2), 232–242 (2010). https://doi.org/10.1002/wcc.30

15. Spangenberg, J.H., Settele, J.: Value pluralism and economic valuation - defendable if well done. Ecosyst. Serv. **18**, 100–109 (2016). https://doi.org/10.1016/j.ecoser.2016.02.008

16. Wahab, N.A.A., Zakariya, K., Ibrahim, P.H., Ibrahim, I.: Mapping the Landscape Characters Along a Rural Route for Tourism. Plan. Malaysia **16**(2), 131–140 (2018). https://doi.org/10.21837/PM.V16I6.468

17. Troy, A., Wilson, M.A.: Mapping ecosystem services: practical challenges and opportunities in linking GIS and value transfer. Ecol. Econ. **60**(2), 435–449 (2006). https://doi.org/10.1016/j.ecolecon.2006.04.007

18. Crossman, N.D., et al.: A blueprint for mapping and modelling ecosystem services. Ecosyst. Serv. **4**, 4–14 (2013). https://doi.org/10.1016/j.ecoser.2013.02.001

19. Fisher, B., Turner, R.K., Morling, P.: Defining and classifying ecosystem services for decision making. Ecol. Econ. **68**(3), 643–653 (2009). https://doi.org/10.1016/j.ecolecon.2008.09.014

20. Bastian, O., Grunewald, K., Syrbe, R.U.: Space and time aspects of ecosystem services, using the example of the EU Water Framework Directive. Int. J. Biodivers. Sci. Ecosyst. Serv. Manag. **8**(1–2), 5–16 (2012). https://doi.org/10.1080/21513732.2011.631941

21. Bawa, K.S., Kaufman, L.: Nature's Services: Societal Dependence on Natural Ecosystems (1997). https://www.researchgate.net/publication/37717461

22. Costanza, R., et al.: The value of the world's ecosystem services and natural capital. Ecol. Econ. **25**(1), 3–15 (1998). https://doi.org/10.1016/s0921-8009(98)00020-2

23. "Ecosystems and Human Well-being: A Framework for Assessment."

24. Levin, S., Steiner, A.: A landmark study on one of the most pressing problems facing society, balancing economic growth and ecological protection to achieve a sustainable future

25. Haines-Young, R., Potschin, M.: Common International Classification of Ecosystem Services (CICES): 2011 Update European Environment Agency (2011)

26. Hauck, J., et al.: 'Maps have an air of authority': potential benefits and challenges of ecosystem service maps at different levels of decision making. Ecosyst. Serv. **4**, 25–32 (2013). https://doi.org/10.1016/j.ecoser.2012.11.003

27. Díaz, S., et al.: The IPBES Conceptual Framework - connecting nature and people (2015). Elsevier. https://doi.org/10.1016/j.cosust.2014.11.002

28. Pascual, U., et al.: Valuing nature's contributions to people: the IPBES approach (2017). Elsevier B.V. https://doi.org/10.1016/j.cosust.2016.12.006

29. Wu, J.: Urban ecology and sustainability: the state-of-the-science and future directions. Landsc. Urban Plan. **125**, 209–221 (2014). https://doi.org/10.1016/j.landurbplan.2014.01.018

30. Bastian, O., Grunewald, K., Syrbe, R.U., Walz, U., Wende, W.: Landscape services: the concept and its practical relevance. Landsc. Ecol. **29**(9), 1463–1479 (2014). https://doi.org/10.1007/s10980-014-0064-5

31. Zhang, S.: Applying the Landscape Services Concept in Landscape Research: A Review (2022). Grassroots Institute. https://doi.org/10.33002/nr2581.6853.050401

32. Termorshuizen, J.W., Opdam, P.: Landscape services as a bridge between landscape ecology and sustainable development. Landsc. Ecol. **24**(8), 1037–1052 (2009). https://doi.org/10.1007/s10980-008-9314-8

33. Hermann, A., Schleifer, S., Wrbka, T.: The concept of ecosystem services regarding landscape research: a review (2011). Leibniz Centre for Agricultural Landscape Research. https://doi.org/10.12942/lrlr-2011-1

34. Vallés-Planells, M., Galiana, F., Van Eetvelde, V.: A classification of landscape services to support local landscape planning. Ecol. Soc. **19**(1) (2014). https://doi.org/10.5751/ES-06251-190144

35. Costanza, R.: Ecosystem services: multiple classification systems are needed (2008). https://doi.org/10.1016/j.biocon.2007.12.020

36. Aertsen, W., Kint, V., Muys, B., Van Orshoven, J.: Effects of scale and scaling in predictive modelling of forest site productivity. Environ. Model. Softw. **31**, 19–27 (2012). https://doi.org/10.1016/j.envsoft.2011.11.012

37. Antrop, M.: Interpreting diversity in the European landscape. A comment on perspective essays by Agnoletti and Schnitzler (2014). Elsevier B.V. https://doi.org/10.1016/j.landurbplan.2014.02.013

38. Van Eetvelde, V., Antrop, M.: Indicators for assessing changing landscape character of cultural landscapes in Flanders (Belgium). Land Use Policy **26**(4), 901–910 (2009). https://doi.org/10.1016/j.landusepol.2008.11.001

39. Lu, Y., Xu, S., Liu, S., Wu, J.: An approach to urban landscape character assessment: linking urban big data and machine learning. Sustain. Cities Soc. **83** (2022). https://doi.org/10.1016/j.scs.2022.103983

40. Jellema, A., Stobbelaar, D.J., Groot, J.C.J., Rossing, W.A.H.: Landscape character assessment using region growing techniques in geographical information systems. J. Environ. Manag. **90**(SUPPL. 2) (2009). https://doi.org/10.1016/j.jenvman.2008.11.031

41. Swanwick, C.: Society's attitudes to and preferences for land and landscape. Land Use Policy **26**(SUPPL), 1 (2009). https://doi.org/10.1016/j.landusepol.2009.08.025

42. Gormus, S., Oguz, D.: Role of Landscape Character Analysis in Evaluation Interaction Between Rural Settlement and Protected Area: Kapisuyu Basin Sample. https://www.researchgate.net/publication/297440488

43. Gottero, E., Cassatella, C.: Landscape indicators for rural development policies. application of a core set in the case study of Piedmont Region. Environ. Impact Assess. Rev. **65**, 75–85 (2017). https://doi.org/10.1016/j.eiar.2017.04.002

44. Brown, G., Brabyn, L.: An analysis of the relationships between multiple values and physical landscapes at a regional scale using public participation GIS and landscape character classification. Landsc. Urban Plan. **107**(3), 317–331 (2012). https://doi.org/10.1016/j.landurbplan.2012.06.007

45. Muhamad, D., et al.: Living close to forests enhances people[U+05F3]s perception of ecosystem services in a forest-agricultural landscape of West Java, Indonesia. Ecosyst. Serv. **8**, 197–206 (2014). https://doi.org/10.1016/j.ecoser.2014.04.003

46. Morrison, R., Barker, A., Handley, J.: Systems, habitats or places: evaluating the potential role of landscape character assessment in operationalising the ecosystem approach. Landsc. Res. **43**(7), 1000–1012 (2018). https://doi.org/10.1080/01426397.2017.1415314

47. Snyder, H.: Literature review as a research methodology: an overview and guidelines. J. Bus. Res. **104**, 333–339 (2019). https://doi.org/10.1016/j.jbusres.2019.07.039

48. Wong, G., et al.: RAMESES publication standards: Meta-narrative reviews. BMC Med. **11**(1) (2013). https://doi.org/10.1186/1741-7015-11-20

49. Lieskovský, J., Rusňák, T., Klimantová, A., Izsóf, M., Gašparovičová, P.: Appreciation of landscape aesthetic values in Slovakia assessed by social media photographs. Open Geosci. **9**(1), 593–599 (2017). https://doi.org/10.1515/geo-2017-0044

50. Hearn, K.P.: Mapping the past: using ethnography and local spatial knowledge to characterize the Duero River borderlands landscape. J. Rural. Stud. **82**, 37–53 (2021). https://doi.org/10.1016/j.jrurstud.2021.01.024

51. Martín, B., Ortega, E., Otero, I., Arce, R.M.: Landscape character assessment with GIS using map-based indicators and photographs in the relationship between landscape and roads. J. Environ. Manage. **180**, 324–334 (2016). https://doi.org/10.1016/j.jenvman.2016.05.044

52. Cerreta, M., Panaro, S., Poli, G.: A spatial decision support system for multifunctional landscape assessment: a transformative resilience perspective for vulnerable inland areas. Sustainability (Switzerland) **13**(5), 1–23 (2021). https://doi.org/10.3390/su13052748

53. Baylan, E., Karadeniz, N.: Identifying landscape values and stakeholder conflicts for the protection of landscape multifunctionality: the case of ekŞisu wetlands (Turkey). Appl. Ecol. Environ. Res. **16**(1), 199–223 (2018). https://doi.org/10.15666/aeer/1601_199223

54. Darvishi, A., Yousefi, M., Dinan, N.M., Angelstam, P.: Assessing levels, trade-offs and synergies of landscape services in the Iranian province of Qazvin: towards sustainable landscapes. Landsc. Ecol. **37**(1), 305–327 (2022). https://doi.org/10.1007/s10980-021-01337-0

55. Bi, Y.: Coupling relationship between urbanization and water-related ecosystem services in China's Yangtze River economic Belt and its socio-ecological driving forces: a county-level perspective. Ecol. Indic. **146** (2023). https://doi.org/10.1016/j.ecolind.2023.109871

56. Longato, D., et al.: Bioenergy and ecosystem services trade-offs and synergies in marginal agricultural lands: a remote-sensing-based assessment method. J. Clean Prod. **237** (2019). https://doi.org/10.1016/j.jclepro.2019.117672

57. Villoslada Peciña, M., et al.: Country-scale mapping of ecosystem services provided by semi-natural grasslands. Sci. Total Environ. **661**, 212–225 (2019). https://doi.org/10.1016/j.scitotenv.2019.01.174

58. Palola, P., Bailey, R., Wedding, L.: A novel framework to operationalise value-pluralism in environmental valuation: environmental value functions. Ecol. Econ. **193** (2022). https://doi.org/10.1016/j.ecolecon.2021.107327

High-Resolution Coastal Vulnerability Assessment: Integrating Ecosystem Services Mapping for Sustainable Urban Management in the Naples Coastline

Ivan Murano, Giuliano Poli$^{(\boxtimes)}$, Maria Somma, and Mattia Federico Leone

Department of Architecture, University of Naples Federico II, via Toledo 402, Naples, Italy
i.murano@studenti.unina.it, {giuliano.poli,maria.somma,
mattia.leone}@unina.it

Abstract. Environmental stresses of coastal zones becoming more intense due to natural processes and anthropogenic pressures are increasing. Now more than ever, the need for robust environmental management is crucial in urban areas where critical interplay of economic development, infrastructure growth, and environmental protection have to be struck at the right balance. Also using low-resolution data in a great many coastal vulnerability assessment models impairs their skill to identify fine-scale risk hotspots within high-density regions. This study presents a methodology supported by *InVEST* model for identifying high-risk and highly vulnerable coastal areas by integrating spatial analysis with ecosystem services mapping. The approach is applied to the city of Naples as a case study, utilizing high-resolution data to assess the protective role of coastal ecosystems, particularly *Posidonia oceanica,* in mitigating flood risks and stabilizing the shoreline. The findings indicate that highly urbanized areas exhibit the greatest vulnerability, whereas regions with well-preserved natural features provide enhanced coastal protection. By using this approach the decision makers will set a priority list of recommended management strategies that will both inform tradeoffs in regional planning between urbanization and environmental sustainability. Given the continued magnification of coastal fringe risks with climate change, advanced analysis tools play an even greater role. The method described here is a reusable framework that can be applied to other urban coastal areas to implement data-driven decision-making and resilience planning. Additionally, the peri-urban urban area on and around the central region is already fulfilling an ecological function thus highlighting the necessity of balancing and including nature-based solutions in coastal management.

Keywords: Ecosystem Services mapping · Regulating Services · Coastal Vulnerability Assessment · INVEST

O. Gervasi et al. (Eds.): ICCSA 2025 Workshops, LNCS 15887, pp. 84–100, 2026.
https://doi.org/10.1007/978-3-031-97589-9_7

1   Introduction

Coastal cities worldwide are increasingly exposed to both natural and anthropogenic stressors, necessitating structured approaches for vulnerability assessment, planning and management. According to IPCC, vulnerability is the degree to which a system is susceptible to, and unable to cope with, adverse effects of climate change, including climate variability and extremes. Vulnerability is a function of the character, magnitude, and rate of climate change and variation to which a system is exposed, its sensitivity, and its adaptive capacity.

Vulnerability in the context of coastal systems refers to the degree to which a system (e.g., a community, an ecosystem, or infrastructure) is likely to experience harm due to exposure, sensitivity, and limited adaptive capacity to coastal hazards. More formally, vulnerability can be broken down into three key components:

- Exposure: The extent and magnitude to which a system is in the path of potential threats like coastal flood or erosion.
- Sensitivity: The degree to which a system is affected by those threats, such as structural fragility or ecological health.
- Adaptive Capacity: The system's ability to respond, cope, or reorganize in ways that mitigate damage and capitalize on new opportunities.

In coastal urban areas, vulnerability manifests through high population density, infrastructure at or near sea level, and the complexity of balancing economic growth with environmental protection [1].

Ecosystem Services (ES) concept refers to the direct and indirect benefits that ecosystems provide to humans, encompassing provisioning, regulating, supporting, and cultural services [2, 3]. These services are vital for human well-being and sustainability, and their evaluation and management are critical for effective policy and conservation efforts to reduce vulnerability of socio-ecological systems [4]. The regulating function of ecosystem services can be described as the capacity of natural and semi-natural ecosystems to regulate essential ecological processes and life support systems through biogeochemical cycles and other biospheric processes [5]. In addition to maintaining ecosystem health, these regulation functions provide many services that have direct and indirect benefits to humans [6]. Coastal vulnerability-related ecosystem services, in particular, perform the function of disturbance prevention, i.e. the influence of ecosystem structure on dampening environmental disturbances [7, 8].

The assessment of coastal vulnerability has become essential for effective planning and management of coastal zones, especially in light of climate change and increasing coastal hazards [9–11]. Scientific community has been relying for long years on different methods to assess vulnerability and develop effective adaptation strategies.

Nevertheless, some gaps recur in scientific literature on current assessment approaches. First, they rely on physical and social data, simple models, and expert judgment. This suggests that existing methods may not be comprehensive or robust enough to address the complexities of coastal vulnerabilities [12]. Another gap points out that there is currently no universal method for accurately assessing coastal vulnerability, which can lead to inconsistencies across different regions [13]. At least, data lacking emerges as one of the most recurring gaps which prevents decision-makers in some countries from obtaining consistent information about coastal risks and, thus, to address comprehensive climate plans [14].

From this research perspective, Spatial Decision Support Systems (SDSS) are positioned as an advanced category of Decision Support Systems (DSS) [15], integrating Geographic Information Systems (GIS) technologies to collect, analyse, and organise spatial data in support of territory-related decision-making [16]. The SDSS has proven to be useful tool not only to solve resource allocation problem but also in other different fields, such as environmental management, urban planning, emergency response, and infrastructure optimization [18]. In particular, the integration of GIS capabilities into the DSS enables the collection, processing, and visualisation of geospatial data through maps, three-dimensional models [23], and scenario simulation by allowing Decision Makers to understand the impacts of specific decisions on a territory [17].

Recently, SDSS has evolved through the use of advanced spatial analysis capabilities, which include simulations, AI support, and predictive algorithms. As an example, an SDSS can integrate historical rainfall data with hydrological model to predict flood risks, while enhanced visualisation allowing users to explore several scenarios and DMs to make informed decisions for risk reduction [19].

In this study, an SDSS for scenario simulation of natural disasters, such as floods, was suggested to provide critical insights for preventing damage and avoiding costs through the preservation and valorisation of Ecosystem Services.

In conclusion, the effectiveness of SDSS depends not only on the quality and regular updating of spatial data, but also on their capacity to integrate other methodologies and tools used for assessing urban dynamics. In this context, the study presents an integrated Spatial Decision Support System (SDSS) developed to evaluate coastal vulnerability by combining ecosystem services mapping with high-resolution data analysis. This methodology provides a foundation for advancing an SDSS that offers more refined support to policymakers, proposing alternative strategies to help adapt to and reduce risks affecting the built heritage of urban areas and their communities.

2   State-of-Art on Coastal Vulnerability Assessment Methods

A short survey of coastal vulnerability assessment approaches has highlighted that spatial assessments through GIS and Ecosystem Services mapping are the most recurring approaches to detect the vulnerability levels of coastal zones [20, 21]. Indeed, essential tools in coastal vulnerability assessment are Geographic Information Systems (GIS) since they allow users to visualize which areas are most at risk from rising sea levels, coastal erosion, and habitat loss [9, 11]. Through spatial analysis and mapping functions, GIS not only helps identify vulnerable locations but also supports planners and policymakers in making informed decisions [16, 23] about conservation efforts, disaster risk reduction, and development of Nature-Based Solutions [7, 23, 25].

Another broad and integrated approach relates to the Integrated Assessment Models (IAMs) [27], which bring together multidimensional factors to assess the cumulative effects of different stressors by identifying their intercations in a cross-cutting perspective [28]. In a nutshell, IAMs help decision-makers explore long-term effects and assess the most effective adaptation strategies [29]. A particularly fitting form of IAM relates to ES mapping approach, which is a good practice for identifying, assessing, and managing the direct and indirect benefits provided by ecosystems. By employing empirical models, remote sensing, and GIS mapping, IAMs allows specialists to classify specific typology of services and their spatial distribution to inform decision-making towards integrated sustainability strategies [30].

On the other hand, DMs can recur to risk assessment framework to evaluate the probability of adverse events impacts by combining qualitative and quantitative data to prioritize intervention areas. These models can be integrated with Multi-Criteria Decision Analysis (MCDA) to produce composite vulnerability indices to benchmark the susceptibility of different regions [20, 31]. Composite indices can aggregate factors like exposure to hazards, sensitivity to environmental changes, and the ability to adapt. In this way, the vulnerability indices can provide a standardized way to identify the most at-risk regions while prioritising mitigation efforts and fundings [24]. Moreover, involving local communities in the vulnerability assessment process is essential for developing effective, place-based solutions that respect and reflect territorial values [32]. Coastal residents possess firsthand experience of environmental changes and previous climate-related events. Their knowledge can enrich scientific findings, contributing to more practical and locally tailored strategies. Such engagement also nurtures a sense of ownership and motivates communities to take an active role in coastal protection initiatives [33].

Additionally, scenario analysis supports decision-makers in exploring a variety of strategic options. By simulating different future scenarios—including variations in climate change, human activity, and policy interventions—experts can better anticipate the outcomes of potential decisions. This approach promotes flexible and adaptive planning, helping ensure that coastal management strategies remain responsive to emerging challenges [26].

The integration of above-mentioned methods can promote a deeper understanding of coastal risks by sparking proactive strategies to preserve and manage the socio-ecological landscape system.

3   The Case Study: Naples Coastal Areas and Marine Ecosystem Services

Naples exemplifies coastal vulnerability due to its convergence of high urban density, extensive economic infrastructure, and exposure to extreme weather events. Population data from the Italian Statistical Institute shows Naples as the most densely populated area in Italy. This coastal city include a variety of infrastructures such as commercial and tourist ports, urban waterfronts, and areas of ecological importance. With the combination of these elements and the rising climate-induced threats such as storm surges and sea-level rise, there is a need for a systematic coastal risk assessment and resilience planning.

The Gulf of Naples, located in the Tyrrhenian Sea, is a semi-enclosed basin characterized by a unique coastal landscape that includes sandy beaches, rocky cliffs, and densely urbanized shorelines. Equally worth mentioning are the marine protected areas existing in the region such as the Parco Sommerso di Gaiola where high maritime traffic can be observed, as well as the Port of Naples, the Port of Pozzuoli, and other touristic harbors. The continuous transformation of the coastal area mainly due to urban and port development negatively affects the ecosystems, making them more vulnerable to climate change.

Severe weather incidents recorded in history serve as a reminder of the vulnerability of the Naples coastline to natural extreme events. The storm surge that occurred on December 28, 2020, combined with several infrastructural problems, severe urban flooding, and economic disruptions, showed how much these events have increased their frequency and apprehensiveness. Similar incidents from past decades justify the need for a comprehensive risk assessment approach based on physical infrastructure and ecosystem functions of both types. Posidonia oceanica (hereafter *P. oceanica*) meadows are among the natural protections created by the plants that are not robotic. They are wave attenuators, sediment stabilizers, and shoreline preservatives. However, these critical ecosystems are increasingly impacted by excessive human activities like boat anchoring, coastal development, and habitat degradation, which calls for the implementation of biodiversity conservation plans.

The highly urbanized Naples coastline, which is becoming more prone to coastal risks, needs an integrated spatial decision-support system (SDSS) to plan and manage coastal risks. The use of GIS-based modeling tools, like the InVEST Coastal Vulnerability Model, allows the quantification of numerous risk factors, leading to a data-driven approach to urban planning and policymaking for coastal management. These frameworks can also be used to promote the introduction of nature-based adaptation strategies taking advantage of *P. oceanica* as a coastal defense biological asset. The disappearance of these meadows means that not only the coastal protection is undermined but also the ecosystem services like habitat provision and water quality maintenance are compromised. The incorporation of an SDSS into the decision-making process within the regional planning framework would promote the adaptive, informed management, thus leading to a more resilient Naples' coastal areas.

P. oceanica is a vital seagrass species existing in the Mediterranean marine environment mainly due to its ecological significance. It is well-known for its part in sediment stabilization, water quality regulation, and biodiversity support, as proved by numerous studies made by science practitioners. Found mainly in the shallow coastal zone, this species of seagrass forms dense meadows that are an essential part of the ecosystem and increase its function.

3.1 Posidonia Oceanica as an Ecosystem Service

In the Gulf of Naples, *P. oceanica* colonizes a variety of locations along the coastal ecosystem. As reported by ISPRA, this seagrass generally colonizes depths between 1 and 40 m, depending on the water's transparency and the substrate's characteristics. These meadows are sensitive to multiple environmental variables, including anchoring, discharges, and coastal modifications, exerting their pressure on them. This study seeks to determine the particular contribution of *P. oceanica* to wave propagation reduction and resilience in the Gulf of Naples coastal area. Previous studies have demonstrated the species' capacity to mitigate hydrodynamic forces and lower the rate of erosion but the real impact of the species in the study area still has to be established. With the coming together of geographical research and ecological studies, it is intended to discover how much *P. oceanica* forester class meadows are equally a part of the adaptive ecological features and thus create a new knowledge base for the development of coastal conservation policies and their implementation. The high urban density and extensive reliance on coastal infrastructure in Naples necessitate a data-driven approach to risk mitigation. Integrating spatial data analytics, long-term monitoring, and conservation strategies within an SDSS framework provides a comprehensive method for managing vulnerability.

4 Material and Methods

A structured methodological framework, built on the foundational research questions, was established to guide the development of the SDSS, setting a clear objective and organizing the process into three distinct phases: intelligence, design, and choice (Fig. 1).

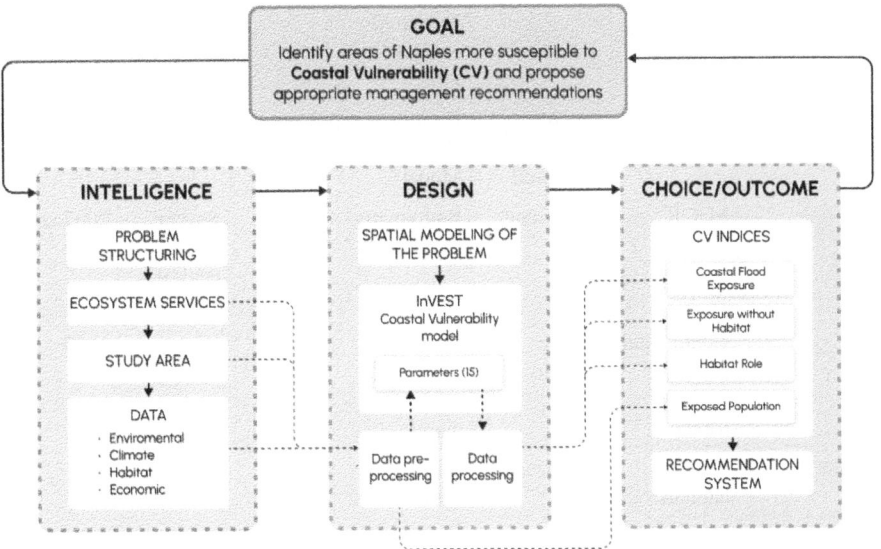

Fig. 1. Methodological framework of the SDSS

In the intelligence phase, the decision problem is defined, and the necessary data are compiled—encompassing local ecosystem services and key parameters for the InVEST© model. The design phase centers on spatial modeling through the Coastal Vulnerability tool, supported by meticulous data preprocessing and analysis of model outputs. During the choice phase, the computed indices are compared, and a preliminary recommendation system is outlined, equipping decision-makers with evidence-based strategies for coastal management interventions.

4.1 Intelligence Phase

To implement the InVEST Coastal Vulnerability model, a diverse set of spatial and numerical parameters was prepared (Table 1), often requiring non-trivial data acquisition and processing.

Table 1. Datasets description and sources.

Category	Dataset	Source	Content	Spatial resolution	Spatial extension	Timeframe
Economy	POIs	Overture Maps Foundation	Commercial activities location	n/a	Global	2025
Climate	Wind speed & direction	Rete Mareografica Nazionale	Wind speed and direction measured every 10 min	Single point	Port of Naples	2010–2025
Environmental	DTM	Campania Region Geoportal	Digital Terrain Model	86 cm	Campania region	2008–2013
	MaGIC	Protezione Civile	Bathymetry	10 to 50 m	Several Italian coastal areas	2007–2012
	Continental Shelf Contour	Marine Regions	Shallow submerged continental margin	n/a	Global	2009
Habitat	Seabed habitats	EMODnet	Marine habitats	n/a	Europe	2021

First, all raster and vector datasets were projected to the same coordinate system (WGS84/UTM zone 33N) to ensure proper overlay and distance measurement.

High-resolution bathymetric data from the MaGIC project allowed for a detailed representation of the seafloor, addressing one of the common challenges in coastal modeling—the lack of adequate bathymetric resolution.

The digital terrain model (DTM) used for emerged land underwent quality checks to ensure consistency with the study area and correct any small-scale inaccuracies.

Marine habitats, particularly the Mediterranean seagrass *P. Oceanica,* were sourced from EMODnet's Seagrass Cover in European Waters and assigned a protective rank informed by research demonstrating its relevance in shallow-water coastal defense.

Wind and wave data were adapted to reflect NOAA's WaveWatchIII outputs, using a 90th-percentile threshold derived from historical observations at the port of Naples (ISPRA) to capture high-energy storm events.

Furthermore, InVEST's "Human Population" field was repurposed to reflect economic exposure by converting Overture Maps Foundation POI datasets into a 50-m raster showing commercial activity density within 50 m inland from the coastline.

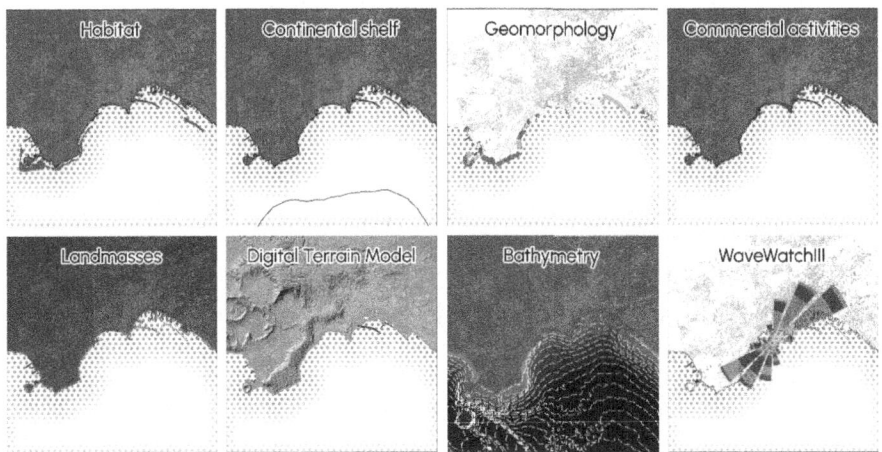

Fig. 2. Pre-processed geographical datasets to suit the InVEST model

These processes (Fig. 2) ensured that all inputs were harmonized, georeferenced, and calibrated to local conditions, in so doing enhancing the model's reliability for coastal vulnerability assessment and scenario testing.

4.2 Design Phase

The InVEST Coastal Vulnerability model quantifies the relative exposure of coastal areas to wave energy, coastal erosion, and flooding by integrating multiple spatial datasets—such as shoreline geometry, bathymetry, wave exposure, and habitat distribution—to generate a coastal vulnerability index that highlights the regulating function of coastal habitats. In this study, the focus is on *P. oceanica* for two main reasons: it is recognized as a key seagrass species in the Mediterranean (forming extensive meadows along much of the Gulf of Naples) and broader Mediterranean research indicates that its meadows significantly mitigate wave impact, particularly in shallow waters. Mechanistically, *P. oceanica* rhizomes and leaves slow water flow, causing sediment to settle and reducing wave energy before it reaches the shoreline. Information on the distribution of these meadows was obtained from a high-resolution European dataset and refined with local depth measurements; the meadows in the study area predominantly occupy depths between −5 m and −15 m (though *P. oceanica* can thrive as deep as −40 m). The high resolution of the bathymetric data used enabled accurate delineation of shallow-water meadows, which are especially relevant for wave attenuation. By default, the InVEST model assigns a protective rank of 4 to marine habitats, indicating low protective capacity, but Mediterranean-wide studies [1, 34] suggest a stronger protective effect for *P. oceanica* compared to that baseline. Indeed, Infantes et. al. (2012) have highlighted that: "*Root mean squared wave height (Hrms) is reduced by around 50% for incident waves of 1.1 m propagating over ~ 1,000 m of a meadow of P. oceanica with shoot density of ~ 600 shoots m − 2.*". At the same time, rank 1 is typically reserved for habitats like mangroves, whose protective impact is exceptionally high; for this reason, assigning rank 1 to *P. oceanica* would have been unrealistically high for this context.

Consequently, two intermediate scenarios (rank 2 and rank 3) were explored to capture a plausible range of protection offered by *P. oceanica* in shallow Mediterranean waters, accounting for ecological attributes and studies reporting its influence on nearshore hydrodynamics.

- In Scenario 1, the meadows receive rank 2, reflecting evidence that dense and shallow *P. oceanica* meadows can dissipate a significant portion of wave energy.
- In Scenario 2, the meadows are assigned rank 3, indicating a moderate protective effect above the default assumption but below the maximum protection.

The model was run using these two rankings, incorporating the high-resolution input layers (shoreline segments, wave exposure indices, localized fetch distances) and adhering to InVEST Coastal Vulnerability guidelines with adjustments for the Gulf of Naples' hydro-geomorphological features. Advanced hydrodynamic modeling and detailed biological analyses were outside the scope, and the approach relies on existing Mediterranean-wide literature rather than direct local measurements. Nonetheless, employing both ranks 3 and 2 provides a bounded exploration of how parameter variations might affect coastal vulnerability outputs, making this method suitable for informing preliminary urban and territorial planning considerations related to coastal exposure and climate resilience.

5   Choice/Outcome Phase

5.1   Coastal Vulnerability Index Maps

The model autonomously computes four outputs: the Coastal Exposure Index with and without the presence of *P. oceanica*, an evaluation of the ecosystem's role in mitigating vulnerability, and an estimate of the exposed commercial activities. These results derive directly from the model's spatial analysis and computational framework, ensuring an objective and data-driven assessment of coastal hazards.

Coastal Vulnerability Index

The Coastal Vulnerability Index, is shown with two variants (Fig. 3) reflecting different classifications for the *P. oceanica* habitat. Differences between the scenarios are minimal, mainly noticeable along the coastal stretch of San Giovanni a Teduccio. Notably, the areas with the highest vulnerability values coincide with zones historically affected by flooding events.

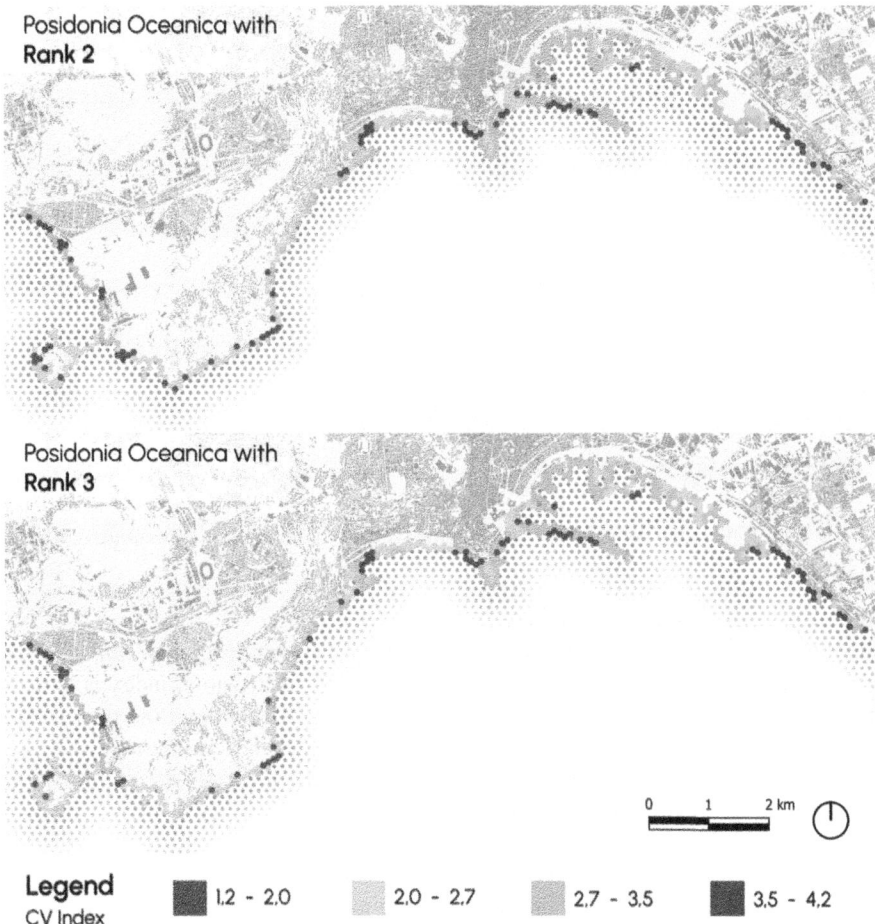

Fig. 3. Coastal Vulnerability Index in the two scenarios of coastal protection provided by *P. oceanica.*

Coastal Vulnerability Index Without Habitat

Figure 4 presents the Coastal Vulnerability Index in the absence of habitat protection. This index is of particular importance to understand what would happen if the habitats of seagrasses currently present disappeared, leaving the coast without protection offered by ecosystem services.

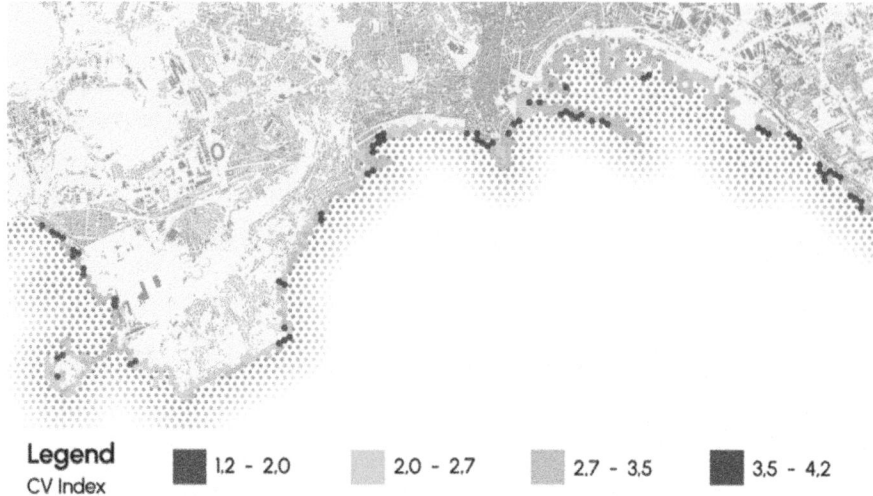

Fig. 4. Coastal Vulnerability Index in the scenario of absence of *P. oceanica.*

Habitat Role in Coastal Protection

Figure 5 quantitatively assesses the role of marine habitats, specifically *P. oceanica* meadows, in mitigating coastal vulnerability. The ecosystem contribution index is derived from the difference between CV indices calculated with and without the presence of these habitats. Although habitat effectiveness logically depends on the assigned rank across the two considered scenarios, this variation occurs uniformly across all coastal cells adjacent to existing marine habitats.

Commercial Activities Exposed to Coastal Hazards

Figure 6 illustrates the distribution of population exposure along the Gulf of Naples, based on the "Human Population" field that was repurposed for this study. The results indicate that densely populated urban areas, particularly those lacking natural protection, are disproportionately exposed to coastal hazards. The integration of demographic and spatial risk data allows for the identification of high-risk zones, supporting targeted adaptation and mitigation strategies.

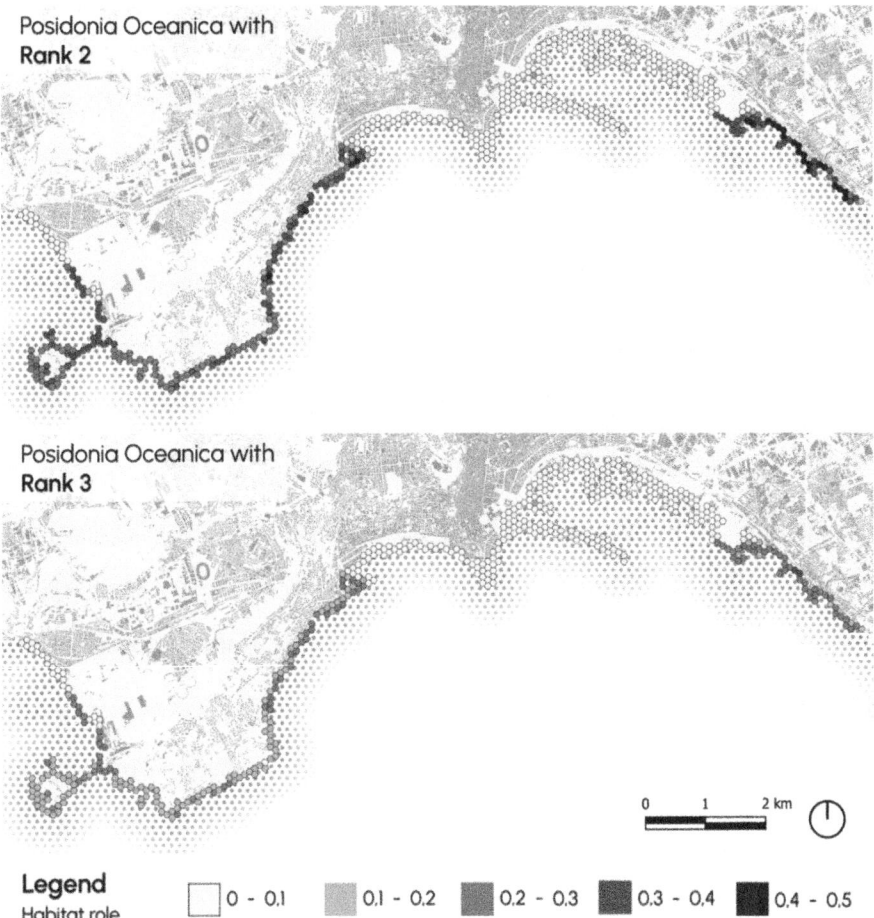

Fig. 5. Comparison of the Habitat Role in the two scenarios of coastal protection provided by *P. oceanica.*

5.2 Scenario Comparison

The graphs (Fig. 7) compare the two scenarios with the arithmetic averages of the entire distribution for the two indices of CV and Habitat Role.

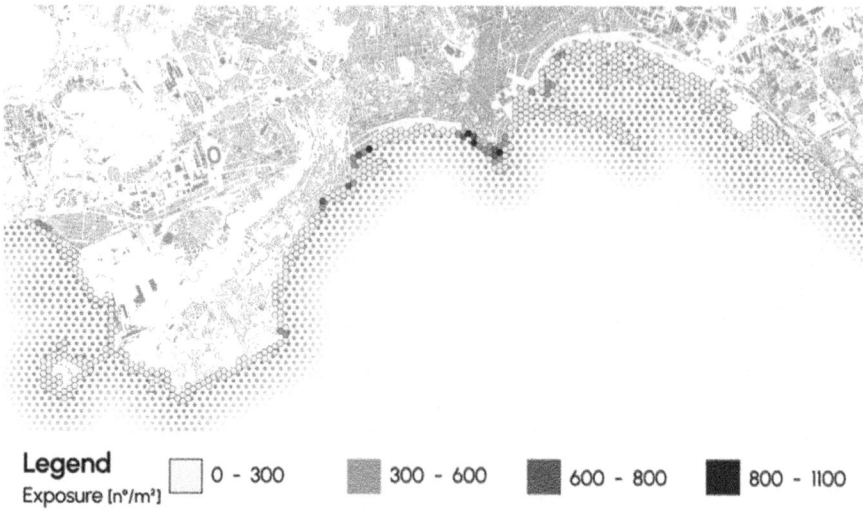

Fig. 6. Concentration of commercial activities in direct proximity to the shoreline.

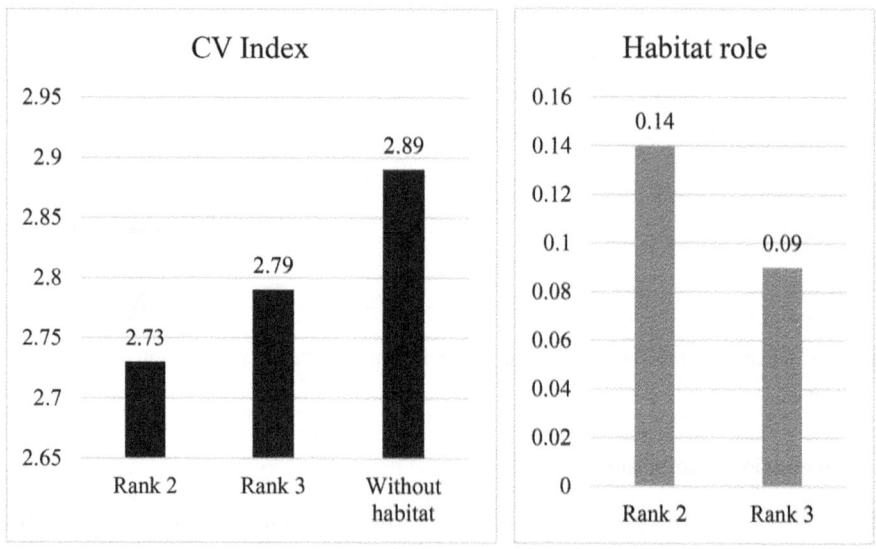

Fig. 7. Quantitative comparison between the different simulated scenarios.

5.3 Data-Driven Preliminary Recommendation System

Building on the spatial modeling outcomes and the analyses of key marine habitats, a preliminary recommendation framework was devised to lower the Coastal Vulnerability Index in the city of Naples. The distribution of *P. oceanica*, primarily observed off the Posillipo coastline and in a smaller meadow about 800 m from San Giovanni a Teduccio, underscores the importance of restoring and expanding seagrass meadows in ecologically suitable areas. Such Nature-Based Solutions (NBS) can provide significant co-benefits by enhancing biodiversity, sequestering "blue carbon," and improving water quality through the mitigation of eutrophication processes.

Three incremental intervention scenarios were thus defined. Scenario 1 entails reinforcing existing Posidonia meadows and establishing new ones where local conditions permit. Scenario 2 enhances coastal resilience by introducing "living breakwaters" in the most vulnerable shoreline segments, effectively reducing wave impacts while preserving ecological function. Lastly, Scenario 3 adds dune systems along San Giovanni a Teduccio and Bagnoli, representing a broader-scale strategy that couples the protective effect of dunes with the ecological benefits of submerged habitats (Fig. 8).

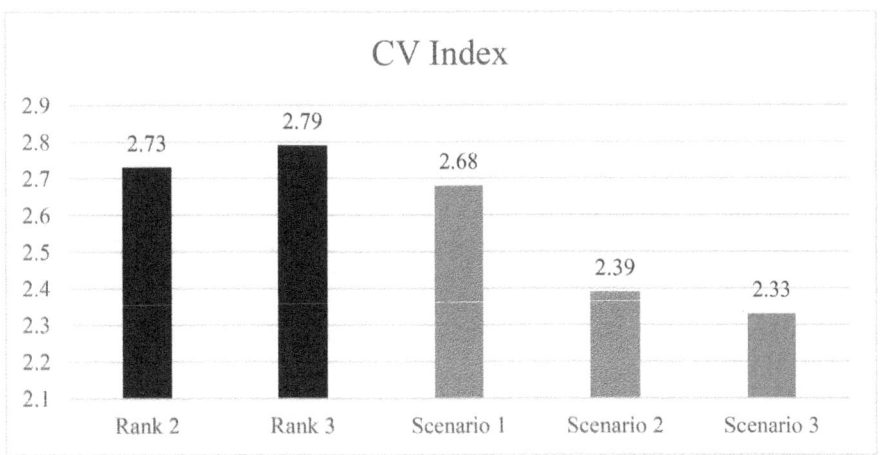

Fig. 8. Quantitative comparison of the CV Index between the actual and proposed state scenarios.

Although the first scenario yields a modest decrease in CVI, Scenario 2 shows a clearer reduction of coastal risk in areas previously identified as highly vulnerable. Scenario 3 further refines these improvements, principally in areas where dune systems were simulated, although the overall change is incremental rather than transformative.

In combining ecological restoration, engineered habitat structures, and soft coastal defenses, this integrated approach aims to deliver measurable benefits for urban coastal resilience, aligning essential protective functions with the co-benefits inherent in healthy marine and coastal ecosystems.

6 Conclusions

Traditionally, the InVEST "Coastal Vulnerability" model has been applied at large scales—with national or regional datasets and correspondingly low spatial resolution—limiting its applicability in urban settings. In contrast, our approach has adapted this model for the urban context of Naples, employing high-resolution input data to capture fine-scale variations in coastal vulnerability and the benefits of ecosystem services. Particular emphasis was placed on regulating services, such as flood mitigation and shoreline stabilization, which are critical for the resilience of urban coastal areas. By integrating detailed ecosystem services mapping within the SDSS framework, this methodology could provide local stakeholders with robust decision-support tools to balance urban development with the preservation of vital coastal functions. The results demonstrated that high-resolution assessments enhance our understanding of coastal dynamics in urban environments, offering a replicable model for improving coastal risk management in cities facing similar challenges.

In conclusion, the conservation and restoration of *P. oceanica* meadows must be prioritized as a core component of adaptive coastal management, bridging ecosystem-based strategies with urban resilience planning. Strengthening these initiatives through multidisciplinary collaboration and policy integration will be essential to ensuring the long-term sustainability of one of Italy's most exposed coastal regions.

References

1. Infantes, E., Orfila, A., Simarro, G., Terrados, J., Luhar, M., Nepf, H.: Effect of a seagrass (Posidonia oceanica) meadow on wave propagation. Mar. Ecol. Prog. Ser. **456**, 63–72 (2012). https://doi.org/10.3354/meps09754
2. Costanza, R.: The value of natural and social capital in our current full world and in a sustainable and desirable future. Sustain. Sci.: Emerg. Paradigm Urban Environ. **9781461431886**, 99–109 (2012). https://doi.org/10.1007/978-1-4614-3188-6_5
3. M.E.A: Millennium ecosystem assessment. Ecosystems and human well - being. Washington, DC, USA (2001)
4. Berrouet, L.M., Machado, J., Villegas-Palacio, C.: Vulnerability of socio—ecological systems: a conceptual framework. Ecol. Indic. **84**, 632–647 (2018). https://doi.org/10.1016/J.ECOLIND.2017.07.051
5. De Groot, R.S., Wilson, M.A., Boumans, R.M.J.: A typology for the classification, description and valuation of ecosystem functions, goods and services. Ecol. Econ. **41**, 393–408 (2002). https://doi.org/10.1016/S0921-8009(02)00089-7
6. Costanza, R., et al.: The value of the world's ecosystem services and natural capital. Nature **387**, 253–260 (1997). https://doi.org/10.1038/387253a0
7. Arkema, K.K., et al.: Embedding ecosystem services in coastal planning leads to better outcomes for people and nature. Proc. Natl. Acad. Sci. U. S. A. **112**, 7390–7395 (2015). https://doi.org/10.1073/PNAS.1406483112/SUPPL_FILE/PNAS.1406483112.SAPP.PDF
8. Mills, M., et al.: Real-world progress in overcoming the challenges of adaptive spatial planning in marine protected areas. Biol. Conserv. **181**, 54–63 (2015). https://doi.org/10.1016/J.BIOCON.2014.10.028
9. Arkema, K.K., et al.: Coastal habitats shield people and property from sea-level rise and storms. Nat. Climate Change **3**, 913–918 (2013). https://doi.org/10.1038/nclimate1944
10. Gornitz, V.: Global and Planetary Change Section). **89**, 379–398 (1991)
11. Bukvic, A., Rohat, G., Apotsos, A., de Sherbinin, A.: A systematic review of coastal vulnerability mapping. Sustainability **12**, 2822 (2020). https://doi.org/10.3390/SU12072822
12. Tanim, A.H., Goharian, E., Moradkhani, H.: Integrated socio-environmental vulnerability assessment of coastal hazards using data-driven and multi-criteria analysis approaches. Sci. Rep. **12**(1), 11625 (2022)
13. Nguyen, T.T., Bonetti, J., Rogers, K., Woodroffe, C.D.: Indicator-based assessment of climate-change impacts on coasts: a review of concepts, methodological approaches and vulnerability indices. Ocean Coast. Manage. **123**, 18–43 (2016)

14. Nichols, C.R., et al.: Collaborative science to enhance coastal resilience and adaptation. Front. Mar. Sci. **6**, 404 (2019)
15. Simon, H.A.: The New Science of Management Decision. Harper & Brothers: New York, NY, USA (1960)
16. Malczewski, J., Rinner, C.: Multicriteria decision analysis in geographic information science. Adv. Geographic Inf. Sci. https://doi.org/10.1007/978-3-540-74757-4_1
17. Malczewski, J., Jankowski, P.: Emerging trends and research frontiers in spatial multicriteria analysis. Int. J. Geogr. Inf. Sci. **34**, 1257–1282 (2020). https://doi.org/10.1080/13658816.2020.1712403
18. Jankowski, P., Richard, L.: Integration of GIS-based suitability analysis and multicriteria evaluation in a spatial decision support system for route selection. Environ. Plann. B. Plann. Des. **21**(3), 323–340 (1994)
19. Heinzlef, C., Becue, V., Serre, D.: A spatial decision support system for enhancing resilience to floods: Bridging resilience modelling and geovisualization techniques. Nat. Hazard. **20**, 1049–1068 (2020). https://doi.org/10.5194/NHESS-20-1049-2020
20. Adger, W.N.: Vulnerability. Glob. Environ. Chang. **16**, 268–281 (2006). https://doi.org/10.1016/J.GLOENVCHA.2006.02.006
21. Renaud, F., Sudmeier-Rieux, K., Estrella, M., Nehren, U.: Ecosystem-Based Disaster Risk Reduction and Adaptation in Practice. Springer International Publishing, Cham (2016). https://doi.org/10.1007/978-3-319-43633-3
22. Malczewski, J., Rinner, C.: Multicriteria decision analysis in geographic information science.(2015). https://doi.org/10.1007/978-3-540-74757-4
23. Cerreta, M., Mele, R., Poli, G.: Urban ecosystem services (UES) assessment within a 3D virtual environment: a methodological approach for the larger urban zones (LUZ) of Naples, Italy. Appl. Sci. **10**, 6205 (2020). https://doi.org/10.3390/APP10186205
24. Smits, J., Huisman, J.: The GDL vulnerability index (GVI). Soc. Indic. Res. **174**(2), 721–741 (2024)
25. Mele, R., Poli, G.: The effectiveness of geographical data in multi-criteria evaluation of landscape services †. Data **2**, 9 (2017). https://doi.org/10.3390/DATA2010009
26. Poli, G., Cuntò, S., Muccio, E., Cerreta, M.: A spatial decision support system for multidimensional sustainability assessment of river basin districts: the case study of Sarno river. Land Use Policy **141**, 107123 (2024)
27. Bosetti, V.: Integrated Assessment Models for Climate Change. https://doi.org/10.1093/acrefore/9780190625979.013.572
28. Crain, C.M., Kroeker, K., Halpern, B.S.: Interactive and cumulative effects of multiple human stressors in marine systems. Ecol. Lett. **11**, 1304–1315 (2008). https://doi.org/10.1111/J.1461-0248.2008.01253.X
29. van Beek, L., Hajer, M., Pelzer, P., van Vuuren, D., Cassen, C.: Anticipating futures through models: the rise of Integrated assessment modelling in the climate science-policy interface since 1970. Glob. Environ. Chang. **65**, 102191 (2020). https://doi.org/10.1016/J.GLOENVCHA.2020.102191
30. Qi, Z.F., Ye, X.Y., Zhang, H., Yu, Z.L.: Land fragmentation and variation of ecosystem services in the context of rapid urbanization: the case of Taizhou city, China. Stoch. Env. Res. Risk Assess. **28**, 843–855 (2014). https://doi.org/10.1007/s00477-013-0721-2
31. Thieler, E.R., Hammar-Klose, H.-K.: National assessment of coastal vulnerability to sea-level rise: preliminary results for the U.S. Atlantic Coast. U.S Geol. Surv. 99–593 (2000)
32. La Rocca, L., Mazzarella, C., Regalbuto, S., Somma, M., Imbriaco, A.: Community archive as place-based decision-making process: a proposal for the "Archivio Atena." In: Lecture Notes in Computer Science (including subseries Lecture Notes in Artificial Intelligence and Lecture Notes in Bioinformatics), pp. 209–225. Springer Science and Business Media Deutschland GmbH (2023). https://doi.org/10.1007/978-3-031-37117-2_16

33. Jennings, V., et al.: Place-based conservation in coastal and marine ecosystems: the importance of engagement with underrepresented communities. Sustainability **16**, 9965 (2024). https://doi.org/10.3390/SU16229965
34. Agulles, M., Marbà, N., Duarte, C.M., Jordà, G.: Mediterranean seagrasses provide essential coastal protection under climate change. Scientific Reports **14**, 1–12 (2024). https://doi.org/10.1038/s41598-024-81026-5

Blockchain and Distributed Ledgers: Technologies and Applications (BDLTA 2025)

Efficient Application of Multi-Layer Data Processing with PBFT and RAFT for Transaction Forecasting Using LSTM

Alexander Bogdanov[1], Jasur Kiyamov[1,4]([envelope]), Valery Khvatov[2], Gennady Dik[1,3], Aleksandr Dik[1,3], Egor Savkov[5], and Aleksandr Shchegolev[6]

[1] St. Petersburg University, St. Petersburg, Russia
{a.v.bogdanov,z.kiyamov,a.dik}@spbu.ru, g.dick@systechnologies.ru
[2] DGT Technologies AG, Montreal, Canada
[3] St. Petersburg LLC "System Technologies", St. Petersburg, Russia
[4] Samarkand branch of Tashkent University of Information Technologies, Samarkand, Uzbekistan
[5] Consern Avrora Scientific and Production Association JSC, St. Petersburg, Russia
[6] St. Petersburg State Marine Technical University, St. Petersburg, Russia

Abstract. The article considers approaches to multi-level data processing using the Practical Byzantine Fault Tolerance (PBFT) and Reliable, Replicated, and Fault-Tolerant (RAFT) consensus algorithms. Their application for organizing efficient processing and aggregation of transactional data in distributed systems is analyzed. The main focus is on the use of recurrent neural networks with long short-term memory (LSTM) for predicting transactions based on data processed by PBFT and RAFT. The results of experiments on improving the accuracy of predictions taking into account various consensus strategies are presented.

Keywords: LSTM · PBFT · RAFT · Blockchain · Consensus Algorithms · Deep Learning

1 Introduction

Accurate forecasting of transactions in a distributed system is crucial in the maintenance of reliability and security [1]. Most contemporary financial and business systems require accuracy on the order of more than 90%, as any inaccuracies may cause users to lose a lot of money and confidence in the organization. Therefore, there is a need to employ information processing methods that not only guarantee data integrity and consistency, but can also aid in predicting future transactions with a high level of accuracy by detecting obscured patterns. An automation method for transaction data issues are the consensus algorithms, like PBFT and RAFT, which guarantee consistency in the presence of a partially reliable network [2,3].

PBFT offers protection from some interfering attacks and system failures, while RAFT makes the consensus process easier and more intuitive. Yet, these methods are insufficient to precisely predict transaction dynamics. The adoption

O. Gervasi et al. (Eds.): ICCSA 2025 Workshops, LNCS 15887, pp. 103–114, 2026.
https://doi.org/10.1007/978-3-031-97589-9_8

of some computer science techniques with particular methods, like the integration of LSTM type neural networks, can noticeably enhance forecasting accuracy.

LSTM networks have proven to be one of the most, if not the single most efficient and effective transactional time series tool alongside with their counterparts. Their capability to account for long-term dependencies makes them indispensable when dealing with predicted noise from distributed systems. This paper demonstrates the advantages of blending.

2 PBFT and RAFT Consensus Algorithms

Two well-liked consensus algorithms that guarantee dependable operation of distributed systems are PBFT and RAFT (Table 1):

– By permitting up to one-third of nodes to be malicious, PBFT (Practical Byzantine Fault Tolerance) is made to function in the face of potential attacks and failures;
– Implementation simplicity is the main goal of RAFT (Reliable, Replicated, and Fault-Tolerant), which is utilized in less hostile environments [4].

These algorithms guarantee high confidence in the input data for the LSTM model by enabling data to be compiled and arranged prior to being provided into a machine learning system [5].

Table 1. Comparison table of PBFT and RAFT

Characteristic	PBFT	RAFT
Failure type	Byzantine (up to 1/3 of nodes may be malicious)	Node failures (only crashes, no malicious behavior)
Operating speed	Slower due to complex approval stages	Faster because it requires fewer messages
Computational costs	Hight	Low
Implementation complexity	Hight	Low
Application area	Highly secure financial systems, blockchains	Cloud services, distributed databases

For distributed systems to be dependable, secure, and resilient to possible failures and anomalies, transaction forecasting is essential. High prediction accuracy is necessary for contemporary business, blockchain, and financial applications since mistakes can result in large losses, erode user trust, and cause the system to become unstable. Transaction forecasting is difficult because of the unpredictability of data flows, noise and anomalous values, and reliance on numerous outside variables like market fluctuations and cyberattacks.

Complex data processing techniques that guarantee the integrity, consistency, and dependability of information are required to produce forecasts with the highest possible accuracy and dependability. The PBFT and RAFT consensus algorithms, which remove duplication, filter out anomalies, and arrange transactions to produce structured time sequences, are crucial to this process. Recurrent neural networks (LSTM) can be used to further analyse this data in order to find deep patterns, model recurrent patterns, and create precise time series forecasts.

When PBFT, RAFT, and LSTM are used together, the model is more resilient to noise, anomaly detection is more effective, and the likelihood of inaccurate predictions is decreased. This method can be used in distributed computing, cybersecurity, blockchain data analysis, and financial transactions. Neural network architecture optimisation, model adaptation to shifting market conditions, and integration with hybrid machine learning techniques are possible future developments of this methodology.

One of the best methods for processing time series, including transaction flows, has been shown to be LSTM networks [6]. They are the best option for transaction prediction tasks in distributed systems because of their capacity to filter noise and take long-term dependencies into account [7]. The advantages of combining PBFT and RAFT with LSTM for transaction data prediction are covered in this paper, along with an analysis of experimental findings that support the efficacy of the suggested methodology. The work algorithm PBFT → RAFT → LSTM (Fig. 1)

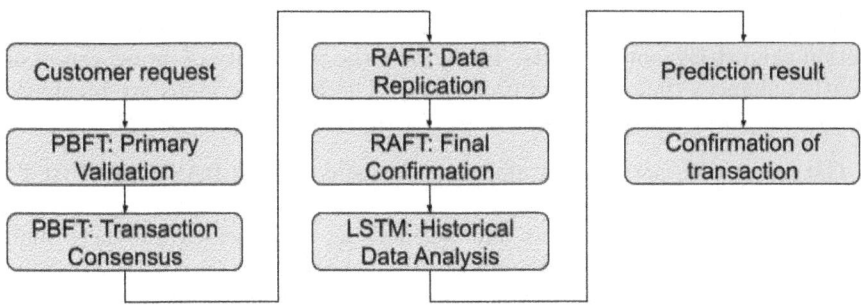

Fig. 1. Block diagram PBFT → RAFT → LSTM

1. PBFT: Attack Defences and Initial Validation
   - To complete a transaction, the client submits a request.
   - PBFT confirms the data's consistency and authenticity.
   - The following stages are carried out: Prepare → Commit → Prepare
   - RAFT receives the consistent data
2. RAFT: Fast Replication and Final Confirmation
   - RAFT receives data validated by PBFT
   - RAFT leader distributes data among nodes

- A majority of nodes confirms the transaction commit
- The finalized data is passed to LSTM
3. LSTM: Forecasting Upcoming Deals
   - Data that has been cleaned and replicated is sent to LSTM.
   - The time series of transactions is analysed by the trained model.
   - LSTM uses historical data to forecast future transactions.
4. The result's output
   - The network is optimised using the predicted data.
   - The client is given a forecast for upcoming operations as well as details regarding the execution of the transaction.

3   Applying LSTM to Transaction Prediction

When it comes to time series forecasting, including transaction flow analysis, recurrent neural networks—particularly their enhanced LSTM model—show excellent efficiency. They are among the most dependable tools for predictive analysis in distributed and financial systems because of their capacity to account for long-term dependencies, eliminate noisy outliers, and adjust to dynamic data changes. However, the quality of the input data, which necessitates pre-processing using trustworthy consensus mechanisms, has a significant impact on forecast accuracy. You can improve the consistency of transaction flows, remove inconsistencies, and filter out anomalies by using PBFT and RAFT before feeding data to the LSTM model (Fig. 2). RAFT ensures data ordering and replication, which lowers the amount of noise in the data, while PBFT ensures protection against Byzantine faults. This lowers the possibility of model errors and greatly enhances the quality of predictions. The following steps are involved in the transaction forecasting process using PBFT, RAFT, and LSTM:

1. Gathering transaction data and pre-processing it with RAFT and PBFT to get rid of inaccurate information.
2. Establishing time sequences and normalising data, which enhances model convergence and lessens the influence of outliers.
3. Optimising the network architecture, number of layers, training window size, and gradient descent parameters when training the LSTM model.
4. To avoid overfitting and improve the model's resistance to anomalies, regularisation (Dropout, L2) is used.
5. Examining the precision of forecasts with the MSE (Mean Squared Error), RMSE (Root Mean Squared Error) and MAE (Mean Absolute Error) measures lets one assess their quality.
6. Results visualisation and testing on actual transaction data let you customise the model to the particular system characteristics.

Since the model operates on structured and pre-agreed data, combining PBFT and RAFT with LSTM improves the dependability and accuracy of predictions. Forecasting mistakes can cause major financial losses in financial platforms, blockchain systems, and distributed computing environments, making this strategy particularly pertinent. Using convolutional neural networks (CNN) to emphasise complex data patterns or implementing hybrid models like LSTM + Transformer could help to increase accuracy even more in the future. Therefore, the combination of consensus algorithms and a deep neural network opens up new possibilities for exact analysis of transaction flows and the development of smart predictive systems.

Recurrent neural networks (RNNs), especially their advanced version LSTM (Long Short-Term Memory), are a powerful tool for time series analysis. In the context of transaction forecasting, LSTM allows you to identify patterns and predict future transactions based on historical data [8].

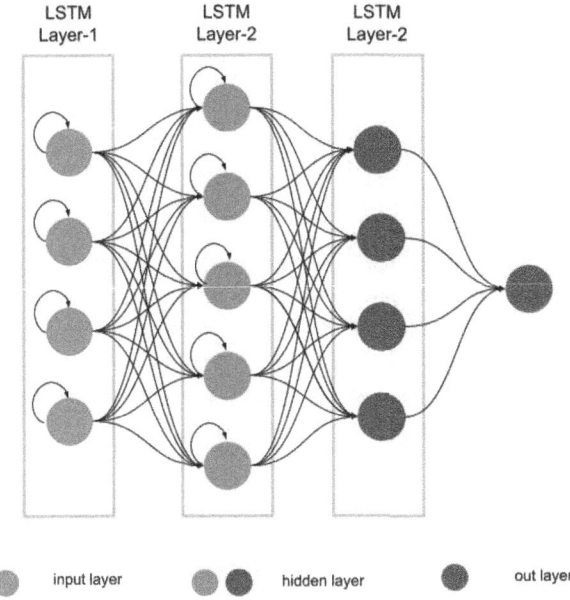

Fig. 2. LSTM architecture

Because PBFT and RAFT consensus algorithms guarantee the consistency and purity of the input data, using pre-processed data greatly increases prediction accuracy.

3.1   Key Steps of LSTM Application in Transaction Forecasting

Filtering, normalising, and structuring time sequences are the goals of the multi-stage processing that the data goes through before being fed into the LSTM model. By doing this, the noise level is decreased, mistakes are removed, and the model's predictions are guaranteed to be highly accurate. Pre-processing's primary objective is to guarantee data consistency and dependability, which is crucial in distributed systems where transactions could be vulnerable to failures or attacks.

1. **Transaction data collection and preprocessing (PBFT and RAFT)**
   Prior to analysis, the PBFT and RAFT consensus algorithms are combined to increase the consistency and dependability of the data. These algorithms improve the stability of transaction data by removing errors brought on by malevolent nodes, network outages [9,10], or random anomalies.
   – By detecting malicious or incorrect transactions, PBFT removes Byzantine errors and offers defence against attacks.
   – Transactional data is organised and replicated by RAFT, which guarantees its synchronisation and integrity amongst system nodes.
   These steps lessen the possibility of noise, duplicates, and inconsistencies by providing LSTM with pre-processed, cleaned, and trustworthy transactional data. Predictions become more accurate and stable as a result, and model convergence is greatly enhanced.
2. **Normalising data and creating time sequences**
   The data is organised and ready for training following pre-processing, which consists of two crucial steps:
   – Data normalisation speeds up model training and lessens the effect of various data scales on the network weight optimisation process by bringing all numerical values into the range [0,1] or [-1,1].
   – creation of time sequences: every transaction is shown as a window of context for earlier occurrences. For instance, when utilising a window of size 10, the model predicts the next transaction after analysing the previous ten.

The removal of anomalous data found through statistical analysis is one of the additional data processing enhancements:

– incorporating a sliding window to take transaction flow dynamics into consideration.
– increasing the training set's diversity through the use of data augmentation techniques.

Transaction data is subjected to deep filtering, normalisation, and structuring through the combined application of PBFT, RAFT, and LSTM. This reduces forecast errors, boosts the model's resilience to noise, and enhances prediction accuracy. This method works particularly well in decentralised, blockchain, and financial systems where transaction accuracy and consistency are crucial (Table 2).

LSTM is trained on the previous values (T-3, T-2, T-1) to predict the next value (T-n).

Table 2. Example of preparing input data for LSTM

Time	Transaction amount	Number of inputs	Number of inputs
T-3	0.32	2	2
T-2	0.45	3	3
T-1	0.38	1	1
T-n	...	...	...

3.2 Training an LSTM Model with Optimized Hyperparameters

Transaction prediction is essential to the efficiency, security, and dependability of contemporary distributed systems. Standard prediction techniques frequently struggle to handle complex temporal dependencies in the presence of high data variability and possible anomalies. RNNs are the best tool for analysing and forecasting transaction flows in this situation, particularly their LSTM variant.

The ability of LSTM to retain information about long-term dependencies is one of its key benefits, this is particularly crucial when examining transaction sequences. Prior to training the model, thorough preprocessing is done, including data normalisation, outlier removal, and time series ordering, because the quality of the input data has a significant impact on prediction accuracy. By removing inconsistencies and guaranteeing high transaction sequence reliability, the preprocessing stage of the preprocessing process can greatly enhance the structure of the input data by utilising the PBFT and RAFT consensus algorithms.

After preparing the data, the LSTM model is trained as follows:

Model Architecture. An LSTM model for transaction prediction consists of several components, each of which performs specific mathematical operations on the data [11,12]:

- Input Layer: The input layer takes in normalized time sequences of data, which represent the transaction time series. Let the input sequence x_t have length T (the total number of time steps) and N (the number of features at each time step), then the input data can be written as a matrix:

$$X = \{x_1, x_2, \ldots, x_T\} \tag{1}$$

where $x_t \in \mathbb{R}^N$
- LSTM Layers: The main computation in LSTM is to update the hidden states h_t and the cell state c_t at each time step t. LSTM uses several operations to process input data and store information in long-term and short-term memory:
  1. Input gate i_t:
$$i_t = \sigma(W_i \cdot [h_{t-1}, x_t] + b_i) \tag{2}$$
  2. Forget gate f_t:
$$f_t = \sigma(W_f \cdot [h_{t-1}, x_t] + b_f) \tag{3}$$

3. Output gate o_t:
$$o_t = \sigma(W_o \cdot [h_{t-1}, x_t] + b_o) \tag{4}$$

4. Candidate for new cells $\tilde{c}_t$:
$$\tilde{c}_t = \tanh(W_c \cdot [h_{t-1}, x_t] + b_c) \tag{5}$$

5. Update state of cell c_t:
$$c_t = f_t \cdot c_{t-1} + i_t \cdot \tilde{c}_t \tag{6}$$

6. Update hidden state h_t:
$$h_t = o_t \cdot \tanh(c_t) \tag{7}$$

In these formulas:
- W_i, W_f, W_o, W_c are weight matrices for input, forget, and output gates, as well as for cell candidates.
- b_i, b_f, b_o, b_c are biases.
- σ is the sigmoid, tanh is the hyperbolic tangent.
- Output Layer: After processing all the input time steps, LSTM passes the result to the output layer, which is a simple linear regressor to predict future transactions:
$$\hat{y}_t = W_y \cdot h_t + b_y \tag{8}$$

where $\hat{y}_t$ is the future transaction prediction, W_y and by b_y are the output parameters.

Optimizing Hyperparameters. To achieve the best results, it is necessary to optimize the hyperparameters of the model:

1. Window Size k: The window size (the number of previous time steps to predict the next one) is determined by the value kk. The window determines the number of inputs that will be fed to the LSTM at each training step.The window size can be defined as:
$$X_{\text{window}} = \{x_{t-k}, x_{t-k+1}, \ldots, x_{t-1}\} \tag{9}$$

where k is the window length.
2. Number of LSTM layers: The number of LSTM layers L controls the depth of the network. Typically 2–3 layers are used, which allows extracting more complex relationships from time series.
3. Activation function:
   - LSTM uses ReLU (Rectified Linear Unit) or tanh for activation.
   - Linear activation is usually used for the output layer.
4. Optimizer: Adam or RMSprop algorithms are often used to optimize the model, which effectively adapt the learning step at each step:
$$\theta_t = \theta_{t-1} - \eta \cdot \frac{m_t}{\sqrt{v_t} + \epsilon} \tag{10}$$

where η is the learning rate, m_t and v_t are the first and second order moments, ϵ is a small value for numerical stability.

Training Process. At each training step, the input data X_{window} is fed to the LSTM, which updates the hidden state h_t and the memory cell c_t based on the previous data. After the model makes a prediction $\hat{y}_t$, the error is calculated:

$$\text{Error} = \hat{y}_t - y_t \tag{11}$$

where y_t is the true value of the transaction. The error is propagated back through the network to adjust the weights using the gradient descent algorithm.The weight matrices W and bias b are updated using gradient descent:

$$W_i = W_i - \eta \cdot \frac{\partial \text{Loss}}{\partial W_i} \tag{12}$$

where η is the learning rate and $\frac{\partial \text{Loss}}{\partial W_i}$ is the gradient of the error with respect to the weights.

This process continues throughout the training epochs until the error becomes minimal and the model begins to make more accurate transaction predictions.

After Training, the accuracy of the model is assessed using error metrics:

– MSE (Mean Squared Error):

$$MSE = \frac{1}{n} \sum_{i=1}^{n} (y_i - \hat{y}_i)^2 \tag{13}$$

The lower the MSE, the more accurate the model's predictions.
– RMSE (Root Mean Squared Error)—the root of the root mean square error:

$$RMSE = \sqrt{\frac{1}{n} \sum_{i=1}^{n} (y_i - \hat{y}_i)^2} \tag{14}$$

RMSE is used to interpret the error in the same units as the original data.

4   Experimental Results of the Work

A number of tests were carried out to assess the suggested method's efficacy. When compared to conventional data processing, the prediction error rate was decreased by using PBFT and RAFT for data preprocessing. According to experimental results, by removing noise and organising transactions, combining these algorithms with LSTM greatly increases prediction accuracy.

4.1   Data Preprocessing

PBFT and RAFT were used to process the data before it was fed into the LSTM model. These algorithms offer:

- PBFT, which removes inaccurate data resulting from malicious or chance errors.
- RAFT lowers the degree of chaos in the input data by organising and coordinating the transaction sequence. LSTM Model Architecture after preprocessing, the data was used to train a multilayer LSTM model with the following parameters:
  - Input layer: normalized transaction time series.
  - Hidden layers: two LSTM layers with 128 and 64 neurons.
  - Output layer: regression for time series prediction.

Model errors were decreased by using PBFT and RAFT for data preprocessing because they decreased noise and improved transaction consistency. The decrease in MSE and RMSE when compared to conventional techniques verified more precise predictions and improved LSTM time series adaptation. By avoiding abrupt changes in values, better data structuring guaranteed the forecasts' stability. Therefore, combining PBFT and RAFT with LSTM improved the model's resilience and the precision of transaction flow forecasting (Table 3).

4.2   Reducing the Error Rate

When comparing data processing methods, the following improvements in model accuracy are observed:

Table 3. Accuracy of the observation model

Data processing method	RMSE	MAE	MAPE
Normal processing (without PBFT and RAFT)	0.082	0.065	8.5%
PBFT + RAFT	**0.047**	**0.032**	**4.1%**

Where:

- RMSE (Root Mean Square Error) – root mean square error;
- MAE (Mean Absolute Error) – mean absolute error;
- MAPE (Mean Absolute Percentage Error) – mean absolute percentage error.

4.3   Impact on Noise Immunity

The model's sensitivity to anomalies was demonstrated by the 15–20% error spikes it experienced in the absence of PBFT and RAFT. Preprocessing was used to stabilise the predicted values and reduce noise.

During the model training process, the Train Loss and Validation Loss graph is displayed in Fig. 3. The number of epochs is displayed on the X axis, and the loss function value is displayed on the Y axis.

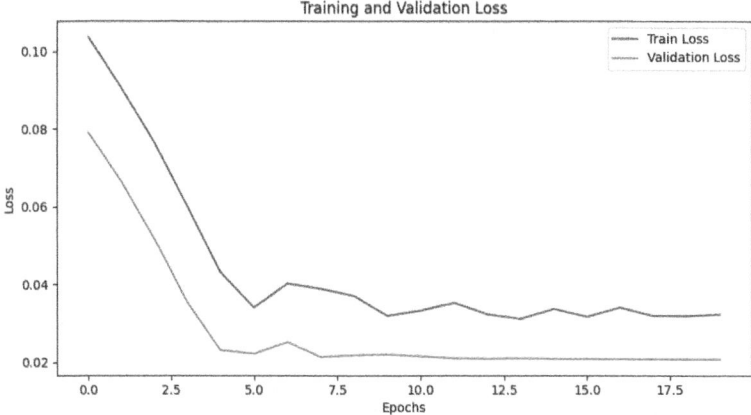

Fig. 3. The process of training the model using P-BFT and RAFT transactions

1. Training Loss - measures how well the model predicts the data it is trained on. Validation
2. Loss - shows how well the model generalizes knowledge to new data.

The graph demonstrates that:

– Effective learning starts when the error rapidly drops in the initial epochs.
– Following the fifth epoch, the decline's dynamics slow down before a mild oscillation starts.
– The fact that the validation error is still less than the training error could be a sign of regularisation techniques being used or of the test data being simple.

Experimental results showed that integrating PBFT and RAFT before processing in the LSTM model allows: Reducing prediction errors (up to 50%), Increasing resistance to noise, Streamlining the transaction sequence

5   Conclusion

When combined with LSTM, the consensus algorithms PBFT and RAFT show great promise for transaction prediction in distributed systems. This method can greatly improve the consistency and dependability of data, which lowers the number of errors and raises prediction accuracy.

By combining PBFT and RAFT, anomalies from potentially malicious or random data failures are removed, and time series are smoothed, increasing the model's resistance to noise and sudden changes in input data. This is particularly crucial in blockchain and financial systems, where prediction accuracy is essential to avoiding mistakes, fraud, and poor choices.

Additionally, temporal dependencies in transaction sequences can be considered when processing ordered and cleaned data using LSTM, which reduces information loss and produces more accurate forecasts. Thus, the model's stability and adaptability to dynamic changes in distributed environments are greatly enhanced by the combination of recurrent neural networks and consensus algorithms.

References

1. Bogdanov, A., et al.: Testing and comparative analysis of the F-BFT-based DLT solution. In: Gervasi, O., et al. (eds.) ICCSA 2021. LNCS, vol. 12952, pp. 31–41. Springer, Cham (2021). https://doi.org/10.1007/978-3-030-86973-1_3
2. Bogdanov, A., et al.: Integration of PBFT and raft algorithms with recurrent neural networks to improve the reliability of distributed systems. In: Gervasi, O., Murgante, B., Garau, C., Taniar, D., Rocha, A.M.A.C., Faginas Lago, M.N. (eds.) ICCSA 2024, pp. 226–237. Springer, Cham (2024). https://doi.org/10.1007/978-3-031-65154-0_14
3. Castro, M., Liskov, B.: Practical byzantine fault tolerance. In: OsDI, vol. 99, pp. 173–186 (1999)
4. Ongaro, D., Ousterhout, J.: In search of an understandable consensus algorithm. In: 2014 USENIX Annual Technical Conference (USENIX ATC 14), pp. 305–319 (2014)
5. Hochreiter, S., Schmidhuber, J.: Long short-term memory. Neural Comput. **9**(8), 1735–1780 (1997)
6. Goodfellow, I., et al.: Deep Learning, vol. 1, no. 2. Cambridge, MIT Press (2016)
7. Li, X., Liu, Q., Wu, Y.: Prediction on blockchain virtual currency transaction under long short-term memory model and deep belief network. Appl. Soft Comput. **116**, 108349 (2022)
8. Kingma, D.P., Ba, J.: Adam: a method for stochastic optimization. arXiv preprint arXiv:1412.6980 (2014)
9. Schmidhuber, J.: Deep learning in neural networks: an overview. Neural Netw. **61**, 85–117 (2015)
10. Vaswani, A., et al.: Attention is all you need. Adv. Neural Inf. Process. Syst. **30** (2017)
11. Brown, T., et al.: Language models are few-shot learners. Adv. Neural Inf. Process. Syst. **33**, 1877–1901 (2020)
12. Wang, B., et al.: Exploring anomaly detection and risk assessment in financial markets using deep neural networks. Int. J. Innov. Res. Comput. Sci. Technol. **12**(4) (2024)

Towards Secure Cross-Organizational Data Transfer: A Blockchain-Enabled Message Broker Approach

Gleb Slepenkov and Vladimir Korkhov(✉)

Saint Petersburg State University, 7-9 Universitetskaya Embankment, St Petersburg, Russia 199034
gslepenkov@gmail.com, v.korkhov@spbu.ru

Abstract. Secure data transfer (SDT) is crucial in modern information societies, particularly for cross-organizational data exchange. This paper investigates the application of blockchain technology to create robust SDT systems, combining the benefits of using blockchain as both a data access interface and a direct data transfer tool. We propose a novel architecture featuring a message broker-like design that overcomes data size limitations present in existing blockchain-based SDT solutions. The architecture incorporates blockchain, internal data storage within organizations, and connectors facilitating interaction between these components. The SDT process relies on smart contracts for managing data access, transfer, and confirmation, while the actual data is stored off-chain. We advocate for a private, two-layered blockchain-based system, employing PBFT consensus within smaller clusters for efficient message transfer and RAFT consensus for system management and data replication. This layered approach enhances both fault tolerance and scalability capabilities in comparison to existing blockchain approaches and traditional message brokers. Furthermore, we explore the potential of integrating Artificial Intelligence (AI) for anomaly detection in smart contract execution and dynamic load balancing across blockchain nodes in order to optimize the security and performance characteristics of the system. We present a system architecture overview and describe key implementation details of proposed system, including potential AI-driven enhancements.

Keywords: Blockchain · Secure Data Transfer (SDT) · Data Security · Distributed Ledger Technology (DLT) · Message Broker · Data Access Control · Fault Tolerance · Artificial Intelligence (AI)

1 Introduction

Nowadays, secure data transfer (SDT) is essential for maintaining data confidentiality and integrity. SDT systems are critical infrastructure components across diverse sectors, including financial institutions, governmental agencies, and enterprises. Implementing robust SDT mechanisms becomes particularly challenging when facilitating cross-organizational data exchange or connecting

O. Gervasi et al. (Eds.): ICCSA 2025 Workshops, LNCS 15887, pp. 115–130, 2026.
https://doi.org/10.1007/978-3-031-97589-9_9

geographically distributed departments within a single organization, i.e., scenarios which require the use of public networks. This fact significantly increases the risk of data loss, data corruption, or unauthorized access to data during the transfer process. Consequently, data integrity verification and counterparty authentication protocols are required. Furthermore, confirmation of data reception is often a critical requirement. The heterogeneity of data transfer technologies utilized by different counterparties further complicates the SDT process.

Blockchain technology has the potential to enhance existing SDT mechanisms. This technology, by design, provides core features essential for SDT, such as fault tolerance, ledger data immutability, and zero trust between blockchain nodes. Moreover, many blockchains are designed to operate in unreliable public networks with nodes running in different, heterogeneous clusters owned by separate stakeholders, which makes this technology especially suitable for cross-organizational data transfer. Furthermore, blockchain platforms often provide smart contracts, which allow implementing custom data transfer logic directly on the blockchain.

The reasons mentioned above have stimulated significant research interest, as evidenced by comprehensive surveys exploring blockchain applications for data sharing and exchange [1] and for specific domains like smart transport [2]. These surveys highlight the potential of blockchain to address the challenges of SDT in diverse and demanding environments.

This study explores existing blockchain application paradigms for the SDT process and proposes a novel approach that integrates their advantages. The result is a blockchain-based SDT system that maintains key features of established approaches while adopting a message broker-like architecture with relaxed data size limitations. Furthermore, we investigate the potential of integrating Artificial Intelligence (AI) to enhance the security and efficiency of this system through anomaly detection and dynamic load balancing. This article presents an architectural overview and describes key implementation details of the proposed system, including potential AI-driven enhancements.

The study is organized in the following way. Section 2 describes existing data transfer paradigms in detail. Section 3 represents the proposed system architecture. Section 4 describes implementation details of the proposed system. Section 5 explores the potential AI-driven enhancements to the system. Finally, Sect. 6 concludes this article and denotes further research directions, including future work on AI integration.

2   Related Work

The integration of blockchain technology into data transfer systems is implemented according to two primary paradigms: blockchain as a data access interface and blockchain as a direct data transfer tool. This section examines the existing literature, classifying studies according to these two distinct roles of blockchain in facilitating data exchange.

2.1   Blockchain as a Data Access Interface

This approach leverages blockchain as a secure and transparent mechanism for managing and controlling access to data that is typically stored off-chain. The blockchain records metadata about the data, access permissions, and transaction histories, thereby ensuring data integrity, audit ability, and secure access control. The data itself is transferred using conventional methods.

Wang et al. introduced BBS, a big data sharing system utilizing blockchain for access control and data integrity management [3]. Similarly, Wang et al. proposed a blockchain-based model for sharing big data in the oil and gas sector, employing blockchain to enable secure data access and provenance tracking [4]. Yang et al. developed a sharing platform for wild bird data based on blockchain and IPFS, where blockchain governs access rights to data residing in IPFS [5]. A cross-organizational data sharing framework that uses blockchain probes to orchestrate and audit data access across various entities was presented by Jia et al. [6]. Gupta et al. explored the application of blockchain for securing data access within e-healthcare applications [7].

2.2   Blockchain as a Data Transfer Tool

This approach employs the blockchain directly to transfer data between participants. While data may occasionally be stored on-chain, it is more common for the blockchain to facilitate the transfer of data stored off-chain, often in conjunction with technologies such as peer-to-peer networks or distributed file systems.

Lin et al. proposed a multi-level blockchain architecture for secure data transfer in the Internet of Vehicles (IoV), directly leveraging blockchain for data exchange [8]. Peng et al. demonstrated the feasibility of building a peer-to-peer file storage and sharing system on a consortium blockchain, where the blockchain assists in discovering and securely transferring file chunks [9]. Priyadarshini et al. introduced a system for secured data transfer between fog nodes utilizing blockchain to enhance the security of the data transfer process itself [10].

2.3   Enabling Technologies and Security Considerations

Regardless of the chosen paradigm, several enabling technologies and security considerations are universally relevant. Kim et al. presented a hybrid decentralized PBFT blockchain framework for OpenStack message queues, aimed at improving fault tolerance and scalability, crucial aspects for reliable data transfer systems [11]. A publish-subscribe architecture to foster interoperability among different blockchain networks, thus facilitating data exchange across heterogeneous systems, was introduced by Ghaemi et al. [12]. Both solutions represent the architecture where blockchain acts as a message broker, data transfer process is organized in publish-subscribe way and data flow is separated into topics. Such an architecture is traditional for message brokers like Apache Kafka [13]. That's why it will be referenced as "message broker-like" architecture in the rest of the paper.

Bagga et al. and Xu et al. explored blockchain-based authentication and key agreement protocols for IoV, enhancing the security of data transfer in vehicular contexts [14,15]. Bogdanov et al. focused on the consensus mechanism, exploring a combination of PBFT and Raft [16], while Ai et al. proposed a Proof-of-Transactions consensus protocol [17], both striving for efficient and scalable agreement in distributed ledgers.

2.4   Comparison of Approaches

The two approaches, blockchain as a data access interface and blockchain as a data transfer tool, offer distinct advantages and disadvantages depending on the specific use case and requirements.

Table 1. Comparison of Blockchain Approaches for Data Transfer

Feature	Blockchain as Data Access Interface	Blockchain as Data Transfer Tool
Data Storage	Primarily Off-Chain	Often Off-Chain, but metadata on-chain
Data Transfer	Traditional methods	Blockchain or Blockchain-assisted
Scalability	Higher, as data transfer is off-chain	Potentially Lower, dependent on blockchain throughput
Complexity	Lower	Higher
On-Chain Footprint	Smaller (Metadata only)	Larger (Metadata and potentially data chunks)
Suitability	Large datasets, access control focus	Smaller datasets, secure and direct transfer focus

As illustrated in Table 1, the choice between these two approaches hinges on factors such as data size, scalability requirements, security priorities, and the level of on-chain transparency desired. The data access interface approach is generally more suitable for scenarios involving large datasets and a primary focus on secure access control, while the data transfer tool approach is better suited for scenarios demanding secure and direct data transfer, even if it potentially introduces limitations in terms of scalability.

3   System Architecture Overview

3.1   System Components

This section describes the architecture of the proposed system. The architecture aims to combine two dominant blockchain integration paradigms for data transfer systems, as identified in Sect. 2. By integrating these approaches, our system seeks to achieve a message broker-like architecture that facilitates convenient data transfer while mitigating the data size limitations inherent in individual solutions.

Our architecture leverages the following trends observed in recent research:

1. **Blockchain as a message broker:** (e.g., [11,12]). This approach utilizes the blockchain ledger for direct message transfer.
2. **Blockchain as an interface to off-chain data:** (e.g., [3,6]). This paradigm employs the blockchain to manage access and pointers to data stored off-chain.

While each of these trends offers unique advantages, they also present limitations:

1. **Limitations of Blockchain as a Message Broker:** Relying on the blockchain ledger for message transfer significantly restricts system scalability and the size of transmissible data due to the inherent constraints of blockchain technology.
2. **Limitations of Blockchain as an Interface to Off-Chain Data:** Solutions implementing this approach often lack native notification mechanisms, making efficient message retrieval a challenge and requiring external polling or other complex notification strategies.

The proposed system addresses these individual limitations by combining the strengths of both paradigms. This integrated approach allows us to leverage the blockchain for both message brokering and off-chain data referencing, effectively relaxing the constraints on data size and enabling efficient notification mechanisms.

The proposed architecture assumes that the system should contain the following components:

- Blockchain as the core system component responsible for data transfer process orchestration. Blockchain nodes act as interfaces to data storages, while smart contracts implement all data transfer mechanisms like data transformation (e.g. message encryption / signing), data verification and message notifications.
- Data storages internally used by counterparties (organizations) to store the data to be sent.
- Connectors—some application used by SDT process counterparties in order to create a connection between their data storages and blockchain nodes owned by the organization (mainly inspired by blockchain probes described in [6]).

A sample of such an architecture for SDT between two organizations is presented in Fig. 1.

3.2   SDT Process Scheme

The SDT process scheme is illustrated in Fig. 2 and involves data transfer between two organizations (Org1 and Org2) using a blockchain-mediated system.

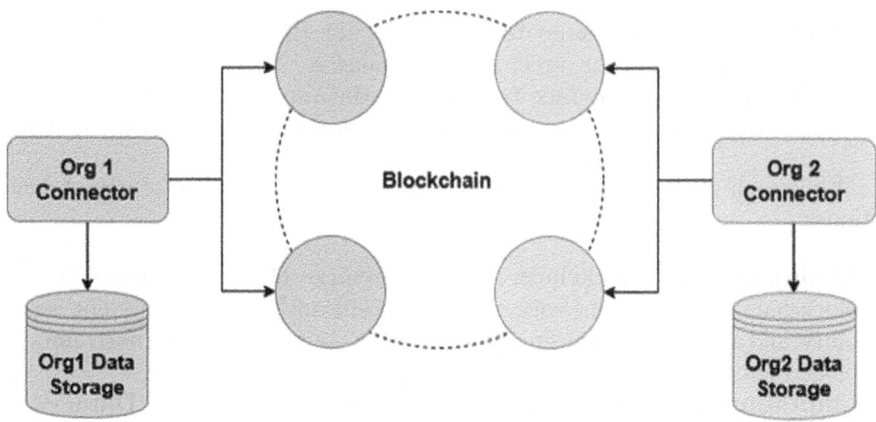

Fig. 1. System architecture for two organizations

The process can be separated into following stages:

Data Sending (Org1)

1. **Initiate Transfer (1):** The data sender (Org1) initiates a data transfer request to its connector.
2. **Data Persistence and Metadata Collection (2):** The Org1 connector persists the data in Org1's storage and gathers associated metadata.
3. **Smart Contract Invocation (3):** The Org1 connector queries the blockchain to initiate the execution of the SDT smart contract.
4. **Metadata Validation and Recording (4):** The smart contract validates the provided metadata and records it on the ledger.
5. **Notification (5–6):** Upon successful metadata validation, the smart contract notifies the Org2 connector about the availability of a new message and acknowledges message acceptance to Org1.

Data Retrieval (Org2)

1. **Data Request and Smart Contract Execution (7):** The Org2 connector queries the blockchain nodes and executes the SDT smart contract.
2. **Receiver Authentication (8):** The smart contract verifies Org2's permissions to the requested data.
3. **Data Retrieval from Org1 (9–12):** If authorized, the smart contract requests the data from the Org1 connector. Upon receiving the request, the Org1 connector retrieves the data from Org1's storage and transmits it back to the smart contract.
4. **Data Preparation (13):** The smart contract prepares the data for transfer, potentially involving encryption and digital signing.
5. **Data Delivery to Org2 (14–16):** The prepared data is returned to the Org2 connector, which then stores the received data in Org2's storage.

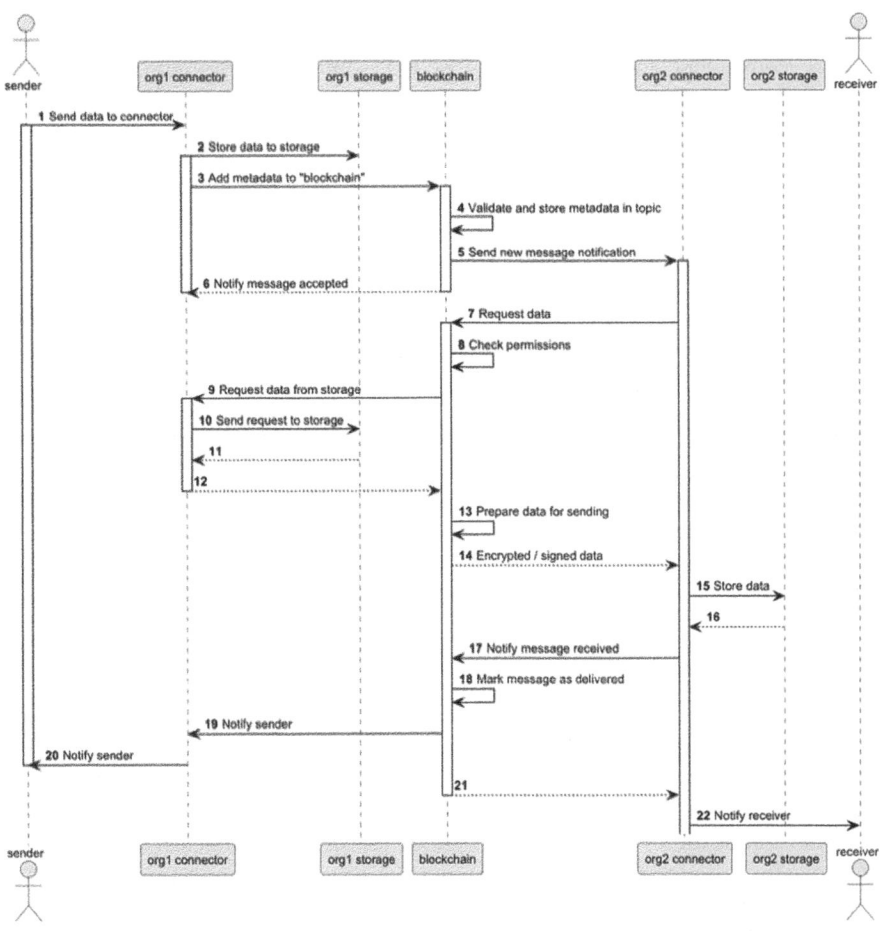

Fig. 2. SDT process scheme

Process Finalization

1. **Message Reception Notification (17):** The Org2 connector notifies the blockchain about the message reception via the smart contract.
2. **Message Registry Update (18):** The smart contract updates the message registry, marking the message as delivered.
3. **Confirmation Notifications (19–22):** The smart contract notifies the Org1 and Org2 connectors about the successful completion of the message delivery process, and the connectors inform the data sender and data receiver about the completion of the data transfer process respectively.

Such an algorithm has the following important features:

1. Loose coupling between sender and receiver due to blockchain usage as a message broker.

2. Better fault tolerance compared to regular message brokers.
3. More convenient message broker-like SDT interface compared to existing blockchain solutions.
4. Greater SDT process customization capabilities due to smart contract usage.

4   Implementation Details

4.1   Blockchain Selection

Blockchain technology constitutes the core component of the SDT system. Consequently, the specific blockchain implementation exerts a significant influence on key system parameters, including:

- **Throughput:** The volume of data the system can transfer within a defined time interval.
- **Fault Tolerance:** The types of faults the system can withstand and the maximum number of node failures the system can accommodate while maintaining functionality.
- **Scalability:** The maximum permissible number of nodes within the system.

The parameters delineated above are primarily governed by the blockchain type and the employed consensus algorithm.

A review of the existing literature reveals a prevalent trend favoring private blockchain solutions. This preference arises from the necessity for controlled access, enhanced privacy, and the potential for higher throughput in many SDT scenarios, particularly within applications such as IoT and vehicular networks. While several studies mention the potential use of public blockchains, they are not typically presented as the primary option. Specific examples include:

- Peng et al. [9] propose a peer-to-peer file storage and sharing system based on a consortium blockchain.
- Jia et al. [6] present a cross-organizational data sharing framework based on blockchain-probes, indicative of a permissioned setting.
- Numerous papers addressing IoT applications (e.g., [7,17]) often implicitly or explicitly assume a permissioned blockchain context to address security and scalability constraints.

Therefore, this paper posits that a private blockchain is the most suitable option for SDT system implementation.

In addition to selecting the appropriate blockchain type, employing the correct consensus algorithm is crucial. To enhance the SDT system's fault tolerance, this paper proposes the utilization of the Practical Byzantine Fault Tolerance (PBFT) algorithm, aligning with observed trends in the literature. However, PBFT is known to have inherent performance limitations.

Firstly, PBFT implementations necessitate the transfer of substantial data volumes between blockchain nodes to achieve consensus. For instance, the BFT-SMaRT algorithm, employed by Hyperledger Fabric [18], requires each node to transmit 80 MB of data to achieve a performance of 2500 transactions per second. This implies a total traffic volume of 720 MB within a cluster of only 10 nodes during all consensus algorithm stages.

Furthermore, the throughput of such a consensus algorithm is contingent upon the number of nodes within the system. Research [18] indicates that BFT-SMaRT achieves maximum throughput when the system comprises 7 nodes (Fig. 3).

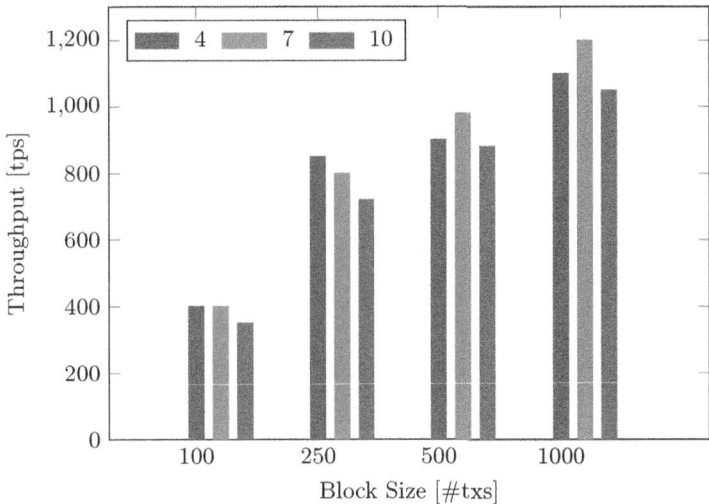

Fig. 3. BFT-SMaRT performance in global networks (measured by Barger et al. [18])

Increasing the number of nodes beyond this optimum leads to a degradation in throughput. The maximum permissible number of nodes, according to research [19], is limited to approximately 100.

For the reasons articulated above, a pure PBFT blockchain is not ideally suited for the creation of scalable and fault-tolerant systems. Fortunately, this limitation can be addressed by leveraging the multi-layered blockchain architecture described in [8,16], coupled with the data flow separation into topics and partitions, a common practice in message brokers such as Apache Kafka [13].

This paper proposes the use of a two-layered blockchain architecture. The first layer employs the PBFT consensus algorithm. Given the algorithm's known limitations, this layer will be constructed from multiple, relatively small clusters, each consisting of up to 7 nodes. This layer embodies the concept of a partition, representing the smallest system component directly responsible for the execution of SDT smart contracts.

The subsequent layer leverages the RAFT consensus algorithm [20]. This layer is designed for two primary functions: system management (detailed in Sect. 4.2) and asynchronous data replication following PBFT consensus rounds (described in Sect. 4.3). Consequently, this layer is analogous to the topic concept found in message brokers.

This architecture allows for the preservation of all fault-tolerance characteristics inherent in the PBFT consensus algorithm while simultaneously enhancing system scalability. Scaling the system does not necessitate an increase in the PBFT cluster size. Instead, a new, smaller PBFT layer-1 cluster is created and connected to the existing RAFT layer-2 cluster, which has a less stringent limit on the maximum number of nodes.

4.2   Data Flow Separation

This section delineates the proposed data flow separation scheme. As previously mentioned, the data flow of the SDT system is partitioned into topics and partitions.

A topic is defined as a data stream unified by a common theme or a list of consumers. To address the limitations outlined earlier, each topic is further subdivided into a list of partitions. An illustrative example of such a data flow separation into two partitions is depicted in Fig. 4.

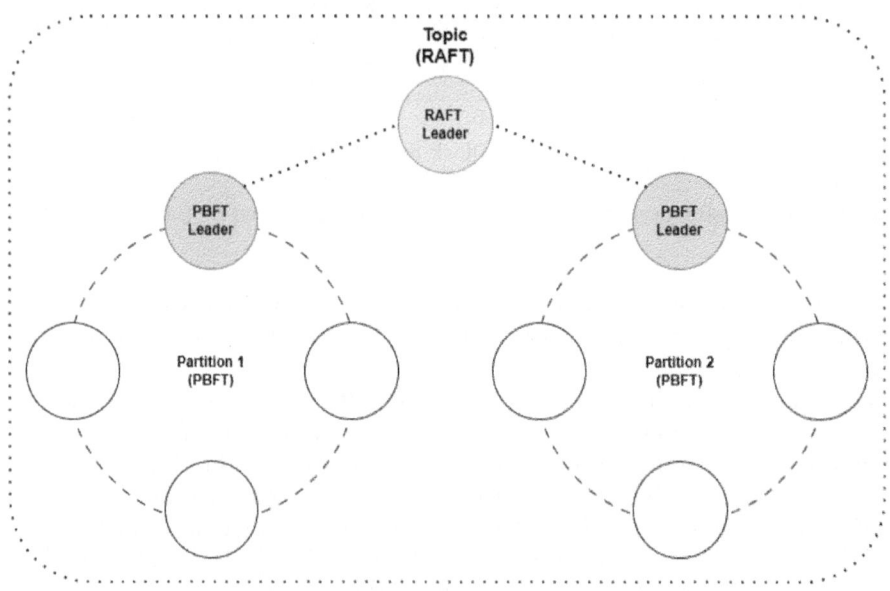

Fig. 4. Structure of a topic with two partitions

Two primary challenges must be addressed to implement this data flow separation:

- How to select a specific blockchain node for SDT process initialization while ensuring effective load balancing?
- How to select the appropriate partition for a specific message?

The selection of a specific load balancing algorithm constitutes a separate area of research and, therefore, falls outside the scope of this article.

Concerning the second challenge, this paper proposes the utilization of hash partitioning, a technique employed by Apache Kafka, for partition selection. The partition is determined by calculating the remainder of dividing the key's hash value by the total number of partitions.

To store the topic configuration data, the layer-2 ledger of the blockchain is proposed. Each node within this blockchain layer stores a list of partitions and a corresponding list of nodes for each partition. Any structural modifications within a topic, such as the creation of a new partition, are to be executed via a dedicated smart contract.

A key advantage of this approach lies in the replication of configuration data across all blockchain nodes. Consequently, data senders can retrieve this data from any topic node. This eliminates the need for dedicated control nodes, such as Apache Zookeeper nodes in Apache Kafka, thereby enhancing system fault tolerance by mitigating the risk of a single point of failure.

4.3   Data Replication

As previously discussed, a primary advantage of utilizing blockchain technology in a data transfer system is its ability to provide verifiable evidence of message delivery by immutably recording the data transfer history within its ledger. Given the system's separation into multiple partitions, verifying message delivery necessitates identifying the specific partition used for the message's transfer. This task is complicated by the fact that the system configuration may evolve over time, potentially requiring an iterative search across all existing partitions. To streamline the message delivery verification process, data replication to all topic nodes is essential.

To facilitate this data replication mechanism, this article introduces the concepts of global and local ledgers. The global ledger, maintained at the topic level, essentially represents the union of all partition-specific ledgers, which we term local ledgers. The global ledger is updated asynchronously with data from the local ledgers through a dedicated periodic task. This task implements the following algorithm:

1. Retrieve the list of partitions from the topic configuration ledger.
2. For each partition:
   (a) Identify the key of the last replicated block.
   (b) Query the local partition ledger to ascertain the presence of new data.
   (c) If new data is found, copy all new data blocks to the global ledger.

An illustrative example of this algorithm's execution for two partitions is presented in Fig. 5. In the figure, the last replicated blocks are highlighted in yellow, while the blocks slated for replication are depicted in green. Prior to the algorithm's execution, there are three blockchain nodes awaiting replication: one from Partition 1 and two from Partition 2. Following the replication process, these blocks are appended to their corresponding blockchains within the global ledger.

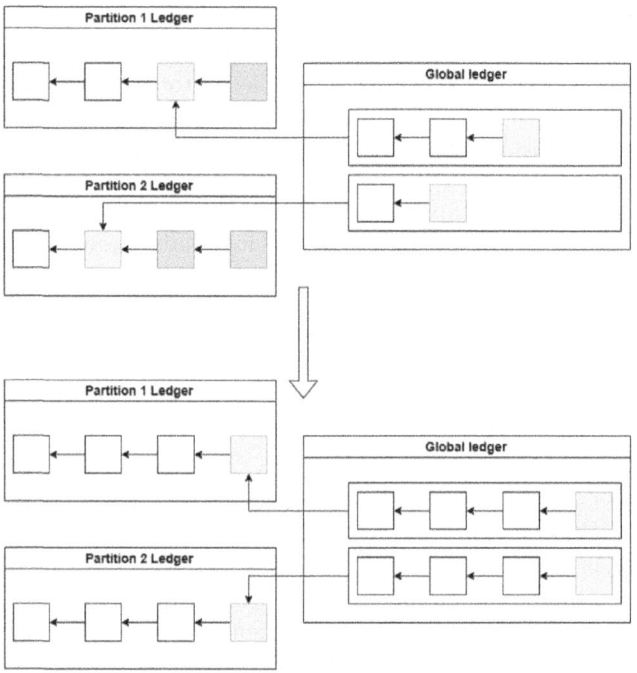

Fig. 5. Data replication to global ledger

Given that the algorithm operates on the second blockchain layer, all modifications to the global ledger are, again, governed by the RAFT consensus algorithm.

5   Potential AI-Driven Enhancements

Building upon the architecture and implementation details described in previous sections, the integration of Artificial Intelligence (AI) offers substantial opportunities to further optimize and enhance the SDT system. Specifically, AI can be instrumental in improving the efficiency and security of smart contract execution, as well as in dynamically managing the workload across the blockchain nodes.

5.1   AI-Powered Anomaly Detection

As outlined in Sect. 3, smart contracts play a central role in managing data access, transfer, and message delivery confirmation within the SDT process. However, vulnerabilities in these contracts can compromise the entire system. Drawing inspiration from [21], AI, and particularly deep learning techniques, can be employed to create a real-time anomaly detection system tailored to the nuances of the SDT process.

This AI system would continuously monitor the execution of SDT smart contracts, learning the expected behavior patterns for each stage of the data transfer process (as depicted in Fig. 2). Deviations from these established patterns, such as:

– **Unvalidated Metadata Changes:** Detecting attempts to alter metadata recorded on the ledger without proper authorization.
– **Unexpected Data Transformation:** Identifying unauthorized or incorrect data encryption/signing operations.
– **Abnormal Access Patterns:** Recognizing unauthorized data retrieval attempts or suspicious data requests from connector applications.

These deviations would be flagged as potential anomalies, triggering alerts and potentially halting the SDT process until the issue is investigated. This proactive approach significantly strengthens the security of the SDT system by mitigating risks associated with malicious or compromised smart contracts.

5.2   AI-Driven Dynamic Load Balancing

As described in Sect. 4, the two-layered blockchain architecture, coupled with data flow separation into topics and partitions, is designed to enhance the scalability and throughput of the SDT system. However, the efficient allocation of smart contract execution requests across the cluster nodes is crucial to maximizing performance.

Inspired by the work of Singh et al. [22] and Tsang et al. [23], we propose integrating an AI-powered dynamic load balancing mechanism that considers a multitude of factors to intelligently route SDT smart contract execution requests:

– **Node Availability and Capacity:** Monitoring the real-time availability and computational capacity of each node within the PBFT clusters in layer 1.
– **Network Latency:** Assessing the network latency between the requesting connectors and the potential execution nodes.
– **Current Workload:** Evaluating the current workload of each node to avoid overloading.
– **Data Localization:** Prioritizing the selection of nodes that have already replicated relevant metadata from the topic, as described in Sect. 4.3, minimizing data transfer overhead.

The AI algorithm, potentially employing reinforcement learning techniques, would continuously learn from past performance data to optimize the routing decisions, ensuring that SDT smart contract execution requests are directed to the most suitable node based on the prevailing conditions. This dynamic load balancing would lead to improved network throughput, reduced latency, and enhanced overall system efficiency.

6   Conclusions and Future Work

Blockchain technology is, by design, a promising solution for enhancing the security and performance characteristics of SDT systems. However, existing blockchain application paradigms have either strict transferred data size limitations or interfaces inconvenient for SDT process implementation. That's why we propose a novel approach, which is basically a combination of existing paradigms enhanced by a message broker-like architecture. Such an approach allows us to combine the strengths of existing solutions in order to achieve better security and performance characteristics, combined with familiar data transfer interfaces and data flow separation into topics and partitions. The core component of the proposed system is a two-layered blockchain. The first blockchain layer utilizes small PBFT clusters (named partitions) directly for data transfer. These small clusters are then combined into a second layer blockchain with a RAFT consensus algorithm (named topics), utilized for system management and asynchronous data replication across topic nodes. Such a two-layered architecture allows us to overcome known PBFT cluster size limitations while preserving fault tolerance capabilities. For further system improvements, we explored the potential integration of Artificial Intelligence (AI) for anomaly detection and dynamic load balancing. To summarize, the proposed system architecture provides loose coupling between sender and receiver, improved fault tolerance compared to traditional message brokers, a more convenient message broker-like SDT interface, greater SDT process customization capabilities through smart contract usage, and the prospect of AI-driven enhancements, which makes it a practical and secure solution for cross-organizational data sharing.

Future research will focus on several directions. The main research direction is the implementation and evaluation of the proposed system's functional prototype in order to measure its performance characteristics. The list of additional research directions includes the selection of specific, optimized consensus algorithm implementations, the development of a dynamic load balancing mechanism for smart contract execution node selection, and the integration of AI-driven SDT process anomaly detection.

Acknowledgments. Supported by Saint Petersburg State University, project ID: 95438429.

References

1. Song, R., et al.: A survey of blockchain-based schemes for data sharing and exchange. IEEE Trans. Big Data (2023)
2. Bagga, P., Das, A.K.: Blockchain for smart transport applications. In: Advances in Blockchain Technology for Cyber Physical Systems, pp. 125–154. Springer, Cham (2022)
3. Wang, S., et al.: BBS: a secure and autonomous blockchain-based big-data sharing system. J. Syst. Architect. **150**, 103133 (2024)
4. Wang, Y.Y., Huang, S., Yu, X.: An oil and gas big data sharing model based on blockchain technology. IOP Conf. Ser. Earth Environ. Sci. **651**(3), 032105 (2021)
5. Yang, H., et al.: A research on the sharing platform of wild bird data in Yunnan province based on blockchain and interstellar file system. Sensors **22**(18), 6961 (2022)
6. Jia, X., et al.: Cross-organisational data sharing framework based on blockchain-probes. IET Netw. **12**(2), 77–85 (2023)
7. Gupta, S., Yadav, B., Gupta, B.: Security of IoT-based e-healthcare applications using blockchain. In: Advances in Blockchain Technology for Cyber Physical Systems, pp. 79–107. Springer, Cham (2022)
8. Lin, H.Y.: Secure data transfer based on a multi-level blockchain for internet of vehicles. Sensors **23**(5), 2664 (2023)
9. Peng, S., et al.: A peer-to-peer file storage and sharing system based on consortium blockchain. Futur. Gener. Comput. Syst. **141**, 197–204 (2023)
10. Priyadarshini, R., Malarvizhi, N.: Secured data transfer between fog nodes using blockchain. In: Proceedings of the 2nd International Conference on Computational and Bio Engineering: CBE 2020, pp. 417–422. Springer Singapore (2021)
11. Kim, Y., Park, J.: Hybrid decentralized PBFT blockchain framework for Open-Stack message queue. HCIS **10**(1), 31 (2020)
12. Ghaemi, S., et al.: A pub-sub architecture to promote blockchain interoperability. arXiv preprint arXiv:2101.12331 (2021)
13. Foundation, A.S.: Apache Kafka documentation. https://kafka.apache.org/documentation/ Accessed 9 March 2025
14. Bagga, P., et al.: Blockchain-based batch authentication protocol for internet of vehicles. J. Syst. Architect. **113**, 101877 (2021)
15. Xu, Z., et al.: A blockchain-based roadside unit-assisted authentication and key agreement protocol for internet of vehicles. J. Parallel Distrib. Comput. **149**, 29–39 (2021)
16. Bogdanov, A., et al.: Combining PBFT and Raft for scalable and fault-tolerant distributed consensus. Phys. Part. Nucl. **55**(3), 418–420 (2024)
17. Ai, Z., Cui, W.: A proof-of-transactions blockchain consensus protocol for large-scale IoT. IEEE Internet Things J. (2022). https://doi.org/10.1109/JIOT.2021.3108621
18. Barger, A., et al.: A byzantine fault-tolerant consensus library for hyperledger fabric. In: 2021 IEEE International Conference on Blockchain and Cryptocurrency (ICBC), pp. 1–9. IEEE (2021)
19. Ke, Z., Park, N.: Performance modeling and analysis of hyperledger fabric. Clust. Comput. **26**(5), 2681–2699 (2023)
20. Ongaro, D., Ousterhout, J.: The Raft consensus algorithm. Lecture Notes CS **190**, 2022 (2015)

21. Demertzis, K., Iliadis, L., Tziritas, N., Kikiras, P.: Anomaly detection via blockchained deep learning smart contracts in industry 4.0. Neural Comput. Appl. **32**(23), 17361–17378 (2020). https://doi.org/10.1007/s00521-020-05189-8
22. Singh, A.R., Kumar, R.S., Madhavi, K.R., Alsaif, F., Bajaj, M., Zaitsev, I.: Optimizing demand response and load balancing in smart EV charging networks using ai integrated blockchain framework. Sci. Rep. **14**(1), 31768 (2024)
23. Tsang, Y.P., Lee, C., Zhang, K., Wu, C.H., Ip, W.: On-chain and off-chain data management for blockchain-internet of things: a multi-agent deep reinforcement learning approach. J. Grid Comput. **22**(1), 16 (2024)

Computational and Applied Mathematics (CAM 2025)

Two Families of W-Methods: Analysis and Application on Battery Models

Dajana Conte[1]([✉])[ID] and Giovanni Pagano[2][ID]

[1] Department of Mathematics, University of Salerno, 84084 Fisciano, Italy
`dajconte@unisa.it`
[2] Department of Agricultural Sciences, University of Naples Federico II,
80055 Portici, Italy
`giovanni.pagano5@unina.it`

Abstract. This paper focuses on the efficient numerical solution of stiff initial value problems arising from the spatial discretization of Partial Differential Equations (PDEs). In particular, this work shows an efficient implementation of two families of linearly implicit numerical methods recently introduced in the scientific literature: the TASE-W methods and the singly TASE-Runge-Kutta methods. These methods are derived exploiting the so-called TASE (Time-Accurate and highly Stable Explicit) operators, and are particular cases of W-methods. We deeply analyze the properties of consistency, stability, and computational cost of TASE-W and singly TASE-Runge-Kutta methods, employing them for the solution of a system of two coupled PDEs for the description of the charge/discharge processes in electric batteries.

Keywords: W-methods · TASE-W methods · singly
TASE-Runge-Kutta methods · stiff problems · PDEs · battery
modeling

1 Introduction

This work focuses on the numerical solution of large stiff initial value problems (IVPs)

$$y'(t) = f(t, y), \quad y_0 = y(t_0), \qquad t \in [t_0, t_{\text{end}}], \quad y, f \in \mathbb{R}^m. \qquad (1)$$

Stiff IVPs are characterized by the presence of rapidly changing components, and often require very small discretization step-sizes unless a stable numerical method is employed for their solution. Stiff systems often arise in fields like chemical kinetics or control theory, where some components evolve much faster than others. Stiff IVPs can also arise from the spatial semi-discretization of Partial Differential Equations (PDEs), that are widely used in engineering and physics to describe phenomena characterized by several independent variables, such as temperature distribution in a solid, evolution of different plant species in arid or semi-arid environments, corrosion of materials [30], charge/discharge processes in electric batteries involving several chemical substances [31]. Models of recent interest are also constituted by stochastic differential equations [16],

O. Gervasi et al. (Eds.): ICCSA 2025 Workshops, LNCS 15887, pp. 133–149, 2026.
https://doi.org/10.1007/978-3-031-97589-9_10

which introduce randomness into a system of ordinary differential equations, representing phenomena influenced by unpredictable noise, often used in finance, biology and physics to describe uncertain dynamics. Among the stiff problems of great interest in the deterministic and stochastic fields we mention, for example, Hamiltonian systems, for which it is known that the design of numerical methods capable of ensuring energy conservation on long time scales is very important [3,17,18,22]. Otherwise, small errors in numerical integration could accumulate, leading to unrealistic results. Currently, also stochastic partial differential equations, that combine the complexities of both randomness and spatial variability, are highly regarded in the field of numerical modeling [19]. For stiff deterministic problems several numerical methods have been proposed that attempt to combine low error coefficients and computational effort with good stability properties, in order to get an efficient solution [5,10,13,23,24,29]. Furthermore, an effort has been made in the construction of methods adapted to the problem, capable of unconditionally preserving the most important properties of the analytical solution in the discrete setting [11,25–28]. The extension of some of these methods to the stochastic case has also been considered [6,12,20,21].

Among the numerical methods for stiff IVPs recently introduced in the scientific literature, the so-called TASE-RK (Time-Accurate and highly Stable Explicit Runge-Kutta) schemes [4,9], which constitute a subclass of the linearly implicit W-methods [33], have garnered significant attention, see [1,2,7, 8,14,15,32]. TASE-RK methods are indeed very simple to implement, as they require a slight modification of an explicit RK scheme through the so-called TASE operators. Also, TASE-RK methods have good stability properties and low computational cost. This makes them quite attractive for large stiff IVPs arising e.g. from the semi-discretization in space of PDEs. The main computational cost of the original s-stage TASE-RK methods [4,9] is given by the solution of s^2 linear systems at each time-step, to reach a given order of consistency $p = s = 2, 3, 4$. Such linear systems involve s different coefficient matrices, which are of the type $(I - h\theta J)$, being: I the identity of size m, h the time step-size used by the method to provide the solution $y_n \approx y(t_n)$ at the points of the discrete grid $\{t_n = t_0 + nh, \ n = 0, \ldots, N, \ t_N = t_{\text{end}}\}$, θ a positive parameter, J the Jacobian, i.e. $J = J(t, y) := \frac{\partial f}{\partial y}(t, y)$. To avoid trivial cases, we assume from now on that the Jacobian J is not constant.

To improve the computational cost of the original TASE-RK methods [4, 9], new operators and numerical schemes have been proposed that attempt to reduce the number of overall linear systems to be solved, and/or the number of coefficient matrices involved. In particular, by exploiting the connections between the TASE-RK methods and the W-methods, the family of TASE-W methods [32] has been proposed, which allows to reduce the overall number of linear systems to be solved to reach order $2, 3, 4$, involving only two coefficient matrices. A further improvement from this last point of view has been given by the so-called singly TASE operators [7], which used in the context of explicit RK methods allow to consider linear systems at any time-step where a single coefficient matrix is involved. In particular, the resulting singly TASE-RK methods [7] require the solution of s^2 linear systems at each step where the coefficient matrix is always the same. Unlike the original TASE-RK methods [4,9], which have a relatively simple structure, the TASE-W [32] and singly TASE-RK methods [7] involve a rather intricate formulation. In this work, therefore, we show in detail the structure of the various stages of these methods, and highlight the steps required for an efficient computation of the time-marching solution.

The structure of this paper is as follows. In Sect. 2 we recall the family of TASE-W methods, propose a strategy for an efficient implementation, and analyze the properties of accuracy, stability, and computational cost of numerical schemes of order 2, 3, and 4. In Sect. 3 we do the same for the singly TASE-RK methods. In Sect. 4 we use the two considered families of methods for the solution of a PDEs model for the description of the electrodeposition process in batteries. Section 5 concludes the manuscript with comments on the results obtained and ideas for future research.

2   The Family of TASE-W Methods

TASE-W methods [32] were introduced taking inspiration from the connections between TASE-RK methods and W-methods, with the aim of reaching a given order p, up to $p = 4$, solving the smallest possible number of linear systems at each step, while still obtaining good stability properties. For reminders of stability definitions, see e.g. [32, p. 131]. The general formulation of TASE-W methods is as follows:

$$
\begin{cases}
(I - \theta_q hW) K_i^{[q]} = hf\left(t_n + c_i h, y_n + \sum_{j=1}^{i-1} a_{ij} K_j\right) + \sum_{j=1}^{i-1} \ell_{ij} K_j, \quad q = 1, \ldots, r, \\[2ex]
K_i = \sum_{q=1}^{r} \omega_q K_i^{[q]}, \quad i = 1, \ldots, s, \\[2ex]
y_{n+1} = y_n + \sum_{i=1}^{s} b_i K_i.
\end{cases}
$$

$$(2)$$

The matrix W can be arbitrary (also constant throughout the numerical integration) without affecting the order of consistency of the methods. That is, the order conditions of these methods have been studied for arbitrary W. However, for stability reasons W should correspond to the Jacobian of the problem at the current step, i.e. $W = J_n$ with $J_n = J(t_n, y_n)$, or at least to the Jacobian of the stiff part of the vector field. Indeed, the good stability properties of these methods have been proved under the assumption $W = J_n$.

Remark 1. Actually, solving non-autonomous problems (1) requires a slight modification of the formulation (2) of TASE-W methods, which consists in adding the term $\tilde{v}h^2 k_i^{[q]}$ in the right-hand side of the linear system that leads to determining $K_i^{[q]}$, being $k_i^{[q]}$ a given coefficient and $\tilde{v} \approx v(t_n, y_n)$, with $v(t, y) = \frac{\partial f}{\partial t}(t, y)$, see [32, Subsec. 3.2]. However, the order of consistency of the methods on non-autonomous problems is independent of the choice of $\tilde{v}$. Thus,

$\tilde{v}$ is typically considered equal to $\mathbf{0}$ [32, Subsec. 3.2], being $\mathbf{0}$ the vector of zeros of length m. In this way we recover formulation (2) also for non-autonomous problems.

The coefficients of the TASE-W methods (2) can be organized defining the following matrices and vectors:

$$A = (a_{ij})^s_{i,j=1} \in \mathbb{R}^{s \times s} \text{ strictly lower triangular,} \tag{3}$$
$$L = (\ell_{ij})^s_{i,j=1} \in \mathbb{R}^{s \times s} \text{ strictly lower triangular,}$$
$$b = (b_i)^s_{i=1} \in \mathbb{R}^s, \quad c = (c_i)^s_{i=1} \in \mathbb{R}^s, \quad \theta = (\theta_i)^r_{i=1} \in \mathbb{R}^r, \quad w = (w_i)^r_{i=1} \in \mathbb{R}^r.$$

From now on, we consider $c_1 = 0$. Also, we take $r = 2$ according to the following result, which can be directly deduced from [32, Th. 1 and Rem. 4].

Proposition 1. *TASE-W methods reach order of consistency $p = s = 2, 3, 4$ with $r = 2$. TASE-W methods cannot reach order $p = s = 3, 4$ with $r = 1$.*

As can be seen from (2), the more the value of r increases, the more the number of linear systems to be solved increases. The choice $r = 2$ is therefore preferable, since it allows to work with small computational effort to reach order $p = 3, 4$, and also as we will show it allows to obtain L-stable methods.

For clarity and to highlight the steps required by the TASE-W methods (2), below we express them in full with $r = 2$.

$$f_1 = f(t_n, y_n),$$
$$(I - h\theta_1 W) K_1^{[1]} = hf_1, \quad (I - h\theta_2 W) K_1^{[2]} = hf_1,$$
$$K_1 = w_1 K_1^{[1]} + w_2 K_1^{[2]},$$

$$f_2 = f(t_n + c_2 h, y_n + a_{21} K_1),$$
$$(I - h\theta_1 W) K_2^{[1]} = hf_2 + \ell_{21} K_1, \quad (I - h\theta_2 W) K_2^{[2]} = hf_2 + \ell_{21} K_1,$$
$$K_2 = w_1 K_2^{[1]} + w_2 K_2^{[2]},$$

$$\vdots$$

$$f_s = f\left(t_n + c_s h, y_n + \sum_{j=1}^{s-1} a_{sj} K_j\right),$$

$$(I - h\theta_1 W) K_s^{[1]} = hf_s + \sum_{j=1}^{s-1} \ell_{sj} K_j, \quad (I - h\theta_2 W) K_s^{[2]} = hf_s + \sum_{j=1}^{s-1} \ell_{sj} K_j,$$

$$K_s = w_1 K_s^{[1]} + w_2 K_s^{[2]},$$

$$y_{n+1} = y_n + \sum_{j=1}^{s} b_j K_j.$$

From here it is clear that the main computational effort of TASE-W methods is given by the solution of $2s$ linear systems at each step, involving 2 different coefficient matrices $(I - h\theta_1 W)$ and $(I - h\theta_2 W)$.

The next subsections discuss in detail an efficient implementation strategy of such methods, and show examples of L-stable TASE-W methods of order $p = 2, 3, 4$, with low error coefficients.

2.1   Implementation Steps

At a given grid point t_n, to compute the numerical solution at t_{n+1}, we perform the following steps.

1. Possible evaluation of the Jacobian of the problem at the current point, if the user chooses to select $W = J_n$.
2. Computation of the LU factorization of all the coefficient matrices involved in the linear systems to be solved: using the Matlab notation for employing the related $\mathtt{lu}$ built-in function, we thus write

$$[L_{\theta_1}, U_{\theta_1}] = \mathtt{lu}\,(I - h\theta_1 W)\,, \quad [L_{\theta_2}, U_{\theta_2}] = \mathtt{lu}\,(I - h\theta_2 W)\,.$$

   If the above coefficient matrices do not admit pure LU factorization, we compute a PLU one. As discussed below, this does not alter the implementation structure and main computational cost of the method.
3. Computation of the stages K_i, $i = 1, \ldots, s$: using the Matlab notation for employing the related backslash command, we derive K_i as shown in the following Algorithm 1, solving 4 triangular linear systems.

Algorithm 1. Computation of K_i in TASE-W methods.

1: evaluate $f_i = f\left(t_n + c_i h, y_n + \sum_{j=1}^{i-1} a_{ij} K_j\right)$

2: compute

$$K_i = \omega_1 \cdot \left(U_{\theta_1} \backslash (L_{\theta_1} \backslash (h f_i + \sum_{j=1}^{i-1} \ell_{ij} K_j))\right) + \omega_2 \cdot \left(U_{\theta_2} \backslash (L_{\theta_2} \backslash (h f_i + \sum_{j=1}^{i-1} \ell_{ij} K_j))\right)$$

---

4. Computation of the time-marching solution:

$$y_{n+1} = y_n + b_1 K_1 + \ldots + b_s K_s.$$

This implementation involves at each t_n: 2 LU factorizations and $4s$ triangular linear systems, see the above steps 2 and 3. We underline that when $(I - h\theta_i W)$ does not admit pure LU factorization (for some i or W), but only PLU, the above algorithm can still be used, provided that the coefficient vector of the linear system to be solved is premultiplied by the permutation matrix. In this way, the computational cost of the proposed implementation is almost unchanged, since the linear systems to be solved remain of triangular form.

Finally, we observe that if the user chooses W constant for the whole numerical integration, steps 1 and 2 need to be performed only once and not for each n: in this case the method would require 2 LU factorizations in total, and at each t_n the solution of $4s$ triangular systems.

2.2   Examples of 2nd, 3rd and 4th Order TASE-W Methods

We now list efficient methods reporting the coefficients as in (3) of the TASE-W family of order 2, 3 and 4, from [32, p. 140]. For all the methods considered below, ω is as follows:

$$\omega = \left(-\frac{\theta_2}{\theta_1 - \theta_2}, \frac{\theta_1}{\theta_1 - \theta_2} \right)^T .$$

2nd Order Method: TASEW2
The coefficients of the method are as

$$b = (1,1)^T , \; c = \left(0, \frac{1}{2} \right)^T , \; \theta = \left(\frac{1}{2}, \frac{\sqrt{2}}{2} \right)^T , \; A = \begin{pmatrix} 0 & 0 \\ \frac{1}{2} & 0 \end{pmatrix}, \; L = \begin{pmatrix} 0 & 0 \\ -1 & 0 \end{pmatrix} .$$

3rd Order Method: TASEW3
The coefficients of the method are as

$$b = \left(b_1, b_2, \frac{4}{9} \right)^T , \; c = \left(0, \frac{1}{2}, \frac{3}{4} \right)^T , \; \theta = \left(\frac{1}{2}, \frac{7}{10} \right)^T ,$$

$$A = \begin{pmatrix} 0 & 0 & 0 \\ \frac{1}{2} & 0 & 0 \\ a_{31} & \frac{3}{4} & 0 \end{pmatrix}, \; L = \begin{pmatrix} 0 & 0 & 0 \\ \ell_{21} & 0 & 0 \\ \ell_{31} & \ell_{32} & 0 \end{pmatrix} ,$$

with

$$b_1 = 1.6351578675654365735, \quad b_2 = 0.92024060176023148028,$$
$$a_{31} = 1.2776842708687388139, \quad \ell_{21} = -1.7035790278249849372,$$
$$\ell_{31} = -1.9014209311534939761, \quad \ell_{32} = -1.3205413539605210804.$$

4th Order Method: TASEW4
The coefficients of the method are as

$$b = \left(b_1, b_2, b_3, \frac{1}{6} \right)^T , \; c = \left(0, \frac{1}{2}, \frac{1}{2}, 1 \right)^T , \; \theta = \left(\frac{1}{2}, \frac{7}{10} \right)^T ,$$

$$A = \begin{pmatrix} 0 & 0 & 0 & 0 \\ \frac{1}{2} & 0 & 0 & 0 \\ a_{31} & \frac{1}{2} & 0 & 0 \\ a_{41} & a_{42} & 1 & 0 \end{pmatrix}, \; L = \begin{pmatrix} 0 & 0 & 0 & 0 \\ \ell_{21} & 0 & 0 & 0 \\ \ell_{31} & \ell_{32} & 0 & 0 \\ \ell_{41} & \ell_{42} & \ell_{43} & 0 \end{pmatrix} ,$$

with

$$b_1 = 2.2125690141456160198, \quad b_2 = 1.0480568967728132179,$$
$$b_3 = 0.86264453466476542776, \quad a_{31} = 1.8930871174773045151,$$
$$a_{41} = 0.49836947454490920784, \quad a_{42} = 0.46104213203322702563,$$
$$\ell_{21} = -3.7861742349546090303, \quad \ell_{31} = -0.49836947454490920784,$$
$$\ell_{32} = -0.46104213203322702563, \quad \ell_{41} = -3.7063266658746600868,$$
$$\ell_{42} = -3.3662571165704262555, \quad \ell_{43} = -3.1758672079885927886.$$

Properties of the Considered Methods

Table 1 reports the properties of the above-listed TASE-W methods, in terms of stability, computational cost and error terms.

Table 1. Properties of the considered TASE-W methods: stability, number of triangular linear systems (N. tr. sys.) and LU factorizations (N. LU) required at each time-step, and maximum error coefficient (Err. coeff.) in absolute value. The symbol * refers to the choice $W = J_n$.

Method	Stability*	N. tr. sys.	N. LU*	Err. coeff.
TASEW2	L-stability	8	2	0.1667
TASEW3	L-stability	12	2	0.07229
TASEW4	L-stability	16	2	0.05210

The properties of stability and the number of LU factorizations required at each time-step refer to the choice $W = J_n$. Indeed, as already highlighted, if W is selected as a constant matrix different from J_n, the number of factorizations is reduced to 2 in total, and not at each time-step. However, the stability study of TASE-W methods has been carried out under the assumption $W = J_n$. If the reader is interested in techniques for the study of stability with inexact Jacobian, in the work [15] the authors analyzed it for a particular family of TASE-RK methods.

3   Runge-Kutta Methods with Singly TASE Operators

The original TASE-RK methods [4,9] require the solution of s^2 linear systems at each time-step to reach order $p = s = 2, 3, 4$, involving s different coefficient matrices. In [7], the authors proposed the so-called singly TASE operators, which allow considering only one coefficient matrix at each time-step, thus also improving the TASE-W methods on this aspect. From [7, pp. 5–6], the resulting singly TASE-RK methods have the general formulation

$$\begin{cases} K_i = \left(\sum_{q=1}^{s} \omega_q \left(I - h\theta W \right)^{-q} \right) hf \left(t_n + c_i h, y_n + \sum_{j=1}^{i-1} a_{ij} K_j \right), \quad i = 1, \ldots, s, \\ y_{n+1} = y_n + \sum_{i=1}^{s} b_i K_i. \end{cases}$$

$$(4)$$

As for TASE-W methods, also for singly TASE-RK methods the matrix W can be arbitrary without affecting the order of consistency, but for stability reasons it is advisable that it corresponds to J_n, or at least to the Jacobian of the stiff part of the vector field.

Similarly to TASE-W methods (2), we organize the coefficients of singly TASE-RK methods (4) defining the following matrices and vectors:

$$A = (a_{ij})_{i,j=1}^s \in \mathbb{R}^{s\times s} \text{ strictly lower triangular,} \tag{5}$$

$$b = (b_i)_{i=1}^s \in \mathbb{R}^s, \quad c = (c_i)_{i=1}^s \in \mathbb{R}^s, \quad w = (w_i)_{i=1}^s \in \mathbb{R}^s, \quad \theta \in \mathbb{R}.$$

We rewrite the singly TASE-RK methods (4) in full below, with the purpose of highlighting: the steps needed to compute the solution, the connections with the TASE-W methods (2). From now on, we consider $c_1 = 0$.

$$f_1 = f(t_n, y_n),$$
$$(I - h\theta W)^q K_1^{[q]} = hf_1, \quad q = 1, \ldots, s,$$
$$K_1 = w_1 K_1^{[1]} + \ldots + w_s K_1^{[s]},$$

$$f_2 = f(t_n + c_2 h, y_n + a_{21} K_1),$$
$$(I - h\theta W)^q K_2^{[q]} = hf_2, \quad q = 1, \ldots, s,$$
$$K_2 = w_1 K_2^{[1]} + \ldots + w_s K_2^{[s]},$$

$$\vdots$$

$$f_s = f\left(t_n + c_s h, y_n + \sum_{j=1}^{s-1} a_{sj} K_j\right),$$
$$(I - h\theta W)^q K_s^{[q]} = hf_s, \quad q = 1, \ldots, s,$$
$$K_s = w_1 K_s^{[1]} + \ldots + w_s K_s^{[s]},$$

$$y_{n+1} = y_n + \sum_{j=1}^s b_j K_j.$$

Note that, for each stage K_i, $i = 1, \ldots, s$, we need to compute $K_i^{[q]}$ from

$$(I - h\theta W)^q K_i^{[q]} = hf_i, \quad q = 1, \ldots, s.$$

This corresponds to perform the following Algorithm 2.

Therefore, the main computational effort of singly TASE-RK methods is given by the solution of s^2 linear systems at each step (s linear systems for each stage) involving just 1 coefficient matrix $(I - h\theta W)$.

Algorithm 2. Computation of $K_i^{[q]}$, $q = 1, \ldots, s$, in singly TASE-RK methods.

1: compute $K_i^{[1]}$ by solving $(I - h\theta W) K_i^{[1]} = hf_i$
2: **for** $q = 2, \ldots, s$ **do**
3:    solve $(I - h\theta W) K_i^{[q]} = K_i^{[q-1]}$
4: **end for**

Remark 2. Note that Algorithm 2 involves computing the i-th stage K_i in (4) by sequential solution of the linear systems $(I - h\theta W) K_i^{[q]} = K_i^{[q-1]}$, $q = 2, \ldots, s$, starting from $K_i^{[1]}$ by $(I - h\theta W) K_i^{[1]} = hf_i$. Then, $K_i = \sum_{q=1}^{s} \omega_q K_i^{[q]}$. In [7, Subsec. 6], the authors propose to compute the i-th stage K_i via a slightly different Horner-type algorithm, which can be well understood through an example. Let us fix e.g. $s = 4$, and consider the computation of the i-th stage K_i in (4), which reads

$$K_i = \left(\sum_{q=1}^{4} \omega_q (I - h\theta W)^{-q} \right) hf_i, \quad f_i = \left(t_n + c_i h, y_n + \sum_{j=1}^{i-1} a_{ij} K_j \right).$$

This can be expressed as

$$K_i = \Big((I - h\theta W)^{-1} \big(\omega_1 I + (I - h\theta W)^{-1} \big(\omega_2 I +$$

$$(I - h\theta W)^{-1} (\omega_3 I + \omega_4 \cdot (I - h\theta W)^{-1})) \big) \Big) hf_i.$$

Therefore, it is possible to determine the stage K_i starting from the solution of the linear system

$$(I - h\theta W)\tilde{K}_i^{[4]} = \omega_4 hf_i.$$

Then, computing

$$(I - h\theta W)\tilde{K}_i^{[3]} = \omega_3 hf_i + \tilde{K}_i^{[4]},$$
$$(I - h\theta W)\tilde{K}_i^{[2]} = \omega_2 hf_i + \tilde{K}_i^{[3]},$$
$$(I - h\theta W)\tilde{K}_i^{[1]} = \omega_1 hf_i + \tilde{K}_i^{[2]},$$

note that the stage K_i corresponds to $\tilde{K}_i^{[1]}$. We emphasize that this algorithm does not imply changes in the number of linear systems to be solved at each time-step, but as mentioned in [7] it can bring advantages from a stability point of view.

3.1   Implementation Steps

According to [7, Sec. 2], to simplify some notation we make the change of variable $d = \theta^{-1}$. This leads to equivalently getting the stages K_i, $i = 1, \ldots, s$, of the method (4) as

$$(dI - hW)^q \, K_i^{[q]} = h f_i, \quad q = 1, \ldots, s,$$
$$K_i = \beta_1 K_i^{[1]} + \ldots + \beta_s K_i^{[s]}. \tag{6}$$

Here, the new β_q coefficients and the ω_q coefficients in (4) are related as follows:

$$\beta_q = \omega_q \theta^{-q}, \quad q = 1, \ldots, s. \tag{7}$$

Using this, we report below the steps for an efficient implementation of the singly TASE-RK methods.

At a given grid point t_n, to compute the numerical solution at t_{n+1}, we perform the following steps.

1. Possible evaluation of the Jacobian of the problem at the current point, if the user chooses to select $W = J_n$.
2. Computation of the LU factorization of the only coefficient matrix involved in all the linear systems to be solved:

$$[L_d, U_d] = \mathrm{lu}\,(dI - hW).$$

3. Computation of the stages K_i, $i = 1, \ldots, s$: according to Remark 2 and the change of variable $d = \theta^{-1}$ implying (6) and (7), we use the following Algorithm 3, leading to the solution of $2s$ triangular systems for each K_i.

Algorithm 3. Computation of K_i in singly TASE-RK methods.

1: evaluate $f_i = f\left(t_n + c_i h, y_n + \sum_{j=1}^{i-1} a_{ij} K_j\right)$

2: initialize $\tilde{K}_i^{[s+1]} = \mathbf{0}$

3: **for** $q = s, \ldots, 1$ with step -1 **do**

4:     compute $\tilde{K}_i^{[q]} = \left(U_d \backslash \left(L_d \backslash \left(\tilde{K}_i^{[q+1]} + \beta_q h f_i\right)\right)\right)$

5: **end for**

6: set $K_i = \tilde{K}_i^{[1]}$

---

4. Computation of the time-marching solution:

$$y_{n+1} = y_n + b_1 K_1 + \ldots + b_s K_s.$$

This implementation involves at each t_n: 1 LU factorization and $2s^2$ triangular linear systems, see the above steps 2 and 3. Similarly to the previous section, if $(dI - hW)$ does not admit pure LU factorization, we compute a PLU one and still use the above algorithm, premultiplying the coefficient vector of the linear system to be solved by the permutation matrix.

Finally, we observe that if the user chooses W constant for the whole numerical integration, steps 1 and 2 need to be performed only once and not for each n: in this case the method would require 1 LU factorizations in total.

3.2   Examples of 2nd, 3rd and 4th Order Singly TASE-RK Methods

Below we report examples of efficient singly TASE-RK methods from [9, Subsecs. 3–5], by indicating the coefficients as in (5) where, instead of w and θ, we consider

$$\beta = (\beta_i)_{i=1}^s \in \mathbb{R}^s, \quad d = \theta^{-1} \in \mathbb{R},$$

according to the used change of variable and relations (7). For reasons of consistency, for all the methods considered below the β_i coefficients are as follows [7, p. 6]:

$$\beta_i = \binom{s}{s-i} d^i (-1)^{-1+i}, \quad i = 1, \ldots, s.$$

2nd Order Method: Singly-TRK2
The coefficients of the method are as

$$d = \frac{1}{2}, \; \beta = \left(1, -\frac{1}{4}\right)^T, \; b = (0,1)^T, \; c = \left(0, \frac{1}{2}\right)^T, \; A = \begin{pmatrix} 0 & 0 \\ \frac{1}{2} & 0 \end{pmatrix}.$$

3rd Order Method: Singly-TRK3
The coefficients of the method are as

$$b = \left(\frac{1}{6}, \frac{3}{10}, \frac{8}{15}\right)^T, \; c = \left(0, \frac{1}{3}, \frac{3}{4}\right)^T, \; A = \begin{pmatrix} 0 & 0 & 0 \\ \frac{1}{3} & 0 & 0 \\ -\frac{3}{16} & \frac{15}{16} & 0 \end{pmatrix},$$

and

$$d = 0.532023879327774, \quad \beta_1 = 1.596071637983322,$$
$$\beta_2 = -0.849148224524921, \quad \beta_3 = 0.150589044178680.$$

4th Order Method: Singly-TRK4
The coefficients of the method are as

$$b = \left(\frac{1}{6}, \frac{1}{3}, \frac{1}{3}, \frac{1}{6}\right)^T, \; c = \left(0, \frac{1}{2}, \frac{1}{2}, 1\right)^T, \; A = \begin{pmatrix} 0 & 0 & 0 & 0 \\ \frac{1}{2} & 0 & 0 & 0 \\ 0 & \frac{1}{2} & 0 & 0 \\ 0 & 0 & 1 & 0 \end{pmatrix},$$

and

$$d = 0.399017909495830,$$
$$\beta_1 = 1.596071637983322, \quad \beta_2 = -0.955291752590537,$$
$$\beta_3 = 0.254119012051523, \quad \beta_4 = -0.025349509237986.$$

Table 2. Properties of the considered singly TASE-RK methods: stability, number of triangular linear systems (N. tr. sys.) and LU factorizations (N. LU) required at each time-step, and maximum error coefficient (Err. coeff.) in absolute value. The symbol * refers to the choice $W = J_n$.

Method	Stability*	N. tr. sys.	N. LU*	Err. coeff.
singly-TRK2	strong A-stab.	8	1	4
singly-TRK3	L(α)-stab., $\alpha = 88.99$	18	1	6.64
singly-TRK4	strong A(α)-stab., $\alpha = 87.17$	32	1	39.45

Properties of the Considered Methods

Table 2 reports the properties of the above-listed singly TASE-RK methods, in terms of stability, computational cost and error terms.

In Table 2, the properties of stability and the number of LU factorizations required at each time-step refer to the choice $W = J_n$. Indeed, as already highlighted, if W is chosen as a constant matrix different from J_n, the number of factorizations is reduced to 1 in total, and not at each time-step. However, as for the TASE-W methods, the stability study of singly TASE-RK methods has been carried out under the assumption $W = J_n$. Finally, we recall that strong A-stability or strong A(α)-stability means that the value assumed by the stability function of the methods at infinity is strictly less than 1. In particular, for the singly-TRK2 and singly-TRK4 this value is 0.5 and 0.27, respectively.

4   Experiments on the DIB System for Battery Modeling

In this section, we apply the methods illustrated in this paper to solve the 2D DIB model, which was introduced to characterize the electrodeposition process in batteries [31]. It is given by the following system of coupled PDEs:

$$\begin{cases} \dfrac{\partial \eta_1}{\partial t} = \Delta \eta_1 + \rho \left(A_1(1 - \eta_2)\eta_1 - A_2\eta_1^3 - B(\eta_2 - a) \right), \\ \dfrac{\partial \eta_2}{\partial t} = d\Delta\theta + \rho\big(C\left(1 + k_2\eta_1\right)\left(1 - \eta_2\right)\left(1 - \gamma\left(1 - \eta_2\right)\right) - \\ \qquad\qquad D\eta_2\left(1 + \gamma\eta_1\right)\left(1 + k_3\eta_1\right)\big). \end{cases}$$

Here, $\eta_1 : \Omega \times [0, t_{\text{end}}] \to \mathbb{R}$ and $\eta_2 : \Omega \times [0, t_{\text{end}}] \to [0, 1]$. We consider $\Omega = [0, 5]^2$, zero Neumann boundary conditions, and as initial condition

$$\eta_1(x_1, x_2, t_0) = 10^{-5} \text{ rand}(x_1, x_2), \quad \eta_2(x_1, x_2, t_0) = a + 10^{-5} \text{ rand}(x_1, x_2).$$

Above, **rand** refers to the Matlab function that generates uniformly distributed random numbers. We consider the following values for the parameters: $a = 0.5$, $\gamma = 0.2$, $\rho = 1$, $A_1 = 10$, $A_2 = 30$, $B = 66$, $C = 3$, $d = 20$, $D = 2.4545$, $k_2 = 2.5$, $k_3 = 1.5$. We carry out the space discretization with order-two finite differences, using the same number of points in both directions x_1 and x_2. The Neumann conditions are imposed introducing ghost points, see [34]. For the space discretization, we consider step-size $\Delta x = 0.5$, thus obtaining

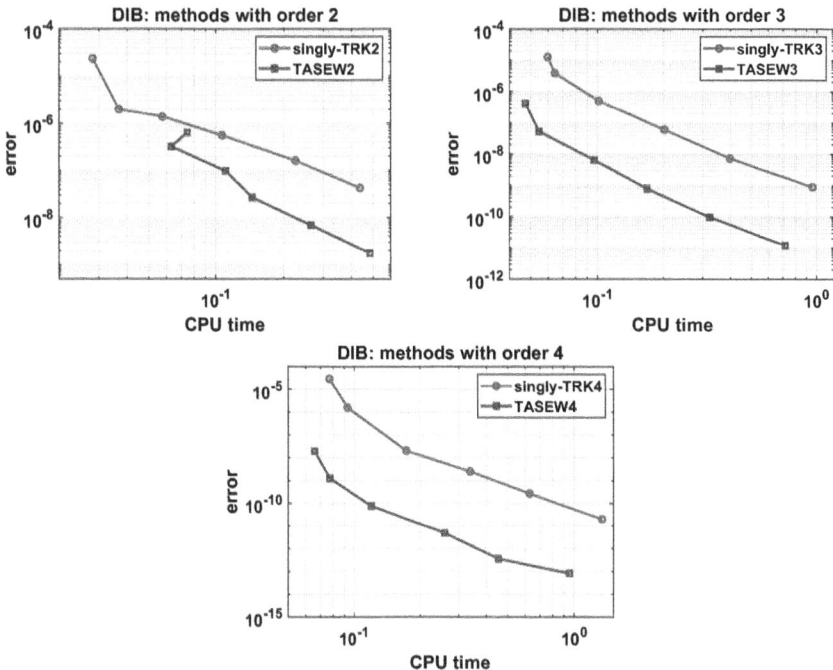

Fig. 1. Performance of the TASE-W and singly TASE-RK methods of order $p = 2, 3, 4$ on the DIB model for $h = (t_{end} - t_0)/N$, $N = 2^5, \ldots, 2^{10}$, with $W = J_0$.

Table 3. CPU times in seconds used by methods for different values of N for $W = J_0$.

Method	$N = 2^5$	$N = 2^6$	$N = 2^7$	$N = 2^8$	$N = 2^9$	$N = 2^{10}$
singly-TRK2	0.03	0.04	0.06	0.11	0.23	0.44
TASEW2	0.07	0.06	0.11	0.15	0.26	0.48
singly-TRK3	0.06	0.06	0.10	0.20	0.40	0.96
TASEW3	0.05	0.05	0.10	0.17	0.32	0.72
singly-TRK4	0.08	0.09	0.17	0.34	0.63	1.33
TASEW4	0.07	0.08	0.12	0.26	0.45	0.95

11 grid points in each direction. Therefore, the resulting system of ODEs has size $m = 2 \cdot 11^2 = 242$. We apply the TASE-W and singly TASE-RK methods for several values of $h = (t_{end} - t_0)/N$, $N = 2^5, \ldots, 2^{10}$, selecting both constant W corresponding to the Jacobian only at the initial point, namely $W = J_0$, and W corresponding exact Jacobian at each time-step, namely $W = J_n$.

The results are reported in Figs. 1 and 2, where we compare the CPU time used by the methods in seconds, and the absolute error in infinity norm computed at the last point of the time grid. The reference solution has been computed with the MATLAB function ode15s, setting AbsTol= RelTol= 10^{-14}. In particular, Fig. 1 shows the case $W = J_0$, while Fig. 2 shows the case $W = J_n$. Also,

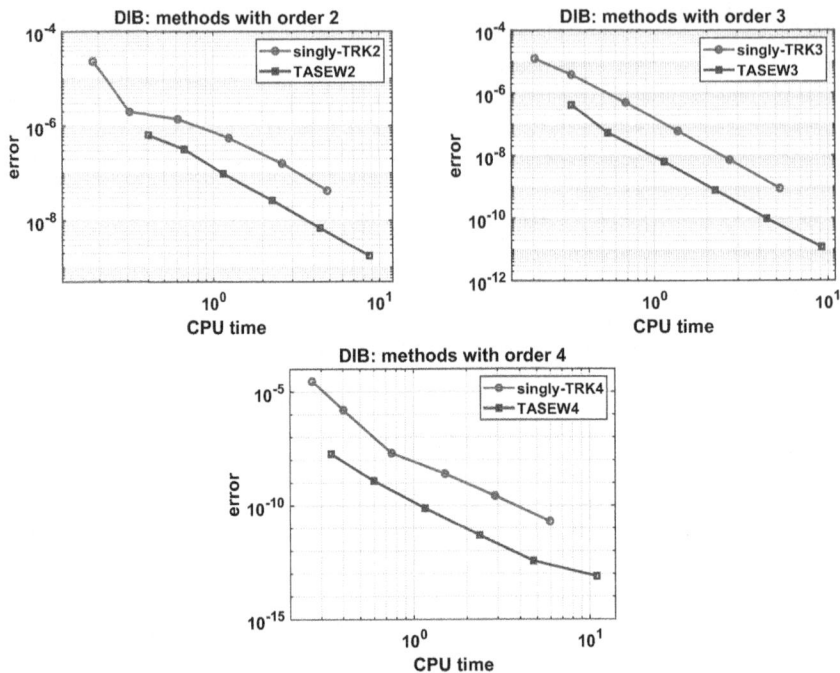

Fig. 2. Performance of the TASE-W and singly TASE-RK methods of order $p = 2, 3, 4$ on the DIB model for $h = (t_{end} - t_0)/N$, $N = 2^5, \ldots, 2^{10}$, with $W = J_n$.

Tables 3 and 4 report the values of the computing times used by the methods for $W = J_0$ and $W = J_n$, respectively. Note that, for $W = J_0$, the TASE-W and singly TASE-RK methods exhibit comparable computing times, but the former provide the solution with the lowest errors. This is consistent with the maximum error coefficients of the methods given in Tables 1 and 2. Note also that, although we are not using exact Jacobian in this case, all the methods are stable for any considered value of the step-size h. For $W = J_n$, clearly the computing times of the methods increase, but the singly TASE-RK schemes become faster than the TASE-W schemes, for the same step-size h. This is consistent with the fact that, if $W = J_n$, we need to compute at each step a factorization of the coefficient matrices of the linear systems to be solved. In this case, it is more convenient to work with the smallest possible number of coefficient matrices. From this point of view, as explained in the paper, singly TASE-RK methods are advantageous over TASE-W methods.

All the tests have been done using the version R2023b of MATLAB and a laptop with processor Intel(R) Xeon(R) CPU E3-1245 v5 3.50 GHz, RAM of 16 Gb, on Windows 10 Enterprise 64–bit 22H2.

Table 4. CPU times in seconds used by methods for different values of N for $W = J_n$.

Method	$N = 2^5$	$N = 2^6$	$N = 2^7$	$N = 2^8$	$N = 2^9$	$N = 2^{10}$
singly-TRK2	0.18	0.31	0.61	1.25	2.61	4.86
TASEW2	0.40	0.67	1.15	2.28	4.39	8.71
singly-TRK3	0.20	0.33	0.69	1.37	2.71	5.27
TASEW3	0.33	0.54	1.14	2.24	4.42	9.20
singly-TRK4	0.27	0.40	0.75	1.50	2.90	5.94
TASEW4	0.34	0.60	1.16	2.36	4.76	10.98

5 Conclusions

In this work, we have described in detail the TASE-W and singly TASE-RK methods, recently introduced in the scientific literature for the efficient solution of large stiff IVPs. In particular, we have analyzed their properties of consistency, stability and computational cost, proposing an efficient implementation strategy. Numerical tests on a system of PDEs modeling charge/discharge processes in electric batteries have shown the good performance of both families of methods. In particular, they have shown that the TASE-W methods are advantageous for obtaining a solution with high accuracy, even with large step-size h. Instead, to obtain a stable solution by sacrificing great accuracy, in order to use low computing times, for the same step-size the singly TASE-RK methods are advantageous compared to the TASE-W methods.

Acknowledgments. The authors are members of the research group GNCS-INdAM. This work has been supported by GNCS-INdAM projects and by the Italian Ministry of University and Research (MUR), through the PRIN PNRR 2022 projects BAT-MEN (P20228C2PP, CUP: F53D23010020001) and MatForPat (P2022WC2ZZ, CUP: E53D23018030001).

Disclosure of Interests. The authors have no competing interests to declare that are relevant to the content of this article.

References

1. Aceto, L., Conte, D., Pagano, G.: On a generalization of time-accurate and highly-stable explicit operators for stiff problems. Appl. Numer. Math. **200**, 2–17 (2024). https://doi.org/10.1016/j.apnum.2023.04.001
2. Aceto, L., Conte, D., Pagano, G.: Modified TASE Runge-Kutta methods for integrating stiff differential equations. SIAM J. Sci. Comput. **47**(3), A1652–A1680 (2025). https://doi.org/10.1137/24M1667336
3. Amodio, P., Brugnano, L., Frasca-Caccia, G., Iavernaro, F.: Arbitrarily high-order energy-conserving methods for Hamiltonian problems with quadratic holonomic constraints. J. Comput. Math. **42**(4), 1145–1171 (2024). https://doi.org/10.1016/j.cam.2024.115826

4. Bassenne, M., Fu, L., Mani, A.: Time-accurate and highly-stable explicit operators for stiff differential equations. J. Comput. Phys. **424**, 109847 (2021). https://doi.org/10.1016/j.jcp.2020.109847

5. Brugnano, L., Frasca-Caccia, G., Iavernaro, F., Vespri, V.: A new framework for polynomial approximation to differential equations. Adv. Comput. Math. **48**(6), 76 (2022). https://doi.org/10.1007/s10444-022-09992-w

6. Buckwar, E., D'Ambrosio, R.: Exponential mean-square stability properties of stochastic linear multistep methods. Adv. Comput. Math. **47**(4), 1–14 (2021). https://doi.org/10.1007/s10444-021-09879-2

7. Calvo, M., Fu, L., Montijano, J.I., Rández, L.: Singly TASE operators for the numerical solution of stiff differential equations by explicit Runge-Kutta schemes. J. Sci. Comput. **96**(1) (2023). https://doi.org/10.1007/s10915-023-02232-3

8. Calvo, M., Montijano, J.I., Rández, L.: Modified Singly-Runge–Kutta-TASE methods for the numerical solution of stiff differential equations. J. Sci. Comput. **103**(1) (2025). https://doi.org/10.1007/s10915-025-02813-4

9. Calvo, M., Montijano, J.I., Rández, L.: A note on the stability of time-accurate and highly-stable explicit operators for stiff differential equations. J. Comput. Phys. **436**, 110316 (2021). https://doi.org/10.1016/j.jcp.2021.110316

10. Cardone, A., Conte, D., Paternoster, B.: Stability of two-step spline collocation methods for initial value problems for fractional differential equations. Commun. Nonlinear Sci. Numer. Simul. **115**, 106726 (2022). https://doi.org/10.1016/j.cnsns.2022.106726

11. Cardone, A., Frasca-Caccia, G.: Numerical conservation laws of time fractional diffusion PDEs. Fract. Calc. Appl. Anal. **25**(4), 1459–1483 (2022). https://doi.org/10.1007/s13540-022-00059-7

12. Citro, V., D'Ambrosio, R.: Long-term analysis of stochastic theta-methods for damped stochastic oscillators. Appl. Numer. Math. **150**, 18–26 (2020). https://doi.org/10.1016/j.apnum.2019.08.011

13. Conte, D., D'Ambrosio, R., Jackiewicz, Z.: Two-step Runge-Kutta methods with quadratic stability functions. J. Sci. Comput. **2**, 191–218 (2010). https://doi.org/10.1007/s10915-010-9378-x

14. Conte, D., González-Pinto, S., Hernández-Abreu, D., Pagano, G.: On approximate matrix factorization and TASE W-methods for the time integration of parabolic partial differential equations. J. Sci. Comput. **100**(2), 34 (2024). https://doi.org/10.1007/s10915-024-02579-1

15. Conte, D., Martin-Vaquero, J., Pagano, G., Paternoster, B.: Stability theory of TASE–Runge–Kutta methods with inexact Jacobian. SIAM J. Sci. Comput. **46**(6), A3628–A3657 (2024). https://doi.org/10.1137/24M1631869

16. R. D'Ambrosio: Numerical Approximation of Ordinary Differential Problems - From Deterministic to Stochastic Numerical Methods. Springer (2023). https://doi.org/10.1007/978-3-031-31343-1

17. D'Ambrosio, R., Di Giovacchino, S.: Strong backward error analysis of symplectic integrators for stochastic Hamiltonian systems. Appl. Math. Comput. **467**, 128488 (2024). https://doi.org/10.1016/j.amc.2023.128488

18. D'Ambrosio, R., Di Giovacchino, S.: Long-term analysis of stochastic Hamiltonian systems under time discretizations. SIAM J. Sci. Comput. **45**(2), A257–A288 (2023). https://doi.org/10.1137/21M1458612

19. D'Ambrosio, R., Di Giovacchino, S.: Numerical conservation issues for the stochastic Korteweg-de Vries equation. J. Comput. Appl. Math. **424**, 114967 (2023). https://doi.org/10.1016/j.cam.2022.114967

20. D'Ambrosio, R., Di Giovacchino, S.: Mean-square contractivity of stochastic theta-methods. Commun. Nonlinear Sci. Numer. Simul. **96**, 105671 (2021). https://doi.org/10.1016/j.cnsns.2020.105671

21. D'Ambrosio, R., Di Giovacchino, S.: Nonlinear stability issues for stochastic Runge-Kutta methods. Commun. Nonlinear Sci. Numer. Simul. **94**, 105549 (2021). https://doi.org/10.1016/j.cnsns.2020.105549

22. D'Ambrosio, R., Giordano, G., Paternoster, B., Ventola, A.: Perturbative analysis of stochastic Hamiltonian problems under time discretizations. Appl. Math. Lett. **120**, 107223 (2021). https://doi.org/10.1016/j.aml.2021.107223

23. D'Ambrosio, R., Izzo, G., Jackiewicz, Z.: Search for highly stable two-step Runge-Kutta methods for ODEs. Appl. Numer. Math. **62**(10), 1361–1379 (2012). https://doi.org/10.1016/j.apnum.2012.06.012

24. D'Ambrosio, R., Paternoster, B.: Multivalue collocation methods free from order reduction. J. Comput. Appl. Math. **387**, 112515 (2021). https://doi.org/10.1016/j.cam.2019.112515

25. Frasca-Caccia, G.: Finite difference schemes with non polynomial local conservation laws. J. Comput. Appl. Math. **458**, 116330 (2025). https://doi.org/10.1016/j.cam.2024.116330

26. Frasca-Caccia, G., Hydon, P.E.: A new technique for preserving conservation laws. Found. Comput. Math. **22**(2), 477–506 (2022). https://doi.org/10.1007/s10208-021-09511-1

27. Frasca-Caccia, G., Hydon, P.E.: Numerical preservation of multiple local conservation laws. Appl. Math. Comput. **403**, 126203 (2021). https://doi.org/10.1016/j.amc.2021.126203

28. Frasca-Caccia, G., Hydon, P.E.: Simple bespoke preservation of two conservation laws. IMA J. Numer. Anal. **40**(2), 1294–1329 (2020). https://doi.org/10.1093/imanum/dry087

29. Frasca-Caccia, G., Singh, P.: Optimal parameters for numerical solvers of PDEs. J. Sci. Comput. **97**(1), 11 (2023). https://doi.org/10.1007/s10915-023-02324-0

30. Frasca-Caccia, G., Valentino, C., Colace, F., Conte, D.: An overview of differential models for corrosion of cultural heritage artefacts. Math. Model. Nat. Phenom. **18**, 27 (2023). https://doi.org/10.1051/mmnp/2023031

31. Frittelli, M., Sgura, I.: Matrix-oriented FEM formulation for reaction-diffusion PDEs on a large class of 2D domains. Appl. Numer. Math. **200**, 286–308 (2024). https://doi.org/10.1016/j.apnum.2023.07.010

32. González-Pinto, S., Hernández-Abreu, D., Pagano, G., Pérez-Rodríguez, S.: Generalized TASE-RK methods for stiff problems. Appl. Numer. Math. **188**, 129–145 (2023). https://doi.org/10.1016/j.apnum.2023.03.007

33. Hairer, E., Wanner, G.: Solving ordinary differential equations II - Stiff and Differential Algebraic Problems. Springer Series in Computational Mathematics (14), Springer, Berlin (1996). https://doi.org/10.1007/978-3-642-05221-7

34. Hundsdorfer, W., Verwer, J.: Numerical Solution of Time-Dependent Advection Diffusion-Reaction Equations. Springer (2007). https://doi.org/10.1007/9783-662-09017-6

The Mandelbrot Set for a Coquaternionic Family of Quadratics

Maria Irene Falcão⬤, Fernando Miranda⬤, and Ricardo Severino$^{(\boxtimes)}$⬤

CMAT and Departamento de Matemática, Universidade do Minho, Braga, Portugal
{mif,fmiranda,ricardo}@math.uminho.pt
http://www.cmat.uminho.pt

Abstract. The Mandelbrot set stands as one of the most fascinating and visually striking mathematical objects ever discovered, representing a fundamental milestone in dynamical systems theory and fractal geometry. Extending this set into the coquaternionic domain introduces significant mathematical challenges and unveils structures of remarkable complexity. In this work, we investigate the generalization of the Mandelbrot set from the quadratic mapping family $x^2 + bx$ in the complex plane to the coquaternionic space $\mathbb{H}_{\text{coq}}$, examining its mathematical properties, visualization techniques, and theoretical implications.

Keywords: Coquaternions · Iteration of quadratic maps · Mandelbrot set

1 Introduction

The Mandelbrot set, first studied by French mathematicians Pierre Fatou and Gaston Julia in the early 20th century, gained significant attention in the 1980s when Benoit Mandelbrot used computers to visualize it. The resulting structure revealed infinite complexity, with patterns repeating at progressively smaller scales, exemplifying the self-similarity characteristic of fractals [7]. These properties, combined with its aesthetic appeal and the ability to generate intricate visual complexity from simple iterative rules, contributed to its popularity beyond mathematical circles.

Given its profound impact and the rich mathematical structures it unveiled, researchers soon began exploring generalizations of the Mandelbrot set beyond the complex plane, aiming to extend its principles to higher-dimensional spaces. To understand how such generalizations can be pursued, we first examine the definition of the Mandelbrot set.

Traditionally, the Mandelbrot set is defined as the set of points c in the complex plane for which the iteration of $z = 0$ under the quadratic map $z^2 + c$ remains bounded. Here, $z = 0$ serves as the critical point of the mapping. This specific choice within the one-parameter family of quadratic maps arises from a fundamental equivalence in dynamical behavior: every quadratic mapping in the complex plane is dynamically conjugate to $z^2 + c$ for some complex parameter

O. Gervasi et al. (Eds.): ICCSA 2025 Workshops, LNCS 15887, pp. 150–162, 2026.
https://doi.org/10.1007/978-3-031-97589-9_11

c. This equivalence establishes the complex Mandelbrot set as a unique object of study, encapsulating essential dynamical properties of all complex quadratic mappings.

The first generalization of this set to higher-dimensional spaces was achieved for a family of quaternionic quadratics, see [1,2,8]. While this yielded interesting results, it did not introduce fundamentally new dynamics.

In this work, we propose studying the Mandelbrot set for a family of quadratic mappings in the four-dimensional space of coquaternions $\mathbb{H}_{coq}$, also referred to as split-quaternions in literature. This endeavor is inherently challenging due to the non-commutative nature of coquaternionic multiplication. Nevertheless, we are motivated by the diversity and complexity observed in coquaternionic dynamics, see [3–5], which provide strong justification for this study. Specifically, we focus on a family of quadratic mappings previously shown to be dynamically non-equivalent to simpler families [5].

This paper is organized as follows: Sect. 2 provides an overview of fundamental concepts related to coquaternions. Section 3 introduces key concepts from discrete dynamical systems in coquaternionic contexts. Section 4 presents a generalization of the complex Mandelbrot set to coquaternions and discusses visualization methods. Finally, Sect. 5 summarizes our findings and comments on their implications.

2   Basic Definitions and Results on Coquaternions

Let $\{1, i, j, k\}$ form an orthonormal basis of the Euclidean vector space $\mathbb{R}^4$, endowed with a bilinear product defined by:

$$\begin{cases} i^2 = -1, \qquad j^2 = k^2 = 1, \\ ij = -ji = k \end{cases}$$

A straightforward computation shows that this product generates an associative but non-commutative real algebra, denoted $\mathbb{H}_{coq}$, whose elements are called coquaternions. Notably, unlike Hamilton quaternions, $\mathbb{H}_{coq}$ is not a division algebra, as it contains both zero divisors and nilpotent elements.

We identify $\mathbb{R}^4$ with $\mathbb{H}_{coq}$ through the correspondence

$$(q_0, q_1, q_2, q_3) \leftrightarrow q_0 + q_1 i + q_2 j + q_3 k.$$

For $q = q_0 + q_1 i + q_2 j + q_3 k \in \mathbb{H}_{coq}$, we define:

the *conjugate* $\bar{q} = q_0 - q_1 i - q_2 j - q_3 k$;

the *real part* $re(q) = q_0$;

the *vector part* $vec(q) = q_1 i + q_2 j + q_3 k$.

Coquaternions with zero vector part are naturally identified with real numbers.

An important result for the coquaternions is the fact that the algebra $\mathbb{H}_{coq}$ is isomorphic to the algebra of real 2×2 matrices via:

$$\Phi(q_0 + q_1\mathrm{i} + q_2\mathrm{j} + q_3\mathrm{k}) = \begin{pmatrix} q_0 + q_3 & q_1 + q_2 \\ q_2 - q_1 & q_0 - q_3 \end{pmatrix}$$

The *determinant* of q, denoted $\det q$, is defined as:

$$\det q = q_0^2 + q_1^2 - q_2^2 - q_3^2 = q\bar{q}$$

A coquaternion q is invertible if and only if $\det q \neq 0$, with inverse:

$$q^{-1} = \frac{\bar{q}}{\det q}.$$

Definition 1. *Two coquaternions* q *and* p *are* similar *(*q ∼ p*) if there exists an invertible* h *such that* $p = hqh^{-1}$.

This equivalence relation partitions $\mathbb{H}_{coq}$ into similarity classes, denoted by [q]. One can show that, $[q] = \{q\}$ if and only if q is real.

For invertible h, the *similarity map* $\phi_h : \mathbb{H}_{coq} \to \mathbb{H}_{coq}$ defined by:

$$\phi_h(q) = h^{-1}qh \qquad (1)$$

constitutes an algebra automorphism.

Unlike Hamilton quaternions, coquaternions require three distinct representative forms for non-real elements, see [3] and the references cited therein:

Theorem 1. *For a non-real coquaternion* $q = q_0 + \text{vec}\, q$ *with* $r = \det(\text{vec}\, q) = q_1^2 - q_2^2 - q_3^2$, *we have:*

if $r > 0$, $\exists \phi_h$ *such that* $\phi_h(q) = q_0 + \sqrt{r}\mathrm{i}$;

if $r < 0$, $\exists \phi_h$ *such that* $\phi_h(q) = q_0 + \sqrt{-r}\mathrm{j}$;

if $r = 0$, $\exists \phi_h$ *such that* $\phi_h(q) = q_0 + \mathrm{i} + \mathrm{j}$.

Next, we recall some basic definitions of discrete dynamical systems.

3   Basic Definitions on Coquaternionic Discrete Dynamical Systems

Let us consider a coquaternionic map $f : \mathbb{H}_{coq} \to \mathbb{H}_{coq}$. For $k \in \mathbb{N}$, we shall denote by f^k the k-th iterate of f, inductively defined by

$$\begin{cases} f^0 = \mathrm{id}_{\mathbb{H}_{coq}} \\ f^k = f \circ f^{k-1}. \end{cases}$$

For a given initial point $q_0 \in \mathbb{H}_{coq}$, the orbit of q_0 under the map f is the sequence

$$\mathcal{O}(q_0) := \left(f^k(q_0) \right)_{k \in \mathbb{N}_0}.$$

In the context of dynamical systems, the orbit of a point under a map f represents the time evolution of a specific quantity. Next, we focus on particular types of orbits, which correspond to distinctive patterns in the system's time evolution.

A point $q \in \mathbb{H}_{coq}$ is said to be a periodic point of f, with period $n \in \mathbb{N}$, if we have $f^n(q) = q$, with $f^k(q) \neq q$ for $0 < k < n$; in this case, we say that the set

$$\mathcal{C} = \{q, f(q), \ldots, f^{n-1}(q)\}$$

is a n-cycle for f, usually written as

$$\mathcal{C} : q_0 \xrightarrow{f} q_1 \xrightarrow{f} \cdots \xrightarrow{f} q_{n-1}$$

with $q_i = f^i(q)$. Periodic points of period one are usually called fixed points.

Finally, there is one last definition relevant for the rest of the paper:

Definition 2. *We say that two maps* $f : \mathbb{H}_{coq} \to \mathbb{H}_{coq}$ *and* $g : \mathbb{H}_{coq} \to \mathbb{H}_{coq}$ *are conjugate if there exists an invertible map* $\phi : \mathbb{H}_{coq} \to \mathbb{H}_{coq}$ *such that*

$$f \circ \phi = \phi \circ g.$$

In this case, we say that the corresponding dynamical systems $(\mathbb{H}_{coq}, f)$ and $(\mathbb{H}_{coq}, g)$ are dynamically equivalent, since they share the same dynamical characteristics.

4   The Coquaternionic Mandelbrot Set of a Family of Quadratics

Prior to examining the coquaternionic generalization, it is instructive to review foundational results concerning the classical complex Mandelbrot set.

While the family of complex quadratic maps $z^2 + bz$ is topologically conjugate to the standard quadratic family $z^2 + c$, its associated Mandelbrot set remains underrepresented in canonical literature due to this structural equivalence. This conjugacy implies dynamical equivalence between the two families, rendering distinct visualizations of their Mandelbrot sets superfluous in most analyses. However, given the pedagogical and comparative objectives of this work, we deem it methodologically pertinent to explicitly illustrate the Mandelbrot set for the $z^2 + bz$ parametrization. Such a representation not only reinforces the foundational principles governing quadratic complex dynamics but also provides a conceptual bridge to the non-commutative coquaternionic extension discussed subsequently.

Consider the family of complex quadratic maps $R_b(z) = z^2 + bz$. It is known that the Möbius transformation $\phi(z) = z + b/2$ establishes a conjugacy between

R_b and the simpler quadratic family $Q_c(z) = z^2 + c$ (see the following diagram)

$$\begin{array}{ccc} \mathbb{C} & \xrightarrow{R_b} & \mathbb{C} \\ \phi \downarrow & & \downarrow \phi \\ \mathbb{C} & \xrightarrow{Q_b} & \mathbb{C} \end{array}$$

Specifically, the inverse transformation $\phi^{-1}(z) = z - b/2$ facilitates the construction of the Mandelbrot set for R_b and enables the translation of properties from the classical complex Mandelbrot set to this parameterized family.

The mapping conjugacy induces a relationship between parameters b and c, given by

$$c = \frac{1}{4} b(2 - b),$$

with the inverse transformation

$$b = 1 \pm \sqrt{1 - 4c}.$$

This result implies that the Mandelbrot set for the quadratics R_b bifurcates into two symmetric components along the parameter axis re $b = 1$, intersecting at the point $b = 1$. These components are not mere geometric reflections but retain full dynamical equivalence to the classical Mandelbrot set under topological conjugacy.

A key consequence of the conjugacy is the derivation of the boundary curve for the Mandelbrot set of R_b, which takes the form of a Cassini oval:

$$|b(2 - b)| = 8.$$

This curve encloses both symmetric components of the Mandelbrot set, forming a unified topological structure.

The conjugacy further induces an obvious correspondence between critical points: $\phi^{-1}(0) = -b/2$. Consequently, the Mandelbrot set for R_b can be characterized in two equivalent ways: either by mapping points from the classical Mandelbrot set via ϕ^{-1}, or by identifying parameters $b \in \mathbb{C}$ for which

$$\lim_{k \to \infty} \left| R_b^k(-b/2) \right| \not\to \infty.$$

Figure 1 illustrates the resulting Mandelbrot set alongside its bounding Cassini oval.

In subsequent analysis, we concentrate on the right component defined as the subset of parameters $b = b_0 + b_1 \mathring{\imath}$ with $b_0 \geq 1$. This component retains dynamical equivalence to the classical Mandelbrot set and serves as the foundation for our generalization to coquaternionic mappings.

Since the Mandelbrot set for R_b is topologically conjugate to the classical complex Mandelbrot set, we can conclude that it inherits the properties of being both bounded and connected. We now turn our focus to analyzing the Mandelbrot set arising from the generalization of this quadratic family to coquaternions.

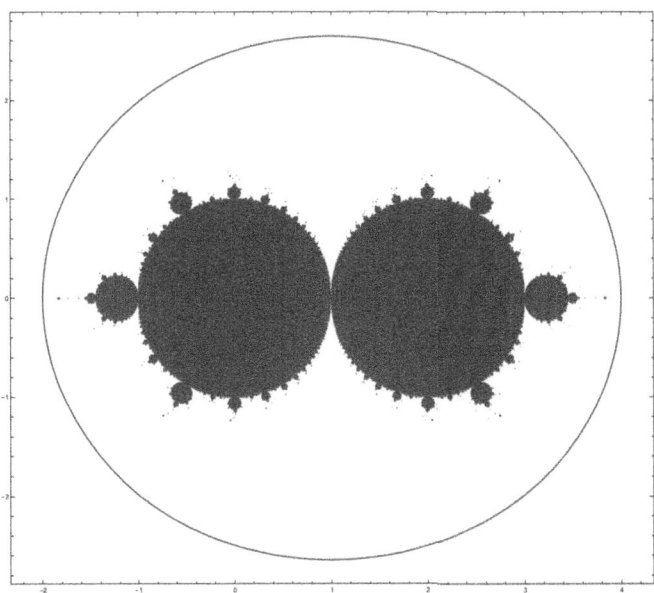

Fig. 1. The Mandelbrot set for the family of complex quadratics $R_b(z) = z^2 + bz$, bounded by the Cassini oval $|b(2 - b)| = 8$. This Mandelbrot set bifurcates into two symmetric components along the parameter axis $\mathrm{re}\, b = 1$, intersecting at the point $b = 1$.

Consider the one-parameter family of quadratic maps

$$f_b : \mathbb{H}_{coq} \to \mathbb{H}_{coq}$$
$$q \mapsto q^2 + b\, q$$

where b is a fixed parameter in $\mathbb{H}_{coq}$, such that $\mathrm{re}\, b > 1$. We introduce the following definition:

Definition 3. *The coquaternionic Mandelbrot set of the family* f_b *is the set of parameters* $b \in \mathbb{H}_{coq}$ *for which the map* f_b *has an attractor* Γ *such that the point* $-b/2$ *belongs to its basin of attraction.*

We denote this coquaternionic Mandelbrot set as $\mathcal{M}_b$.

Remark 1. The proposed definition of the coquaternionic Mandelbrot set for the family f_b differs from the standard one. The inclusion of a second restriction – requiring the existence of an attractor for the map f_b – is necessary due to results reported in [6], which indicate that there are complex attractors for R_b that are not attractors for f_b, where $b = b_0 + b_1 i$. Including such parameters in the coquaternionic Mandelbrot set $\mathcal{M}_b$ would be inconsistent. In the context of complex quadratic maps, this additional restriction would be excessive, as the existence of an attractor is guaranteed by the non-divergence of the orbit of the map's critical point.

The following results are crucial in guiding our approach to studying and obtaining the Mandelbrot set $\mathcal{M}_b$.

Lemma 1. *Let ϕ_h be the similarity map defined by (1) for a given invertible coquaternion h. The dynamical system $(\mathbb{H}_{coq}, f_b)$ is dynamically equivalent to the dynamical system $(\mathbb{H}_{coq}, f_{\phi_h(b)})$.*

Proof. We have

$$
\begin{aligned}
(\phi_h \circ f_b \circ \phi_h^{-1})(q) &= (\phi_h \circ f_b)(hqh^{-1}) \\
&= \phi_h((hqh^{-1})^2 + b\,hqh^{-1}) \\
&= \phi_h(hq^2h^{-1} + b\,hqh^{-1}) \\
&= h^{-1}(hq^2h^{-1} + b\,hqh^{-1})h \\
&= q^2 + h^{-1}bh\,q = f_{\phi_h(b)}(q).
\end{aligned}
$$

$\square$

As a consequence of Lemma 1 above and of Theorem 1, we immediately obtain the result contained in the following theorem.

Theorem 2. *To study the dynamics of the quadratic map f_b, there is no loss of generality in assuming that the parameter b assumes one of the following forms, where $b_0, b_1, b_2 \in \mathbb{R}$:*

$\mathcal{B}_0 \qquad b = b_0$

$\mathcal{B}_1 \qquad b = b_0 + b_1 i, \quad b_1 > 0$

$\mathcal{B}_2 \qquad b = b_0 + b_2 j, \quad b_2 > 0$

$\mathcal{B}_3 \qquad b = b_0 + i + j$

We will refer to the four different forms of the parameter b given above as the *canonical forms*.

As an illustration of the dynamical implications of the existence of a conjugacy transformation between maps with similar parameters, consider the following example.

Example 1. Consider the set of parameters

$$
b = 2.632 + 1.2\,i + b_2 j + b_3 k
$$

such that $0 < b_2^2 + b_3^2 < 1.2$. Then, we computed the subsets of these parameters for which the orbit of the point $-b/2$ converges to cycles of periods 6, 3, 14, and 1, respectively. The obtained results can be represent graphically on the (j, k) plane, see Fig. 2. As we expected, the subsets of parameters corresponding to the orbit of $-b/2$ being attracted to a n-cycle are given as circular annuli in the (j, k) plane.

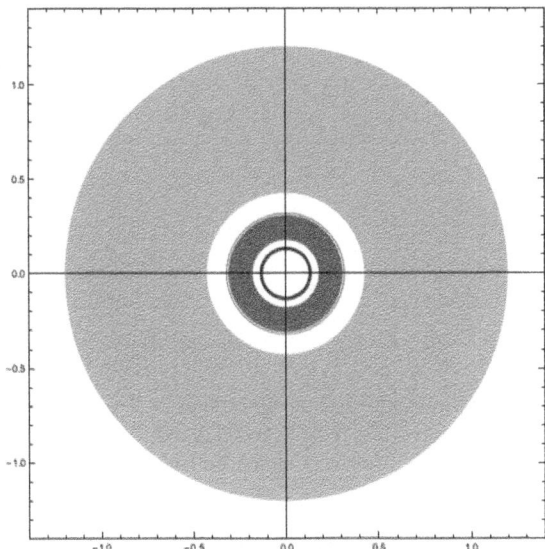

Fig. 2. The four gray circular annuli in the $(\mathbb{j}, \mathbb{k})$ plane indicate parameters $b = 2.632 + 1.2\mathbb{i} + b_2\mathbb{j} + b_3\mathbb{k}$ for which the orbits of $-b/2$ under f_b are attracted to cycles of period 6 (dark gray), 3 (medium gray), 14 (gray), and 1 (light gray), from the center outward, respectively. (Color figure online)

The circular parameter regions exhibiting equivalent dynamical behavior for orbits of the point $-b/2$ directly result from the similarity transformation $f_b \sim f_{b'}$, where

$$b = b_0 + b_1\mathbb{i} + b_2\mathbb{j} + b_3\mathbb{k}$$

and

$$b' = b_0 + b_1\mathbb{i} + b_2'\mathbb{j} + b_3'\mathbb{k}$$

satisfy $b_2^2 + b_3^2 = b_2'^2 + b_3'^2$. This symmetry allows us to study $\mathcal{M}_b$ by fixing $b_3 = 0$, with the understanding that these results extend to all possible b_3 values. The following result, a direct demonstration of map similarity, reveals the unbounded nature of the set $\mathcal{M}_b$.

Lemma 2. *Given any parameter* $b = b_0 + b_1\mathbb{i}$ *belonging to* $\mathcal{M}_b$, *all parameters* $b' = b_0 + b_1'\mathbb{i} + b_2'\mathbb{j} + b_3'\mathbb{k}$ *satisfying* $b_1'^2 - b_2'^2 - b_3'^2 = b_1^2$ *are similar to* b. *This infinite family of similar parameters demonstrates that the Mandelbrot set* $\mathcal{M}_b$ *cannot be bounded.*

In Fig. 3 we can see the curve of points corresponding to similar parameters $b' = 2.82 + b_1'\mathbb{i} + b_2'\mathbb{j}$ of a given parameter $b = 2.82 + 0.59\mathbb{i} \in \mathcal{M}_b$, being easy to conclude from this example that, unlike its complex counterpart, the Mandelbrot set $\mathcal{M}_b$ is not bounded.

Given its role in analyzing $\mathcal{M}_b$, next we introduce the set corresponding to its intersection with the complex plane (denoted $\mathcal{M}_0$), as shown in Fig. 4.

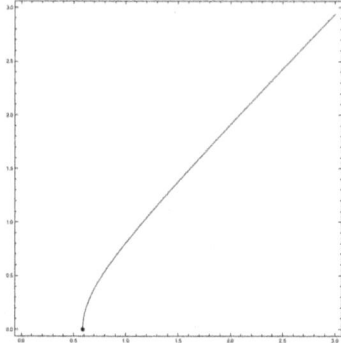

Fig. 3. Curve in the $(\mathtt{i}, \mathtt{j})$ plane showing parameters $\mathsf{b}' = 2.82 + b_1' \mathtt{i} + b_2' \mathtt{j}$ with $b_1'^2 - b_2'^2 = 0.59^2$. Since they are similar to $\mathsf{b} = 2.82 + 0.59\,\mathtt{i} \in \mathcal{M}_\mathsf{b}$, they also belong to $\mathcal{M}_\mathsf{b}$ and thus the coquaternionic Mandelbrot set cannot be bounded.

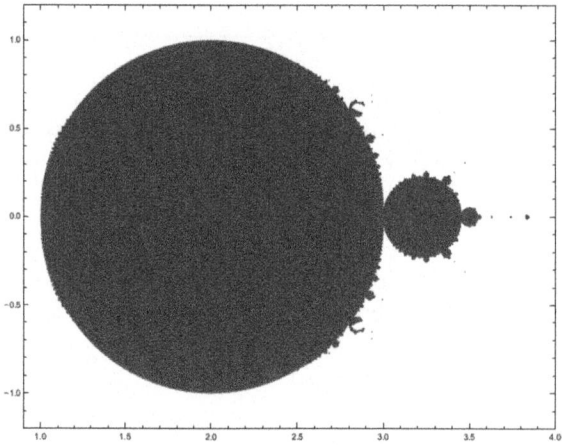

Fig. 4. Visualization of $\mathcal{M}_0$, the complex planar section of $\mathcal{M}_\mathsf{b}$.

As commonly recognized, the coquaternionic Mandelbrot set $\mathcal{M}_\mathsf{b}$ exists in 4-dimensional space, rendering complete visualization fundamentally impossible. However, our preceding analysis demonstrates that its projection onto the $(1, \mathtt{i}, \mathtt{j})$ subspace provides a structurally representative approximation. Nevertheless, even three-dimensional projections of such intricate mathematical objects inevitably obscure certain fine details. We therefore propose an alternative visualization strategy: by fixing $1 \leq b_0 \leq 4$, we can effectively represent parameters $\mathsf{b} = b_0 + b_1\mathtt{i} + b_2\mathtt{j}$ (within the $(\mathtt{i}, \mathtt{j})$ plane) belonging to $\mathcal{M}_\mathsf{b}$. Conceptually, the Mandelbrot set $\mathcal{M}_\mathsf{b}$ then becomes the topological union of all such cross-sectional slices.

For fixed $1 \leq b_0 \leq 4$, consider the set of parameters $(b_0, b_1) \in \mathcal{M}_0$. These manifest along the $b_2 = 0$ axis in the $(\mathtt{i}, \mathtt{j})$ plane. Through the equivalence of maps with similar parameters, we can say that points (b'_1, b'_2) satisfying $b'^2_1 - b'^2_2 = b^2_1$ correspond to parameters $b' = b_0 + b'_1 i + b'_2 j$ belonging to the coquaternionic Mandelbrot set $\mathcal{M}_b$. Noticeably, all such solutions reside in the region $b_2 \leq b_1$.

Following a similar reasoning, let us compute the set of values b_2 such that parameters $b = b_0 + b_2 j$ belong to $\mathcal{M}_b$. This time, these parameters correspond to points appearing along the $b_1 = 0$ axis. Then, the points (b'_1, b'_2) satisfying $b'^2_1 - b'^2_2 = -b^2_2$ represent parameters $b' = b_0 + b'_1 i + b'_2 j$ similar to $b = b_0 + b_2 j$, therefore also belonging to $\mathcal{M}_b$. We can easily conclude that these points are constrained to the region $b_2 \geq b_1$.

Thus, each slice of $\mathcal{M}_b$ is formed by combining both parameter sets through union operation. An illustration of such slices are given in Fig. 5, Fig. 6, and Fig. 7.

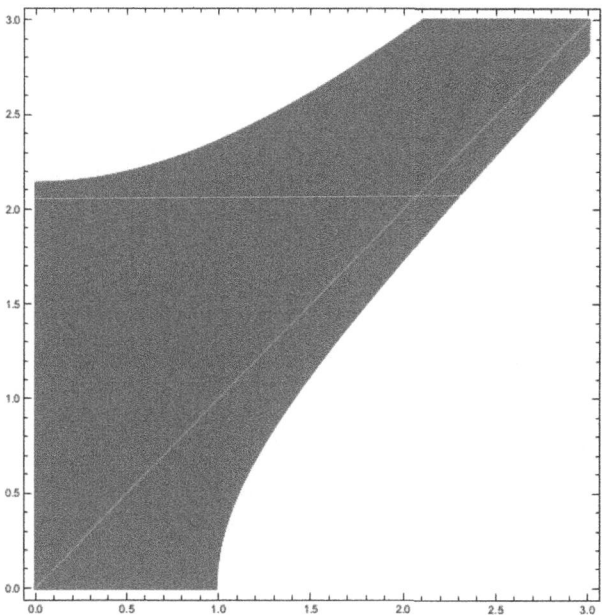

Fig. 5. The slice of the Mandelbrot set $\mathcal{M}_b$ in the (i, j) plane corresponding to parameters $b = 1.850 + b_1 i + b_2 j$.

The visualization of three coquaternionic Mandelbrot set $\mathcal{M}_b$ slices yields two key observations: the first one concerns the complexity amplification: the intricate structure observed in the complex Mandelbrot set of quadratic maps $z^2 + bz$ becomes inherently amplified when generalized to coquaternions. This amplification arises because each point in the classical Mandelbrot set generates a curve of equivalent parameters in the (i, j) plane, preserving the original complexity while expanding its geometric representation.

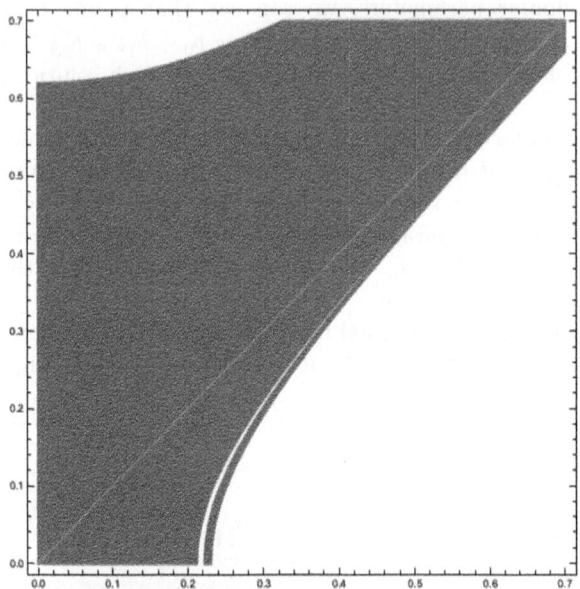

Fig. 6. The slice of the Mandelbrot set $\mathcal{M}_\mathsf{b}$ in the $(\mathtt{i}, \mathtt{j})$ plane corresponding to parameters $\mathsf{b} = 3.380 + b_1\mathtt{i} + b_2\mathtt{j}$.

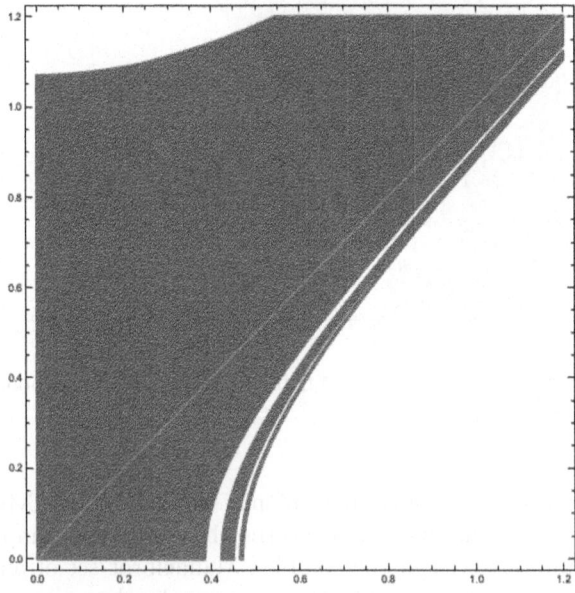

Fig. 7. The slice of the Mandelbrot set $\mathcal{M}_\mathsf{b}$ in the $(\mathtt{i}, \mathtt{j})$ plane corresponding to parameters $\mathsf{b} = 2.923 + b_1\mathtt{i} + b_2\mathtt{j}$.

The second one is about the upper-region simplicity: for parameters satisfying $b_2 > b_1$, upper regions correspond to coquaternionic parameters similar to $b_0 + b_2\mathtt{j} \in \mathcal{M}_\mathtt{b}$. These exhibit a direct correspondence with iterations of real quadratic maps, implying such regions derive from intervals of real parameters. Consequently, these upper subsets manifest as fundamentally simple geometric structures within the $(\mathtt{i}, \mathtt{j})$ plane.

5 Conclusions

The Mandelbrot set remains one of the most captivating and visually striking mathematical objects ever discovered. Defined by a simple criterion in the iteration of quadratic complex maps within the framework of complex discrete dynamical systems, it presents a significant challenge to generalize this concept to the four-dimensional space of coquaternions.

Extending the Mandelbrot set into the coquaternionic domain introduces profound mathematical challenges and reveals structures of remarkable complexity.

In this work, we explored the generalization of the Mandelbrot set from the quadratic mapping family $x^2 + b\,x$ in the complex plane to the coquaternionic space $\mathbb{H}_{\mathrm{coq}}$. One of the first observations is the necessity of redefining the Mandelbrot set for this higher-dimensional context. Additionally, leveraging the equivalence of maps for similar parameters, we demonstrated that, unlike its complex counterpart, the coquaternionic Mandelbrot set is not a bounded set.

Using specialized visualization techniques, we concluded that, strictly speaking, the complexity of the coquaternionic Mandelbrot set $\mathbb{H}_{\mathrm{coq}}$ mirrors that of its complex counterpart. While each point in the complex Mandelbrot set corresponds to a curve in the $(\mathtt{i}, \mathtt{j})$ plane for coquaternions, this geometric expansion preserves the same underlying complexity.

However, our final observation is that the Mandelbrot set does not fully capture the diversity and intricacy inherent in the dynamics generated by coquaternionic quadratic mappings. The apparent simplicity of upper-region slices conceals a deeper complexity in the dynamics associated with these parameter choices. This limitation arises because the only information encoded by the coquaternionic Mandelbrot set is whether or not the orbit of the critical point $-b/2$ escapes to infinity. As such, it does not fully reflect the richness of dynamical behaviors present in this system.

Acknowledgments. Research at CIDMA has been supported by FCT (Portuguese Foundation for Science and Technology) Multi-Annual Financing Program for R&D Units. Research at CMAT was partially financed by Portuguese funds through FCT within the Projects UID/00013. Research at CISE has been financed by FCT within the Projects UIDB/04131/2020 and UIDP/04131/2020.

References

1. Boily, V., Rochon, D.: On the algebraic foundation of the Mandelbulb. Fractals **31**(5), 2350062 (2023)
2. Brouillette, G., Rochon, D.: Characterization of the principal 3d slices related to the multicomplex Mandelbrot set. Adv. Appl. Clifford Algebras **29**(3), 1–18 (2019). https://doi.org/10.1007/s00006-019-0956-1
3. Falcão, M.I., Miranda, F., Severino, R., Soares, M.J.: Iteration of quadratic maps on coquaternions. Int. J. Bifurcation Chaos **27**(12), 1730039 (2017)
4. Falcão, M.I., Miranda, F., Severino, R., Soares, M.J.: Basins of attraction for a quadratic coquaternionic map. Chaos, Solitons Fractals **104**, 716–724 (2017)
5. Falcão, M.I., Miranda, F., Severino, R., Soares, M.J.: Dynamics of the coquaternionic maps $x^2 + bx$. Rend. Circ. Mat. Palermo, II. Ser **72**, 959–975 (2023)
6. Falcão, M.I., Miranda, F., Severino, R., Soares, M.J.: The stability of complex dynamics for two families of coquaternionic quadratic polynomials. In: Gervasi, O., et al. (eds.) Computational Science and its Applications – ICCSA 2023 Workshops. ICCSA 2023. LNCS, vol. 14104. Springer (2023). https://doi.org/10.1007/978-3-031-37105-9_48
7. Peitgen, H.-O., Jürgens, H., Saupe, D.: Chaos and Fractals. Springer, New York (1992). https://doi.org/10.1007/978-1-4757-4740-9
8. Wang, X.-Y., Sun, Y.-Y.: The general quaternionic M-J sets on the mapping $z \leftarrow z^\alpha + c \, (\alpha \in \mathbb{N})$. Comput. Math. Appl. **53**, 1718–1732 (2007)

Mixed Integer Linear Formulation for the Multiple Trip Aircraft Refueling Problem of a Brazilian Company

Karyne Alves Zampirolli[1]([✉])(iD) and André Renato Sales Amaral[2](iD)

[1] Graduate School of Computer Science (PPGI), Federal University of Espírito Santo, Vitória ES 29075-910, Brazil
karyne.zampirolli@ufes.br
[2] Graduate School of Computer Science (PPGI), Federal University of Espírito Santo, Vitória ES 29075-910, Brazil
amaral@inf.ufes.br

Abstract. This work presents a study on a problem faced by a Brazilian fuel distribution company, which aims to develop a decision system to minimize the operational costs of tanker trucks that refuel aircraft at airports. This is called the Aircraft Refueling Problem (ARP). ARP is related to the vehicle routing problem but focuses on the practical aspects of actual operations. The ARP variant discussed allows trucks to make multiple trips, which is called the Multiple Trip Aircraft Refueling Problem (MTARP). A Mixed-Integer Linear Programming Model (MILP) was developed to address the problem. A diverse set of instances was generated based on real-world operational constraints, simulating refueling scenarios at Brazilian airports. The model was solved using the CPLEX solver, and computational experiments were conducted to evaluate solution quality under different time limits. Two key analyzes were performed: (1) identifying instance characteristics that increase problem complexity and (2) assessing solution quality within a 30-min time limit. For smaller instances, CPLEX quickly finds optimal solutions, while for larger, constrained cases, optimality gaps remain significant. These findings offer insights into MTARP's scalability and demonstrate that even under strict computational limits, CPLEX can provide useful solutions. However, for highly complex instances, hybrid approaches, such as heuristics or decomposition methods, may be necessary. These findings offer valuable guidance for optimizing aircraft refueling operations in real-world applications.

Keywords: Mixed-integer linear programming · Aircraft refueling problem · Vehicle routing

1 Introduction

At Brazilian airports, tanker trucks are typically used to refuel aircraft before they take off for their next destination. Poor management of this refueling service can lead to flight delays. A Brazilian company, which is the country's main

O. Gervasi et al. (Eds.): ICCSA 2025 Workshops, LNCS 15887, pp. 163–180, 2026.
https://doi.org/10.1007/978-3-031-97589-9_12

aviation fuel distributor and responsible for the refueling service, aims to plan routes for its tanker trucks, ensuring that aircraft receive fuel within predetermined time windows, minimizing the total distance traveled by the trucks. This is called the Aircraft Refueling Problem (ARP). ARP is a type of Vehicle Routing Problem (VRP) [5, 10, 11, 17, 23, 27]. Finding the optimal solution to a real-size vehicle routing problem is a complex task since these problems are NP-hard [8]. Thus, depending on the size of the problem, no optimization algorithm can achieve the optimal solution of the problem in a feasible time.

Although the ARP is related to the vehicle routing problem, ARP differs by considering the unique characteristics of a real airport refueling operation. This distinction makes ARP a new and promising object of study. When reviewing the literature, no studies were found that completely represented the Brazilian company's aircraft refueling problem. A few authors have examined the use of tanker trucks for aircraft fuel supply service [3, 9, 12, 15, 18, 20, 21, 24, 25, 28] but the problems they considered differ from the ARP in some objectives or by not including ARP assumptions, such as the aircraft refueling rate, the average speed of the trucks, the rate of reloading trucks at the depot, the fuel sedimentation time after truck reloading at the depot for a new trip, heterogeneous fleet, aircraft being serviced by a single truck without compatibility restrictions, and trucks without maximum travel distance restrictions, among other factors.

When dealing with the ARP, we can investigate two variants: the Single Trip Aircraft Refueling Problem (STARP) and the Multiple Trip Aircraft Refueling Problem (MTARP). STARP was introduced in [26], where the authors propose a mathematical model and heuristic methods to solve it. The STARP focuses on the refueling service of aircraft using a fleet of non-homogeneous tanker trucks with capacity and time window constraints, where each truck makes only one trip within a given time horizon. This problem is related to the Vehicle Routing Problem with Time Windows (VRPTW) [7]. On the other hand, the MTARP allows trucks to make multiple trips, requiring them to return to the depot to refuel before starting new trips, and is, therefore, closely related to the Multi-Trip Vehicle Routing Problem with Time Windows (MTVRPTW) [2]. However, STARP and MTARP add application-specific restrictions.

In this paper, we will address the MTARP variant. We present a Mixed-Integer Linear Programming Model (MILP) for the MTARP and test it on a set of instances constructed based on several airport scenarios for the study of the ARP. The instances span two distinct categories: one where aircraft are parked in a straight line and another where they are not.

The main contributions of this article are: the introduction of a practical problem of a fuel distribution company, called MTARP; the development of a MILP formulation tailored to the operational constraints and objectives of the company under study; the generation of a diverse set of instances to analyze problem complexity under different scenarios; a computational analysis identifying key instance characteristics that impact problem solvability; insights into the model's scalability, emphasizing its effectiveness for small- and medium-scale problems and its limitations in solving large, highly constrained instances within practical timeframes.

The paper is organized as follows: Sect. 2 presents a brief literature review of studies related to the aircraft fuel supply service and the MTVRPTW problem. Then, Sect. 3 presents the mathematical model proposed for the MTARP. Section 4 describes the characteristics of the instances considered in the study. Computational results are presented in Sect. 5. Finally, some conclusions and suggestions for future research are presented in Sect. 6.

2   Literature Review

This section presents a brief literature review on research related to aircraft fuel supply operations and MTVRPTW.

2.1   Aircraft Fuel Supply Service

The ARP is innovative because, after reviewing the literature, no previous studies have been found to address this problem fully. Some studies address the aircraft fuel supply service by tanker trucks [3,9,12,15,18,20,21,24,25,28], but they differ from the ARP as they do not include some of the ARP assumptions outlined in Sect. 1.

One of the first studies on aircraft fueling service was carried out in [3], where a model suitable for Belgrade airport was presented. The main objective in [3] was to minimize both the number of tanker trucks and the total distance traveled by these trucks. The problem was approached using the *branch-and-bound* technique. Reference [3] assumes that flights are served in increasing order of service start time, that all tanker trucks have the same capacity, and that each aircraft can be served by up to two vehicles, each providing half the required amount of fuel. However, in ARP, the flight service order is not fixed, tanker trucks have different capacities and finally, an aircraft cannot be serviced by more than one truck at the same time.

In [9] a mathematical formulation for the optimization problem known as Airport Ground Service Scheduling (AGSS) is presented. The objective is to minimize several factors, such as the number of tanker trucks used, the sum of the service start times for each flight, and the total travel time of the trucks. To illustrate the problem, the authors considered the Oil Tanker Truck Scheduling (OTTS) problem. The objective of OTTS is to obtain a feasible solution that assigns tanker trucks to fuel aircraft and provides the start time of each service operation. In this formulation, preference was given to fueling aircraft with earlier service start times, shorter travel times, shorter waiting times, shorter service times, and earlier service end times. In addition, the study considered the use of non-homogeneous vehicles, where each could serve up to $G(\in \mathbb{Z})$ aircraft. In ARP, unlike this work, a truck can serve as many aircraft as needed, as long as it does not violate the vehicle's capacity. As for the solution method, the authors used an Ant Colony Optimization (ACO) algorithm. A heuristic called Earliest Due Date First (EDD) was incorporated into ACO as a comparative ant to improve the algorithm's performance. A case study was conducted considering data from a domestic airport.

The study in [21] investigated the Dynamic Capacitated Vehicle Routing Problem with Time Windows, (partial) Split Delivery and Heterogeneous fleets (DVRPTWSD), applied to the aircraft fuel supply activity using trucks at an airport. The objective is to optimize response capacity, that is, to complete the fuel supply as quickly as possible within the time window, allowing the vehicle to return to its activities as quickly as possible. In constructing the routes of the tanker trucks, the problem considers that each vehicle has a specific capacity, a service time and a list of incompatibilities according to which some trucks are not suitable to serve certain aircraft. Furthermore, in the DVRPTWSD, a single aircraft can be served by different trucks. In the ARP, the trucks do not have a list of incompatibilities and an aircraft cannot be served by more than one truck. The author proposed an algorithm based on ant colony optimization to solve DVRPTWSD. This approach was tested in a real case in the air transport area, demonstrating the effectiveness of the proposed algorithm.

Reference [15] conducted a study on route scheduling for aircraft fuel supply at Juanda Airport in Surabaya. This was called Airport Ground Service Scheduling (AGSS). The authors assume that an aircraft can only be serviced by one truck. They also considered the use of non-homogeneous vehicles with a maximum service restriction of G aircraft. The objective of the study was to determine the minimum number of trucks required for the refueling service. To solve the problem, they developed a solution approach based on the ACO algorithm.

In [20], a mathematical model is presented to address the dynamic scheduling problem of fueling vehicles at airports, formulating it as a variant of the Vehicle Routing Problem with Time Windows (VRPTW). In the study, the authors considered tanker trucks with maximum travel distance constraints. Unlike the assumption of this work, in ARP, trucks do not have a travel distance limitation. The objective is to minimize both the number of service routes for refueling vehicles and the number of vehicles needed to complete the aircraft refueling service. To solve this problem, the authors proposed a hybrid multi-strategy approach. This approach combines a Genetic Algorithm (GA) with a crossover method inspired by particle swarm optimization and a local search strategy based on Simulated Annealing (SA). Additionally, they developed a local replanning strategy based on a dynamic time window. The effectiveness of this method was validated through a real case study carried out at an airport.

2.2   Multi-Trip Vehicle Routing Problem with Time Windows

In the Multi-Trip Vehicle Routing Problem with Time Windows (MTVRPTW) vehicles can be scheduled to make more than one trip during a working day, and the customers must be served by these vehicles within specific time windows. The need for multiple trips arises when the vehicle fleet is limited. The problem consists of optimizing the working day of each vehicle, aiming at minimizing transportation costs. The working day of a vehicle is made up of a sequence of customers to be visited. The vehicle can return to the distribution center to be reloaded and then start a new trip. The maximum number of trips for a vehicle is predefined. Each customer must be served only once, within a predetermined time [1, 2, 4, 13, 16, 19].

According to [1], MTVRPTW has received little attention in the literature, despite its importance in practice. Most existing studies on solving this problem have addressed the use of meta-heuristics. In the literature, the research in [13] is considered the first study to address the concept of multiple trips in the vehicle routing problem without time windows. The author used an economy algorithm to construct the routes and a heuristic for the *bin-packing* problem to combine them into vehicles. The proposed approach was used to solve examples between 68 and 361 customers.

In [4], the authors divide MTVRPTW into two easier problems and develop two heuristics to solve them. The first heuristic deals with the creation of a set of routes, while the second deals with the *bin-packing* problem, in which routes are aggregated into multiple trips. The complete algorithm is iterative and is based on an adaptive guidance strategy, which directs the route heuristic to calculate only routes capable of improving the solution.

In [22], the MTVRPTW is addressed in the context of a company that distributes loaded pallets to designated customers. They proposed a mathematical model that considers heterogeneous fleet, total route time, and accessibility constraints between vehicles and customers. As a solution method, the authors used a constructive heuristic and a meta-heuristic based on Tabu Search (TS). To evaluate the performance of the heuristic, they presented a column generation algorithm, integrating a *branch-and-bound* procedure.

The work in [6] surveyed mathematical formulations and research exploring exact and heuristic approaches in the context of MTVRP and its extensions. The study also addresses other variants of VRP, where multiple trips are sometimes allowed. In this scenario, the authors highlight the motivations for linking multiple trips to vehicles and discuss the consequences of this approach on solution methods.

3   Problem Description and Modeling

In this section, we will present a Mixed Integer Linear Programming (MILP) formulation for the problem of the Brazilian fuel distribution company, called the Multiple-Trip Aircraft Refueling Problem (MTARP).

3.1   MTARP Description

Consider an airport with a depot (distribution center - DC) that houses tanker trucks responsible for supplying fuel to aircraft. The MTARP is defined on a complete directed graph $G(N, A)$ where $N = N_A \cup \{0, n+1\}$. $N_A = \{1, 2, ..., n\}$ is the set of aircraft. 0 and $n+1$ are the origin and destination vertices, both corresponding to the depot. The set A is the set of arcs that join two distinct vertices of G. No arc ends at vertex 0 and no arc originates at vertex $n + 1$.

Thus, MTARP can be described as follows: let N_A be the set of aircraft waiting for refueling service, K be the set of non-homogeneous tanker trucks and R be the set of trips, where $n = |N_A|$, $\bar{k} = |K|$ e $\bar{r} = |R|$. For each aircraft i that requires a quantity of fuel c_i ($i \in N_A$), the refueling service must occur in the time interval $[a_i, b_i]$. A truck k, with capacity Q_k ($k \in K$), cannot arrive to refuel aircraft i after time b_i. Furthermore, if the truck arrives before time a_i, it must wait until a_i to start the service. Each aircraft i can only be served once and by a single truck.

During aircraft refueling service, all tanker trucks are initially located at the depot. A preparation time for reloading a truck is associated with each route. This preparation time is proportional to the sum of the service times on each aircraft along the route. In addition, a fuel sedimentation time after truck reloading at the depot is considered. Each truck can service several aircraft. The truck leaves the depot and heads to aircraft i to refuel it, after which it can travel to another aircraft j or return to the depot to be reloaded and start a new trip. Thus, a route consists of a feasible sequence of trips $r \in R$, where each trip starts and ends at the depot. The maximum number of trips is predefined. The fuel demand for each trip cannot exceed the tanker truck's maximum load capacity. Trucks that are not used follow a fictitious route, starting and ending at the depot, without visiting any aircraft. The objective is to minimize the total distance traveled by the trucks. To formulate the problem as a MILP model, indices, parameters and decision variables are described in Table 1. The conditions to be considered are the following: $a_0 = a_{n+1} = 0$; $b_0 = b_{n+1} = b_{CD}$, $D_{0,n+1} = 0$.

3.2   MTARP Mathematical Model

Our model is based on the one proposed in [22]. However, our model does not consider two constraints used in [22]: the total route time constraint and the accessibility constraints between vehicles and customers. Another difference is the way of calculating the preparation time for reloading a truck at the depot for a new trip. In [22], the time for reloading the truck at the depot corresponds to an average vehicle loading time, regardless of the customers to be served along the route. An additional difference is that, in our model, we consider the average speed of the vehicle, the rate of reloading the vehicle at the depot, and for the calculation of the service time at the customer, the rate to refueling customer, which are metrics appropriate to the matter of aircraft refueling operations (e.g., [3]).

The MILP model proposed here for MTARP is formulated as follows:
Minimize:

$$\sum_{k \in K} \sum_{r \in R} \sum_{i \in N} \sum_{j \in N, j \neq i} D_{i,j} X_{i,j,k,r} \tag{1}$$

Subject to:

Table 1. Indices, parameters and decision variables of the MTARP model.

Indices	Description
i, j	aircraft
k	tanker trucks
r	trips
Parameters	Description
n	total number of aircraft
$\bar{k}$	total number of trucks
$\bar{r}$	maximum number of trips allowed for each truck
c_i	amount of fuel requested by aircraft $i \in N_A$
Q_k	maximum fuel capacity of truck $k \in K$
$D_{i,j}$	distance associated with arc $(i,j) \in A$
a_i	earliest start time for refueling aircraft i, $i \in N$
b_i	latest start time for refueling aircraft i, $i \in N$
q_i	rate to refueling aircraft i, $i \in N_A$
V_k	average speed of the truck k, $k \in K$
u	rate to reloading truck k at the depot, $k \in K$
t_σ	fuel sedimentation time after reloading truck k, $k \in K$
M	large positive number for time window constraints
Variables	Description
$X_{i,j,k,r}$	binary variables. Equal to 1 if edge $(i,j) \in A$ is traversed by truck $k \in K$ on trip $r \in R$. Otherwise, equal to 0. Note that when $X_{0,n+1,k,r} = 0$ trip r is empty
$T_{i,k,r}$	non-negative variables. They indicate the time when truck $k \in K$ on trip $r \in R$ starts serving node $i \in N$

$$\sum_{k \in K} \sum_{r \in R} \sum_{j \in N, j \neq i} X_{i,j,k,r} = 1, \quad i \in N_A \tag{2}$$

$$\sum_{i \in N_A} \sum_{j \in N, j \neq i} c_i X_{i,j,k,r} \leq Q_k, \quad k \in K, r \in R \tag{3}$$

$$\sum_{j \in N} X_{0,j,k,r} = 1, \quad k \in K, r \in R \tag{4}$$

$$\sum_{i \in N} X_{i,n+1,k,r} = 1, \quad k \in K, r \in R \tag{5}$$

$$\sum_{i \in N, h \neq i} X_{i,h,k,r} - \sum_{j \in N, j \neq h} X_{h,j,k,r} = 0, \quad h \in N_A, k \in K, r \in R \tag{6}$$

$$T_{j,k,r} \geq T_{i,k,r} + \frac{c_i}{q_i} + \frac{D_{i,j}}{V_k} - M(1 - X_{i,j,k,r}), \quad i,j \in N, i \neq j, k \in K, r \in R \quad (7)$$

$$a_i \leq T_{i,k,r} \leq b_i, \quad i \in N, k \in K, r \in R \quad (8)$$

$$T_{0,k,r} \geq \sum_{i \in N_A} \sum_{j \in N, j \neq i} \frac{c_i}{u} X_{i,j,k,r} + t_\sigma, \quad k \in K, r \in R \quad (9)$$

$$T_{0,k,r} \geq T_{n+1,k,r-1} + \sum_{i \in N_A} \sum_{j \in N, j \neq i} \frac{c_i}{u} X_{i,j,k,r} + t_\sigma, \quad k \in K, r = 2, ..., |R| \quad (10)$$

$$X_{0,n+1,k,r} \leq X_{0,n+1,k,r+1}, \quad k \in K, r = 1, ..., |R| - 1 \quad (11)$$

$$X_{i,j,k,r} \in \{0,1\}, \quad i,j \in N, i \neq j, k \in K, r \in R \quad (12)$$

$$T_{i,k,s} \geq 0, \quad i \in N, k \in K, r \in R \quad (13)$$

The objective function (1) aims to minimize the total distance traveled by tanker trucks. Constraints (2) impose that an aircraft i can only be served by a truck k on a trip r. Constraints (3) state that the total demand on a route cannot exceed the vehicle capacity. In (4), it is imposed that every truck k must depart from each origin on the route. Similarly, constraints (5) impose that every truck k must arrive at each destination on the route.

Constraints (6) ensure that if a truck arrives at an aircraft, it must also depart from it. Constraints (4) to (6) ensure flow conservation, that is, they ensure that routes have their proper sequencing, starting and ending at the depot and visiting all aircraft. Constraints (8) impose that time windows are respected. Constraints (7) establish the relationship between the time a truck leaves an aircraft and the time the next aircraft is serviced. Note that these constraints ensure that when a truck k travels from aircraft i to aircraft j on a trip r, the arrival time at aircraft j must be greater than or equal to the time the truck began servicing aircraft i, plus the service time to refuel aircraft i (c_i/q_i), plus the time to travel from i to j $(D_{i,j}/V_k)$. M is a large constant value.

Constraints (9) impose that the departure time of truck k on trip r is greater than or equal to the time required to reload the truck for it to make trip r plus the fuel sedimentation time after reloading the truck (t_σ). Furthermore, constraints (10) impose that the departure time of truck k at the origin node of trip r must be greater than or equal to the arrival time of truck k at the destination node of trip $r - 1$, plus the time it takes to reload the truck for it to make trip r and the fuel sedimentation time, applicable only when $r \geq 2$. These constraints ensure proper route sequencing.

Constraint (11) ensures that trip $r + 1$ is not taken if trip r has not been taken. Trips that service aircraft are always placed at the beginning of the trucks' route, and empty trips are always taken at the end. This constraint only applies when $|R| \geq 2$, because if a truck k traverses the fictitious arc $(0, n + 1)$ during trip r, then the fictitious arcs of subsequent trips must also be traversed. Finally, constraints (12) and (13) define the domain of the variables.

4   Instance Generation

To simulate real scenarios of Brazilian airports, sets of adapted instances were created. The creation of these instances was motivated by the fact that the ARP is a new problem and, thus, there is no instances available. The construction of these sets was based on premises identified through dialogues and question-naires conducted with employees of the company studied and through data from the FlightAware platform [14]. FlightAware operates the largest flight data and tracking platform in the world, ensuring the quality of the data used.

The company studied does not have data on the location of aircraft parking lots. For this reason, it was necessary to seek this data from other sources to determine the distances. Due to the unavailability of real data, the fuel demand and time windows were estimated based on information collected on the platform FlightAware [14].

The constructed instance sets provide two scenarios for the MTARP investigation: the first set, called *APSL-MT type set*, has aircraft parked in a straight line. The second set, *ANPSL-MT type set*, introduces a scenario of aircraft not parked in a straight line. For the sets of instances with aircraft parked in a straight line, the positions were generated using the following methodology: the distance between the depot and the first aircraft parking position was considered. For each subsequent parking position, the distance of 40 m was added to the previous parking position, determining its position. This process resulted in a set of distances d_i, where $i \in N$, represents the distance between aircraft i and the depot. From d_i, the distance matrix $D_{i,j}$ was calculated as $D_{i,j} = |d_i - d_j|$. This calculation of $D_{i,j}$ follows the methodology described in the work of [3]. For the instance sets with aircraft not parked in a straight line, a distance matrix $D_{i,j}$ was constructed with random values between 99 and 1299.

The time windows $[a_i, b_i]$ represent the first and last moments in which the fueling operation of each aircraft i can occur. These intervals were defined based on data from Brazilian airport operations collected on the FlightAware platform, considering the scheduled departure time of each flight. The upper limit b_i of each window was defined as 10 min before the scheduled departure time, as per the company guidance. The lower limit a_i assumes values between 30 and 40 min before b_i, varying according to the airline, the boarding and baggage handling processes. For this study, a_i was set at 30 min before b_i.

The truck's service time to refuel each aircraft varies according to the amount of fuel requested and the refueling rate. This rate varies according to the type of aircraft, which can be 350, 500 or 700 liters per minute, according to the data from the company studied. However, in this study, only the values of 350 and 500 liters per minute were considered.

The average speed of the trucks was set at 20 km/h, although the maximum permitted speed is 30 km/h. The trucks used have different capacities— 7,500 liters, 13,000 liters, 20,000 liters, 40,000 liters and 50,000 liters— but availability differs across airports. The average amount of fuel requested by a given flight ranges from 800 liters to 24,000 liters.

The time required to reload a truck for a new trip is influenced by the amount of fuel to be loaded and the rate of reloading the truck, which is a pump with an average flow rate of 1,000 liters per minute. After the truck is finished loading, an additional 10 min is considered for the fuel sedimentation. The company reported that, on average, each truck makes three trips per day, which may vary during peak seasons. The value of three was set as the maximum limit for trips in this study.

Tables 2 and 3 provide details about the instance characteristics for MTARP. The first column indicates the name of the instances followed by the number of aircraft (n), the number of available trucks ($\bar{k}$), the number of allowed trips ($\bar{r}$), total demand (liters), demand characteristics, time window characteristics and characteristics of simultaneous arrivals of flights.

Table 2. Characteristics of the APSL-MT type set.

Instance	n	$\bar{k}$	$\bar{r}$	Total Demand (liters)	Demand Characteristics	Time Windows	Simultaneous Arrivals
A1	6	6	3	18,650	Less than truck capacity	Spaced	No
A2	11	6	3	33,650	Less than truck capacity	Spaced	No
A3	15	6	3	41,650	Less than truck capacity	Spaced	Yes
A4	18	6	3	50,100	Less than truck capacity	Some close	Yes
A5	18	6	3	106,850	Close to or exceeding capacity	Close	Yes
A6	25	7	3	172,700	Close to or exceeding capacity	Close	Yes
A7	30	8	3	192,800	Close to or exceeding capacity	Close	Yes
A8	40	10	3	212,500	Close to or exceeding capacity	Close	Yes

Table 3. Characteristics of the ANPSL-MT type set.

Instance	n	$\bar{k}$	$\bar{r}$	Total Demand (liters)	Demand Characteristics	Time Windows	Simultaneous Arrivals
B1	6	10	3	18,650	Less than truck capacity	Spaced	No
B2	15	10	3	69,730	Less than truck capacity	Close	Yes
B3	18	10	3	84,250	Close to truck capacity	Spaced	Yes
B4	25	10	3	109,250	Less than truck capacity	Spaced	Yes
B5	30	10	3	131,600	Close to truck capacity	Close	Yes
B6	45	10	3	182,800	Close to truck capacity	Close	Yes
B7	50	10	3	183,000	Close to or exceeding capacity	Spaced	Yes

5   Computational Results

The MILP model was coded in *Optimization Programming Language* (OPL) and solved by CPLEX 12.8 with default settings and some predefined maximum execution time, running on an Intel Core i5-8250U processor at 1.8 GHz and 12 GB of RAM.

5.1   Computational Performance of the MILP Model for a Time Limit of 18,000 s

In this subsection, we analyze the performance of the MILP model by running the CPLEX solver with a 5-h. time limit (18,000 s). The objective is to assess the ability to find high-quality solutions with the MILP model and to determine which instance characteristics contribute most to problem difficulty. Table 4 presents the results for the APSL-MT instance set, detailing the solutions obtained within the time limit. The first column identifies the name of the instance (I) and the second column presents the number of aircraft that requested service (n). The third and fourth columns show the *lower bound* (LB) and *upper bound* (UB) determined by CPLEX. The fifth column shows the gap (in %) $GAP = (UB - LB)/UB$. The sixth and seventh columns provide the CPLEX execution time in seconds ($Time$) and the number of trucks used in the solution (w), respectively.

Table 4. Experimental results of the application of the MILP proposed for MTARP in the APSL-MT type set.

I	n	LB	UB	GAP(%)	Time	w
		CPLEX 18,000				
A1	6	740.00	740.00	0.00	<1.0	1
A2	11	2,000.00	2,000.00	0.00	<1.0	2
A3	15	1,720.00	1,720.00	0.00	<1.0	1
A4	18	2,880.00	2,880.00	0.00	10,562.45	2
A5	18	2,951.78	3,380.00	12.67	18,000.00	3
A6	25	2,978.09	4,960.00	39.96	18,000.00	5
A7	30	3,209.13	5,760.00	44.29	18,000.00	4
A8	40	3,663.51	8,540.00	57.10	18,000.00	6

From the results for the APSL-MT set in Table 4 it can be seen that smaller instances (6, 11, and 15 aircraft) were solved to optimality in under one second, while larger instances presented progressively greater challenges. Instance A4, containing 18 aircraft, required substantially more computational effort (10,562.45 s) despite reaching optimality. Notably, Instance A5 (also with 18 aircraft) proved more challenging, yielding a 12.67% gap after the 5-h time limit

(18,000 s). This increased difficulty likely stems from several key characteristics: fuel demands exceeding individual tanker truck capacities, a substantially higher total fuel requirement (106,850 liters), and numerous flights with overlapping time windows (see Table 2). The remaining instances (25, 30, and 40 aircraft) exhibited these same challenging characteristics, resulting in progressively larger optimality gaps of 39.96%, 44.29%, and 57.10% respectively. This pattern suggests that problem difficulty scales non-linearly with instance size when combined with these complicating factors.

The experimental results on Table 5 show that for small-scale instances (e.g., B1 with 6 aircraft), the model could be optimally solved within 1.25 s. However, solution quality degraded significantly for larger instances, with optimality gaps ranging from 7.18% to 37.96% when reaching the 18,000-sec time limit. Notably, Instance B5 (30 aircraft) exhibited the worst performance (35.9% gap) among mid-sized instances, suggesting a critical complexity threshold when combining close time windows with demand near truck capacity. Analysis of instance characteristics (Table 3) reveals three primary difficulty factors: (i) simultaneous aircraft arrivals, (ii) tight time windows, and (iii) demand-to-capacity ratios approaching or exceeding 100%. The counterintuitive performance of Instance B3 (18 aircraft), which achieved a relatively low 7.18% gap despite high demand, suggests that spaced time windows can partially mitigate challenges posed by increased fuel requirements. The results particularly emphasize how the convergence of multiple challenging characteristics - rather than just problem size alone - creates particularly difficult cases where exact optimization methods struggle to produce high-quality solutions within reasonable timeframes.

Table 5. Experimental results of the application of the MILP proposed for MTARP in the ANPSL-MT type set.

I	n	CPLEX 18,000				
		LB	UB	$GAP(\%)$	$Time$	w
B1	6	3,335.00	3,335.00	0.00	1.25	2
B2	15	7,763.30	9,926.00	21.79	18,000.00	4
B3	18	7,438.44	8,014.00	7.18	18,000.00	5
B4	25	10,208.79	11,566.00	11.73	18,000.00	6
B5	30	7,493.46	11,690.00	35.90	18,000.00	7
B6	45	14,413.26	19,369.00	25.59	18,000.00	8
B7	50	14,123.00	22,763.00	37.96	18,000.00	9

The initial tests of the MTARP model on both APSL-MT and ANPSL-MT instance sets (Tables 4 and 5) revealed substantial optimization times for larger instances. While these extended computation periods (up to 18,000 s) were valuable for establishing baseline performance, real-world operational scenarios typically demand faster decision-making. To evaluate the model's practical applicability, we conducted additional experiments with a strict 30-min (1,800-s) time limit, as presented in Subsect. 5.2.

5.2 Experimental Analysis with Reduced Time Limits (30 Min)

Let UB(1,800) represent the upper bounds obtained with time limits of 1,800 s. In this subsection, we wish to assess how effective UB(1,800) is in approximating a good solution in practical settings, where only 30 min (1,800 s) are available to solve the problem. Table 6 compares results of the MTARP model on the APSL-MT instance set under time limits of 1,800 s and 18,000 s. The table shows that for instances (A1 to A5), UB(1,800) matches the best-known values or comes very close, making it a reliable guide. For simpler instances (A1 to A3), optimal solutions are found quickly—often within seconds. These instances feature relatively few customers, low total demand (well below truck capacity), and time windows that are well spaced. The number of vehicles used is minimal (usually one or two), and the solver can readily verify optimality. For moderately complex instances A4 and A5, the solution found within 30 min matches the one found in a 5-h run in terms of objective value and number of vehicles used. However, the reported optimality gaps remain above 20%, not because the solutions are of poor quality, but because the solver struggles to improve the lower bounds. These results highlight that as problem complexity grows (more aircraft, tighter constraints, simultaneous arrivals), the solver requires significantly more time to close the optimality gap. This trend becomes more pronounced for more complex instances (A6 to A8), where the number of aircraft, vehicles, and the total demand increase substantially. For Instances A6 and A7, UB(1,800) overestimates the cost by 4.84% and 7.29%, respectively—still under 10%, which is relatively acceptable for operational use. Moreover, the number of vehicles suggested is only one more than in the longer run, which may not be a critical issue in practice. Thus, UB(1,800) appears to remain useful in these cases. Notwithstanding, its limitations should be acknowledged in tightly constrained or highly complex instances. For example, in A8, CPLEX could not produce any feasible solution within 30 min, highlighting that UB(1,800) may not provide guidance at all in very large instances. In such cases, relying solely on a general-purpose MILP solver might not be sufficient, and alternative strategies, such as problem decomposition, matheuristics, or using tailored constructive heuristics, may be necessary to support decision-making. Furthermore, it would be useful to employ methods aimed at improving the lower bound. A tighter lower bound reduces the optimality gap and increases confidence in the quality of feasible solutions found. Techniques such as problem relaxations, dual formulations, or bounding procedures tailored to the problem structure could be explored to strengthen the model's performance under strict time constraints.

The experimental results shown in Table 7 reveal distinct computational phases based on instance characteristics. For small-scale instances (e.g., B1 with 6 aircraft), UB(1,800) consistently achieves optimal solutions (0% gap) in under two seconds while utilizing only two trucks (w = 2). This strong performance aligns with the instance's simple structure: low fuel demand relative to truck capacity, widely spaced time windows, and no simultaneous aircraft arrivals. Such cases demonstrate UB(1,800)'s effectiveness for basic refueling scenarios where operational constraints are minimal. For medium-sized instances (B2-B4, 15-25 aircraft), UB(1,800) becomes increasingly sensitive to time constraints. Instance B2, despite having manageable demand levels (69,730 liters), exhibits a 27.4% gap under 30-min limits most likely due to its challenging combination of close time windows and simultaneous arrivals. Notably, while UB(1,800) remains identical for B2 (9,926.00), both B3 and B4 show modest increases of 3.2% and 1.3% respectively. This confirms that the degraded gaps primarily reflect insufficient time for lower bound improvement rather than substantially poorer solutions. The pattern suggests that UB(1,800) may be operationally acceptable for moderately complex cases despite suboptimal gaps, particularly when spaced time windows (B3, B4) help maintain solution stability. The most significant challenges appear in large-scale instances (B5-B7, 30-50 aircraft),

Table 6. Computational performance of the MILP model for MTARP using APSL-MT instances under different CPLEX time limits (1,800 s and 18,000 s)

I	n	CPLEX 18,000				CPLEX 1,800			
		UB	$GAP(\%)$	w	$Time$	UB	$GAP(\%)$	w	$Time$
A1	6	740.00	0.00	1	<1.0	740.00	0.00	1	<1.0
A2	11	2,000.00	0.00	2	<1.0	2,000.00	0.00	2	<1.0
A3	15	1,720.00	0.00	1	<1.0	1,720.00	0.00	1	<1.0
A4	18	2,880.00	0.00	2	10,562.45	2,880.00	20.77	2	1,800.00
A5	18	3,380.00	12.67	3	18,000.00	3,380.00	20.02	3	1,800.00
A6	25	4,960.00	39.96	5	18,000.00	5,200.00	48.05	6	1,800.00
A7	30	5,760.00	44.29	4	18,000.00	6,180.00	51.74	5	1,800.00
A8	40	8,540.00	57.10	6	18,000.00	-	-	-	1,800.00

Table 7. Computational performance of the MILP model for MTARP using ANPSL-MT instances under different CPLEX time limits (1,800 s and 18,000 s)

I	n	CPLEX 18,000				CPLEX 1,800			
		UB	$GAP(\%)$	w	$Time$	UB	$GAP(\%)$	w	$Time$
B1	6	3,335.00	0.00	2	1.25	3,335.00	0.00	2	1.28
B2	15	9,926.00	21.79	4	18,000.00	9,926.00	27.40	4	1,800.00
B3	18	8,014.00	7.18	5	18,000.00	8,268.00	22.99	5	1,800.00
B4	25	11,566.00	11.73	6	18,000.00	11,719.00	16.03	6	1,800.00
B5	30	11,690.00	35.90	7	18,000.00	14,651.00	50.17	7	1,800.00
B6	45	19,369.00	25.59	8	18,000.00	28,746.00	49.90	9	1,800.00
B7	50	22,763.00	37.96	9	18,000.00	26,961.00	48.54	10	1,800.00

where the interaction of multiple constraints creates compounding complexity. Instance B5's 50.17% gap - accompanied by a 25.3% cost increase in UB(1,800) - highlights how tight scheduling windows combined with near-capacity demand (131,600 liters) strain the solution quality. The effect intensifies for B6, showing a dramatic 48.4% increase in UB(1,800). Both bound quality and feasibility suffer, with B7's UB(1,800) degrading by 18.4% while requiring an additional truck (w goes from 9 to 10). These results underscore that under stringent operational constraints a hybrid solution approach may be necessary.

6   Conclusion

This paper considers a fuel supply problem faced by a Brazilian fuel distribution company, called the Multiple Trip Aircraft Refueling Problem (MTARP). A Mixed-Integer Linear Programming (MILP) model was presented to solve the problem. This model effectively represents the specific characteristics of the aircraft refueling service at Brazilian airports, meeting this crucial activity's operational and logistical needs. Sets of instances were created to provide various scenarios for problem analysis. Two key experiments were conducted: identifying the characteristics that make certain instances more challenging, and evaluating the quality of solutions obtained under a restricted 30-min computational time.

The first experiment analyzed the factors contributing to problem difficulty across different instance sizes and structures. The results showed that problem complexity does not scale linearly with the number of aircraft but is significantly influenced by the interaction of complicating factors. For example, while smaller instances (6, 11, and 15 aircraft) were solved optimally in under one second, instances with similar aircraft counts (e.g., A5 with 18 aircraft) exhibited substantial optimality gaps (12.67% after 18,000 s). This difficulty was attributed to high fuel demand, overlapping time windows, and demand exceeding individual truck capacities. Larger instances (25, 30, and 40 aircraft) exhibited even greater optimality gaps (up to 57.10%), confirming that complexity is compounded by multiple interacting constraints rather than just problem size alone. Furthermore, some mid-sized instances (e.g., B3) performed unexpectedly well due to spaced time windows, highlighting the importance of problem structure in determining computational tractability.

The second experiment evaluated how well solutions obtained in just 30 min (UB(1,800)) approximated those from extended runs. For small and moderately complex instances, UB(1,800) closely matched the best-known solutions, often achieving optimality within seconds (e.g., A1-A3, B1). Even for mid-sized instances like A4, A5, B3, and B4, UB(1,800) produced solutions with minimal deviations, making it a reliable approximation in many operational cases. However, as complexity increased, the solver struggled to refine lower bounds within the time limit, leading to larger optimality gaps, with feasibility also suffering in the most constrained scenarios (e.g., A8, where no feasible solution was found). These results indicate that while UB(1,800) remains useful in many practical settings, it is less reliable for highly constrained, large-scale instances.

It should be noted that large-scale and highly constrained instances may require alternative approaches such as decomposition techniques, matheuristics, or specialized heuristics to improve both solution feasibility and bound quality. Future work should explore these methods while also investigating ways to strengthen lower bounds, ensuring that optimization models remain practical for real-world decision-making.

Acknowledgments. The first author would like to acknowledge the doctoral scholarship provided by FAPES - Fundação de Amparo Pesquisa e Inovação do Espírito Santo (FAPES) (Grant Number 2020-LGJV3). This study was financed in part by the Coordenação de Aperfeiçoamento de Pessoal de Nível Superior - Brasil (CAPES) - Finance Code 001. The authors also acknowledge support from PROAPEM/FAPES - project numbers: 368/2022 - P: 2022-NGKM5; and PDPG/FAPES - project numbers: 129/2021 - P: 2021-GL60J.

Disclosure of Interests. The authors have no competing interests to declare that are relevant to the content of this article.

References

1. Azi, N., Gendreau, M., Potvin, J.Y.: An exact algorithm for a single-vehicle routing problem with time windows and multiple routes. Eur. J. Oper. Res. **178**(3), 755–766 (2007). https://doi.org/10.1016/j.ejor.2006.02.019
2. Azi, N., Gendreau, M., Potvin, J.Y.: An exact algorithm for a vehicle routing problem with time windows and multiple use of vehicles. Eur. J. Oper. Res. **202**(3), 756–763 (2010). https://doi.org/10.1016/j.ejor.2009.06.034
3. Babić, O.: Optimization of refuelling truck fleets at an airport. Transport. Res. Part B: Methodologica **21**(6), 479–487 (1987). https://doi.org/10.1016/0191-2615(87)90042-7
4. Battarra, M., Monaci, M., Vigo, D.: An adaptive guidance approach for the heuristic solution of a minimum multiple trip vehicle routing problem. Comput. Oper. Res. **36**(11), 3041–3050 (2009). https://doi.org/10.1016/j.cor.2009.02.008
5. Braekers, K., Ramaekers, K., Van Nieuwenhuyse, I.: The vehicle routing problem: state of the art classification and review. Comput. Ind. Eng. **99**, 300–313 (2016). https://doi.org/10.1016/j.cie.2015.12.007
6. Cattaruzza, D., Absi, N., Feillet, D.: Vehicle routing problems with multiple trips. 4OR **14**, 223–259 (2016). https://doi.org/10.1007/s10288-016-0306-2
7. Cordeau, J.F., Groupe d'études et de recherche en analyse des décisions Montréal, Q.: The VRP with time windows. Citeseer (2000)
8. Dantzig, G.B., Ramser, J.H.: The truck dispatching problem. Manage. Sci. **6**(1), 80–91 (1959). https://doi.org/10.1287/mnsc.6.1.80
9. Du, Y., Zhang, Q., Chen, Q.: ACO-IH: an improved ant colony optimization algorithm for airport ground service scheduling. In: IEEE International Conference on Industrial Technology, pp. 1–6 (2008). https://doi.org/10.1109/ICIT.2008.4608674
10. Eksioglu, B., Vural, A.V., Reisman, A.: The vehicle routing problem: a taxonomic review. Comput. Ind. Eng. **57**(4), 1472–1483 (2009)
11. Elatar, S., Abouelmehdi, K., Riffi, M.E.: The vehicle routing problem in the last decade: variants, taxonomy and metaheuristics. Procedia Comput. Sci. **220**, 398–404 (2023). https://doi.org/10.1016/j.procs.2023.03.051, the 14th International

Conference on Ambient Systems, Networks and Technologies Networks and The 6th International Conference on Emerging Data and Industry 4.0 (EDI40)

12. Feng, X., Zuo, H., Sun, Q.: Research on collaborative scheduling of aircraft ground service vehicles based on simple temporal network. In: 2021 IEEE 3rd International Conference on Civil Aviation Safety and Information Technology (ICCASIT), pp. 263–269 (2021). https://doi.org/10.1109/ICCASIT53235.2021.9633418

13. Fleischmann, B.: The vehicle routing problem with multiple use of vehicles (1990)

14. FlightAware, E.: Flightaware (2005). https://pt.flightaware.com/

15. Gamayanti, N., Sahal, M., Wibisono, A.: Optimization of vehicle routing problem with tight time windows, short travel time and re-used vehicles (VRPTSR) for aircraft refueling in airport using ant colony optimization algorithm. J. Adv. Res. Electr. Eng. **2**(1), 43–46 (2018). https://doi.org/10.12962/j25796216.v2.i1.40

16. Hernandez, F., Feillet, D., Giroudeau, R., Naud, O.: A new exact algorithm to solve the multi-trip vehicle routing problem with time windows and limited duration. 4OR **12**(3), 235–259 (2013). https://doi.org/10.1007/s10288-013-0238-z

17. Konstantakopoulos, G.D., Gayialis, S.P., Kechagias, E.P.: Vehicle routing problem and related algorithms for logistics distribution: a literature review and classification. Oper. Res. Int. J. **22**(3), 2033–2062 (2022). https://doi.org/10.1007/s12351-020-00600-7

18. Liu, Y., Wu, J., Tang, J., Wang, W., Wang, X.: Scheduling optimisation of multi-type special vehicles in an airport. Transportmetrica B: Transp. Dyn. **10**(1), 954–970 (2022). https://doi.org/10.1080/21680566.2021.1983484

19. Macedo, R., Alves, C., Valério de Carvalho, J., Clautiaux, F., Hanafi, S.: Solving the vehicle routing problem with time windows and multiple routes exactly using a pseudo-polynomial model. Eur. J. Oper. Res. **214**(3), 536–545 (2011). https://doi.org/10.1016/j.ejor.2011.04.037

20. Quan, W., Chen, C., Shao, Z., Meng, K.: Dynamic scheduling for airport special vehicles based on a multi-strategy hybrid algorithm. In: 2022 41st Chinese Control Conference (CCC), pp. 1916–1921 (2022).https://doi.org/10.23919/CCC55666.2022.9901875

21. Schyns, M.: An ant colony system for responsive dynamic vehicle routing. Eur. J. Oper. Res. **245**(3), 704–718 (2015). https://doi.org/10.1016/j.ejor.2015.04.009

22. Seixas, M.P., Mendes, A.B.: Column generation for a multitrip vehicle routing problem with time windows, driver work hours, and heterogeneous fleet. Math. Probl. Eng. **2013** (2013).https://doi.org/10.1155/2013/824961

23. Toth, P., Vigo, D.: The vehicle routing problem. Soc. Ind. Appl. Math. (2002). https://doi.org/10.1137/1.9780898718515

24. Wang, Y., Sun, J., Sun, B., Feng, M.: Research on application of airport tanker truck scheduling based on particle swarm optimization. In: 2021 6th International Conference on Control, Robotics and Cybernetics (CRC), pp. 278–282 (2021). https://doi.org/10.1109/CRC52766.2021.9620157

25. Wang, Z., Li, Y., Hei, X., Meng, H.: Research on airport refueling vehicle scheduling problem based on greedy algorithm. In: Huang, D.-S., Bevilacqua, V., Premaratne, P., Gupta, P. (eds.) ICIC 2018. LNCS, vol. 10954, pp. 717–728. Springer, Cham (2018). https://doi.org/10.1007/978-3-319-95930-6_73

26. Zampirolli, K.A., Amaral, A.R.S.: Simulated annealing and iterated local search approaches to the aircraft refueling problem. In: Gervasi, O., et al. (eds.) ICCSA 2021. LNCS, vol. 12952, pp. 422–438. Springer, Cham (2021). https://doi.org/10.1007/978-3-030-86973-1_30

27. Zhang, H., Ge, H., Yang, J., Tong, Y.: Review of vehicle routing problems: models, classification and solving algorithms. Arch. Comput. Methods Eng. **29**(1), 195–221 (2021). https://doi.org/10.1007/s11831-021-09574-x
28. Zhaohua, Z., Liqi, J.: Research on airport special vehicle scheduling problem. In: 2020 International Conference on Virtual Reality and Intelligent Systems (ICVRIS), pp. 1076–1078 (2020). https://doi.org/10.1109/ICVRIS51417.2020.00262

Symbolic and Numerical Computation of Coquaternionic Functions in *Mathematica*

Maria Irene Falcão[ID], Fernando Miranda[(✉)][ID], and Ricardo Severino[ID]

CMAT, Universidade do Minho, Braga, Portugal
{mif,fmiranda,ricardo}@math.uminho.pt

Abstract. This paper presents an updated version of the *Mathematica* package `Coquaternions`, originally introduced by the authors in 2019. The new release extends the package's functionality by incorporating the definition and manipulation of elementary functions within the algebra of coquaternions. In addition to their implementation in *Mathematica*, several properties of these functions are formally introduced and proved.

Keywords: Coquaternions · Elementary Functions · Computer Algebra System

1 Introduction

Coquaternions, also known as split quaternions, form a number system introduced by James Cockle in 1849 [5] as a generalization of complex numbers. Over time, they have attracted increasing attention and have found applications in various fields, including geometry and physics [1–4, 11–14, 16–19].

In 2019, the authors of [9] introduced a *Mathematica* add-on application, `Coquaternions`, designed to define rules for the symbolic manipulation of coquaternions. Later, in [8], the package functionalities have been extended with a collection of functions, `CoqPolynomial`, for working with polynomials. This paper aims to further update the `Coquaternions` package by incorporating a class of functions of a coquaternionic variable, particularly some elementary functions.

The paper is organized as follows. Section 2 presents the fundamental results on the coquaternion algebra. In Sect. 3, we introduce elementary functions in the coquaternionic context and establish some of their properties. Finally, Sect. 4 details the *Mathematica* implementation of the new functionalities added to the package `Coquaternion`.

2 Basic Results and Notation

In this section, we provide a brief introduction to the algebra of coquaternions, recall some of their key properties, and establish the notation. For a more in-depth discussion of this nondivision algebra, we refer the interested reader to the references [8, 10, 15, 18].

O. Gervasi et al. (Eds.): ICCSA 2025 Workshops, LNCS 15887, pp. 181–194, 2026.
https://doi.org/10.1007/978-3-031-97589-9_13

Let $\{1, i, j, k\}$ be an orthonormal basis for the Euclidean vector space $\mathbb{R}^4$. The algebra of real coquaternions, denoted by $\mathbb{H}_{\mathrm{coq}}$, is generated by the product defined according to the following rules:

$$i^2 = -1, \; j^2 = k^2 = 1, \; ij = -ji = k.$$

Consider a coquaterion of the form

$$q = q_0 + q_1 i + q_2 j + q_3 k.$$

The *conjugate* of q, denoted by $\bar{q}$, is given by

$$\bar{q} = q_0 - q_1 i - q_2 j - q_3 k.$$

Analogous to the complex case, the scalar q_0 is called the *real part* of q, and is denoted by $\operatorname{Re} q$, while the expression

$$\underline{q} = q_1 i + q_2 j + q_3 k$$

is referred to as the *vector part* of q. The subset of elements in $\mathbb{H}_{\mathrm{coq}}$ with zero vector part is identified with $\mathbb{R}$, the set of real numbers.

The *trace* and *determinant* of q are defined, respectively, as

$$\operatorname{tr} q = q + \bar{q} = 2\operatorname{Re} q, \quad \det q = q\bar{q} = q_0^2 + q_1^2 - q_2^2 - q_3^2.$$

We equip $\mathbb{H}_{\mathrm{coq}}$ with the semi-norm

$$\|q\| = \sqrt{|\det q|}$$

and classify a coquaternion as *non-singular* if $\|q\| \neq 0$, and as a *unit coquaternion* if $\|q\| = 1$.

The sign of $\det q$ determines the type of the coquaternion q: q is called *space-like, light-like* or *time-like*, if $\det q < 0$, $\det q = 0$ or $\det q > 0$, respectively; the sets of such coquaternions will be denoted by $\mathbb{S}$, $\mathbb{L}$ and $\mathbb{T}$, respectively.

It is easy to see that any coquaternion q with a non-singular vector part (i.e., $\underline{q} \in \mathbb{S} \cup \mathbb{T}$) can be written in the form

$$q = q_0 + \boldsymbol{\omega}_{\underline{q}} \|\underline{q}\| \tag{1}$$

where

$$\boldsymbol{\omega}_{\underline{q}} = \boldsymbol{\omega}(\underline{q}) = \frac{\underline{q}}{\|\underline{q}\|}$$

is a unit coquaternion satisfying

$$\boldsymbol{\omega}_{\underline{q}}^2 = \begin{cases} 1, & \text{if } \underline{q} \in \mathbb{S} \\ -1, & \text{if } \underline{q} \in \mathbb{T} \end{cases} \tag{2}$$

If $\underline{q} \in \mathbb{L}$, then it can be written in the form

$$q = q_0 + \boldsymbol{\omega}_{\underline{q}} \tag{3}$$

where $\boldsymbol{\omega}_{\underline{q}} = \underline{q}$ satisfies

$$\boldsymbol{\omega}_{\underline{q}}^2 = 0. \tag{4}$$

Remark 1. The following properties of $\omega(\underline{q}) = \omega_{\underline{q}}$ will be useful in the subsequent sections, and their proofs follow immediately from the definition.

1. $\omega(\omega(\underline{q})) = \omega_{\underline{q}}$

2. If $\alpha \in \mathbb{R}$, then

$$
\omega(\alpha\,\underline{q}) = \begin{cases} \operatorname{sgn}(\alpha)\,\omega_{\underline{q}}, & \text{if } \underline{q} \in \mathbb{T} \cup \mathbb{S} \\ \alpha\,\omega_{\underline{q}}, & \text{if } \underline{q} \in \mathbb{L} \end{cases}
$$

where sgn is the usual real sign function.

3   Functions of a Coquaternionic Variable

In the context of quaternionic functions, there are several possible approaches to defining elementary functions, depending on the properties we are seeking. For example, in the case of the exponential function, multiple definitions have been derived over the years. For $x = x_0 + x_1 \mathbb{i} + x_2 \mathbb{j} + x_3 \mathbb{k} \in \mathbb{H}$, the following exponential functions can be found (see [7] and references therein):

$$
\operatorname{Exp}_1(x) = e^{x_0}\left(\cos\frac{x_1+x_2+x_3}{\sqrt{3}} + \frac{\mathbb{i}+\mathbb{j}+\mathbb{k}}{\sqrt{3}}\sin\frac{x_1+x_2+x_3}{\sqrt{3}}\right);
$$

$$
\operatorname{Exp}_2(x) = 2e^{x_0}\left(-\frac{\sin\|\underline{x}\|}{\|\underline{x}\|} + \omega_{\underline{x}}\frac{\|\underline{x}\|\cos\|\underline{x}\| - \sin\|\underline{x}\|}{\|\underline{x}\|^2}\right);
$$

$$
\operatorname{Exp}_3(x) = e^{x_1+x_2+x_3}\left(\cos(x_0\sqrt{3}) - \frac{\mathbb{i}+\mathbb{j}+\mathbb{k}}{\sqrt{3}}\sin(x_0\sqrt{3})\right).
$$

In addition to the above definitions, one of the most commonly used approaches to defining the exponential function in applications is through the standard power series expansion, i.e.,

$$
\operatorname{Exp}(x) := \sum_{k=0}^{\infty} \frac{x^k}{k!} = e^{x_0}(\cos\|\underline{x}\| + \omega_{\underline{x}}\sin\|\underline{x}\|).
$$

In this section, we take a systematic approach to introduce elementary functions, starting from an analytic complex function f and examining the properties of the resulting functions. Since f is analytic, it admits a Taylor series expansion around any real point x. For $z = x + iy$, we write:

$$
f(z) = f(x+iy) = \sum_{n=0}^{\infty} \frac{f^{(n)}(x)}{n!}(iy)^n.
$$

At this stage, we do not concern ourselves with the convergence of the series. To obtain the corresponding coquaternionic function F, we replace the complex variable z with the coquaternion variable $q = q_0 + \underline{q}$, yielding

$$
F(q) = F(q_0 + \underline{q}) = \sum_{n=0}^{\infty} \frac{f^{(n)}(q_0)}{n!}(\underline{q})^n. \tag{5}
$$

Taking into account the nature of the coquaternion q, we can write (see (1))

$$F(q) = F(q_0 + \omega_{\underline{q}}\|\underline{q}\|) = \sum_{n=0}^{\infty} \frac{f^{(n)}(q_0)}{n!}(\omega_{\underline{q}}\|\underline{q}\|)^n, \text{ if } \underline{q} \in \mathbb{T} \cup \mathbb{S},$$

or (see (3))

$$F(q) = F(q_0 + \omega_{\underline{q}}) = \sum_{n=0}^{\infty} \frac{f^{(n)}(q_0)}{n!}(\omega_{\underline{q}})^n, \text{ if } \underline{q} \in \mathbb{L}.$$

Using (2) and (4), the coquaternionic function F can be written as

$$F(q) = \sum_{n=0}^{\infty}(-1)^n \frac{f^{(2n)}(q_0)}{(2n)!}\|\underline{q}\|^{2n} + \omega_{\underline{q}}\sum_{n=0}^{\infty}(-1)^n \frac{f^{(2n+1)}(q_0)}{(2n+1)!}\|\underline{q}\|^{2n+1}, \text{if } \underline{q} \in \mathbb{T}, \quad (6)$$

$$F(q) = \sum_{n=0}^{\infty} \frac{f^{(2n)}(q_0)}{(2n)!}\|\underline{q}\|^{2n} + \omega_{\underline{q}}\sum_{n=0}^{\infty} \frac{f^{(2n+1)}(q_0)}{(2n+1)!}\|\underline{q}\|^{2n+1}, \text{if } \underline{q} \in \mathbb{S}, \quad (7)$$

$$F(q) = f(q_0) + \omega_{\underline{q}}f'(q_0), \text{if } \underline{q} \in \mathbb{L}. \quad (8)$$

Remark 2. When $\underline{q} \in \mathbb{T}$ the coquaternion $q_0 + \omega_{\underline{q}}\|\underline{q}\|$ behaves like a complex, in the sense that $\omega_{\underline{q}}^2 = -1$. The elementary functions can be obtained at once (like in the quaternionic case) from the corresponding complex ones (cf. (6)). In fact, if we write the complex function f as

$$f(x + iy) = u(x, y) + iv(x, y),$$

where u and v are real functions, then the corresponding coquaternionic function is

$$F(q_0 + \omega_{\underline{q}}\|\underline{q}\|) = u(q_0, \|\underline{q}\|) + \omega_{\underline{q}}v(q_0, \|\underline{q}\|).$$

In the particular case where $q = q_0 + q_1 i$, i.e., $q \in \mathbb{C}$, then $F(q) = f(q)$, meaning that all the functions derived from (6) coincide with the corresponding complex functions.

As a consequence of these observations, it suffices to derive the expressions of the functions and analyze their properties for the cases where $\underline{q} \in \mathbb{S}$ or $\underline{q} \in \mathbb{L}$. However, for completeness, we also provide details on the case $\underline{q} \in \mathbb{T}$.

3.1 Exponential Function

Since the power series of the exponential function has an infinite radius of convergence, the use of (6)-(8) leads to the following coquaternionic exponential function.

$$\text{Exp}(q) = \begin{cases} e^{q_0}\left(\cos\|\underline{q}\| + \omega_{\underline{q}}\sin\|\underline{q}\|\right), & \text{if } \underline{q} \in \mathbb{T} \\[2mm] e^{q_0}\left(\cosh\|\underline{q}\| + \omega_{\underline{q}}\sinh\|\underline{q}\|\right), & \text{if } \underline{q} \in \mathbb{S} \\[2mm] e^{q_0}(1 + \omega_{\underline{q}}), & \text{if } \underline{q} \in \mathbb{L} \end{cases} \quad (9)$$

We note that the exponential function derived in [6, Theorem 4] coincides with the one presented here, as it was obtained using a similar approach.

We list some properties of the coquaternionic exponential function, which hold regardless of the nature of the coquaternion.

Property 1. If p and q are coquaternions then:

1. $\mathrm{Exp}(q) \neq 0$.

2. $\|\mathrm{Exp}(q)\| = e^{q_0}$.

3. $\mathrm{Exp}(q_0 + \underline{q}) = e^{q_0}\,\mathrm{Exp}(\underline{q})$.

4. If p and q commute, then

$$\mathrm{Exp}(p + q) = \mathrm{Exp}(p)\,\mathrm{Exp}(q).$$

In particular,

$$\mathrm{Exp}(q)\,\mathrm{Exp}(-q) = 1 \quad \text{and} \quad (\mathrm{Exp}(q))^n = \mathrm{Exp}(nq)$$

Proof. The first three identities are directly derived from (9) and the properties (2) and (4) of $\boldsymbol{\omega}_q$. Consider now the coquaternions $p = p_0 + p_1\mathrm{i} + p_2\mathrm{j} + p_3\mathrm{k}$ and $q = q_0 + q_1\mathrm{i} + q_2\mathrm{j} + q_3\mathrm{k}$. The use of (5) allows to write

$$\mathrm{Exp}(p + q) = e^{p_0 + q_0} \sum_{n=0}^{\infty} \frac{(\underline{p} + \underline{q})^n}{n!}.$$

Since p and q commute, their vector parts also commute, which means that

$$\mathrm{Exp}(p + q) = e^{p_0 + q_0} \sum_{n=0}^{\infty} \sum_{k=0}^{n} \binom{n}{k} \frac{\underline{p}^k \underline{q}^{n-k}}{n!} = e^{p_0 + q_0} \sum_{n=0}^{\infty} \sum_{k=0}^{n} \frac{\underline{p}^k}{k!} \frac{\underline{q}^{n-k}}{(n-k)!}.$$

By recognizing the last expression as the Cauchy product of two series, we can rewrite it as

$$\mathrm{Exp}(p + q) = e^{p_0 + q_0} \sum_{n=0}^{\infty} \frac{\underline{p}^k}{k!} \sum_{n=0}^{\infty} \frac{\underline{q}^k}{k!} = e^{p_0 + q_0}\,\mathrm{Exp}(\underline{p})\,\mathrm{Exp}(\underline{q}).$$

The result follows now at once by using identity 3. of Property 1.   □

3.2   Trigonometric Functions

It is easy to see that the coquaternionic sine function obtained by the use of (6)-(8) is

$$\mathrm{Sin}(q) = \begin{cases} \sin q_0 \cosh \|\underline{q}\| + \boldsymbol{\omega}_q \cos q_0 \sinh \|\underline{q}\|, & \text{if } \underline{q} \in \mathbb{T} \\[2mm] \sin q_0 \cos \|\underline{q}\| + \boldsymbol{\omega}_q \cos q_0 \sin \|\underline{q}\|, & \text{if } \underline{q} \in \mathbb{S} \\[2mm] \sin q_0 + \boldsymbol{\omega}_q \cos q_0, & \text{if } \underline{q} \in \mathbb{L} \end{cases} \qquad (10)$$

while the cosine function is

$$
\mathrm{Cos}(q) = \begin{cases} \cos q_0 \cosh \|\underline{q}\| - \boldsymbol{\omega}_{\underline{q}} \sin q_0 \sinh \|\underline{q}\|, \text{ if } \underline{q} \in \mathbb{T} \\ \cos q_0 \cos \|\underline{q}\| - \boldsymbol{\omega}_{\underline{q}} \sin q_0 \sin \|\underline{q}\|, \text{ if } \underline{q} \in \mathbb{S} \\ \cos q_0 - \boldsymbol{\omega}_{\underline{q}} \sin q_0, \text{ if } \underline{q} \in \mathbb{L} \end{cases} \tag{11}
$$

A direct computation using (10) and (11) establishes several identities for the sine and cosine coquaternionic functions, valid for all coquaternions.

Property 2. If q is a coquaternion then:

1. $\mathrm{Sin}^2(q) + \mathrm{Cos}^2(q) = 1.$

2. $\mathrm{Sin}(q) = \sin q_0 \, \mathrm{Cos}(\underline{q}) + \cos q_0 \, \mathrm{Sin}(\underline{q}).$

3. $\mathrm{Cos}(q) = \cos q_0 \, \mathrm{Cos}(\underline{q}) - \sin q_0 \, \mathrm{Sin}(\underline{q}).$

4. The zeros of the coquaternionic sine and cosine functions reduce to the real ones.

3.3   Hyperbolic Functions

Applying the procedure described by (6)-(8) we obtain the following coquaternionic hyperbolic sine and cosine functions

$$
\mathrm{Sinh}(q) = \begin{cases} \sinh q_0 \cos \|\underline{q}\| + \boldsymbol{\omega}_{\underline{q}} \cosh q_0 \sin \|\underline{q}\|, \text{ if } \underline{q} \in \mathbb{T} \\ \sinh q_0 \cosh \|\underline{q}\| + \boldsymbol{\omega}_{\underline{q}} \cosh q_0 \sinh \|\underline{q}\|, \text{ if } \underline{q} \in \mathbb{S} \\ \sinh q_0 + \boldsymbol{\omega}_{\underline{q}} \cosh q_0, \text{ if } \underline{q} \in \mathbb{L} \end{cases} \tag{12}
$$

$$
\mathrm{Cosh}(q) = \begin{cases} \cosh q_0 \cos \|\underline{q}\| + \boldsymbol{\omega}_{\underline{q}} \sinh q_0 \sin \|\underline{q}\|, \text{ if } \underline{q} \in \mathbb{T} \\ \cosh q_0 \cosh \|\underline{q}\| + \boldsymbol{\omega}_{\underline{q}} \sinh q_0 \sinh \|\underline{q}\|, \text{ if } \underline{q} \in \mathbb{S} \\ \cosh q_0 + \boldsymbol{\omega}_{\underline{q}} \sinh q_0, \text{ if } \underline{q} \in \mathbb{L} \end{cases} \tag{13}
$$

The following properties follow directly from the explicit definitions of the hyperbolic functions (12) and (13).

Property 3. If q is a coquaternion then:

1. $\mathrm{Cosh}^2(q) - \mathrm{Sinh}^2(q) = 1.$

2. $\text{Sin}(q\,\boldsymbol{\omega}_{\underline{q}}) = \begin{cases} \text{Sinh}(q)\,\boldsymbol{\omega}_{\underline{q}}, \text{ if } \underline{q} \in \mathbb{T} \\[2mm] \text{Sin}(q)\,\boldsymbol{\omega}_{\underline{q}}, \text{ if } \underline{q} \in \mathbb{S} \\[2mm] q_0\,\boldsymbol{\omega}_{\underline{q}}, \text{ if } \underline{q} \in \mathbb{L} \end{cases}$

3. $\text{Cos}(q\,\boldsymbol{\omega}_{\underline{q}}) = \begin{cases} \text{Cosh}(q), \text{ if } \underline{q} \in \mathbb{T} \\[2mm] \text{Cos}(q), \text{ if } \underline{q} \in \mathbb{S} \\[2mm] 1, \text{ if } \underline{q} \in \mathbb{L} \end{cases}$

4. Beyond the real zero 0, the hyperbolic sine function has the time-like zeros $k\pi\boldsymbol{\omega}_{\underline{q}}$, while the hyperbolic cosine vanishes at $(k+\frac{1}{2})\pi\boldsymbol{\omega}_{\underline{q}}$, with $\underline{q} \in \mathbb{T}$.

Remark 3. If $\underline{q} \in \mathbb{T}$, the well-known relationship between the complex (or quaternionic) exponential function and the trigonometric and hyperbolic functions has the analogue:

$$\text{Cos}(q) = \frac{\text{Exp}(q\boldsymbol{\omega}_{\underline{q}}) + \text{Exp}(-q\boldsymbol{\omega}_{\underline{q}})}{2}, \qquad \text{Cosh}(q) = \frac{\text{Exp}(q) + \text{Exp}(-q)}{2},$$

$$\text{Sin}(q) = -\boldsymbol{\omega}_{\underline{q}}\frac{\text{Exp}(q\boldsymbol{\omega}_{\underline{q}}) - \text{Exp}(-q\boldsymbol{\omega}_{\underline{q}})}{2}, \qquad \text{Sinh}(q) = \frac{\text{Exp}(q) - \text{Exp}(-q)}{2}.$$

However, when $\underline{q} \in \mathbb{S}$, due to Property 3.3, the relationships involving the sine and cosine functions no longer hold. Only the relations between the exponential function and the hyperbolic functions remain valid.

3.4 Logarithm Function

We derive the expression for the coquaternionic logarithm function as the inverse of the exponential function defined in Sect. 3.1. Consequently, the following identities must hold:

$$\text{Log}(\text{Exp}(q)) = \text{Exp}(\text{Log}(q)) = q. \tag{14}$$

Property 4. The inverse of the exponential function (9) is the following logarithm function:

$$\text{Log}(q) = \begin{cases} \log\|q\| + \boldsymbol{\omega}_{\underline{q}}\,\text{atan2}(q_0, \|\underline{q}\|), \text{ if } \underline{q} \in \mathbb{T} \\[2mm] \log\|q\| + \boldsymbol{\omega}_{\underline{q}}\,\text{arctanh}\,\frac{\|\underline{q}\|}{q_0}, \text{ if } \underline{q} \in \mathbb{S}, \ q \in \mathbb{T}, \text{ and } q_0 > 0 \\[2mm] \log q_0 + \frac{1}{q_0}\boldsymbol{\omega}_{\underline{q}}, \text{ if } \underline{q} \in \mathbb{L}, \text{ and } q_0 > 0 \end{cases}$$

Proof. The case $\underline{q} \in \mathbb{T}$ follows directly from the complex case, as explained in Remark 2. Here, we use the function atan2 to denote the two-argument arctangent, which determines the principal argument of a complex number. Consequently, the derived logarithm function represents the principal value of the coquaternionic logarithm.

If $q = \omega_q \in \mathbb{L}$, then

$$\mathrm{Log}\left(\mathrm{Exp}(q)\right) = \mathrm{Log}\left(e^{q_0} + e^{q_0}\boldsymbol{\omega}_q\right) = \log(e^{q_0}) + \tfrac{1}{e^{q_0}}e^{q_0}\boldsymbol{\omega}_q = q$$

and

$$\mathrm{Exp}\left(\mathrm{Log}(q)\right) = \mathrm{Exp}\left(\log(q_0) + \tfrac{1}{q_0}\boldsymbol{\omega}_q\right) = e^{\log(q_0)}(1 + \tfrac{1}{q_0}\boldsymbol{\omega}_q) = q_0 + \boldsymbol{\omega}_q = q.$$

Consider now the case where $q = \boldsymbol{\omega}_q\|q\| \in \mathbb{S}$. Denoting by $\underline{\mathrm{Exp}}$ the vector part of the exponential function, and considering Remark 2, Property 1, and the condition $q_0 > 0$, we can write

$$\|\mathrm{Exp}(q)\| = e^{q_0}; \quad \boldsymbol{\omega}_{\underline{\mathrm{Exp}}(q)} = \boldsymbol{\omega}_q; \quad \|\underline{\mathrm{Exp}}(q)\| = e^{q_0}\sinh\|\underline{q}\|. \tag{15}$$

Therefore

$$\mathrm{Log}\left(\mathrm{Exp}(q)\right) = \log(e^{q_0}) + \boldsymbol{\omega}_q\,\mathrm{arctanh}\,\frac{e^{q_0}\sinh\|\underline{q}\|}{e^{q_0}\cosh\|\underline{q}\|} = q_0 + \boldsymbol{\omega}_q\|\underline{q}\| = q.$$

Observe that

$$\boldsymbol{\omega}_{\underline{\mathrm{Log}}(q)} = \mathrm{sgn}\left(\mathrm{arctanh}\,\frac{\|\underline{q}\|}{q_0}\right)\boldsymbol{\omega}_q = \boldsymbol{\omega}_q$$

and

$$\|\underline{\mathrm{Log}}(q)\| = \left|\mathrm{arctanh}\,\frac{\|\underline{q}\|}{q_0}\right| = \mathrm{arctanh}\,\frac{\|\underline{q}\|}{q_0}.$$

Therefore we can write

$$\mathrm{Exp}\left(\mathrm{Log}(q)\right) = \mathrm{Exp}\left(\log\|q\| + \boldsymbol{\omega}_q\,\mathrm{arctanh}\,\frac{\|\underline{q}\|}{q_0}\right)$$

$$= \mathrm{Exp}(\log\|q\|)\left(\cosh\left(\mathrm{arctanh}\,\frac{\|\underline{q}\|}{q_0}\right) + \boldsymbol{\omega}_q\sinh\left(\mathrm{arctanh}\,\frac{\|\underline{q}\|}{q_0}\right)\right)$$

$$= \|q\|\left(\cosh\left(\mathrm{arctanh}\,\frac{\|\underline{q}\|}{q_0}\right) + \boldsymbol{\omega}_q\sinh\left(\mathrm{arctanh}\,\frac{\|\underline{q}\|}{q_0}\right)\right).$$

The result follows by using the well-known identities $\cosh(\mathrm{arctanh}\,x) = \frac{1}{\sqrt{1-x^2}}$ and $\sinh(\mathrm{arctanh}\,x) = \frac{x}{\sqrt{1-x^2}}$ and the observation that for any $q \in \mathbb{S}$, we have $\sqrt{q_0^2 - \|\underline{q}\|^2} = \|q\|$. □

Remark 4. The condition $q_0 > 0$ in the definition of the logarithm for $q \in \mathbb{S}$ guarantees that the second condition in Eq. (14) is satisfied. However, we can extend the given definition to the case $q_0 < 0$.

3.5   Other Elementary Functions

Other elementary functions can be derived from the coquaternionic functions defined in the previous sections by employing analogues of the corresponding complex relationships, replacing, if necessary, the imaginary unit by $\omega_{\underline{q}}$. For example, we can define

$$\operatorname{Tanh}(q) = \frac{\operatorname{Sinh}(q)}{\operatorname{Cosh}(q)}$$

or

$$\operatorname{ArcTan}(q) = -\omega_{\underline{q}} \operatorname{Log} \left(\frac{1 + \omega_{\underline{q}} q}{1 - \omega_{\underline{q}} q} \right).$$

Since the numerators and denominators in the previous divisions commute, both left and right divisions can be considered.

4   *Mathematica* Tools

The *Mathematica* package `Coquaternions` [9] provides a foundation for manipulating coquaternions. This work extends this framework by defining and implementing elementary functions in the coquaternionic setting, further enhancing the package's applicability.

All these computational tools, including the release version described in this section, are available and can be freely downloaded from the website, along with their support documentation.

https://w3.math.uminho.pt/Coquaternions/

In the `Coquaternions` package, a coquaternion $q = q_0 + q_1 \mathbf{i} + q_2 \mathbf{j} + q_3 \mathbf{k}$ is an object of the form `Coquaternion[q0,q1,q2,q3]`. The package allows the use of symbolic entries, assuming that all symbols represent real numbers and adds rules to `Plus`, `Times`, `NonCommutativeMultiply`, and `Power`. It also extends several standard functions to support coquaternionic objects, including `Re`, `Abs`, `Norm`, `Det`, `Tr`, among others. Additionally, new functions are available, such as `Vec` for extracting the vector part of a coquaternion, `PolarForm` for obtaining its polar form, and `Nature` for classifying a coquaternion as time-like, light-like, or space-like (as defined in Sect. 2), using the boolean functions `TimelikeQ`, `LightlikeQ`, or `SpacelikeQ`, respectively.

A new function introduced in this release is the `Omega` function for obtaining $\omega_{\underline{q}}$, which is essential for defining the elementary functions. It can be called with either one or two arguments, allowing for numerical or symbolic use, respectively.

```
Coquaternion/:Omega[q_Coquaternion,"Timelike"|"Spacelike"]:=
    Vec[q]Norm[Vec[q]]
```

```
Coquaternion/:Omega[q_Coquaternion,"Lightlike"]:= Vec[q]
```

```
Coquaternion /: Omega[q_Coquaternion]:= Module[{NatVecq = Nature@Vec@q},
  If[MatchQ[NatVecq, "Timelike"|"Spacelike"|"Lightlike"],
  Omega[q, NatVecq], Message[Coquaternion::UndefinedNature]]]
```

We now illustrate the use of the Omega function by considering some simple examples.

In[1]:= <<Coquaternions

In[2]:= lq={Coquaternion[1,2,0,0],Coquaternion[4,0,3,0],
        Coquaternion[1,2,2,0]};

In[3]:= lvq=Vec[lq]

Out[3]= {Coquaternion[0, 2, 0, 0], Coquaternion[0, 0, 3, 0], Coquaternion[0, 2, 2, 0]}

In[4]:= Nature@lvq

Out[4]= {Timelike, Spacelike, Lightlike}

In[5]:= Omega[lvq] // TraditionalForm

Out[5]= {î, ĵ, 2î + 2ĵ}

When q is a coquaternion with symbolic entries, using the Omega function with a single input parameter is not suitable. An additional input is required to clarify the nature of q.

In[6]:= q=Coquaternion[q0,q1,q2,q3];

        $Assumptions=Element[q0|q1|q2|q3,Reals];

In[7]:= Omega[q]

        ⋯ Coquaternion: Unable to determine the nature of the argument.

In[8]:= Omega[q,"Lightlike"]

Out[8]= Coquaternion[0, q1, q2, q3]

In[9]:= Omega[q,"Timelike"]

Out[9]= Coquaternion $\left[0, \dfrac{q1}{\sqrt{\text{Abs}[q1^2-q2^2-q3^2]}}, \dfrac{q2}{\sqrt{\text{Abs}[q1^2-q2^2-q3^2]}}, \dfrac{q3}{\sqrt{\text{Abs}[q1^2-q2^2-q3^2]}}\right]$

Following the same approach, we define each elementary function, using one input argument for numerical values and two for symbolic expressions, with the second parameter specifying the nature of the coquaternion. We do not provide the code for defining all the elementary functions, but instead illustrate only the case of the exponential function, according to the definition (9). The implementation details of the other functions can be found on the previously provided website.

```
Coquaternion/:Exp[q_Coquaternion,"Timelike"]:=
    Module[{Req=Re[q],NormVecq=Norm[Vec[q]],
    Exp[Req](Cos[NormVecq]+Omega[q,"Timelike"]Sin[NormVecq])]

Coquaternion/:Exp[q_Coquaternion,"Spacelike"]:=
    Module[{Req=Re[q],NormVecq=Norm[Vec[q]],
    Exp[Req](Cosh[NormVecq]+Omega[q,"Spacelike"]Sinh[NormVecq])]

Coquaternion/:Exp[q_Coquaternion,"Lightlike"]:=
    Exp[Re[q]](1+Omega[q,"Lightlike"])

Coquaternion /: Exp[q_Coquaternion]:= Module[{NatVecq = Nature@Vec@q},
  If[MatchQ[NatVecq, "Timelike"|"Spacelike"|"Lightlike"],
  Exp[q, NatVecq], Message[Coquaternion::UndefinedNature]]]
```

We now explore how this extended Exp function can be used to compute the coquaternionic exponential in selected examples and verify previously established properties. We use the data from the previous example.

– Numerical computations with Exp function:

In[10]:= Exp[1q]

Out[10]= {Coquaternion[$\mathrm{e}\,$Cos[2], $\mathrm{e}\,$Sin[2], 0, 0],

Coquaternion[e^4Cosh[3], 0, e^4Sinh[3], 0], Coquaternion[e, 2e, 2e, 0]}

– Symbolic computations with Exp function:

In[11]:= Exp[q, "Spacelike"]

Out[11]= Coquaternion$\left[\mathrm{e}^{q0}\mathrm{Cosh}\left[\sqrt{\mathrm{Abs}[q1^2 - q2^2 - q3^2]}\right], \dfrac{\mathrm{e}^{q0}q1\mathrm{Sinh}\left[\sqrt{\mathrm{Abs}[q1^2-q2^2-q3^2]}\right]}{\sqrt{\mathrm{Abs}[q1^2-q2^2-q3^2]}},\right.$

$\dfrac{\mathrm{e}^{q0}q2\mathrm{Sinh}\left[\sqrt{\mathrm{Abs}[q1^2-q2^2-q3^2]}\right]}{\sqrt{\mathrm{Abs}[q1^2-q2^2-q3^2]}}, \dfrac{\mathrm{e}^{q0}q3\mathrm{Sinh}\left[\sqrt{\mathrm{Abs}[q1^2-q2^2-q3^2]}\right]}{\sqrt{\mathrm{Abs}[q1^2-q2^2-q3^2]}}\left.\right]$

– Verification of Identities (15)

In[12]:= Simplify[Omega[Vec[Exp [q,"Spacelike"]],"Spacelike"]==
        Omega[Vec[q],"Spacelike"]]

Out[12]= True

In[13]:= Norm[Vec[Exp[q,"Spacelike"]]] // Simplify

Out[13]= e^{q0}Sinh$\left[\sqrt{\mathrm{Abs}[q1^2 - q2^2 - q3^2]}\right]$

– Verification of relation 4. of Property 1 for $\underline{q} \in \mathbb{T}$

We note that two coquaternions q_1 and q_2, whose vector parts do not vanish, commute if and only if $\boldsymbol{\omega}(q_1) = \pm\boldsymbol{\omega}(q_2)$, i.e., $q_2 = \alpha + \boldsymbol{\omega}(q_1)\beta$, with $\alpha, \beta \in \mathbb{R}$.

```
In[14]:= p = α + Omega[q,"Timelike"] β;
In[15]:= Assuming[Det[Vec[q] > 0 && Element[β,Reals], Simplify @
            Exp[p+q,"Timelike"] - Exp[p,"Timelike"]**Exp[q,"Timelike"]]
Out[15]= Coquaternion[0,0,0,0]
```

We conclude this section by presenting additional examples featuring other elementary functions.
– Numerical computations with Sin function:

```
In[16]:= Sin[1q] // TableForm
Out[16]/TableForm=
        Coquaternion[Sin[1] Cosh[2],Cos[1] Sinh[2],0,0]
        Coquaternion[Sin[4] Cos[3],0,Sin[3] Cos[4],0]
        Coquaternion[Sin[1],2 Cos[1],2 Cos[1],0]
```

– Verification of identity 2. Property 2, for $\underline{q} \in \mathbb{T}$

```
In[17]:= Sin[q,"Timelike"] - Sin[q0] Cos[Vec[q],"Timelike"] -
            Cos[q0] Sin[Vec[q],"Timelike"] // Simplify
Out[17]= Coquaternion[0, 0, 0, 0]
```

– Verification of identity 3. Property 3, for $\underline{q} \in \mathbb{H}_{coq}$

```
In[18]:= Assuming[Det[Vec[q]] > 0,
            Simplify[Cos[q Omega[q,"Timelike"],"Timelike"]] ==
            Simplify[Cosh[q,"Timelike"]]]
Out[18]= True
In[19]:= Assuming[Det[Vec[q]] < 0,
            Simplify[Cos[q**Omega[q,"Spacelike"],"Spacelike"]] ==
            Simplify[Cos[q,"Spacelike"]]]
Out[19]= True
In[20]:= Assuming[Det[Vec[q]] == 0,
            Simplify[Cos[q**Omega[q,"Lightlike"],"Lightlike"]]]
Out[20]= Coquaternion[1,0,0,0]
```

– Numerical computations with Log function:

In[21]:= Log[lq] // TableForm

Out[21]/TableForm=

$\qquad$ Coquaternion $\left[\frac{\text{Log}[5]}{2}, \text{ArcTan}[2], 0, 0\right]$

$\qquad$ Coquaternion $\left[\frac{\text{Log}[7]}{2}, 0, \text{ArcTanh}\left[\frac{3}{4}\right], 0\right]$

$\qquad$ Coquaternion $[0, 2, 2, 0]$

– Numerical computations with Tan function:

In[22]:= Tan[lq] // N // TableForm

Out[22]/TableForm=

$\qquad$ Coquaternion[0.0338128,1.01479,0.,0.]

$\qquad$ Coquaternion[1.21443,0.,-0.34298,0.]

$\qquad$ Coquaternion[1.55741,6.85104,6.85104,0.]

5   Conclusion

We have developed a systematic framework for defining and computing elementary coquaternionic functions through analytic extension. Our implemented *Mathematica* functions support both numerical and symbolic computations, and the examples presented throughout the article confirm the theoretical properties established earlier while underscoring the practical applicability of our approach.

Ackowledgment. Research at CMAT was partially funded by Portuguese funds through FCT - Fundação para a Ciência e a Tecnologia within the Projects UID/00013.

References

1. Adler, S.L.: Quaternionic Quantum Mechanics and Quantum Fields. In: International Series of Monographs of Physics, vol. 88. Oxford University Press, New York (1995)

2. Ata, E., Yayli, Y.: Split quaternions and semi-Euclidean projective spaces. Chaos, Solitons Fractals **41**(4), 1910–1915 (2009)

3. Bekar, M., Yaylı, Y.: Involutions of complexified quaternions and split quaternions. Adv. Appl. Clifford Algebras **23**(2), 283–299 (2013)

4. Brody, D.C., Graefe, E.M.: On complexified mechanics and coquaternions. J. Phys. A Math. Theor. **44**(7), 072001 (2011)

5. Cockle, J.: On systems of algebra involving more than one imaginary; and on equations of the fifth degree. Phil. Mag. **35**(3), 434–435 (1849)

6. Erdoğdu, M., Özdemir, M.: On exponential of split quaternionic matrices. Appl. Math. Comput. **315**, 468–476 (2017)

7. Falcão, M.I., Cruz, J., Malonek, H.R.: Remarks on the generation of monogenic functions. In: 17th International Conference on the Application of Computer Science and Mathematics on Architecture and Civil Engineering, Weimar (2006)

8. Falcão, M.I., Miranda, F., Severino, R., Soares, M.J.: Mathematica tools for coquaternions. In: Gervasi, O., et al. (eds.) ICCSA 2021. LNCS, vol. 12952, pp. 449–464. Springer, Cham (2021). https://doi.org/10.1007/978-3-030-86973-1_32

9. Falcão, M.I., Miranda, F., Severino, R., Soares, M.J.: Symbolic computations over the algebra of coquaternions. In: 4th International Conference on Numerical and Symbolic Computation: Developments and Applications - SYMCOMP 2019 Proceedings, pp. 141–155 (2019)

10. Falcão, M.I., Miranda, F., Severino, R., Soares, M.J.: On the roots of coquaternions. Adv. Appl. Clifford Algebras **28**(5), 97 (2018). https://doi.org/10.1007/s00006-018-0914-3

11. Gao, C., Chen, X., Shen, Y.G.: Quintessence and phantom emerging from the split-complex field and the split-quaternion field. Gen. Relativ. Gravit. **48**(11), 1–23 (2016)

12. Gogberashvili, M.: Split quaternions and particles in (2+1)-space. Eur. Phys. J. C **74**(12), 1–9 (2014). https://doi.org/10.1140/epjc/s10052-014-3200-0

13. Jiang, T., Zhang, Z., Jiang, Z.: Algebraic techniques for Schrödinger equations in split quaternionic mechanics. Comput. Math. Appl. **75**(7), 2217–2222 (2018)

14. Kula, L., Yayli, Y.: Split quaternions and rotations in semi Euclidean space E_2^4. J. Korean Math. Soc. **44**(6), 1313–1327 (2007)

15. Özdemir, M.: The roots of a split quaternion. Appl. Math. Lett. **22**(2), 258–263 (2009)

16. Özdemir, M., Ergin, A.: Some geometric applications of split quaternions. In: Proceedings 16th International Conference Jangjeon Mathematical Society, vol. 16, pp. 108–115 (2005)

17. Özdemir, M., Ergin, A.: Rotations with unit timelike quaternions in Minkowski 3-space. J. Geom. Phys. **56**(2), 322–336 (2006)

18. Serôdio, R., Beites, P.D., Vitória, J.: Intersection of a double cone and a line in the split-quaternions context. Adv. Appl. Clifford Algebras **27**(3), 2795–2803 (2017)

19. Simsek, H., Özdemir, M.: Rotations on a lightcone in Minkowski 3-space. Adv. Appl. Clifford Algebras **27**(3), 2841–2853 (2017)

Pascal Trapezoids as Wigner Numbers and Some Combinatorial Properties

Isabel Cação[2] , M. Irene Falcão[1]([⊠]) , Helmuth R. Malonek[2] ,
and Graça Tomaz[2,3,4]

[1] Centro de Matemática, Universidade do Minho, Braga, Portugal
mif@math.uminho.pt
[2] CIDMA, Universidade de Aveiro, Aveiro, Portugal
{isabel.cacao,hrmalon}@ua.pt
[3] CISE–Electromechatronic Systems Research Centre, University of Beira Interior,
Covilhã, Portugal
[4] Polytechnic of Guarda, Guarda, Portugal
gtomaz@ipg.pt

Abstract. Despite their entirely different origins, the entries of Pascal trapezoids are closely related to Wigner numbers. In this paper, we bridge both approaches, rediscover recurrences using alternative techniques, and establish new combinatorial identities.

Keywords: Pascal trapezoids · Wigner numbers · Combinatorial identities

1 Introduction

A few years ago, some of the authors of this paper generalized the concept of Appell polynomials to the hypercomplex context (cf. [5]), resulting in a class of multidimensional polynomials that can be expressed in various forms using hypercomplex variables. Later, in [3], the authors investigated bijections between the coefficients of two different representations of these generalized Appell polynomials. In that study, they introduced the specific class of integers (Theorems 6 and 7),

$$\sigma_{i,j}^k - \sum_{m=0}^{i} (-1)^m \binom{i}{m}\binom{k-i}{j-m}, \; k = 0, 1, 2, \ldots, j = 0, \ldots, k, \tag{1}$$

that was shown to possess interesting properties, warranting a more in-depth study of its own, which was initiated in that paper. It was proven that these numbers satisfy a Pascal-like relation, forming arrangements in trapezoidal arrays, with the classical Pascal triangle emerging as a particular case within this collection. Moreover, the Catalan triangle, as discussed by Miana et al. [9], is also included. Several combinatorial properties of those numbers were proven, regarding symmetries, closed-form sums, connections to well-known numbers such as the central binomial coefficient as well as a generating function. Closely related numbers appeared later in the theory of angular momentum in quantum

O. Gervasi et al. (Eds.): ICCSA 2025 Workshops, LNCS 15887, pp. 195–207, 2026.
https://doi.org/10.1007/978-3-031-97589-9_14

mechanics, particularly in the development of efficient evaluation methods for the reduced Wigner matrices (cf. [1]). Indeed, for the rotations of particles and systems the so-called Wigner rotation matrices

$$D_{M,M'}^{J}(\alpha,\beta,\gamma) = e^{-\mathrm{i}M\alpha}d_{M,M'}^{J}(\beta)e^{-\mathrm{i}M'\gamma} \qquad (2)$$

play a central role. Here, (α,β,γ) are the Euler rotation angles, the index $J \in \{0,\frac{1}{2},1,\frac{3}{2},2,\frac{5}{2},3,\ldots\}$ stands for the angular momentum and (M,M') are the Z-components of the angular momentum, M, $M' = -J,-J+1,\ldots,J-1,J$. The calculation of the Wigner reduced matrices $d_{M,M'}^{J}(\beta)$ presents several challenges. Although explicit formulas and recurrence relations were known, as observed by Allen [1] none offered a completely satisfactory method for determining the reduced Wigner rotation matrices for large quantum numbers J. Aiming to establish an efficient and numerically stable method for arbitrary J, Allen noticed the emergence of the set of numbers (cf. [1, Eq. 97])

$$W_{m,n}^{J} = \sum_{\sigma=\max\{0,m-n\}}^{\min\{m,2J-n\}} (-1)^{m+\sigma}\binom{2J-n}{\sigma}\binom{n}{m-\sigma}, \ m, \ n = 0,1,2,\ldots,2J,$$

that he called Wigner numbers. He recognized and explored a myriad of combinatorial properties of these numbers in the paper.

As it was noticed in [2, Eq. 2], this formulation is equivalent to

$$W_{m,n}^{J} = \sum_{i=0}^{n}(-1)^{i}\binom{n}{i}\binom{2J-n}{m-i}, \qquad (3)$$

for $J \in \{0,\frac{1}{2},1,\frac{3}{2},2,\frac{5}{2},3,\ldots\}$, $m,n \in [0,2J]$, establishing a connection with the entries of the Pascal trapezoids (1). Also, in [2], the class of Wigner numbers was extended to an ℓ parameter-dependent class of numbers, called ℓth order Wigner numbers, of which the entries of Pascal trapezoids are of first order and the numbers introduced by Allen are of second order.

Although these sets of numbers emerged in two such distinct contexts, they were recognized in both cases as having intrinsic importance due to their interesting combinatorial properties and as worthy of deeper investigation beyond the context in which they arose. In this paper, for the sake of clarity, we begin by revisiting some properties previously established in [3] and introducing new properties of the Wigner numbers of the first order. These new properties include additional recurrence formulas that relate entries in consecutive rows of each trapezoid, as well as consecutive entries within the same row. Some of these properties exhibit structural similarities to those obtained by Allen for the Wigner numbers of the second order, whereas others have not been explored before.

The paper is organized as follows. In Sect. 2, we recall the extension of the Wigner numbers as defined in [2] and identify the Pascal trapezoids (1) as Wigner numbers of the first order, expressing them in terms of Gauss' hypergeometric function. Section 3 focuses on recurrence relations, some of which were previously established in [3], while others resemble those obtained by Allen in [1], but are derived using different techniques. Finally, in Sect. 4, we explore additional combinatorial properties, including symmetries, closed summation formulas, and central coefficients of the Pascal trapezoids.

2   The Entries of Pascal Trapezoids as Wigner Numbers

Following [2], we consider the extension of the Wigner numbers to the ℓ-parameter class defined by

$$W_{m,n}^{J,\ell} = \sum_{i=0}^{n}(-1)^i\binom{n}{i}\binom{\ell J - n}{m - i},$$

for $\ell \in \mathbb{N}$, $J \geq 0$ and $m, n \in [0, \ell J]$.

In this view, the integers (3) are 2nd order Wigner numbers, while the entries of the Pascal trapezoids (1) are 1st order Wigner numbers, by replacing (i, j, k) by (n, m, J), for $\ell = 1$.

As mentioned previously, the numbers in equation (1) emerged from the connection between two distinct representations of a multidimensional polynomial sequence, as briefly outlined below. By extending the concept of Appell polynomials within the framework of hypercomplex function theory in $\mathbb{R}^{n+1}$, the following infinite array of numbers arises as coefficients [5]:

$$T_s^k(n) = \binom{k}{s}\frac{\left(\frac{n+1}{2}\right)_{k-s}\left(\frac{n-1}{2}\right)_s}{(n)_k}, \quad n, k = 1, 2, \ldots, ; s = 0, 1, \ldots, k,$$

where $(a)_r := a(a + 1)\ldots(a + r - 1)$, for any integer $r \geq 1$ is the Pochhammer symbol with $(a)_0 := 1, a \geq 0$. In [6], various properties of these numbers were studied, namely their relationship with the generalized Vietoris numbers (cf. [4]),

$$c_k(n) = \frac{\left(\frac{1}{2}\right)_{\lfloor\frac{k+1}{2}\rfloor}}{\left(\frac{n}{2}\right)_{\lfloor\frac{k+1}{2}\rfloor}}, \quad n \in \mathbb{N}, \ k = 0, 1, 2, \ldots,$$

that can be given by

$$c_k(n) = \sum_{s=0}^{k}(-1)^k T_s^k(n).$$

Later, new relations between $T_s^k(n)$ and $c_k(n)$ were explored, giving rise to (cf. [3], Theorems 6 and 7)

$$\frac{2^k}{\binom{k}{s}}T_s^k(n) = \sum_{j=0}^{k}\sigma_{s,j}^k c_j(n)$$

and

$$\binom{k}{j}c_{k-j}(n) = \sum_{s=0}^{k}(-1)^s \sigma_{s,j}^k T_s^k(n), \quad k = 0, 1, 2, \ldots; \ j = 0, 1, \ldots, k,$$

where the coefficients $\sigma_{s,j}^k$ are precisely the 1st order Wigner numbers (1).

We highlight that for arbitrary nonnegative integers i, j, k with $j \le k$, the numbers $\sigma_{i,j}^k$ can be arranged, for each fixed i, in a triangular array. In this arrangement, the rows associated with k ($k = 0, 1, \dots$) are ordered from $j = 0$ to $j = k$ (see Table 1). The case $i = 0$ corresponds to the ordinary Pascal triangle because $\sigma_{0,j}^k = \binom{k}{j}$. In the other cases we obtain trapezoids, where for each row, the Pascal recurrence is satisfied, justifying the name of Pascal trapezoids (cf. Theorem 1 below). We remark that the case $i = 1$ corresponds to the Catalan triangle numbers (cf. [9]).

Similarly, for each fixed j, $\sigma_{i,j}^k$, can also be expressed as

$$\sigma_{i,j}^k = \sum_{m=0}^{j} (-1)^m \binom{i}{m}\binom{k-i}{j-m}, \tag{4}$$

because $\binom{k-i}{j-m} = 0$, for $m > j$, while $\binom{i}{m} = 0$ when $m > i$. In Table 2, these numbers are displayed as an arithmetic triangle, ordered from $i = 0$ to $i = k$.

The use of appropriate properties of the Pochhammer symbol, enables to express the Wigner numbers of 1st order (1) in terms of the Gauss' hypergeometric function

$$_2F_1(a, b; c; z) = \sum_{s=0}^{\infty} \frac{(a)_s (b)_s}{(c)_s s!} z^s,$$

as

$$\sigma_{i,j}^k = \binom{k-i}{j} {}_2F_1(-i, -j; k - i - j + 1; -1). \tag{5}$$

Remark 1. We remark that representations of the Wigner numbers of 1st order in terms of certain values of Jacobi polynomials can be easily establish, considering (5) and known formulas for the Jacobi polynomials in terms of the hypergeometric function. For instance, the following representation of the Jacobi polynomials,

$$P_n^{(\alpha,\beta)}(x) = \left(\frac{x+1}{2}\right)^n \frac{(n+\alpha)!}{n!\alpha!} {}_2F_1\left(-n, -n - \beta; \alpha + 1; \frac{x-1}{x+1}\right),$$

evaluated at $x = 0$ with (n, α, β) as $(i, k - i - j, j - i)$, yields

$$\sigma_{i,j}^k = 2^i \frac{\binom{k}{j}}{\binom{k}{i}} P_i^{(k-i-j,j-i)}(0).$$

3   Recurrence Relations

In this section, we present different ways to obtain $\sigma_{i,j}^k$ recursively, either by fixing the value of i or by fixing the value of j.

Table 1. Trapezoids associated with $\sigma_{i,j}^k$, $(i = 0, \ldots, 3)$

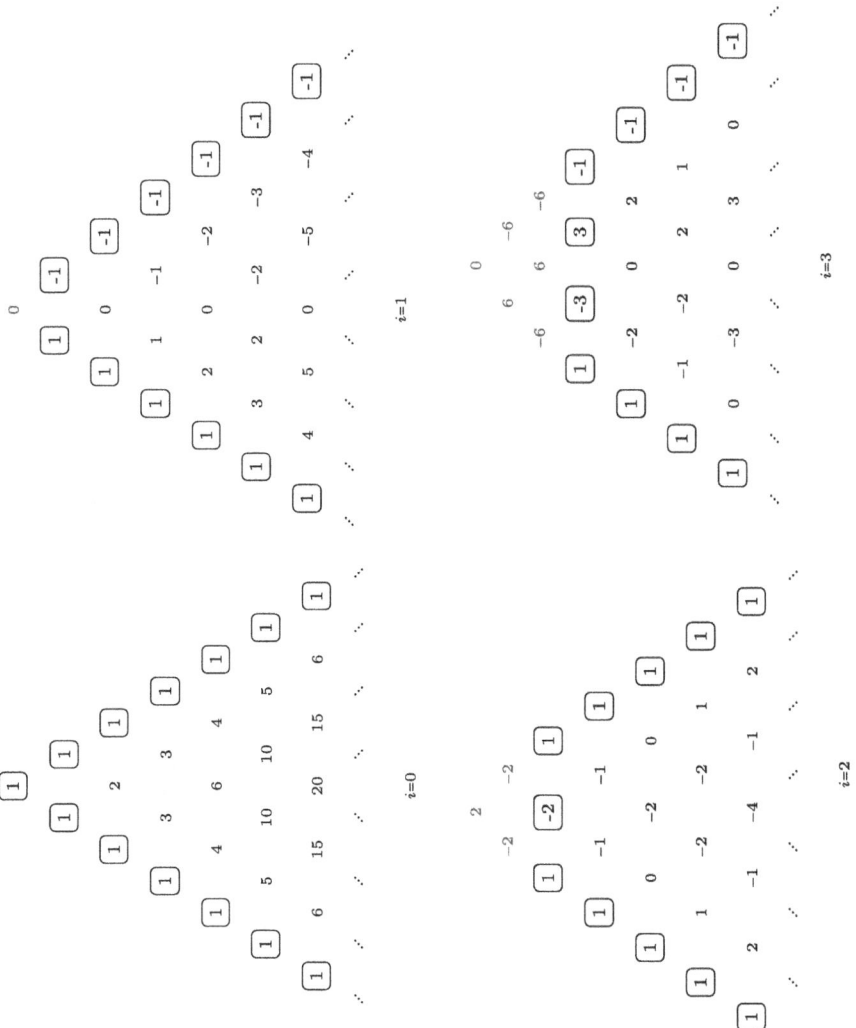

Table 2. Trapezoids associated with $\sigma_{i,j}^k$, $(j = 0, \ldots, 3)$

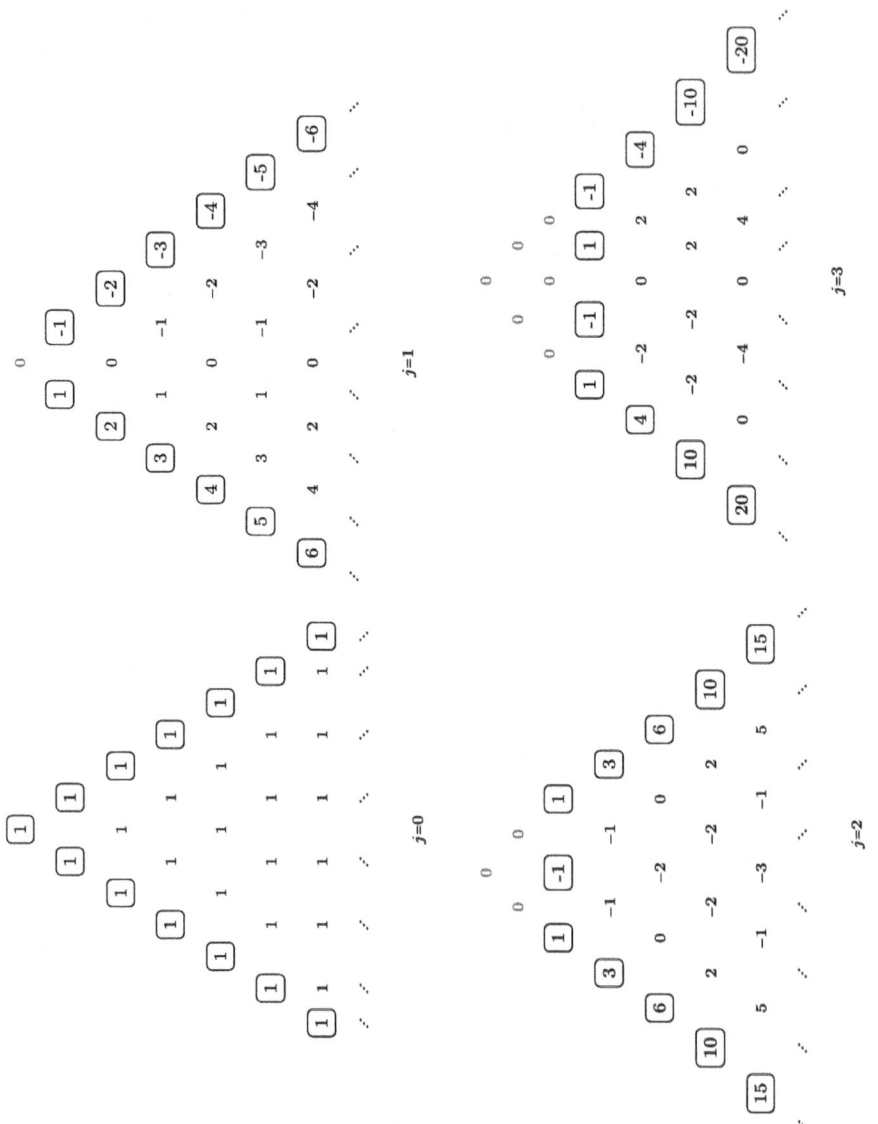

Theorem 1 (Pascal-like recurrences).

(i) *For each fixed value of i, the numbers $\sigma_{i,j}^k$ satisfy the following linear recurrence relation*

$$\sigma_{i,j+1}^{k+1} = \sigma_{i,j}^k + \sigma_{i,j+1}^k, \quad (0 \le j \le k - 1, k \ge i) \tag{6}$$

with boundary conditions

$$\sigma_{i,0}^{k} = 1, \qquad \sigma_{i,k}^{k} = (-1)^{i}, \ (k \geq i) \tag{7}$$

and initial values

$$\sigma_{i,j}^{i} = \binom{i}{j}(-1)^{j}, \ j = 1, \ldots, i-1 \tag{8}$$

(cf. [3, Theorem 10]).

(ii) *For each fixed value of j, the numbers $\sigma_{i,j}^{k}$ satisfy the following linear recurrence relation*

$$\sigma_{i+1,j}^{k+1} = 2\,\sigma_{i,j}^{k} - \sigma_{i,j}^{k+1}, \ (0 \leq i \leq k, \ k \geq j) \tag{9}$$

with boundary conditions

$$\sigma_{0,j}^{k} = \binom{k}{j}, \qquad \sigma_{k,j}^{k} = (-1)^{j}\binom{k}{j}, \ (k \geq j) \tag{10}$$

and initial values

$$\sigma_{i,j}^{j} = (-1)^{i}, \ i = 1, \ldots, j-1. \tag{11}$$

Proof.

(i) Recurrence (6) was obtained in Theorem 10 of [3].

(ii) Considering (5), we get for the numbers $\sigma_{i+1,j}^{k+1}$ and $\sigma_{i,j}^{k+1}$ the form

$$\sigma_{i+1,j}^{k+1} = \binom{k-i}{j}{}_2F_1(-i-1,-j;k-i-j+1;-1),$$

$$\sigma_{i,j}^{k+1} = \binom{k-i+1}{j}{}_2F_1(-i,-j;k-i-j+2;-1),$$

respectively.

The Gauss's relation for contiguous functions (cf. [10]),

$$c\,(1-z)\,{}_2F_1(a,b;c;z) - c\,{}_2F_1(a-1,b;c;z) + (c-b)z\,{}_2F_1(a,b;c+1;z) = 0,$$

with $z = -1$, leads to

$$c\,{}_2F_1(a-1,b;c;-1) = 2c\,{}_2F_1(a,b;c;-1) - (c-b)\,{}_2F_1(a,b;c+1;-1).$$

Setting $a = -i$, $b = -j$, and $c = k-i-j+1$, we obtain

$$(k-i-j+1)\,{}_2F_1(-i-1,-j;k-i-j+1;-1) =$$
$$2(k-i-j+1)\,{}_2F_1(-i,-j;k-i-j+1;-1) - (k-i+1)\,{}_2F_1(-i,-j;k-i-j+2;-1).$$

The result follows after multiplying both sides by $\frac{1}{k-i-j+1}\binom{k-i}{j}$. □

The following result, derived as a consequence of the latest theorem, corresponds to that presented in [1] for the 2nd order Wigner numbers, using different arguments (see [1, Eq. 66]).

Corollary 1. *The numbers $\sigma_{i,j}^k$ satisfy the relation*

$$\sigma_{i+1,j}^{k+1} = \sigma_{i,j}^k - \sigma_{i,j-1}^k, \ (0 \le i, j \le k)$$

with boundary conditions (7)-(10), initial values (8)-(11), and $\sigma_{i,-1}^k = 0$.

Proof. The result follows immediately from (6) and (9), since

$$\sigma_{i+1,j}^{k+1} = 2\sigma_{i,j}^k - (\sigma_{i,j-1}^k + \sigma_{i,j}^k) = \sigma_{i,j}^k - \sigma_{i,j-1}^k.$$

□

While the recurrences in Theorem 1 connect three elements from two consecutive rows of trapezoids (see Table 1 for fixed i and Table 2 for fixed j), the following results establish three-term recurrence relationships among elements within the same row.

Theorem 2. (i) *For each fixed value of i, the numbers $\sigma_{i,j}^k$ satisfy the following relation*

$$(j+1)\sigma_{i,j+1}^k + (2i-k)\sigma_{i,j}^k + (k-j+1)\sigma_{i,j-1}^k = 0, \tag{12}$$

$0 \le j \le k-1, \ k \ge i, \sigma_{i,0}^k = 1,$ *and* $\sigma_{i,-1}^k = 0.$
(ii) *For each fixed value of j, the numbers $\sigma_{i,j}^k$ satisfy the following relation*

$$(k-i)\sigma_{i+1,j}^k + (2j-k)\sigma_{i,j}^k + i\sigma_{i-1,j}^k = 0, \tag{13}$$

$0 \le i \le k-1, \ k \ge j,$ *and* $\sigma_{0,j}^k = \binom{k}{j}.$

Proof.

(i) Considering (5), we can write

$$\sigma_{i,j+1}^k = \binom{k-i}{j+1} \, {}_2F_1(-i,-j-1;k-i-j;-1),$$

$$\sigma_{i,j-1}^k = \binom{k-i}{j-1} \, {}_2F_1(-i,-j+1;k-i-j+2;-1),$$

and taking into account the well-known linear transformation (cf. [10]),

$${}_2F_1(a,b;c;z) = (1-z)^{-a} \, {}_2F_1\left(a,c-b;c;\tfrac{z}{z-1}\right),$$

we get, after making the appropriate substitutions, that

$${}_2F_1\left(-i,-j-1;k-i-j;-1\right) = 2^i \, {}_2F_1\left(-i,k-i+1;k-i-j;\tfrac{1}{2}\right),$$
$${}_2F_1\left(-i,-j;k-i-j+1;-1\right) = 2^i \, {}_2F_1\left(-i,k-i+1;k-i-j+1;\tfrac{1}{2}\right),$$
$${}_2F_1\left(-i,-j+1;k-i-j+2;-1\right) = 2^i \, {}_2F_1\left(-i,k-i+1;k-i-j+2;\tfrac{1}{2}\right).$$

Combining the previous relations, and the combinatorial identities

$$\binom{k-i}{j+1} = \frac{k-i-j}{j+1}\binom{k-i}{j} \quad \text{and} \quad \binom{k-i}{j-1} = \frac{j}{k-i-j+1}\binom{k-i}{j},$$

it follows that

$$(j+1)\sigma_{i,j+1}^k + (2i-k)\sigma_{i,j}^k + (k-j+1)\sigma_{i,j-1}^k = 2^i\binom{k-i}{j}\mathcal{A}_{i,j}^k,$$

where

$$\mathcal{A}_{i,j}^k = (k-i-j)\,_2F_1\left(-i, k-i+1; k-i-j; \tfrac{1}{2}\right)$$
$$+ (2i-k)\,_2F_1\left(-i, k-i+1; k-i-j+1; \tfrac{1}{2}\right)$$
$$+ \tfrac{(k-j+1)j}{k-i-j+1}\,_2F_1\left(-i, k-i+1; k-i-j+2; \tfrac{1}{2}\right).$$

Using the contiguity relation between hypergeometric functions (cf. [10])

$$c(c-1)(z-1)\,_2F_1(a,b;c-1;z) + c(c-1-(2c-a-b-1)z)\,_2F_1(a,b;c;z)$$
$$+ (c-a)(c-b)z\,_2F_1(a,b;c+1;z) = 0,$$

with $z = \frac{1}{2}$, i.e.,

$$c(c-1)_2F_1(a,b;c-1;\tfrac{1}{2}) + c(-a-b+1)_2F_1(a,b;c;\tfrac{1}{2})$$
$$+ (c-a)(b-c)_2F_1(a,b;c+1;\tfrac{1}{2}) = 0, \quad (14)$$

and substituting $a = -i, b = k-i+1, c = k-i-j+1$, we get $\mathcal{A}_{i,j}^k = 0$, and the result follows.

(ii) Analogously to the proof of (i), this time using the linear transformation (cf. [10]),

$$_2F_1(a,b;c;z) = (1-z)^{-b}\,_2F_1\left(c-a,b;c;\tfrac{z}{z-1}\right),$$

with appropriate substitutions, we obtain

$$_2F_1(-i-1,-j;k-i-j;-1) = 2^j\,_2F_1(k-j+1,-j;k-i-j;\tfrac{1}{2}),$$
$$_2F_1(-i,-j;k-i-j+1;-1) = 2^j\,_2F_1(k-j+1,-j;k-i-j+1;\tfrac{1}{2}),$$
$$_2F_1(-i+1,-j;k-i-j+2;-1) = 2^j\,_2F_1(k-j+1,-j;k-i-j+2;\tfrac{1}{2}).$$

Bearing in mind (5),

$$\sigma_{i+1,j}^k = \binom{k-i-1}{j}_2F_1(-i-1,-j;k-i-j;-1),$$

$$\sigma_{i-1,j}^k = \binom{k-i+1}{j}_2F_1(-i+1,-j;k-i-j+2;-1),$$

and the identities

$$\binom{k-i-1}{j} = \frac{k-i-j}{k-i}\binom{k-i}{j} \quad \text{and} \quad \binom{k-i+1}{j} = \frac{k-i+1}{k-i-j+1}\binom{k-i}{j},$$

it follows that

$$(k-i)\sigma_{i+1,j}^k + (2j-k)\sigma_{i,j}^k + i\sigma_{i-1,j}^k = 2^j \binom{k-i}{j}\mathcal{B}_{i,j}^k,$$

where

$$\mathcal{B}_{i,j}^k = (k-i-j)\,_2F_1\left(k-j+1,-j;k-i-j;\tfrac{1}{2}\right)$$
$$+ (2j-k)\,_2F_1\left(k-j+1,-j;k-i-j+1;\frac{1}{2}\right)$$
$$+ \frac{i(k-i+1)}{k-i-j+1}\,_2F_1\left(k-j+1,-j;k-i-j+2;\tfrac{1}{2}\right).$$

Using (14) with $a = k-j+1$, $b = -j$, and $c = k-i-j+1$, we obtain $\mathcal{B}_{i,j}^k = 0$, thus proving the statement. □

The recurrence relations (12) and (13) correspond, respectively, to Eqs. 27 and 55 of [1], which were derived in the context of calculating unknown quantities (the 2nd order Wigner numbers), involved in the reduced Wigner matrices $d_{M,M'}^J(\beta)$ of rotation matrices (2).

4　Other Properties

In this section, we explore and prove additional properties linking the numbers in the previously introduced trapezoids, uncovering deeper connections between various combinatorial structures.

Property 1 (Patterns).

(i) Trapezoids of $i-$ and $j-$even order are symmetric, i.e.,

$$\sigma_{2i,j}^k = \sigma_{2i,k-j}^k \quad \text{and} \quad \sigma_{i,2j}^k = \sigma_{k-i,2j}^k; \tag{15}$$

(ii) Trapezoids of of $i-$ and $j-$odd order are anti-symmetric, i.e.,

$$\sigma_{2i+1,j}^k = -\sigma_{2i+1,k-j}^k \quad \text{and} \quad \sigma_{i,2j+1}^k = -\sigma_{k-i,2j+1}^k. \tag{16}$$

Proof. The identities on the left hand side of (15) and (16) come, respectively, from Property 11 (i) and (ii) derived in [3]. Using the identity (4), one can write

$$\sigma_{k-i,j}^k = \sum_{m=0}^{j}(-1)^m\binom{k-i}{m}\binom{i}{j-m} = \sum_{m=0}^{j}(-1)^{j-m}\binom{k-i}{j-m}\binom{i}{m} = (-1)^j\sigma_{i,j}^k$$

and the result is proved. □

In the next property, we present the central coefficients of the trapezoid of order i and j. These coefficients exhibit a distinct behavior depending on whether the indices i and j are even or odd. Specifically, we derive the explicit expressions for $\sigma_{i,k}^{2k}$ and $\sigma_{k,j}^{2k}$ based on the parity of i and j, revealing their dependency on binomial coefficients and alternating signs.

Property 2 (Central Coefficients). The central coefficients of the trapezoid of order i and j are given, respectively, by

$$\sigma_{i,k}^{2k} = \begin{cases} 0, & \text{if } i \text{ is odd;} \\ (-1)^{\frac{i}{2}} \dfrac{\binom{k}{\frac{i}{2}}}{\binom{2k}{i}} \binom{2k}{k}, & \text{if } i \text{ is even.} \end{cases}$$

and

$$\sigma_{k,j}^{2k} = \begin{cases} 0, & \text{if } j \text{ is odd;} \\ (-1)^{\frac{j}{2}} \binom{k}{\frac{j}{2}}, & \text{if } j \text{ is even.} \end{cases}$$

Proof. The expression for $\sigma_{i,k}^{2k}$ was derived as Property 12 in [3]. The expression for $\sigma_{k,j}^{2k}$ follows from the expansion of $(1-x)^k(1+x)^k$ (cf. [7, Formula 1.19]) by taking identity (4).   □

Next result presents summation formulas for the numbers in the trapezoids, including both the sum and alternating sum of the rows. These formulas depend on the parity of the indices and provide explicit expressions for different cases.

Property 3 (Summation formulas).

(i) Sum of the rows:

$$\sum_{j=0}^{k} \sigma_{i,j}^{k} = 0, \qquad (k \geq i > 0); \tag{17}$$

$$\sum_{i=0}^{k} \sigma_{i,j}^{k} = \begin{cases} 0, & \text{if } j \text{ is odd;} \\ \binom{k+1}{j+1}, & \text{if } j \text{ is even.} \end{cases}, \qquad (k \geq j > 0). \tag{18}$$

(ii) Alternating sum of the rows:

$$\sum_{j=0}^{k} (-1)^{j} \sigma_{i,j}^{k} = 0, \qquad (k > i); \tag{19}$$

$$\sum_{i=0}^{k} (-1)^{i} \sigma_{i,j}^{k} = \begin{cases} 0, & \text{if } k-j \text{ is odd;} \\ \binom{k+1}{j}, & \text{if } k-j \text{ is even.} \end{cases}, \qquad (k > j).$$

Proof.

(i) Relation (17) is the identity obtained in Property 13 (i) of [3]. To prove (18), observe that

$$\sum_{i=0}^{k} \sigma_{i,j}^{k} = \sum_{i=0}^{k} \sum_{m=0}^{i} (-1)^m \binom{i}{m}\binom{k-i}{j-m} = \sum_{m=0}^{k} (-1)^m \sum_{i=0}^{k} \binom{i}{m}\binom{k-i}{j-m}.$$

Since $\binom{k-i}{j-m} = 0$, when $m > j$, one can write

$$\sum_{i=0}^{k} \sigma_{i,j}^{k} = \sum_{m=0}^{j} (-1)^m \sum_{i=0}^{k} \binom{i}{m}\binom{k-i}{j-m}.$$

Using now relation (5.26) of [8] we obtain

$$\sum_{i=0}^{k} \sigma_{i,j}^{k} = \sum_{m=0}^{j} (-1)^m \binom{k+1}{j+1} = \binom{k+1}{j+1} \sum_{m=0}^{j} (-1)^m$$

and the result follows at once.

(ii) Relation (19) is the identity obtained in Property 13 (ii) of [3]. Using the arguments of (i), we can write

$$\sum_{i=0}^{k} (-1)^i \sigma_{i,j}^{k} = \sum_{m=0}^{j} (-1)^m \sum_{i=0}^{k} (-1)^i \binom{i}{m}\binom{k-i}{j-m}.$$

Since $\binom{i}{m} = 0$, for $i < m$ and $\binom{k-i}{j-m} = 0$, when $i > k-j+m$, we can rewrite the inner sum as

$$\sum_{i=m}^{k-j+m} (-1)^i \binom{i}{m}\binom{k-i}{j-m} = \sum_{i=0}^{k-j} (-1)^{i+m} \binom{i+m}{m}\binom{k-i-m}{j-m}.$$

Substituting this into the original sum and rearranging the order of summation, we obtain

$$\sum_{i=0}^{k} (-1)^i \sigma_{i,j}^{k} = \sum_{m=0}^{j} \sum_{i=0}^{k-j} (-1)^i \binom{i+m}{m}\binom{k-i-m}{j-m}$$

$$= \sum_{i=0}^{k-j} (-1)^i \sum_{m=0}^{j} \binom{i+m}{i}\binom{k-i-m}{k-i-j}.$$

Finally, applying identity (5.26) of [8], we conclude that

$$\sum_{i=0}^{k} (-1)^i \sigma_{i,j}^{k} = \sum_{i=0}^{k-j} (-1)^i \binom{k+1}{k-j+1} = \binom{k+1}{j} \sum_{i=0}^{k-j} (-1)^i$$

and the final result follows.   □

5   Conclusion

As is often the case in mathematics, problems that were once considered completely independently and without knowledge of their practical application can also turn out to be practically significant.

The results obtained a few years ago in [3] for purely mathematical reasons in the search for intrinsic combinatorial connections between two different sets of coefficients have been supplemented by new ones, inspired by their connection to the Wigner numbers.

Although some of the results in the present paper correspond to rediscoveries of the "intriguing properties" identified by Allen [1], other cases establish entirely new identities. Regardless of the context or tools used to derive them, these properties are inherently interesting, revealing valuable connections that merit further exploration.

Acknowledgments. Research at CIDMA has been supported by FCT (Portuguese Foundation for Science and Technology) Multi-Annual Financing Program for R&D Units. Research at CMAT was partially financed by Portuguese funds through FCT within the Projects UID/00013. Research at CISE has been financed by FCT within the Projects UIDB/04131/2020 and UIDP/04131/2020.

References

1. Allen, W.D.: Wigner numbers. J. Chem. Phys. **151**, 244122 (2019)
2. Árendás, P., Császár, A.G.: Comment on "Wigner numbers". J. Chem. Phys. **154**, 087101 (2021)
3. Cação, I., Malonek, H.R., Falcão, M.I., Tomaz, G.: Combinatorial identities associated with a multidimensional polynomial sequence. J. Integer Sequences **21**, 18.7.4 (2018)
4. Cação, I., Malonek, H.R., Falcão, M.I.: On generalized Vietoris' number sequences. Discrete Appl. Math. **269**, 77–85 (2019)
5. Falcão, M.I., Cruz, J., Malonek, H.R.: Remarks on the generation of monogenic functions. In: 17th International Conference on the Application of Computer Science and Mathematics in Architecture and Civil Engineering, Weimar (2006)
6. Falcão, M.I., Malonek, H.R.: A note on a one-parameter family of non-symmetric number triangles. Opuscula Math. **32**, 661–673 (2012)
7. Gould, H.W.: Combinatorial identities: table I: intermediate techniques for summing finite series, from the seven unpublished manuscripts (2010). edited and compiled by Jocelyn Quaintance, http://www.math.wvu.edu/~hgould/Vol.4.PDF
8. Graham, R.L., Knuth, D.E., Patashnik, O.: Concrete Mathematics. A Foundation for Computer Science. Addison-Wesley Professional, Reading (1994)
9. Miana, P.J., Ohtsuka, H., Romero, N.: Sums of powers of Catalan triangle numbers. Discrete Math. **340**, 2388–2397 (2017)
10. Olver, F., Lozier, D.W., Boisvert, R.F., Clark, C.W.: NIST Handbook of Mathematical Functions. Cambridge University Press, Cambridge (2010)

Predicting Information Diffusion on Social Media Using an Epidemiological Approach

Dajana Conte$^{(\boxtimes)}$ ⓘ, Samira Iscaro ⓘ, and Beatrice Paternoster ⓘ

Department of Mathematics, University of Salerno, Via Giovanni Paolo II, 132-84084
Fisciano, SA, Italy
{dajconte,siscaro,beapat}@unisa.it
https://www.dipmat.unisa.it/

Abstract. Recent decades have been characterized by deep changes in
our way of communicating thanks to powerful new tools e.g., social networks, that allow a fast spread of information with very limited costs and
control. In this paper, we will show the importance of analyzing information diffusion on social media in the first phases of the news spread, using
a mathematical epidemiological approach. We will highlight the importance of predicting the evolution of the news trend over time before a loss
of interest from social media users is observed. For this reason, firstly, we
will analyze the characteristics of several kinds of mathematical models
from literature to choose the most appropriate for our purposes, showing that a possible choice consists of a model of Ignorant - Spreader -
Exposed - Skeptic (IESZ) type. Then, we will describe a possible strategy
to compute optimized parameters for the chosen model starting from a
dataset of real data. Finally, by exploiting several case studies regarding
both true and fake news shared on X (Twitter) in the last years, we will
show that the proposed strategy is truly applicable to reality.

Keywords: Information diffusion · Epidemiological models · IESZ
model · Parameter estimation · Trust region methods

1 Introduction

The early years of the 21st century have been characterized by a deep change
in communication means. New tools, such as content sharing sites, social networks, forum, blogs, and many other typologies of websites, have completely
changed our social life, from the way of communicating to our way of establishing new relationships. This simplification in communications has led to a series
of economic advantages, since the buying and selling of products has been made
easier. However, also a rapid increase in the spread of false or only partially verified news has been observed. The latter phenomenon is also more worrying if it
is considered that there exists a strict link between public emotions and common

O. Gervasi et al. (Eds.): ICCSA 2025 Workshops, LNCS 15887, pp. 208–224, 2026.
https://doi.org/10.1007/978-3-031-97589-9_15

opinions regarding particular events, as e.g. the outcomes of many social or political events or unusual situations, and the dissemination of information related to them [45, 46]. For this reason, a proper way to analyze information diffusion is required. Several approaches are possible, from machine learning tools and statistical techniques [9, 35], to the use of mathematical models based on systems of differential equations. Among these types of models, epidemiological ones can be considered. Generally based on a system of ordinary differential equations (ODE_S), these models describe the evolution in time of epidemics. In fact, their application to the field of the analysis of information diffusion is due to the possibility of considering a news, that is spread on a social network, in the same way as a virus that affects the human population. Just as a virus spreads through encounters between individuals, information spreads when a social media user reads a piece of news and decides to share it. In [26, 32], D'Ambrosio et al. carried out an analysis of this kind considering two well known epidemiological models from literature, the Susceptible-Infectious-Recovered (SIR) and the Susceptible-Exposed-Infectious-Recovered ($SEIR$) model respectively, and linked their parameters to two indexes related to the grade of access to the web of a population and its ability to recognize fake news. In [7], Cardone et al. showed the importance of considering the age of individuals in the model formulation process, showing that the possibility that a news is spread is strictly related to the age of individuals who share it. Worthy of consideration is also the work carried out in [50] by Muhlmeyer et al. Here they show different possible mathematical models for studying the diffusion of information, presenting models suitable for the diffusion of fake news or highly debated news where two opposed groups of news spreaders are involved in the process of news sharing, or for situations in which there is first of all an initial interest in the news, then a phase when the news is in trend and popular, and a final phase in which there is a loss of interest in this news. Note that, since the scope of these kind of analyses is the description of real case studies, it is necessary to built a dataset by extracting data from a certain social network. However, this action is not trivial and can led to errors in the row data extracted. To take in consideration the noise in the data, stochastic models can be considered [50]. In particular, more details regarding stochastic differential equations can be found in [5, 11, 14, 25, 27–31, 33, 36]. Furthermore, the popularity of a news does not only depend on how many people are interested in it, but also by whom it is shared. If the person sharing the news in question is famous, the probability that this news will be seen by a large number of people is undoubtedly greater. For this reason, several studies related to the analysis of the information diffusion through mathematical models also require an accurate study of the main characteristics of the social network where the news is spread. In particular, these studies make use of graph theory and the possible use of centrality measures of a graph to determine the most influential users who can influence the outcome of the diffusion process of the considered news (see [4] for more details and references therein). Moreover, taking in consideration a possible spatial distribution of the social network users, also model based on partial differential equations (PDE_S) can be employed [55].

Researches in this field, however, is widespread. Epidemiological models, in fact, are characterized by positive solution, and by some invariant quantities, as for e.g. equilibrium points. For this reason, it is fundamental to apply proper numerical methods. For example, recent works in which a description of numerical methods able to preserve positivity and invariant quantities of ODE_S or PDE_S based models are [3,8,15,16,37–43]. Furthermore, in the specific case where models involving PDE_S are considered, it is important to know how to handle large-scale problems during the model resolution phase. In this sense, there are countless works in the literature in which numerical techniques for this kind of situations are presented. Among the most recent works, for example, we can mention [1,2,6,17,21,23,24,44,51].

According to the main features of the news, the most suitable typology of model should be considered. However, the only description of the evolution of the news popularity will not be useful in the long term. We are interested in predicting this evolution by observing the phenomenon just in the early phases of the news spread. An example of possible strategies to predict the evolution of news can be found in [10,20], where a strategy to predict the moment of maximum interest towards a news from social media users, starting from real data, is exploited. Certainly, one of the possible advantages of these studies is the possibility of blocking a fake news before it becomes popular. Moreover, also companies can benefit from these studies, since knowing the moment in which there is interest in their products can allow them to maximize earnings through a proper advertisement campaign. However, it is also true that news shared on a social network are not in trend for a long period of time, so in order to benefit from these kinds of analyses, it is also important to know in advance the possible total number of individuals that will share something related to the considered news after a short period of time since the start of the news spreading, and before the loss of interest towards it is observed. For this purposes, the aforementioned models are not suitable. Thus, in this work, we want to highlight the possible use of another mathematical model present in literature [47]: the Susceptible-Exposed-Infectious-Skeptic ($SEIZ$) model. To achieve this goal, starting from datasets of real data extracted from the social network X (Twitter), a parameter estimation phase (or data fitting phase), based on a trust-region method, will be employed.

The work will be organized as follows. *Section* 2, is dedicated to the description of the used mathematical model and its main features. *Section* 3 is dedicated to the experimental phase: in particular, we will describe both the strategy followed for the parameter estimation phase and the case studies being analyzed showing, to confirm the reliability of our strategies, the obtained numerical results. Finally, *Section* 4 will be dedicated to concluding remarks and future works.

2   Epidemiological Models for Information Diffusion

As above mentioned, a possible approach to analyze and possibly predict the spread out of information consists in the use of ODE_S based model of epidemiological type. These models, in particular, are of compartmental type, i.e. they divide the population in classes or compartments, and study their evolution using ordinary differential equations [48]. Certainly according to the features of the epidemic being described, several classes can be considered, as for example:

- *Susceptibles* $S(t)$, i.e. the individuals that can be infected by the virus;
- *Infectious* $I(t)$, i.e. the individuals affected by the disease;
- *Exposed* $E(t)$, i.e. the individuals that have been exposed to the disease but that are not yet infectious;
- *Recovered* $R(t)$, i.e. the individuals that recovered from the disease.

Actually in the epidemiological context many other classes can be considered as hospitalized, individuals in quarantine, dead, vaccinated and so on. As aforementioned, news can be analyzed in the same way of diseases: however, it should be taken in consideration that the two contexts are different and that the meaning given to the above mentioned classes slightly changes. Thus, following the terminology of [50], we will refer to the following classes during the model formulation process. We will refer to:

- *Ignorants*, to describe the counterpart of the susceptible class of epidemics, i.e. all the individuals that can see a news and share it;
- *Spreaders*, to describe the counterpart of infectious class, i.e. the individuals that share the news;
- *Recovered* to describe individuals, that exactly as the Recovered of the epidemics, are no longer interested in the process being considered.

Moreover, in addition to these classes, new others can be introduced. For example, if the shared news is fake or related to an highly debated topic, it is reasonable to consider two classes of spreaders: one that shares the news and which is still addressed as the Spreader class and another class, the *Counter Spreader* class generally indicated with $C(t)$, of individuals that contrast the diffusion of news spread by spreaders by sharing news with the opposite content [50]. Using the above mentioned classes, the Ignorant-Spreader-Recovered (ISR) model [10,50] and the Ignorant-Spreader-Counter Spreader-Recovered (ISCR) model [50] can be formulated.

The ISR model can be formulated by considering that, when individuals of the ignorant class read a news shared by spreaders, they automatically believe in the news and decide to share it, while after a certain period of time, they will lose interest in the news, consequently transiting into the recovered class. These transitions, that happen respectively at rate β and γ and that are also influenced by the average number of connections κ among individuals, are summarized by the following graph (Fig. 1).

Specifically, the ISR model is formulated through the following system:

$$\begin{cases} I'(t) = -\beta\kappa I(t)S(t), \\ S'(t) = \beta\kappa I(t)S(t) - \gamma\kappa S(t)S(t), \\ R'(t) = \gamma\kappa S(t)S(t). \end{cases} \tag{1}$$

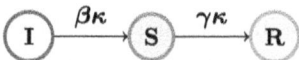

Fig. 1. Graph summarizes transitions among classes in the ISR model [50].

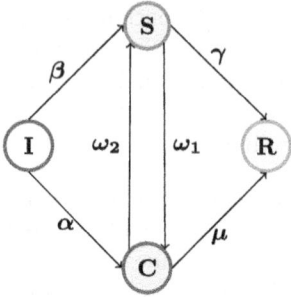

Fig. 2. Graph that shows possible transions among classes into the ISCR model [50].

Note that this is not the only way to formulate a model of ISR type for information diffusion. In fact, this model originally presented in [50] is specific for social media. Other possible formulations can be found also in [50] or in [32] and references therein.

On the contrary, the ISCR model that consider two opposed classes of individuals that share conflicting news items on the same topic, can be formulated as follows:

$$
\begin{cases}
I'(t) = -\beta\kappa I(t)S(t) - \alpha\kappa I(t)C(t), \\
S'(t) = \beta\kappa I(t)S(t) - (\omega_1 - \omega_2)\kappa S(t)C(t) - \gamma\kappa S(t)[S(t) + R(t)], \\
C'(t) = \alpha\kappa I(t)C(t) + (\omega_1 - \omega_2)\kappa S(t)C(t) - \mu\kappa C(t)[C(t) + R(t)], \\
R'(t) = \gamma\kappa S(t)[S(t) + R(t)] + \mu\kappa C(t)[C(t) + R(t)].
\end{cases}
\tag{2}
$$

Note that, in this case, apart from transitions from the ignorant class to the spreader or counter spreader class that respectively happen at rate β and α, and the corresponding transitions into the recovered class at rates γ and μ when a loss of interest in the news occurs, also other interactions are considered. In fact, parameters ω_1 and ω_2 that describe the transition rates from spreaders to counter spreaders class and vice versa have been introduced into the model formulation (Fig. 2).

Exhaustive examples of applications of these two models are given in [10, 50]. As can be seen by results described there, both the two models take in consideration a possible loss of interest by spreaders, or by counter spreaders when present, towards the news. So, the function that represents the Spreaders, is firstly an increasing functions, that at a certain point reaches a peak, before decreasing.

Although results described in these works are good, in some situations it can be more advantageous to analyze the spread of news only in the early phases of their spread. In fact, since we are at the beginning of the spread, it is reasonable

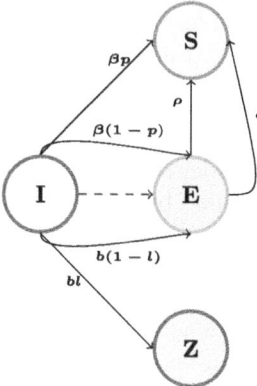

Fig. 3. Graph of the ISEZ model [47].

that the considered news is not well known. So, it could happen that not every social media user that reads it will immediately share something related to it. Moreover, it could also happen that some individuals will not show any particular reaction towards the news item. In this case, a more specific model can be adopted: the Ignorant-Exposed-Spreader-Skeptic (IESZ) model, also known in literature with the classical terminology of $SEIZ$ model. Described and analyzed in depth in [47] this model, born to describe information diffusion, provides a division of the population in four classes. Apart from Ignorant $(I(t))$ and Spreaders $(S(t))$ previously described, the classes of Exposed $(E(t))$ and Skeptic $(Z(t))$ are considered, and both refer to individuals who have seen a news but have not shared anything about it yet. However, in the model formulation, it is assumed that exposed believe in the news and so, sooner or later, will share something related to it, while skeptic have not showed any interest towards the news, choosing to ignore it. Note that, skeptic individuals seem to be similar to the recovered of the previous two models, however they have a completely different role. In fact, they have never had any reaction towards a certain news, while recovered believed in the news and shared it, before loosing interest. By indicating with N the total number of individuals of the population, computed as the sum of all the individuals of the four compartments in which it has been divided, the IESZ model reads as follows:

$$\begin{cases} I'(t) = -\beta I(t)\frac{S(t)}{N} - bI(t)\frac{Z(t)}{N}, \\ E'(t) = (1-p)\beta I(t)\frac{S(t)}{N} + (1-l)bI(t)\frac{Z(t)}{N} - \rho E(t)\frac{S(t)}{N} - \epsilon E(t), \\ S'(t) = p\beta I(t)\frac{S(t)}{N} + \rho E(t)\frac{S(t)}{N} + \epsilon E(t), \\ Z'(t) = lbI(t)\frac{Z(t)}{N}. \end{cases} \tag{3}$$

Transitions between different classes of the population are illustrated by the graph in Fig. 3.

As it can be seen from the model formulation in (3), a major number of parameters is involved. In particular, we take:

- β, the transition rate from the ignorant class to the spreader class: in this case, when individuals of the ignorant class read a news, spread by a spreader, they can transit into the spreader class with probability p, or into the exposed class, if they believe in the news but don't share anything, with probability $1 - p$.
- b, the transition rate from the ignorant class to the skeptic class. As it happens for transitions from the ignorant class to the spreader class, it can happen that ignorant individuals decide to ignore the news, transiting into the skeptic class with probability l, or they can be affected by it, transiting into the exposed class with probability $1 - l$. Note that, once in the exposed class, it is not possible to come back into the skeptic compartment anymore, since the only allowed transition is into the spreader class.
- ρ, the contact rate between an exposed individual and a spreader individual. This parameter is used to rule all the transitions from the exposed class to the spreader class, that happen when exposed individuals get in contact with news shared by spreaders, such that they directly transit into the spreader class.
- ϵ, the transition rate from the exposed class to the spreader class. Observe that, contrary to ρ, the part of exposed population that transits into the spreader class at rate ϵ is the one that transits there after a period of uncertainty relating to whether or not to believe the considered news. In this case, the exposed are not further influenced by news spread by spreaders.

In particular, in the IESZ model graph, there is a dotted line that describes the passage between classes of ignorant and exposed. This is due to the fact that individuals from the ignorant class can pass into the exposed class either because of the influence of a spreader or because, even if initially skeptical, they have then believed in the news.

Note that, from a modeling point of view, the above described IESZ model is suitable to analyze the initial phase of news spread, particularly if we want to predict the total number of individuals interested in the news after a short period of time since the beginning of its spread. Moreover, it should be noticed that, if we want to analyze real case studies, we need data to be used for the model validation phase. However, in this case, it is not possible to extract data regarding the initial number of exposed or skeptic, since it is not known who, of all the possible users interested by the news, has read it and decided to ignore it, or that has believed in it but without sharing anything yet. For this reason, a data fitting phase involving not only model parameters but also the initial conditions of the problem, is essential to obtain good results, as we will show in the next Section.

3   Parameter Estimation and Numerical Results

As previously anticipated, in order to analyze the process of information spread considering real case studies using the IESZ model, we need both to extract real data from a chosen social network and an adequate parameter estimation phase. Several techniques are available for these kinds of problems. For example, in [49], Physics Informed Neural Network (PINN) are used to optimize parameters involved into a model of SIR type (see also [54] for other possible uses of PINN). In [53] a parameter estimation phase is carried out solving a nonlinear least squares problem. Moreover, also in [47], a similar approach is presented. The authors, there, used the IESZ model to analyze the spread of a fake news, spread on X (Twitter) with the hashtag #DCBlackout, related to possible interruption of communications in the city of Washington D.C on June 1st, 2020 due to the Black Lives Matter movement. In particular, the IESZ model is employed using a parameter estimation strategy that allows to compute optimized parameters, such that the error between real data and the ones computed using the ODE_S solvers routine of MATLAB is minimum. However, in the case study presented in literature, all data are used for the fitting phase. So, in that case, it is possible just to describe the evolution of a news over time, but it is not possible to have predictions. For this reason, we follow two strategies. First of all we check that the IESZ model is suitable for describing information diffusion, employing it to describe the news trend of different case studies, other than the already mentioned #DCBlackout. Then, we will try to carry out the parameter estimation phase using just few data to compute optimized parameters, trying to make real predictions, and employing the remaining part of the dataset just to check if the outcomes are good or if they need to be improved. Note also that in our numerical experiments the IESZ model will be solved using the MATLAB ODE_S solver routine $ode45$, since we want to focus on the parameter estimation phase. Nevertheless, also other numerical methods can be used, as e.g. structure-preserving methods with good stability properties presented in [18, 19, 22, 25] and reference therein.

3.1   Case Studies and Dataset Construction Process

For our purposes, firstly, we need to extract data from a social network and build datasets. Using tools as the *Twitter Developer Option* (www.developer.twitter.com) or the Python data scraper *Tweepy* (https://docs.tweepy.org/en/latest/), it has been possible to collect data from the social network X (Twitter) regarding news spread during the period 2020–2022. In particular, data extracted consist of qualitative information regarding a news spread with a certain hashtag: among these, the ID of users who shared a tweet, the date when they tweeted, the text of the tweet they shared. Then, in order to organize data in such a way that the acquired information can be used for our aims, we build our datasets, by modifying the algorithm construction process described in [10], where a similar process has been made to employ a model of ISR type, and organizing data in minutes.

The following case studies will be taken in considerations:

- #DCBlackout: the already mentioned fake news regarding possible trubles due to Black Lives Matter movement [47];
- #NoVaxDjokovic: fake news regarding a declaration of a "No-Vax" position by the serbian tennis player Novak Djokovic, after his refusal of getting vaccinated against the COVID-19 virus in order to play the Australian Open 2022 tennis tournament [12];
- #NovakDjokovic: true pieces of news spread on X with this hashtag after the 2022 edition of the Australian Open tennis tournament regarding the tennis player Novak Djokovic;
- #Macron: true news spread after Emmanuel Macron was reelected President of France in 2022. Note that tweets regarding this piece of news have also been collected by searching shared tweets containing the phrase "*Emmanuel Macron réélù Président de la République*".

Observe that since the model we want to employ is of IESZ type, where we consider classes of individuals that have seen a news and have been possibly influenced by it but that have not shared anything yet, it is possible to determine numerically data only for the Spreader class. Data for all the other classes, especially at the starting time of the observation of the phenomenon, have to be optimized as well as the model parameters, as we will show in the next section.

3.2   Parameter Estimation

As anticipated, we will carry out the phase of numerical experiments twice, following two different strategies. In particular:

- *first strategy*: it consists of using the entire dataset for parameter estimation. In this way, the reliability of the IESZ model for describing different kinds of news will be tested. We will make simulations also using the #DCBlackout news. In fact, this piece of news has already been analyzed in [47]. However, tweets can be modified or removed. So, it is reasonable to think that our dataset is slightly different from the one used in [47], due to the fact that our data were extracted after a year since that work had been released.
- *second strategy*: it consists of using just a part of the dataset to compute optimized parameters. After that, solving again the model with them, the accuracy of our predictions will be checked.

Note that, during both the two numerical experiments, all the model parameters and the initial values for ignorants I_0, exposed E_0 and skeptics Z_0 will be optimized. The initial value for spreaders, on the contrary, is taken from the initial dataset, while for the population size, which is assumed as constant in the model, a simplifying assumption is made. We will assume it equal, during the entire period of the observation of the phenomenon, to the sum of the initial values of all the involved classes.

Regarding the parameter estimation process, it is carried out by solving a nonlinear least squares problem. In fact, we compute the set of optimized parameters as the value that minimizes the following function:

$$f(param) = \sum_{j=1}^{n}(S_j - S_{data}(t_j))^2, \tag{4}$$

where $param$ is a vector containing the parameters to be optimized, S_j is the number of spreaders at time t_j computed by solving the IESZ model, while $S_{data}(t_j)$ is the corresponding value for spreaders taken from the dataset. From an implementation point of view, the fitting phase will be carried out using the MATLAB built in function $lsqnonlin$. It solves nonlinear least squares problems allowing users to choose two kind of algorithms: the $Levemberg\text{-}Marquardt$ algorithm and the $trust\text{-}region\text{-}reflective$ algorithm. In particular, we will use the second one. This algorithm, in fact, permits to find the set of parameters that minimizes a function within a certain region of the space where parameters are defined (see [52] for more details). In this way, it allows to choose a lower and an upper bound for the parameters to be optimized, giving us the possibility to avoid meaningless physical situations in which negative parameters or population values are obtained.

3.3 Numerical Results

Table 1. Optimized parameters and initial conditions for the IESZ model, obtained when all data are used for the fitting phase.

News	β	b	p	l	ρ	ϵ	$I0$	$E0$	$Z0$
#DCBlackout	0.9451	0.36684	0.96331	0.96309	0.010493	0.031694	300000	2222	90775
#NoVaxDjokovic	0.26669	0.093984	0.7038	0.97469	0.01	0.01	186850	100	35786
#NovakDjokovic	0.10003	0.019876	0.012391	0.0123981	0.010017	0.01010	132240	809	215610
#Macron		0.18513	0.900036	0.29056	1	0.024875	0.025308	110910	2803	295630

Table 2. Optimized parameters and initial conditions for the IESZ model, obtained few data are used for the fitting phase.

News	β	b	p	l	ρ	ϵ	$I0$	$E0$	$Z0$
#DCBlackout	0.59597	0.66732	0.99979	0.94191	0.010003	0.043369	210310	1491	4013
#NoVaxDjokovic	0.33615	0.25249	0.011234	0.9665	0.11749	0.033041	153950	197	1000
#NovakDjokovic	0.13323	0.073073	0.011967	0.99924	0.5886	0.010044	144140	465	9197
#Macron		0.99999	0.93747	1	1	0.010427	0.017207	200580	1391	24163

Results regarding the first strategy are summarized in Table 1 and displayed in Fig. 4, while results regarding the second strategy are summarized in Table 2 and displayed in Fig. 5.

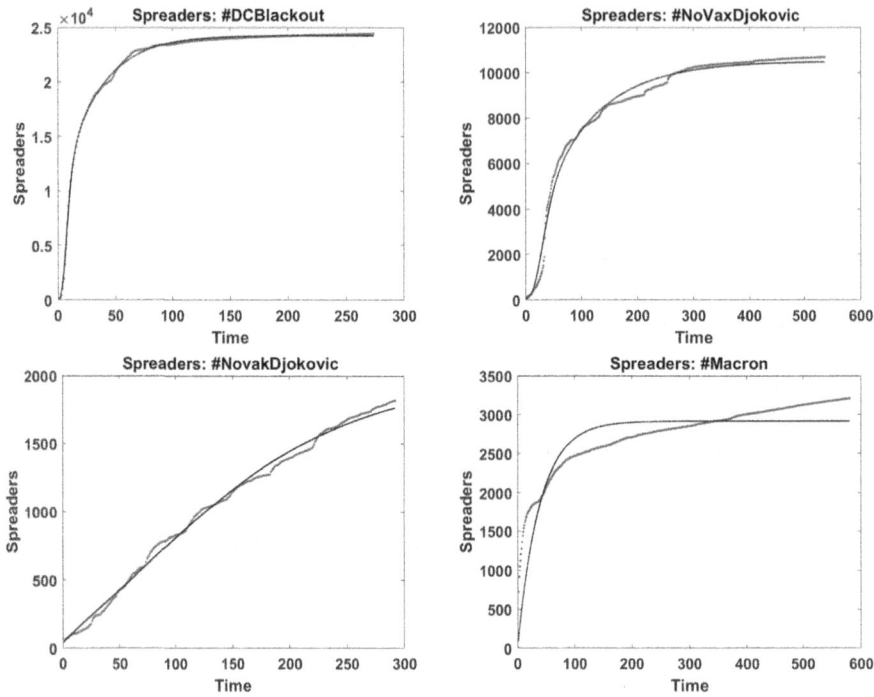

Fig. 4. Time evolution of news trend for all the case studies under consideration. Note *: data used for the fitting phase; -: estimated number of spreaders (Color figure online)

Observing results obtained using all data for the parameters estimation, it can be seen that the IESZ model is useful to describe the evolution of news spread over time, since the fashion of the curve of data extracted from X is similar, or in some cases even overlying, the one obtained solving the problem with the MATLAB ODE_S solver routine *ode45*. However, also the second strategy seem to be applicable. Even if there is an underestimation in the number of spreaders, due to oscillations and inaccuracies of the dataset caused by the fact that we are not analyzing the text of extracted tweets but we only consider the presence in them of the hashtag linked to the news, the estimated curve is similar to the real one. Note that in particular for fake news, as the one spread with hashtag #NoVaxDjokovic, the underestimation is more evident, despite the great number of data (the green *) used for the fitting phase. This is explainable by considering that this fake news is linked to a relevant figure of a worldwide followed sport. So, it is reasonable that in the first phases of the diffusion of the news, the number of spreaders rises quickly, thanks also to external influences as televisions or newspapers that publish news related to the figure of the tennis player, creating hype and increasing possible fake news regarding his opinion on vaccines. Nevertheless, in all the analyzed cases, the trend of the data is still respected.

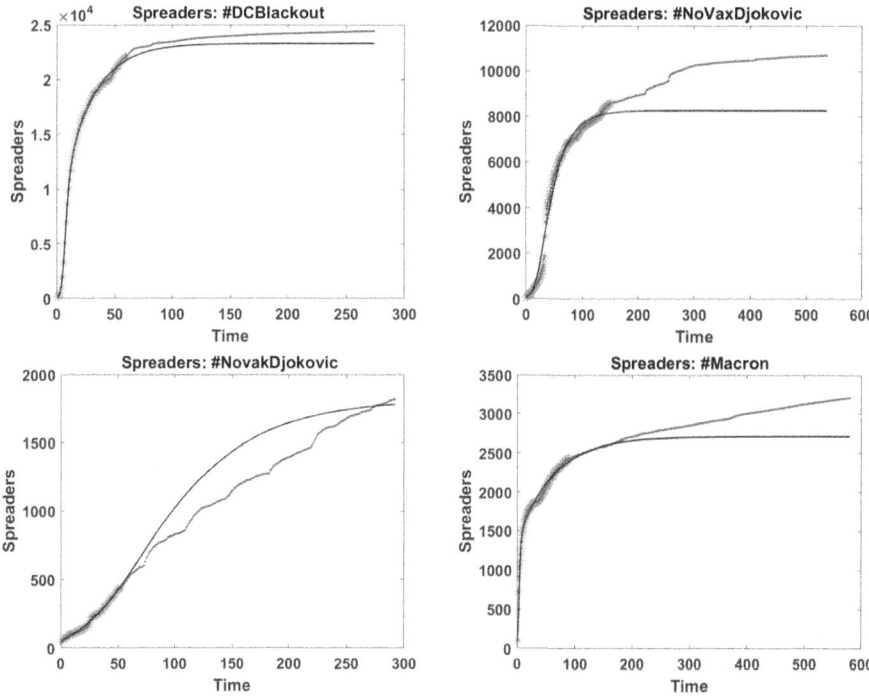

Fig. 5. Time evolution of news trend for all the case studies under consideration. Note ⋅ : data used for the fitting phase •: data used for predictions; -: estimated number of spreaders (Color figure online)

Table 3. Relative errors in norm two on spreaders obtained employing the second strategy for parameter estimation for all the news items

News	Error
#DCBlackout	0.0412
#NoVaxDjokovic	0.1831
#NovakDjokovic	0.1519
#Macron	0.1073

To have a quantitative representation of the performance of this second strategy, Table 3 can be considered, where for each of the news items, the value in norm two of the relative error computed on all the available data for spreaders is reported.

As it can be observed, this strategy can truly be used to describe the initial phase of a news spread, both in the case of true or fake news. This feature is not trivial: in fact, before the news is spread and analyzed by experts, we do not know if it is real or not, so at least in this initial phase of the spread, it is

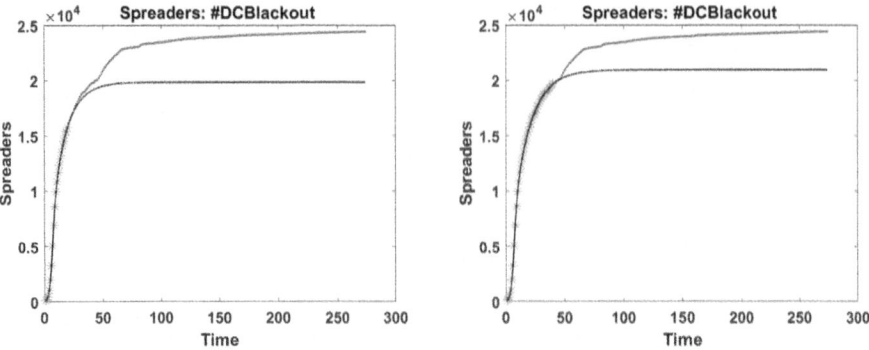

Fig. 6. Tests of parameter estimation carried out on the #DCBlackout news using data related to, respectively, 20 and 40 instants of time.

fundamental to model the phenomenon of dissemination of information by using an efficient model that can be adapted whatever type of news is considered.

Note, also, that in the case in which the second strategy is used, it becomes essential to determine the minimum number of data from the dataset to be employed for parameter estimation. For the news being analyzed, in fact, we use a number of data variable from 25 to 150 instants of time, corresponding to values from 10% to 30% of the dataset. Specifically, the minimum number of data that allows us to obtain good predictions, can be determined employing several approaches. In particular, we decided to avoid using a greater number of values for a simple reason. Since we are interested in predictions, it would not be very useful to optimize parameters using a very large part of the dataset. Moreover, in a real scenario, we are interested in predicting the evolution of a news before it is spread, so it is very probable that we will not have much time to observe it and extract data. Thus, starting from available dataset, we determined the number of data to be used for parameter estimation empirically. As example, consider Fig. 6, where taking into account the dataset related to the #DCBlackout news, two more tests of parameter estimation are exploited using respectively data related to 20 and 40 instants of time. In both these two cases, a stronger underestimation of the total number of spreaders can be observed in comparison to the results obtained using 60 instants of time, as showed in the first figure of Fig. 5.

4   Conclusions and Future Works

In this paper a possible use of a mathematical epidemiological model to describe information diffusion on social media has been analyzed. We have showed that the Ignorant-Exposed-Spreader-Skeptic model, when combined with a proper parameter estimation phase, can be applicable to describe the initial phase of the spread of a news, independently if true or false, before that a loss of interest of users towards it is observed.

Many research developments relating to this topic are possible. Certainly, an analysis of the type of tweets collected could lead to a better construction of the dataset and therefore to greater regularity in the data used for fitting. Furthermore, it would be interesting to carry out a description of the phenomenon in which the model presented here is used to describe what happens in the early stages of information diffusion, while a second model is used to describe any future developments. Note, also, that to solve the ODE_S system we employed the MATLAB routine $ode45$, because we want to focus on the parameter estimation strategy. However, several efficient numerical methods for this kind of systems are available in literature [13, 18, 22, 34], so possible developments can consist in the implementation of the methods there described.

Acknowledgments. The authors are members of the research group GNCS-INdAM. This work has been supported by GNCS–INdAM projects and by the Italian Ministry of University and Research (MUR), through the PRIN PNRR 2022 project BAT-MEN (P20228C2PP, CUP: F53D23010020001).

Disclosure of Interests. The authors have no competing interests to declare that are relevant to the content of this article.

References

1. Aceto, L., Conte, D., Pagano, G.: On a generalization of time-accurate and highly-stable explicit operators for stiff problems. Appl. Numer. Math. **200**, 2–17 (2024). https://doi.org/10.1016/j.apnum.2023.04.001
2. Aceto, L., Conte, D., Pagano, G.: Modified TASE Runge-Kutta methods for integrating stiff differential equations. SIAM J. Sci. Comput. **47**(3), A1652–A1680 (2025). https://doi.org/10.1137/24M1667336
3. Amodio, P., Brugnano, L., Frasca-Caccia, G., Iavernaro, F.: Arbitrarily high-order energy-conserving methods for Hamiltonian problems with quadratic holonomic constraints. J. Comput. Math. **42**(4), 1145–1171 (2024). https://doi.org/10.4208/jcm.2301-m2022-0065
4. Benzi, M., Boito, P.: Matrix functions in network analysis. GAMM-Mitteilungen **43**(3), e202000012 (2020). https://doi.org/10.1002/gamm.202000012
5. Buckwar, E., D'Ambrosio, R.: Exponential mean-square stability properties of stochastic linear multistep methods. Adv. Comput. Math. **47**(4), 1–14 (2021). https://doi.org/10.1007/s10444-021-09879-2
6. Cardone, A., Conte, D., Paternoster, B.: Stability of two-step spline collocation methods for initial value problems for fractional differential equations. Commun. Nonlinear Sci. Numer. Simul. **115**, 106726 (2022). https://doi.org/10.1016/j.cnsns.2022.106726
7. Cardone, A., Diaz de Alba, P., Paternoster, B.: Analytical properties and numerical preservation of an age-group susceptible-infected-recovered model: application to the diffusion of information. J. Comput. Nonlinear Dyn. **19**(6), 061006 (2024). https://doi.org/10.1115/1.4065437
8. Cardone, A., Frasca-Caccia, G.: Numerical conservation laws of time fractional diffusion PDEs. Fract. Calc. Appl. Anal. **25**(4), 1459–1483 (2022). https://doi.org/10.1007/s13540-022-00059-7

9. Casillo, M., Colace, F., Conte, D., De Santo, M., Lombardi, M., Mottola, S., San-taniello, D.: A multi-feature Bayesian approach for fake news detection. In: Chellappan, S., Choo, K.-K.R., Phan, N.H. (eds.) CSoNet 2020. LNCS, vol. 12575, pp. 333–344. Springer, Cham (2020). https://doi.org/10.1007/978-3-030-66046-8_27

10. Castiello, M., Conte, D., Iscaro, S.: Using epidemiological models to predict the spread of information on Twitter. Algorithms **16**(8), 391 (2023). https://doi.org/10.3390/a16080391

11. Citro, V., D'Ambrosio, R.: Long-term analysis of stochastic theta-methods for damped stochastic oscillators. Appl. Numer. Math. **150**, 18–26 (2020). https://doi.org/10.1016/j.apnum.2019.08.011

12. CNN (Cable News Network). https://edition.cnn.com/2022/01/20/sport/djokovic-serbia-national-hero-intl-spt/index.html. Accessed 1 Mar 2025

13. Conte, D., D'Ambrosio, R., Jackiewicz, Z.: Two-step Runge-Kutta methods with quadratic stability functions. J. Sci. Comput. **2**, 191–218 (2010). https://doi.org/10.1007/s10915-010-9378-x

14. Conte, D., D'Ambrosio, R., Paternoster, B.: Improved θ-methods for stochastic Volterra integral equations. Commun. Nonlinear Sci. Numer. Simul. **93**, 105528 (2021). https://doi.org/10.1016/j.cnsns.2020.105528

15. Conte, D., Frasca-Caccia, G.: Exponentially fitted methods that preserve conservation laws. Commun. Nonlinear Sci. Numer. Simul. **109**, 106334 (2022). https://doi.org/10.1016/j.cnsns.2022.106334

16. Conte, D., Frasca-Caccia, G.: Exponentially fitted methods with a local energy conservation law. Adv. Comput. Math. **49**(4), 49 (2023). https://doi.org/10.1007/s10444-023-10049-9

17. Conte, D., González-Pinto, S., Hernández-Abreu, D., Pagano, G.: On approximate matrix factorization and TASE W-methods for the time integration of parabolic partial differential equations. J. Sci. Comput. **100**(2), 34 (2024). https://doi.org/10.1007/s10915-024-02579-1

18. Conte, D., Guarino, N., Pagano, G., Paternoster, B.: Positivity-preserving and elementary stable nonstandard method for a COVID-19 SIR model. Dolomites Res. Notes Approx. **15**(5), 65–77 (2022). https://doi.org/10.14658/pupj-drna-2022-5-7

19. Conte, D., Guarino, N., Pagano, G., Paternoster, B.: On the advantages of non-standard finite difference discretizations for differential problems. Numer. Anal. Appl. **15**(3), 219–235 (2022). https://doi.org/10.1134/S1995423922030041

20. Conte,D., Iscaro,S., Pagano,G., Paternoster,B.: Adapted numerical modeling for fake news diffusion on social networks. Submitted

21. Conte, D., Martin-Vaquero, J., Pagano, G., Paternoster, B.: Stability theory of TASE–Runge–Kutta methods with inexact Jacobian. SIAM J. Sci. Comput. **46**(6), A3628–A3657 (2024). https://doi.org/10.1137/24M1631869

22. Conte, D., Pagano, G., Paternoster, B.: Nonstandard finite differences numerical methods for a vegetation reaction–diffusion model. J. Comput. Appl. Math. **419**, 114790 (2023). https://doi.org/10.1016/j.cam.2022.114790

23. Conte, D., Pagano, G., Paternoster, B.: Two-step peer methods with equation-dependent coefficients. Comput. Appl. Math. **41**(4), 140 (2022). https://doi.org/10.1007/s40314-022-01844-z

24. Conte, D., Pagano, G., Paternoster, B.: Time-accurate and highly-stable explicit peer methods for stiff differential problems. Commun. Nonlinear Sci. Numer. Simul. **119**, 107136 (2023). https://doi.org/10.1016/j.cnsns.2023.107136

25. D'Ambrosio, R.: Numerical Approximation of Ordinary Differential Problems: From Deterministic to Stochastic Numerical Methods. Springer (2023). https://doi.org/10.1007/978-3-031-31343-1

26. D'Ambrosio, R., Díaz de Alba, P., Giordano, G., Paternoster, B.: A modified SEIR model: stiffness analysis and application to the diffusion of fake news. In: Gervasi, O., Murgante, B., Hendrix, E.M.T., Taniar, D., Apduhan, B.O. (eds.) ICCSA, 90-103, Springer International Publishing (2022). https://doi.org/10.1007/978-3-031-10522-7_7

27. D'Ambrosio, R., Di Giovacchino, S.: Mean-square contractivity of stochastic theta-methods. Comm. Nonlin. Sci. Numer. Simul. **96**, 105671 (2021). https://doi.org/10.1016/j.cnsns.2020.105671

28. D'Ambrosio, R., Di Giovacchino, S.: Nonlinear stability issues for stochastic Runge-Kutta methods. Comm. Nonlin. Sci. Numer. Simul. **94**, 105549 (2021). https://doi.org/10.1016/j.cnsns.2020.105549

29. D'Ambrosio, R., Di Giovacchino, S.: Strong backward error analysis of symplectic integrators for stochastic Hamiltonian systems. Appl. Math. Comput. **467**, 128488 (2024). https://doi.org/10.1016/j.amc.2023.128488

30. D'Ambrosio, R., Di Giovacchino, S.: Long-term analysis of stochastic Hamiltonian systems under time discretizations. SIAM J. Sci. Comput. **45**(2), A257–A288 (2023). https://doi.org/10.1137/21M1458612

31. D'Ambrosio, R., Di Giovacchino, S.: Numerical conservation issues for the stochastic Korteweg-de Vries equation. J. Comput. Appl. Math. **424**, 114967 (2023). https://doi.org/10.1016/j.cam.2022.114967

32. D'Ambrosio, R., Giordano, G., Mottola, S., Paternoster, B.: Stiffness analysis to predict the spread out of fake information. Future Internet **13**(9), 222 (2021). https://doi.org/10.3390/fi13090222

33. D'Ambrosio, R., Giordano, G., Paternoster, B., Ventola, A.: Perturbative analysis of stochastic Hamiltonian problems under time discretizations. Appl. Math. Lett. **120**, 107223 (2021). https://doi.org/10.1016/j.aml.2021.107223

34. D'Ambrosio, R., Izzo, G., Jackiewicz, Z.: Search for highly stable two-step Runge-Kutta methods for ODEs. Appl. Numer. Math. **62**(10), 1361–1379 (2012). https://doi.org/10.1016/j.apnum.2012.06.012

35. Giordano, G., Mottola, S., Paternoster, B.: A short review of some mathematical methods to detect fake news. Circuits Syst. Signal Process **14**, 255–265 (2020). https://doi.org/10.46300/9106.2020.14.37

36. D'Ambrosio, R., Paternoster, B.: Multivalue collocation methods free from order reduction. J. Comput. Appl. Math. **387**, 112515 (2021). https://doi.org/10.1016/j.cam.2019.112515

37. Frasca-Caccia, G.: Finite difference schemes with non polynomial local conservation laws. J. Comput. Appl. Math. **458**, 116330 (2025). https://doi.org/10.1016/j.cam.2024.116330

38. Frasca-Caccia, G., Hydon, P.E.: A new technique for preserving conservation laws. Found. Comput. Math. **22**(2), 477–506 (2022). https://doi.org/10.1007/s10208-021-09511-1

39. Frasca-Caccia, G., Hydon, P.E.: Simple bespoke preservation of two conservation laws. IMA J. Numer. Anal. **40**(2), 1294–1329 (2020). https://doi.org/10.1093/imanum/dry087

40. Frasca-Caccia, G., Hydon, P.E.: Numerical preservation of multiple local conservation laws. Appl. Math. Comput. **403**, 126203 (2021). https://doi.org/10.1016/j.amc.2021.126203

41. Frasca-Caccia, G., Hydon, P.E.: Locally conservative finite difference schemes for the modified KdV equation. J. Comput. Dyn. **6**(2), 307–323 (2019). https://doi.org/10.3934/jcd.2019015

42. Frasca-Caccia, G., Singh, P.: Optimal parameters for numerical solvers of PDEs. J. Sci. Comput. **97**(1), 11 (2023). https://doi.org/10.1007/s10915-023-02324-0

43. Frasca-Caccia, G., Valentino, C., Colace, F., Conte, D.: An overview of differential models for corrosion of cultural heritage artefacts. Math. Model. Nat. Phenom. **18**, 27 (2023). https://doi.org/10.1051/mmnp/2023031

44. González-Pinto, S., Hernández-Abreu, D., Pagano, G., Pérez-Rodríguez, S.: Generalized TASE-RK methods for stiff problems. Appl. Numer. Math. **188**, 129–145 (2023). https://doi.org/10.1016/j.apnum.2023.03.007

45. Lazer, D., et al.: The science of fake news. Science **359**(6380), 1094–1096 (2018). https://doi.org/10.1126/science.aao2998

46. Mahdikhani, M.: Predicting the popularity of tweets by analyzing public opinion and emotions in different stages of Covid-19 pandemic. Int. J. Inf. Manage. Data Insights **2**(1), 100053 (2022). https://doi.org/10.1016/j.jjimei.2021.100053

47. Maleki, M., Mead, E., Arani, M., Agarwal, N.: Using an epidemiological model to study the spread of misinformation during the black lives matter movement. Preprint arXiv:2103.12191 (2021). https://doi.org/10.48550/arXiv.2103.12191

48. Martcheva, M.: An Introduction to Mathematical Epidemiology. TAM, vol. 61. Springer, Boston, MA (2015). https://doi.org/10.1007/978-1-4899-7612-3

49. Millevoi, C., Pasetto, D., Ferronato, M.: A physics-informed neural network approach for compartmental epidemiological models. PLoS Comput. Biol. **20**(9),e1012387 (2024). https://doi.org/10.1371/journal.pcbi.1012387

50. Muhlmeyer, M., Agarwal, S.: Information Spread in a Social Media Age: Modeling and Control. CRC Press (2021). https://doi.org/10.1201/9780429263842

51. Pagano, G.: Stabilized explicit peer methods with parallelism across the stages for stiff problems. Appl. Numer. Math. **207**, 156–173 (2025). https://doi.org/10.1016/j.apnum.2024.08.023

52. Quarteroni, A., Saleri, F., Gervasio, P.: Metodi numerici per problemi ai limiti stazionari ed evolutivi. In: Calcolo Scientifico. U, vol. 105, pp. 373–433. Springer, Milano (2017). https://doi.org/10.1007/978-88-470-3953-7_9

53. Treibert, S. M.: Mathematical Modelling and Nonstandard Schemes for the Corona Virus Pandemic. Springer Spektrum (2021). https://doi.org/10.1007/978-3-658-35932-4

54. Valentino, C., Pagano, G., Conte, D., Paternoster, B., Colace, F., Casillo, M.: Step-by-step time discrete physics-informed neural networks with application to a sustainability PDE model. Math. Comput. Simul. **230**, 541–558 (2025). https://doi.org/10.1016/j.matcom.2024.10.043

55. Wang, H., Wang, F., Xu, K.: Modeling information diffusion in online social networks with partial differential equations, vol. 7. Springer Nature (2020). https://doi.org/10.1007/978-3-030-38852-2

Discrete Gradient θ-Methods for Port-Hamiltonian Systems

Raffaele D'Ambrosio$^{(\boxtimes)}$ and Simone Di Donato

Department of Information Engineering and Computer Science and Mathematics,
University of L'Aquila, Via Vetoio, Loc. Coppito - 67100, L'Aquila (AQ), Italy
raffaele.dambrosio@univaq.it, simone.didonato@student.univaq.it

Abstract. The paper is focused on the geometric numerical integration of port-Hamiltonian problems, via discrete gradient θ-methods. The ability of this method to retain inherent dissipativity properties of the exact dynamics is considered, as well as the stability properties of the numerical scheme with respect to a test problem based on a controlled pendulum are treated. The analysis is also equipped by selected numerical experiments.

Keywords: Port-Hamiltonian problems · Discrete gradient method · Geometric numerical integration

1 Introduction

Geometric numerical integration is nowadays a well established paradigm in Numerical Analysis, aiming to preserve qualitative and quantitative aspects of the exact dynamics along its discretization via suitable numerical schemes.

As highlighted, for instance, in [23], the denomination *geometric numerical integration* traces the vision of geometry given by Felix Klein in his outstanding Erlangen program, where he describes geometry as the study of invariants under suitable transformations. Accordingly, a numerical methods is geometric when it retains relevant properties of a dynamical system along the numerical dynamics. Building blocks of geometric numerical integration have been first placed in the scientific literature for structure-preservation in the framework of Hamiltonian problems, then conveyed to the numerical treament of evolutive problems of various kind. For a general treatment of geometric numerical methods a non-exhaustive list of relevant references is given, for instance, by [3, 4, 6, 23, 37, 40, 41, 43, 45, 46, 50] and references therein.

Out of Runge-Kutta methods, nearly-conserving linear multistep methods exhibiting excellent long-time behaviors have been developed [34, 36, 37], as well as a theory of nearly-preserving multivalue methods [9, 10, 29, 30] and energy-preserving numerical integrators (see, for instance, [4, 14] and references therein). Principles of geometric numerical integration for stochastic differential equations have also been treated in recent scientific literature, for instance in the

O. Gervasi et al. (Eds.): ICCSA 2025 Workshops, LNCS 15887, pp. 225–236, 2026.
https://doi.org/10.1007/978-3-031-97589-9_16

conservation of invariance laws characteristic properties of stochastic oscillators [8,16,26,28,31,35,51,52,56], in nonlinear SDEs with one-sided Lipschitz drift leading to mean-square contractive dynamics [5,24,25,38], in stochastic Hamiltonian and Poisson problems [2,7,15,17,18,27,32,39,44,48,49,53] and related issues.

In this paper, we aim to focus our attention on some aspects regarding the geometric numerical integration of port-Hamiltonian problems, that are controlled systems of ODEs of fundamental importance in several fields of applications: for instance, we refer to [11,47,55,57] and references therein. As well highlighted, for instance, in [54], port-Hamiltonian dynamics is an extension of Hamiltonian canonical approach to motion, combined with the network point of view, useful in modelling and simulation of complex systems. Moreover, port-Hamiltonian systems are able to convey the interaction with their environment through specific ports, as well as to describe energy dissipation.

Under a more specific numerical point of view, it is worth preserving the peculiar dissipativity features characterizing port-Hamiltonian systems along their numerical discretization with accuracy. In particular, inspired by [13], this paper pursues the aim to study when discrete gradient θ-methods are able to retain inherent properties of the dynamics of systems with dissipation in the Hamiltonian, together with the stability properties of the numerical scheme with respect to a test problem based on a controlled pendulum. Moreover, selected numerical experiments complement the theoretical investigation.

2   Basics on Port-Hamiltonian Systems

A port-Hamiltonian problem is modelled by the following system of ODEs:

$$
\begin{aligned}
\dot{x} &= B(x)\nabla H(x) + G(x)u, \\
x(0) &= x_0, \\
y &= G(x)^{\mathsf{T}}\nabla H(x),
\end{aligned}
\tag{1}
$$

having denoted by $x \in \mathbb{R}^n$ the state variable of the system, $u \in \mathbb{R}^m$ the input and $y \in \mathbb{R}^m$ the output. The matrix $B(x)$ is assumed to be skew-symmetric and $H(x)$ is the Hamiltonian function of the system.

Problem (1) falls in the more general framework of controlled systems of ODEs

$$
\begin{aligned}
\dot{x} &= f(x,u), \\
y &= h(x),
\end{aligned}
\tag{2}
$$

whose vector field $f : \mathbb{R}^n \times \mathbb{R}^m \to \mathbb{R}^n$ is supposed to be locally Lipschitz. A relevant property for problem (2) is given by its *passivity*, occurring if there exists a continuously differentiable positive semidefinite function $V(x)$ such that

$$
u^{\mathsf{T}}y \geq \nabla V(x)^{\mathsf{T}}f(x,u),
\tag{3}
$$

for any $(x,u) \in \mathbb{R}^n \times \mathbb{R}^m$. The function $V(x)$ is denoted as *storage function*. If (3) is satisfied as an equality, the system is said to be *lossless*, i.e., $u^{\mathsf{T}}y = \dot{V}$.

We observe that the condition of passivity can be recast in integral form. Indeed, side-by-side integrating Equation (3) yields

$$\langle y, u \rangle_{L^2} \geq V(t) - V(0),$$

for any $t \geq 0$, with

$$\langle y, u \rangle_{L^2} = \int_0^t y^{\mathsf{T}} u \, ds.$$

One can easily check that system (1) is lossless with respect to the Hamiltonian function as storage function. Indeed,

$$\dot{H} = \nabla H(x)^{\mathsf{T}} \dot{x}$$
$$= \nabla H(x)^{\mathsf{T}} B(x) \nabla H(x) + \nabla H(x)^{\mathsf{T}} G(x) u.$$

Since $\nabla H(x)^{\mathsf{T}} B(x) \nabla H(x) = 0$, due to the skew-symmetry of $B(x)$, we have

$$\dot{H} = \nabla H(x)^{\mathsf{T}} G(x) u = y^{\mathsf{T}} u.$$

Then, in terms of L^2 product, the property of lossless with respect to the Hamiltonian function reads as

$$\langle y, u \rangle_{L^2} = H(t) - H(0).$$

3   Discrete Gradient θ-Methods

Following [13], we use a first order discretization of the gradient, defined as

$$\overline{\nabla} H(x_n, x_{n+1})^{\mathsf{T}} (x_{n+1} - x_n) = H(x_{n+1}) - H(x_n).$$

Correspondingly, we introduce the following discrete gradient θ-method of problem (1)

$$x_{n+1} = x_n + h(1 - \theta) \Big(B(x_n) \overline{\nabla} H(x_{n-1}, x_n) + G(x_n) u_n \Big)$$
$$+ h\theta \Big(B(x_{n+1}) \overline{\nabla} H(x_n, x_{n+1}) + G(x_{n+1}) u_{n+1} \Big), \qquad (4)$$

$$y_{n+1} = G(x_{n+1})^{\mathsf{T}} \overline{\nabla} H(x_n, x_{n+1}),$$

over the grid of equispaced points

$$\mathcal{I}_h = \left\{ t_n = nh, \quad n = 0, 1, \ldots, N, \quad h = \frac{T}{N} \right\},$$

supposing that $[0, T]$ is the selected time window.

Let us compute $\overline{\nabla}H(x_n, x_{n+1})^\mathsf{T}(x_{n+1} - x_n)$, using the hyphotesis of skew-simmetry for the matrix $B(x)$:

$$\overline{\nabla}H(x_n, x_{n+1})^\mathsf{T}(x_{n+1} - x_n) = h(1-\theta)\left(\overline{\nabla}H(x_n, x_{n+1})^\mathsf{T}B(x_n)\overline{\nabla}H(x_{n-1}, x_n)\right.$$

$$\left. + \overline{\nabla}H(x_n, x_{n+1})^\mathsf{T}G(x_n)u_n\right) + h\theta y_{n+1}^\mathsf{T}u_{n+1}.$$

We aim to satisfy, along the numerical dynamics, a discrete balance law, i.e., we aim to express the Hamiltonian deviation $\Delta H(x_{n+1}) = H(x_{n+1}) - H(x_n)$ as a quantity proportional to $y_{n+1}^\mathsf{T}u_{n+1}$.

For $\theta = 1$, we have

$$\overline{\nabla}H(x_n, x_{n+1})^\mathsf{T}(x_{n+1} - x_n) = h y_{n+1}^\mathsf{T}u_{n+1},$$

i.e., the only θ-method satisfying a discrete balance law is the implicit Euler method. For all other θ-methods with $\theta \neq 1$, the defect is equal to

$$h(1-\theta)\left(\overline{\nabla}H(x_n, x_{n+1})^\mathsf{T}B(x_n)\overline{\nabla}H(x_{n-1}, x_n) + y_n^\mathsf{T}u_n\right)$$

and, under suitable regularity, it can be negligible in a left neighborhood of $\theta = 1$, where unconditionally stability is also acknowledgeable.

Let us consider as test problem the port-Hamiltonian controlled pendulum [13], i.e., problem (1) with

$$B = \begin{bmatrix} 0 & 1 \\ -1 & 0 \end{bmatrix}, \quad G = \begin{bmatrix} 0 \\ 1 \end{bmatrix}, \quad H(q, p) = \frac{p^2}{2} + 1 - \cos(q),$$

and input $u(y) = -\alpha \arctan(y)$, with $\alpha > 0$, leading to

$$\begin{bmatrix} \dot{q} \\ \dot{p} \end{bmatrix} = \begin{bmatrix} 0 & 1 \\ -1 & 0 \end{bmatrix}\begin{bmatrix} -\sin(q) \\ p \end{bmatrix} - \begin{bmatrix} 0 \\ \alpha \arctan(p) \end{bmatrix}. \tag{5}$$

Figs. 1 and 2 show the corresponding solution orbits, arising from the numerical dynamics of (4) for selected values of θ and α. One can appreciate that the choices of the parameters θ and α have a direct influence on the stability of the numerical dynamics, that deserves being properly analyzed.

4   Stability Issues

Let us perform the analysis of stability of the numerical scheme (4), assuming as discrete gradient operator the averaged vector field discrete gradient, i.e.,

$$\overline{\nabla}H(x_n, x_{n+1}) = \int_0^1 \nabla H(\rho(\alpha))d\alpha,$$

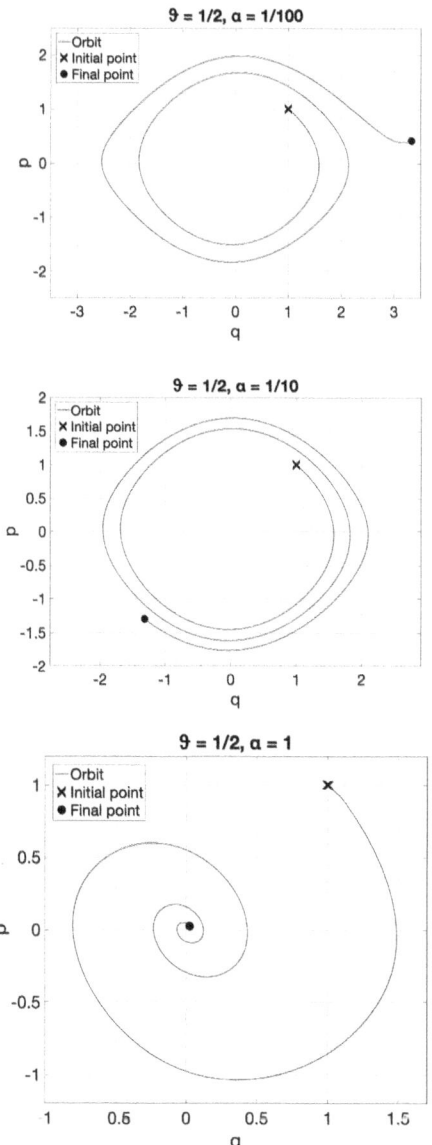

Fig. 1. Solution orbits related to the controlled pendulum (5) with the discrete gradient θ-method (4), for the highlighted values of θ and α.

with $\rho(\tau) = x_n(1 - \tau) + x_{n+1}\tau$. For the approximation of the integral, we use the trapezoidal rule, i.e.,

$$\overline{\nabla}H(x_n, x_{n+1}) \approx \frac{1}{2} \left(\nabla H(x_{n+1}) + \nabla H(x_n) \right).$$

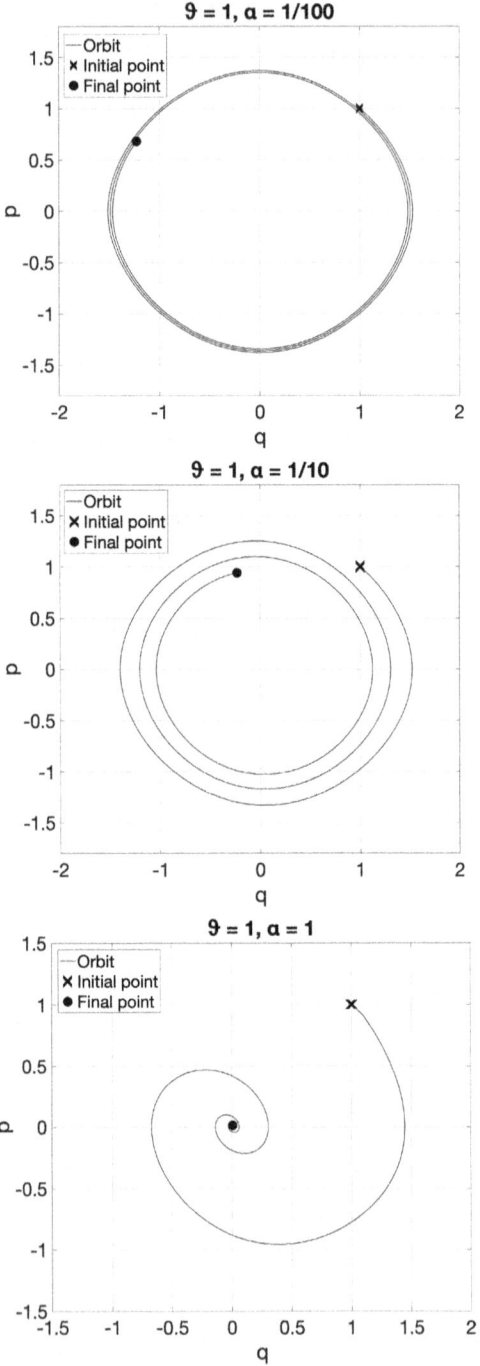

Fig. 2. Solution orbits related to the controlled pendulum (5) with the discrete gradient θ-method (4), for the highlighted values of θ and α.

We consider as test problem the port-Hamiltonian controlled pendulum (5). Considering that, in this case,

$$\overline{\nabla} H(x_n, x_{n+1}) \approx \frac{1}{2} \begin{bmatrix} \sin(q_{n+1}) + \sin(q_n) \\ p_{n+1} + p_n \end{bmatrix},$$

applying the discrete gradient θ-method (4) to the controlled pendulum (5) leads to

$$\begin{bmatrix} q_{n+1} \\ p_{n+1} \end{bmatrix} = \begin{bmatrix} q_n \\ p_n \end{bmatrix} + \frac{h}{2}(1-\theta) \begin{bmatrix} p_n + p_{n-1} \\ -\sin(q_{n-1}) - \sin(q_n) - \alpha \arctan(p_n) \end{bmatrix}$$
$$+ \frac{h}{2}\theta \begin{bmatrix} p_{n+1} + p_n \\ -\sin(q_n) - \sin(q_{n+1}) - \alpha \arctan(p_{n+1}) \end{bmatrix}.$$

Since $p_{n+1} = p_n + \mathcal{O}(h)$ and $q_{n+1} = q_n + \mathcal{O}(h)$ and via local linearization of the circular functions in last equation, we obtain

$$\begin{bmatrix} q_{n+1} \\ p_{n+1} \end{bmatrix} = \begin{bmatrix} q_n \\ p_n \end{bmatrix} + \frac{h}{2}(1-\theta) \begin{bmatrix} p_n + p_{n-1} \\ -q_{n-1} - q_n - \alpha p_n \end{bmatrix}$$
$$+ \frac{h}{2}\theta \begin{bmatrix} p_{n+1} + p_n \\ -q_n - q_{n+1} - \alpha p_{n+1} \end{bmatrix} + \mathcal{O}(h^2).$$

Neglecting the remainder term $\mathcal{O}(h^2)$, the aforestated equation is a system of second order difference equations, that we can write in compact form as

$$x_{n+1} = A x_n + B x_{n-1}, \tag{6}$$

with

$$A = \frac{1}{h^2\theta^2 + 2\alpha h\theta + 4} \begin{bmatrix} h^2\theta(\theta - 1) + 4h\theta\alpha + 4 & h\left(\alpha h\theta^2 + 2\theta + 2\right) \\ -4h(\theta + 1) & -h^2\theta + 2\alpha h(\theta - 1) + 4 \end{bmatrix},$$

$$B = \frac{h(\theta - 1)}{h\theta(2\alpha + h\theta) + 4} \begin{bmatrix} h\theta & -h\theta\alpha - 2 \\ 2 & h\theta \end{bmatrix}, \qquad x_n = \begin{bmatrix} q_n \\ p_n \end{bmatrix}.$$

Let us recast Eq. (6) as a system of first order difference equations, by employing the auxiliary discrete state variable $z_n = x_{n-1}$, leading to

$$\begin{bmatrix} x_{n+1} \\ z_{n+1} \end{bmatrix} = C \begin{bmatrix} x_n \\ z_n \end{bmatrix}, \qquad C = \begin{bmatrix} A & B \\ I & \mathbf{0} \end{bmatrix}, \tag{7}$$

being I the 2×2 identity matrix and $\mathbf{0}$ the zero matrix of the same dimension.

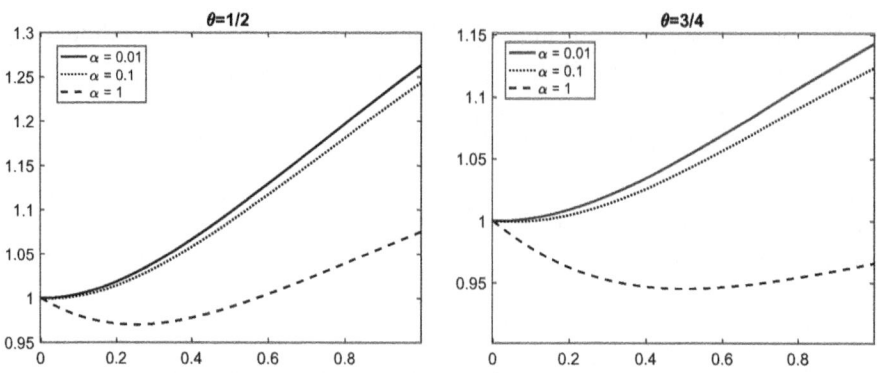

Fig. 3. Stability radii of the matrix C in (7) with respect to the stepsize, for the highlighted values of θ and α.

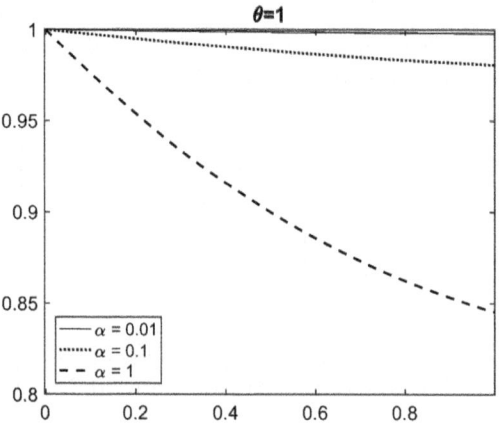

Fig. 4. Stability radii of the matrix D in (8) with respect to the stepsize, for $\theta = 1$ and selected values of α.

A degenerate case occurs for $\theta = 1$ since, in correspondence of this value, the matrix B is the zero matrix and, as a consequence, the second order system (6) reduces to the first order system of difference equations $x_{n+1} = Dx_n$, with

$$D = \frac{1}{h(2\alpha + h) + 4} \begin{bmatrix} 4(\alpha h + 1) & h(\alpha h + 4) \\ -8h & 4 - h^2 \end{bmatrix}. \tag{8}$$

Stability radii of the matrices C and D are depicted in Figs. 3 and 4, for selected values of θ and α and depicted as functions of h. As visible, for $\theta = \frac{1}{2}$, the stability radius is smaller than 1 only for selected values of α and for h satisfying a restriction. For $\theta = \frac{3}{4}$, larger values of α lead to a stable pattern, considering the stability radius behaviour displayed in Fig. 3, without stepsize restrictions. For $\theta = 1$, the behaviour displayed in Fig. 4 shows unconditional stability, since the spectral radius is always smaller than 1, even if it goes closer and closer to 1 for smaller values of α. Indeed, for α tending to 0, both matrices C and D in (7) and (8) tends to the identity matrix.

It is also worth observing that the unstable behaviour of the matrix C for small values of α is also coherent with the corresponding phase portraits shown in Figs. 3 and 4.

5   Concluding Remarks

We have focused our attention on the geometric numerical integration of port-Hamiltonian problems, assuming that the exact dynamics is approximated by means of the discrete gradient θ-method. In particular, the analysis has revealed the ability of this method in numerically retaining peculiar dissipativity features of the problem, such as a discrete balance law. In other terms, the discrete gradient θ-method provides Hamiltonian deviations $\Delta H(x_{n+1})$ proportional to $y_{n+1}^{\mathsf{T}} u_{n+1}$.

The analysis has also included the investigation of some stability issues for the discrete gradient θ-method, given with respect to the controlled pendulum. Stability properties have then been given in terms of spectral properties of the involved stability matrices, highlighting their connection with the value of the parameter θ characterizing the method and additional parameters visible in the problem.

This research may be extended to the geometric numerical integration of many significant evolution problems exhibiting peculiar dissipative dynamics, such as deterministic and stochastic reaction-diffusion problems or non-local problems described by integral and fractional differential equations. [1, 12, 19–22, 33, 42].

Acknowledgements. The authors are grateful to the anonymous reviewers for their careful and useful suggestions, allowing an attentive revision of the paper. The author RD is member of the INdAM Research group GNCS (Gruppo Nazionale per il Calcolo Scientifico). This work is supported by GNCS-INDAM project, by PRIN-MUR 2022 project 20229P2HEA "Stochastic numerical modelling for sustainable innovation" (CUP: E53C24002280006) and by the European Union - NextGenerationEU under the Italian Ministry of University and Research (MUR) National National Centre for HPC, Big Data and Quantum Computing (CN 00000013 - CUP: E13C22001000006).

References

1. Aceto, L., Conte, D., Pagano, G.: Modified TASE Runge-Kutta methods for integrating stiff differential equations. SIAM J. Sci. Comput. **47**(3), A1652–A1680 (2025)
2. Anton, C., Deng, J., Wong, Y.S.: Weak symplectic schemes for stochastic Hamiltonian equations. Electron. Trans. Numer. **43**, 1–20 (2014)

3. Blanes, S., Casas, F.: A Concise Introduction to Geometric Numerical Integration. CRC Press, New York (2016)
4. Brugnano, L., Iavernaro, F.: Line Integral Methods for Conservative Problems. CRC Press, New York (2016)
5. Buckwar, E., D'Ambrosio, R.: Exponential mean-square stability properties of stochastic linear multistep methods. Adv. Comput. Math. **47**(4), 1–14 (2021). https://doi.org/10.1007/s10444-021-09879-2
6. Budd, C.J., Pigott, M.D.: Geometric integration and its applications. In: Handbook of Numerical Analysis, Vol. XI, pp. 35–139. North-Holland, Amsterdam (2003)
7. Burrage, K., Burrage, P.M.: Structure-preserving Runge-Kutta methods for stochastic Hamiltonian equations with additive noise. Numer. Algorithms **65**(3), 519–532 (2014)
8. Burrage, K., Lenane, I., Lythe, G.: Numerical methods for second-order stochastic differential equations. SIAM J. Sci. Comput. **29**, 245–264 (2007)
9. Butcher, J.C., D'Ambrosio, R.: Partitioned general linear methods for separable Hamiltonian problems. Appl. Numer. Math. **117**, 69–86 (2017)
10. Butcher, J.C., Habib, Y., Hill, A.T., Norton, T.: The control of parasitism in G-symplectic methods. SIAM J. Numer. Anal. **52**(5), 2440–2465 (2014)
11. Camlibel, M.K., Van Der Schaft, A.J.: Port-Hamiltonian systems theory and monotonicity. SIAM J. Control. Optim. **61**(4), 2193–2221 (2023)
12. Cardone, A., Frasca-Caccia, G.: Numerical conservation laws of time fractional diffusion PDEs. Fract. Calc. Appl. Anal. **25**(4), 1459–1483 (2022)
13. Celledoni, E., Høiseth, E.H.: Energy-preserving and passivity-consistent numerical discretization of port-Hamiltonian systems. arXiv:1706.0862 (2017)
14. Celledoni, E., et al.: Energy-preserving Runge-Kutta methods. ESAIM: Math. Model. Numer. Anal. **43**(4), 645–649 (2009)
15. Chen, C., Cohen, D., D'Ambrosio, R., Lang, A.: Drift-preserving numerical integrators for stochastic Hamiltonian systems. Adv. Comput. Math. **46**(2), 1–22 (2020). https://doi.org/10.1007/s10444-020-09771-5
16. Cohen, D.: On the numerical discretisation of stochastic oscillators. Math. Comput. Simul. **82**, 1478–1495 (2012)
17. Cohen, D., Dujardin, G.: Energy-preserving integrators for stochastic Poisson systems. Comm. Math. Sci. **12**, 1523–1539 (2014)
18. Cohen, D., Vilmart, G.: Drift-preserving numerical integrators for stochastic Poisson systems. Int. J. Comput. Math. **99**, 4–20 (2022)
19. Conte, D., D'Ambrosio, R., Paternoster, B.: Improved θ-methods for stochastic Volterra integral equations. Commun. Nonlinear Sci. Numer. Simul. **93**, 105528 (2021)
20. Conte, D., D'Ambrosio, R., Paternoster, B.: On the stability of θ-methods for stochastic volterra integral equations. Discr. Contin. Dyn. Syst. B **23**(7), 2695–2708 (2018)
21. Conte, D., Frasca-Caccia, G.: Exponentially fitted methods with a local energy conservation law. Adv. Comput. Math. **49**(4), 49 (2023)
22. Conte, D., Frasca-Caccia, G.: Exponentially fitted methods that preserve conservation laws. Commun. Nonlinear Sci. Numer. Simul. **109**, 106334 (2022)
23. D'Ambrosio, R.: Numerical Approximation of Ordinary Differential Problems - From Deterministic to Stochastic Numerical Methods. Springer (2023). https://doi.org/10.1007/978-3-031-31343-1
24. D'Ambrosio, R., Di Giovacchino, S.: Mean-square contractivity of stochastic ϑ-methods. Comm. Nonlinear Sci. Numer. Simul. **96**, 105671 (2021)

25. D'Ambrosio, R., Di Giovacchino, S.: Nonlinear stability issues of stochastic Runge-Kutta methods. Comm. Nonlinear Sci. Numer. Simul. **94**, 105549 (2021)
26. D'Ambrosio, R., Di Giovacchino, S.: Numerical preservation issues in stochastic dynamical systems by θ-methods. J. Comput. Dyn. **9**(2), 123–131 (2022)
27. D'Ambrosio, R., Di Giovacchino, S.: Long-term analysis of Hamiltonians under time discretizations. SIAM J. Sci. Comput. **45**(2), A257–A288 (2023)
28. D'Ambrosio, R., Scalone, C.: On the numerical structure preservation of nonlinear damped stochastic oscillators. Numer. Algorithms **86**(3), 933–952 (2021)
29. D'Ambrosio, R., Hairer, E.: Long-term stability of multi-value methods for ordinary differential equations. J. Sci. Comput. **60**(3), 627–640 (2014)
30. D'Ambrosio, R., Hairer, E., Zbinden, C.J.: G-symplecticity implies conjugate-symplecticity of the underlying one-step method. BIT Numer. Math. **53**(4), 867–872 (2013). https://doi.org/10.1007/s10543-013-0437-1
31. de la Cruz, H., Jimenez, J.C., Zubelli, J.P.: Locally linearized methods for the simulation of stochastic oscillators driven by random forces. BIT **57**(1), 123–151 (2017)
32. Deng, J., Anton, C., Wong, Y.S.: High-order symplectic schemes for stochastic Hamiltonian systems. Commun. Comput. Phys. **16**(1), 169–200 (2014)
33. E, W., Di, L.: Gibbsian dynamics and invariant measures for stochastic dissipative PDEs. J. Amer. Math. Soc. **15**(4), 1125–1156 (2002)
34. Eirola, T., Sanz-Serna, J.M.: Conservation of integrals and symplectic structure in the integration of differential equations by multistep methods. Numer. Math. **61**, 281–290 (1992)
35. Gitterman, M.: The Noisy Oscillator. From Einstein Until Now. World Scientific, The First Hundred Years (2005)
36. Hairer, E., Lubich, C.: Symmetric multistep methods over long times. Numer. Math. **97**, 699–723 (2004)
37. Hairer, E., Lubich, C., Wanner, G.: Geometric Numerical Integration: Structure-preserving Algorithms for Ordinary Differential Equations, 2nd edn. Springer, Berlin (2006). https://doi.org/10.1007/3-540-30666-8
38. Higham, D.J., Mao, X., Stuart, A.: Exponential mean-square stability of numerical solutions to stochastic differential equations. LMS J. Comput. Math. **6**, 297–313 (2013)
39. Hong, J., Ruan, J., Sun, L., Wang, L.: Structure-preserving numerical methods for stochastic Poisson systems. Commun. Comput. Phys. **29**(3), 802–830 (2021)
40. Iserles, A.: A First Course in the Numerical Analysis of Differential Equations, 2nd edn. Cambridge University Press, Cambridge (2008)
41. Kang, F., Mengzhao, Q.: Symplectic Geometric Algorithms for Hamiltonian Systems. Springer, Berlin (2010). https://doi.org/10.1007/978-3-642-01777-3
42. Kloeden, P.E.: An elementary inequality for dissipative Caputo fractional differential equations. Fract. Calc. Appl. Anal. **26**, 2166–2174 (2023)
43. Leimkuhler, B., Reich, S.: Geometric Integrators in Hamiltonian Mechanics. Cambridge University Press, Cambridge (2003)
44. Luesink, E., Ephrati, S., Cifani, P., Geurts, B.: Casimir preserving stochastic Lie–Poisson integrators. Adv. Cont. Discr. Mod. **2024**, 1 (2024)
45. McLachlan, R.I.: Perspectives on geometric numerical integration. J. Roy. Soc. New Zeal. **49**(2), 114–125 (2019)
46. McLachlan, R.I., Quispel, G.: Geometric integrators for ODEs. J. Phys. A: Math. Gen. **39**(19), 5251–5285 (2006)
47. Mehrmann, V., van Dooren, P.M.: Optimal robustness of port-Hamiltonian systems. SIAM J. Matrix Anal. Appl. **41**(1), 134–151 (2020)

48. Milstein, G.N., Repin, Y.M., Tretyakov, M.V.: Numerical methods for stochastic systems preserving symplectic structure. SIAM J. Numer. Anal. **40**, 1583–1604 (2002)
49. Misawa, T.: Energy conservative stochastic difference scheme for stochastic Hamiltonian dynamical systems. Japan J. Indust. Appl. Math. **17**, 119–128 (2000)
50. Sanz-Serna, J.M., Calvo, M.P.: Numerical Hamiltonian Problems. Chapman & Hall (1994)
51. Schurz, H.: The invariance of asymptotic laws of linear stochastic systems under discretization. Z. Angew. Math. Mech. **6**, 375–382 (1999)
52. Ströhmen Melbö, A.H., Higham, D.J.: Numerical simulation of a linear stochastic oscillator with additive noise. Appl. Numer. Math. **51**, 89–99 (2004)
53. Talay, D.: Stochastic Hamiltonian systems: exponential convergence to the invariant measure, and discretization by the implicit Euler scheme. Markov Processes Relat. Fields **8**, 1–36 (2002)
54. Van Der Schaft, A.: Port-Hamiltonian systems: an introductory survey. In: Proceedings of the International Congress of Mathematicians, Madrid, Spain, 2006, Volume III - Invited Lectures, European Mathematical Society, pp. 1339–1365 (2007)
55. Van Der Schaft, A., Jeltsema, D.: Port-Hamiltonian systems theory: an introductory overview. Found. Trends Syst. Control **1**(2–3), 173–378 (2014)
56. Vilmart, G.: Weak second order multi-revolution composition methods for highly oscillatory stochastic differential equations with additive or multiplicative noise. SIAM J. Sci. Comput. **36**, 1770–1796 (2014)
57. Wang, L., Maschke, B., van der Schaft, A.: Port-Hamiltonian modeling of non-isothermal chemical reaction networks. J. Math. Chem. **56**(6), 1707–1727 (2018). https://doi.org/10.1007/s10910-018-0882-9

Mean-Square Monotonicity Analysis of θ-Maruyama Methods

Helena Biščević[1($\boxtimes$)] and Raffaele D'Ambrosio[2]

[1] Gran Sasso Science Institute, L'Aquila (AQ), Italy
`helena.biscevic@gssi.it`
[2] Department of Information Engineering and Computer Science and Mathematics,
L'Aquila (AQ), Italy
`raffaele.dambrosio@univaq.it`

Abstract. The paper focuses on the analysis of mean-square contractivity of the numerical dynamics arising from the application of θ-Maruyama methods to stochastic differential equations (SDEs) with linear affine drift and diffusion coefficients. We prove that the numerical deviation between two distinct solutions of the SDE is monotonically non-increasing under the same stepsize restrictions needed for mean-square stability or holds unconditionally for certain values of θ. A selection of numerical experiments complements the theoretical investigation.

Keywords: Stochastic differential equations · θ-Maruyama numerical methods · Numerical monotonicity

1 Introduction

This paper aims to analyse the behavior of the numerical dynamics resulting from discretizations of stochastic differential equations (SDEs) with linear affine drift and diffusion coefficients, i.e.,

$$\mathrm{d}X(t) = (\mu X(t) + \nu)\,\mathrm{d}t + (\sigma X(t) + \tau)\,\mathrm{d}W(t), \quad t \geq 0, \tag{1}$$

with $\mu, \nu, \sigma, \tau \in \mathbb{R}$ and $X(t) \in \mathbb{R}$. $\{W(t),\ t \geq 0\}$ is a Wiener process, with independent increments $W(\tau_{j+1}) - W(\tau_j)$, identically distributed as $\sqrt{h} \cdot \mathcal{N}(0, 1)$, $\mathcal{N}(0, 1)$ being a standard normal random variable.

The problem is intended in Itô sense, i.e., Eq. (1) is the shorthand notation for the integral equation

$$X(t) = \int_0^t (\mu X(s) + \nu)\,\mathrm{d}s + \int_0^t (\sigma X(s) + \tau)\,\mathrm{d}W(s), \quad t \geq 0,$$

where the integral of the drift is intended in Riemann sense along each path, while the integral of the diffusion is here meant in Itô sense, that is, for a given integrable function g,

$$\int_0^t g(X(s))\mathrm{d}W(s) = \lim_{n \to \infty} \sum_{j=0}^{n-1} g(X(\tau_j))\left(W(\tau_{j+1}) - W(\tau_j)\right).$$

O. Gervasi et al. (Eds.): ICCSA 2025 Workshops, LNCS 15887, pp. 237–248, 2026.
https://doi.org/10.1007/978-3-031-97589-9_17

This limit is intended in mean-square sense, on the set of equidistant points

$$\mathcal{I}_h = \left\{ \tau_\ell = \ell h, \quad \ell = 0, 1, \ldots, n, \quad h = \frac{t}{n} \right\}.$$

For a general overview of the theory of SDEs, including Itô and Stratonovich calculi, results of existence and uniqueness of solutions in strong and weak senses, stability issues, the interested reader can consider, for instance, [3,17,25,28] and references therein.

It is worth observing that the existing literature on numerical methods for SDEs has addressed several significant aspects, such as convergence in strong and weak senses, the analysis of linear stability, principles of geometric numerical integration. For the presentation of a selection of relevant numerical methods for SDEs, as well as of their aforementioned aspects, one can consider [12,20,24,27] and references therein.

In particular, nonlinear stability analysis in exponential mean-square sense has been investigated in [6,12–14,21,22] and references therein. Stability analysis in exponential mean-square sense implies estimates for the mean-square deviation between two distinct solutions of (1), obtained by choosing two distinct initial values $X_0 \neq Y_0 \in \mathbb{R}$, leading to

$$\mathbb{E}\left[\|X(t) - Y(t)\|^2\right] \leq \mathbb{E}\left[\|X_0 - Y_0\|^2\right] e^{\alpha t},$$

with exponential rate $\alpha = 2\mu + \sigma$. Supposing that α is negative, consequently the mean-square deviation $\mathbb{E}\left[\|X(t) - Y(t)\|^2\right]$ is monotone over each time interval $[t, t + \Delta t]$ and, specifically, non-increasing, i.e.,

$$\mathbb{E}\left[\|X(t + \Delta t) - Y(t + \Delta t)\|^2\right] \leq \mathbb{E}\left[\|X(t) - Y(t)\|^2\right]. \tag{2}$$

Analysing the monotonicity of mean-square deviations of (2) is useful, for instance, when approaching the numerical modelling of dissipative stochastic partial differential equations [5,15], semi-discretized along the spatial variables and leading to a system of SDEs of large dimension. Indeed, condition (2) formalizes the mean-square contractivity of the numerical dynamics, highlighting the mean-square dissipative character of the problem.

We aim to understand if monotonicity condition (2) is accurately preserved by θ-Maruyama numerical methods [4,7,12,19,20,29], whose expression, with reference to the discrete set

$$\mathcal{I}_{\Delta t} = \left\{ t_n = n\Delta t, \quad n = 0, 1, \ldots, N, \quad \Delta t = \frac{T}{N} \right\},$$

providing a discretisation of the interval $[0, T]$ and applied to problem (1), is given by

$$X_{n+1} = X_n + (1 - \theta)\Delta t(\mu X_n + \nu) + \theta \Delta t(\mu X_{n+1} + \nu) + (\sigma X_n + \tau)\Delta W_n, \tag{3}$$

for $\theta \in [0, 1]$. Here X_n represents the approximate value for $X(t_n)$ and ΔW_n is discretisation of the Wiener increment in the interval $[t_n, t_{n+1}]$. We observe that, to make discretised Wiener increments computable in $\mathcal{I}_{\Delta t}$, usually Δt is taken proportional to the steplength h in concordance with the partition $\mathcal{I}_h$.

As proved in [19], the choice of the parameter $\theta \in [0, 1]$ has a direct influence on the mean-square stability properties of the corresponding θ-Maruyama method (3). Indeed, for any $\theta \in [\frac{1}{2}, 1]$, the corresponding method is mean-square A-stable, i.e., it unconditionally preserves the mean-square stability properties of the problem. For $\theta \in [0, \frac{1}{2})$, this preservation occurs under a prescribed stepsize restriction.

In the context of SDEs with linear affine coefficients (1), in the following section we prove that condition (2) is well maintained along the numerical dynamics of θ-Maruyama methods (3), under a suitable stepsize restriction and, for some values of θ, the condition is preserved unconditionally.

2   Monotone Mean-Square Deviation

Let us apply the θ-Maruyama method (3) to the SDE with linear affine coefficients (1), for the approximation of two distinct solutions of (1), obtained with initial values $X_0 \neq Y_0$. Therefore, we obtain

$$X_{n+1} = X_n + (1 - \theta)\Delta t(\mu X_n + \nu) + \theta \Delta t(\mu X_{n+1} + \nu) + (\sigma X_n + \tau)\Delta W_n,$$

$$Y_{n+1} = Y_n + (1 - \theta)\Delta t(\mu Y_n + \nu) + \theta \Delta t(\mu Y_{n+1} + \nu) + (\sigma Y_n + \tau)\Delta W_n.$$

Subtraction of these two solutions yields

$$X_{n+1} - Y_{n+1} = \frac{1 + (1 - \theta)\Delta t\mu + \sigma \Delta W_n}{1 - \theta \Delta t\mu}(X_n - Y_n),$$

and, passing to mean-square, gives

$$\mathbb{E}\left[\|X_{n+1} - Y_{n+1}\|^2\right] = \frac{(1 + (1 - \theta)\Delta t\mu)^2 + \sigma^2 \Delta t}{(1 - \theta \Delta t\mu)^2}\mathbb{E}\left[\|X_n - Y_n\|^2\right].$$

In other terms, focusing on a single step of the θ-Maruyama method, from the step point t_n to t_{n+1}, the numerical mean-square deviation is non-increasing if

$$\frac{(1 + (1 - \theta)\Delta t\mu)^2 + \sigma^2 \Delta t}{(1 - \theta \Delta t\mu)^2} \leq 1, \tag{4}$$

that is the condition of mean-square stability for stochastic θ-methods [12, 19, 20]. In summary, we have proved the following result.

Theorem 1. *For θ-Maruyama methods (3), monotonicity of the mean-square deviation of two distinct solutions of the SDE (1), obtained in correspondence to two distinct initial values, occurs over a single step as in (2) for all the values of the stepsize such that the method is mean-square stable.*

As a consequence of Theorem 1, we observe the following two cases.

Corollary 1. *For any $0 \leq \theta < \frac{1}{2}$, monotonicity of the mean-square deviation over a single step of* (3) *applied to* (1) *occurs as in* (2) *if the following stepsize restriction is satisfied*

$$\Delta t \leq -\frac{2\mu + \sigma^2}{(1 - 2\theta)\mu^2}. \tag{5}$$

Corollary 2. *For any $\frac{1}{2} \leq \theta \leq 1$, monotonicity of the mean-square deviation over a single step of* (3) *applied to* (1) *occurs as in* (2) *without any restriction on the stepsize.*

Proof. Condition (4) is equivalent to $f(\Delta t) \leq 0$, with

$$f(\Delta t) = 2\mu + \sigma^2 + (1 - 2\theta)\mu^2\Delta t.$$

We observe that $f'(\Delta t) = (1 - 2\theta)\mu^2 \leq 0$, for any value of $\theta \in [\frac{1}{2}, 1]$, and $f(0) = 2\mu + \sigma^2$, which is negative based on the hypothesis of mean-square stability for the SDE. Therefore, we have $f(\Delta t) \leq 0$, for any Δt, if $\theta \in [\frac{1}{2}, 1]$, leading to the thesis. □

As regards the unconditional conservation of monotonicity given by Corollary 2, we observe that all mean-square A-stable θ-Maruyama methods preserve both mean-square monotonicity and mean-square deviations between two distinct solutions of the linear problem (1). In the next section, we will illustrate these results using two examples.

3   Numerical Experiments

The literature contains numerous applications of SDEs with linear affine coefficients. Despite their simplicity, these models represent a valuable contribution to their respective application areas, often providing strong motivation to analyse their numerical behaviour. Before presenting examples that connect them with our theoretical results, we briefly present some of the most interesting applications discussed in the literature. Among the most widely considered are geometric Brownian motion as well as arithmetic Brownian motion, used, for instance, to model precipitation [2] as well as various financial models, including the Ornstein-Uhlenbeck process, mean-reverting models, and stochastic volatility models [23, 25]. We will present two examples to illustrate the aforementioned theory: geometric Brownian motion and a mean-reverting model.

3.1   Geometric Brownian Motion

Geometric Brownian motion (GBM) is given by the following equation [25]:

$$dX(t) = \mu X(t)dt + \sigma X(t)dW(t), \tag{6}$$

where μ is the drift and σ is the volatility.

The most common application of GBM is in modelling stock prices. Therefore, the numerical experiments presented below will be conducted with this application in mind. GBM is preferred over the Brownian motion model in financial applications since it cannot take negative values and maintains stock movements proportional to the value of the stock—a consequence of its exponential nature—thus making it a more appropriate model of price dynamics. It is worth pointing out that, despite its simplicity and usefulness, this model is valid only over short time intervals, since it implies that the stock price over time follows a normal distribution, with mean μt and variance $\sigma^2 t$. It has been thoroughly investigated that stock price behaviour over long time does not follow a normal distribution, but rather a lognormal distribution [26].

In the context of financial applications, the modelled variable $X(t)$ represents the current asset price, μ is the expected return (usually represented as a percentage value) and σ is the standard deviation of returns [26]. To satisfy the monotonicity condition derived in the theoretical result, the drift must be negative. This special case will corresponds to negative market growth or bankruptcy. However, according to the properties of GBM, even though a negative drift drives the asset price downward, it will not fall below zero, as observed in real markets. To remain faithful to the model's statistical interpretation, volatility should not be assigned a negative value. Finally, when choosing parameters, it is important to ensure that the condition $2\mu + \sigma < 0$ is satisfied.

The parameters used in the numerical experiments are as follows: $\mu = -0.7$, $\sigma = 0.5$. In Fig. 1, the behaviour of the mean-square deviations is illustrated for three methods that are not A-stable, for $\theta = 0$, 0.2, 0.3, and hence have an upper bound on the timestep which, when surpassed, results in a blow-up. Under each subfigure, the method and the corresponding upper bound are indicated. In Fig. 1a, corresponding to Euler-Maruyama method, monotone behaviour of the mean-square deviation is observed for $\Delta t = 2$, since it is below the monotonicity bound 2.34. However, a blow-up occurs for $\Delta t = 3.33$ as this value goes over the bound. In Fig. 1b, corresponding to the method for $\theta = 0.2$, the value of $\Delta t = 3.33$ is below the monotonicity bound 3.91, but we can notice that even though no blow-up is observed, the obtained numerical deviation fails to exhibit the monotonicity characterizing the underlying exact dynamics. A similar situation is evident for the same timestep in Fig. 1c for $\theta = 0.3$. Overall, an improvement in monotonicity properties is observed as the value of θ increases.

In Fig. 2, by contrast, mean-square contractivity is demonstrated for three A-stable methods with $\theta = 0.5$, 0.7, 1. These methods are unconditionally monotone for all general linear SDEs, and therefore impose no restriction on the timestep.

3.2   Mean Reverting Model

The mean-reverting model (MRM) is given by the following equation [25]:

$$dS(t) = r(\mu - S(t))dt + \sigma S(t)dW(t), \qquad (7)$$

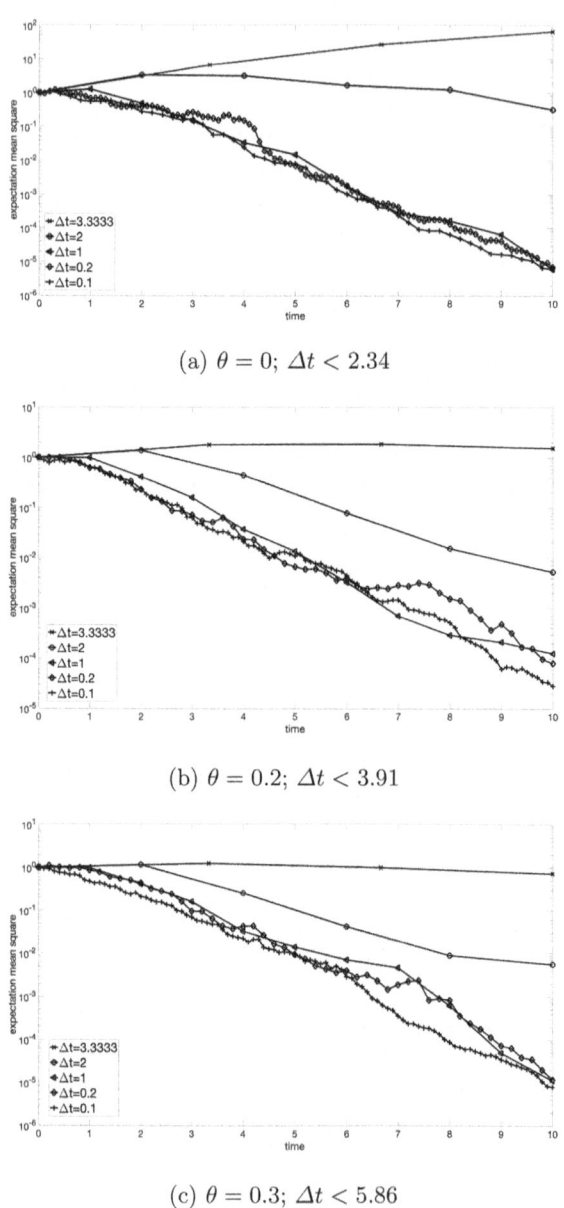

(a) $\theta = 0$; $\Delta t < 2.34$

(b) $\theta = 0.2$; $\Delta t < 3.91$

(c) $\theta = 0.3$; $\Delta t < 5.86$

Fig. 1. Mean-square deviations associated to θ-Maruyama method (3) applied to GBM problem (6), for selected values of θ corresponding to methods that are not mean-square A-stable, emphasising the timestep restriction for each method to preserve monotonicity

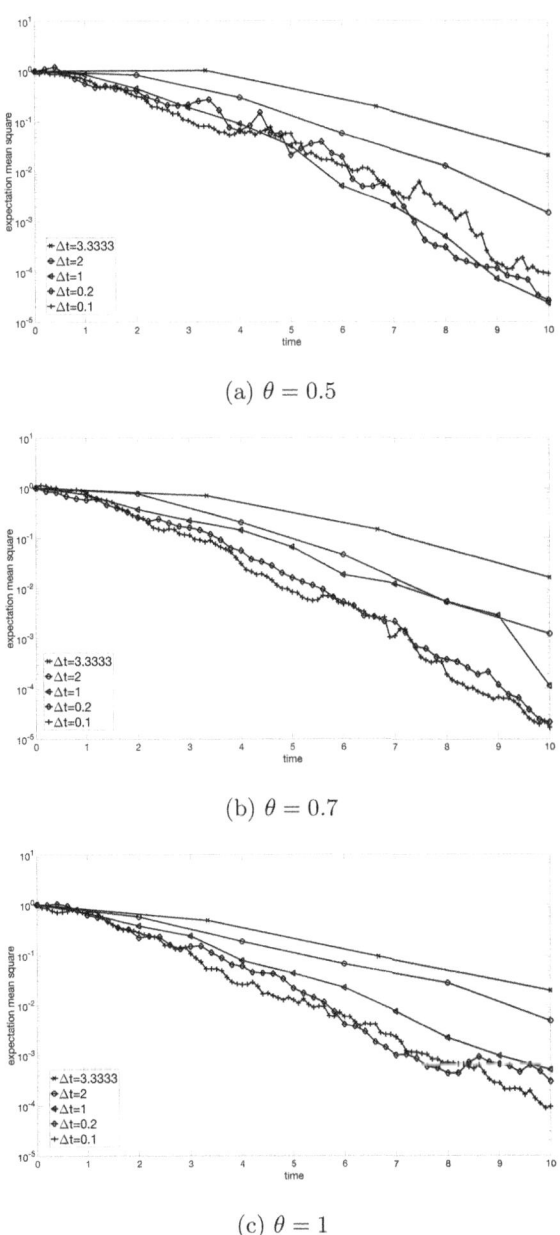

(a) $\theta = 0.5$

(b) $\theta = 0.7$

(c) $\theta = 1$

Fig. 2. Mean-square deviations associated to θ-Maruyama method (3) applied to GBM problem (6), for selected values of θ corresponding to methods that are mean-square A-stable

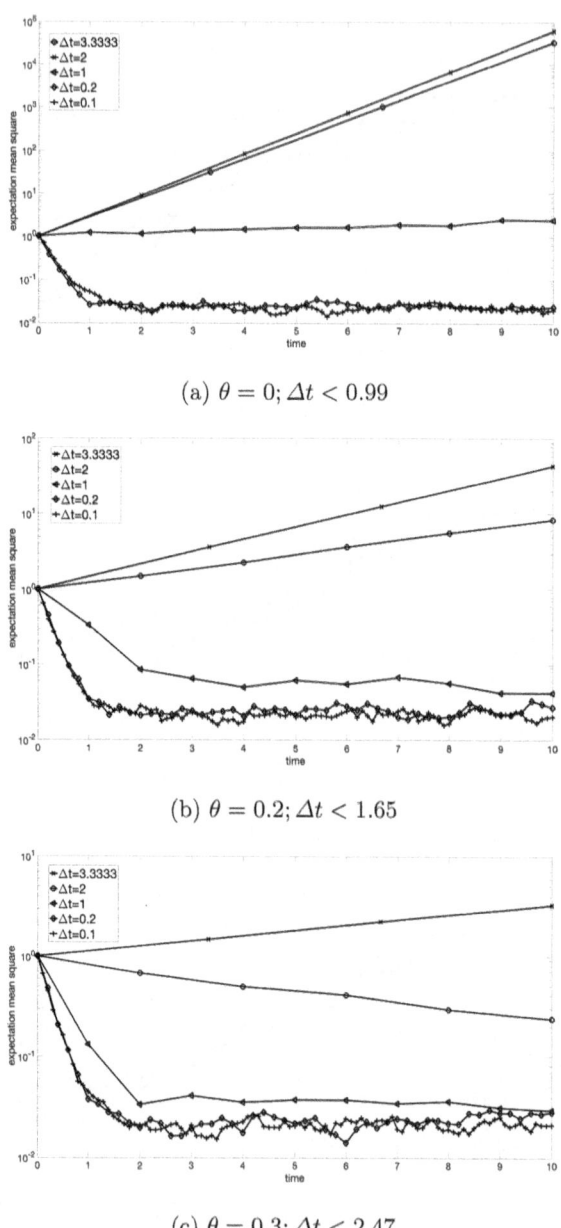

(a) $\theta = 0;\ \Delta t < 0.99$

(b) $\theta = 0.2;\ \Delta t < 1.65$

(c) $\theta = 0.3;\ \Delta t < 2.47$

Fig. 3. Mean-square deviations associated to θ-Maruyama method (3) applied to MRM problem (7), for selected values of θ corresponding to methods that are not mean-square A-stable, emphasising the timestep restriction for each method to preserve monotonicity

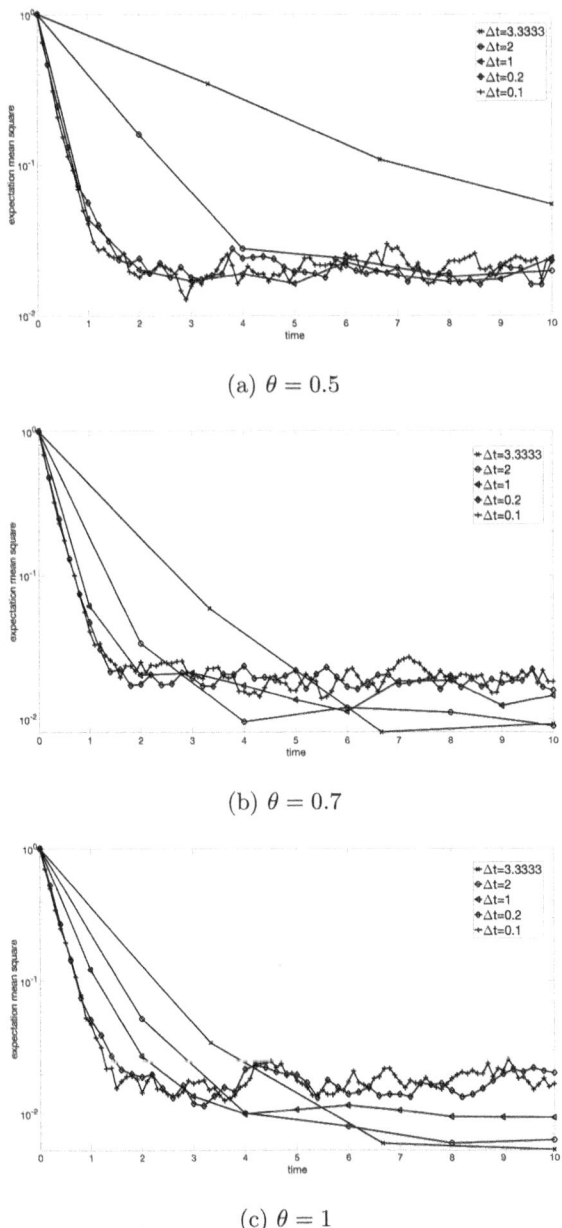

(a) $\theta = 0.5$

(b) $\theta = 0.7$

(c) $\theta = 1$

Fig. 4. Mean-square deviations associated to θ-Maruyama method (3) applied to MRM problem (7), for selected values of θ corresponding to methods that are mean-square A-stable

where r is the reversion rate, μ is the long-run mean price and σ is the volatility as before.

This model is similar to GBM, but it additionally accounts for mean reversion, introduced through the reversion parameter r. Following the stochastic dynamics described previously, it includes a tendency for the process to revert toward the its mean. It is typically used to model interest rate dynamics.

To explain the role of reversion, we first examine the behaviour of the model. By construction, it is evident that when $S(t)$ rises above (or falls below) the mean value μ, the drift function becomes negative (or positive), causing $dS(t)$ more likely to become negative (or positive) and therefore leading $S(t)$ to decrease (or increase) [25]. As the dynamics evolve, $S(t)$ will repeatedly revert toward the mean, but the previous deviations from the mean, known as excursions, are going to occur each time the process returns to the mean. The duration of excursions is governed by the reversion rate r [23].

The parameters used in the numerical experiments are as follows: $r = 2$, $\mu = 1$, $\sigma = 0.2$. Figure 3, illustrates the behaviour of mean-square deviations for three methods that are not A-stable with $\theta = 0$, 0.2, 0.3, and hence exhibit an upper bound on the timestep, beyond which numerical blow-up occurs. Below each subfigure, the method and the corresponding upper bound are indicated. We observe that, for decreasing values of Δt, the methods exhibit a monotone decrease of the mean-square deviation between two solutions up to a plateau, due to accuracy demands. For each subfigure, similar considerations to those discussed in the previous example apply with respect to both the blow-up behaviour and the monotone decay.

In Fig. 4, by contrast, monotonicity is demonstrated for three A-stable methods with $\theta = 0.5$, 0.7, 1. These methods are unconditionally monotone for all general linear SDEs, implying that the time step is unrestricted and the mean-square deviations remain monotone. As demonstrated for all three methods, this monotone behaviour is consistently preserved, along with the characteristic shape of the decay.

4   Conclusions

We have analysed the ability of stochastic θ-methods to provide monotone mean square deviations between two solutions of SDEs with linear affine drift and diffusion coefficients (1), obtained with two distinct initial values. The investigation revealed that the conservation of the monotone character of such mean-square deviations is given in terms of stepsize restrictions when $\theta < \frac{1}{2}$ and it occurs unconditionally when $\theta \geq \frac{1}{2}$. Moreover, the analysis revealed that all stepsize values ensuring mean-square stability also satisfy the monotonicity condition (2). This issue has been confirmed by selected numerical experiments.

Future developments of this research may establish the connection between analogous stability and monotonicity properties of θ-methods also for systems of SDEs, involving spectral or pseudospectral properties of the coefficient matrices. The results may also be extended to other evolution problems, also regarding non-local problems with memory or stiff problems arising from the spatial discretization of reaction-diffusion partial differential equations [1,8–11,16,18,30].

Acknowledgements. The authors are members of the INdAM Research group GNCS (Gruppo Nazionale per il Calcolo Scientifico). This work is supported by GNCS-INDAM project and by PRIN-MUR 2022 project 20229P2HEA "Stochastic numerical modelling for sustainable innovation" (CUP: E53C24002280006).

References

1. Aceto, L., Conte, D., Pagano, G.: On a generalization of time-accurate and highly-stable explicit operators for stiff problems. Appl. Numer. Math. **200**, 2–17 (2024)
2. Allen, E.: Modeling with Itô Stochastic Differential Equations. Springer (2007)
3. Arnold, L.: Stochastic Differential Equations: Theory and Applications. John Wiley & Sons, New York (1973)
4. Biščevic, H., D'Ambrosio, R., Di Giovacchino, S.: Contractivity of stochastic θ-methods under non-global Lipschitz conditions. Appl. Math. Comput. **505**, article number 129527 (2025)
5. Biščevic, H., D'Ambrosio, R.: Time integration of dissipative stochastic PDEs. In preparation
6. Buckwar, E., D'Ambrosio, R.: Exponential mean-square stability properties of stochastic linear multistep methods. Adv. Comput. Math. **47**(4), 1–14 (2021). https://doi.org/10.1007/s10444-021-09879-2
7. Buckwar, E., Sickenberger, T.: A comparative linear mean-square stability analysis of Maruyama- and Milstein-type methods. Math. Comput. Simul. **81**, 1110–1127 (2011)
8. Cardone, A., Frasca-Caccia, G.: Numerical conservation laws of time fractional diffusion PDEs. Fract. Calc. Appl. Anal. **25**(4), 1459–1483 (2022)
9. Conte, D., D'Ambrosio, R., Paternoster, B.: Improved θ-methods for stochastic Volterra integral equations. Commun. Nonlinear Sci. Numer. Simul. **93**, 105528 (2021)
10. Conte, D., D'Ambrosio, R., Paternoster, B.: On the stability of θ-methods for stochastic Volterra integral equations. Discrete Contin. Dyn. Syst. - B **23**(7), 2695–2708 (2018)
11. Conte, D., Frasca-Caccia, G.: Exponentially fitted methods that preserve conservation laws. Commun. Nonlinear Sci. Numer. Simul. **109**, 106334 (2022)
12. D'Ambrosio, R.: Numerical Approximation of Ordinary Differential Problems - From Deterministic to Stochastic Numerical Methods. Springer (2023)
13. D'Ambrosio, R., Di Giovacchino, S.: Nonlinear stability issues for stochastic Runge-Kutta methods. Comm. Nonlinear Sci. Numer. Simul. **94**, 105549 (2021)
14. D'Ambrosio, R., Di Giovacchino, S.: Mean-square contractivity of stochastic theta-methods. Comm. Nonlinear Sci. Numer. Simul. **96**, 105671 (2021)
15. E, W., Di, L.: Gibbsian dynamics and invariant measures for stochastic dissipative PDEs. J. Amer. Math. Soc. **15**(4), 1125–1156 (2002)
16. Frasca-Caccia, G.: Finite difference schemes with non polynomial local conservation laws. J. Comput. Appl. Math. **458**, 116330 (2025)
17. Gard, T.C.: Introduction to Stochastic Differential Equations. Marcel Dekker Inc., New York-Basel (1988)

18. González-Pinto, S., Hernández-Abreu, D., Pagano, G., Pérez-Rodríguez, S.: Generalized TASE-RK methods for stiff problems. Appl. Numer. Math. **188**, 129–145 (2023)

19. Higham, D.: Mean-square and asymptotic stability of the stochastic θ-method. SIAM J. Numer. Anal. **38**, 753–769 (2000)

20. Higham, D., Kloeden, P.: An Introduction to the Numerical Simulation of Stochastic Differential Equations. SIAM, Philadelphia (2021)

21. Higham, D., Kloeden, P.: Numerical methods for nonlinear stochastic differential equations with jumps. Numer. Math. **101**, 101–119 (2005)

22. Higham, D., Mao, X., Stuart, A.: Exponential mean-square stability of numerical solutions to stochastic differential equations. LMS J. Comput. Math. **6**, 297–313 (2013)

23. Hirsa, A., Neftci, S. N.: An Introduction to the Mathematics of Financial Derivatives. 3rd Edn., Elsevier (2014)

24. Kloeden, P.E., Platen, E.: Numerical solution of stochastic differential equations. Springer-Verlag, Berlin (1992)

25. Mao, X.: Stochastic Differential Equations and Applications, 2nd edn. Horwood, Chichester (2007)

26. Mastro, M.: Financial Derivative and Energy Market Valuation: Theory and Implementation in MATLAB. Wiley (2013)

27. Milstein, G.N., Tretyakov, M.V.: Stochastic Numerics for Mathematical Physics. Springer-Verlag, Berlin (2004)

28. Øksendal, B.: Stochastic Differential Equations. An Introduction with Applications. 6th edn. Springer-Verlag, Berlin Heidelberg (2003)

29. Scalone, C.: Positivity preserving stochastic-methods for selected SDEs. Appl. Numer. Math. **172**, 351–358 (2022)

30. Zhang, Z., Kaniadakis, G.E.: Numerical Methods for Stochastic Partial Differential Equations with White Noise. AMS, vol. 196. Springer, Cham (2017). https://doi.org/10.1007/978-3-319-57511-7_12

Solution of Quaternion Equations with Imprecisely Defined Coefficients

Rogério Serôdio[1]([✉])[ID] and José Vitória[2][ID]

[1] Department of Mathematics and CMA-UBI, University of Beira Interior,
Covilhã, Portugal
`rserodio@ubi.pt`
[2] Department of Mathematics, University of Coimbra, Coimbra, Portugal
`jvitoria@mat.uc.pt`

Abstract. In this paper we investigate quaternion polynomial equations with imprecisely defined coefficients, an area not previously explored. To address this uncertainty, we introduce the concept of a closed quaternion ball and develop arithmetic operations for these sets. Within this framework, we analyze specific classes of equations and identify the conditions under which solutions exist. The approach allows us to represent the solution sets within closed quaternion balls, thereby capturing the range of all possible values. In particular, we examine quadratic and cubic equations in detail and derive a quaternionic analogue of the de Moivre formula, providing explicitly the n-th roots of a closed quaternion ball.

Keywords: Closed quaternion ball · algebraic structure · quaternion polynomial equation

1 Introduction

A quaternion polynomial equation is an equation of the form $f(x) = g(x)$, where

$$f(x) = x^m + a_{m-1}x^{m-1} + \cdots + a_1 x + a_0 \tag{1}$$

and

$$g(x) = x^n + b_{n-1}x^{n-1} + \cdots + b_1 x + b_0, \tag{2}$$

are polynomials with quaternionic coefficients. The solution set

$$S = \{x \in \mathbb{H} \ : \ f(x) = g(x)\}. \tag{3}$$

consists of the zeros of the quaternion polynomial $p(x) = f(x) - g(x)$, which can be computed using known techniques. This problem has received considerable attention in recent years; see, for example, [14] for a historical overview.

Motivated by the studies in [3–5,7,10,12,13,15–18,20], we investigate the setting in which certain coefficients in quaternion polynomial equations are not known precisely and lie within specified bounds. To the best of our knowledge,

O. Gervasi et al. (Eds.): ICCSA 2025 Workshops, LNCS 15887, pp. 249–266, 2026.
https://doi.org/10.1007/978-3-031-97589-9_18

quaternion polynomial equations with uncertain coefficients and independent terms have not been previously studied in the literature.

Representing and computing the corresponding solution sets under such uncertainty presents significant challenges. To address this, we enclose the solution set S within a closed quaternion ball and develop arithmetic operations specific to this structure. The uncertainty in each quaternion component can be modeled either by assigning intervals of the form $[a, b]$ to each component, resulting in a hypercube, or by treating the quaternion as the center of a hypersphere. In this work, we adopt the latter model.

In this work, operations on closed quaternion balls are considered in Sect. 2. First, we start with a revision on quaternion algebra, focusing on quaternion polynomials and their zeros; this is given in Subsect. 2.1. In Subsect. 2.2, we define closed quaternion balls and give two binary operations: addition and multiplication; some of their properties are established. In Sect. 3 we present some results related to some specific equations with imprecisely defined coefficients and independent term. Finally, in Sect. 4, some examples are given.

2 Preliminaries

This section presents preliminary results on quaternion algebras and closed quaternion balls.

2.1 Quaternion Algebra

Let $\mathbb{H} = \{q_0 + q_1 i + q_2 j + q_3 k : q_0, q_1, q_2, q_3 \in \mathbb{R}\}$ denote the quaternion field, where $i^2 = j^2 = k^2 = -1$, $ij = -ji = k$, $jk = -kj = i$, and $ki = -ik = j$. For $q = q_0 + q_1 i + q_2 j + q_3 k \in \mathbb{H}$, the conjugate of q is given by $\overline{q} = q_0 - q_1 i - q_2 j - q_3 k$. The **trace** of q, denoted by $t(q)$, is twice its real part: $t(q) \equiv 2q_0 = q + \overline{q}$. The **norm** of q is defined by $|q| \equiv \sqrt{q\overline{q}} = \sqrt{\overline{q}q} = \sqrt{q_0^2 + q_1^2 + q_2^2 + q_3^2} \in \mathbb{R}$. If $q \neq 0$, then its inverse is $q^{-1} = \overline{q}/|q|$.

We recall some basic properties and definitions.

Theorem 1. *For any $q_1, q_2 \in \mathbb{H}$, $\overline{q_1 + q_2} = \overline{q_1} + \overline{q_2}$, and $\overline{q_1 q_2} = \overline{q_2}\,\overline{q_1}$.*

We now introduce the notion of similarity.

Definition 1. *Given $q, q' \in \mathbb{H}$, $q \sim q'$ if there exists $\sigma \in \mathbb{H}$ such that $q' = \sigma q \sigma^{-1}$.*

This defines an equivalence relation on $\mathbb{H}$. The **conjugacy class** of a quaternion q is denoted by $[q] = \{x \in \mathbb{H} : x \sim q\}$. All elements of $[q]$ satisfy the same characteristic polynomial:

$$\Delta_q(x) = x^2 - t(q)x + |q|^2 \tag{4}$$

Let $\mathbb{H}[x]$ denote the ring of left-unilateral polynomials with quaternionic coefficients, where the variable x commutes with elements of $\mathbb{H}$. A polynomial

$p(x) = \sum_{i=0}^{n} a_i x^i \in \mathbb{H}[x]$ is said to have degree n if $a_n \neq 0$, and is called **monic** if $a_n = 1$. The conjugate of $p(x)$ is given by $\overline{p}(x) = \sum_{i=0}^{n} \overline{a}_i x^i$.

For $p(x) \in \mathbb{H}[x]$ and $q \in \mathbb{H}$, the **evaluation** of $p(x)$ at q is defined as:

$$p(q) = \sum_{i=0}^{n} a_i q^i, \tag{5}$$

where the expression must be rewritten in standard form before substitution (see p. 262 in [8]).

Although addition and multiplication in $\mathbb{H}[x]$ mimic those in the commutative case, it is important to note that in general:

$$f(x)g(x) = p(x) \Rightarrow f(q)g(q) \neq p(q). \tag{6}$$

We say that $q \in \mathbb{H}$ is a *zero* of $p(x)$ if $p(q) = 0$. The set of all such zeros is denoted by $\mathrm{Zero}(p)$.

Note that if $a_n \neq 0$, then $p(q) = 0$ if and only if $a_n^{-1} p(q) = 0$, so we may assume without loss of generality that $p(x)$ is monic.

We now present key theorems about the zeros of quaternion polynomials.

Let $p(x), q(x), r(x) \in \mathbb{H}[X]$. We define $r(x)$ as a **right divisor** of $p(x)$ if there exists a polynomial $q(x)$ such that $p(x) = q(x)r(x)$.

Theorem 2 (pp. 262 [8]). *Let $q \in \mathbb{H}$ and $p(x) \in \mathbb{H}[x]$. Then $q \in \mathrm{Zero}(p)$ if and only if $x - q$ is a right divisor of $p(x)$.*

Theorem 3 (pp. 263 [8]). *Let $q \in \mathbb{H}$ and $p(x), q(x), r(x) \in \mathbb{H}[X]$ be such that $p(x) = q(x)r(x)$. If $\gamma = r(q) \neq 0$, then $p(q) = q(\gamma q \gamma^{-1}) r(q)$.*

Theorem 4 (Factorization Theorem, pp. 658 [6]). *All non-constant quaternion polynomial of degree m can be factorized into a product of m linear factors.*

The above theorems provide a theoretical foundation for locating the zeros of quaternion polynomials. However, due to the noncommutativity of the quaternion algebra, the computation of these zeros requires specific methods. One such approach, combining both classical and quaternion-specific techniques, is described below.

Let $p(x) = \sum_{i=0}^{n} a_i x^i$ be a quaternion polynomial of degree n. The following algorithm, adapted from [19], outlines a systematic procedure for computing all zeros of $p(x)$:

1. Compute the polynomial $n_p(x) = p(x)\overline{p}(x)$. This is a polynomial of degree $2n$ with real coefficients.
2. Find the complex roots z_i of $n_p(x)$. These roots occur in conjugate pairs. The zeros of the original polynomial $p(x)$ will lie within the conjugacy classes $[z_i] \subset \mathbb{H}$.
3. For each complex root z_i, use Niven's algorithm [11] to extract the quaternion zeros from the class $[z_i]$. Specifically:

(a) Divide $p(x)$ on the right by the characteristic polynomial $\Delta_{z_i}(x)$, obtaining:

$$p(x) = q(x)\Delta_{z_i}(x) + \alpha x + \beta. \tag{7}$$

(b) if $\alpha = \beta = 0$, then $[z_i] \subset \text{Zero}(p)$;
(c) otherwise, the unique zero in the class is given by $q = -\alpha^{-1}\beta$.

2.2   Closed Quaternion Balls

In this subsection, we introduce the notion of closed quaternion balls, adapting the definitions from [2] to the quaternionic setting. These sets serve as the foundational structure for representing uncertainty in quaternion polynomial equations.

Definition 2. *Let $q \in \mathbb{H}$ and let $r \in \mathbb{R}_0^+$. The closed ball in $\mathbb{H}$, called* **a closed quaternion ball** *is defined by*

$$\langle q, r \rangle = \{x \in \mathbb{H} : |x - q| \leq r\}. \tag{8}$$

*If $Q = \langle q, r \rangle$ then the **center** and the **radius** of Q are denoted by $C(Q) = q$ and $R(Q) = r$, respectively.*

*The set of all closed quaternion balls is denoted by $\mathcal{H}$. The zero-radius elements in $\mathcal{H}$ are called **scalars** and correspond to the quaternions themselves.*

Definition 3. *Let $Q_1, Q_2 \in \mathcal{H}$. The closed quaternion balls Q_1 and Q_2 are* **concentric** *if $C(Q_1) = C(Q_2)$.*

If Q_1 and Q_2 are concentric and $R(Q_1) = R(Q_2)$, then Q_1 and Q_2 are equal.
We now state a useful characterization of inclusion between closed quaternion balls.

Lemma 1. *Let $Q_1, Q_2 \in \mathcal{H}$ such that $Q_1 = \langle q_1, r_1 \rangle$ and $Q_2 = \langle q_2, r_2 \rangle$. Then $Q_1 \subseteq Q_2$ if and only if $|q_1 - q_2| \leq r_2 - r_1$. In particular, if Q_1 and Q_2 are concentric, then $Q_1 \subseteq Q_2$ if and only if $r_1 \leq r_2$.*

Proof.

[⇒] Let $Q_1 \subseteq Q_2$. The most distant $x \in Q_1$ from q_2 is located at the boundary of Q_1, along the line that extends through q_1 and q_2. Consequently, $|x - q_2| = |q_2 - q_1| + |x - q_1| \leq r_2$, leading us to deduce that $|q_2 - q_1| \leq r_2 - r_1$.
[⇐] Suppose that $|q_1 - q_2| \leq r_2 - r_1$ and that $x \in Q_1$. Then

$$|x - q_2| = |x - q_1 + q_1 - q_2| \leq |x - q_1| + |q_2 - q_1| \leq r_1 + r_2 - r_1 = r_2. \tag{9}$$

Hence, $x \in Q_2$, and $Q_1 \subseteq Q_2$.

In the special case where $q_1 = q_2$, the condition reduces to $r_1 \leq r_2$.   □

Next we define algebraic operations on closed quaternion balls and study their properties.

Addition: We begin by defining a natural addition operation on closed quaternion balls and examining its algebraic properties.

Definition 4. *The binary operation* $+ : \mathcal{H} \times \mathcal{H} \to \mathcal{H}$, *from now on referred to as* **addition**, *is defined by the equation*

$$\langle \boldsymbol{q}_1, r_1 \rangle + \langle \boldsymbol{q}_2, r_2 \rangle := \langle \boldsymbol{q}_1 + \boldsymbol{q}_2, r_1 + r_2 \rangle. \tag{10}$$

Proposition 1. *Addition in* $\mathcal{H}$ *is both commutative and associative. Furthermore,* $\langle 0, 0 \rangle$ *is the addition identity.*

Proof. The result follows immediately from the commutativity and associativity of addition in $\mathbb{H}$ and $\mathbb{R}$, and from the addition identity elements $0 \in \mathbb{H}$ and $0 \in \mathbb{R}$. □

Corollary 1. *The elements in* $\mathcal{H}$ *that have an additive inverse are the zero-radius closed quaternion balls. Moreover, the reciprocal of* $\langle \boldsymbol{q}, 0 \rangle$ *is* $\langle -\boldsymbol{q}, 0 \rangle$.

Proof. A direct consequence of Definition 4 and Proposition 1. □

We now provide a geometric interpretation of the addition operation.

Lemma 2. *Let* $\boldsymbol{Q}_1, \boldsymbol{Q}_2 \in \mathcal{H}$. *Then* $\boldsymbol{Q}_1 + \boldsymbol{Q}_2 = \{\boldsymbol{x}_1 + \boldsymbol{x}_2 : \boldsymbol{x}_1 \in \boldsymbol{Q}_1 \text{ and } \boldsymbol{x}_2 \in \boldsymbol{Q}_2\}$.

Proof. Let $\boldsymbol{y}_i \in \boldsymbol{Q}_i = \langle \boldsymbol{q}_i, r_i \rangle$, for $i \in \{1, 2\}$. Then $\boldsymbol{y}_1 + \boldsymbol{y}_2 \in \{\boldsymbol{x}_1 + \boldsymbol{x}_2 : \boldsymbol{x}_1 \in \boldsymbol{Q}_1 \text{ and } \boldsymbol{x}_2 \in \boldsymbol{Q}_2\}$, and

$$\begin{aligned}
|\boldsymbol{y}_1 + \boldsymbol{y}_2 - (\boldsymbol{q}_1 + \boldsymbol{q}_2)| &= |\boldsymbol{y}_1 - \boldsymbol{q}_1 + \boldsymbol{y}_2 - \boldsymbol{q}_2| \\
&\leq |\boldsymbol{y}_1 - \boldsymbol{q}_1| + |\boldsymbol{y}_2 - \boldsymbol{q}_2| \\
&= r_1 + r_2.
\end{aligned} \tag{11}$$

Hence, $\boldsymbol{y}_1 + \boldsymbol{y}_2 \in \boldsymbol{Q}_1 + \boldsymbol{Q}_2$, and $\{\boldsymbol{x}_1 + \boldsymbol{x}_2 : \boldsymbol{x}_1 \in \boldsymbol{Q}_1 \text{ and } \boldsymbol{x}_2 \in \boldsymbol{Q}_2\} \subseteq \boldsymbol{Q}_1 + \boldsymbol{Q}_2$.
Conversely, for any $\boldsymbol{q} \in \boldsymbol{Q}_1 + \boldsymbol{Q}_2$, we can write $\boldsymbol{q} = \boldsymbol{y}_1 + \boldsymbol{y}_2$, where $\boldsymbol{y}_1 = \frac{r_1}{r_1 + r_2}(\boldsymbol{q} - \boldsymbol{q}_2) + \frac{r_2}{r_1 + r_2}\boldsymbol{q}_1$, and $\boldsymbol{y}_2 = \frac{r_2}{r_1 + r_2}(\boldsymbol{q} - \boldsymbol{q}_1) + \frac{r_1}{r_1 + r_2}\boldsymbol{q}_2$. Then

$$\begin{aligned}
|\boldsymbol{y}_1 - \boldsymbol{q}_1| &= \left| \frac{r_1}{r_1 + r_2}(\boldsymbol{q} - \boldsymbol{q}_2) + \frac{r_2}{r_1 + r_2}\boldsymbol{q}_1 - \boldsymbol{q}_1 \right| \\
&= \left| \frac{r_1}{r_1 + r_2}(\boldsymbol{q} - \boldsymbol{q}_2) - \frac{r_1}{r_1 + r_2}\boldsymbol{q}_1 \right| \\
&= \frac{r_1}{r_1 + r_2}|\boldsymbol{q} - \boldsymbol{q}_1 - \boldsymbol{q}_2| \\
&\leq \frac{r_1}{r_1 + r_2}(r_1 + r_2) = r_1.
\end{aligned} \tag{12}$$

Consequently, $\boldsymbol{y}_1 \in \boldsymbol{Q}_1$. Swapping indices 1 and 2, we can also conclude that $\boldsymbol{y}_2 \in \boldsymbol{Q}_2$. Hence, $\boldsymbol{q} \in \{\boldsymbol{x}_1 + \boldsymbol{x}_2 : \boldsymbol{x}_1 \in \boldsymbol{Q}_1 \text{ and } \boldsymbol{x}_2 \in \boldsymbol{Q}_2\}$ and $\boldsymbol{Q}_1 + \boldsymbol{Q}_2 \subseteq \{\boldsymbol{x}_1 + \boldsymbol{x}_2 : \boldsymbol{x}_1 \in \boldsymbol{Q}_1 \text{ and } \boldsymbol{x}_2 \in \boldsymbol{Q}_2\}$. □

We now introduce a monotonicity property under inclusion.

Definition 5. *Let $\diamond : \mathcal{B} \times \mathcal{B} \to \mathcal{B}$ be a binary operation in $\mathcal{B}$. The operation $\diamond$ is **inclusion monotonic** if, for all $\boldsymbol{a}_m, \boldsymbol{b}_m \in \mathcal{B}$ such that $\boldsymbol{a}_m \subseteq \boldsymbol{b}_m$, $m \in \{1,2\}$, $\boldsymbol{a}_1 \diamond \boldsymbol{a}_2 \subseteq \boldsymbol{b}_1 \diamond \boldsymbol{b}_2$.*

Proposition 2. *The addition in $\mathcal{H}$ is inclusion monotonic.*

Proof. Let $\boldsymbol{Q}_m, \boldsymbol{R}_m \in \mathcal{H}$ such that $\boldsymbol{Q}_m \subseteq \boldsymbol{R}_m$, $m \in \{1,2\}$. By Lemma 2, $\boldsymbol{Q}_1 + \boldsymbol{Q}_2 = \{\boldsymbol{x} + \boldsymbol{y} : \boldsymbol{x} \in \boldsymbol{Q}_1 \text{ and } \boldsymbol{y} \in \boldsymbol{Q}_2\} \subseteq \{\boldsymbol{x} + \boldsymbol{y} : \boldsymbol{x} \in \boldsymbol{R}_1 \text{ and } \boldsymbol{y} \in \boldsymbol{R}_2\} = \boldsymbol{R}_1 + \boldsymbol{R}_2$. □

Multiplication: We now define and study multiplication of closed quaternion balls. This operation is not commutative and does not distribute over addition but retains important structural properties.

Definition 6. *The binary operation $* : \mathcal{H} \times \mathcal{H} \to \mathcal{H}$, referred to as **multiplication**, is defined by*

$$\langle q_1, r_1 \rangle * \langle q_2, r_2 \rangle \equiv \langle q_1, r_1 \rangle \langle q_2, r_2 \rangle := \langle q_1 q_2, r_1 |q_2| + r_2 |q_1| + r_1 r_2 \rangle. \quad (13)$$

Scalar multiplication by $\alpha \in \mathbb{H}$ is defined as:

$$\alpha \langle q, r \rangle \equiv \langle \alpha, 0 \rangle \langle q, r \rangle = \langle \alpha q, |\alpha| r \rangle. \quad (14)$$

Proposition 3. *There exists a multiplicative identity in $\mathcal{H}$, namely the zero-radius ball $\langle 1, 0 \rangle$.*

Proof. For any $\langle q, r \rangle \in \mathcal{H}$, we have $\langle q, r \rangle \langle 1, 0 \rangle = \langle 1, 0 \rangle \langle q, r \rangle = \langle q, r \rangle$. □

Definition 7. *Let $\boldsymbol{Q} \in \mathcal{H}$. We define the **powers of $\boldsymbol{Q}$** $\neq \langle 0, 0 \rangle$ by*

$$\boldsymbol{Q}^0 = \langle 1, 0 \rangle \text{ and } \boldsymbol{Q}^k = \boldsymbol{Q}^{k-1} \boldsymbol{Q} \text{ for } k \in \mathbb{N}. \quad (15)$$

If $\boldsymbol{Q} = \langle 0, 0 \rangle$, then $\boldsymbol{Q}^k = \langle 0, 0 \rangle$, for all $k \in \mathbb{N}$.

Definition 8. *The multiplication operation is **power-associative** if, for all $\boldsymbol{Q} \in \mathcal{H}$ and for all $m, s \in \mathbb{N}$, $\boldsymbol{Q}^s \boldsymbol{Q}^m = \boldsymbol{Q}^{s+m}$.*

Proposition 4. *The multiplication in $\mathcal{H}$ is power-associative.*

Proof. Let $\boldsymbol{Q} = \langle q, r \rangle \in \mathcal{H}$. On one hand,

$$\boldsymbol{Q}^2 \boldsymbol{Q} = \langle q^2, 2 |q| r + r^2 \rangle \langle q, r \rangle \quad (16)$$
$$= \left\langle q^3, 3 |q|^2 r + 3 |q| r^2 + r^3 \right\rangle,$$

and

$$\boldsymbol{Q} \boldsymbol{Q}^2 = \langle q, r \rangle \langle q^2, 2 |q| r + r^2 \rangle \quad (17)$$
$$= \left\langle q^3, 3 |q|^2 r + 3 |q| r^2 + r^3 \right\rangle,$$

which implies $Q^2Q = QQ^2$.

On the other hand, we have

$$(Q^2Q)\,Q = \left\langle q^3, 3\,|q|^2\,r + 3\,|q|\,r^2 + r^3 \right\rangle \langle q, r \rangle \qquad (18)$$
$$= \left\langle q^4, 4\,|q|^3\,r + 6\,|q|^2\,r^2 + |q|\,r^3 + r^4 \right\rangle$$

and

$$Q^2Q^2 = \left\langle q^2, 2\,|q|\,r + r^2 \right\rangle \left\langle q^2, 2\,|q|\,r + r^2 \right\rangle \qquad (19)$$
$$= \left\langle q^4, 4\,|q|^3\,r + 6\,|q|^2\,r^2 + |q|\,r^3 + r^4 \right\rangle.$$

As $Q^2Q = QQ^2$ and $(Q^2Q)\,Q = Q^2Q^2$, invoking [1], the result follows.   □

Proposition 5. *Let* $\langle q, r \rangle \in \mathcal{H}$. *Then, for all* $k \in \mathbb{N}$ *with* $k \geq 1$,

$$\langle q, r \rangle^k = \left\langle q^k, (|q| + r)^k - |q|^k \right\rangle. \qquad (20)$$

Proof. Let $\langle q, r \rangle \in \mathcal{H}$. We will prove by induction. For $k = 1$, the equation states

$$\langle q, r \rangle = \langle q, |q| + r - |q| \rangle = \langle q, r \rangle, \qquad (21)$$

which is clearly true. Suppose that the proposition is true for k. Then, for $k+1$ we have

$$\langle q, r \rangle^{k+1} = \langle q, r \rangle^k\,\langle q, r \rangle$$
$$= \left\langle q^k, (|q| + r)^k - |q|^k \right\rangle \langle q, r \rangle \qquad (22)$$
$$= \left\langle q^{k+1}, |q|\left((|q| + r)^k - |q|^k \right) + |q|^k\,|\,r + \left((|q| + r)^k - |q|^k \right) r \right\rangle$$
$$= \left\langle q^k, |q|\,(|q| + r)^k - |q|^{k+1} + |q|^k\,r + (|q| + r)^k\,r - |q|^k\,r \right\rangle$$
$$= \left\langle q^{k+1}, (|q| + r)^{k+1} - |q|^{k+1} \right\rangle.$$

By mathematical induction, it is proved that for all $k \geq 1$ the statement is true.
□

Proposition 6. *The multiplication in* $\mathcal{H}$ *is not distributive with respect to the addition.*

Proof. Let $Q_1 = \langle i, 1 \rangle$, $Q_2 = \langle j, 1 \rangle$, and $Q_3 = \langle k, 1 \rangle$. Then

$$Q_1\,(Q_2 + Q_3) = \langle i, 1 \rangle\,\langle j + k, 2 \rangle = \left\langle k - j, 4 + \sqrt{2} \right\rangle \qquad (23)$$

and

$$Q_1Q_2 + Q_1Q_3 = \langle i, 1 \rangle\,\langle j, 1 \rangle + \langle i, 1 \rangle\,\langle k, 1 \rangle = \langle k, 3 \rangle + \langle -j, 3 \rangle = \langle k - j, 6 \rangle. \qquad (24)$$

Hence,

$$Q_1\,(Q_2 + Q_3) \neq Q_1Q_2 + Q_1Q_3. \qquad (25)$$

□

We have seen that the set $\{\boldsymbol{x}_1 + \boldsymbol{x}_2 : \boldsymbol{x}_i \in \boldsymbol{Q}_i,\ i = 1, 2\}$ remains a closed quaternion ball. However, the set $\{\boldsymbol{x}_1 \boldsymbol{x}_2 : \boldsymbol{x}_i \in \boldsymbol{Q}_i,\ i = 1, 2\}$ is generally not a closed quaternion ball. Nonetheless, it is bounded. Among all closed quaternion balls centered at $C(\boldsymbol{Q}_1)C(\boldsymbol{Q}_2)$, containing the set $\{\boldsymbol{x}_1 \boldsymbol{x}_2 : \boldsymbol{x}_i \in \boldsymbol{Q}_i,\ i = 1, 2\}$, we will demonstrate that the one with the minimal radius is the closed quaternion ball $\boldsymbol{Q}_1 \boldsymbol{Q}_2$.

Proposition 7. *The set of all products of two quaternions from distinct closed quaternion balls is not necessarily a closed quaternion ball.*

Proof. It is sufficient to consider a counterexample. Let $\boldsymbol{Q}_1 = \langle -5 - 2\boldsymbol{i}, 2 \rangle$ and $\boldsymbol{Q}_2 = \langle 5 + 2\boldsymbol{j}, 4 \rangle$. Then $\boldsymbol{Q}_1\boldsymbol{Q}_2 = \langle -25 - 10\boldsymbol{i} - 10\boldsymbol{j} - 4\boldsymbol{k}, 8 + 6\sqrt{29} \rangle$. Given that $|-25 - 10\boldsymbol{i} - 10\boldsymbol{j} - 4\boldsymbol{k}| \leq 8 + 6\sqrt{29}$, we deduce that $0 \in \boldsymbol{Q}_1\boldsymbol{Q}_2$, while $0 \notin \boldsymbol{Q}_1$ and $0 \notin \boldsymbol{Q}_2$. □

Lemma 3. *Let $\boldsymbol{Q}_1, \boldsymbol{Q}_2 \in \mathcal{H}$. Then $\{\boldsymbol{x}_1 \boldsymbol{x}_2 : \boldsymbol{x}_i \in \boldsymbol{Q}_i,\ i = 1, 2\} \subseteq \boldsymbol{Q}_1 \boldsymbol{Q}_2$.*

Proof. Let $\boldsymbol{Q}_1, \boldsymbol{Q}_2 \in \mathcal{H}$, $\boldsymbol{x}_1 \in \boldsymbol{Q}_1 = \langle q_1, r_1 \rangle$, and $\boldsymbol{x}_2 \in \boldsymbol{Q}_2 = \langle q_2, r_2 \rangle$. Then

$$
\begin{aligned}
|\boldsymbol{x}_1\boldsymbol{x}_2 - q_1 q_2| &= |\boldsymbol{x}_1\boldsymbol{x}_2 - \boldsymbol{x}_1 q_2 + \boldsymbol{x}_1 q_2 - q_1 q_2| \\
&= |\boldsymbol{x}_1(\boldsymbol{x}_2 - q_2) + (\boldsymbol{x}_1 - q_1)q_2| \\
&= |\boldsymbol{x}_1(\boldsymbol{x}_2 - q_2) - q_1(\boldsymbol{x}_2 - q_2) + q_1(\boldsymbol{x}_2 - q_2) + (\boldsymbol{x}_1 - q_1)q_2| \\
&= |(\boldsymbol{x}_1 - q_1)(\boldsymbol{x}_2 - q_2) + q_1(\boldsymbol{x}_2 - q_2) + (\boldsymbol{x}_1 - q_1)q_2| \qquad (26) \\
&\leq |\boldsymbol{x}_1 - q_1|\,|\boldsymbol{x}_2 - q_2| + |q_1|\,|\boldsymbol{x}_2 - q_2| + |\boldsymbol{x}_1 - q_1|\,|q_2| \\
&= r_1 r_2 + |q_1|\,r_2 + |q_2|\,r_1.
\end{aligned}
$$

Hence, $\boldsymbol{x}_1\boldsymbol{x}_2 \in \boldsymbol{Q}_1\boldsymbol{Q}_2$. □

Proposition 8. *Given the closed quaternion balls $\boldsymbol{Q}_i = \langle q_i, r_i \rangle$, for $i = 1, 2$, the closed quaternion ball centered at $q_1 q_2$ with the smallest radius that contains $\{\boldsymbol{x}_1\boldsymbol{x}_2 : \boldsymbol{x}_i \in \boldsymbol{Q}_i,\ i = 1, 2\}$ is $\boldsymbol{Q}_1 \boldsymbol{Q}_2$.*

Proof. Let $\boldsymbol{Q}_1 = \langle q_1, r_1 \rangle$, $\boldsymbol{Q}_2 = \langle q_2, r_2 \rangle$, and $\boldsymbol{y} = \boldsymbol{x}_1\boldsymbol{x}_2$. If $q_1 = q_2 = 0$, then $\boldsymbol{x}_i = \frac{\sigma_i}{|\sigma_i|}r_i \in \boldsymbol{Q}_i$, for any $0 \neq \sigma_i \in \mathbb{H}$, $i = 1, 2$. Furthermore, $|\boldsymbol{x}_1\boldsymbol{x}_2| = r_1 r_2$, from where we conclude that $\boldsymbol{y}$ belongs to the border of $\boldsymbol{Q}_1\boldsymbol{Q}_2$.

If only one of the balls is centered at 0, and without loss of generality, suppose that $q_1 = 0$, then $\boldsymbol{x}_1 = \frac{\sigma}{|\sigma|}r_1 \in \boldsymbol{Q}_1$, for any $0 \neq \sigma \in \mathbb{H}$, and $\boldsymbol{x}_2 = \left(1 + \frac{r_2}{|q_2|}\right)q_2 \in \boldsymbol{Q}_2$. Since $\boldsymbol{x}_1\boldsymbol{x}_2 = \frac{\sigma}{|\sigma|}\left(|q_2|\,r_1 + r_1 r_2\right)\frac{q_2}{|q_2|}$ and

$$
\boldsymbol{Q}_1\boldsymbol{Q}_2 = \{\boldsymbol{x} \in \mathbb{H} : |\boldsymbol{x}| \leq |q_2|\,r_1 + r_1 r_2\}, \qquad (27)
$$

we also conclude that $\boldsymbol{y}$ belongs to the border of $\boldsymbol{Q}_1\boldsymbol{Q}_2$.

If both balls are not centered at 0, then $\boldsymbol{x}_i = \left(1 + \frac{r_i}{|q_i|}\right)q_i \in \boldsymbol{Q}_i$, for $i = 1, 2$.

But

$$y = x_1 x_2$$

$$= \left(1 + \frac{r_1}{|q_1|}\right) q_1 \left(1 + \frac{r_2}{|q_2|}\right) q_2 \tag{28}$$

$$= q_1 q_2 + \frac{|q_1| r_2 + |q_2| r_1 + r_1 r_2}{|q_1| |q_2|} q_1 q_2.$$

Since

$$Q_1 Q_2 = \{x \in \mathbb{H} : |x - q_1 q_2| \le |q_1| r_2 + |q_2| r_1 + r_1 r_2\}, \tag{29}$$

one can verify that y belongs again to the border of $Q_1 Q_2$. Since y belongs to the border in all cases, and taking into account Lemma 3, we conclude the proposition. □

Proposition 9. *The multiplication in $\mathcal{H}$ is inclusion monotonic.*

Proof. Let $Q_1 = \langle q_1, r_1 \rangle$, $Q_2 = \langle q_2, r_2 \rangle$, $Q_3 = \langle q_3, r_3 \rangle$, and $Q_4 = \langle q_4, r_4 \rangle$, such that $Q_1 \subseteq Q_3$ and $Q_2 \subseteq Q_4$. Then

$$Q_1 Q_2 = \langle q_1 q_2, |q_1| r_2 + |q_2| r_1 + r_1 r_2 \rangle. \tag{30}$$

Let $x \in Q_1 Q_2$. Then

$$
\begin{aligned}
|x - q_3 q_4| &= |x - q_1 q_2 + q_1 q_2 - q_3 q_4| \\
&\le |x - q_1 q_2| + |q_1 q_2 - q_3 q_4| \\
&\le |q_1| r_2 + |q_2| r_1 + r_1 r_2 + |q_1 q_2 - q_1 q_4 + q_1 q_4 - q_3 q_4| \\
&\le |q_1| r_2 + |q_2| r_1 + r_1 r_2 + |q_1| |q_4 - q_2| + |q_4| |q_3 - q_1|.
\end{aligned} \tag{31}
$$

Since $Q_1 \subseteq Q_3$ and $Q_2 \subseteq Q_4$, by Lemma 1,

$$
\begin{aligned}
|x - q_3 q_4| &\le |q_1| r_2 + |q_2| r_1 + r_1 r_2 + |q_1| (r_4 - r_2) + |q_4| (r_3 - r_1) \\
&= (|q_2| - |q_4|) r_1 + r_1 r_2 + |q_1| r_4 + |q_4| r_3 \\
&\le |q_4 - q_2| r_1 + r_1 r_2 + |q_1| r_4 + |q_4| r_3.
\end{aligned} \tag{32}
$$

Again, by Lemma 1,

$$
\begin{aligned}
|x - q_3 q_4| &\le (r_4 - r_2) r_1 + r_1 r_2 + |q_1| r_4 + |q_4| r_3 \\
&= r_4 r_1 + |q_1| r_4 + |q_4| r_3.
\end{aligned} \tag{33}
$$

Since $Q_1 \subseteq Q_3$, we know that $|q_3 - q_1| \le r_3 - r_1$. Thus

$$|q_1| - |q_3| \le |q_3 - q_1| \le r_3 - r_1 \tag{34}$$

from where we conclude that

$$|q_1| \le r_3 - r_1 + |q_3|. \tag{35}$$

Substituting in Eq. (33), we obtain

$$
\begin{aligned}
|x - q_3 q_4| &\le r_4 r_1 + (r_3 - r_1 + |q_3|) r_4 + |q_4| r_3 \\
&= |q_4| r_3 + |q_3| r_4 + r_3 r_4.
\end{aligned} \tag{36}
$$

Hence, $x \in Q_3 Q_4$, and $Q_1 Q_2 \subseteq Q_3 Q_4$. □

3   Polynomial Equations in Closed Quaternion Balls

In this section, we present our main results concerning quaternion polynomial equations with imprecisely defined coefficients. We focus on determining conditions under which a closed quaternion ball contains all solutions of such equations, and we provide explicit bounds for the radius of the solution ball. We also derive a formula analogous to the de Moivre's theorem, suitable for computing powers and roots of closed quaternion balls.

Solving such equations involves subtleties that may not be immediately apparent. For instance, the solution set of equation

$$A_2 X^2 = A_1 X + A_0, \tag{37}$$

where $A_2, A_1, A_0 \in \mathcal{H}$, is not the same solution set of equation

$$A_2 X^2 - A_1 X = A_0. \tag{38}$$

Since only closed quaternion balls with zero radius, i.e., scalar quaternions, possess additive inverses in $\mathcal{H}$, only such terms can be freely moved from one side of an equation to the other without altering the solution set. As a result, caution is required when manipulating these expressions, particularly when rearranging terms. Nonetheless, within this limitation, it is still possible to obtain meaningful results for certain specific cases.

Proposition 10. *Consider the equation*

$$A_n X^n + A_{n-1} X^{n-1} + \cdots + A_1 X + A_0 = 0_\alpha, \tag{39}$$

where $A_i = \langle a_i, r_i \rangle \in \mathcal{H}$, for $i = 0, \ldots, n$ and $0_\alpha = \langle 0, \alpha \rangle \in \mathcal{H}$. Then $\langle q, r \rangle$ is a solution of (39) if and only if

$$|q|^n r_n + |q|^{n-1} r_{n-1} + \cdots + |q| r_1 + r_0 \leq \alpha, \tag{40}$$

where q is a zero of the quaternion polynomial

$$p(x) = a_n x^n + a_{n-1} x^{n-1} + \cdots + a_1 x + a_0. \tag{41}$$

Moreover, for each q, the solution is unique.

Proof. Let $X = \langle q, r \rangle$ and $A_k = \langle a_k, r_k \rangle$. Calling upon Proposition 5, we have

$$
\begin{aligned}
A_k X^k &= \langle a_k, r_k \rangle \left\langle q^k, (|q| + r)^k - |q|^k \right\rangle \\
&= \left\langle a_k q^k, |q^k| r_k + (|a_k| + r_k) \left((|q| + r)^k - |q|^k \right) \right\rangle \\
&= \left\langle a_k q^k, (|a_k| + r_k)(|q| + r)^k - |a_k q^k| \right\rangle.
\end{aligned}
\tag{42}
$$

Thus,

$$\sum_{k=0}^{n} A_k X^k = \sum_{k=0}^{n} \left\langle a_k q^k, (|a_k| + r_k)(|q| + r)^k - |a_k q^k| \right\rangle$$

$$= \left\langle \sum_{k=0}^{n} a_k q^k, \sum_{k=0}^{n} \left((|a_k| + r_k)(|q| + r)^k - |a_k q^k| \right) \right\rangle \qquad (43)$$

$$= \left\langle \sum_{k=0}^{n} a_k q^k, \sum_{k=0}^{n} \left(\sum_{i=0}^{k} (|a_k| + r_k) \binom{k}{i} |q|^{k-i} r^i - |a_k q^k| \right) \right\rangle$$

From equation $\sum_{k=0}^{n} A_k X^k = \langle 0, \alpha \rangle$, we get two equations, one for the center

$$\sum_{k=0}^{n} a_k q^k = 0, \qquad (44)$$

and another for the radius

$$\alpha = \sum_{k=0}^{n} \left(\sum_{i=0}^{k} (|a_k| + r_k) \binom{k}{i} |q|^{k-i} r^i - |a_k q|^k \right). \qquad (45)$$

The RHS of this last equation is a polynomial in r where all the coefficients and the independent term are positive. From $r \geq 0$, we conclude that

$$\alpha \geq \sum_{k=0}^{n} |q|^k r_k. \qquad (46)$$

Furthermore, if this final condition is satisfied, then for each quaternion root of Eq. (44), the associated Eq. (45) has all coefficients positive except for the constant term, which is negative. Consequently, by Descartes' Rule of Signs, the equation admits exactly one positive real solution. □

We next study second-degree quaternion polynomial equations of the form $f(x) = g(x)$, where both f and g have degree two.

Proposition 11. *Consider the second-degree closed quaternion ball equation*

$$\langle a_2, r_2 \rangle X^2 + \langle a_1, r_1 \rangle X + \langle a_0, r_0 \rangle = \langle b_2, r_2 \rangle X^2 + \langle b_1, r_1 \rangle X + \langle b_0, r_0 \rangle, \qquad (47)$$

where $|b_2| \neq |a_2|$, *and let* q *be a zero of the quaternion polynomial*

$$p(x) = (a_2 - b_2)x^2 + (a_1 - b_1)x + a_0 - b_0. \qquad (48)$$

For each q, *the solutions of* (47) *are the closed quaternion balls* $\langle q, 0 \rangle$, *and* $\langle q, \beta - 2|q| \rangle$, *where*

$$\beta = -\frac{|a_1| - |b_1|}{|a_2| - |b_2|} \qquad (49)$$

provided that $\beta \geq -2|q|$, *which ensures the radius is non-negative and thus defines a valid closed quaternion ball.*

Proof. Applying the closed quaternion ball arithmetic

$$\langle a_2, r_2 \rangle X^2 + \langle a_1, r_1 \rangle X + \langle a_0, r_0 \rangle = \langle b_2, r_2 \rangle X^2 + \langle b_1, r_1 \rangle X + \langle b_0, r_0 \rangle, \quad (50)$$

and putting $X = \langle x, r \rangle$, we get two equations: one for the center

$$a_2 x^2 + a_1 x + a_0 = b_2 x^2 + b_1 x + b_0; \quad (51)$$

and another for the radius, which, after canceling equal terms from both sides, takes the form

$$|a_2| R^2 + |a_1| R - |a_2 q^2| - |a_1 q| = |b_2| R^2 + |b_1| R - |b_2 q^2| - |b_1 q| \quad (52)$$

where $R = |q| + r$. These equations can be expressed as follows:

$$p(x) = \alpha_2 x^2 + \alpha_1 x + \alpha_0 \quad (53)$$

and

$$\alpha_2 (R^2 - |q|^2) + \alpha_1 (R - |q|) = 0, \quad (54)$$

where $\alpha_i = |a_i| - |b_i|$.

If q is a solution of the first equation, then for the second equation

$$(\alpha_2 (R + |q|) + \alpha_1)(R - |q|) = 0 \iff (\alpha_2 (r + 2|q|) + \alpha_1) r = 0, \quad (55)$$

there are two solutions: $r = 0$, and $r = -\alpha_1/\alpha_2 - 2|q|$, provided $\alpha_1/\alpha_2 \le 2|q|$.
□

Proposition 12. *Consider the closed quaternion ball polynomial equation*

$$A_n X^n + \cdots + A_1 X + A_0 = B_n X^n + \cdots + B_1 X + B_0, \quad (56)$$

where $A_i = \langle a_i, r_i \rangle$ and $B = \langle b_i, r_i \rangle$, for $i = 0, \ldots, n$, and A_n and B_n are not concentric. Then the scalar $\langle q, 0 \rangle$ is a solution, where q a zero of the quaternion polynomial

$$p(x) = (a_n - b_n)x^n + \cdots + (a_1 - b_1)x + a_0 - b_0. \quad (57)$$

Furthermore, any other solution, if it exists, is independent of the r_i's.

Proof. In the proof of Proposition 11, we note that the closed quaternion ball polynomial equation inherently produces two distinct equations: one for the center, which determines the roots of the corresponding quaternion polynomial, and another for the radius. The radii of the coefficients for terms of similar degree are the same on both sides of the equation, resulting in their cancellation and rendering the radius equation independent of these terms. Furthermore, it is evident that $r = 0$ consistently constitutes a valid solution for any root q of the central equation. As the radius equation is not dependent of r_i, it consequently follows that any other solution for the radius will also be independent of them.□

A classical problem associated with polynomial equations is the computation of n-th roots, here, in the context of closed quaternion balls. Specifically, an n-th root of a closed quaternion ball $\boldsymbol{A}$ is another closed quaternion ball $\boldsymbol{X}$ such that $\boldsymbol{X}^n = \boldsymbol{A}$. As shown in the following result, this leads to a quaternionic analogue of the de Moivre's formula, from which we derive an explicit expression for the n-th root of a closed quaternion ball.

Proposition 13. *Let* $a \in \mathbb{H}$ *be given in the polar form*

$$a = |a| \left(\cos\theta + \hat{u}_a \sin\theta\right), \tag{58}$$

with $\hat{u}_a \equiv \frac{a}{|a|} \neq 0$. *Then* $\boldsymbol{A} = \langle a, r_a \rangle \in \mathcal{H}$ *has exactly* n *n-th roots given by*

$$\sqrt[n]{\boldsymbol{A}} = \left\langle \sqrt[n]{|a|} \left(\cos\left(\frac{\theta + 2k\pi}{n}\right) + \hat{u}_a \sin\left(\frac{\theta + 2k\pi}{n}\right)\right), \sqrt[n]{|a| + r_a} - \sqrt[n]{|a|} \right\rangle, \tag{59}$$

for $k = 0, \ldots, n - 1$.

Proof. Let $\boldsymbol{X} = \langle q, r \rangle$ and $\boldsymbol{A} = \langle a, r_a \rangle$. The n-th roots of $\boldsymbol{A}$ can be obtained by the closed quaternion ball equation $\boldsymbol{X}^n = \boldsymbol{A}$. Substituting $\boldsymbol{X}$ and $\boldsymbol{A}$ in this equation, we obtain two equations:

$$\begin{cases} q^n = a \\ (|q| + r)^n - |q|^n = r_a \end{cases}. \tag{60}$$

The solution for the first equation is wellknown and can be found in [9], and is given by

$$q = \sqrt[n]{|a|} \left(\cos\left(\frac{\theta + 2k\pi}{n}\right) + \hat{u}_a \sin\left(\frac{\theta + 2k\pi}{n}\right)\right), \tag{61}$$

for $k = 0, \ldots, n - 1$.

For the second equation there is only one real positive solution, namely,

$$r = \sqrt[n]{|a| + r_a} - \sqrt[n]{|a|}. \tag{62}$$

Hence, the n solutions for the n-th roots of the closed quaternion ball $\boldsymbol{A}$ are given by

$$\sqrt[n]{\boldsymbol{A}} = \left\langle \sqrt[n]{|a|} \left(\cos\left(\frac{\theta + 2k\pi}{n}\right) + \hat{u}_a \sin\left(\frac{\theta + 2k\pi}{n}\right)\right), \sqrt[n]{|a| + r_a} - \sqrt[n]{|a|} \right\rangle, \tag{63}$$

for $k = 0, \ldots, n - 1$. $\qquad\square$

4   Examples

In this section, we will present some examples illustrating our findings.

For the first three examples, the quaternion polynomial equation is the same. For the sake of clarity, we will illustrate how the zeros of this equation are computed using Niven's algorithm.

We need to solve the polynomial equation

$$p(x) = x^3 - (i + 2j + 3k)x^2 + (6i - 3j + 2k)x + 6 = 0. \tag{64}$$

Following the zero-finding algorithm adapted from Niven's method (see Subsect. 2.1):

1. compute $n_p(x) = p(x)\overline{p}(x) = x^6 + 14x^4 + 49x^2 + 36$;
2. compute the complex zeros of $n_p(x)$: $\pm i, \pm 2i, \pm 3i$;
3. (a) for $z_1 = \pm i$, $\Delta_{z_1}(x) = x^2 + 1$; dividing $p(x)$ by $\Delta_{z_1}(x)$, we obtain

$$p(x) = q(x)\Delta_{z_1}(x) + \alpha x + \beta \tag{65}$$

where $\alpha = -1 + 6i - 3j + 2k$ and $\beta = 6 + i + 2j + 3k$, which gives the zero $q_1 = -\alpha^{-1}\beta = \dfrac{1}{25}(12i - 16j + 15k)$;
   (b) for $z_2 = \pm 2i$, $\Delta_{z_2}(x) = x^2 + 4$; dividing $p(x)$ by $\Delta_{z_2}(x)$, we obtain

$$p(x) = q(x)\Delta_{z_2}(x) + \alpha x + \beta \tag{66}$$

where $\alpha = -4 + 6i - 3j + 2k$ and $\beta = 6 + 4i + 8j + 12k$, which gives the zero $q_2 = -\alpha^{-1}\beta = \dfrac{1}{13}(-10j + 24k)$;
   (c) for $z_3 = \pm 3i$, $\Delta_{z_3}(x) = x^2 + 9$; dividing $p(x)$ by $\Delta_{z_3}(x)$, we obtain

$$p(x) = q(x)\Delta_{z_3}(x) + \alpha x + \beta \tag{67}$$

where $\alpha = -9 + 6i - 3j + 2k$ and $\beta = 6 + 9i + 18j + 27k$, which gives the zero $q_3 = -\alpha^{-1}\beta = 3k$.

The following example demonstrates the basic use of the solution from Proposition 10 for a cubic equation with uncertainty in the right-hand side.

Example 1. Let $X = \langle q, r \rangle$.

$$X^3 + a_2 X^2 + a_1 X = \langle -a_0, 1 \rangle, \tag{68}$$

where

$$
\begin{aligned}
a_2 &= -(i + 2j + 3k) \\
a_1 &= 6i - 3j + 2k \\
a_0 &= 6
\end{aligned} \tag{69}
$$

From the closed quaternion ball polynomial equation, we obtain two equations, one for the center and the other for the radius:

$$
\begin{cases}
q^3 + a_2 q^2 + a_1 q + a_0 = 0 \\
r^3 + (3\,|q| + \sqrt{14})r^2 + (3\,|q|^2 + 2\sqrt{14}\,|q| + 7)r = 1
\end{cases} \tag{70}
$$

The zeros of the first equation where already calculated. It is easy to see that $q_1 \in [i]$, $q_2 \in [2i]$, and $q_3 \in [3i]$. Hence, $|q_1| = 1$, $|q_2| = 2$, and $|q_3| = 3$. For each of these zeros, there exists only one radius. Solving the second equation, we obtain $r_1 \approx 0.055979$, $r_2 \approx 0.029195$, and $r_3 \approx 0.017644$, respectively. Thus, Eq. (68) has three solutions:

$$
\begin{aligned}
X_1 &\approx \left\langle \frac{1}{25}(12i - 16j + 15k), 0.055979 \right\rangle \\
X_2 &\approx \left\langle \frac{1}{13}(-10j + 24k), 0.029195 \right\rangle \\
X_3 &\approx \langle 3k, 0.017644 \rangle.
\end{aligned}
\tag{71}
$$

◇

The following example illustrates Proposition 12. The equation is structurally similar to that in Example 1, except that the linear term has been moved to the opposite side, leading to a different solution due to the algebraic asymmetry of closed quaternion balls.

Example 2. Let $X = \langle q, r \rangle$.

$$
X^3 + A_2 X^2 = -A_1 X - B,
\tag{72}
$$

where

$$
\begin{aligned}
A_2 &= \langle -(i + 2j + 3k), 0 \rangle \\
A_1 &= \langle 6i - 3j + 2k, 0 \rangle \\
B &= \langle -a_0, 1 \rangle \\
a_0 &= 6
\end{aligned}
\tag{73}
$$

From the closed quaternion ball polynomial equation, we obtain two equations, one for the center and the other for the radius:

$$
\begin{cases}
q^3 + a_2 q^2 + a_1 q + a_0 = 0 \\
r^3 + (3|q| - \sqrt{14})r^2 + (3|q|^2 - 2\sqrt{14}|q| + 7)r - 1 = 0
\end{cases}
\tag{74}
$$

The zeros of the first equation are the same as in Example 1. For each of these zeros, there exists only one radius. Solving the second equation, we obtain $r_1 \approx 0.41989$, $r_2 \approx 0.21859$, and $r_3 \approx 0.083365$, respectively. Thus, Eq. (72) has three solutions:

$$
\begin{aligned}
X_1 &\approx \left\langle \frac{1}{25}(12i - 16j + 15k), 0.41989 \right\rangle \\
X_2 &\approx \left\langle \frac{1}{13}(-10j + 24k), 0.21859 \right\rangle \\
X_3 &\approx \langle 3k, 0.083365 \rangle.
\end{aligned}
\tag{75}
$$

The third example also relates to Proposition 12. The equation is similar to that in Example 1, but the coefficients now have nonzero radii. This affects the radial part of the solution, altering the admissible values and causing one of the previously valid solutions to disappear.

Example 3. Let $X = \langle q, r \rangle$.

$$X^3 + A_2 X^2 + A_1 X + A_0 = \langle 0, 1 \rangle, \tag{76}$$

where

$$\begin{aligned}
A_2 &= \langle -(i + 2j + 3k), 0.1 \rangle \\
A_1 &= \langle 6i - 3j + 2k, 0.2 \rangle \\
A_0 &= \langle 6, 0.1 \rangle
\end{aligned} \tag{77}$$

From the closed quaternion ball polynomial equation, we obtain two equations, one for the center and the other for the radius:

$$\begin{cases}
q^3 + a_2 q^2 + a_1 q + a_0 = 0 \\
R^3 + (|a_2| + r_2) R^2 + (|a_1| + r_1) R + r_0 - 1 - |q^3| - |a_2 q^2| - |a_1 q| = 0
\end{cases}, \tag{78}$$

where $R = |q| + r$.

The zeros of the first equation are the same as in Example 1. The condition (40) of Proposition 10 is not satisfied for q_3, so it does not correspond to a valid solution. For q_2 and q_1 the condition is verified. Solving the second equation, we obtain $r'_1 \approx 0.0331229$, and $r'_2 \approx 0.00289056$. Thus, Eq. (76) has two solutions:

$$\begin{aligned}
X_1 &\approx \left\langle \frac{1}{25}(12i - 16j + 15k), 0.0331229 \right\rangle \\
X_2 &\approx \left\langle \frac{1}{13}(-10j + 24k), 0.00289056 \right\rangle.
\end{aligned} \tag{79}$$

$\Diamond$

The following example illustrates Proposition 11 by considering a quadratic equation in which corresponding terms on both sides have the same radius, allowing the radius components to cancel and yielding a purely algebraic condition on the centers.

Example 4. Consider the equation

$$\langle 2, 2 \rangle X^2 + \langle 1, 10 \rangle X + \langle 2, 1 \rangle = \langle 1, 2 \rangle X^2 + \langle 4, 10 \rangle X + \langle 5, 1 \rangle. \tag{80}$$

From the closed quaternion ball polynomial equation, we obtain two equations, one for the center and the other for the radius:

$$\begin{cases}
q^2 - 3q - 3 = 0 \\
(r + 2|q| - 3)r = 0
\end{cases}. \tag{81}$$

From the first equation, we get

$$q_1 = \frac{3 - \sqrt{21}}{2} \quad \text{and} \quad q_2 = \frac{3 + \sqrt{21}}{2}. \tag{82}$$

From Proposition 11, we have $\beta = 3$. For q_1, the quantity $\beta - 2\,|q_1| = 6 - \sqrt{2} > 0$. Hence, for this root, there are two solutions:

$$X_1 = \langle q_1, 0 \rangle \quad \text{and} \quad X_2 = \left\langle q_1, 6 - \sqrt{21} \right\rangle. \tag{83}$$

For q_2, the quantity $\beta - 2\,|q_2| < 0$. Therefore, for this root, there is only one solution:

$$X_3 = \langle q_2, 0 \rangle. \tag{84}$$

$\Diamond$

Finally, the next example illustrates Proposition 13 by applying the quaternionic de Moivre formula to compute the cube roots of a closed quaternion ball. The result demonstrates how both the center and radius transform under root extraction in this setting.

Example 5. Let $A = \langle 4(1 + i + j + k), 19 \rangle$. The quaternion $a = 4(1 + i + j + k)$ written in polar form is given by $a = 8\,(\cos \theta + \hat{u}_a \sin \theta)$, where $\theta = \frac{\pi}{3}$ and $\hat{u}_a = \frac{1}{\sqrt{3}}(i + j + k)$. Applying the de Moivre's formula, the cube roots of A are:

$$
\begin{aligned}
Q_1 &= \left\langle 8 \left(\cos \left(\frac{\pi}{9} \right) + \sin \left(\frac{\pi}{9} \right) \frac{i + j + k}{\sqrt{3}} \right), 1 \right\rangle \\
Q_2 &= \left\langle 8 \left(\cos \left(\frac{7\pi}{9} \right) + \sin \left(\frac{7\pi}{9} \right) \frac{i + j + k}{\sqrt{3}} \right), 1 \right\rangle \\
Q_3 &= \left\langle 8 \left(\cos \left(\frac{13\pi}{9} \right) + \sin \left(\frac{13\pi}{9} \right) \frac{i + j + k}{\sqrt{3}} \right), 1 \right\rangle.
\end{aligned} \tag{85}
$$

It can easily be checked that $Q_i^3 = A$, for $i = 1, 2, 3$. $\Diamond$

Acknowledgments. R. Serôdio is supported by FCT (Fundação para a Ciência e a Tecnologia, Portugal), research project UIDB/00212/2020 of CMA-UBI (Centro de Matemática e Aplicações, Universidade da Beira Interior, Portugal).

Disclosure of Interests. The authors have no competing interests to declare that are relevant to the content of this article.

References

1. Albert, A.A.: Power-associative rings. Trans. Amer. Math. Soc. **64**, 552–593 (1948). https://doi.org/10.1090/S0002-9947-1948-0027750-7
2. Alefeld, G., Herzberger, J.: Introduction to Interval Computations, 1st edn. Academic Press, New York (1983)

3. Beites, P.D., Nicolás, A.P., Vitória, J.: Multiplication of closed balls in $\mathbb{C}^n$. Turkish J. Math. **47**, 1899–1914 (2023). https://doi.org/10.55730/1300-0098.3471

4. Berti, S.: On the interval equation $AX + B = CX + D$. J. Numer. Anal. Approx. Theory **2**, 11–2 (1973). https://doi.org/10.33993/jnaat21-7

5. Gargantini, I., Henrici, P.: Circular arithmetic and the determination of polynomial zeros. Numer. Math. **18**, 305–320 (1972). http://eudml.org/doc/132111

6. Gentili, G., Stoppato, C.: Zeros of regular functions and polynomials of a quaternionic variable. Michigan Math. J. **56**, 655–667 (2008). https://doi.org/10.1307/mmj/1231770366

7. Hansen, E.: On the solution of linear algebraic equations with interval coefficients. Linear Algebra Appl. **2**, 153–165 (1969). https://doi.org/10.1016/0024-3795(69)90024-X

8. Lam, T.Y.: A First Course in Noncommutative Rings, 1st edn. Springer, Berlin (1991). https://doi.org/10.1007/978-1-4419-8616-0

9. Leite, F.S., Vitoria, J.: Generalization of the de Moivre formulas for quaternions and octonions. Math. studies in the honour of Luis de Albuquerque, Universidade de Coimbra, Coimbra (1994)

10. Neumaier, A.: Further results on linear interval equations. Linear Algebra Appl. **87**, 155–179 (1987). https://doi.org/10.1016/0024-3795(87)90164-9

11. Niven, I.: Equations in quaternions. Amer. Math. Monthly **48**, 654–661 (1941). https://doi.org/10.1080/00029890.1941.11991158

12. Oettli, W., Prager, W.: Compatibility of approximate solution of linear equations with given error bounds for coefficients and right-hand sides. Numer. Math. **6**, 405–409 (1964). https://doi.org/10.1007/BF01386090

13. Oettli, W.: On the solution set of a linear system with inaccurate coefficients. SIAM J. Numer. Anal. **2**, 115–118 (1965). https://doi.org/10.1137/0702009

14. Opfer, G., Janovská, D.: A note on the computation of all zeros of simple quaternionic polynomials. SIAM J. Numer. Anal. **48**(1), 244–256 (2010). https://doi.org/10.1137/090748871

15. Polyak, B.T., Nazin, S.A.: Interval solutions for interval algebraic equations. Math. Comput. Simulat. **66**, 207–217 (2004). https://doi.org/10.1016/j.matcom.2003.11.006

16. Ratschek, H., Sauer, W.: Linear interval equations. Computing **28**, 105–115 (1982). https://doi.org/10.1007/BF02241817

17. Rohn, J.: A Fakras-type theorem for linear interval equations. Computing **43**, 93–95 (1989). https://doi.org/10.1007/BF02243809

18. Seif, N.P., Hussein, S.A., Deif, A.S.: The interval Sylvester equation. Computing **52**, 233–244 (1994). https://doi.org/10.1007/BF02246505

19. Serôdio, R., Siu, L.-S.: Zeros of quaternion polynomials. Appl. Math. Lett. **14**, 237–239 (2001). https://doi.org/10.1016/S0893-9659(00)00142-7

20. Singh, S., Panda, G.: Bounding the solution set of overdetermined system of interval linear equations. B. Iran. Math. Soc., 51–23 (2025). https://doi.org/10.1007/s41980-024-00943-3

Computational and Applied Statistics
(CAS 2025)

Predicting Obstetric Outcome Through a Web Application Using a Multinomial Logistic Regression Model

Márcia Oliveira[1]([✉]) [iD], Ana Cristina Braga[2] [iD], and Rosete Nogueira[3,4] [iD]

[1] School of Engineering, University of Minho, 4710-057 Braga, Portugal
marcia27999@gmail.com
[2] ALGORITMI Research Centre, LASI, University of Minho, Campus de Gualtar, 4710-057 Braga, Portugal
[3] Life and Health Sciences Research Institute (ICVS), ICVS/3B's - PT Government Associate Laboratory, Campus de Gualtar, 4710-057 Braga/Guimarães, Portugal
[4] CGC Genetics, Unilabs, Embryo-fetal Pathology Laboratory, R. Sá da Bandeira, 706, 5o, 4000-432 Porto, Portugal

Abstract. Accurately predicting obstetric outcome is a critical challenge in maternal-fetal medicine, with significant implications for improving healthcare practices and minimizing adverse events. A dataset comprising fetoplacental biometric features was used, with the response variable stratified into three distinct categories: newborn, intrauterine fetal death, and neonatal death. In this context, the present paper aimed to develop an application capable of predicting one of the three possible obstetric outcomes. Multinomial logistic regression models are commonly used to identify the most influential predictors, as they enable the modeling of relationships between independent variables and a categorical dependent variable with more than two categories. In that regard, within the scope of model determination, various variable selection techniques were implemented, with the *Elastic net* method, using an alpha of 0.1, showing the best performance. For the intrauterine fetal death category, the model identified four significant variables, achieving an AUC-ROC of 0.841, with female fetal gender emerging as the most contributive factor. Regarding the neonatal death category, seven relevant variables were selected, with the model yielding an AUC-ROC of 0.620. The most impactful variables in this category were Diameter2, male gender, and maternal age. Following this stage, the chosen model, integrating the multinomial logistic regression algorithm with the *Elastic net* technique, was employed in the development of a web application, which is available at https://obstetricoutcome.shinyapps.io/mo_uminho/. This platform can be a significant contribution to obstetric practice, providing an intuitive tool for healthcare professionals.

Keywords: Obstetric outcome · Multinomial logistic regression · Variable selection · Application

This work has been supported by FCT Fundação para a Ciência e Tecnologia within the R&D Units Project Scope: UID/00319/2023.

O. Gervasi et al. (Eds.): ICCSA 2025 Workshops, LNCS 15887, pp. 269–286, 2026.
https://doi.org/10.1007/978-3-031-97589-9_19

1 Introduction

Obstetrics plays a crucial role in maternal and fetal health, significantly impacting pregnancy outcomes [17]. The ability to accurately predict obstetric outcomes is vital for providing personalized medical care during gestation, minimizing adverse effects, and optimizing healthcare delivery [30].

Despite decades of intensive research in this area, predicting obstetric outcomes and associated complications, such as intrauterine growth restriction, preeclampsia, and stillbirth, remains a significant medical challenge [11]. Furthermore, placenta-mediated pregnancy complications are among the leading causes of maternal, fetal, and neonatal morbidity and mortality in developed countries, with increased risks of recurrence in subsequent pregnancies [20].

Placenta serves as the gateway and it is responsible for providing vital nutrients and oxygen supply to the fetus, while also produces hormones for maintaining pregnancy. It is essential to ensure that the fetus receives the appropriate supplement, being crucial for promoting optimal fetal growth. A successful pregnancy depends on a well-functioning placenta, and any compromise in its function has been suggested as a potential factor contributing to fetal demise. It is believed that a key determinant of placental function is its surface area, which facilitates the exchange of respiratory gases and nutrients necessary for optimal growth and well-being of the fetus during the gestational period [6,18,31]. Impaired placental function can lead to inadequate fetal growth, making it a focus of research aimed at understanding and mitigating these risks.

Over the past years, fetal and neonatal measurements have been widely used as indicators of fetal development. More recently, however, there has been growing interest in exploring placental biometric parameters and their relationship with obstetric outcomes [22,27]. Among these, placental weight (PW) has emerged as a potential indicator of placental function, reflecting both maternal and fetal environments, and varying in response to different pregnancy-related circumstances [18,24].

A linear relationship between fetal weight (FW) and PW has been documented in humans, and the Fetal Weight/Placental Weight Ratio (FPW-R) has garnered increasing interest on obstetricians, since it can indicate some conditions associated with certain placental disorders. Deviations in FPW-R have been associated with growth restriction, perinatal death, non-reassuring fetal status, and low Apgar scores. Any deviation in these processes can compromise the placenta's ability to support healthy fetal growth, highlighting its role as a focus of clinical and scientific research aimed at preventing potential adverse pregnancy outcomes. These findings emphasize the importance of understanding fetoplacental biometric features in preventing complications and improving pregnancy results, thereby enabling more precise and effective medical interventions [24,31].

This study aimed to explore fetoplacental biometric data during the viability period of pregnancy, with the goal of understanding the obstetric outcome. This period was specifically chosen as it corresponds to the stage of pregnancy when the fetus has reached a level of development sufficient to survive outside the womb after birth. The final purpose was to develop a web application that enables professionals to obtain real-time estimates of obstetric outcome. To achieve this, multinomial logistic regression (MLR) techniques were employed for predictive modeling.

The structure of this paper is organized into four sections. Section 2 provides a comprehensive overview of the dataset utilized, accompanied by the preprocessing steps applied, the study variables and the statistical analysis conducted. Section 3 presents the obtained results and offers a critical analysis of the findings, highlighting their implications and relevance in this context. Lastly, Sect. 4 summarizes the main conclusions drawn from the study and emphasizes potential directions for future research.

2   Material and Methods

2.1   Dataset

The data utilized in this study comprises fetoplacental biometric features collected at Embryofetal and Placental Pathology Laboratory, situated at CGC Genetics, in Unilabs, Porto, Portugal. Parameters were obtained from autopsy reports of placentas and fetuses collected over an eleven-year period, 2014 to 2024. These reports covered a wide range of gestational age (GA), from 12 to 41 weeks, and focused on the portuguese population. The initial sample comprised 7321 histopathological reports, which underwent rigorous preprocessing as part of a previous study conducted in 2019 by Nogueira *et al.* [28]. This procedure refined the dataset to 1951 samples. Subsequently, a study carried out in 2023 by Lemos included additional cases, adhering to the initially defined criteria, resulting in an expanded dataset of 2092 reports [23]. For the present study, further cases were added, culminating in a final dataset of 2278 samples used to determine the model that aims to predict the obstetric outcome.Considering the study's scope, 12 of the 25 available variables were selected based on their contextual significance and research objectives. These included "local", "Processnumber" (hospital process number), "MaternalAge" (mother's age), "GA" (gestational age), "Fetalweight" (fetal weight), "Fetalgender" (fetal gender), "Pregnancyoutcome" (pregnancy outcome), "Placentalweight" (placental weight), "Diameter1" (largest diameter of the placenta), "Diameter2" (smallest diameter of the placenta), "Placentalthickness" (placental thickness) and"ratio" (FPW-R).

2.2   Data Preprocessing

A comprehensive dataset preprocessing process emerges as the initial and crucial step in implementing a predictive model. This phase involves applying preparation and transformation techniques that precede statistical analyses, resulting in a dataset that is ready for analysis. In this study, all stages were performed using R, allowing for efficient data handling and transformation. The dataset underwent two more filtering steps to align with the criteria established for this work. In that regard, the study focused on the phase corresponding to the period of viability. Consequently, only samples with GA $\geq$ 22 weeks were selected. Also to ensure the validity and reliability of the results, samples categorized as medical termination of pregnancy under the "Pregnancyoutcome" variable were excluded. After this, the "local" and "Processnumber" columns were removed to optimize subsequent analysis. This approach helps prevents potential biases and distortions in the interpreting of results.

Data Cleaning. One of the key tasks carried out was data cleaning, which involves the process of identifying and correcting missing or incorrect values in the raw data. The number of missing values was assessed using the `is.na` function, resulting in the identification of 18 missing entries (1.3% of the total dataset). Additionally, the `missmap` function from the *Amelia* package was employed to visualize missing data patterns. The presence of duplicate observations can introduce significant issues in statistical analysis and modeling and therefore, identifying and removing such data is paramount. The `duplicated` function was applied to detect these values, and the `sum` function was subsequently utilized to quantify the number of duplicate rows identified. A total of 5 duplicate rows were found and eliminated.

Correlation. Analyzing correlation effects between variables can significantly influence machine learning modeling in several ways, particularly in the context of feature selection. When two variables exhibit a high degree of correlation, it may be redundant to include them together in the model, as one of them may provide similar information to the other. Consequently, a correlation analysis was conducted among key variables, such as FW, PW, and FPW-R. Based on the results, FW and PW were excluded from the model, as their strong correlation could introduce unnecessary redundancy.

Data Transformation. Given the presence of numerical variables with divergent scales in the database, a direct comparison between them becomes challenging. To mitigate this disparity, a data normalization technique was applied, specifically Min-Max scaling, which rescales all numerical variables to a uniform range of 0 to 1. The values are adjusted according to the minimum and maximum observed value, using the transformation described in Eq. 1:

$$z = \frac{x - \min}{\max - \min} \tag{1}$$

Here, z is the normalized value, while x is the original value. The terms *min* and *max* represent the minimum and maximum observed values, respectively.

Proper encoding of categorical variables is crucial when applying MLR to maintain the accuracy and interpretability of the model. To achieve this, dummy variables are created to represent the distinct categories of a categorical variable. By creating only $k - 1$ dummies for k categories, we ensure that the variables are not linearly dependent on each other.

2.3   Study Variables: Predictors and Outcomes

After completing the data preprocessing and transformation steps, the resulting dataset is expected to be cleaner, more refined, free of missing values and standardized. Therefore, Table 1 presents the final dataset, outlining its attributes, the ranges of registered values for numerical variables, and the absolute frequency along with the corresponding codification for categorical variables. In this approach, the response variable ("outcome") was multicategorical, with the newborn as the reference category, while the remaining classes corresponded to intrauterine fetal death and neonatal death.

Table 1. Summary of variables, both numeric and categorical used in the study.

Numeric variable	Range/Codification	Frequency
MaternalAge	15.1 − 48.2 years	-
GA	22 - 41 weeks	-
Diameter1	5.5 - 32 cm	-
Diameter2	5 - 30 cm	-
Placentalthickness (PT)	0.8 − 13.5 cm	-
FPW-R	1.33 - 11.51	-
Categorical variable		
Fetalgender	0 - Female	496
	1 - Male	547
	2 - Unknown	277
Outcome	0 - Newborn	841
	1 - Intrauterine Fetal Death	453
	2 - Neonatal Death	26

2.4   Statistical Analysis

Machine learning algorithms are used to extract knowledge from diverse data and generate effective prediction and classification models [5]. Regression analysis is a statistical tool that examines the relationship between two or more variables and the logistic regression model is important to analyze categorical data [9]. MLR can be used to predict the categorical placement or the probability of belonging to a category on a dependent variable, considering several independent variables [21]. With this concept in mind, in this paper an MLR model was used to aid in the prediction of the obstetric outcome, taking into account the 7 independent variables and the response variable.

In a model that considers a categorical response variable with multiple categories (nominal), where Y is the response variable and J represents the different categories it can take, the probability of Y taking each of the J categories is denoted by $\pi_j(x)$, where $\sum \pi_j(x) = 1$. The model described by Eq. 2 considers the logarithm of the odds ratio (OR) $\pi_j(x)/\pi_J(x)$, where $\pi_J(x)$ is the probability of the reference category. The model simultaneously describes the effects of the explanatory variables x on these J - 1 logits. The J - 1 equations determine the parameters for the logits with other pairs of response categories. In this context, in a MLR model, the logit can be expressed by the following Eq. 2 [1]:

$$\log \frac{\pi_j(x)}{\pi_J(x)} = \alpha_j + \beta_j x, \quad \text{for } j = 1, \ldots, J - 1 \tag{2}$$

Here, $\pi_j(x)$ represents the probability of the response variable Y being assigned to category j, while $\pi_J(x)$ denotes the probability of Y belonging to the reference category J. The term α_j corresponds to the intercept for category j, and β_j is the vector of coefficients associated with the explanatory variables x.

Split the Dataset. A common practice in data analysis involves dividing the dataset into two distinct subsets: one for model training and the other for model evaluation [3,26]. In this approach, the training dataset was utilized to construct the model, while the testing dataset was reserved for assessing the model's predictive performance [26]. For this particular study, a split ratio of 0.7 was applied, which means that 70% of the data were allocated for training purposes, and the remaining 30% was designated for testing. Consequently, the resulting training dataset consisted of 589 samples from the newborn class, 318 samples from the intrauterine fetal death class, and 19 samples from the neonatal death class.

Balance the Dataset. The issue of unequal class distribution presents a notable challenge in many machine learning applications. This arises from the scarcity of training examples for the minority classes, which leads to models that tend to favor the prediction of the majority classes, due to the availability of abundant data for these classes [32]. To handle the significant class imbalance, the Synthetic Minority Oversampling Technique (SMOTE) was employed and evaluated in the training set. This approach generates synthetic samples through an oversampling approach, which was identified as the most effective method in the context of limited data, aiming to create samples in the minority classes to equalize the number of examples across different categories. It is important to highlight that these balancing techniques were applied exclusively to the training dataset, preventing biased or overestimated model performance. After applying SMOTE, the training set was expanded to 1496 samples: 589 newborn, 318 intrauterine fetal death, and 589 neonatal death instances.

Feature Selection. Variable selection is a critical and challenging phase in model construction, often considered the most intricate aspect of the process. This step involves removing redundant or irrelevant features, in order to select those that are best suited to optimize the model's performance. Additionally, it is crucial to prevent the inclusion of noise variables that may degrade the model's effectiveness [8]. However, identifying the most appropriate algorithm for this task is not straightforward as different algorithms apply distinct criteria to determine the most representative variables. Feature selection methods can be categorized into two main approaches: wrapper, and embedded techniques [7].

- *Wrapper Method*. Incorporate a predictive model during training and evaluate variable subsets to optimize feature selection [7]. The effectiveness of these methods depends on the choice of classification algorithms and search strategies [15]. Commonly employed techniques include Sequential Forward Selection (SFS), an iterative approach that progressively adds variables in a step-by-step process, Sequential Backward Elimination (SBE), which removes variables iteratively starting from the full model, and bidirectional search, which combines the addition and removal of features in each iteration, beginning with an initial set of features [4, 8, 25, 33].

In this modeling approach, the `multinom` function from the *nnet* package in R was employed to fit the initial model, specifically designed for MLR, which is well-suited for classification tasks involving response variables with more than two categories. Following this step, variable selection in MLR can be performed using one of three sequential search techniques, leveraging the *MASS* package and utilizing the fitted model as input.

- *Embedded Method*. The core principle of embedded techniques lies in introducing a penalization of the model coefficients, forcing some of them to approach zero or be exactly zero, gradually reducing their importance. This can lead to model simplification without the need to eliminate variables. Among the key regularization techniques are *Ridge*, Least Absolute Shrinkage and Selection Operator (*LASSO*), and *Elastic net* [2]. *Ridge* regularization applies an L_2 penalty, shrinking coefficient magnitudes proportionally toward zero without eliminating them. *LASSO* regularization, using a L_1 penalty, reduces some coefficients exactly to zero, selecting only the most relevant variables [13, 29]. *Elastic net* combines *Ridge* (L_2) and *LASSO* (L_1) regularization, making it particularly advantageous in scenarios involving highly correlated variables [13].

In this approach, the *glmnet* and *caret* packages were employed to implement *Ridge*, *LASSO*, and *Elastic net* regularization techniques efficiently [13]. Within the *glmnet* framework in R, the parameter alpha controls the type of penalty applied in regression models. Specifically, alpha is set to 0 for *Ridge* regularization, equals 1 for *LASSO*, and takes values between 0 and 1 to represent *Elastic net*. This method fits models with different penalty values (lambda) and uses lambda as the key hyperparameter for regularizing model coefficients [29]. For tuning regularization, 10-fold cross-validation was applied to determine the optimal lambda value [10].

Assessment Metrics. To compare the performance of different predictive models in forecasting obstetric outcomes using the dataset variables, several assessment metrics were used to select the best model:

- *Accuracy:* It is defined as the proportion of correctly classified cases relative to the total number of instances in the dataset. Thus, the precision formula considers the rates of True Positive (TP) and True Negative (TN) [16, 19].

- **F1-Score:** It provides a balanced relationship between precision and recall, where their relative contributions are equally weighted in the F1-Score. This formula takes into account both false positives (FP) and false negatives (FN) [16,19].

- **Precision:** It measures the proportion of instances that were correctly classified as positive relative to the total number of instances predicted as belonging to the positive class [19]. Precision indicates how much we can trust the model when it predicts a case as positive [16].

- **Recall:** Also known as sensitivity, represents the proportion of actual positive instances that were correctly identified by the model. The formula involves TP divided by the total number of units classified as positive [16,19].

- **AUC-PR/AUC-ROC:** Metrics such as Area Under a Receiver Operating Characteristic Curve (AUC-ROC) and Area Under a Precision-Recall Curve (AUC-PR) can be adapted for multiclass problems through two methodologies: One versus One, and One versus All [12,14]. The ROC curve summarizes the test's ability to discriminate between positive and negative classes across all possible threshold values, balancing trade-offs between sensitivity and specificity [34]. The PR curve can evaluate various types of classifiers across the entire spectrum of thresholds, which illustrates a trade-off between precision and recall. AUC-PR is particularly useful in datasets with class imbalance [14].

3   Results and Discussion

To better understand the distribution and behavior of these variables across obstetric outcomes, a detailed statistical analysis was conducted for each category. Additionally, Kruskal-Wallis and Chi-squared tests were applied to assess

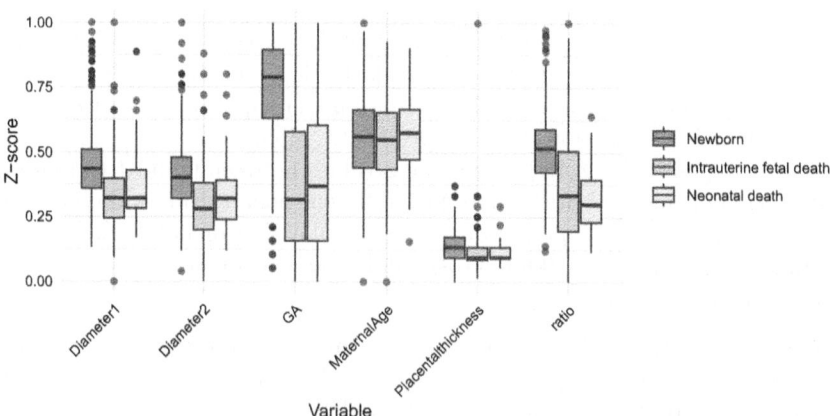

Fig. 1. Boxplots illustrating the distribution of numerical variables values across the three obstetric outcomes, highlighting the median, interquartile ranges, and potential outliers within each group.

differences among groups, with p-values below 0.05 indicating statistical significance. Variables such as GA, PT, placental diameters, FPW-R, and fetal gender
showed significant differences among obstetric outcome classes.

Beyond statistical analysis, Fig. 1 provides a visual representation of the distribution of normalized numerical variables among the three outcome categories.
The observed differences in GA, placental diameters, PT, and FPW-R also suggest potential trends that may be crucial for understanding their impact on
obstetric results. In contrast, maternal age exhibits no marked differences, indicating a less pronounced impact when considered in isolation.

3.1 Model Selection

Despite the previously mentioned class imbalance, an MLR model was implemented using the unbalanced dataset, achieving an accuracy of 83%. While the
model performs well for the majority class (newborn), it struggles significantly
with the minority classes, particularly neonatal death. This issue stems from
the unequal class distribution, resulting in a bias towards the majority class.
Therefore, implementing a balancing strategy was crucial to addressing this class
imbalance to improve the model's generalization across all categories.

Based on the above, after applying the SMOTE technique, the MLR model
was trained, and predictions were made on the test data. Compared to the unbalanced training set, the balancing technique led to overall performance improvements, as shown in Table 2. It yielded superior results in most cases, particularly
in precision, recall, AUC-PR, and AUC-ROC metrics for the neonatal death category. These findings highlight SMOTE as an effective technique for improving
model performance when applied to the training dataset.

Table 2. Performance metrics of the MLR model for the unbalanced dataset and the
SMOTE technique.

Class	Accuracy	F1	Precision	Recall	AUC-PR	AUC-ROC
	Unbalanced dataset					
Intrauterine fetal death	0.830	0.756	0.733	0.780	0.781	0.884
Neonatal death	0.830	NaN	0.000	NaN	0.020	0.571
	SMOTE					
Intrauterine fetal death	0.617	0.259	0.163	0.629	0.645	0.812
Neonatal death	0.617	0.037	0.286	0.020	0.022	0.600

Variable selection methods analyzed and compared in detail included the
wrapper and embedded approaches. In this type of regression, one category of the
response variable was designated as the reference, while the remaining categories
were compared against it. In this framework, the coefficients associated with the
reference category were set to zero, whereas the coefficients for the other classes

represented the logarithm of the OR of belonging to each category relative to the reference.

In this context of imbalanced datasets, the AUC-ROC metric was particularly relevant, as it plays a crucial role in discriminating between classes and should be considered. To compare various MLR models with different subsets of variables, a reference model (designated as model 0) was used, which included all seven available variables without any selection technique.

In relation to the wrapper method, as observed in the analysis of Table 3, the models developed through sequential search did not show improvements in predictive performance compared to the reference model. Specifically, none of the three methods demonstrated any improvement, yielding the same or even lower estimates than those obtained with the model without variable selection. It was worth noting that none of these methods reduced the number of attributes used in the process. Therefore, the application of these methods did not bring noticeable benefits to the model.

Table 3. Performance metrics obtained after applying wrapper methods for variable selection in MLR.

Model	Accuracy	F1	Precision	Recall	AUC-PR	AUC-ROC	Variables
0	Method without variable selection						
Intrauterine fetal death	0.617	0.259	0.163	0.629	0.645	0.812	7
Neonatal death	0.617	0.037	0.286	0.020	0.022	0.600	7
1	Forward						
Intrauterine fetal death	0.612	0.249	0.156	0.618	0.645	0.811	7
Neonatal death	0.612	0.036	0.286	0.019	0.022	0.601	7
2	Backward						
Intrauterine fetal death	0.612	0.249	0.156	0.618	0.645	0.811	7
Neonatal death	0.612	0.036	0.286	0.019	0.022	0.601	7
3	Bidirectional						
Intrauterine fetal death	0.612	0.249	0.156	0.618	0.645	0.811	7
Neonatal death	0.612	0.036	0.286	0.019	0.022	0.601	7

Concerning the embedded method, about the results obtained for the different regularization techniques using the dataset obtained through SMOTE, as shown in Table 4. It was noteworthy that the *Ridge* regularization model resulted in a total number of variables (7), which was expected given its more generalized nature aimed at avoiding overfitting. The *LASSO* regularization approach using the minimum lambda (lambda min) showed a reduction in the number of variables, with estimates like those of the reference model without variable selection. *LASSO* regularization with the one standard error lambda (lambda 1se) also significantly reduced the number of variables and showed improvements in some metrics compared to the reference model.

For *Elastic net* regularization, different alpha values were tested. This was an important aspect since low alpha values retain more variables, offering a more comprehensive model, though potentially more complex. In contrast, higher alpha values result in a potentially simpler model with fewer variables, which can better handle multicollinearity and focus on the most relevant variables. Models with alpha values of 0.1 and 0.9 showed better results compared to others, with higher values for AUC-PR and AUC-ROC metrics. Although model 8 demonstrated similar results to model 7, the latter was chosen due to its superior performance in evaluation metrics, particularly in AUC-PR and AUC-ROC values. This was a decisive criterion for the decision.

Table 4. Performance metrics obtained after applying regularization techniques for variable selection in MLR.

series Model	series Accuracy	series F1	series Precision	series Recall	series AUC-PR	series AUC-ROC	series Variables
0	Method without variable selection						
Intrauterine fetal death	0.617	0.259	0.163	0.629	0.645	0.812	7
Neonatal death	0.617	0.037	0.286	0.020	0.022	0.600	7
4	Ridge Regularization						
Intrauterine fetal death	0.594	0.085	0.044	0.857	0.720	0.846	7
Neonatal death	0.594	0.062	0.571	0.033	0.023	0.622	7
5	LASSO Regularization (lambda min)						
Intrauterine fetal death	0.609	0.229	0.141	0.613	0.652	0.816	2
Neonatal death	0.609	0.036	0.286	0.019	0.021	0.597	6
6	LASSO Regularization (lambda 1se)						
Intrauterine fetal death	0.596	0.170	0.096	0.722	0.683	0.840	1
Neonatal death	0.596	0.063	0.571	0.034	0.022	0.603	4
7	Elastic net Regularization (alpha = 0.1)						
Intrauterine fetal death	0.602	0.098	0.052	0.875	0.715	0.841	4
Neonatal death	0.602	0.064	0.571	0.034	0.023	0.620	7
8	Elastic net Regularization (alpha = 0.9)						
Intrauterine fetal death	0.612	0.205	0.119	0.762	0.680	0.838	2
Neonatal death	0.612	0.067	0.571	0.035	0.022	0.601	5

In this regard, the chosen model showed a relatively reasonable AUC-ROC value, with scores of 0.841 for intrauterine fetal death and 0.620 for neonatal death. On the other hand, the AUC-PR metric yielded values of 0.715 and 0.023 for intrauterine fetal death and neonatal death, respectively. This means that the predictive model performed reasonably well in identifying true positives for the first class, demonstrating high sensitivity. However, it showed low precision. Furthermore, the model faced significant difficulty in classifying cases of neonatal death, revealing both poor sensitivity and a limited ability to correctly distinguish this specific class.

The results could be attributed to the low proportion of the minority classes, which negatively impacts the model's performance. Out of the 1 320 samples available in the records, only 24.09% correspond to intrauterine fetal death, and 1.44% pertain to neonatal death. In turn, the similarity in performance metrics between wrapper methods and regularization techniques (Tables 3 and 4) suggests that both strategies extract a similar level of predictive signal from the variables. This may indicate that the most informative features are consistently selected across methods, or that the overall signal is weak and redundant, thereby reducing the effectiveness of more complex selection strategies. While regularization approaches (e.g., *LASSO* and *Elastic net*) simplified the models by selecting fewer variables, this did not consistently translate into improved predictive performance, possibly due to inherent data limitations such as low signal-to-noise ratio and class imbalance.

3.2 Variable Importance and Estimated Coefficients

Intrauterine Fetal Death. The *Elastic net* method with alpha = 0.1 in the MLR classifier selected four key variables. As illustrated in Fig. 2, fetal female sex category was found to be the most contributive to intrauterine fetal death, exhibiting the highest positive coefficient. This suggests a strong association between female fetuses and an increased risk of intrauterine fetal death compared to newborns, potentially due to biological differences between the genders where hormonal and developmental factors could make female fetuses more susceptible to adverse conditions. Conversely, Diameter2, Diameter1, and GA play a protective role, reducing the likelihood of this outcome.

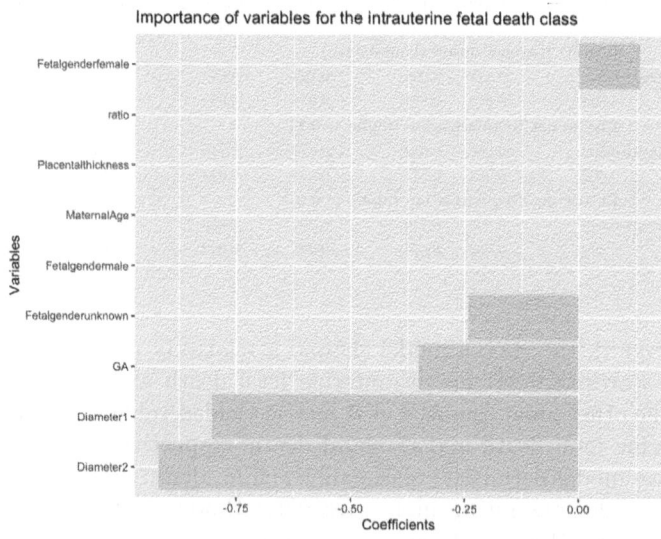

Fig. 2. Graph representing the importance of variables based on their respective coefficients for the intrauterine fetal death class, obtained through variable selection using the *Elastic net* regularization method with alpha=0.1.

Table 5 reveals that female infants have 1.140 times higher odds of intrauterine fetal death. In contrast, each additional unit of GA decreases this probability by 29.6. Similarly, increases in Diameter1 and Diameter2 lower the risk by 55.2%

and 60.1%, respectively. These findings emphasize the differential impact of these predictors on intrauterine fetal death, offering valuable insights into obstetric risk assessment.

Table 5. Demonstration of the estimated coefficients for the independent variables in the selected model and the respective OR for the intrauterine fetal death category.

series Variables	series Estimated coefficients	series OR
Intercept	0.582	1.789
GA	−0.351	0.704
Fetalgender (female)	0.131	1.140
Fetalgender (unknown)	−0.242	0.785
Diameter1	−0.803	0.448
Diameter2	−0.920	0.399

Neonatal Death. Seven original variables were identified for this category, as illustrated in Fig. 3. The most contributory factors for neonatal death include Diameter2, male sex, and maternal age. Among these, Diameter2 emerges as the most influential predictor, with higher values strongly associated with an increased likelihood of neonatal death compared to newborn. On the other hand, FPW-R and GA exhibit the strongest negative coefficients, suggesting that greater values significantly reduce the probability of this type of death. These results highlight potential fetal development concerns linked to Diameter2, the increased vulnerability of male infants during critical neonatal stages, and the increased risk of obstetric complications associated with advanced maternal age.

The results presented in Table 6 show that each additional year of maternal age increases the probability of neonatal death by 21.2%. Similarly, an OR of 1.241 suggests that male sex is associated with a 24.1% higher probability of neonatal death. An increase of one unit in Diameter1 and Diameter2 raises the risk of neonatal death by 1.098 and 1.666 times, respectively, compared to the newborn category. In contrast, a one-unit increase in GA reduces the probability of neonatal death by approximately 60%, while higher PT values reduce the risk by 0.524 times relative to the reference class. Furthermore, an increase in FPW-R dramatically decreases the probability of neonatal death by 84.4%, highlighting its strong protective effect. These observations provide valuable insights into both risk and protective factors for neonatal mortality, offering critical information for potential clinical interventions.

3.3   Web Application

After selecting the best MLR model (model 7) for predicting obstetric outcome, a web application was developed using the *shiny* package. Aligned with the study's

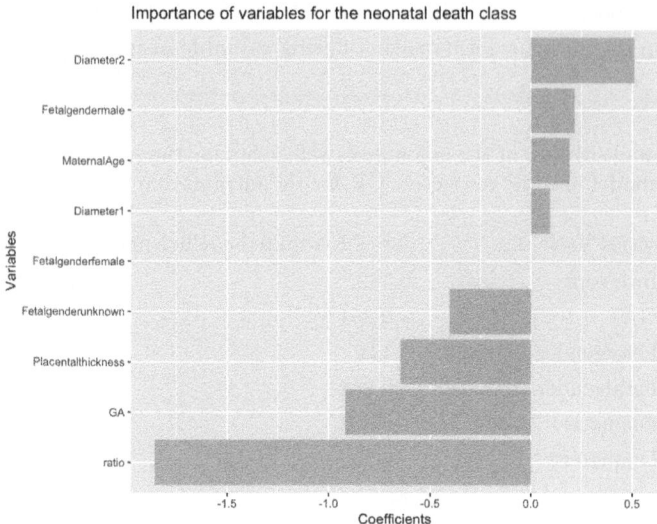

Fig. 3. Graph illustrating the importance of variables based on the coefficients obtained through *Elastic net* regularization with alpha = 0.1, in which the variables were selected to predict the neonatal death class.

objectives, this tool enables healthcare professionals to estimate fetal outcomes based on fetoplacental biometric features.

The "ObstetricOutcome" application has carefully designed to provide an intuitive and accessible experience, catering to the needs of healthcare professionals and other users. Its interface has been crafted to be user-friendly and easy to navigate, allowing for efficient interaction with the available tools and resources. The application enables real-time access to obstetric outcome predictions by filling in the required fields in the designated form, estimating the probability of each possible outcome. The platform is structured into four main sections - Home, About, Form, and Results - accessible through a navigation bar, each offering distinct functionalities. It is available at the following link: https://obstetricoutcome.shinyapps.io/mo_uminho/.

Hypothetical Case Study. To illustrate the application developed for predicting obstetric outcomes, consider the case of a 20-year-old pregnant woman in her third trimester, at 31 weeks of gestation. During a consultation, she presented the following clinical data: Diameter1 of 10 cm, Diameter2 of 8 cm, PT of 2 cm, FW of 440 g, PW of 120 g, and a female fetal gender. This information about the pregnant woman, the fetus, and the pregnancy was entered into the corresponding fields of the form available in the application. After submitting the data, the application generated a prediction of neonatal death (Fig. 4). Based on this result, the medical team can assess the implications of the outcome, emphasizing the importance of regular monitoring and early interventions, if necessary. This

Table 6. Presentation of the estimated coefficients for the predictor variables in the selected model, along with the corresponding OR for the neonatal death category.

series Variables	series Estimated coefficients	series OR
Intercept	1.111	3.037
MaternalAge	0.192	1.212
GA	−0.917	0.400
Fetalgender (male)	0.216	1.241
Fetalgender (unknown)	−0.406	0.666
Diameter1	0.094	1.098
Diameter2	0.511	1.666
Placentalthickness	−0.646	0.524
FPW-R	−1.857	0.156

approach allows better planning and the implementation of measures aimed at improving the health and well-being of both the mother and the newborn.

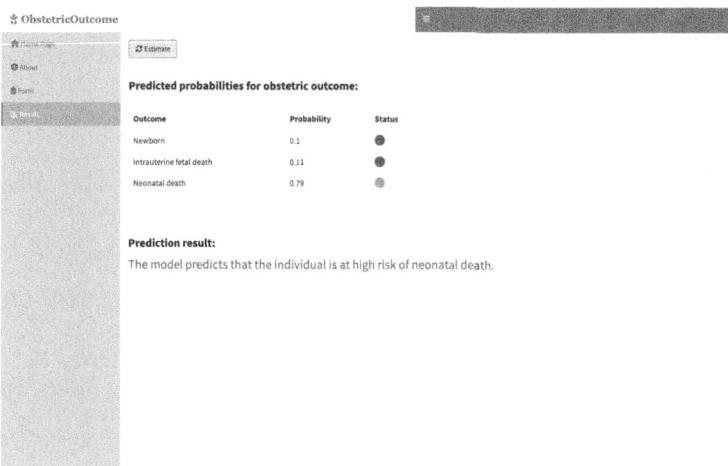

Fig. 4. Example of the obstetric outcome prediction result based on the data entered by the user in the hypothetical case.

4   Conclusion

Throughout this study, a comprehensive approach was employed to predict three different obstetric outcomes based on placental and fetal parameters. To carry out this process, MLR models were implemented to identify the most contributive variables in determining fetal health across different gestational scenarios. Furthermore, the use of R packages such as *nnet* and *glmnet* demonstrated the versatility of the R environment in developing robust predictive solutions.

Although the classifier demonstrates reasonable predictive capability, its performance is constrained by the limited number of cases in certain outcome categories. It is hypothesized that a substantial increase in records for minority classes, particularly for neonatal death, would improve model's reliability. This could improve classification precision, strengthen predictive robustness, and enhance overall model effectiveness.

From a future perspective, expanding the dataset with additional maternal and fetoplacental biometric records could significantly improve the model's ability. Moreover, exploring alternative feature selection techniques and diverse machine learning algorithms, such as Random Forest or Support Vector Machines, could be an alternative to provide valuable insights for optimizing predictive outcomes.

In conclusion, this research could significantly contribute to the medical community in the field of obstetrics, offering support to assist healthcare professionals in making critical real-time decisions. They have great potential to facilitate the early detection of complications related to maternal and fetal health, while also transforming care into a more proactive and personalized approach. This could lead to more effective interventions, promoting a healthy and safe pregnancy.

References

1. Agresti, A.: Categorical Data Analysis, vol. 792. John Wiley & Sons (2012)
2. Altelbany, S.: Evaluation of ridge, elastic net and lasso regression methods in precedence of multicollinearity problem: a simulation study. J. Appl. Econ. Bus. Studies **5**(1), 131–142 (2021)
3. Baldi, P., Brunak, S.: Bioinformatics: The Machine Learning Approach. MIT Press (2001)
4. Bashir, S., Khattak, I.U., Khan, A., Khan, F.H., Gani, A., Shiraz, M.: A novel feature selection method for classification of medical data using filters, wrappers, and embedded approaches. Complexity **2022**(1), 8190814 (2022)
5. Birba, D.E.: A comparative study of data splitting algorithms for machine learning model selection (2020)
6. Bonds, D.R., Gabbe, S.G., Kumar, S., Taylor, T.: Fetal weight/placental weight ratio and perinatal outcome. Am. J. Obstet. Gynecol. **149**(2), 195–200 (1984)
7. Chen, C.W., Tsai, Y.H., Chang, F.R., Lin, W.C.: Ensemble feature selection in medical datasets: combining filter, wrapper, and embedded feature selection results. Expert. Syst. **37**(5), e12553 (2020)
8. Chowdhury, M.Z.I., Turin, T.C.: Variable selection strategies and its importance in clinical prediction modelling. Family Med. Comm. Health **8**(1) (2020)
9. El-Habil, A.M.: An application on multinomial logistic regression model. Pakistan J. Stat. Oper. Res. **8**(2), 271–291 (2012)

10. Friedman, J., Hastie, T., Tibshirani, R.: Regularization paths for generalized linear models via coordinate descent. J. Stat. Softw. **33**(1), 1 (2010)
11. Gaccioli, F., Lager, S., Sovio, U., Charnock-Jones, D.S., Smith, G.C.: The pregnancy outcome prediction (pop) study: investigating the relationship between serial prenatal ultrasonography, biomarkers, placental phenotype and adverse pregnancy outcomes. Placenta **59**, S17–S25 (2017)
12. Galar, M., Fernández, A., Barrenechea, E., Bustince, H., Herrera, F.: An overview of ensemble methods for binary classifiers in multi-class problems: experimental study on one-vs-one and one-vs-all schemes. Pattern Recogn. **44**(8), 1761–1776 (2011)
13. García-Nieto, P.J., Garcia-Gonzalo, E., Paredes-Sánchez, J.P.: Prediction of the critical temperature of a superconductor by using the woa/mars, ridge, lasso and elastic-net machine learning techniques. Neural Comput. Appl. **33**, 17131–17145 (2021)
14. Gong, M.: A novel performance measure for machine learning classification. Int. J. Manag. Inf. Technol. (IJMIT) **13** (2021)
15. González, J., Ortega, J., Damas, M., Martín-Smith, P., Gan, J.Q.: A new multi-objective wrapper method for feature selection-accuracy and stability analysis for BCI. Neurocomputing **333**, 407–418 (2019)
16. Grandini, M., Bagli, E., Visani, G.: Metrics for multi-class classification: an overview. arXiv preprint arXiv:2008.05756 (2020)
17. Grobman, W.A.: Obstetric patient safety: an overview. Am. J. Perinatol. **29**(01), 03–06 (2012)
18. Haavaldsen, C., Samuelsen, S.O., Eskild, A.: Fetal death and placental weight/birthweight ratio: a population study. Acta Obstet. Gynecol. Scand. **92**(5), 583–590 (2013)
19. Hossin, M., Sulaiman, M.N.: A review on evaluation metrics for data classification evaluations. Int. J. Data Mining Knowl. Manag. Process **5**(2), 1 (2015)
20. Jeppegaard, M., Rasmussen, S.C., Anhøj, J., Krebs, L.: Winter, spring, summer or fall: temporal patterns in placenta-mediated pregnancy complications–an exploratory analysis. Arch. Gynecol. Obstet. **309**(5), 1991–1998 (2024)
21. Kwak, C., Clayton-Matthews, A.: Multinomial logistic regression. Nurs. Res. **51**(6), 404–410 (2002)
22. Lemos, D., Braga, A.C., Nogueira, R.: Nonlinear regression on growth curves for placental parameters in R. In: International Conference on Optimization, Learning Algorithms and Applications, pp. 575–590. Springer (2023)
23. Lemos, D.F.M.: Regressão não linear em curvas de crescimento para parâmetros placentares em R. Master's thesis, Universidade do Minho (Portugal) (2023)
24. Matsuda, Y., et al.: Impact of placental weight and fetal/placental weight ratio z score on fetal growth and the perinatal outcome. Int. J. Med. Sci. **15**(5), 484 (2018)
25. Mlambo, W., Cheruiyot, W.K., Kimwele, M.W.: N,"a survey and comparative study of filter and wrapper feature selection techniques". Int. J. Eng. Sci. **5**(8), 57–67 (2016)
26. Muraina, I.: Ideal dataset splitting ratios in machine learning algorithms: general concerns for data scientists and data analysts. In: 7th International Mardin Artuklu Scientific Research Conference, pp. 496–504 (2022)
27. Njeze, N.R., Ogbochukwu, J.O., Chinawa, J.M.: Correlation of ultrasound placental diameter and thickness with gestational age. Pak. J. Med. Sci. **36**(5), 1058 (2020)

28. Nogueira, R., et al.: Placental biometric parameters: the usefulness of placental weight ratio and birth/placen-tal weight ratio percentile curves for singleton gestations as a function of gestational age. J. Clin. Anat. Pathol. **4**, 1–15 (2019)
29. Ogutu, J.O., Schulz-Streeck, T., Piepho, H.P.: Genomic selection using regularized linear regression models: ridge regression, lasso, elastic net and their extensions. In: BMC Proceedings, vol. 6, pp. 1–6. Springer (2012)
30. Pettker, C.M., Grobman, W.A.: Obstetric safety and quality. Obstet. Gynecol. **126**(1), 196–206 (2015)
31. Salavati, N., Gordijn, S.J., Sovio, U., Zill-E-Huma, R., Gebril, A., Charnock-Jones, D., Scherjon, S.A., Smith, G.C.: Birth weight to placenta weight ratio and its relationship to ultrasonic measurements, maternal and neonatal morbidity: a prospective cohort study of nulliparous women. Placenta **63**, 45–52 (2018)
32. Susan, S., Kumar, A.: The balancing trick: optimized sampling of imbalanced datasets–a brief survey of the recent state of the art. Eng. Rep. **3**(4), e12298 (2021)
33. Wah, Y.B., Ibrahim, N., Hamid, H.A., Abdul-Rahman, S., Fong, S.: Feature selection methods: case of filter and wrapper approaches for maximising classification accuracy. Pertanika J. Sci. Technol. **26**(1) (2018)
34. Zou, K.H., O'Malley, A.J., Mauri, L.: Receiver-operating characteristic analysis for evaluating diagnostic tests and predictive models. Circulation **115**(5), 654–657 (2007)

The Mediating Role of Occupational Self-efficacy in the Relationship Between Employees' Perceived Trust and Work Engagement

Karma Lhaden ⓘ and Isabel Dórdio Dimas⁽⊠⁾ ⓘ

CeBER, Faculty of Economics, University of Coimbra, Coimbra, Portugal
idimas@fe.uc.pt

Abstract. Although trust is crucial in enhancing positive attitudes and behaviour, trust signals are not explicit. Hence, trust recipients must cognitively process the trust cues to translate into positive outcomes. This study innovates by examining how employees' perceived trust indirectly influences their work engagement through its influence on occupational self-efficacy. We collected a sample of 335 employees from three major companies in Bhutan over a two-wave survey on the Lime survey platform. Data were analyzed using structural equation modeling on IBM SPSS AMOS (29). The results supported the positive impact on occupational self-efficacy of cognitive trust but the influence of affective trust was not significant. Occupational self-efficacy presented a strong positive impact on work engagement. Additionally, the results revealed an indirect effect of cognitive trust on work engagement through occupational self-efficacy. Therefore, our findings posit cognitive trust as an important resource to foster a positive work attitude, however, requires individual resources. Nonetheless, the role of affective trust remains less active. Organizations must capitalize on cognitive trust to foster employees' self-belief and enhance engagement levels.

Keywords: Cognitive and Affective trust · Occupational self-efficacy · Work engagement

1 Introduction

Interpersonal trust is a vital socio-emotional resource, a foundation of social exchange mechanisms, fostering positive workplace attitudes and behaviours (Blau 1964; Dirks and De Jong 2022; Legood et al. 2021). Trust is typically classified into two dimensions: cognitive trust, which reflects reliance on and belief in the trustee's perceived traits that ensure competent job performance (McAllister 1995; Mayer et al. 1995; Yang and Mossholder, 2010), and affective trust, which involves a willingness to confide in the trustee's supportive nature, thereby strengthening relational ties (McAllister 1995; Tomlinson et al. 2020).

While trust has been extensively studied, its conceptual complexity continues to reveal new avenues for exploration (Dirks and De Jong, 2022). Traditional theories,

O. Gervasi et al. (Eds.): ICCSA 2025 Workshops, LNCS 15887, pp. 287–299, 2026.
https://doi.org/10.1007/978-3-031-97589-9_20

such as social exchange theory, posit that trust inherently enhances positive exchanges at work, with trustworthiness seen as undeniably beneficial (Legood et al. 2021; Brower et al. 2009). However, this assumption has been increasingly challenged. For instance, Baer et al. (2015) demonstrated that trust can sometimes be emotionally taxing, and subsequent work by Baer et al. (2021) questioned the universal desirability of being trusted. These findings highlight the nuanced and multifaceted nature of trust, emphasizing the need for further theoretical refinement.

Building on this foundation, the present study seeks to advance trust theory by addressing how trust translates into positive attitudinal and behavioural outcomes. Drawing on prior research linking trust to self-efficacy (Zheng et al., 2019) and work engagement (Gill et al. 2019), we propose that trust cues are not always explicit and must be psychologically processed by employees to stimulate desired outcomes (Campagna et al. 2020). This process requires personal resources, such as occupational self-efficacy, which refers to an individual's belief in their ability to meet job demands successfully. On this basis, the study explores the indirect effects of cognitive and affective trust on work engagement, mediated by occupational self-efficacy.

1.1 Employees Perceived Cognitive and Affective Trust

Trust is conceptualized as "the willingness of a party to be vulnerable to the actions of another party based on the expectation that the other will perform a particular action important to the trustor, irrespective of the ability to monitor or control that other party" (Mayer et al. 1995, p. 712). Employees' perceived trust is the extent to which they feel their leader trust them. Employees' felt or perceived trust activates psychological mechanisms that influence work attitudes and behaviours (Baer et al. 2015; Gill et al. 2019; Lau et al. 2014). In today's increasingly complex and challenging workplaces, employees' ability to navigate uncertainties (Ferguson et al. 2022) and to add value to their organizations (Dimas et al. 2023) has become essential. Perceived trust plays a pivotal role in this context, fostering positive attitudes and behaviours while establishing strong workplace relationships (Mayer et al. 1995; McAllister 1995).

Trust has been conceptualized considering two dimensions: cognitive and affective (Dirks and DeJong, 2022). Cognitive trust involves relying on another's task-related abilities and it is based on assessments of the trustee's levels of ability and integrity (Karma Lhaden and Dimas 2024; McAllister 1995; Tomlinson et al. 2020). Previous studies reveal that this trust dimension is positively related to task performance outcomes, such as in-role achievements (Mayer and Gavin, 2005), by reducing perceived risks of deception (Mayer et al. 1995; Colquitt et al. 2012).

Affective trust, on the other hand, is related to emotional reliance and arises from perceptions of benevolence (Tomlinson et al. 2020) and actions that go beyond formal duties (Karma Lhaden and Dimas 2024). Affective trust improves the quality of the relational exchanges that take place in the organizational context (Colquitt et al. 2012) and has been shown to positively influence group motivation and organizational citizenship behaviour (Carter and Mossholder 2015).

The impact of trust on work attitudes and behaviours is mediated through psychological states such as empowerment (Gill et al. 2019), self-efficacy (Zheng et al. 2019), and self-esteem (Lau et al. 2014). Trust enhances employees' self-evaluation processes, leading to improved cognitive functioning, heightened self-esteem, and increased self-efficacy (Lau et al. 2014; Zheng et al. 2019). Furthermore, when employees perceive they are trusted, they feel valued and empowered at work (Gill et al. 2019).

Although trust signals may be indirect (Campagna et al. 2020), they consistently foster positive workplace behaviours and outcomes (Dirks and DeJong, 2022). Trust remains a basis of effective workplace dynamics by providing both a cognitive assurance of reliability and an emotional foundation of support.

1.2 Perceived Trust and Occupational Self-efficacy

Bandura (1977) described self-efficacy as an individual's confidence in their ability to effectively perform a specific behaviour necessary to achieve desired outcomes. Previous studies have distinguished between different categories of self-efficacy, such as content-specific self-efficacy, task-specific self-efficacy, or occupational self-efficacy (Guarnaccia et al. 2018; Lent and Brown 2006). Occupational self-efficacy is defined as a domain specific form of self-efficacy and refers to an individual's confidence and belief in their own capacities to succeed in their work context (Guarnaccia et al. 2018; Ozyilmaz et al. 2018; Zheng et al. 2019). This dimension differs from general self-efficacy in that it is specific to the occupational context, focusing on the processes of occupational adaptation and coping with occupational obstacles (Çetin, and Aşkun 2018; Schyns and von Collani 2002). Occupational self-efficacy draws on emotional and psychological resources available in the workplace (Bandura 2006). It emerges from an individual's capacity to perform tasks successfully (Guarnaccia et al. 2018; Schyns and von Collani 2002).

Self-efficacy develops through experiences such as personal attainments, modeling, verbal persuasion, and physiological arousal, which allow individuals to cognitively appraise their perceptions and determine their self-efficacy levels (Bandura 2006; Gist and Mitchell 1992). This makes self-efficacy a judgment of one's workplace capabilities. Among these experiences, social persuasion plays a crucial role in enhancing self-efficacy because it strengthens individual's belief that they can succeed at relevant tasks (Bandura 2006; Zheng et al. 2019). For example, Biron and Bamberger (2010) highlight that providing employees with task flexibility and autonomy can boost their self-efficacy by increasing their confidence in their capabilities.

Trust, a fundamental workplace factor, is built by assessing the trustee's ability, integrity, and benevolence (Mayer et al. 1995; Karma Lhaden and Dimas 2024). It reflects the judgment of someone's capability and can result in autonomy and positive feedback in the workplace (Lau et al. 2014; Karma Lhaden and Dimas 2024). Trust serves as a source of social persuasion, influencing self-efficacy through both cognitive and emotional pathways (Bandura 2006; Zheng et al. 2019). Specifically, employees who feel that their skills are being relied upon (i.e., perceived cognitive trust) are likely to interpret this as positive feedback from the supervisor about their work abilities (e.g., Biron and Bamberger 2010; Zheng et al. 2019). Similarly, the sharing of personal issues or work-related sensitive information (i.e., perceived affective trust) indicates the leader's willingness to have a close relationship with the employee, which in turn is expected to increase employees' occupational self-efficacy by suggesting that they are valued (Zheng et al. 2019). Employees whose skills are trusted by their leaders (cognitive trust) and who feel that their leaders lean on them to share challenges (affective trust) are more likely to believe in their own abilities to carry out tasks effectively. Thus, trust provides the psychological safety and encouragement necessary to build occupational self-efficacy.

Accordingly, we hypothesize:

Hypothesis 1: Perceived cognitive (H1a) and affective trust (H1b) are positively associated with occupational self-efficacy.

1.3 Occupational Self-efficacy and Work Engagement

Work engagement is a positive and fulfilling psychological state, defined by high energy, vigor, and dedication to one's job responsibilities (Bakker et al. 2008; Schaufeli and Bakker 2004). Previous studies have consistently shown that work engagement is influenced significantly by the availability of job and personal resources (Bakker 2009; Bakker and Demerouti 2007; Bakker et al. 2008). Job resources, such as constructive feedback, social support, and coaching, are critical in mitigating stress that emerges as a result of job demands (Crawford et al. 2010; Schaufeli and Bakker 2004). When employees perceive they are valued this shapes their psychological conditions. Respect and recognition contribute to a sense of meaningfulness, psychological availability, and safety—factors crucial for fostering engagement at work (Beltrán-Martín et al. 2023; Tóth-Király et al. 2023). When employees feel valued and supported, they are more likely to be deeply engaged in the work they do.

Additionally, personal resources, such as occupational self-efficacy, are critical in determining engagement levels (Schaufeli and Bakker 2004). Occupational self-efficacy acts as a self-motivating mechanism that directs time and energy towards performing productive tasks (Agarwal 2014; Li et al. 2017). Halbesleben's (2010) meta-analysis shows a strong association between self-efficacy and work engagement, which is reinforced by recent empirical studies (e.g., Albrecht and Marty 2020; Guarnaccia et al. 2018; Li et al. 2017).

Employees with high levels of occupational self-efficacy are better prepared to manage workplace challenges (Schyns and von Collani 2002) and to overcome obstacles to task performance. As they feel more capable and motivated to fulfil their job responsibilities, this increased confidence translates into a greater emotional connection with their work (Albrecht and Marty 2020; Çetin and Aşkun 2018; Guarnaccia et al. 2018). By fostering perseverance and focus, occupational self-efficacy not only improves task outcomes but also enhances engagement by reinforcing an individual's belief in their capacity to succeed.

Based on this, we propose the following hypothesis:

Hypothesis 2: Occupational self-efficacy is positively associated with work engagement.

1.4 The Indirect Effects of Trust on Work Engagement

Trust is a critical socio-emotional resource in the workplace that enhances positive attitudes and behaviours (Brower et al. 2009; Baer et al. 2021). Trust reflects confidence in the abilities, integrity, and benevolence of others, creating a foundation for supportive workplace relationships. However, trust can function as a double-edged sword. While it typically encourages positive dynamics, excessive trust can lead to emotional exhaustion (Baer et al. 2015) or even exploitation, as it may be seen as an opportunity for deception (Skinner et al. 2014). In addition, the impact of trust on workplace outcomes is dependent on the ability of individuals to interpret its indirect cues, which are often nuanced (Campagna et al. 2020; van der Werff and Buckley 2017).

Work engagement is influenced not only by environmental resources but also by personal resources that enable individuals to psychologically process workplace experiences (Zheng et al. 2019). Trust contributes to this process as a source of social persuasion, enhancing employees' self-efficacy (Bandura 2006; Zheng et al. 2019). High levels of occupational self-efficacy enable employees to feel more emotionally connected to their job responsibilities, thereby fostering higher levels of engagement (Guarnaccia et al. 2018; Schaufeli and Bakker 2004; Schyns and von Collani 2002).

Based on this, we expect that cognitive trust (reliance on competence) and affective trust (emotional connection) indirectly influence work engagement by strengthening occupational self-efficacy (Zheng et al. 2019). Trust gives employees a sense of acknowledgment and validation and reinforces their confidence in their capabilities (de Jong et al. 2024). This confidence, in turn, leads to heightened motivation and perseverance, crucial drivers of work engagement (Bakker et al. 2023).

Accordingly, we propose the following hypothesis:

Hypothesis 3: The influence of perceived cognitive (H3a) and affective trust (H3b) on work engagement will be indirect and fully mediated by occupational self-efficacy.

2 Method

2.1 Participants and Procedures

The survey data was collected through the Lime survey platform from the employees and leaders of three major companies in Bhutan. These companies were mainly the public companies operating under Royal Government of Bhutan's investment arm, the Druk Holdings and Investments (DHI). Therefore, to conduct our survey, we had to first seek permission from the DHI, and then from each company management. These companies appointed focal persons who shared with us employee details such as email addresses, departments, and supervisors and facilitated the survey by providing email heads up during each survey moment.

This research was assessed and approved by the ethical committee of the authors' institution. Emails were sent to 1,406 employees to invite them to participate in the study. Although company managers permitted our survey and encouraged the employees, their participation was voluntary. By seeking their informed consent, we assured the anonymity and confidentiality of their responses. A pilot study assessed the items' clarity and adequacy to respondents.

The survey was conducted over two waves. At time 1, employees rated perceived cognitive and affective trust, and at time 2, occupational self-efficacy and work engagement.

Each survey moment was separated by two weeks. Although we received 450 responses for trust measures, only 335 employees responded in the second moment. Therefore, the final data is based on 335 responses, which corresponds to a 23.8% response rate. On average, employees were 34.1 years old, with the eldest being 57 and the youngest being 29. They were predominantly male (55%), and holding at least a bachelor's degree (46.3%). On average, employees have been supervised by their respective leaders for 5.97 years.

2.2 Measures

Because English is the working language in Bhutan, the measures did not need to be translated.

Trust. We used Yang and Mossholder's (2010) ten-item scale to measure cognitive and affective trust. The items are rated on a 5-point Likert scale (1 = strongly disagree, 5 = strongly agree). A sample item for cognitive trust is "My supervisor depends on me to meet the work responsibilities" and for affective trust is "My supervisor is confident about sharing work difficulties with me."

Occupational Self-efficacy. To measure occupational self-efficacy, we adapted a scale developed by Schyns and Von Collani (2002), which is composed of eight items. A sample item is "I can remain calm when facing difficulties in my job because I can rely on my abilities" and is measured on a 6-point Likert type (1 = Not at all true, 6 = Completely true).

Work Engagement. We used the scale by Schaufeli et al. (2019) to evaluate work engagement. A sample of this three-item scale is "At work; I feel bursting with energy." Employees rated this measure on a six-point Likert-type scale (1 = never, 6 = almost every day).

2.3 Data Analysis

We have used structural equation modeling (SEM) with maximum likelihood estimation on IBM SPSS AMOS (version 29 to examine the relationships among our study variables. SEM has several advantages compared to regression analysis as it provides more robust results in examining direct and indirect effects by indicating how well the data fit the proposed model (Collier 2020). Additionally, SEM provides explicit estimates of error variance parameters, thereby improving the accuracy of the data analysis (Byrne 2010). The significance of the indirect effects was tested with bootstrapping.

3   Results

3.1 Preliminary Analysis

We conducted a confirmatory factor analysis (CFA) to examine the convergent and discriminant validity of our measurement model. We implemented an item parcelling approach, allocating items randomly on different parcels of the latent variables (Little et al. 2002). Such an approach is noted for greater reliability, a higher ratio of common-to-unique factor variance (Little et al. 2013) and greater communality (MacCallum et al. 2001). In addition, parcels are beneficial for studies based on smaller samples because they can minimise errors among items within the same construct, providing better-fit solutions (Bandalos 2002), which is the case in our study. The following indicators were used to assess the model fit: χ^2 Goodness of fit statistic, Goodness of Fit Index (GFI), Normed Fit Index (NFI), Tucker–Lewis Index (TLI), Comparative Fit Index (CFI), and root mean square error of approximation (RMSEA).

Table 1. Model fit indices

Models	$\chi2$	df	GFI	NFI	TLI	CFI	RMSEA
4 Factor Model (CT, AT, OSE, WE)	111.3	59	.953	.960	.975	.981	.052
3 Factor Model (CT + AT, OSE, WE)	368.1	62	.835	.869	.859	.888	.122
2 Factor Model (CT + AT, OSE + WE)	575.5	64	.670	.795	.771	.812	.155
1 Factor Model (CT + AT + OSE + WE)	1495.8	65	.542	.466	.370	.475	.257

Abbreviations
CT: Cognitive trust, AT: Affective trust, OSE: Occupational self-efficacy, WE: Work engagement.

The four-factor model (shown in Table 1) yielded an acceptable fit to the data (χ^2 = 111.3, df = 59, GFI = .953, NFI = .960, TLI = .975, CFI = .981, and RMSEA = .05). The results indicated that each of the alternative models had a worse fit than the predicted four-factor model – the $\Delta\chi^2$s are all statistically significant. Hence, the results provide evidence of the convergent and discriminant validity of the study's measures.

Table 2 shows the variables' mean, standard deviation, and bivariate correlations and the validity and reliability of latent variables. Both Cronbach's alpha and composite reliability values were above.70, and average variance extracted values above.50. The results ensure the scale's reliability and validity. Furthermore, correlation results provide initial support for our hypothesized relationships. Cognitive trust (r = .39, p < 0.01) and affective trust (r = .31, p < 0.01) are positively correlated with occupational self-efficacy. With work engagement, trust dimensions (CT = .21, p < 0.01, CT = .18, p < 0.05) and occupational self-efficacy (r = .37, p < 0.01) are also positively correlated. As our results revealed a significant positive correlation between cognitive and affective trust (r = .59, p < 0.01), we combined the two measures in our CFA. However, the model fit indices reduced drastically, thus we proceeded with separate variables.

Table 2. Descriptive statistics, intercorrelations matrix, Cronbach alpha values, CR, and AVE.

Factors	CT	AT	OSE	WE	CR	AVE
CT	*.825*				.83	.63
AT	.597**	*.924*			.93	.82
OSE	.396**	.308**	*.911*		.91	.72
WE	.208**	.175**	.374**	*.753*	.77	.53
Mean	3.931	3.789	4.815	4.839		
SD	.547	.687	.629	.947		

Note: Significance level (2-tailed), ** $p < 0.01$, Cronbach's alphas are presented diagonally and in Italics and bold. Abbreviations: CT: Cognitive trust, AT: Affective trust, OSE: Occupational self-efficacy, WE: Work engagement, CR: Composite reliability; AVE: average variation extracted

3.2 Hypotheses Testing

To test the hypothesized relationships, we conducted structural equation modeling on IBM SPSS AMOS 29.

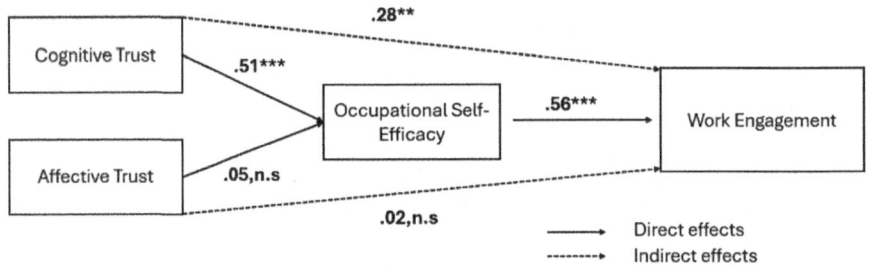

Note: Significance level (2-tailed), ** p< 0.01, *** p< 0.001

Fig. 1. SEM output. Note: Significance level (2-tailed), **p < 0.01, ***p < 0.001

The fit indices of the SEM model were adequate: $\chi^2 = 111.3$, df $= 59$, NFI $= .960$, TLI $= .975$, CFI $= .981$, and RMSEA $= .05$.

In hypothesis 1, we predicted a positive association between trust and occupational self-efficacy. The path to occupational self-efficacy from cognitive trust (B $= .51$, p < 0.001) was positive and significant, while from affective trust (B $= .05$, ns) was not significant. Thus, support was found for H1a but not for H1b. Hypothesis 2 tested for a positive association between occupational self-efficacy and work engagement (B $= .56$, p < 0.001). The results are significant, supporting H2. Finally, to test for indirect effects, we estimated paths from trust to work engagement mediated by occupational self-efficacy in hypothesis 3. H3a results revealed that the indirect effect of cognitive trust to work engagement via occupational self-efficacy (B $= .28$, p < 0.01) was positive and significant, while the indirect effect of affective trust was not (B $= .02$, ns). Thus, support was found for H3a and not H3b. Results are presented in Fig. 1.

4   Discussions and Conclusions

This study investigated the influence of perceived cognitive and affective trust on work engagement, considering occupational self-efficacy as a mediator. The findings reveal a significant positive association between cognitive trust and occupational self-efficacy, which, in turn, positively impacts work engagement. The mediating role of occupational self-efficacy highlights the importance of cognitive trust to enhance engagement levels. On the contrary, the results indicate no significant associations between affective trust and occupational self-efficacy or work engagement.

Cognitive trust plays a pivotal role as a positive evaluation of employees' task abilities, which enhances confidence and belief in their competence (Mayer et al. 1995). Our findings align with prior research suggesting that cognitive trust fosters an environment where employees feel assured about their capabilities and task performance (McAllister 1995). Conversely, affective trust, which involves emotional trust and disclosing sensitive information, can act as a stressor Baer et al. (2015). This result sheds light on the potential double-edged nature of affective trust. Indeed, depending on contextual factors, affective trust can either support or hinder workplace dynamics.

The strong positive relationship between occupational self-efficacy and work engagement can be explained by Bandura's (2006) social cognitive theory. Occupational self-efficacy, which reflects an individual's confidence in successfully executing job-related tasks, emerges as a critical in promoting work engagement. Employees with high self-efficacy are better prepared to overcome workplace challenges and maintain focus on achieving goals, fostering resilience and intrinsic motivation (Zheng et al. 2019). These qualities enable them to be emotionally connected with their workplace roles, leading to higher levels of vigor, dedication, and absorption (Schaufeli and Bakker 2004).

Furthermore, this study supports the indirect positive relationship of cognitive trust with work engagement via occupational self-efficacy. When employees perceive that their leaders trust in their task-related abilities, they feel more self-confident in their skills, which acts as a motivational mechanism enabling them to engage deeply with their work. However, as Campagna et al. (2020) point out, because the effects of trust are not always explicit, translating trust into commitment relies on individual psychological resources such as self-efficacy. Employees with high self-efficacy perceive challenges as opportunities rather than threats, which enable them to direct their effort toward achieving positive outcomes and maintaining high levels of engagement (Albrecht and Marty 2020).

Cognitive trust is a crucial enabler of occupational self-efficacy, which subsequently fosters work engagement. This mediating relationship emphasizes the need for organizations to create environments that promote trust and recognize employees' competencies. Conversely, the lack of significant results for affective trust suggests that its role in fostering engagement is context-dependent and warrants further exploration.

From a practical perspective, organizations should prioritize building cognitive trust through transparent communication, fair evaluations, and acknowledgment of employees' contributions. Timely and constructive feedback can reinforce employees' self-efficacy and motivate them to immerse themselves in their work. Tools such as employee engagement surveys and trust assessments can help monitor and reinforce trust dynamics within the workplace. Future research should explore the nuanced effects of affective trust. Longitudinal studies could also provide insights into the evolving nature of trust and its impact on self-efficacy and engagement over time.

While we carried out the study in a unique, yet an understudied context, we must acknowledge a few limitations. Bhutan is known for prioritizing happiness of the people over economic development through Gross National Happiness (Centre for Bhutan Studies & GNH Research 2017). Blending Buddhist and Western principles, the country focuses on upholding family relationship, freedom and most importantly conducting business with integrity (Sonnenberg et al. 2021). Thus, our study enables the applicability of western and Confucian tested theories in a broader and unique context (Henrich et al. 2010). However, we must acknowledge a few limitations. Firstly, adopting pre-validated scales could have possibly limited in gaining unique perspectives from our respondents. Secondly, single source survey responses may implicate the issue of common method bias, even though we have adopted measures to avoid this threat such as conducting survey over three different moments (Podsakoff et al. 2012). And thirdly, adopting other strategies of data collection along with the existing method could have helped in strengthening the findings of our work. For instance, conducting qualitative and focus group interviews could have provided us with richer and context specific insights.

Acknowledgments. This work has been supported by the Fundação para a Ciência e a Tecnologia (FCT) under project grant UIDB/05037/2020.

Disclosure of Interests. We declare no conflicts of interest to disclose regarding the research presented in this manuscript.

References

Agarwal, U.A.: Linking justice, trust and innovative work behaviour to work engagement. Pers. Rev. **43**(1), 41–73 (2014)

Albrecht, S.L., Marty, A.: Personality, self-efficacy and job resources and their associations with employee engagement, affective commitment and turnover intentions. Int. J. Hum. Resource Manag. **31**(5), 657–681 (2020)

Baer, M.D., Dhensa-Kahlon, R.K., Colquitt, J.A., Rodell, J.B., Outlaw, R., Long, D.M.: Uneasy lies the head that bears the trust: the effects of feeling trusted on emotional exhaustion. Acad. Manag. J. **58**(6), 1637–1657 (2015)

Baer, M.D., Frank, E.L., Matta, F.K., Luciano, M.M., Wellman, N.: Under trusted, over trusted, or just right? The fairness of (in)congruence between trust wanted and trust received. Acad. Manag. J. **64**(1), 180–206 (2021)

Bakker, A.: Building engagement in the workplace. In: Burke, R.J., Cooper, C.L. (eds.) The Peak Performing Organisations. Routledge (2009)

Bakker, A.B., Demerouti, E.: The job demands-resources model: state of the art. J. Manag. Psychol. **22**, 309–328 (2007)

Bakker, A.B., Demerouti, E., Sanz-Vergel, A.: Job demands–resources theory: ten years later. Annu. Rev. Organ. Psych. Organ. Behav. **10**, 25–53 (2023)

Bakker, A.B., Schaufeli, W.B., Leiter, M.P., Taris, T.W.: Work engagement: an emerging concept in occupational health psychology. Work Stress. **22**, 187–200 (2008)

Bandalos, D.L.: The effects of item parcelling on goodness of fit and parameter estimate bias in structural equation modelling. Struct. Equ. Model. **9**(1), 78–102 (2002)

Bandura, A.: Self-efficacy: Toward a unifying theory of behavioral change. Psychol. Rev. **84**, 191–215 (1977)

Bandura, A.: Toward a psychology of human agency. Perspect. Psychol. Sci. **1**(2), 164–180 (2006)

Blau, P.M.: Exchange and Power in Social Life. John Wiley & Sons, Inc (1964)

Beltrán-Martín, I., Guinot-Reinders, J., Rodríguez-Sánchez, A.M.: Employee psychological conditions as mediators of the relationship between human resource management and employee work engagement. Int. J. Hum. Resour. Manag. **34**(11), 2331–2365 (2023)

Biron, M., Bamberger, P.: The impact of structural empowerment on individual well-being and performance: taking agent preferences, self-efficacy and operational constraints into account. Hum. Relat. **63**(2), 163–191 (2010)

Brower, H.H., Lester, S.W., Korsgaard, A.M., Dineen, B.R.: A closer look at trust between managers and subordinates: understanding the effects of both trusting and being trusted on subordinate outcomes. J. Manag. **35**(2), 327–347 (2009)

Byrne, B. M. Structural Equation Modeling with AMOS: Basic Concepts, Applications, and Programming, 2nd ed. Routledge/Taylor & Francis Group (2010)

Campagna, R.L., Dirks, K.T., Knight, A.P., Crossley, C., Robinson, S.L.: On the relation between felt trust and actual trust: examining pathways to and implications of leader trust meta-accuracy. J. Appl. Psychol. **105**(9), 994–1012 (2020)

Carter, M.Z., Mossholder, K.W.: Are we on the same page? The performance effects of congruence between supervisor and group trust. J. Appl. Psychol. **100**(5), 1349–1363 (2015)

Centre for Bhutan Studies & GNH Research. Proposed GNH in Business, 1st ed. Centre for Bhutan Studies & GNH (2017)

Çetin, F., Aşkun, D.: The effect of occupational self-efficacy on work performance through intrinsic work motivation. Manag. Res. Rev. **41**, 186–201 (2018)

Collier, J.E.: Applied Structural Equation Modeling Using AMOS: Basic to Advanced Techniques. Routledge (2020)

Colquitt, J.A., LePine, J.A., Piccolo, R.F., Zapata, C.P., Rich, B.L.: Explaining the justice-performance relationship: trust as exchange deepener or trust as uncertainty reducer? J. Appl. Psychol. **97**(1), 1–15 (2012)

Crawford, E.R., LePine, J.A., Rich, B.L.: Linking job demands and resources to employee engagement and burnout: a theoretical extension and meta-analytic test. J. Appl. Psychol. **95**(5), 834–848 (2010)

de Jong, B., Lee, A., Gill, H., Zheng, X.: Felt trust: Added baggage or added value? A critical review, constructive redirection, and exploratory meta-analysis. J. Organ. Behavior 1–26 (2024)

Dimas, I.D., Torres, P., Rebelo, T., Lourenço, P.R.: Paths to team success: a configurational analysis of team effectiveness. Hum. Perform. **36**(4), 155–179 (2023)

Dirks, K.T., De Jong, B.: Trust within the workplace: a review of two waves of research and a glimpse of the third. Annu. Rev. Organ. Psych. Organ. Behav. **9**, 247–276 (2022)

Gill, H., Cassidy, S.A., Cragg, C., Algate, P., Weijs, C.A., Finegan, J.E.: Beyond reciprocity: the role of empowerment in understanding felt trust. Eur. J. Work Organ. Psy. **28**(6), 845–858 (2019)

Gist, M.E., Mitchell, T.R.: Self-efficacy: a theoretical analysis of its determinants and malleability. Acad. Manag. Rev. **17**(2), 183–211 (1992)

Guarnaccia, C., Scrima, F., Civilleri, A.: The role of occupational self-efficacy in mediating the effect of job insecurity on work engagement. Satisfac. General Health. Curr. Psychol. **37**, 488–497 (2018)

Halbesleben, J.R.B.: A meta-analysis of work engagement: relationships with burnout, demands, resources, and consequences. In: Bakker, A.B. , Leiter, M.P. (eds.) Work Engagement: A Handbook of Essential Theory and Research, pp. 102–117. Psychology Press (2010)

Henrich, J., Heine, S.J., Norenzayan, A.: The weirdest people in the world? Behav. Brain Sci. **33**(2–3), 61–83 (2010)

Karma, L., Dimas, I.D.: Why do I (not) trust my employees? Predicting factors for leaders' trust in employees. Int. Stud. Manag. Organ. 1–19 (2024)

Lau, D.C., Lam, L.W., Wen, S.S.: Examining the effects of feeling trusted by supervisors in the workplace: a self-evaluative perspective. J. Organ. Behav. **35**(1), 112–127 (2014)

Legood, A., van der Werff, L., Lee, A., Den Hartog, D.: A meta-analysis of the role of trust in the leadership- performance relationship. Eur. J. Work Organ. Psy. **30**(1), 1–22 (2021)

Lent, R.W., Brown, S.D.: On conceptualizing and assessing social cognitive constructs in career research: a measurement guide. J. Career Assess. **14**(1), 12–35 (2006)

Li, M., Wang, Z., Gao, J.: Proactive Personality and Job Satisfaction: the mediating effects of self-efficacy and work engagement in teachers. Curr. Psychol. **36**, 48–55 (2017)

Little, T.D., Cunningham, W.A., Shahar, G., Widaman, K.F.: To parcel or not to parcel; exploring the question, weighing the merits. Struct. Equ. Modeling **9**(2), 151–173 (2002)

Little, T.D., Rhemtulla, M., Gibson, K., Schoemann, A.M.: Why the items versus parcels controversy needn't be one. Psychol. Methods **18**(3), 285–300 (2013)

Ferguson, S., Smith, C., Kietzmann, J.: Hands-off? Lessons from high-touch professionals about going virtual. Bus. Horiz. **65**(3), 303–313 (2022)

MacCallum, R.C., Widaman, K.F., Preacher, K.J., Hong, S.: Sample size in factor analysis: the role of model error. Multivar. Behav. Res. **36**(4), 611–637 (2001)

Mayer, R.C., Gavin, M.B.: Trust in management and performance: who mind that shop while the employees watch the boss? Acad. Manag. J. **48**(5), 874–888 (2005)

Mayer, R.C., Davis, J.H., David Schoorman, F.: An integrative model of organizational trust. Acad. Manag. J. **20**(3), 709–734 (1995)

McAllister, D.J.: Affect- and cognition-based trust as foundations for interpersonal cooperation in organizations. Acad. Manag. J. **38**(1), 24–59 (1995)

Ozyilmaz, A., Erdogan, B., Karaeminogullari, A.: Trust in organization as a moderator of the relationship between self-efficacy and workplace outcomes: a social cognitive theory-based examination. J. Occup. Organ. Psychol. **91**, 181–204 (2018)

Podsakoff, P.M., MacKenzie, S.B., Podsakoff, N.P.: Sources of method bias in social science research and recommendations on how to control it. Annu. Rev. Psychol. **63**, 539–569 (2012)

Schaufeli, W.B., Bakker, A.B.: Job demands, job resources, and their relationship with burnout and engagement: a multi-sample study. J. Organ. Behav. **25**(3), 293–315 (2004)

Schaufeli, W.B., Shimazu, A., Hakanen, J., Salanova, M., De Witte, H.: An ultra-short measure for work engagement: the UWES-3 validation across five countries. Eur. J. Psychol. Assess. **35**(4), 577–591 (2019)

Skinner, D., Dietz, G., Weibel, A.: The dark side of trust: When trust becomes a 'poisoned chalice.' Organization **21**(2), 206–224 (2014)

Schyns, B., von Collani, G.: A new occupational self-efficacy scale and its relation to personality constructs and organizational variables. Eur. J. Work Organ. Psy. **11**(2), 219–241 (2002)

Sonnenberg, S., Bernstorff, A., Namgay, T.: Finding the right path: towards a Buddhist sense of corporate ethics in Bhutan. Asia Review **11**(3), 125–164 (2021)

Tomlinson, E.C., Schnackenberg, A.K., Dawley, D., Ash, S.R.: Revisiting the trustworthiness–trust relationship: exploring the differential predictors of cognition- and affect-based trust. J. Organ. Behav. **41**(6), 535–550 (2020)

Tóth-Király, I., Gillet, N., Inhaber, J., Houle, S.A., Vandenberghe, C., Morin, A.J.S.: Job engagement trajectories: their associations with leader–member exchange and their implications for employees. J. Occup. Organ. Psychol. **96**(3), 545–574 (2023)

van der Werff, L., Buckley, F.: Getting to know you: a Longitudinal examination of trust cues and trust development during socialisation. J. Manag. **43**(3), 742–770 (2017)

Yang, J., Mossholder, K.W.: Examining the effects of trust in leaders: a bases-and-foci approach. Leadersh. Quart. **21**(1), 50–63 (2010)

Zheng, X., Hall, R.J., Schyns, B.: Investigating follower felt trust from a social cognitive perspective. Eur. J. Work Organ. Psy. **28**(6), 873–885 (2019)

RidGME Estimation and Inference in Ill-Conditioned Models

Pedro Macedo[1] ⓘ, Jorge Cabral[1] ⓘ, Vera Afreixo[1] ⓘ, Francisco Macedo[2] ⓘ, and Mario Angelelli[3(✉)] ⓘ

[1] Center for Research and Development in Mathematics and Applications (CIDMA), Department of Mathematics, University of Aveiro, Aveiro 3810-193, Portugal
{pmacedo,jorgecabral,vera}@ua.pt
[2] Department of Informatics Engineering, Faculty of Science and Technology, University of Coimbra, Pólo II, 3030-290 Coimbra, Portugal
fmacedo@student.uc.pt
[3] Department of Human and Social Sciences, Centre of Applied Mathematics and Physics for Industry (CAMPI), University of Salento, Via Valesio, 73100 Lecce, Italy
mario.angelelli@unisalento.it

Abstract. The selection of statistical methods that can operate even on ill-conditioned problems, providing accurate estimation and supporting general inference tasks, is a central need in several applications in different domains. In this setting, two major approaches are the methods from the bridge estimation family, such as ridge regression, and the entropy-based methods, such as generalized maximum entropy estimation. Regarding these two methods, on the one hand, the appropriate choice of the shrinkage parameter in ridge regression is not always an easy task, and, on the other hand, the choice of supports for the parameters of the model is a usual difficulty with the generalized maximum entropy estimator. The RidGME estimator proposed in this work, using generalized maximum entropy with supports defined with information from the ridge trace, mitigates the weaknesses of both methodologies, revealing itself as an alternative to ridge regression on ill-conditioned models. The results from an empirical application reveal that the RidGME estimator is competitive with the *best* optimal choice of ridge estimators and outperforms the ordinary least squares estimator in a cross-validation root mean squared error sense. Its implementation is illustrated, and computational codes are made available to practitioners.

Keywords: Generalized maximum entropy · Ridge regression · Ridge trace · Shrinkage estimation

1 Introduction

The quality of analyses exploring relationships between multiple variables may be critically affected by redundant information shared by such variables. Specifically, the presence of strong collinearity in regression models makes them ill-conditioned (or ill-posed in a broader sense) [4, pp. 85–98]. In turn, this situation

O. Gervasi et al. (Eds.): ICCSA 2025 Workshops, LNCS 15887, pp. 300–313, 2026.
https://doi.org/10.1007/978-3-031-97589-9_21

may invalidate or prevent the use of traditional estimation methods, as they may lead to highly unstable estimates in this circumstance.

Ridge regression proposed by Hoerl and Kennard [9] is an estimation procedure to handle collinearity without removing variables from the regression model; although biased, the ridge estimator can be substantially more precise than unbiased estimators under collinearity problems. Regarding the usual concern with the use of biased estimators, note that the unknown parameters in a regression model are assumed finite to be well-defined. Such parameters constitute the components of a vector β and, under the finiteness hypotesis, we can assume an upper bound on $\beta'\beta$ and apply the ordinary least squares (OLS) estimator subject to this restriction. This *constrained* optimization problem returns the general form of the ridge regression [21, p. 470]. Although the standardization of the variables is usually recommended to practitioners, this decision should always be evaluated on a case-by-case basis, depending on the data (e.g., measurement scales), the theoretical model (e.g., the model includes an intercept or not; whether the intercept is involved in the collinearity issue or not), and the purpose of the regularization process (e.g., prediction, precision, interpretation).

The selection of the shrinkage (tuning or ridge) parameter that controls the additional constraint on the coefficient vector's norm remains a challenge in ridge regression. In addition to other possibilities (e.g., formal methods, cross-validation), one straightforward approach is based on the analysis of the ridge trace – a plot with the path of each estimate as a function of several possible values for the shrinkage parameter –, i.e., the analysis of the paths of the estimates [8,9,16,25]. Then a value for the shrinkage parameter is chosen in the region where the estimates "become more stable," but the formalization of this notion of stability is usually considered somewhat arbitrary. It is commonly accepted that this choice should be made in the interval between zero and one for the shrinkage parameter, providing a compromise between the reduction of variance and the increase of bias [16]. This means that, assuming this interval (or even a larger one), each parameter space is clearly established with the analysis of the ridge trace.

On the other hand, a different approach to deal with collinearity (and, in general, with ill-posed models) was proposed by Golan et al. [7] through the *generalized maximum entropy* (GME) estimator. This approach extends the maximum entropy (ME) principle established by Jaynes [10,11] based on Shannon entropy [23]. The concept of entropy appeared in the 19th century as a central notion at the foundations of thermodynamics, later connected with a probabilistic formulation in statistical physics [12]. The concept of entropy acquires a new meaning beyond its original purpose in 1948, with Claude Shannon [23], as a measure of information (or uncertainty) in information theory. The GME and other information-theoretic estimation techniques are included in a research area at the intersection of statistics, computer science, and decision theory, that is, Info-Metrics [6]. Some concerns regarding the use of the GME estimator are usually related to the specification of the support spaces for the parameters of the regression model, an issue that remains an open question from a formal statistical perspective [5–7,19], but also has practical interpretations, e.g., in relation to inequivalent knowledge representations as a source of epistemic uncertainty [3].

The Ridge-GME shrinkage parameter estimator [13,15] is a procedure that combines the ridge and the GME estimators, in order to choose an adequate shrinkage parameter. The ridge trace provides information for the selection of the supports for the parameters in the regression model, which is the main difficulty with the GME estimator; on the other hand, the use of the GME estimator tries to solve the arbitrariness in the selection of the shrinkage parameter based on the visual analysis of the ridge trace. This work moves the initial purpose of the Ridge-GME shrinkage parameter estimator from choosing the shrinkage parameter for ridge regression to the objective of being itself as an alternative to ridge regression estimation, including confidence intervals for inference purposes.

The remainder of the paper is laid out as follows: in Sect. 2, a brief overview of OLS, ridge, GME and Ridge-GME estimators is presented. The new RidGME estimator is discussed in Sect. 3. An illustration is accomplished in Sect. 4. Finally, some concluding remarks are given in Sect. 5.

2   Overview of the Estimators

The linear regression model is usually defined by

$$y = X\beta + u, \tag{1}$$

where y denotes a $(N \times 1)$ vector of noisy observations, β is a $(K \times 1)$ vector of unknown parameters to be estimated, X is a known $(N \times K)$ matrix of explanatory variables, and u is a $(N \times 1)$ vector of random errors, usually assumed to have a conditional expected value of 0 and representing spherical disturbances, i.e., $E[u|X] = 0$ and $E[uu'|X] = \sigma^2 I$, where I is the $(N \times N)$ identity matrix and σ^2 is the error variance. Different instances of the generating model (1) can be considered, for example, including the intercept – if this aligns with the theoretical framework and the nature of data –, by extending both the parameter vector $\overline{\beta} := (\beta_0, \beta)$ and the matrix of explanatory variables $\overline{X} := (1_{N \times 1} \ X)$, where 1 is the $(N \times 1)$-dimensional vector with all components equal to 1.

From these premises, we can formalize the different parameter estimators $\widehat{\beta}$ considered in this work:

Definition 1. *The ordinary least squares estimator, $\widehat{\beta}_{\mathrm{OLS}}$, of β in model (1) is given by*

$$\widehat{\beta}_{\mathrm{OLS}} = (X'X)^{-1}X'y. \tag{2}$$

As mentioned in the Introduction section, the ridge estimator, by adding a small shrinkage parameter to the diagonal of $X'X$, introduces some bias, although it reduces the variance of the OLS estimator.

Definition 2. *The ridge estimator, $\widehat{\beta}_{\mathrm{ridge}}$, of β in model (1) is given by*

$$\widehat{\beta}_{\mathrm{ridge}} = (X'X + \lambda I)^{-1}X'y, \tag{3}$$

where $\lambda \geq 0$ *denotes the shrinkage parameter and* $\boldsymbol{I}$ *is the* $(K \times K)$ *identity matrix.*

Among the advantages of the OLS and ridge estimators, we briefly discuss their closed forms (2) and (3). The real and symmetric matrices $\boldsymbol{X}'\boldsymbol{X}$ and $\lambda \cdot \boldsymbol{I}$ can be simultaneously diagonalized, and the eigenvalues of their sum $\boldsymbol{X}'\boldsymbol{X} + \lambda \cdot \boldsymbol{I}$ have the form $\Lambda_k + \lambda$, where Λ_k denotes the eigenvalues of $\boldsymbol{X}'\boldsymbol{X}$, $k \in \{1, \ldots, K\}$. Therefore, in cases where $\Lambda_k \approx 0$ for some $k \in \{1, \ldots, K\}$, i.e., when $\boldsymbol{X}'\boldsymbol{X}$ is (nearly) singular, we can choose a *generic* value of the shrinkage parameter λ to get a non-singular sum $\boldsymbol{X}'\boldsymbol{X} + \lambda \cdot \boldsymbol{I}$. This means that at least one of the two estimators (2) or (3) is well-defined; furthermore, when they both exist, it follows from Definition 2 that the ridge estimator approaches the OLS estimator when $\lambda \to 0$, while it approaches the zero vector when $\lambda \to \infty$.

On the other hand, we stress once again that, when $\boldsymbol{X}'\boldsymbol{X}$ is (nearly) singular, ridge regression introduces arbitrariness in the estimates due to the freedom in choosing λ. The variance of $\widehat{\beta}_{\text{ridge}}$ decreases as λ increases, but the bias increases with λ. Since the range of values for which the ridge estimator is superior to the OLS estimator depends on the unknown β and σ^2, the challenge is to select an estimate of λ such that the ridge estimator has a smaller mean squared error (MSE) than the OLS estimator. As we will see, this arbitrariness can be handled efficiently through maximum entropy methods, specifically, the GME estimator introduced in the following.

Definition 3. *The generalized maximum entropy estimator,* $\widehat{\beta}_{\text{GME}}$*, of* β *in model (1) is given by*

$$\widehat{\beta}_{\text{GME}} = \boldsymbol{Z}\widehat{\boldsymbol{p}}, \tag{4}$$

where $\widehat{\boldsymbol{p}}$ *is obtained from the optimization problem described by*

$$\underset{\boldsymbol{p},\boldsymbol{w}}{\operatorname{argmax}} \left\{ -\boldsymbol{p}' \ln \boldsymbol{p} - \boldsymbol{w}' \ln \boldsymbol{w} \right\}, \tag{5}$$

subject to the model constraints,

$$\boldsymbol{y} = \boldsymbol{X}\boldsymbol{Z}\boldsymbol{p} + \boldsymbol{V}\boldsymbol{w}, \tag{6}$$

and the additivity constraints for $\boldsymbol{p}$ *and* $\boldsymbol{w}$*, respectively,*

$$\boldsymbol{1}_K = (\boldsymbol{I}_K \otimes \boldsymbol{1}'_M)\boldsymbol{p}, \quad \boldsymbol{1}_N = (\boldsymbol{I}_N \otimes \boldsymbol{1}'_J)\boldsymbol{w}, \tag{7}$$

where $\otimes$ *represents the Kronecker product,* $\boldsymbol{Z}$ *and* $\boldsymbol{V}$ *are the matrices of supports, and* $\boldsymbol{p} > \boldsymbol{0}$ *and* $\boldsymbol{w} > \boldsymbol{0}$ *(componentwise) are probability vectors to be estimated.*

The algebraic structure for β in Definition 3 is given by

$$\beta = \boldsymbol{Z}\boldsymbol{p} = \begin{bmatrix} \boldsymbol{z}'_1 & \boldsymbol{0} & \cdots & \boldsymbol{0} \\ \boldsymbol{0} & \boldsymbol{z}'_2 & \cdots & \boldsymbol{0} \\ \vdots & \vdots & \ddots & \vdots \\ \boldsymbol{0} & \boldsymbol{0} & \cdots & \boldsymbol{z}'_K \end{bmatrix} \begin{bmatrix} \boldsymbol{p}_1 \\ \boldsymbol{p}_2 \\ \vdots \\ \boldsymbol{p}_K \end{bmatrix}, \tag{8}$$

where Z is the $(K \times KM)$ matrix of supports for β and p is the $(KM \times 1)$ vector of unknown probabilities; here, Z is a block-diagonal matrix where each row corresponds to a parameter in the model, and the associated block on the principal diagonal comprises a finite number (M) of points as representatives of a closed and bounded interval in which the parameter is expected to be contained. Regarding the error terms, they are modelled as follows:

$$u = Vw = \begin{bmatrix} v_1' & 0 & \cdots & 0 \\ 0 & v_2' & \cdots & 0 \\ \vdots & \vdots & \ddots & \vdots \\ 0 & 0 & \cdots & v_N' \end{bmatrix} \begin{bmatrix} w_1 \\ w_2 \\ \vdots \\ w_N \end{bmatrix}, \tag{9}$$

where J is the number of points in each support of V, V is the $(N \times NJ)$ matrix of supports for u (representing a closed and bounded interval in which each error is expected to be contained), and w is the $(NJ \times 1)$ vector of unknown probabilities. The number of points, M and J, are usually between three and five because there is no significant improvement in the estimation with more points in the supports [7].

The supports in matrices Z and V should be constructed with prior information, which unfortunately is not always available. As mentioned before, the main criticism in this regard is the specification of the support spaces for the model parameters, as the bounds and the center of supports are problem-specific and should be chosen with care. If no prior information exists, which is the most common scenario in practice, the supports are usually defined with equally spaced points between arbitrarily chosen lower and upper bounds, with the centre set at zero. Due to the lack of a universally accepted criterion, arbitrariness in the choice of bounds is usually managed based on theoretical constraints, data from previous works, or confidence intervals with high confidence levels from other estimation techniques.

Despite their differences, both the ridge and GME estimators can be applied under very mild conditions, even for ill-conditioned problems. Having two distinct methods provides us with a *"self-consistency"* criterion that guides the selection of the ridge parameter, mitigating its indeterminacy by minimizing the distance between the two estimators.

Definition 4. *The Ridge-GME shrinkage parameter estimator of λ is given by*

$$\widehat{\lambda} = \underset{\lambda}{\operatorname{argmin}} \left\| Z\widehat{p} - (X'X + \lambda I)^{-1} X'y \right\|_{\infty}, \tag{10}$$

where the vector $\widehat{p}$ is obtained from the GME estimator, the matrix Z is a $(K \times KM)$ matrix of supports with limits given by

$$z_k = \left[\min \left\{ \widehat{\beta}_{k_{\mathrm{ridge}(\lambda)}} \right\}, \max \left\{ \widehat{\beta}_{k_{\mathrm{ridge}(\lambda)}} \right\} \right], \tag{11}$$

for all the possible values of λ in the domain of ridge values, which is considered $[0, 1]$ by default.

With the Ridge-GME shrinkage parameter estimator, an estimate for λ is obtained without the need for any arbitrary choice from visual analysis of the ridge trace.

As a final remark, Golan et al. [7] defined normalized entropy for the signal $X\beta$ in the model (1) as

$$S(\widehat{p}) = \frac{-\widehat{p}' \ln \widehat{p}}{K \ln M},\tag{12}$$

where $S(\widehat{p}) = 1$ indicates perfect uncertainty and $S(\widehat{p}) = 0$ indicates no uncertainty. Even if this normalization involves a constant scaling factor, it affects the optimization process by changing the relative weights attributed to the signal and error terms in the GME objective function. Furthermore, it is important to note that there is empirical evidence that different supports for Z and for V, as well as different values for M and J, provide different results in terms of variable selection, which means that variable selection through normalized entropy should be interpreted and tested with caution [14]. More generally, in a probabilistic setting, different supports describe different event spaces, and a lack of information on a well-defined event space can be framed as a form of ambiguity [17, Sec. 1]. In turn, inconsistency may arise when combining or comparing results from different specifications, as previous studies explored both at a conceptual level, e.g., in knowledge representations [3], and in practical applications requiring the definition of robust measures for ranking accuracy under such forms of ambiguity [2]. These implications further stress the role of an appropriate choice of supports, taking into account the sources of uncertainty and their potential effects. In this work, we take advantage of the combination of ridge and GME estimators to bound the supports in a data-driven way, devoting to future work the exploration of other information measures, such as normalized entropy, and their use for variable selection within the RidGME estimator.

3   RidGME Estimator

Based on the previous discussion, we can now present the RidGME estimator, as an alternative to ridge regression in ill-conditioned models, starting with the choice of supports for both parameters and errors, which are the basic objects to enable the GME estimation step. This choice may substantially affect the estimation process; in our proposal, the derivation of the supports takes advantage of the ridge estimation step as a robust data-driven procedure, also mitigating the arbitrariness of this choice.

3.1   Step 1: Definition of Parameter and Error Supports

The first step involves choosing the domain $\mathcal{D}_\lambda$ for the shrinkage parameter λ in the ridge regression. We can consider the whole $[0, 1]$ range; alternatively, we can adopt a more parsimonious criterion and select an interval $[a, b] \subseteq [0, 1]$ based on the evaluation of the ridge trace. However, the case $\lambda = 0$ trivially returns the standard OLS estimates, which may be affected by the same collinearity issues we are addressing. Then, we exclude this occurrence by selecting a small regularization value $\varepsilon > 0$ for the domain $\mathcal{D}_\lambda \subseteq [\varepsilon, 1]$ of the shrinkage parameters involved in this step.

The information from the ridge trace is instrumental in finding, for each $k \in \{1, \ldots, K\}$, the bounds

$$z_{\max}^{(\beta_k)} := \max\{\widehat{\beta}_k^{(\lambda)}, \lambda \in \mathcal{D}_\lambda\},$$
$$z_{\min}^{(\beta_k)} := \min\{\widehat{\beta}_k^{(\lambda)}, \lambda \in \mathcal{D}_\lambda\}. \tag{13}$$

These bounds allow us to define the data-driven support in the RidGME algorithm. First, we choose the number of support points for both parameters and error terms, say M and J, respectively. Then, we can identify two specifications for the parameter supports:

– the *asymmetric support* specification, setting

$$Z_{\text{asym}}^{(k)} := \left\{ z_{\min}^{(\beta_k)} + \frac{z_{\max}^{(\beta_k)} - z_{\min}^{(\beta_k)}}{M - 1} \cdot t, \, t \in \{0, \ldots, M - 1\} \right\}, \, k \in \{1, \ldots, K\};$$
$$\tag{14}$$

– the *symmetric support* specification, setting

$$z_\star^{(k)} := \max \left\{ \left| z_{\min}^{(\beta_k)} \right|, \left| z_{\max}^{(\beta_k)} \right| \right\},$$

$$Z_{\text{symm}}^{(k)} := \left\{ -z_\star^{(k)} + \frac{2t}{M - 1} \cdot z_\star^{(k)}, \, t \in \{0, \ldots, M - 1\} \right\}, \, k \in \{1, \ldots, K\}.$$
$$\tag{15}$$

Both the specifications generate equally spaced points in the supports; the former (14) provides narrower supports, hence, it tends to reduce the possible variability of parameter estimates in the subsequent GME step, as they are obtained as convex combinations of the points in the support. Also note that each parameter has its own support, which aligns with the data-driven approach proposed in this work.

Even with respect to the support of error terms, we can use two distinct specifications:

– the first approach is the extension of the well-known three-sigma rule [20] to a different number of points (e.g., user-defined) of the support. Formally, we define the support for error terms as

$$V^{(n)} := \left\{ -3\text{sd}(\boldsymbol{y}) + \frac{2\,s}{J - 1} \cdot 3\text{sd}(\boldsymbol{y}), \, s \in \{0, \ldots, J - 1\} \right\}, \, n \in \{1, \ldots, N\},$$
$$\tag{16}$$

where $\text{sd}(\boldsymbol{y})$ stands for the standard deviation of $\boldsymbol{y}$;
– the second approach leverages the information in the previous phase. Indeed, after conducting ridge regression with multiple values of λ to generate the parameter supports, we can also use the estimates to evaluate the residuals

$$\boldsymbol{\eta}_\lambda := \boldsymbol{y} - \boldsymbol{X}\widehat{\boldsymbol{\beta}}_{\text{ridge}(\lambda)}, \tag{17}$$

and generate the support as

$$\eta_\star^{(n)} := \max\{|\boldsymbol{\eta}_\lambda|, \lambda \in \mathcal{D}_\lambda\}, \ n \in \{1, \dots, N\},$$

$$V^{(n)} := \left\{ -\eta_\star^{(n)} + \frac{2s}{J-1} \cdot \eta_\star^{(n)}, s \in \{0, \dots, J-1\} \right\}, \ n \in \{1, \dots, N\}. \quad (18)$$

The different approaches to estimating the supports reflect the distinguished roles of the parameters (signal) and error terms (statistical noise). Such a distinction is instrumental in different applications [13], even when data exhibit a temporal dimension and a specific update rule is needed for probability distributions to take into account memory effects for parameters, e.g., in the case of streaming data [1].

In terms of numerical implementation, we point out that the maximization in (13) and (18) is carried out over a *discretization* of the support $\mathcal{D}_\lambda \subseteq [\varepsilon, 1]$, namely, we select a given number of points, n_{ridge}, whose default value is set equal to 1000, and generate an equally spaced grid of n_{ridge} points in $\mathcal{D}_\lambda$.

3.2 Step 2: GME Estimation and Residual Bootstrapping

This second step carries out GME estimation based on the supports $Z^{(k)}$, $k \in \{1, \dots, K\}$, and $V^{(n)}$, $n \in \{1, \dots, N\}$, obtained in the previous step. The strategy for this step is the same independent on the choice of asymmetric (14) or symmetric (15) supports for the parameters, as well as variable-based (16) or residual-based (18) supports for the error terms.

Specifically, this step combines GME estimation with the well-known procedure for residual bootstrapping:

- conduct GME estimation by solving the optimization problem (5), with consistency constraints (6) and the normalization conditions (7). From the probability distributions $\widehat{\boldsymbol{p}}$ and $\widehat{\boldsymbol{w}}$ obtained from this optimization step, we get the GME parameter estimates $\widehat{\boldsymbol{\beta}}_{\mathrm{GME}}$ through (4);
- calculate the estimated responses $\widehat{\boldsymbol{y}}_{\mathrm{GME}} := \boldsymbol{X}\widehat{\boldsymbol{\beta}}_{\mathrm{GME}}$ and the corresponding GME residuals $\boldsymbol{\eta}_{\mathrm{GME}} := \boldsymbol{y} - \widehat{\boldsymbol{y}}_{\mathrm{GME}}$;
- conduct residual bootstrapping by selecting (with replacement) $n_{\mathrm{boot}} = 1000$ N-dimensional samples from the vector of residuals $\boldsymbol{\eta}_{\mathrm{GME}}$. For each $b \in \{1, \dots, n_{\mathrm{boot}}\}$, denote the corresponding residual sample as $\boldsymbol{\eta}_{\mathrm{GME}}^{(b)}$, which serves as a means to construct a new vector of observations $\boldsymbol{y}_{\mathrm{boot}}^{(b)} := \widehat{\boldsymbol{y}}_{\mathrm{GME}} + \boldsymbol{\eta}_{\mathrm{GME}}^{(b)}$. Then, iterate the GME algorithm to obtain a new parameter estimate $\widehat{\boldsymbol{\beta}}_{\mathrm{GME}}^{(b)}$ starting with the same supports $Z^{(k)}$, $k \in \{1, \dots, K\}$, and $V^{(n)}$, $n \in \{1, \dots, N\}$, along with the same data matrix $\boldsymbol{X}$ while using the new vector of observations $\boldsymbol{y}_{\mathrm{boot}}^{(b)}$ for the b-th iteration;
- from the n_{boot} iteration of the residual bootstrap procedure, we obtain an empirical distribution for all quantities of interest, including the parameter GME estimates $\widehat{\beta}_{k,\mathrm{boot}}^{(b)}$, $b \in \{1, \dots, n_{\mathrm{boot}}\}$, $k \in \{1, \dots, K\}$. The percentile method is used to infer confidence intervals at a given significance level (e.g., two-sided 95% CI).

We point out that our data-driven procedure derives the supports for the parameters and error terms from the original data; in particular, it relies on the original vector of observations y_n, $n \in \{1, \ldots, N\}$. Therefore, the aforementioned procedure for this step of the RidGME algorithm implicitly relies on the assumption that the distributional properties of the ridge and GME residuals hold approximately even for the bootstrapped distribution in terms of support estimation. On the other hand, the main focus of this work is on potential collinearity issues, which are encoded in the data matrix X that is not modified in the bootstrapping step.

4   Empirical Application

The well-known Portland cement model [18, 22, 24] is used to illustrate the RidGME estimator. The response variable is the heat evolved per gram of cement, and the four explanatory variables, β_k, $k = 1, 2, 3, 4$, are the amounts of tricalcium aluminate, tricalcium silicate, tetracalcium aluminoferrite and β-dicalcium silicate. The data set includes 13 observations. The original linear model (without intercept) has a $\text{cond}_2 \, X \approx 21$, where X is the matrix of explanatory variables and cond_2 is the 2-norm condition number. Interestingly, since the sum of each row is approximately equal to 100 in the original X matrix, adding an intercept, β_0, to the original linear model is obtained $\text{cond}_2 \, X \approx 6056$, with X representing now the matrix of explanatory variables with the first column of ones.

Table 1 presents the OLS estimates for the model with and without intercept, β_0, including the bootstrap confidence intervals at 95% (CI95). All values are rounded to four decimals.

Table 1. OLS estimates for the models with and without intercept.

	$\widehat{\beta}_k$	CI95	$\widehat{\beta}_k$	CI95
$\widehat{\beta}_0$	–	–	62.4054	$(-43.0052, 166.1128)$
$\widehat{\beta}_1$	2.1930	$(1.8797, 2.5288)$	1.5511	$(0.4563, 2.6931)$
$\widehat{\beta}_2$	1.1533	$(1.0688, 1.2315)$	0.5102	$(-0.5596, 1.5814)$
$\widehat{\beta}_3$	0.7585	$(0.4923, 1.0378)$	0.1019	$(-0.9918, 1.2609)$
$\widehat{\beta}_4$	0.4863	$(0.4202, 0.5550)$	-0.1441	$(-1.1881, 0.9025)$

Table 2 and Table 3 present the estimates and bootstrap confidence intervals at 95% (CI95) from the RidGME estimator for the parameters of the model with intercept, considering $\varepsilon = 0$. In Table 2, the RidGME estimator is performed with asymmetric supports (14), considering the three-sigma rule (16), on the left, and the residuals from ridge (18), on the right, to define the supports for the error component. On the other hand, in Table 3, the RidGME estimator is performed with symmetric supports (15), considering the three-sigma rule (16), on the left, and the residuals from ridge (18), on the right, to define the supports for the error component. All values are rounded to four decimals.

Table 2. RidGME estimates; asymmetric; 3σ (left), residuals ridge (right); $\varepsilon = 0$.

$\widehat{\beta}_k$	CI95	$\widehat{\beta}_k$	CI95
$\widehat{\beta}_0$ 31.2334	(30.5811, 31.9154)	31.9373	(27.3898, 34.7482)
$\widehat{\beta}_1$ 1.8685	(1.8658, 1.8714)	1.8788	(1.7780, 1.9894)
$\widehat{\beta}_2$ 0.8324	(0.8263, 0.8395)	0.8281	(0.7668, 0.9170)
$\widehat{\beta}_3$ 0.4271	(0.4239, 0.4304)	0.4113	(0.3144, 0.5175)
$\widehat{\beta}_4$ 0.1714	(0.1644, 0.1789)	0.1621	(0.1043, 0.2339)

Table 3. RidGME estimates; symmetric; 3σ (left), residuals ridge (right); $\varepsilon = 0$.

$\widehat{\beta}_k$	CI95	$\widehat{\beta}_k$	CI95
$\widehat{\beta}_0$ 44.1554	(43.5700, 46.3365)	47.4432	(41.1803, 51.0497)
$\widehat{\beta}_1$ 0.9155	(0.5672, 0.8608)	1.6544	(1.3682, 1.8530)
$\widehat{\beta}_2$ 0.7838	(0.7534, 0.8376)	0.6834	(0.6175, 0.8130)
$\widehat{\beta}_3$ 0.0629	(0.0583, 0.1169)	0.1978	(−0.0302, 0.3502)
$\widehat{\beta}_4$ 0.0937	(0.0783, 0.1339)	0.0174	(−0.0366, 0.1180)

With the same structure as before, Table 4 and Table 5 present the estimates and bootstrap confidence intervals at 95% (CI95) from the RidGME estimator for the parameters of the model with intercept, considering now $\varepsilon = 0.01$. All values are rounded to four decimals.

Table 4. RidGME estimates; asymmetric; 3σ (left), residuals ridge (right); $\varepsilon = 0.01$.

$\widehat{\beta}_k$	CI95	$\widehat{\beta}_k$	CI95
$\widehat{\beta}_0$ 3.4679	(3.4129, 3.5225)	3.5146	(2.7886, 4.1267)
$\widehat{\beta}_1$ 2.1544	(2.1543, 2.1544)	2.1554	(2.1499, 2.1601)
$\widehat{\beta}_2$ 1.1191	(1.1188, 1.1195)	1.1210	(1.1097, 1.1300)
$\widehat{\beta}_3$ 0.7195	(0.7195, 0.7196)	0.7183	(0.7141, 0.7252)
$\widehat{\beta}_4$ 0.4523	(0.4521, 0.4525)	0.4507	(0.4406, 0.4629)

Figure 1 illustrates the results from the previous tables, including the results from the ridge estimator with $\lambda = 0.3$, an acceptable shrinkage parameter from the analysis of the ridge trace, ridge$_{0.3}$, and with the value of λ that provides the

Table 5. RidGME estimates; symmetric; 3σ (left), residuals ridge (right); $\varepsilon = 0.01$.

$\widehat{\beta}_k$	CI95	$\widehat{\beta}_k$	CI95
$\widehat{\beta}_0$	2.5959	$(2.5081, 2.7404)$	4.1958	$(3.8777, 5.5966)$
$\widehat{\beta}_1$	1.6065	$(1.5133, 1.6403)$	2.0736	$(1.8891, 2.1715)$
$\widehat{\beta}_2$	1.1303	$(1.1290, 1.1385)$	1.1389	$(1.1125, 1.1552)$
$\widehat{\beta}_3$	0.3536	$(0.3341, 0.3810)$	0.6229	$(0.4585, 0.7009)$
$\widehat{\beta}_4$	0.3390	$(0.3172, 0.3454)$	0.4539	$(0.4081, 0.4846)$

lowest cross-validation root mean squared error (CV.RMSE), ridge$_{\min}$. Table 6 presents the CV.RMSE, the standard deviation (sd), and the root mean squared error (RMSE) of the RidGME, ridge and OLS estimators. All values are rounded to four decimals.

Table 6. CV.RMSE, sd and RMSE of RidGME, ridge and OLS estimators.

	CV.RMSE	sd	RMSE
RidGME$_{\text{asym};3\sigma;0.01}$	2.4464	0.6743	2.0026
ridge$_{\min}$	2.4503	0.6284	1.9793
RidGME$_{\text{symm};\eta;0}$	2.4553	0.4548	1.9476
ridge$_{0.3}$	2.4592	0.6418	2.0109
RidGME$_{\text{asym};\eta;0.01}$	2.4705	0.7206	2.0071
RidGME$_{\text{asym};3\sigma;0}$	2.5025	0.5688	1.9425
RidGME$_{\text{asym};\eta;0}$	2.5170	0.6013	1.9529
RidGME$_{\text{symm};\eta;0.01}$	2.5422	0.5064	2.0475
OLS	2.7099	0.4310	1.9188
RidGME$_{\text{symm};3\sigma;0}$	6.2382	2.4842	5.1230
RidGME$_{\text{symm};3\sigma;0.01}$	14.7594	2.5972	12.4214

Except in two scenarios, both using symmetric support specification and the three-sigma rule, the results reveal that the RidGME estimator is competitive with the *best* choice of ridge estimators (namely, the one associated with λ returning the lowest cross-validation RMSE) and outperforms OLS in terms of CV.RMSE. In particular, the lowest cross-validation error is obtained for the asymmetric support approach, not including the OLS estimates ($\epsilon = 0$) and with the three-sigma rule. Generally, when $\varepsilon = 0$, the in-sample error decreases, with the exception mentioned before, and the lowest RMSE is obtained precisely for the OLS. A good balance between in- and out-of-sample errors seems to be obtained when the symmetric support specification is used alongside the OLS estimation and the residuals. The same finding is verified by analyzing the estimates and bootstrap confidence intervals, by taking the estimates of the param-

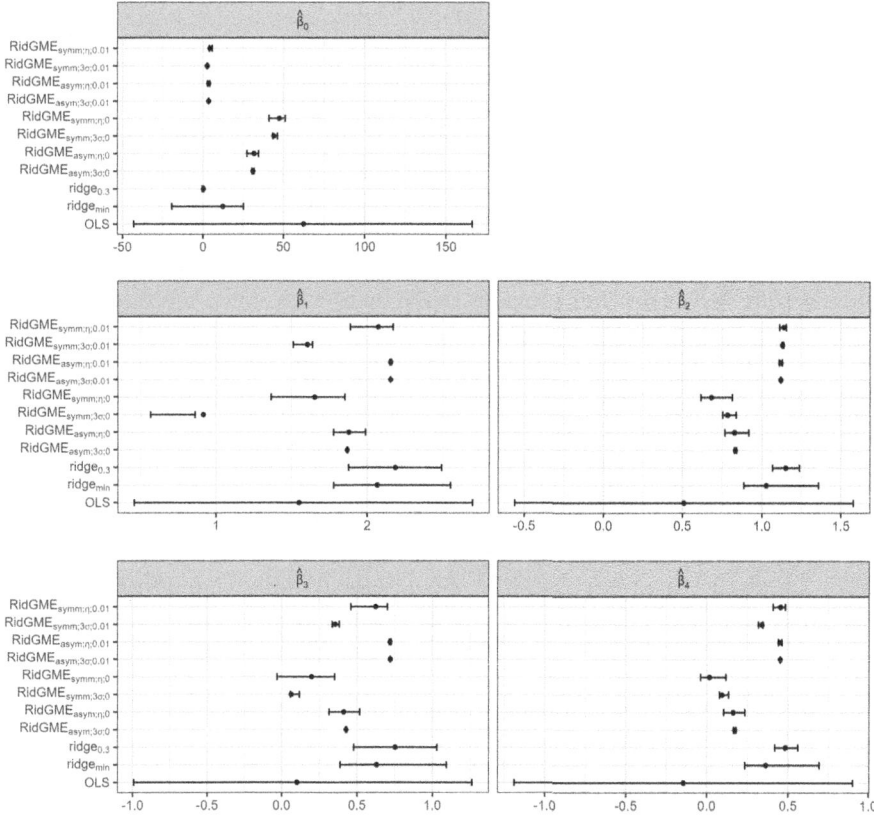

Fig. 1. Estimates and bootstrap CI for the RidGME, ridge and OLS estimators.

eters of the model without constant – the original model without collinearity – as a reference for the accuracy of the estimates. As expected, the OLS confidence intervals are the widest. Note that, for each estimate, these intervals contain all of the others. Asymmetric supports generally produce narrower confidence intervals. The intercept estimate is consistently lower when $\varepsilon = 0.01$. On the other hand, the remaining estimates are generally higher, with some ambiguity for the combination of specifications that produce the worst performance results. The RidGME estimator, although involving the GME estimator through the ridge trace information, is an alternative to the ridge estimator, so the analysis was carried out only in this context. An exhaustive simulation study, including a comparison with the traditional GME estimator, which involves arbitrary choices of supports (its main criticism that is avoided when it is inserted into the RidGME estimator), is left for future research.

5   Concluding Remarks

This work discusses the RidGME estimator as an alternative to ridge regression in ill-conditioned models. In terms of performance in deriving parameter estimates and confidence intervals, the outcomes of our analysis show that RidGME may represent a robust and interpretable approach to deal with the arbitrariness in the choice of the shrinkage parameter in ridge regression, yielding results that are comparable with its optimal choices. However, compared with different procedures available in the literature with a similar purpose, it should be stressed that the RidGME algorithm provides researchers with much more information besides estimation and inference. Indeed, the primary output of the GME steps in RidGME are the parameter, $\hat{p}$, and the error, $\hat{w}$, distributions; these distributions can be used as a means to compare the information-theoretic contributions of different parameters beyond their explained variance, e.g., selecting appropriate statistical divergences (e.g., Kullback-Leibler, chi-squared) or metrics defined between probability distributions. The relevance in highlighting individual and joint contributions is key in different application fields, including psychometrics, where multiple factors or latent variables/constructs may be combined to explain or predict manifest variables. Some user-friendly computational codes (MATLAB, R or Python) will be available upon request to the authors and will soon be available at GitHub.

Acknowledgments. This research is supported by the CIDMA (Center for Research and Development in Mathematics and Applications) under the FCT (Portuguese Foundation for Science and Technology) Multi-Annual Financing Program for R&D Units. M.A. also acknowledges the support provided by the project Small Area Estimation for data Quality in Health – SAEQHealth (Bando a cascata Programma PE GRINS – GRINS – Growing Resilient, Inclusive and Sustainable).

Disclosure of Interests. The authors have no competing interests to declare that are relevant to the content of this article.

References

1. Angelelli, M., Ciavolino, E., Pasca, P.: Streaming generalized cross entropy. Soft. Comput. **24**(18), 13837–13851 (2020)
2. Angelelli, M., Arima, S., Catalano, C., Ciavolino, E.: A robust statistical framework for cyber-vulnerability prioritisation under partial information in threat intelligence. Expert Syst. Appl. **255**, 124572 (2024)
3. Angelelli, M., Gervasi, M., Ciavolino, E.: Representations of epistemic uncertainty and awareness in data-driven strategies. Soft. Comput. **28**, 13763–13780 (2024). https://doi.org/10.1007/s00500-024-09661-8
4. Belsley, D.A., Kuh, E., Welsch, R.E.: Regression Diagnostics - Identifying Influential Data and Sources of Collinearity. Wiley, Hoboken, New Jersey (2004)
5. Caputo, M.R., Paris, Q.: Comparative statics of the generalized maximum entropy estimator of the general linear model. Eur. J. Oper. Res. **185**, 195–203 (2008)

6. Golan, A.: Foundations of Info-Metrics: Modeling, Inference, and Imperfect Information. Oxford University Press, New York (2018)
7. Golan, A., Judge, G., Miller, D.: Maximum Entropy Econometrics: Robust Estimation with Limited Data. Wiley, Chichester (1996)
8. Hoerl, A.E., Kennard, R.W.: Ridge regression: applications to nonorthogonal problems. Technometrics **12**(1), 69–82 (1970)
9. Hoerl, A.E., Kennard, R.W.: Ridge regression: biased estimation for nonorthogonal problems. Technometrics **12**(1), 55–67 (1970)
10. Jaynes, E.T.: Information theory and statistical mechanics. Phys. Rev. **106**(4), 620–630 (1957)
11. Jaynes, E.T.: Information theory and statistical mechanics II. Phys. Rev. **108**(2), 171–190 (1957)
12. Landau, L.D., Lifshitz, E.M.: Statistical Physics, vol. 5. Elsevier (2013)
13. Macedo, P.: Ridge regression and generalized maximum entropy: an improved version of the Ridge-GME parameter estimator. Commun. Stat. Simul. Comput. **46**(5), 3527–3539 (2017)
14. Macedo, P., Costa, M.C., Cruz, J.P.: Normalized entropy: a comparison with traditional techniques in variable selection. In: Simos, T.E., Tsitouras, C. (eds.) Symposium on Mathematical Methods for Artificial Intelligence. vol. 2425, p. 190002. AIP Conference Proceedings (2022)
15. Macedo, P., Scotto, M., Silva, E.: On the choice of the ridge parameter: a maximum entropy approach. Commun. Stat. Simul. Comput. **39**(8), 1628–1638 (2010)
16. McDonald, G.C.: Ridge regression. Wiley Interdiscip. Rev. Comput. Stat. **1**(1), 93–100 (2009)
17. Mukerji, S.: Understanding the nonadditive probability decision model. Econ. Theor. **9**, 23–46 (1997)
18. Muniz, G., Kibria, B.: On some ridge regression estimators: an empirical comparisons. Commun. Stat. Simul. Comput. **38**(3), 621–630 (2009)
19. Preckel, P.V.: Least squares and entropy: a penalty function perspective. Am. J. Agr. Econ. **83**(2), 366–377 (2001)
20. Pukelsheim, F.: The three sigma rule. Am. Stat. **48**(2), 88–91 (1994)
21. Ryan, T.P.: Modern Regression Methods, 2nd edn. Wiley, Hoboken, New Jersey (2009)
22. Sakallıoğlu, S., Kaçıranlar, S.: A new biased estimator based on ridge estimation. Stat. Pap. **49**(4), 669–689 (2008)
23. Shannon, C.E.: A mathematical theory of communication. Bell System Tech. J. **27**(3), 379–423 (1948)
24. Woods, H., Steinour, H.H., Starke, H.R.: Effect of composition of Portland cement on heat evolved during hardening. Ind. Eng. Chem. **24**(11), 1207–1214 (1932)
25. Zhang, R., McDonald, G.C.: Characterization of ridge trace behavior. Commun. Stat. Theory Methods **34**(7), 1487–1501 (2005)

Development of Reference Percentile Growth Curves for Placental Parameters Using Advanced Statistical Models

Daniela Lemos[1]([✉]) [iD], Ana Cristina Braga[1,2][iD], and Rosete Nogueira[3,4,5] [iD]

[1] School of Engineering, University of Minho, 4710-057 Braga, Portugal
danielalemos.research@gmail.com
[2] ALGORITMI Research Centre, LASI, University of Minho, Campus de Gualtar,
4710-057 Braga, Portugal
acb@dps.uminho.pt
[3] School of Medicine, University of Minho, Surgical Sciences Domain Research,
Campus de Gualtar, 4710-057 Braga, Portugal
rosete.nogueira@med.uminho.pt
[4] Life and Health Sciences Research Institute (ICVS), ICVS/3B's - PT Government
Associate Laboratory, Campus de Gualtar, 4710-057 Braga/Guimarães, Portugal
[5] CGC Genetics, Unilabs, Embryo-fetal Pathology Laboratory, R. Sá da Bandeira,
706, 1o, 4000-431 Porto, Portugal

Abstract. There has been a growing interest in assessing placental biometric parameters and their relationship with obstetric outcomes, highlighting their utility in reflecting changes in fetal development and long-term health. However, research focus on fetal development over the placental has caused many gaps in our knowledge about the biological role of placental abnormalities. This study aims to establish reference percentile curves for placental and fetal biometric parameters using data from Portuguese parturients. Nonlinear regression models, including Generalized Additive Models for Location, Scale, and Shape (GAMLSS) and Lambda-Mu-Sigma (LMS) methods, were chosen due to their flexibility in handling diverse statistical distributions. The application of the GAMLSS method with Box-Cox t (BCT) distribution and P-splines to Diameter 1, Diameter 2, Placental Volume, and FW/PW Ratio parameters, and LMS Box-Cox t (LMST) method to Placental Thickness, Placental Weight, and Fetal Weight parameters, results in representative percentile growth curves. This study successfully developed placental growth curves using nonlinear regression models, providing valuable information on placental development and its clinical implications in obstetrics. The reference growth curves enhance the monitoring of maternal-fetal health and can guide clinical decisions, especially in addressing contemporary challenges, such as low birth rates and increasing maternal age.

This work has been supported by FCT–Fundação para a Ciência e Tecnologia within the R and D Units Project Scope: UID/00319/2023.

Keywords: Placenta · Growth curves · Nonlinear regression · GAMLSS · LMST

1 Introduction

In the initial phases of fetal development, a complex interaction between genes and environment is found to be partly responsible for shaping human behaviour and susceptibility to diseases [6]. It is imperative to acknowledge the role of early detection of growth anomalies, especially those related to the functioning of the placenta, to minimize the risks associated with fetal disorders and illnesses in adulthood.

Recently, a growing focus has been placed on using different indices to examine fetal development, particularly in evaluating the biometric parameters of the placenta and their relationship to obstetric outcomes [21,26,28]. Research findings imply that some pregnancy complications, such as decreased fetal activity, intrauterine size deficits, and later individual health problems, are linked with the structure of the placenta [19,24,48].

When properly studied, the parameters of the placenta can be useful in narrowing down cases of perinatal mortality and neonatal diseases. There is a growing demand for pathological placental studies, and their understanding is crucial for expanding the use of placental examinations and measures [3,22]. Parameters like placental diameter (D1—larger or D2—smaller), placental thickness (PT), placental weight (PW), placental volume ($D1 \times D2 \times PT$) (PV), fetal weight (FW) and FW/PW ratio (R-FW) are acknowledged as vital in evaluating placental function and fetal growth [18,21,26]. Consequently, advancements in understanding these parameters in relation to gestational age (GA) can significantly contribute to the early recognition of fetal disorders.

Research focus on fetal development over the placental has caused many gaps in our knowledge about the biological role of placental abnormalities during childbirth and the first weeks after birth [26]. This emphasizes the importance of increased attention to studies and tools that are tailored to differentiate challenging placental characteristics. Growth curve models specifically stand out for this purpose, as they are valuable for monitoring variations in placental weight and diameter throughout GA. While birth weight percentile curves are extensively used to monitor fetal growth and classify the risk of certain fetal conditions [20], studies focusing on percentile curves for placental data, such as, D1, D2, PT, PW, PV and R-FW, are scarce. Existing studies on fetal and placental percentile curves primarily refer to GA above 24 weeks, and some of this information may be outdated. Therefore, it is imperative to study and update information related to these growth curves. Despite the need for additional evidence, percentile curves remain relevant for monitoring fetal growth, and optimizing their understanding can enable early intervention in adverse fetal conditions.

The use of percentile growth curves is important to determine and measure placental characteristics. Nonlinear regression models tend to be the preferred choice in this analysis because they usually outperform linear models. Several researchers investigated the nonlinear model's ability to accurately describe different growth patterns [8, 21, 27]. In our study, we propose employing semiparametric regression models under the framework of Generalized Additive Models for Location, Scale, and Shape (GAMLSS) [33], as well as Lambda-Mu-Sigma (LMS) models [11, 12, 32, 34], to model various parameters such as D1, D2, PT, PW, PV, FW and R-FW.

This study makes a substantial contribution to understanding placental metrics and growth curve modelling. It underlines the vital role of placental biometric data in predicting the outcomes of pregnancy and fetus health. Besides, it presents the applicability of GAMLSS framework for accurate and flexible estimation of percentile growth curves based on placental metrics. The study results highlight the reliability of these curves, especially at the distribution tails, which are particularly important for clinical assessments.

The primary aim of this study is to improve early detection of fetal growth deviations by developing accurate placental growth reference curves. Thus, diverse growth curve models were implemented, and their performance was compared to identify the model that best represents each parameter under study. These models hold the potential to be useful in various ways, promoting advances in placental and fetal monitoring, and thereby enhancing the evaluation of placental function and perinatal care. Consequently, this research may offer psychosocial relief to families and contribute to an increase in perinatal success and birth rates.

This paper is divided into five sections. Section 2 describes the dataset and explains the methods used to model the growth curves. Section 3 presents the results, while Sect. 4 discusses their significance. Finally, Sect. 5 summarizes the findings and suggests future research directions.

2   Material and Methods

2.1   Dataset

In this study, growth curves for various placental parameters were modelled as a function of gestational age (GA) for the Portuguese population. The dataset used to develop and test the generated models partly overlapped with two previous studies [21, 26]. It began with an analysis of 7321 placental samples that were meticulously processed at the Embryonic-Fetal Pathology Laboratory, located at Centro de Genética Clínica (CGC), Unilabs, Porto, Portugal, and were preprocessed (details can be found in [26]). The information collected from the placental pathological reports spanned a four-year period, from January 1, 2014, to December 31, 2017. The reports encompassed a broad range of GA, ranging from 12 to 41 weeks.

For this study, the dataset was extended, incorporating new cases that adhered to the criteria initially outlined by [26]. The final dataset under study, post-preprocessing, comprised a set of $n = 2092$ placental samples. The variables modelled included the following placental parameters: D1, D2, PT, PW, PV, FW, and R-FW.

2.2   Modelling Strategies for Placental Growth Curves

The development of growth curves requires a selection of methods that consider the characteristics of the dataset under analysis and its future applications. The methodology for implementing the curves was divided into several interconnected sections, outlining the process from method review to fit quality assessment. In a previous study by the authors [21], this methodology was analyzed in detail for modelling a placental parameter, D2. Therefore, this study should be referred to for additional information.

All analyses and the development of growth curves were conducted in R using the `gamlss` and `ggplot2`, and `dplyr` packages, which provided a flexible framework for statistical modelling, visualization, and data manipulation.

Figure 1 provides a summary of the methodology used in developing the growth curves. Initially, a critical review of existing methods for modelling growth curves was conducted. Subsequently, based on this review and considering the criteria outlined in Subsect. 2.2, several methods were selected: GAMLSS, LMS, Lambda-Mu-Sigma Box-Cox t (LMST), and Lambda-Mu-Sigma Box-Cox-Power-Exponential (LMSP). Each of these methods offers unique approaches to modelling growth curves.

Within each method, specific distributions that best suit the context of this study were explored. This includes the Box-Cox Cole-Green (BCCG), Box-Cox t (BCT), Box-Cox Power Exponential (BCPE), and Johnson's SU (JSU) distributions. These distributions play a fundamental role in representing the data characteristics. Four smoothing techniques were selected: P-splines, Cubic Splines, Neural Networks, and Loess. Each of these techniques is designed to capture different growth patterns. Finally, several goodness-of-fit criteria were selected, including the Coefficient of Determination (R^2), Mean Square Error (MSE), Akaike's Information Criterion (AIC), Bayesian Information Criterion (BIC), Z-Statistics, Worm plots, and Residual plots.

This methodology was then applied to various models, aiming to identify the most appropriate model for each of the placental parameters under study, namely D1, D2, PT, PW, PV, FW, and R-FW. It is noteworthy that it followed a specific order of procedures. Initially, various smoothing functions were evaluated in a GAMLSS model without imposing a specific distribution for the model. These smoothing functions are known for their flexibility in fitting curves without the need to predefine a specific form for the underlying function [14]. The purpose of this approach lies in simplifying the modelling process. Simultaneously incorporating smoothing functions and distributions would significantly increase the complexity of the modelling process. Subsequently, various distributions were tested in combination with the chosen smoothing function, using different methods. Finally, the fit quality of each model was evaluated.

Criteria for Method Selection. In this study, several criteria were considered to guide the selection of methods for developing the percentile growth curves. Accuracy in estimating extreme percentiles was prioritized due to data scarcity in this region, necessitating methods that rely on an underlying distribution.

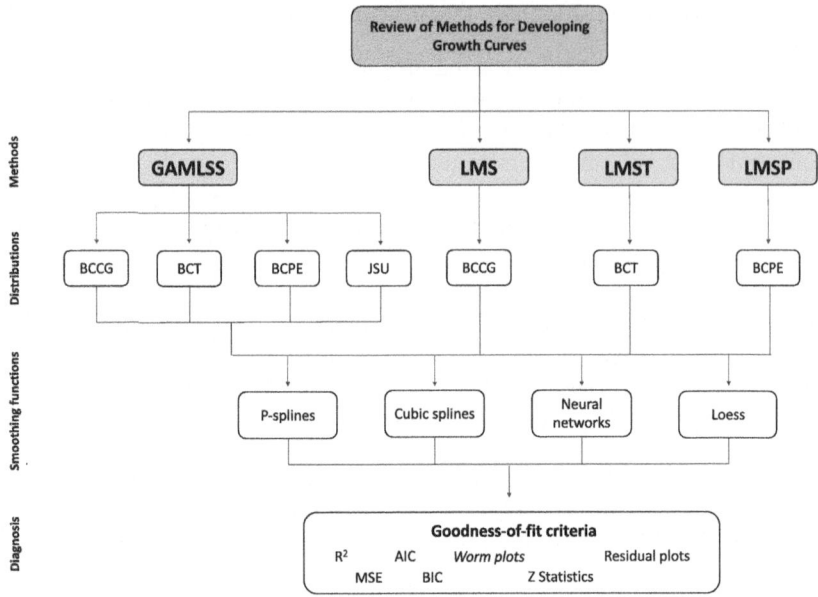

Fig. 1. Workflow illustrating the methodology for developing placental growth curves. Steps include: (1) Reviewing growth curve methods, (2) Selecting methods, (3) Choosing distributions, (4) Applying smoothing functions, and (5) Evaluating Goodness-of-fit criteria. Models were applied to placental parameters D1, D2, PT, PW, PV, FW and R-FW.

Preventing percentile curve crossing was crucial, requiring simultaneous calculation to ensure interpretable percentiles. Facilitating retrotransformations was essential for the direct calculation of percentiles and z-scores, and handling kurtosis alongside skewness was important to preserve the integrity of adjusted percentiles.

In addition to these main criteria, secondary criteria were also considered. Compatibility with diagnostic tools ensures reliable results by evaluating fit quality. Computational efficiency is important for efficient curve construction when comparing methods. Applicability flexibility allows the method to be applied to various measurements, making growth curves applicable in diverse contexts.

GAMLSS, LMS and Its Extensions LMST and LMSP. Introduced by Rigby and Stasinopoulos [33], along with contributions from Akantziliotou *et al.* [2], GAMLSS are semi-parametric regression models. They exhibit parametric characteristics, as they require an assumption of a parametric distribution for the response variable. However, they are considered semi-parametric because the modelling of distribution parameters, in relation to explanatory variables, can incorporate non-parametric smoothing functions [40]. They allow the use of a wide range of distributions, including continuous and discrete distributions with significant skewness and kurtosis [45]. What distinguishes GAMLSS is its ability to model not only the mean (or location) but also other critical distribution parameters, such as scale, skewness, and kurtosis [41].

For the statistical model of GAMLSS, let's assume that the response variable Y follows a four-parameter distribution $Y \sim D(\boldsymbol{\theta})$ with $\boldsymbol{\theta} = (\mu, \sigma, \nu, \tau)$ [40]. Where μ and σ are generally referred to as location and scale parameters, while ν and τ are considered shape parameters, e.g. skewness and kurtosis. The Eq. 1 specifies $g_k(\boldsymbol{\theta}_k)$ as the linear predictor $\boldsymbol{\eta}_k$, which combines fixed effects $\mathbf{X}_k \boldsymbol{\beta}_k$ and potentially non-linear and random effects $\sum_{j=1}^{J_k} \mathbf{Z}_{jk} \boldsymbol{\gamma}_{jk}$. Here, $\mathbf{X}_k$ represents the design matrix for fixed effects, $\boldsymbol{\beta}_k$ is the parameter vector, $\mathbf{Z}_{jk}$ is the design matrix for random effects, and $\boldsymbol{\gamma}_{jk}$ are the corresponding random effect parameters [40].

$$g_k(\boldsymbol{\theta}_k) = \boldsymbol{\eta}_k = \mathbf{X}_k \boldsymbol{\beta}_k + \sum_{j=1}^{J_k} \mathbf{Z}_{jk} \boldsymbol{\gamma}_{jk} \quad \text{for } k = 1, 2, 3, 4 \tag{1}$$

Estimation in GAMLSS is typically performed by maximizing a penalized likelihood function. There are two fundamental algorithms for this purpose, however, during this study, RS was exclusively used due to its effectiveness in treating a wide range of distribution families and its computational efficiency. The Rigby and Stasinopoulos algorithm (RS) is an approach derived from the algorithm used in fitting Mean and Dispersion Additive Models (MADAM) models by [30,31].

The LMS method, developed by Cole [13] and subsequently refined by Cole and Green [12], is a tool for modelling a response variable Y against a single explanatory variable x (e.g., age) [42]. It supports specific distributional assumptions for Y, enabling simultaneous estimation of multiple percentiles without crossings. In GAMLSS, the LMS method integrates assuming Y follows the BCCG distribution for data exhibiting skewness with $Y > 0$. Rigby and Stasinopoulos [32,34] extended the LMS method by introducing the BCT and BCPE distributions for Y, facilitating percentile estimation methods LMST and LMSP.

The final GAMLSS and LMST models for all studied placental parameters utilized the BCT distribution and P-splines as the smoothing function. Further information on this distribution and smoothing function can be found in the authors' previous study [21].

Goodness-of-Fit Criteria. The goodness-of-fit evaluation is crucial in statistical analysis, ensuring the reliability of estimates and the accuracy of the developed reference growth curves. This study used the following quantitative criteria and graphical tools to evaluate the models:

- **Determination Coefficient** (R^2): quantifies how well a model fits data, ranging from 0 to 1, with higher values indicating better fit [10,47].

- **Mean Square Error (MSE):** measures predictive model accuracy, with lower values indicating better fit by minimizing squared differences between predicted and actual values [10,37].
- **Akaike's Information Criterion (AIC):** is a fundamental tool for model selection, balancing model complexity with fit quality based on a mathematical framework that includes a penalty for the number of parameters [1,7].
- **Schwarz Bayesian Information Criterion (BIC):** similar to AIC but penalizing more complex models, aids in selecting parsimonious models [25, 38].
- **Worm plot:** visually assesses model fit by plotting standardized residuals against expected values, indicating the adequacy of the model fit based on deviations from a standard normal distribution [9,42].
- **Z-statistics:** assess residual normality across age groups, crucial in percentile estimation [36,42].
- **Residual plots:** assess model fit quality and identify potential model assumption violations [42]. In this study, four key residual plots were analyzed, including quantile residuals against fitted values of the parameter μ, against specified indices or covariates, kernel density estimation of residuals, and Normal Q-Q plot.

3   Results

3.1   Exploratory Analysis

Exploratory analysis plays a fundamental role in understanding the data underlying the development of growth curves for placental parameters as a function of GA.

Table 1 presents descriptive statistics such as mean, standard deviation (SD), minimum (Min), maximum (Max), median, skewness, and kurtosis of the placental parameters under study. These statistics offer a comprehensive understanding

Table 1. Descriptive statistics of D1, D2, PT, PW, PV, FW, and R-FW. The table includes the mean, standard deviation (SD), minimum (Min), maximum (Max), median, skewness, and kurtosis for each placental parameter in the study.

Placental parameter	Mean	SD	Min	Max	Median	Skewness	Kurtosis
Placental Diameter 1	13.39	4.90	2.00	32.00	13.00	0.50	3.23
Placental Diameter 2	11.21	4.47	1.50	30.00	11.00	0.29	2.87
Placental Thickness	2.10	0.70	0.30	5.00	2.00	0.71	4.02
Placental Weight	229.77	158.08	6.00	995.00	190.00	0.81	3.25
Placental Volume	387.80	327.15	4.80	2345.25	305.70	1.45	6.05
Fetal Weight	1229.58	1152.07	5.70	4880.00	736.50	0.74	2.34
Ratio-FW	4.24	2.41	0.21	11.51	4.12	0.18	2.03

of trends, variability, and distributional characteristics, demonstrating the complexities of placental development and its implications for fetal health.

The mean values for Diameter 1 and Diameter 2 were 13.39 cm (SD = 4.90 cm, range = 2.00–32.00 cm) and 11.21 cm (SD = 4.47 cm, range = 1.50–30.00 cm), respectively. Both diameters exhibited a slight rightward skew (Skewness = 0.50 for D1 and 0.29 for D2) and had kurtosis values suggestive of a leptokurtic distribution (Kurtosis = 3.23 for D1 and 2.87 for D2). Placental thickness had a mean of 2.10 cm (SD = 0.70 cm, range = 0.30–5.00 cm) and displayed a more pronounced skewness (0.71) and high kurtosis (4.02), indicating a distribution with heavier tails than a normal distribution. Placental weight had a mean of 229.77 g (SD = 158.08 g, range = 6.00–995.00 g) and exhibited a skewness of 0.81 and a kurtosis of 3.25. The volume demonstrated the most significant variability and skewness (Skewness = 1.45, Kurtosis = 6.05) with a mean of 387.80 cm^3 (SD = 327.15 cm^3, range = 4.80–2345.25 cm^3), suggesting a highly skewed distribution with a long right tail. Fetal weight showed a broader distribution with a mean of 1229.58 g (SD = 1152.07 g, range = 5.70–4880.00 g), a skewness of 0.74, and a kurtosis of 2.34. The Ratio-FW had a mean of 4.24 (SD = 2.41, range = 0.21–11.51), indicating the least skewness (0.18) and the lowest kurtosis (2.03) among all variables, which suggests a distribution that is closest to normal.

3.2   Significance Tests Between Genders

Statistical analysis was performed using the Student's t-test (respecting the criterion of normality and/or the conditions of applicability of the Central Limit Theorem) with a 5% significance level to identify statistically significant differences between the means of placental parameters D1, D2, PT, PW, and FW for female and male fetuses at each GA. See Fig. 2 for a visual representation of the mean values and their 95% confidence intervals.

Significant differences were found for certain placental parameters at specific GAs. For example, D1 showed significance at week 39 (p-value = 0.04), while D2 at weeks 12 (p-value = 0.009), 14 (p-value = 0.03), and 39 (p-value = 0.006). PT had significant differences at weeks 14 (p-value = 0.02), 20 (p-value = 0.04), and 40 (p-value = 0.02), while FW showed significance at weeks 16 (p-value = 0.009) and 40 (p-value = 0.002). It is noteworthy that PW did not present significant differences at any GA.

3.3   Growth Curves

In this study, the relationship between various placental parameters such as D1, D2, PT, PW, PV, FW and R-FW with GA was analysed to produce reference percentile growth curves at specific percentiles ($3^{rd}, 10^{th}, 25^{th}, 50^{th}, 75^{th}, 90^{th}, 97^{th}$).

Due to the extensive analysis of evaluation criteria, which includes a large number of figures and tables, it was decided to include only the metrics values for the final model of each placental parameter and diagnostic graphical analyses only for the PV in this document, as the diagnostic graphical analysis for the

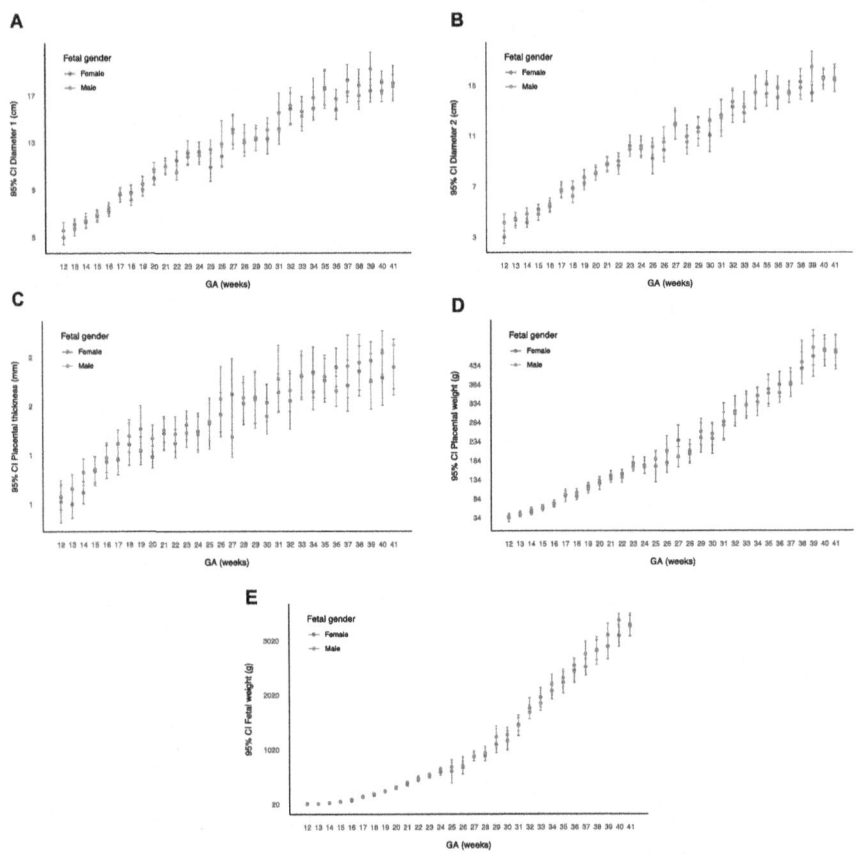

Fig. 2. Mean values and 95% confidence intervals for D1, D2, PT, PW, and FW across gestational age (GA) for female and male fetuses. Statistical significance was evaluated using Student's t-test ($\alpha = 0.05$).

final models of the remaining placental parameters is similar. The other figures and tables, covering all analysed quality criteria, are available in the GitHub [1] repository.

The final models for each placental parameter were selected by choosing the model that achieved the highest R^2 and the lowest MSE, AIC, and BIC among all models evaluated, as summarized in Table 2.

For D1, the model with the best performance was GAMLSS with the BCT distribution, with a R^2 value of 0.755. This indicates a good fit to the data, with

---

[1] https://github.com/daniellalemos/Growth_curves.

minimal deviation between predicted and observed values, as reflected in the MSE of 4.593. Additionally, the AIC and BIC values of 9439 and 9529, respectively, suggest a good fit for the model. Similarly, for D2, GAMLSS with the BCT distribution stood out as the optimal model, with a R^2 value of 0.765 and a relatively low MSE of 4.398. The AIC and BIC values of 9029 and 9142, respectively, further support the adequacy of this model in capturing the variability in D2 measurements over GA. For PT, PW, and FW, the LMST model was identified as the best fit. Despite a lower R^2 value of 0.390 for PT, the LMST model showed satisfactory performance, especially considering the complex nature of the data. For PW, a good fit was observed with a R^2 value of 0.852 and AIC and BIC values of 22281 and 22403, respectively. For FW, a R^2 value of 0.962 and AIC and BIC values of 26679 and 26874 were obtained. Finally, for PV and R-FW, GAMLSS with the BCT distribution was again identified as the best fit, with R^2 values of 0.824 and 0.845, respectively. R-FW showed a relatively low MSE value of 2.621. The AIC values of 25112 and 5394 and the BIC values of 25220 and 5529, respectively, further support the adequacy of these models in capturing variability over GA.

Table 2. Summary of model performance metrics (R^2, MSE, AIC, and BIC) for the final models developed.

Placental parameter - Model	R^2	MSE	AIC	BIC
Placental Diameter 1 - GAMLSS	0.755	4.593	9439	9529
Placental Diameter 2 - GAMLSS	0.765	4.398	9029	9142
Placental Thickness - LMST	0.390	1.552	3210	3288
Placental Weight - LMST	0.852	10.890	22281	22403
Placental Volume - GAMLSS	0.824	12.262	25112	25220
Fetal weight - LMST	0.962	13.110	26679	26874
Ratio-FW - GAMLSS	0.845	2.621	5394	5529

In addition to these metrics, an evaluation of the fit quality was also performed using graphical diagnostic criteria, such as Z-statistics, worm plots, and residual plots. Figure 3 shows these metrics for the final model of the PV. The remaining placental parameters exhibited very similar metrics. Looking at the worm plot, a good fit to the data is notable, as the points and the fitting line are very close to the horizontal reference line, and more than 95% of these points are within the confidence intervals. Z-statistics also indicated a good fit, with no $|Z| > 2$ values.

Regarding the residuals, they indicate acceptable behaviour in the graph concerning the indices, but in the plot relative to the fitted values, there is a pattern of vertical lines, indicating that the variability of the errors is not constant along the range of predicted values. Additionally, an approximation to normality was observed, as evidenced by the two lower residual plots.

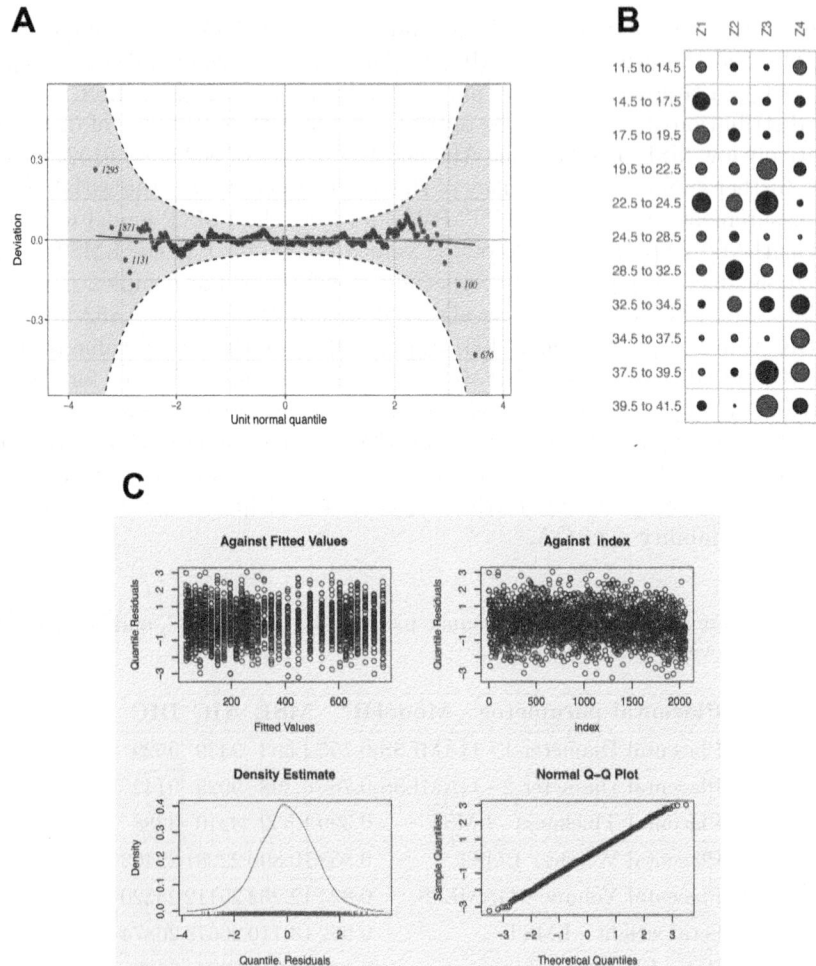

Fig. 3. Goodness-of-fit criteria (worm plot, Z-statistics, and residual plots) for the Placental volume using the GAMLSS model with P-splines and the BCT distribution.

The growth percentile curves for the final models of each placental parameter are represented in Fig. 4. It is evident that these curves accurately capture the data behaviour. As a final diagnostic of the models, the percentages of the sample located at or below each fitted curve are presented in Table 3. The close agreement between the nominal and sample percentiles for the various models suggests a good fit of the percentile curves.

Table 3. Nominal percentiles (%) of the sample located at or below each fitted curve for the placental parameters D1, D2, PT, PW, PV, FW and R-FW.

Nominal percentile	3	10	25	50	75	90	97
Placental Diameter 1	3.05	10.37	25.05	50.29	75.63	90.02	96.75
Placental Diameter 2	3.00	9.21	24.37	49.08	74.61	90.07	96.56
Placental Thickness	3.59	8.67	27.33	49.32	74.37	89.83	96.27
Placental Weight	3.44	10.37	24.32	49.32	75.39	90.55	97.43
Placental Volume	3.30	9.69	24.81	49.76	75.15	90.12	96.95
Fetal weight	3.30	11.39	25.44	48.35	74.81	90.65	97.63
Ratio-FW	2.91	10.13	24.32	50.48	74.81	89.87	96.56

4 Discussion

Throughout the years, researchers have developed percentile growth curves for FW, offering important information for healthcare professionals and parents about fetal and neonatal growth patterns [5,17]. The current study's findings show the feasibility of developing similar percentile growth curves for placental metrics such as D1, D2, PT, PW, PV, and R-FW. These charts can be beneficial for a more detailed examination of fetal health because, as discussed in the literature, there is a correlation between placental morphology and size with pregnancy complications and subsequent health of the child [23,39].

The exploratory data analysis, presented in Sect. 3.1, has provided the basis for developing these percentile curves. There was a progressive growth in all placental parameters, which suggests a positive correlation between them and GA. The skewness and kurtosis values indicate that most placental parameters have distributions that deviate from normality, with a tendency to have a rightward skew and leptokurtic characteristics, particularly in PV and FW. This implies that while most of the placentas and fetuses are within their expected sizes, some extreme values could be attributed to certain health risks or developmental abnormalities. There was also significant variability for FW, indicated by the high SD values, which is expected as pregnancy progresses and there are greater differences between fetuses and placentas. The observed results for all measured placental parameters are consistent with previous research emphasizing the continuous growth of the placenta and fetus during pregnancy [15,44]. The data's positive kurtosis suggests the necessity for techniques capable of handling this issue, like the implemented GAMLSS method, to prevent skewed adjusted percentiles [8].

Since fetal gender is acknowledged to be related to birth weight, it may be important to have separate curves for female and male genders. While some studies indicate no significant gender differences in placental weight [4,26,43], some differences were found in a small percentage (6.2%) of cases. This scenario implies that, in general, percentile curves for placental parameters can be applied

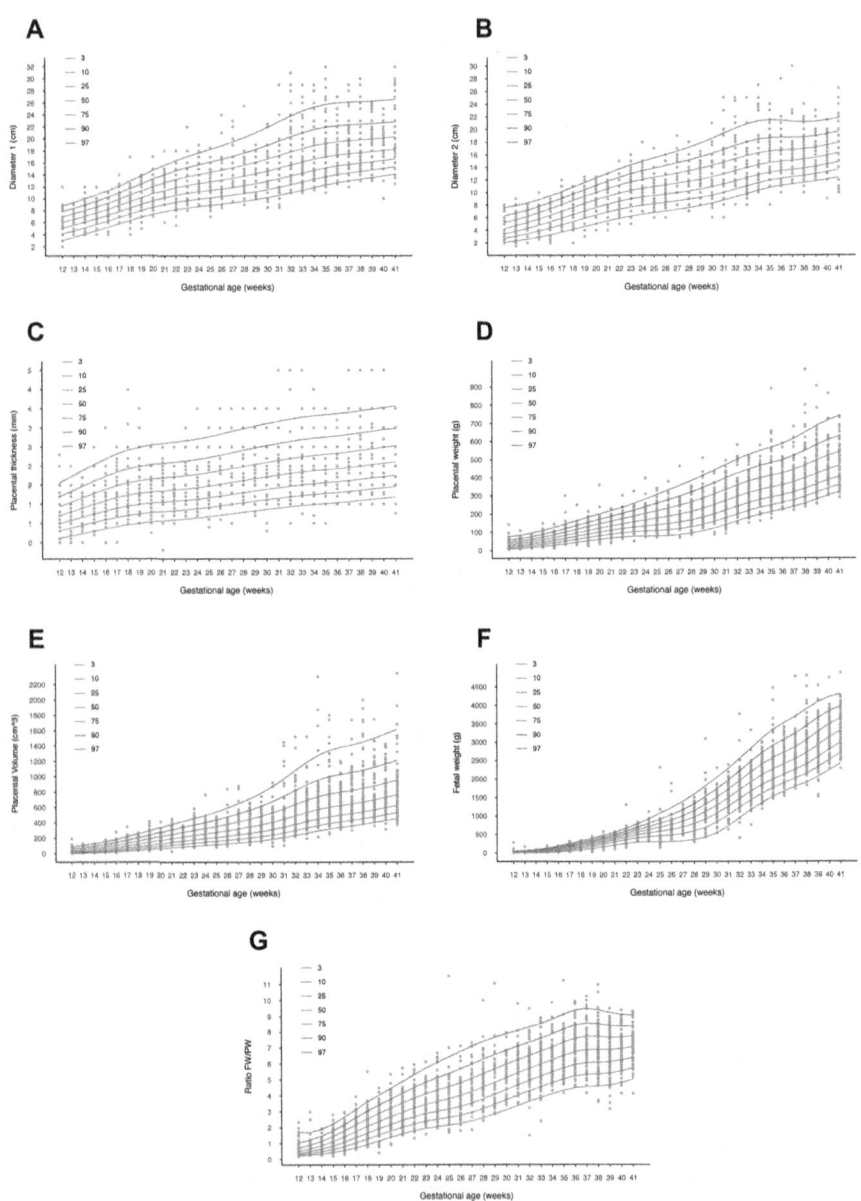

Fig. 4. Observed Diameter 1 (A), Diameter 2 (B), Placental thickness (C), Placental weight (D), Placental volume (E), Fetal weight (F) and Ratio FW/PW (G) values represented as a function of GA (12–41 weeks), with seven adjusted percentile curves (3rd, 10th, 25th, 50th, 75th, 90th and 97th).

without gender differentiation, and therefore, it was chosen not to categorize the curves by gender.

Selecting the most suitable data-fitting method was crucial to creating accurate growth curves. Based on the criteria detailed in Subsect. 2.2, the chosen methods were GAMLSS, LMS, LMST, and LMSP. These methods used P-splines, which are more computationally efficient than other smoothing functions, like cubic spiles [14]. Various distributions were tested using different methods for each placental parameter in the study. In the context of the D1, D2, R-FW and PV, the GAMLSS model with the BCT distribution was chosen to represent the percentile growth curve, due to its good performance. For the PT, PW and FW the LMST model was selected. This prominence is based on the high R^2 values and the reduction in errors, reflected in the relatively low values of MSE, AIC, and BIC. Furthermore, the analysis of the diagnostic plots and the agreement between the nominal and sample percentages confirmed the quality of this model.

These reference curves provide healthcare professionals with valuable tools to assess placental development clinically. By comparing placental parameters like D1 with the 3rd percentile curve for a given GA, it is possible to identify placental underdevelopment, crucial for the early detection of complications and monitoring maternal and fetal health. This methodology has broader applications and can be used to develop growth curves in various contexts. For more detailed information, see [35, 42], which offers foundational guidance for future studies.

A significant challenge in this investigation was the scarcity of data and studies that allow for comparison and contextualization of the results of this investigation within the context of placental parameters. Over the years, reference percentile curves have been produced, mainly for FW in relation to GA, but these graphs are generally restricted to the third trimester of pregnancy and take into account specific cases such as fetal gender, parity, and ethnicity [16, 29, 46]. These conditions do not align with this study, as it explored various GA, including earlier stages such as 12 weeks, did not categorize by gender or parity, and only used data from the Portuguese population.

However, despite this lack of comparative data, some notable studies were identified that effectively explored placental parameters. One example is the study of [26] where the authors analyzed part of the dataset used in this investigation to construct growth curves for the placental parameters PW and FW. Comparing the percentile values and graphs, there are differences in the estimated values for each percentile at each GA and in the shape of the percentile curves. Since no metrics or diagnostic graphs are presented, it is not possible to compare the quality of fit with the curves of this study.

Another study that uses part of the dataset from this investigation is [21] where it was developed a percentile growth curve for the placental parameter D2 that is very similar to this study once it was used the same methodology.

The recent study of [16] demonstrates the successful use of the GAMLSS method to create reference curves related to PW, as they achieved a good quality of fit. The results of this study clearly illustrate the effectiveness of the GAMLSS approach in analysing placental parameters, providing a valuable precedent for this work. However, since the study is done by categorizing by gender and parity for GAs between 28 and 42 weeks, no comparisons can be made with the curves developed in this investigation. Furthermore, the study by [8] is also relevant. This study played a fundamental role in the construction of the World Health Organization's child growth standards. The authors highlighted the feasibility of using GAMLSS, LMS, LMST, and LMSP models, due to their potential to produce promising results when age is treated as a continuous variable, similar to GA.

Therefore, although there is a lack of direct references, these cited studies demonstrate that the analysis of placental parameters, especially using methods such as GAMLSS, has the potential and capacity to produce significant results.

5   Conclusions

This study comprehensively explored placental parameters and their implications on maternal and fetal health, resulting in the development of reference growth curves for 12 to 41 weeks of gestation.

As contemporary challenges related to low birth rates and increasing maternal age are faced, promoting placental and fetal health becomes a fundamental priority. The developed percentile curves offer a detailed understanding of how the placental parameters D1, D2, PT, PW, PV, FW and R-FW evolve throughout pregnancy. Using GAMLSS and LMST models with P-splines and the BCT distribution proved effective for creating accurate reference curves. Specifically, the application of the GAMLSS method to model the D1, D2, R-FW and PV and the LMST method to model PT, PW and FW.

The scarcity of studies on placental biometric parameters, particularly for GAs between 12 and 41 weeks, for the Portuguese population, and the placental parameters in study, posed a significant challenge. However, the pioneering approach of this research fills a crucial gap in the literature, offering valuable information on placental growth patterns and their clinical significance. Despite the accomplishments, this work faces limitations and there are paths for future investigations. It is essential to continue refining methodologies and expanding study samples to enhance the applicability of placental reference growth curves.

For future work, a broader investigation could be conducted to improve the accuracy of the reference growth curves. Including more diverse samples of pregnant women, covering different ethnic groups, gestational ages, and medical conditions. Also, study the relationship of other variables with placental development, such as parity or maternal age, to understand if other factors influence placental parameters. However, the final goal of this research is to develop a web application to consolidate all the work done with the growth curves and make them accessible for easy and effective analysis.

Ultimately, this study reinforces the importance of investigating placental parameters and demonstrates how statistical and mathematical modelling can lead to significant advancements in medicine. Despite the challenges faced, the results demonstrated the feasibility of the developed approach. It is hoped that this work will inspire future research and, at the same time, directly benefit the lives of pregnant women and their babies, promoting a healthy and safe pregnancy.

References

1. Akaike, H.: Information theory and an extension of the maximum likelihood principle. In: 2nd International Symposium on Information Theory, pp. 267–281 (1973)
2. Akantziliotou, C., Rigby, R., Stasinopoulos, D.: A framework for modelling overdispersed count data, including the poisson-shifted generalized inverse gaussian distribution. Comput. Stat. Data Anal. **53**, 381–393 (2008)
3. Akhavan, S., Borna, S., Abdollahi, A., Shariat, M., Zamani, N.: Pathologic examination of the placenta and its benefits in treatment plan or follow-up of patients: a cross-sectional study. Eur. J. Med. Res. **27**, 1–5 (2022)
4. Asgharnia, M., Esmailpour, N., Poorghorban, M., Atrkar-Roshan, Z.: Placenta weight and its association with maternal and neonatal characteristics. Acta Med. Iran. **46**, 467–472 (2008)
5. Aybuke, Y., Mehmet, B., Fatma Nur, S., Mustafa Senol, A., Omer, E., Evrim, A.D.: Comparison of different growth curves in the assessment of extrauterine growth restriction in very low birth weight preterm infants. Arch. Pediatr. **30**, 31–35 (2023)
6. Balasundaram, P., Avulakunta, I.D.: Human Growth and Development. StatPearls Publishing, Treasure Island (FL) (2022)
7. Bonakdari, H., Zeynoddin, M.: Chapter 5 - Goodness-of-Fit and Precision Criteria. Elsevier (2022)
8. Borghi, E., et al.: Construction of the world health organization child growth standards: selection of methods for attained growth curves. Stat. Med. **25**, 247–265 (2006)
9. Buuren, S.v., Fredriks, M.: Worm plot: a simple diagnostic device for modelling growth reference curves. Statist. Med. **20**, 1259–1277 (2001)
10. Chicco, D., Warrens, M.J., Jurman, G.: The coefficient of determination r-squared is more informative than SMAPE, MAE, MAPE, MSE and RMSE in Regression Analysis Evaluation. PEERJ Comput. Sci. **7** (2021)
11. Cole, T.J.: Do growth chart centiles need a face lift? BMJ **308**, 641–642 (1994)
12. Cole, T.J., Green, P.J.: Smoothing reference centile curves: the LMS method and penalized likelihood. Stat. Med. **11**, 1305–1319 (1992)
13. Cole, T.J.: Fitting smoothed centile curves to reference data. J. R. Stat. Soc. A. Stat. Soc. **151**, 385–406 (1988)
14. Currie, I.D., Durban, M.: Flexible smoothing with p-splines: a unified approach. Stat. Model. **2**, 333–349 (2002)
15. DiPietro, J.A., Costigan, K.A., Voegtline, K.M.: Studies in fetal behavior: revisited, renewed, and reimagined. Monogr. Soc. Res. Child Dev. **80**, vii (2015)
16. Flatley, C., et al.: Placental weight centiles adjusted for age, parity and fetal sex. Placenta **117**, 87–94 (2022)
17. Grantz, K.L.: Fetal growth curves: is there a universal reference? Obstet. Gynecol. Clin. North Am. **48**, 281–296 (2021)

18. Hayward, C.E., et al.: Placental adaptation: What can we learn from birthweight: placental weight ratio? Front. Physiol. **7**, 28 (2016)
19. Hendrix, M., Bons, J., Alers, N., Severens-Rijvers, C., Spaanderman, M., Al-Nasiry, S.: Maternal vascular malformation in the placenta is an indicator for fetal growth restriction irrespective of neonatal birthweight. Placenta **87**, 8–15 (2019)
20. Imamoğlu, E.Y., et al.: Birth weight reference percentiles by gestational age for Turkish twin neonates. Turk. Archiv. Pediatr. **56**(4), 316 (2021)
21. Lemos, D., Braga, A.C., Nogueira, R.: Nonlinear regression on growth curves for placental parameters in r. In: Pereira, A.I., Mendes, A., Fernandes, F.P., Pacheco, M.F., Coelho, J.P., Lima, J. (eds.) Optimization, Learning Algorithms and Applications, pp. 575–590. Springer Nature Switzerland (2024)
22. Loverro, M.T., et al.: Pregnancy complications, correlation with placental pathology and neonatal outcomes. Front. Clin. Diab. Healthc. **2** (2022)
23. Mitsuda, N., et al.: Association between maternal hemoglobin concentration and placental weight to birthweight ratio: the Japan environment and children's study (JECS). Placenta **101**, 132–138 (2020)
24. Murdaugh, K.L., Florescue, H.: Small estimated placental volume (EPV) in the setting of decreased fetal movement. Clin. Imaging **104**, 110027 (2023)
25. Neath, Andrew A. e Cavanaugh, J.E.: The Bayesian information criterion: background, derivation, and applications. WIREs Comput. Stat. **4**, 199–203 (2012)
26. Nogueira, R., et al.: Placental biometric parameters: the usefulness of placental weight ratio and birth/placental weight ratio percentile curves for singleton gestations as a function of gestational age journal of clinical and anatomic pathology. J. Clin. Anat. Pathol. **4**, 104 (1–15) (2019)
27. Numan, S., Asad, A., Imran, M., Nisar, A.: Evaluation of nonlinear models to define growth curve in Lohi sheep. Small Rumin. Res. **205**, 106564 (2021)
28. Olaleye, O.A., Olatunji, O.O., Jimoh, K.O., Olaleye, A.O.: Bland–Altman plot: agreement between ultrasound-measured placenta thickness and other biometric parameters in the determination of gestational age. J. West Afr. College Surg. **12**, 46–51 (2022)
29. Panti, A.A., Ekele, B.A., Nwobodo, E.I., Yakubu, A.: The relationship between the weight of the placenta and birth weight of the neonate in a nigerian hospital. Niger. Med. J. J. Niger. Med. Assoc. **53**, 80 (2012)
30. Rigby, R.A., Stasinopoulos, D.M.: A semi-parametric additive model for variance heterogeneity. Stat. Comput. **6**, 57–65 (1996)
31. Rigby, R.A., Stasinopoulos, D.M.: Statistical Theory and Computational Aspects of Smoothing (1996)
32. Rigby, R.A., Stasinopoulos, D.M.: Smooth centile curves for skew and kurtotic data modelled using the box–cox power exponential distribution. Stat. Med. **23**, 3053–3076 (2004)
33. Rigby, R.A., Stasinopoulos, D.M.: Generalized additive models for location, scale and shape. J. Roy. Stat. Soc.: Ser. C (Appl. Stat.) **54**, 507–554 (2005)
34. Rigby, R.A., Stasinopoulos, D.M.: Using the box-cox t distribution in GAMLSS to model skewness and kurtosis. Stat. Model. **6**, 209–229 (2006)
35. Rigby, R.A., Stasinopoulos, M.D., Heller, G.Z., De Bastiani, F.: Distributions for Modeling Location, Scale, and Shape: Using GAMLSS in R. CRC Press (2019)
36. Royston, P., Wright, E.M.: Goodness-of-fit statistics for age-specific reference intervals. Stat. Med. **19**, 2943–2962 (2000)
37. Schluchter, M.D.: Mean Square Error. John Wiley & Sons, Ltd (2005)
38. Schwarz, G.: Estimating the dimension of a model. Ann. Stat. **6**, 461–464 (1978)

39. Shehata, F., Levin, I., Shrim, A., Ata, B., Weisz, B., Gamzu, R., Almog, B.: Placenta/birthweight ratio and perinatal outcome: a retrospective cohort analysis. BJOG Int. J. Obst. Gynaecol. **118**, 741–747 (2011)

40. Stasinopoulos, D.M., Rigby, R.A.: Generalized additive models for location scale and shape (GAMLSS) in R. J. Stat. Softw. **23**, 1–46 (2007)

41. Stasinopoulos, M., Rigby, B., Akantziliotou, C.: Instructions on How to Use the GAMLSS Package in R Second Edition (2008)

42. Stasinopoulos, M.D., Rigby, R.A., Heller, G.Z., Voudouris, V., De Bastiani, F.: Flexible Regression and Smoothing. Chapman & Hall/CRC (2017)

43. Tamayev, L., Schreiber, L., Marciano, A., Bar, J., Kovo, M.: Are there gender-specific differences in pregnancy outcome and placental abnormalities of pregnancies complicated with small for gestational age? Arch. Gynecol. Obstet. **301**(5), 1147–1151 (2020). https://doi.org/10.1007/s00404-020-05514-5

44. Turco, M.Y., Moffett, A.: Development of the Human Placenta. Development (Cambridge) **146** (2019)

45. Voudouris, V., Gilchrist, R., Rigby, R., Sedgwick, J., Stasinopoulos, D.: Modelling skewness and kurtosis with the BCPE density in GAMLSS. J. Appl. Stat. **39**, 1279–1293 (2012)

46. Wallace, J., Bhattacharya, S., Horgan, G.: Gestational age, gender and parity specific centile charts for placental weight for singleton deliveries in Aberdeen, UK. Placenta **34**, 269–274 (2013)

47. Wright, S.: Correlation and Causation (1921)

48. Wu, P., Green, M., Myers, J.E.: Hypertensive disorders of pregnancy. BMJ **381** (2023)

Comparison of Different Estimators for the Rayleigh Gamma Gompertz's Parameters and Reliability Function

Nadia Hashim Al-Noor[1] , Rafida M. Elobaid[2] , and Suzan J. Obaiys[3]($\boxtimes$)

[1] Department of Mathematics, College of Science, Mustansiriyah University, Baghdad, Iraq
nadialnoor@uomustansiriyah.edu.iq
[2] Faculty of Communication, Arts and Sciences, Canadian University Dubai, Dubai, United Arab Emirates
rafida@cud.ac.ae
[3] Department of Computer System and Technology, Faculty of Computer Science and Information Technology, University of Malaya, 50603 Kuala Lumpur, Malaysia
suzan@um.edu.my

Abstract. Estimating parameters and reliability features in various situations is a key challenge for statistical researchers in many disciplines. The prime goal of this paper is to investigate the flexibility of the newly compound three-parameter Rayleigh Gamma Gompertz for estimating unknown parameters and the reliability function under different estimation methods, sample sizes, and datasets. Simulation experiments are presented to investigate how the different estimators behave under various sample sizes and parameter values. The estimators' performance is measured using mean squared error. The empirical results demonstrated the outperforming, flexibility, and consistency of maximum likelihood and maximum product of spacing estimates to estimate the parameters and reliability function, with marked superiority of maximum likelihood for estimating the reliability function, confirming that this approach is still the most often used estimating technique due to its theoretical and practical features.

Keywords: Rayleigh Gamma Gompertz · Estimation Methods · Simulation

1 Introduction

Reliability is defined as a system's or component's ability to fulfill required functions under specified conditions over time [1]. Reliability theory looks at many facets of dependability, probability, statistics, and stochastic modeling to design and scientifically explain failure mechanisms using engineering concepts. Data from various fields, including engineering, biology, medicine, ecology, economics, sociology, and the social sciences, have been examined using reliability analysis [2–4]. In some contexts, reliability data analysis is also known as lifetime, failure-time, survival, or event-time data analysis [2]. In the examination of reliability data, reliability attributes are frequently specified using the mean time to failure, reliability function, and failure rate function.

O. Gervasi et al. (Eds.): ICCSA 2025 Workshops, LNCS 15887, pp. 332–346, 2026.
https://doi.org/10.1007/978-3-031-97589-9_23

Accordingly, reliability theory is adopted to study and analyze the behavior of failures and the factors behind such failures. To achieve this, the parameter estimators of failure models or probability distributions, with good performance and efficiency, are required to estimate the reliability function. Therefore, it is of keen significance to study the methods and techniques for getting the parameter estimators.

One of the most widely used distributions is the one-scale parameter Rayleigh distribution (RD) introduced by Rayleigh [5]. The origins and properties of RD are investigated by Siddiqui [6], while Sinha and Howlader [7] looked at RD inferences. Reports on RD have been increasing since 1993. It is used in applied statistics, diagnostic imaging, physical sciences, clinical subjects, survival and reliability theory, and lifetime data modeling and analysis. Furthermore, this distribution has applications in a variety of domains, including astronomy [8], medicine [9], and environmental science [10]. Much research has utilized RD to evaluate wind speeds and wind potential at different sites throughout the world because of its capacity to precisely characterize wind regimes [11–13]. As a result, this distribution has acquired prominence as a model for a variety of situations. In actuality, models with monotone hazard rates can be well modeled using the RD, while those with non-monotone hazard rates cannot be effectively modeled using this distribution. Therefore, RD has been modified by several authors for use in situations with non-monotone hazard rates. Numerous noteworthy generalized versions related to RD have been introduced in the literature (see [14–23]), and they all share the trait of having more parameters. When additional parameters are included in an existing distribution, the distribution's tail properties improve, and its goodness of fit is enhanced. Furthermore, based on different strategies, the RD is employed as a generator (family) to introduce several modified, extended, and generalized versions of different distributions to improve their flexibility to deal with the different natures of data. Among them, Rayleigh Rayleigh [24, 25], Rayleigh Generalized Gamma [26], Rayleigh Gamma Gompertz [27], Rayleigh Weibull and Rayleigh Inverted Weibull [28], Rayleigh Gompertz [29], Rayleigh Lomax [30], Rayleigh Exponential Gamma [31], Rayleigh Exponential and Rayleigh Generalized Log-Logistic [32].

Motivated by the possibility of estimating the unknown parameters and reliability function, this paper aims to perform seven estimation methods that have not been implemented for the newly flexible compound three-parameter Rayleigh Gamma Gompertz. Simulation experiments are presented to investigate how the different estimators behave under various sample sizes and parameter values. The remainder of the paper is structured as follows. Section 2 briefly describes the essential functions of the considered distribution. Seven approaches for estimating the parameters and reliability function are described in Sect. 3. Simulation results and discussions are provided in Sect. 4. Section 5 contains some concluding remarks.

2   Newly Compound Rayleigh Gamma Gompertz

The cumulative distribution function (CDF) and the probability density function (PDF) of the Rayleigh family of distributions are defined by [27]

$$F(x; a, \varphi) = e^{-\frac{a}{2}(\ln G(x; \varphi))^2}; x > 0 \tag{1}$$

and

$$f(x; a, \varphi) = a\frac{g(x; \varphi)}{G(x; \varphi)}(-\ln G(x; \varphi))e^{-\frac{a}{2}(-\ln G(x;\varphi))^2}; x > 0 \tag{2}$$

where $a > 0$, $g(x; \varphi)$ and $G(x; \varphi)$ are the PDF and CDF of the baseline distribution with vector parameters φ.

According to (1) and (2), with Gamma Gompertz as baseline distribution, the compound three-parameter Rayleigh Gamma Gompertz (RGGo) is defined by the following CDF and PDF

$$F(x) = F(x; a, b, c) = e^{-\frac{a}{2}\left(\ln\left(1-e^{-bcx}\right)\right)^2} \tag{3}$$

$$f(x) = f(x; a, b, c) = \frac{abce^{-bcx}}{1 - e^{-bcx}}\left(-\ln\left(1 - e^{-bcx}\right)\right)e^{-\frac{a}{2}\left(\ln\left(1-e^{-bcx}\right)\right)^2} \tag{4}$$

where $a, b > 0$ are scale parameters and $c > 0$ is a shape parameter.

The reliability and failure rate functions of the failure-time random variable X can be represented as

$$R(x) = 1 - F(x) = 1 - e^{-\frac{a}{2}\left(\ln\left(1-e^{-bcx}\right)\right)^2} \tag{5}$$

$$h(x) = \frac{f(x)}{R(x)} = \frac{abce^{-bcx}\left(-\ln\left(1 - e^{-bcx}\right)\right)e^{-\frac{a}{2}\left(\ln\left(1-e^{-bcx}\right)\right)^2}}{\left(1 - e^{-bcx}\right)\left(1 - e^{-\frac{a}{2}\left(\ln\left(1-e^{-bcx}\right)\right)^2}\right)} \tag{6}$$

The quantile function can be obtained from the inverted CDF in (3) as

$$Q(u) = -\frac{1}{bc}\ln\left(1 - e^{-\left(-\frac{2}{a}\ln(u)\right)^{\frac{1}{2}}}\right); u \in (0,1) \tag{7}$$

Some visualizations of the essential RGGo functions defined in (3)–(6) are shown in Figs. 1 and 2. The CDF and reliability function features are exhibited in Fig. 1. The PDF and failure rate function's various shapes are evident in Fig. 2, confirming that this novel distribution is highly suitable for simulating a variety of positive data.

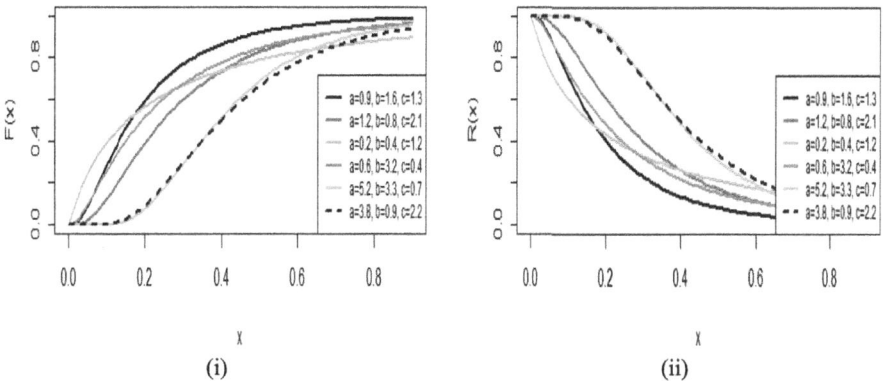

Fig. 1. The *RGGo* (i) CDF (ii) Reliability function plots with different parameter values

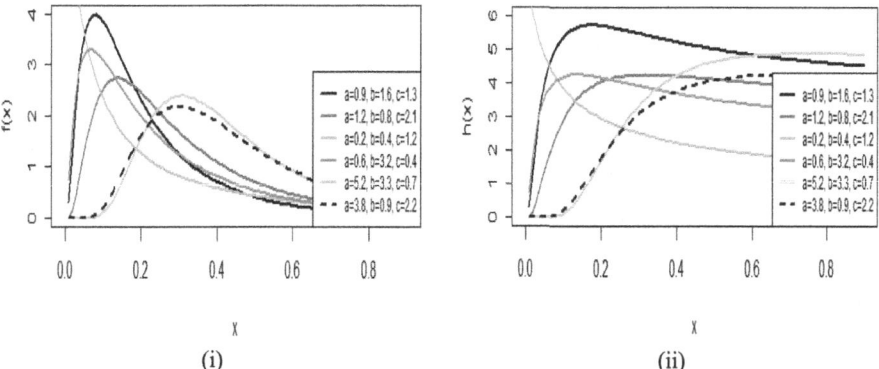

Fig. 2. The *RGGo* (i) PDF (ii) failure rate function plots with different parameter values

3 Different Estimators

This section investigates the estimators of RGGo parameters $\Delta = (a, b, c)$ and the reliability function by different estimation methods. For the purposes of this paper, related to the failure-time random variable X, $(x_1, x_2, \ldots, x_n)$ denotes a random sample of size n that follows the RGGo distribution. Thus, $x_1, x_2, \ldots, x_n$ represent the data, and their ascending ordering values are denoted by $x_{(1)}, x_{(2)}, \ldots, x_{(n)}$. For more details on the considered methods, one can review [33, 34].

3.1 Maximum Likelihood (ML) Estimators

The ML estimators of the vector parameters Δ are given by $\widehat{\Delta}^{ML} = \underset{\Delta}{\text{argmax}} \, L(\Delta)$ or, equivalently $\widehat{\Delta}^{ML} = \underset{\Delta}{\text{argmax}} \, \ell(\Delta)$ where $L(\Delta) = \prod_{i=1}^{n} f(x_i; \Delta)$ and $\ell(\Delta) = \ln(L(\Delta))$ represent the likelihood and natural log likelihood functions.

Now, related to (4), the L(Δ) and $\ell(\Delta)$ are

$$L(\Delta) = (abc)^n \prod_{i=1}^{n} \frac{e^{-bcx_i}}{1-e^{-bcx_i}} \left(-\ln\left(1-e^{-bcx_i}\right)\right) e^{-\frac{a}{2}\left(\ln\left(1-e^{-bcx_i}\right)\right)^2}$$

$$\ell(\Delta) = n\ln(abc) - bc\sum_{i=1}^{n} x_i - \sum_{i=1}^{n} \ln\left(1-e^{-bcx_i}\right) - \sum_{i=1}^{n} \ln\left(\ln\left(1-e^{-bcx_i}\right)\right)$$
$$- \frac{a}{2}\sum_{i=1}^{n} \left(\ln\left(1-e^{-bcx_i}\right)\right)^2$$

(8)

The differentiability of (8) can offer the requested estimators of vector Δ $\left(\hat{a}^{ML}, \hat{b}^{ML}, \hat{c}^{ML}\right)$ by simultaneously solving the following three non-linear equations corresponding to $\partial\ell(\Delta)/\partial\Delta = 0$ with respect to Δ, where

$$\frac{\partial\ell(\Delta)}{\partial a} = \frac{n}{a} - \frac{1}{2}\sum_{i=1}^{n} \left(\ln\left(1-e^{-bcx_i}\right)\right)^2$$

$$\frac{\partial\ell(\Delta)}{\partial b} = \frac{n}{b} - c\sum_{i=1}^{n} x_i - c\sum_{i=1}^{n} \frac{xe^{-bcx_i}}{1-e^{-bcx_i}} - c\sum_{i=1}^{n} \frac{xe^{-bcx_i}}{\left(1-e^{-bcx_i}\right)\ln\left(1-e^{-bcx_i}\right)}$$
$$- ac\sum_{i=1}^{n} \frac{xe^{-bcx_i}}{\left(1-e^{-bcx_i}\right)}\ln\left(1-e^{-bcx_i}\right)$$

$$\frac{\partial\ell(\Delta)}{\partial c} = \frac{n}{c} - b\sum_{i=1}^{n} x_i - b\sum_{i=1}^{n} \frac{xe^{-bcx_i}}{1-e^{-bcx_i}} - b\sum_{i=1}^{n} \frac{xe^{-bcx_i}}{\left(1-e^{-bcx_i}\right)\ln\left(1-e^{-bcx_i}\right)}$$
$$- ab\sum_{i=1}^{n} \frac{xe^{-bcx_i}}{\left(1-e^{-bcx_i}\right)}\ln\left(1-e^{-bcx_i}\right)$$

In the sequel, the ML estimator of the reliability function at each observation of failure time $x_{(i)}$; $i = 1,2,\ldots,n$ can be gained based on (5) by employing the invariant property as

$$\hat{R}^{ML}\left(x_{(i)}\right) = 1 - e^{-\frac{\hat{a}^{ML}}{2}\left(\ln\left(1-e^{-\hat{b}^{ML}\hat{c}^{ML}x_{(i)}}\right)\right)^2}$$

(9)

3.2 Ordinary Least Squares (OLS) Estimators

The OLS estimators of Δ are given by $\hat{\Delta}^{OLS} = \operatorname*{argmin}_{\Delta} OLS(\Delta)$, where.

$OLS(\Delta) = \sum_{i=1}^{n} \left[F\left(x_{(i)}; \Delta\right) - \frac{i}{n+1}\right]^2$.

Related to RGGo distribution, recall (3), the OLS(Δ) is

$$OLS(\Delta) = \sum_{i=1}^{n} \left[e^{-\frac{a}{2}\left(\ln\left(1-e^{-bcx_{(i)}}\right)\right)^2} - \frac{i}{n+1}\right]^2$$

(10)

The OLS estimators $(\hat{a}^{OLS}, \hat{b}^{OLS}, \hat{c}^{OLS})$ can be obtained by solving simultaneously the three non-linear equations summarized as $\partial OLS(\Delta)/\partial\Delta = 0$ with respect to Δ. Also, the estimators can be found by solving the following non-linear equation.

$$\sum_{i=1}^{n}\left[e^{-\frac{q}{2}\left(\ln\left(1-e^{-bcx_{(i)}}\right)\right)^2}-\frac{i}{n+1}\right]K_k\left(x_{(i)};\Delta\right)=0 \text{ for } k=1,2,3, \text{ where}$$

$$K_1\left(x_{(i)};\Delta\right)=\frac{\partial F\left(x_{(i)};\Delta\right)}{\partial a}=-\frac{1}{2}\sum_{i=1}^{n}\left(\ln\left(1-e^{-bcx_{(i)}}\right)\right)^2 e^{-\frac{q}{2}\left(\ln\left(1-e^{-bcx_{(i)}}\right)\right)^2} \quad (11)$$

$$K_2\left(x_{(i)};\Delta\right)=\frac{\partial F\left(x_{(i)};\Delta\right)}{\partial b}=-\frac{acx_{(i)}e^{-\frac{q}{2}\left(\ln\left(1-e^{-bcx_{(i)}}\right)\right)^2}}{e^{bcx_{(i)}}-1}\ln\left(1-e^{-bcx_{(i)}}\right) \quad (12)$$

$$K_3\left(x_{(i)};\Delta\right)=\frac{\partial F\left(x_{(i)};\Delta\right)}{\partial c}=-\frac{abx_{(i)}e^{-\frac{q}{2}\left(\ln\left(1-e^{-bcx_{(i)}}\right)\right)^2}}{e^{bcx_{(i)}}-1} \quad (13)$$

The OLS estimator of reliability function can be obtained approximately based on (5) as

$$\widehat{R}^{OLS}\left(x_{(i)}\right)\cong 1-e^{-\frac{\widehat{a}^{OLS}}{2}\left(\ln\left(1-e^{-\widehat{b}^{OLS}\widehat{c}^{OLS}x_{(i)}}\right)\right)^2} \quad (14)$$

3.3 Weighted Least Squares (WLS) Estimators

The WLS estimators of Δ are defined by $\widehat{\Delta}^{WLS}=\underset{\Delta}{\operatorname{argmin}}WLS(\Delta)$ where.

$WLS(\Delta)=\sum_{i=1}^{n}\frac{(n+1)^2(n+2)}{i(n-i+1)}\left[F\left(x_{(i)};\Delta\right)-\frac{i}{n+1}\right]^2.$

Related to RGGo, recall (3), the $WLS(\Delta)$ is

$$WLS(\Delta)=\sum_{i=1}^{n}\frac{(n+1)^2(n+2)}{i(n-i+1)}\left[e^{-\frac{q}{2}\left(\ln\left(1-e^{-bcx_{(i)}}\right)\right)^2}-\frac{i}{n+1}\right]^2 \quad (15)$$

Based on (15), the WLS estimators $(\widehat{a}^{WLS},\widehat{b}^{WLS},\widehat{c}^{WLS})$ can be obtained, in a similar manner to the OLS, by solving simultaneously the three non-linear equations summarized as $\partial WLS(\Delta)/\partial\Delta=0$ with respect to Δ which follow by solving

$$\sum_{i=1}^{n}\frac{(n+1)^2(n+2)}{i(n-i+1)}\left[e^{-\frac{q}{2}\left(\ln\left(1-e^{-bcx_{(i)}}\right)\right)^2}-\frac{i}{n+1}\right]K_k\left(x_{(i)};\Delta\right)=0; k=1,2,3$$

with $K_k\left(x_{(i)};\Delta\right)$ for $k=1,2,3$ as given in (11), (12), (13).

The WLS estimator of the reliability function is obtain approximately based on (5) as

$$\widehat{R}^{WLS}\left(x_{(i)}\right)\cong 1-e^{-\frac{\widehat{a}^{WLS}}{2}\left(\ln\left(1-e^{-\widehat{b}^{WLS}\widehat{c}^{WLS}x_{(i)}}\right)\right)^2} \quad (16)$$

3.4 Cramér-Von Mises Minimum Distance (CM) Estimators

The CM estimators of Δ are given by $\widehat{\Delta}^{CM} = \underset{\Delta}{\text{argmin}} CM(\Delta)$, where.

$CM(\Delta) = \frac{1}{12n} + \sum_{i=1}^{n} \left[F\left(x_{(i)}; \Delta\right) - \frac{2i-1}{2n} \right]^2$.

Related to RGGo distribution with CDF given in (3), the $CM(\Delta)$ is

$$CM(\Delta) = \frac{1}{12n} + \sum_{i=1}^{n} \left[e^{-\frac{a}{2}\left(\ln\left(1-e^{-bcx_{(i)}}\right)\right)^2} - \frac{2i-1}{2n} \right]^2 \qquad (17)$$

Based on (17), the CM estimators $(\widehat{a}^{CM}, \widehat{b}^{CM}, \widehat{c}^{CM})$ can be obtained by solving simultaneously the three non-linear equations summarized as $\partial CM(\Delta)/\partial \Delta = 0$ with respect to Δ.

The CM estimator of the reliability function can be obtained approximately based on (5) as

$$\widehat{R}^{CM}\left(x_{(i)}\right) \cong 1 - e^{-\frac{\widehat{a}^{CM}}{2}\left(\ln\left(1-e^{-\widehat{b}^{CM}\widehat{c}^{CM}x_{(i)}}\right)\right)^2} \qquad (18)$$

3.5 Maximum Product of Spacing (MP) Estimators

The MP estimators of Δ are given by $\widehat{\Delta}^{MP} = \underset{\Delta}{\text{argmax}} MP(\Delta)$, where.

$MP(\Delta) = \left[\prod_{i=1}^{n+1} (S_i(\Delta)) \right]^{\frac{1}{n+1}}$ where $S_i(\Delta) = F\left(x_{(i)}; \Delta\right) - F\left(x_{(i-1)}; \Delta\right)$ with $F\left(x_{(0)}; \Delta\right) = 0$ and $F\left(x_{(n+1)}; \Delta\right) = 1$. Further, the MP estimators of Δ can be equivalent given by $\widehat{\Delta}^{MP} = \underset{\Delta}{\text{argmax}} LMP(\Delta)$ where $LMP(\Delta) = \ln(S_i(\Delta)) = \frac{1}{n+1} \sum_{i=1}^{n+1} \ln(S_i(\Delta))$.

Related to RGGo distribution, recall (3), the $MP(\Delta)$ and $LMP(\Delta)$ are given by

$$MP(\Delta) = \left[\prod_{i=1}^{n+1} \left(e^{-\frac{a}{2}\left(\ln\left(1-e^{-bcx_{(i)}}\right)\right)^2} - e^{-\frac{a}{2}\left(\ln\left(1-e^{-bcx_{(i-1)}}\right)\right)^2} \right) \right]^{\frac{1}{n+1}} \qquad (19)$$

$$LMP(\Delta) = \frac{1}{n+1} \sum_{i=1}^{n+1} \ln\left(e^{-\frac{a}{2}\left(\ln\left(1-e^{-bcx_{(i)}}\right)\right)^2} - e^{-\frac{a}{2}\left(\ln\left(1-e^{-bcx_{(i-1)}}\right)\right)^2} \right) \qquad (20)$$

The MP estimators $(\widehat{a}^{MP}, \widehat{b}^{MP}, \widehat{c}^{MP})$ can be obtained by solving simultaneously the three non-linear equations summarized as $\partial MP(\Delta)/\partial \Delta = 0$ or equivalently $\partial LMP(\Delta)/\partial \Delta = 0$ with respect to Δ.

The MP estimator of the reliability function is obtain approximately by

$$\widehat{R}^{MP}\left(x_{(i)}\right) \cong 1 - e^{-\frac{\widehat{a}^{MP}}{2}\left(\ln\left(1-e^{-\widehat{b}^{MP}\widehat{c}^{MP}x_{(i)}}\right)\right)^2} \qquad (21)$$

3.6 Percentile (PC) Estimators

The PC estimators of Δ are given by $\widehat{\Delta}^{PC} = argminPC(\Delta)$, where $PC(\Delta) = \sum_{i=1}^{n}\left[x_{(i)} - Q(p_i; \Delta)\right]^2$.

Related to RGGo distribution, recall (7) with $p_i = \frac{i}{n+1}$, the PC(Δ) is

$$PC(\Delta) = \sum_{i=1}^{n}\left[x_{(i)} + \frac{1}{bc}\ln\left(1 - e^{-\left(-\frac{2}{a}\ln(p_i)\right)^{\frac{1}{2}}}\right)\right]^2 \qquad (22)$$

The PC estimators $(\widehat{a}^{PC}, \widehat{b}^{PC}, \widehat{c}^{PC})$ can be obtained by solving simultaneously the three non-linear equations summarized as $\partial PC(\Delta)/\partial\Delta = 0$ with respect to Δ.

The PC estimator of reliability function is obtain approximately by

$$\widehat{R}^{PC}\left(x_{(i)}\right) \cong 1 - e^{-\frac{\widehat{a}^{PC}}{2}\left(\ln\left(1 - e^{-\widehat{b}^{PC}\widehat{c}^{PC}x_{(i)}}\right)\right)^2} \qquad (23)$$

3.7 Anderson Darling (AD) Estimators

The AD estimators of Δ are given by $\widehat{\Delta}^{AD} = argminAD(\Delta)$, where.

$AD(\Delta) = -n + \frac{1}{n}\sum_{i=1}^{n}(2i - 1)\xi$, and $\xi = \ln F\left(x_{(i)}; \Delta\right) + \ln\left(1 - F\left(x_{(n+1-i)}; \Delta\right)\right)$.

Related to RGGo distribution, the AD(Δ) is

$$AD(\Delta) = -n + \frac{1}{n}\sum_{i=1}^{n}(2i - 1)\xi \qquad (24)$$

and

$$\xi = -\frac{a}{2}\left(\ln\left(1 - e^{-bcx_{(i)}}\right)\right)^2 + \ln\left(1 - e^{-\frac{a}{2}\left(\ln\left(1-e^{-bcx_{(n+1-i)}}\right)\right)^2}\right) \qquad (25)$$

The AD estimators $(\widehat{a}^{AD}, \widehat{b}^{AD}, \widehat{c}^{AD})$ can be obtained by solving simultaneously the three non-linear equations summarized as $\partial AD(\Delta)/\partial\Delta = 0$ with respect to Δ.

The AD estimator of the reliability function is obtain approximately by

$$\widehat{R}^{AD}\left(x_{(i)}\right) \cong 1 - e^{-\frac{\widehat{a}^{AD}}{2}\left(\ln\left(1 - e^{-\widehat{b}^{AD}\widehat{c}^{AD}x_{(i)}}\right)\right)^2} \qquad (26)$$

4 Simulation and Results

This section includes simulation experiments to evaluate the behavior of the ML, OLS, WLS, CM, MP, PC, AD estimators for the parameters and reliability function presented above under various sample sizes and configurations. The following procedure is considered with the R software.

1. Generate 1000 Random Samples of the Type $(x_1, x_2, \ldots, x_n)$ from the RGGo Distribution via the So-Called Inverse Transform Sampling Based on the Quantile Function Given by (7) as

$$x_i = -\frac{1}{bc} \ln\left(1 - e^{-\left(-\frac{2}{a}\ln(u_i)\right)^{\frac{1}{2}}}\right); i = 1, 2, \ldots, n \qquad (27)$$

where $u_i; i = 1, 2, \ldots, n$ represents a sample of values drawn from the standard uniform distribution.
2. Investigate different sample sizes as, $n = 25, 50, 100$, and 200.
3. Select three distinct configurations for the vector of parameters (a, b, c) as,
   I.(0.9, 1.6, 1.3); II.(0.2, 0.4, 1.2); and III.(3.8, 0.9, 2.2).
4. For the configurations under consideration, the three parameters' average estimates (AEP) related to ML, OLS, WLS, CM, MP, PC, AD are computed, as well as their mean squared errors (MSEP) and mean squared errors of reliability (MSER).

Numerical results are listed in Tables 1, 2, and 3. Further, the best estimation method of the parameters and reliability function associated with the lowest values of MSEP and MSER are listed in Tables 4 and 5.

The most important empirical results can be summarized as follows:

- As the sample size increases, the AEP values often become closer to the default values.
- For all sample sizes, the parameter's lowest MSEP value corresponds to its lowest default value.
- As the sample size increases, the performance of the estimation methods tends to align more closely.
- The MSEP and MSER values seem to decline with increasing sample size, indicating the estimators' consistency.
- The MP method performed the best when estimating the first parameter across a range of sample sizes and datasets.
- The ML method always performed the best when estimating the second parameter across a range of sample sizes and the III dataset. It also performed the best for the other datasets besides the MP method.
- The ML method always performed the best when estimating the third parameter across a range of sample sizes and datasets, except for a single appearance of the AD method when $n = 200$ with the I dataset and the MP method when $n = 25$ with the III dataset.
- The ML method always performed the best for estimating the reliability function across a range of sample sizes and datasets, except for the MP method's two appearances when $n = 25$ related to I and II datasets.

Table 1. The values of *AEP* corresponding to each configuration

n	$\widehat{\Delta}$	ML	OLS	WLS	CM	MP	PC	AD
I. (0.9, 1.6, 1.3)								
25	$\hat{a}$	1.13148	1.02615	1.02882	1.23547	0.81919	0.91255	1.03489
	$\hat{b}$	1.54534	1.59526	1.59060	1.52914	1.65478	1.69776	1.58040
	$\hat{c}$	1.41754	1.42973	1.40753	1.39957	1.48267	1.44558	1.42797
50	$\hat{a}$	0.97968	0.93226	0.93966	1.01579	0.80987	0.82263	0.94294
	$\hat{b}$	1.58803	1.61085	1.60657	1.57809	1.65344	1.73300	1.60380
	$\hat{c}$	1.44307	1.43581	1.44014	1.41129	1.47936	1.47153	1.43310
100	$\hat{a}$	0.94749	0.92769	0.93306	0.96738	0.84718	0.83074	0.93117
	$\hat{b}$	1.58693	1.59664	1.59334	1.57990	1.62698	1.69595	1.59375
	$\hat{c}$	1.44161	1.43469	1.43744	1.42567	1.45972	1.44482	1.43282
200	$\hat{a}$	0.92007	0.91108	0.91469	0.92999	0.86234	0.83848	0.91262
	$\hat{b}$	1.60184	1.60495	1.60371	1.59658	1.62520	1.68097	1.60437
	$\hat{c}$	1.43739	1.43318	1.42983	1.42644	1.45146	1.44895	1.42731
II. (0.2, 0.4, 1.2)								
25	$\hat{a}$	0.24661	0.22319	0.22661	0.25813	0.18966	0.22046	0.22644
	$\hat{b}$	0.41720	0.39134	0.39666	0.40801	0.38123	0.37220	0.40333
	$\hat{c}$	1.28665	1.32432	1.31451	1.29164	1.33231	1.31024	1.31526
50	$\hat{a}$	0.21516	0.20380	0.20643	0.21835	0.18412	0.19123	0.20647
	$\hat{b}$	0.40970	0.39769	0.40181	0.40716	0.38573	0.39266	0.40294
	$\hat{c}$	1.29882	1.32814	1.31914	1.31153	1.32682	1.31192	1.31444
100	$\hat{a}$	0.20795	0.20162	0.20393	0.20853	0.18967	0.18332	0.20374
	$\hat{b}$	0.40534	0.39922	0.40173	0.40403	0.39099	0.40841	0.40195
	$\hat{c}$	1.30211	1.31977	1.31539	1.31199	1.32130	1.30536	1.31178
200	$\hat{a}$	0.20343	0.20015	0.20153	0.20353	0.19288	0.18574	0.20121
	$\hat{b}$	0.40057	0.39713	0.39869	0.39955	0.39221	0.40675	0.39847
	$\hat{c}$	1.30292	1.31809	1.31545	1.30987	1.31697	1.30278	1.30952
III. (3.8, 0.9, 2.2)								
25	$\hat{a}$	5.08310	4.50637	4.55605	5.71466	3.38162	3.78575	4.55088
	$\hat{b}$	0.92759	0.88353	0.89214	0.92692	0.84393	0.83944	0.90093
	$\hat{c}$	2.47578	2.66155	2.61975	2.44447	3.10244	2.71506	2.40753
50	$\hat{a}$	4.40682	4.23950	4.23352	4.73492	3.47259	3.57327	4.20369

(*continued*)

Table 1. (*continued*)

n	$\widehat{\Delta}$	ML	OLS	WLS	CM	MP	PC	AD
	$\hat{b}$	0.91668	0.89941	0.90413	0.92110	0.86634	0.85695	0.90474
	$\hat{c}$	2.51190	2.59480	2.57113	2.32585	3.02081	2.75859	2.61021
100	$\hat{a}$	4.06552	3.89513	3.95695	4.10228	3.54143	3.60048	3.94173
	$\hat{b}$	0.90714	0.89419	0.89963	0.90478	0.87762	0.87311	0.89929
	$\hat{c}$	2.61617	2.74884	2.75445	2.68774	2.91313	2.75791	2.71057
200	$\hat{a}$	3.91868	3.86716	3.88936	3.96850	3.61716	3.57208	3.87402
	$\hat{b}$	0.90279	0.89785	0.90026	0.90321	0.88552	0.87948	0.89962
	$\hat{c}$	2.59134	2.74460	2.63975	2.65203	2.79387	2.85113	2.69336

Table 2. The values of *MSEP* corresponding to each configuration

n	$\widehat{\Delta}$	ML	OLS	WLS	CM	MP	PC	AD
I. (0.9, 1.6, 1.3)								
25	$\hat{a}$	0.35418	0.91416	0.62239	1.72802	0.14521	0.44576	0.35146
	$\hat{b}$	0.11449	0.13165	0.12304	0.14345	0.10858	0.26457	0.11579
	$\hat{c}$	0.06553	0.37434	0.99632	1.12120	0.07121	0.32875	0.10520
50	$\hat{a}$	0.08874	0.12258	0.09856	0.16515	0.06144	0.19016	0.08957
	$\hat{b}$	0.05339	0.06504	0.05870	0.06756	0.05406	0.18790	0.05732
	$\hat{c}$	0.03391	0.06085	0.04447	0.06880	0.04348	0.14164	0.04509
100	$\hat{a}$	0.03545	0.05552	0.04474	0.06550	0.02839	0.10245	0.04000
	$\hat{b}$	0.02477	0.02977	0.02678	0.03059	0.02481	0.09791	0.02627
	$\hat{c}$	0.02711	0.03719	0.03075	0.03586	0.03242	0.06031	0.02921
200	$\hat{a}$	0.01673	0.02430	0.01961	0.02634	0.01550	0.06037	0.01861
	$\hat{b}$	0.01469	0.01668	0.01546	0.01674	0.01515	0.05936	0.01532
	$\hat{c}$	0.02362	0.02704	0.02380	0.02454	0.02721	0.06769	0.02282
II. (0.2, 0.4, 1.2)								
25	$\hat{a}$	0.00935	0.03516	0.03338	0.05500	0.00405	0.02748	0.00770
	$\hat{b}$	0.01542	0.01737	0.01603	0.01826	0.01377	0.01560	0.01563
	$\hat{c}$	0.01353	0.09403	0.07423	0.09161	0.02419	0.05382	0.02552
50	$\hat{a}$	0.00254	0.00408	0.00326	0.00520	0.00188	0.01350	0.00258
	$\hat{b}$	0.00719	0.00836	0.00781	0.00865	0.00677	0.00894	0.00756
	$\hat{c}$	0.01322	0.03446	0.02566	0.02486	0.01966	0.02413	0.01990
100	$\hat{a}$	0.00108	0.00167	0.00132	0.00189	0.00093	0.00772	0.00122
	$\hat{b}$	0.00364	0.00437	0.00397	0.00446	0.00350	0.00661	0.00393

(*continued*)

Table 2. (*continued*)

n	$\hat{\Delta}$	ML	OLS	WLS	CM	MP	PC	AD
	$\hat{c}$	0.01263	0.02262	0.01955	0.02031	0.01764	0.01852	0.01709
200	$\hat{a}$	0.00055	0.00086	0.00067	0.00090	0.00053	0.00460	0.00065
	$\hat{b}$	0.00166	0.00207	0.00185	0.00208	0.00168	0.00376	0.00182
	$\hat{c}$	0.01188	0.01929	0.01816	0.01672	0.01532	0.01683	0.01523

III. (3.8, 0.9, 2.2)

n	$\hat{\Delta}$	ML	OLS	WLS	CM	MP	PC	AD
25	$\hat{a}$	12.5427	21.5825	17.9790	44.76931	4.33821	12.1620	10.3980
	$\hat{b}$	0.01437	0.01958	0.01728	0.02155	0.01560	0.02536	0.01494
	$\hat{c}$	5.22534	14.0249	9.74865	35.7509	3.34283	7.21264	7.19477
50	$\hat{a}$	3.56113	5.63766	4.18173	8.16952	1.93357	4.46351	3.52512
	$\hat{b}$	0.00727	0.01025	0.00852	0.01110	0.00780	0.01486	0.00778
	$\hat{c}$	1.86306	7.03200	5.13464	8.48300	2.39344	3.84600	4.31666
100	$\hat{a}$	1.14066	1.76167	1.41664	2.09099	0.84262	2.04212	1.26210
	$\hat{b}$	0.00332	0.00494	0.00398	0.00501	0.00367	0.00690	0.00379
	$\hat{c}$	0.89823	2.86871	1.81010	2.08994	1.99767	1.82369	1.65567
200	$\hat{a}$	0.45762	0.75369	0.59100	0.82507	0.40178	1.05355	0.54802
	$\hat{b}$	0.00155	0.00235	0.00189	0.00237	0.00172	0.00357	0.00181
	$\hat{c}$	0.55086	2.62489	1.88195	1.77239	0.93217	1.89191	1.28415

Table 3. The values of *MSER* corresponding to each configuration

n	ML	OLS	WLS	CM	MP	PC	AD
I. (0.9, 1.6, 1.3)							
25	0.004300	0.004912	0.004561	0.005034	0.004261	0.008547	0.004432
50	0.002039	0.002446	0.002221	0.002463	0.002086	0.004969	0.002185
100	0.000994	0.001185	0.001083	0.001195	0.001005	0.002388	0.001066
200	0.000561	0.000651	0.000601	0.000653	0.000566	0.001346	0.000596
II. (0.2, 0.4, 1.2)							
25	0.003775	0.004419	0.004044	0.004563	0.003631	0.014120	0.003904
50	0.001888	0.002331	0.002112	0.002349	0.001915	0.012360	0.002052
100	0.000993	0.001215	0.001093	0.001220	0.001008	0.007622	0.001079
200	0.000486	0.000601	0.000536	0.000601	0.000496	0.004050	0.000533
III. (3.8, 0.9, 2.2)							
25	0.004275	0.004931	0.004607	0.005000	0.004325	0.005657	0.004445
50	0.002111	0.002409	0.002236	0.002440	0.002137	0.003014	0.002180
100	0.001100	0.001280	0.001172	0.001282	0.001117	0.001574	0.001163
200	0.000515	0.000617	0.000558	0.000618	0.000525	0.000762	0.000553

Table 4. The best estimation method for the parameters

n	$\widehat{\Delta}$	I. (0.9, 1.6, 1.3)	II. (0.2, 0.4, 1.2)	III. (3.8, 0.9, 2.2)
25	$\hat{a}$	MP	MP	MP
	$\hat{b}$	MP	MP	ML
	$\hat{c}$	ML	ML	MP
50	$\hat{a}$	MP	MP	MP
	$\hat{b}$	ML	MP	ML
	$\hat{c}$	ML	ML	ML
100	$\hat{a}$	MP	MP	MP
	$\hat{b}$	ML	MP	ML
	$\hat{c}$	ML	ML	ML
200	$\hat{a}$	MP	MP	MP
	$\hat{b}$	ML	ML	ML
	$\hat{c}$	AD	ML	ML

Table 5. The best estimation method for the reliability function

n	I. (0.9, 1.6, 1.3)	II. (0.2, 0.4, 1.2)	III. (3.8, 0.9, 2.2)
25	MP	MP	ML
50	ML	ML	ML
100	ML	ML	ML
200	ML	ML	ML

5   Conclusion

The one-scale parameter Rayleigh distribution is one of the most extensively utilized. It has gained popularity as a model for various situations involving monotone hazard rates. It is also employed as a generator family to introduce many notable generalized variants of different probability distributions. This paper focused on Rayleigh Gamma Gompertz (RGGo) as one of these distributions. The RGGo's capabilities and flexibility in estimating unknown parameters and the reliability function are investigated under various sample sizes and datasets by employing seven estimation methods: ML, OLS, WLS, CM, MP, PC, and AD. The estimators' performance is measured using mean squared error. The simulation results generally demonstrated the outperforming, flexibility, and consistency of ML and MP estimates, which deal with maximizing specific objective functions for estimating the parameters for various datasets, while PC, CM, and OLS, which deal with minimizing specific objective functions, have recorded the lowest performance depending on certain configurations. Regarding estimating the reliability function, the ML and MP are the most performed methods, while the least performed is always associated with PC. Consequently, for estimating the parameters and reliability function of RGGo, it is recommended to use ML and MP rather than utilizing PC. In the same context, as an open topic for future research, other generalized and extended distributions may be examined.

References

1. Safari, M.A.M., Masseran, N., Abdul Majid, M.H.: Robust reliability estimation for Lindley distribution-a probability integral transform statistical approach. Mathematics **8**, 1634 (2020)
2. Meeker, W.Q., Escobar, L.A.: Statistical Methods for Reliability Data. John Wiley and Sons, New York (2014)
3. Blischke, W.R., Murthy, D.N.P.: Reliability: Modeling, Prediction, and Optimization. John Wiley and Sons, New York (2000)
4. Lee, E.T., Wang, J.: Statistical Methods for Survival Data Analysis, 3rd edn., p. 476. John Wiley and Sons, New York (2003)
5. Rayleigh, J.W.S.: On the resultant of a large number of vibrations of the same pitch and of arbitrary phase. London Edinburgh and Dublin Philos. Mag. J. Sci. - 5th Ser. **10**, 73–78 (1880)
6. Siddiqui, M.M.: Some problems connected with Rayleigh distributions. J. Res. Natl. Bureau Standard **66D**, 167–174 (1962)
7. Sinha, S.K., Howlader, H.A.: Credible and HPD intervals of the parameter and reliability of Rayleigh distribution. IEEE Trans. Reliab. **32**, 217–220 (1993)
8. Bovaird, T., Lineweaver, C.H.: A flat inner disc model as an alternative to the Kepler dichotomy in the Q1–Q16 planet population. Mon. Not. R. Astron. Soc. **468**, 1493–1504 (2017)
9. Belaid, A., Boukerroui, D.: Local maximum likelihood segmentation of echocardiographic images with Rayleigh distribution. SIViP **12**, 1087–1096 (2018)
10. Casas-Prat, M., Holthuijsen, L.H.: Short-term statistics of waves observed in deep water. J. Geophys. Res.: Oceans **115**, 1–20 (2010)
11. Morgan, E.C., Lackner, M., Vogel, R.M., Baise, L.G.: Probability distributions for offshore wind speeds. Energy Convers. Manage. **52**, 15–26 (2011)
12. Sohoni, V., Gupta, S., Nema, R.: A comparative analysis of wind speed probability distributions for wind power assessment of four sites. Turk. J. Electr. Eng. Comput. Sci. **24**, 4724–4735 (2016)
13. Bidaoui, H., El Abbassi, I., El Bouardi, A., Darcherif, A.: Wind speed data analysis using Weibull and Rayleigh distribution functions, case study: five cities northern Morocco. Procedia Manuf. **32**, 786–793 (2019)
14. Bekker, A., Roux, J.J.J., Mosteit, P.J.: A generalization of the compound Rayleigh distribution: using a Bayesian method on cancer survival times. Commun. Stat.-Theory Methods **29**(7), 1419–1433 (2000)
15. Kundu, D., Raqab, M.Z.: Generalized Rayleigh distribution: different methods of estimations. Comput. Stat. Data Anal. **49**(1), 187–200 (2005)
16. Dey, S., Dey, T., Kundu, D.: Two-parameter Rayleigh distribution: different methods of estimation. Am. J. Math. Manag. Sci. **33**(1), 55–74 (2014)
17. Merovci, F., Elbatal, I.: Weibull Rayleigh distribution: theory and applications. Appl. Math. Inf. Sci. **9**(4), 2127–2137 (2015)
18. Almongy, H.M., Almetwally, E.M., Aljohani, H.M., Alghamdi, A.S., Hafez, E.H.: A new extended Rayleigh distribution with applications of COVID-19 data. Results Phys. **23**, 104012 (2021)

19. Bhat, A.A., Ahmad, S.P., Almetwally, E.M., Yehia, N., Alsadat, N., Tolba, A.H.: The odd Lindley power Rayleigh distribution: properties, classical and Bayesian estimation with applications. Sci. Afr. **20**, e01736 (2023)

20. Hilal, O.A., Al-Noor, N.H.: Theory and applications of truncated exponential Topp Leone Rayleigh distribution. AIP Conf. Proc. **2414**, 040055 (2023)

21. Abd El-Raouf, M.M., AbaOud, M.: A novel extension of generalized Rayleigh model with engineering applications. Alexandria Eng. J. **73**, 269–283 (2023)

22. Kalaf, B.A., Jabar, N.A.A., Madaki, U.Y.: Truncated inverse generalized Rayleigh distribution and some properties. Ibn AL-Haitham J. Pure Appl. Sci. **36**(4), 414–428 (2023)

23. Haj Ahmad, H., Ramadan, D.A., Almetwally, E.M.: Evaluating the discrete generalized Rayleigh distribution: statistical inferences and applications to real data analysis. Mathematics **12**(2), 183 (2024)

24. Ateeq, K., Qasim, T.B., Alvi, A.R.: An extension of Rayleigh distribution and applications. Cogent Math. Stat. **6**(1), 1–16 (2019)

25. Al-Noor, N.H., Assi, N.K.: Rayleigh-Rayleigh distribution: properties and applications. J. Phys.: Conf. Ser. IOP Publ. **1591**, 1–15 (2020)

26. Bentoumi, A., Mezache, A., Oudira, H.: Parameter estimation of Rayleigh-generalized gamma mixture model. Instrum. Mesure Métrologie **19**(1), 59–64 (2020)

27. Al-Noor, N.H., Assi, N.K.: Rayleigh gamma Gompertz distribution: properties and applications. AIP Conf. Proc. **2334**(1), 090003 (2021)

28. Smadi, M.M., Alrefaei, M.H.: New extensions of Rayleigh distribution based on inverted-Weibull and Weibull distributions. Int. J. Electr. Comput. Eng. **11**(6), 5107–5118 (2021)

29. Al-Noor, N.H., Khaleel, M.A., Assi, N.K.: The Rayleigh Gompertz distribution: theory and real applications. Int. J. Nonlinear Anal. Appl. **13**(1), 3505–3516 (2022)

30. Fatima, K., Jan, U., Ahmad, S.P.: Statistical properties of Rayleigh Lomax distribution with applications in survival analysis. J. Data Sci. **16**(3), 531–548 (2022)

31. Michael, A.T., Ayobami, A.I., Ayooluwa, O.E.: Rayleigh-exponential-gamma distribution: theory and properties. Int. J. Res. Publ. Rev. **4**(8), 33–39 (2023)

32. Farhin, S., Khan, A.A.: Bayesian survival analysis of Rayleigh-X family with time varying covariate. Appl. Math. E-Notes **23**, 124–145 (2023)

33. Hassan, E.A.A., Elgarhy, M., Eldessouky, E.A., Hassan, O.H.M., Amin, E.A., Almetwally, E.M.: Different estimation methods for new probability distribution approach based on environmental and medical data. Axioms **12**, 220 (2023)

34. Afify, A.Z., Hussein, E.A., Al-Mofeh, H., Alsultan, R., Aljohani, H.M.: The flexible Frechet distribution: properties, inference, and medical applications. J. Math. **2600560**, 1–27 (2024)

Pricing Models in Individual Health Insurance

Ângelo Cunha[1] and A. Manuela Gonçalves[1,2(✉)] (iD)

[1] Department of Mathematics, University of Minho, Guimarães, Portugal
mneves@math.uminho.pt
[2] University of Minho, Centre of Mathematics, Guimarães, Portugal

Abstract. Accurate premium estimation is fundamental in insurance pricing, ensuring both fairness for policyholders and financial stability for insurers. Generalized Linear Models (GLMs) have been widely adopted due to their interpretability and compliance with regulatory standards. However, recent advancements in Machine Learning (ML) offer improved predictive accuracy by capturing non-linear relationships and complex risk structures. This study evaluates the performance of GLMs against ML models such as Decision Trees, Random Forest, Gradient Boosting (GBM), and XGBoost in predicting claim frequency and severity. Results demonstrate that GBM and XGBoost outperform GLMs in predictive accuracy, yet challenges remain in ensuring model interpretability and regulatory transparency. While GLMs provide an established actuarial framework, ML techniques offer optimization potential, leading to enhanced risk assessment and fairer pricing. The findings highlight the trade-off between predictive accuracy and interpretability in insurance pricing, emphasizing the need for hybrid approaches that integrate the strengths of both GLMs and ML models. This study contributes to the ongoing evolution of actuarial science by demonstrating how data-driven techniques can complement traditional methodologies while maintaining compliance with industry regulations.

Keywords: Actuarial Science · Generalized Linear Models · Machine Learning · Predictive Modeling · Pricing

1 Introduction

Insurance pricing is a critical process that balances fairness for policyholders with financial stability for insurers. Traditionally, Generalized Linear Models (GLMs) [11] have been the industry standard due to their interpretability and widespread acceptance by regulators [?]. GLMs provide a structured framework for modeling claim frequency and severity while maintaining transparency in pricing methodologies [4]. However, recent advancements in Machine Learning (ML) techniques, such as tree-based models and deep learning, offer promising alternatives that enhance predictive accuracy by capturing non-linear relationships and complex risk structures [15].

© The Author(s), under exclusive license to Springer Nature Switzerland AG 2026
O. Gervasi et al. (Eds.): ICCSA 2025 Workshops, LNCS 15887, pp. 347–364, 2026.
https://doi.org/10.1007/978-3-031-97589-9_24

This study focuses on individual health insurance pricing, comparing GLMs with ML techniques, specifically Decision Trees, Random Forest, Gradient Boosting (GBM), and XGBoost. The primary goal is to evaluate whether ML models can improve claim frequency and severity predictions, leading to more precise pricing strategies. Prior research highlights the benefits of ML in actuarial science, including applications in frequency and severity modeling [8]. Despite their strong predictive capabilities, ML models pose challenges related to interpretability, regulatory compliance, and potential bias [14].

Regulatory bodies require transparent pricing methodologies, which traditional GLMs provide but ML models often lack [14]. The use of black-box models in a highly regulated industry raises concerns about fairness, bias, and accountability [13]. As Olhede and Wolfe (2018) [14] point out, predictive models must adhere to strict guidelines ensuring that decision-making processes remain explainable and justifiable.

Given these challenges, this research aims to identify the best-performing models while ensuring they remain practical for actuarial and regulatory applications. This study contributes to the evolving field of actuarial science and data-driven risk assessment by exploring the trade-off between accuracy and explainability in insurance pricing. Moreover, it highlights the potential of hybrid approaches that integrate ML techniques with traditional actuarial methods to optimize predictive performance while preserving interpretability.

2   Generalized Linear Models: Application to Pricing

Insurance pricing relies on a tariff system that evaluates historical claims data and policyholder characteristics to determine fair premiums. The cost associated with a policy i can be divided into two primary components:

- **Frequency** (N_i): Number of claims per exposure unit.
- **Severity** (X_{ij}): Total loss amount per claim.

The total loss for policy i is given by:

$$S_i = \sum_{j=1}^{N_i} X_{ij}. \tag{1}$$

The expected loss or pure premium is computed as:

$$E[S_i] = E[N_i] \cdot E[X_i]. \tag{2}$$

For an insurance portfolio of n policies, the total expected loss and variance are:

$$\mu_S = \sum_{i=1}^{n} E[S_i], \tag{3}$$

$$\sigma_S^2 = \sum_{i=1}^{n} \text{Var}[S_i]. \tag{4}$$

Frequency Modeling

Claim frequency is often modeled using the **Poisson distribution**, given by:

$$P(N = x) = \frac{e^{-\lambda}\lambda^x}{x!}, \quad E[N] = \lambda, \quad \text{Var}[N] = \lambda. \tag{5}$$

When overdispersion is present ($\text{Var}[N] > E[N]$), the **Negative Binomial distribution** is preferred:

$$P(N = x) = \frac{\Gamma(x + \kappa)}{\Gamma(x + 1)\Gamma(\kappa)} \left(\frac{\kappa}{\kappa + \mu}\right)^{\kappa} \left(\frac{\mu}{\kappa + \mu}\right)^{x}. \tag{6}$$

Severity Modeling

Claim severity is commonly modeled using the **Gamma distribution**:

$$f(y) = \frac{y^{\alpha-1}e^{-y/\theta}}{\theta^\alpha \Gamma(\alpha)}, \quad E[Y] = \theta\alpha, \quad \text{Var}[Y] = \theta^2\alpha. \tag{7}$$

An alternative is the **Inverse Gaussian distribution**, useful for heavy-tailed severity data:

$$f(y) = \sqrt{\frac{\lambda}{2\pi y^3}} \exp\left(-\frac{\lambda(y - \mu)^2}{2\mu^2 y}\right), \quad E[Y] = \mu, \quad \text{Var}[Y] = \frac{\mu^3}{\lambda}. \tag{8}$$

GLM Framework for Pricing

Generalized Linear Models (GLMs) are used to estimate claim frequency and severity. The **log-link function** is commonly applied:

$$\ln(\mu_i) = \beta_0 + \sum_{j=1}^{p} \beta_j x_{ij}. \tag{9}$$

This results in a **multiplicative model**:

$$\mu_i = e^{\beta_0} \times e^{\beta_1 x_{1i}} \times \ldots \times e^{\beta_p x_{pi}}. \tag{10}$$

Exposure, Offsets, and Weights

Exposure (Exposure_i) accounts for varying risk durations. In GLMs, exposure can be incorporated as an **offset**:

$$g(\mu_i) = \beta_0 + \sum_{j=1}^{p} \beta_j x_{ij} + \log(\text{Exposure}_i). \qquad (11)$$

Alternatively, exposure can be included as a **weight variable** to adjust for variance:

$$\text{Var}(y_i) = V(\mu_i) \cdot a(\phi) \cdot \omega_i. \qquad (12)$$

Where:

- $\text{Var}(y_i)$ is the variance of the ith observation.
- $V(\mu_i)$ is the variance function.
- $a(\phi)$ is a function of the dispersion parameter ϕ.
- ω_i is the weight assigned to observation i, commonly related to exposure in insurance data.

Premium Components

The total premium charged consists of:

- **Pure Premium**: Expected loss.
- **Security Margin**: Covers uncertainty.
- **Other Charges**: Administrative costs and taxes.

Policyholders with similar risk factors are grouped into **tariff classes** and charged the same premium.
Using GLMs, insurers can improve risk segmentation, optimize pricing strategies, and enhance financial stability.

3   Methodologies

Preprocessing

The following preprocessing steps were applied using R: Data anonymization: Removed personally identifiable information and regional identifiers for privacy compliance. Handling missing values and unrealistic data points: Ensured data integrity by removing incomplete or implausible records. Although alternative imputation strategies—such as mean substitution or model-based imputation— were considered, they were ultimately deemed inappropriate for this specific dataset. Imputing values without a strong underlying justification could have introduced artificial patterns or noise, particularly in an actuarial context where reliability and explainability are critical. Normalization: Applied to numerical features for ML models to enhance training stability. Encoding categorical variables: Converted categorical data into numerical formats. Outlier handling. These preprocessing techniques ensured that the dataset was optimized for both GLMs and ML models, allowing for a robust comparison of pricing methodologies.

Generalized Linear Models (GLMs)

GLMs were used as the baseline models for health insurance pricing due to their interpretability and regulatory acceptance.

For claim frequency, the Poisson and Negative Binomial distributions were evaluated. The Negative Binomial GLM was selected as the best model, as it effectively handled overdispersion (i.e., when the variance exceeds the mean), which was a key issue in the dataset.

For claim severity, models suited for positive, right-skewed continuous distributions were considered, including Gamma GLM, Inverse Gaussian GLM, and Gaussian GLM. Given the skewed nature of incurred claims, the Gaussian model was ruled out, and the Inverse Gaussian GLM was selected as the best-performing model.

The primary goal in GLM modeling is not to achieve a perfect fit to the data's distribution but to identify the distribution that best approximates the observed data while ensuring interpretability and business applicability.

To determine the best GLM models, the following techniques were applied:

- Stepwise Akaike Information Criterion (AIC) – sequentially removed non-significant predictors to balance model goodness-of-fit and complexity;
- Bayesian Information Criterion (BIC) – used to prioritize simpler models when differences in fit were marginal;
- Deviance analysis – assessed how well each model explained variability in the data;
- Residual analysis – identified systematic patterns that could indicate model misspecification;
- 10-fold cross-validation - ensured robustness of model predictions on unseen data;
- Performance metrics (MSE and MAE) – used to quantitatively compare model accuracy.

To refine the rating structure, multiple models were tested, some including interaction effects between categorical variables (e.g., Age Band * Gender). Only interactions that significantly improved predictive accuracy were retained in the final models.

Machine Learning Models (MLM)

To explore improvements in predictive accuracy, four machine learning (ML) models were tested:

Decision Tree Regression, Random Forest, Gradient Boosting Machine (GBM), XGBoost.

To ensure ML models could effectively process the dataset, the following preprocessing steps were applied:

- Feature Engineering – created Claim Frequency (Number of Claims / Exposure) and Claim Severity (Incurred Claims / Exposure), as ML models do not incorporate exposure as an offset;
- Normalization – applied to improve convergence of algorithms sensitive to data scaling, such as GBM and XGBoost;
- Categorical Encoding – converted categorical features (Age Band, Gender, Region, Benefit Type) into a numerical format;
- Handling Imbalanced Data – removed INS. D (Benefit Type) due to having only one observation, which could bias the model and disrupt cross-validation;
- Train-Test Split – data was split into 80% training and 20% testing to ensure robust model evaluation;
- Hyperparameter Tuning – conducted manually.

Regarding the hyperparameter tuning, it is important to notice that, unlike GLMs, ML models require this to optimize performance. Hyperparameters were adjusted manually by iterating through different configurations and selecting those with the best performance metrics on validation data. The key parameters adjusted for each model were:

- **Decision Tree** – complexity parameter (to prevent overfitting);
- **Random Forest** – number of trees, maximum depth, and minimum samples per split;
- **GBM** – learning rate, number of boosting iterations, maximum depth, and minimum samples per leaf;
- **XGBoost** – learning rate, number of boosting rounds, maximum tree depth, and subsampling ratio.

Model Evaluation and Cross-Validation

To ensure model generalizability and reduce the risk of overfitting, **10-fold cross-validation** was employed. In this approach, the dataset was randomly partitioned into ten approximately equal-sized subsets (folds). Each model was trained on nine of these folds and validated on the remaining one, rotating the validation fold through all ten combinations. This process ensured that every observation was used for both training and validation exactly once, providing a more reliable estimate of model performance. The final performance metrics were calculated by averaging the results across all ten iterations, offering a robust assessment of how the model would perform on unseen data. The evaluation included: The final performance was assessed using: Mean Squared Error (MSE) Mean Absolute Error (MAE) Additionally, cross-validation MAE boxplots and line plots were analyzed to assess the stability and consistency of each model across folds.

The test dataset was used to compare model performance at the end.

4   Case Study

4.1   Data Collection and Methods

In this section, the data sources and methodologies employed are described, providing a comprehensive account of the research approach undertaken in the project.

The dataset used in this study was obtained from Grupo Actuarial and consists of 233,745 individual health insurance policies. To ensure confidentiality, all regional identifiers and specific insurance details were anonymized. Additionally, records containing missing, erroneous, or nonsensical values were excluded to maintain data integrity and ensure the dataset was suitable for analysis.

The dataset includes nine variables: Age Band, which categorizes individuals into different age groups, Gender, which specifies the policyholder's gender, Benefit Type, which defines the type of insurance coverage, and Region, which provides geographical context. Additionally, Exposure represents the time an individual has been at risk, Commercial Premium denotes the amount paid for the insurance policy, Sum Insured reflects the total coverage amount under the policy, Incurred Claims measures the total amount claimed by the policyholder, and Number of Claims indicates the count of claims filed.

To prepare the dataset for modeling, several preprocessing steps were applied. First, data cleaning was performed by removing records with missing or unrealistic values. Feature engineering was then carried out by creating two key variables: Claim Frequency, calculated as the number of claims divided by exposure, and Claim Severity, obtained by dividing incurred claims by exposure. Categorical variables were converted into numerical representations to facilitate machine learning applications, and normalization was applied to improve model convergence and performance, particularly for gradient boosting algorithms.

By implementing these preprocessing steps, the final dataset was optimized for developing and evaluating Generalized Linear Models (GLMs) and Machine Learning (ML) models in insurance pricing.

4.2   Exploratory Data Analysis Response Variables

In insurance pricing, response variables represent the key financial risks associated with policyholders. This study models claim frequency using the **Number of Claims** and claim severity using **Incurred Claims**. Both variables exhibit highly skewed distributions, which require specialized statistical models for accurate prediction.

Number of Claims (Frequency Model). is a discrete variable representing the count of claims reported per policyholder. The distribution is highly right-skewed, with most policyholders not submitting any claims during the observed period. The mean number of claims per policy is 0.0419, with a standard deviation of 0.4583, indicating a large disparity between policyholders. The minimum and first three quartiles (Q1, Q2, and Q3) are all zero, confirming that the vast majority of policyholders do not file claims. However, the maximum recorded number of claims is 53, highlighting the presence of a small subset of individuals who submit significantly more claims than the average.

The skewness of this variable is 32.61, indicating extreme asymmetry, while the kurtosis is 2238.62, suggesting a heavy-tailed distribution with significant outliers. This distribution pattern is typical for insurance claim data, where a small proportion of policyholders generate most of the claims. Given the high variance relative to the mean, a Poisson regression model may not be appropriate, as it assumes equality between mean and variance. Instead, the Negative Binomial model, which accommodates over-dispersion, provides a more suitable alternative.

Incurred Claims (Severity Model). represents the total monetary amount paid in claims per policyholder. Like the Number of Claims, this variable is also highly skewed, with a mean of 184.7 monetary units (m.u.) and a standard deviation of 787.9 m.u. The minimum, first quartile, and median values are all zero, reinforcing the observation that most policyholders do not incur claims. However, the maximum recorded claim reaches nearly 10,000 m.u., demonstrating the presence of extreme cases.

The analysis of percentiles reveals that 80% of policies have incurred claims equal to zero, while the 90th percentile reaches 296.1 m.u., and the top 1% of claims exceed 4,292.3 m.u. This confirms that a small fraction of policyholders accounts for a disproportionately large share of total claim costs. The skewness value of 6.67 and kurtosis of 56.61 further confirm that the distribution is heavily right-skewed with extreme values. Given these properties, standard Gaussian models are unsuitable, and severity is better modeled using the Gamma or Inverse Gaussian distributions, both of which are designed for strictly positive and right-skewed data.

Exposure (Offset Variable). represents the total duration of risk coverage per policyholder and serves as an offset variable in Generalized Linear Models (GLMs). This ensures that claim frequency estimates account for differences in policy duration, enabling fair comparisons across policyholders with varying coverage periods. The dataset reveals that 76.6% of policies have full-year exposure, meaning they were active for an entire 12-month period. A significant proportion, 20.2%, has an exposure of less than 0.2 years, reflecting policyholders who had coverage for a much shorter duration.

Adjusting for exposure is crucial, as policies with longer coverage periods are naturally more likely to generate claims than those with shorter durations. Incorporating exposure as an offset variable in GLMs ensures that claim frequencies are evaluated on a per-unit-time basis, preventing bias in the estimation of risk factors (Table 1).

Table 1. Summary of Response Variables

Variable	Type	Mean	Std. Dev.	Max	Distribution Considerations
Number of Claims	Discrete	0.0419	0.4583	53	Highly skewed, requires Poisson or Negative Binomial models.
Incurred Claims	Continuous	184.7 m.u.	787.9 m.u.	9999.6 m.u.	Heavy-tailed, modeled with Gamma or Inverse Gaussian.
Exposure	Offset	-	-	1 (full year)	Adjusts claim frequency for varying policy durations.

4.3 Exploratory Data Analysis Feature Variables and Bivariate Analysis

The feature variables in this dataset include Age Band, Gender, Benefit Type, and Region, each providing key insights into the characteristics of policyholders.

Age Band: This variable categorizes individuals into six age groups. The dataset is skewed towards younger individuals, with the "25 to 35" years category being the most populous, followed by the "36 to 45" years group. Older age bands have fewer individuals, especially those above 65 years.

Gender: There is a significant gender imbalance, with male policyholders almost doubling the number of female policyholders. This disparity should be considered when analyzing gender-specific trends.

Benefit Type: The majority of individuals have "INS. A" (69.44%) and "INS. B" (30.38%) benefits. Other benefit types have very few individuals, indicating a strong preference for these two insurance types.

Region: The dataset is predominantly concentrated in Region A, which has 53.66% of the individuals. Other regions, such as Region B and Region C, follow but with significantly fewer individuals. "Region F" has an almost negligible number of individuals.

In terms of **bivariate analysis**, it was conducted in order to identify relationships between variables, revealing trends that may have impact in claim frequency and severity and looking for possible variable interactions. For pricing models, understanding these dependencies is crucial for setting fair premiums, detecting risk patterns, and improving model accuracy. For example, analyzing the correlation between exposure and incurred claims can refine risk assessment, while relationships between sum insured and claims frequency help adjust pricing strategies effectively and also help avoiding multicollinearity that can complicate the interpretation of coefficients and destabilize the model.

The correlation matrix showed weak or negligible correlations between most variables, except for a strong positive correlation (0.40) between Incurred Claims and Number of Claims. This indicates that as the number of claims increases, the total amount incurred also rises, which aligns with expectations.

The analysis also highlighted that Commercial Premium had little correlation with both Incurred Claims and Number of Claims, suggesting that policyholders who pay higher premiums do not necessarily file more claims. Exposure exhibited a weak negative correlation with the number of claims, implying that individuals with longer coverage periods do not always report more claims (Table 2).

Table 2. Correlation Matrix of the Variables

	Exposure	Commercial Premium	Sum Insured	Incurred Claims	Number Claims
Exposure	1.0000	0.0110	0.0677	0.0108	−0.1103
Commercial Premium	-	1.0000	0.0709	0.0034	0.0016
Sum Insured	-	-	1.0000	0.0779	0.0591
Incurred Claims	-	-	-	1.0000	0.4025
Number Claims	-	-	-	-	1.0000

To confirm the significance of these relationships, a Pearson's Correlation Test was conducted. Most correlations were statistically significant, except for those involving Commercial Premium, reinforcing that some variables may contribute little to predictive modeling.

4.4 Modeling The Claim Frequency and Severity Finding the Most Parcimonious GLM Model

Claim Frequency: Link Function: Logarithm

$$
\begin{aligned}
\eta(\text{estimated}) = & -5.3200 \\
& + 0.3598 \cdot \text{Age\_Band25 to 35} + 0.7135 \cdot \text{Age\_Band36 to 45} \\
& + 0.9851 \cdot \text{Age\_Band46 to 55} + 3.9480 \cdot \text{Age\_Band56 to 65} \\
& + 5.3880 \cdot \text{Age\_BandAbove 65} - 0.0433 \cdot \text{GenderMale} \\
& + 2.1580 \cdot \text{Benefit\_TypeINS. B} + 2.1300 \cdot \text{Benefit\_TypeINS. C} \\
& - 29.8100 \cdot \text{Benefit\_TypeINS. E} - 0.0716 \cdot \text{Region B} + 1.2230 \cdot \text{Region C} \\
& + 0.1318 \cdot \text{Region D} + 0.6810 \cdot \text{Region E} - 28.8800 \cdot \text{Region F}
\end{aligned}
$$

Offset: Log of Exposure

The Negative Binomial GLM was identified as the optimal model for predicting claim frequency, selected through a comprehensive evaluation using AIC, BIC, deviance, and residual analysis. While the variable "Gender" was not statistically significant, as indicated by the Wald and ANOVA tests (p-value = 0.3425), it was retained in the model to ensure interpretability and relevance for business applications. Its inclusion did not substantially affect the model's parsimony, as the AIC and BIC values remained nearly identical with or without it.

The model analysis revealed a strong positive relationship between age and claim frequency, with individuals aged 56 to 65 filing approximately 52.93 times more claims than those in the 0 to 25 age group. This effect became even more pronounced for policyholders aged above 65, who exhibited a 216.55-fold increase in claims compared to the baseline. Gender differences were also examined, with females demonstrating a 5.8% higher claim frequency than males, although this effect was not statistically significant.

The type of insurance coverage was another crucial factor influencing claim frequency. Policies under INS. B and INS. C showed a substantial increase in claim frequency, estimated at 8.65 and 8.41 times higher, respectively, compared to INS. A. In contrast, INS. E exhibited a drastic decrease in claims, with a claim frequency nearly 29.81 times lower than the baseline. This extreme reduction suggests potential data anomalies or unique characteristics associated with this benefit type.

Regional variations were also evident in the model. Region C exhibited the most significant increase in claim frequency, approximately 3.40 times higher than Region A. Meanwhile, Region B and Region D displayed only moderate deviations. A particularly striking result was observed for Region F, where claim frequency decreased drastically, likely due to data sparsity or insufficient policy representation in this category.

These findings reinforce the significance of age, benefit type, and region as key rating factors in insurance pricing. The insights gained from this model support better risk segmentation and more accurate premium calculations, ensuring that insurers can refine their pricing strategies based on data-driven decision-making. Additionally, even though the variable "Gender" was not statistically significant, it was retained in the frequency model due to business interpretability and regulatory considerations. An ANOVA test confirmed that including "Gender" did not significantly improve model fit (p-value = 0.3425). Despite its lack of predictive power, gender was retained to align with business applications and industry standards.

Claim Severity: Link Function: Logarithm
   Estimated Model:

$$\eta(\text{estimated}) = 6.76541$$
$$+ 0.08226 \cdot \text{Region1 B} - 0.10544 \cdot \text{Region1 C}$$
$$+ 0.05213 \cdot \text{Region1 D} + 0.11703 \cdot \text{Region1 E}$$
$$+ 0.01820 \cdot \text{Age1 25 to 35} + 0.25587 \cdot \text{Age1 36 to 45}$$
$$+ 0.44167 \cdot \text{Age1 46 to 55} + 1.06005 \cdot \text{Age1 56 to 65}$$
$$+ 1.49170 \cdot \text{Age1 Above 65} + 0.49103 \cdot \text{BenType1 INS. B}$$
$$+ 0.63113 \cdot \text{BenType1 INS. C} - 0.47847 \cdot \text{BenType1 INS. E}$$
$$- 0.08005 \cdot \text{Gender1 Male}$$

Offset: Log of Exposure

To model claim severity, an Inverse Gaussian GLM with a log-link function was applied. The model incorporated key predictors such as age, region, benefit type, and gender, with log exposure included as an offset to adjust for varying policy durations.

The results showed that region, age, and benefit type significantly influenced claim severity. Policyholders from Region B had an 8.6% increase in expected claim amounts, whereas those in Region C had a 10% decrease, both statistically significant. Regions D and E showed modest increases of 5.3% and 12.4%, respectively.

Age had a strong effect on severity, with claim costs rising as age increased. Compared to the baseline group (ages 0–25), individuals aged 36–45 had 29.2% higher claim amounts, while those aged 46–55 and 56–65 had increases of 55.5% and 106%, respectively. The oldest policyholders (65+) exhibited the highest severity, with a 149% increase in incurred claims.

Benefit type was also a key driver of claim severity. INS. B and INS. C increased expected claim amounts by 63.4% and 88%, respectively, relative to the baseline (INS. A). Conversely, INS. E showed a 38.1% reduction, though this effect was not statistically significant.

These findings reinforce the importance of demographic and policy-related factors in determining claim severity, highlighting the value of GLMs in risk assessment and premium calculation.

4.5 Pure Premium Model Using GLM

As stated previously, the Pure Premium is calculated as the product of the Frequency and Severity models. Given that both models are in the form of a log-link function, the linear predictors can be added together. The final model for Pure Premium is obtained by taking the exponential of the combined linear predictors. for this project, using GLM models, the combined linear predictor for the Pure Premium is:

$$
\begin{aligned}
\eta_{\text{Pure Premium}} = {} & 1.44541 \\
& + 0.44206 \cdot \text{Age\_Band25 to 35} + 0.96937 \cdot \text{Age\_Band36 to 45} \\
& + 1.42677 \cdot \text{Age\_Band46 to 55} + 5.00805 \cdot \text{Age\_Band56 to 65} \\
& + 6.87970 \cdot \text{Age\_BandAbove 65} + 0.44773 \cdot \text{GenderMale} \\
& + 2.64903 \cdot \text{Benefit\_TypeINS. B} + 2.76113 \cdot \text{Benefit\_TypeINS. C} \\
& - 30.28847 \cdot \text{Benefit\_TypeINS. E} + 0.04543 \cdot \text{Region B} \\
& + 1.30526 \cdot \text{Region C} + 0.18393 \cdot \text{Region D} \\
& + 0.79803 \cdot \text{Region E} - 29.35847 \cdot \text{Region F}
\end{aligned}
$$

Finally, the Pure Premium model is given by:

$$
\text{Pure Premium} = \exp(\eta_{\text{Pure Premium}})
$$

4.6 Machine Learning Models for Frequency and Severity

The study explores the use of Machine Learning (ML) techniques alongside Generalized Linear Models (GLMs) to improve predictive accuracy in claim frequency modeling. Data preprocessing included renaming columns, converting categorical variables into factors, and creating "Frequency" and "Severity" variables to accommodate the absence of an offset in ML models. Normalization was applied to enhance model performance, and an 80-20 train-test split ensured robust evaluation. Due to insufficient observations, the "INS. D" category was excluded to prevent bias in cross-validation.

Four ML models—Decision Tree Regression, Random Forest, Gradient Boosting Machine (GBM), and XGBoost—were tested. Hyperparameter tuning played a crucial role in optimizing model performance. For Decision Trees, complexity was controlled to prevent overfitting. Random Forest tuning focused on the number of trees, depth, and minimum samples per split. GBM optimization involved tuning boosting iterations, learning rate, and tree depth to balance underfitting and overfitting. Similarly, XGBoost fine-tuned boosting rounds, tree depth, learning rate, and subsampling ratio to improve stability and generalization.

Overall, careful data preprocessing, feature engineering, and model-specific hyperparameter tuning contributed to robust model performance and better risk estimation in health insurance pricing.

Comparison of Model Performance During "training": Cross-Validation MAE for Different Frequency and Severity Models.

To deepen the model evaluation, analyzing graphics with, for example, the MAE values across folds recorded during cross-validation. These plots enable to examine not only overall performance but also variability across folds, giving a fuller view of model consistency. This analysis is essential because a model may perform well on average yet exhibit high variability across folds, which could suggest potential instability when applied to new data. By doing this, it is possible to assess the stability and consistency of the model.

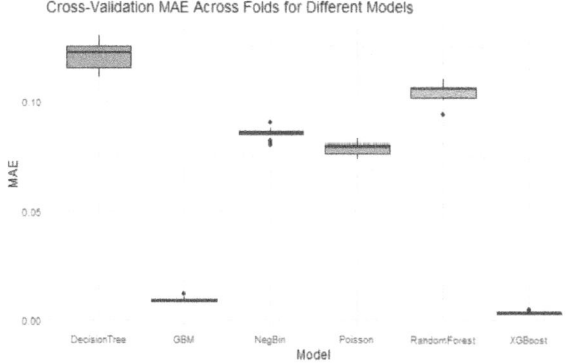

Fig. 1. Cross-Validation MAE Boxplot for the different Frequency Models.

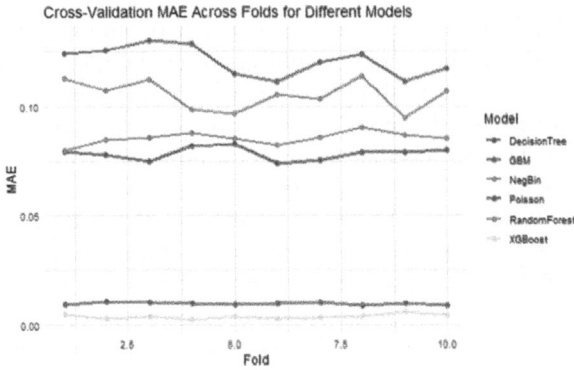

Fig. 2. Cross-Validation MAE Line plot for the different Frequency Models.

Figure 1 and Fig. 2 show that the Frequency Models using GBM and XGBoost have the lowest MAE, and are very consistent and stable across folds, indicating they perform better in terms of predictive accuracy compared to the other models. Decision Tree and Random Forest has the highest MAE, meaning it performs the worst among these models. The Negative Binomial and Poisson Models perform somewhere in between but not as well as GBM and XGBoost.

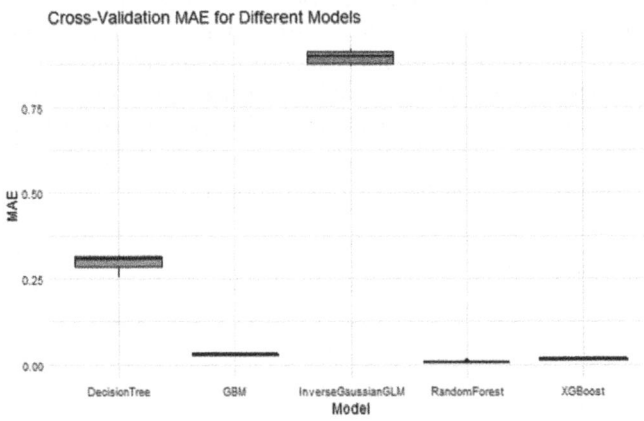

Fig. 3. Cross-Validation MAE Boxplot for the different Severity Models.

Figure 3 and Fig. 4 show that the severity Models using Random Forest, GBM and XGBoost have the lowest MAE, and are very consistent and stable across folds, indicating they perform better in terms of predictive accuracy compared to the other models. Decision Tree has the highest MAE, among the machine learning models, meaning it performs the worst among these models. The Inverse Gaussian model performs poorly when compared with the machine learning models.

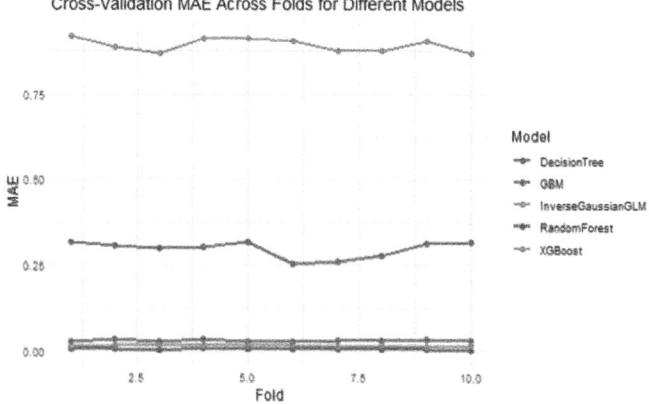

Fig. 4. Cross-Validation MAE Line plot for the different Severity Models.

Assessment of Model Accuracy in Test Phase

The performance of each model was evaluated using the Test Data. The Table 3 summarizes the results for each model, indicating the Mean Squared Error (MSE) and Mean Absolute Error (MAE) for the Frequency Models.

Table 3. Performance Metrics for Different Frequency Models

Model	MSE	MAE
Poisson GLM	0.2152	0.0798
Negative Binomial GLM	0.4716	0.0865
Decision Tree	0.2111	0.0717
Random Forest	0.2055	0.0700
GBM	0.1976	0.0626
XGBoost	0.1620	0.0493

Based on the metrics, is easy to notice that XGBoost has the lowest MSE (0.1620), and MAE (0.0493), making it the best performing model according to the metrics. GBM follows as the next best model with the second lowest MSE (0.1976), and MAE (0.0626). Random Forest and Decision Tree also perform relatively well but are outperformed by GBM and XGBoost. The Poisson GLM and Negative Binomial GLM models show higher error rates across all metrics, indicating lower performance compared to the other models. Among the models evaluated, XGBoost emerges as the best model due to its superior performance across all the considered metrics: MSE, RMSE, and MAE. Therefore, XGBoost is recommended as the optimal choice.

As for the Severity, the Table 4 summarizes the results for each model, indicating the Mean Squared Error (MSE) and Mean Absolute Error (MAE) for the Frequency Models.

Table 4. Performance Metrics for Different Severity Models

Model	MSE	MAE
Inverse Gaussian GLM	2.2340	1.3711
Decision Tree	0.3394	0.3143
Random Forest	0.0025	0.0044
GBM	0.0118	0.0275
XGBoost	0.0024	0.0150

Based on the metrics, Random Forest and XGBoost stand out as the best-performing models. The Random Forest Model has the second lowest MSE (0.0025) and the lowest MAE (0.0044). XGBoost follows closely with a slightly lower MSE (0.0024) and an MAE of 0.0150. GBM also performs well with an MSE of 0.0118 and an MAE of 0.0275. The Decision Tree shows moderate performance, while the Inverse Gaussian GLM has a substantially higher MSE (2.2340) and MAE (1.3711), indicating lower predictive accuracy compared to the machine learning models. Overall, Random Forest and XGBoost are the recommended models due to their superior performance in both MSE and MAE.

5   Conclusions

This study analyzed different pricing models for individual health insurance, comparing Generalized Linear Models (GLMs) with Machine Learning (ML) techniques to improve premium estimation accuracy. While GLMs remain widely used due to their interpretability, results show that ML models, particularly Random Forest, GBM, and XGBoost, provide higher predictive accuracy for claim frequency and severity modeling.

By integrating ML into insurance pricing, insurers can better align premiums with underlying risks, ensuring a fairer pricing structure that benefits both insurance companies and policyholders. The improved predictive performance of ML models also enhances financial stability and competitive positioning in an evolving market.

A major challenge was the availability of high-quality data, highlighting the need for stronger collaborations with companies to obtain richer datasets while reducing noise and outliers.

This research emphasizes the importance of continuous innovation in actuarial science. As insurance risks and regulatory requirements evolve, pricing methodologies must adapt to ensure accuracy and fairness. The findings lay the groundwork for future advancements in the use of ML for insurance pricing, reinforcing its practical applications and industry adoption.

6   Future Work

This study highlights several directions for future research in insurance pricing models. While Generalized Linear Models (GLMs) and Machine Learning (ML) techniques (Decision Trees, Random Forest, GBM, and XGBoost) were analyzed, further advancements can be made by incorporating neural networks and deep learning methods. These models may improve predictive accuracy but pose challenges in terms of interpretability, which is critical for regulatory compliance in insurance.

Future research should focus on enhancing model explainability while maintaining high predictive power. Methods such as permutation feature importance and partial dependence plots (PDPs) can provide deeper insights into model behavior, improving transparency in decision-making. These techniques can help identify key risk factors, making ML models more interpretable and applicable in real-world insurance pricing.

Another promising avenue is hybrid modeling approaches [10], which integrate GLMs with ML models to balance accuracy and interpretability. The combination of actuarial expertise with modern ML tools could refine risk assessment methodologies, ensuring robust, fair, and transparent pricing structures.

Additionally, the methodologies developed in this study can be extended beyond individual health insurance to other sectors, such as life, automobile, and property insurance. Each insurance line presents unique risk factors, creating opportunities for further optimization and adaptation of ML-based pricing models.

By addressing these challenges, future research can drive the evolution of insurance pricing strategies, enhancing both predictive performance and regulatory transparency while expanding ML applications in actuarial science.

Acknowledgements. I would like to express my sincere gratitude to Doutora A. Manuela Gonçalves for the invaluable support and mentorship throughout the course of this research. Lastly, I would like to express my heartfelt gratitude to my family, friends and colleagues for all the support and encouragement shown throughout my academic journey. Their belief in my abilities has been a constant source of motivation, and I am truly grateful for their enduring support. A. Manuela Gonçalves was partially financed by Portuguese Funds through FCT (Fundação para a Ciência e a Tecnologia) within the Project UID/00013: Centro de Matemática da Universidade do Minho (CMAT/UM).

References

1. Breiman, L.: Random forests. Mach. Learn. **45**(1), 5–32 (2001)
2. Chen, T., Guestrin, C.: XGBoost: a scalable tree boosting system. In: Proceedings of the 22nd ACM SIGKDD International Conference on Knowledge Discovery and Data Mining, pp. 785–794 (2016)
3. Ferrario, A., Candelieri, A., Archetti, F.: Integrating neural networks and generalized linear models to predict health insurance claims. Artif. Intell. Med. **107**, 101877 (2020)

4. Frees, E.W., Valdez, E.A.: Hierarchical insurance claims modeling. J. Am. Stat. Assoc. **103**(484), 1457–1469 (2008)
5. Friedman, J.H.: Greedy function approximation: a gradient boosting machine. Ann. Stat. **29**(5), 1189–1232 (2001)
6. Haberman, S., Renshaw, A. E.: Generalized Linear Models and Actuarial Science. J. Royal Stat. Soc. Ser. D Stat. **45**(4), 407 (1996)
7. Hastie, T., Tibshirani, R., Friedman, J.: The Elements of Statistical Learning: Data Mining, Inference, and Prediction. 2nd edn. Springer (2009). https://doi.org/10.1007/978-0-387-84858-7
8. Henckaerts, R., Antonio, K., Clijsters, M., Verbelen, R.: A data science perspective on predicting insurance claims using generalized linear models. Insurance Math. Econ. **100**, 402–418 (2021)
9. Kohavi, R.: A study of cross-validation and bootstrap for accuracy estimation and model selection. In: International Joint Conference on Artificial Intelligence (IJCAI), pp. 1137–1145 (1995)
10. Kuo, Y.-C., Yao, C.-C.: Hybrid modeling approach in insurance pricing: combining GLMs with machine learning. J. Risk Finan. Manage. **15**(2), 95 (2022). https://doi.org/10.3390/jrfm15020095
11. Nelder, J.A., Wedderburn, R.: Generalized linear models. J. Royal Stat. Soc. Ser. A (General) **135**(3), 370–384 (1972)
12. De Jong, P., Heller, G. Z.: Generalized Linear Models for Insurance Data. Cambridge University Press (2008)
13. Spedicato, G., Dutang, C., Petrini, L.: Machine learning methods to perform pricing optimization: a comparison with standard generalized linear models. Casualty Actuarial Soc. (2023)
14. Olhede, S.C., Wolfe, P.J.: The growing ubiquity of algorithms in society: implications, impacts, and innovations. Proc. Natl. Acad. Sci. **115**(50), 12516–12523 (2018)
15. Wüthrich, M. V., Buser, C.: Tree-based machine learning methods in actuarial science. Scandinavian Actuarial J., 159–179 (2021)
16. Yang, J., Zhang, Y., Zhou, X.: Direct modeling of total loss using gradient boosting and Tweedie distribution. Ann. Actuarial Sci. **12**(1), 73–91 (2018)

Revisiting the Fail-Safe Number in Meta-analysis: Insights from a Simulation Study

Vera Afreixo[1]([✉]) [iD], Vanusa Rocha[1] [iD], Filipa Rocha[1] [iD], and Miguel Felgueiras[1,2] [iD]

[1] Center for Research and Development in Mathematics and Applications (CIDMA), Department of Mathematics, University of Aveiro, 3810-193 Aveiro, Portugal
{vera,vanusa,filipasarreira}@ua.pt, mfelg@ipleiria.pt
[2] ESTG, Polytechnic Institute of Leiria and CEAUL – Centro de Estatística e Aplicações, Universidade de Lisboa, Lisbon, Portugal

Abstract. Publication bias remains a major challenge in meta-analysis, posing a significant threat to the validity of synthesized evidence. The fail-safe number (FSN) is commonly employed to assess the robustness of meta-analytic findings by estimating the number of unpublished studies with null or opposing results needed to nullify an observed effect, that is, to shift a statistically significant result to a nonsignificant one. However, the performance capacity of different FSN estimators may vary across meta-analytic conditions, potentially raising concerns about their reliability and interpretability.

This study presents a simulation-based evaluation of the most commonly used FSN estimators: the Rosenthal FSN and the Rosenberg FSN and several modifications. We examine their performance availability by analyzing their behavior under controlled scenarios with null, weak, and moderate true effects within selective pressure. As a case study, we focus on the standardized mean difference using Cohen's d as the effect size measure. Additionally, we explore the usability of these methods, discussing their strengths and limitations in meta-analytic applications. The validity and applicability of commonly used rules of thumb for interpreting FSN values are also assessed.

Our findings provide a clearer understanding of when and how these FSN estimators yield meaningful insights, offering guidance about their appropriate use in evaluating the robustness of meta-analyses.

Keywords: Fail-safe number · Meta-analysis · Simulation · Performance · Standardized Mean Difference · Cohen's d

1 Introduction

A systematic literature review identifies, selects, and critically appraises research to answer a formulated question [1]. An important step in a systematic review is to carefully analyze whether it is suitable to combine the numerical findings of the studies [2]. Meta-analysis is a study design used to systematically evaluate previous research studies to

© The Author(s), under exclusive license to Springer Nature Switzerland AG 2026
O. Gervasi et al. (Eds.): ICCSA 2025 Workshops, LNCS 15887, pp. 365–376, 2026.
https://doi.org/10.1007/978-3-031-97589-9_25

derive conclusions [3]. By doing a meta-analysis, a single overall estimate statistic can be obtained to determine whether an effect exists or to determine whether the effect is positive or negative [2, 3].

Although systematic reviews and meta-analyses are invaluable for synthesizing available evidence, they are susceptible to multiple forms of bias [4].

Publication bias arises when the possibility of a study being published is not independent of its results, which prevents the production of valid evidence. One type of this bias is selective reporting, defined as reporting results from only a selection of studies. It refers to the tendency only to publish studies with positive results or statistically significant findings [5], suggesting that studies with a p-value > 0.05 (the more commonly used significance level) may not get published. It can be caused by factors such as rejection by editors or reviewers, lack of interest in revising the study, competing interests, or simply a lack of motivation to write up the study [6].

When publication bias is present, the estimated average effect sizes obtained in meta-analysis tend to be inflated to an unknown and potentially significant extent. Additionally, this bias can skew the evidence favoring the dominant theory [7].

Several techniques can be used for evaluating the possibility of publication bias and its impact. To conduct these types of analyses, it is recommended to have a reasonable number of studies (minimum of 10), at least one study with a significant effect and relevant heterogeneity should be avoided [8].

The fail-safe number (FSN) is a procedure that allows the impact of potential publication bias to be partially discussed by answering the question, "How many studies would it take to 'nullify' the combined effect". It only applies to meta-analyses that lead to combined effects with a p-value < 0.05 or confidence intervals that do not contain the value that translates the null effect size. This procedure can be used as a sensitivity analysis of meta-analytical results to include studies with effects that somehow compensate for potential publication bias [9].

There are different ways of calculating FSN. In practice, authors propose calculating the number of additional studies with a nonsignificant effect (null/negative effects) that modifies the meta-analytical response. This procedure is limited as it does not allow the meta-analytical effect to be adjusted for potential publication bias or to measure this effect [9].

1.1 Rosenthal's FSN

Rosenthal's method discusses if the meta-analytical effect is robustly significant, assuming that a positive and significant meta-analytical overall effect is estimated [10].

Rosenthal's FSN considers the null hypothesis.

$H_0 : \theta_1 = \theta_2 = \cdots = \theta_k = 0,$

and the test statistic,

$$Z_i = \frac{T_i}{\sqrt{v_i}} \sim N(0,1) \Rightarrow \frac{\sum Z_i}{\sqrt{k}} \sim N(0,1), \tag{1}$$

with T_i the effect size obtained from study i ($i = 1, \ldots, k$ and k the number of studies in the meta-analysis) and $\sqrt{v_i}$ the corresponding standard error.

Assuming that there are N_α additional studies with null effect that were not considered, then the previous test statistic has the following formulation,

$$\frac{\sum Z_i}{\sqrt{k + N_\alpha}} \sim N(0,1), \tag{2}$$

with $i = 1, \ldots, k$. To find the minimum number of null effect studies to change the significant effect into a non-significant, solve the following equation in order to N_α

$$\frac{\sum Z_i}{\sqrt{k + N_\alpha}} = z_{1-\alpha} \tag{3}$$

with $z_{1-\alpha}$ the quantile of order $1 - \alpha$ of the standard normal distribution. The solution of the previous equation is Rosenthal's FSN (**Rt**),

$$N_\alpha = \left[\frac{\sum Z_i}{z_\alpha}\right]^2 - k \tag{4}$$

Rosenthal proposed a cut-off value (one rule of thumb), $5k + 10$, to determine the robustness of a meta-analysis result. A smaller N_α may indicate that the effect being analyzed might not be robustly significant. A larger N_α suggests the effect is significant.

1.2 Rosenthal's FSN Based on Counting

Rosenthal also proposed an alternative procedure, described as "probably less powerful," which estimates the FSN by considering the number of studies with statistically significant results (n_s) and those with non-significant results ($n_{ns} = k - n_s$) [10]. This approach assumes that, under the normal assumption and the null effect hypothesis, the proportion of significant results vs the non-significant results ratio is known. Figure 1 presents a graphical illustration of both proportions, given the alpha level (α) and considering the effect size distribution. If the number of true non significative studies is $N_\alpha + n_{ns}$, the number of observed non significative studies is ns and the number of significative studies is s the following equality is obtained,

$$\frac{N_\alpha + n_{ns}}{n_s} = \frac{1 - \alpha}{\alpha} \tag{5}$$

Then, Rosenthal's FSN based on counting is then estimated using the formula (**Rtc**):

$$N_\alpha = n_s \frac{1 - \alpha}{\alpha} - n_{ns} = \frac{n_s}{\alpha} - k \tag{6}$$

1.3 Rosenthal's FSN Modification

Rosenthal's proposal reinforces that the missing studies observe null effect values, which may be an inappropriate assumption. With the same type of approach, Iyengar and

Normal curve

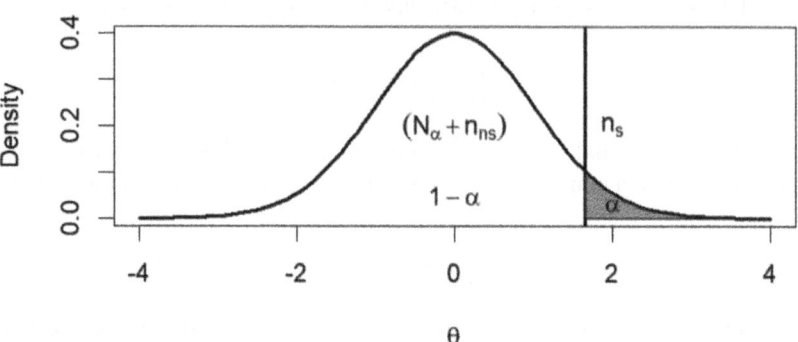

Fig. 1. Graphical illustration of the proportion of significant vs non-significant results, under the null effect hypothesis, for α significance level.

Greenhouse proposed an alternative FSN (N_α), here denominated by Rosenthal's FSN modified (**Rtm**)

$$\frac{\sum Z_i + N_\alpha M_\alpha}{\sqrt{k + N_\alpha}} = z_{1-\alpha} \tag{7}$$

where the statistics from additional studies are not considered null but the mean value of the standard normal distribution truncated at $z_{1-\alpha}$ [11]. Recall that the density function of the standard normal distribution truncated at $z_{1-\alpha}$ is given by

$$f(x) = \begin{cases} \frac{\phi(x)}{\Phi(z_{1-\alpha})}, x \leq z_{1-\alpha} \\ 0, x > z_{1-\alpha} \end{cases} \tag{8}$$

with ϕ as the standard normal density function and Φ as the standard normal distribution function, and the corresponding mean value is given by

$$M_\alpha = E[X] = \int_{-\infty}^{+\infty} xf(x) = -\frac{\phi(z_{1-\alpha})}{\Phi(z_{1-\alpha})} = -\frac{\phi(z_{1-\alpha})}{1-\alpha}. \tag{9}$$

In practice, N_α is computed as the smallest non-negative integer that satisfies the condition $\frac{\sum Z_i + N_\alpha M_\alpha}{\sqrt{k + N_\alpha}} \leq z_{1-\alpha}$,

$$N_\alpha = argmin\{N \in \mathbb{N}_0 \mid \frac{\sum Z_i + N_\alpha M_\alpha}{\sqrt{k + N_\alpha}} \leq z_{1-\alpha}\} \tag{10}$$

1.4 Rosenberg's FSN

Rosenberg's FSN is similar to Rosenthal's FSN with differences in the test statistic [12]. In Rosenberg's FSN approach, test statistic's uses the overall meta-analytic estimate,

$\hat{\theta} = \frac{\sum_{i=1}^{k}\left(w_i \times \hat{\theta}_i\right)}{\sum_{i=1}^{k} w_i}$, considering the individual studies weights (w_i), and considers the global null hypothesis $H_0 : \theta = 0$. The test statistic for Rosenberg's FSN is

$$\hat{\theta}/SE \sim N(0,1), \tag{11}$$

with $SE^2 = \frac{1}{\sum_{i=1}^{k} w_i}$.

Let us consider that additional null-effect studies are missing. These studies are capable of reducing the value of the test statistic to the critical value and their weight assumes the average value of the studies published. Therefore, the FSN can be obtained from:

$$z_{1-\alpha}^2 = \frac{\left(\sum_{i=1}^{k}\left(w_i \times \hat{\theta}_i\right)\right)^2}{N_\alpha \frac{\sum_{i=1}^{k} w_i}{k} + \sum_{i=1}^{k} w_i} \tag{12}$$

Explicitly, N_α is given by the following equation:

$$N_\alpha = \frac{\left(\sum_{i=1}^{k}\left(w_i \times \hat{\theta}_i\right)\right)^2}{\sum_{i=1}^{k} w_i} - k. \tag{13}$$

2 Methods

In this section we present a simulation procedure where the new functions were implemented in RStudio (2022.07.1 + 554) using R (version 4.2.2). Several meta-analytic scenarios were simulated and the different FSN were computed. Rosenthal's FSN and Rosenberg's FSN were implemented in *metafor* package through the fsn function. The functions to calculate the modified Rosenthal's FSN and Rosenthal's FSN based on counting were programed. Association between several features of meta-analytic studies (heterogeneity level, I^2, number of studies, effect size strangeness) and the FSN levels were explored graphically.

2.1 Simulation Procedure

Different conditions were implemented for each meta-analysis study. Table 1 summarizes these conditions.

Standard Deviation Between Studies
To generate the set of effect sizes to each meta-analytic study we randomly generated n values from a normal distribution with a fixed mean from the set $\{0, 0.1, 0.2, 0.5\}$ and one fixed standard deviation from the set $\{0.05, 0.1, 0.2, 0.5\}$. This simulation allows for the evaluation of scenarios with null, weak, and moderate effect sizes.

Standard Error of Each Individual Effect Size (Sample Unity of Each Meta-analysis)

For each individual meta-analytic study, we generated for each effect size one corresponding standard error. The standard error (SE) was generated assuming the effect size under analysis is a Cohen's d (d) for the mean difference of two independent sample, which is obtained by

$$SE = \sqrt{\frac{1}{n_1} + \frac{1}{n_2} + \frac{d^2}{2(n_1 + n_2)}} \tag{14}$$

With n_1 and n_2 the samples sizes of each group from one fixed study. Values n_1 and n_2 are randomly generated from 20 to 200.

Other Simulation Parameters

Each different scenario was simulated 100 times, with the number of studies per meta-analysis ranging from 15 to 60. When the number of studies with null or weak effect sizes was lower than 15, the meta-analytic overall effect in high number of scenarios was non-significant; therefore, these results are not presented.

After the data generation procedure, three scenarios of selective pressure (publication bias) were considered:

- without selective pressure - a control scenario;
- total pressure through the non-significative studies; in this case some meta-analytic scenarios are null meta-analytic scenarios (scenarios without studies);
- partial pressure through the non-significative studies; 1/3 of studies without positive results and p-values > 0.05 were deleted (1/3 of studies with highest p-values).

Table 1. Different conditions for each simulation/meta-analysis unit.

Simulation runs	100
Number of studies by each meta-analysis study (n)	15, 30, and 60
Effect size (ES)	0, 0.1, 0.2, and 0.5
Standard deviation between studies	0.05, 0.1, 0.2, and 0.5
Proportion of deleted studies whose p-values > 0.05	0, until 1/3, and until 1
Standard error of each study - Eq. (11), n_1 and n_2	Integer between 20 and 200

Table 2 synthesizes the values that were extracted from the simulation that was carried out. For each simulation we perform a meta-analysis, and the overall effect was estimated (effect size and corresponding confidence interval) with heterogeneity estimated by I^2 index. When the overall effect was significant the fail-safe numbers under analysis were extracted. The number of studies eliminated by pressure selection through non-significative studies was also registered (number of deleted studies).

We also count in each simulation scenario the number of meta-analytic studies with non-significant overall effect size or null meta-analytic scenarios. Since FSNs can only be

Table 2. Extracted results.

Classic methods	Rosenthal's FSN (**Rt**) Rosenberg's FSN (**Rb**)
Method based on counting	Rosenthal's FSN counting (**Rtc**)
Methods with modification from Iyengar & Greenhouse 1988	Rosenthal's FSN modified (**Rtm**)
Other results	Number of deleted studies Heterogeneity I-squared (I^2) Overall ES and CI

calculated in meta-analyses with a significant overall effect, it is important to determine in how many simulation scenarios the FSNs calculation was applied.

2.2 Performance Evaluation

To evaluate the performance of each FSN approach, the Root Mean Square Error (RMSE) was used to measure the difference between the number of deleted studies and the estimated value by the FSNs. So, the bias of FSN estimators was quantified using the square root of the mean squared error.

The cut-off criteria, proposed by Rosenthal, for determining the robustness of meta-analytic findings were examined under described scenarios.

The distribution of FSN values was analyzed, considering variations in the number of studies and different levels of selective pressure. For each selective pressure condition, key metrics were reported, including the number of true eliminated studies, the median FSN values, the proportion of meta-analyses yielding a p-value below 0.05 and the number of cases where FSN met or exceeded the true number of true removed studies.

To provide a straightforward guideline for interpreting the robustness of null hypothesis rejection in meta-analysis, several cut-off rules were evaluated, offering insights into their applicability across different scenarios.

3 Results

Figure 2 shows that the different FSNs present similar patterns even with different levels of selective pressure and different numbers of studies involved in each meta-analysis/simulation unit. We can observe greater dispersion and higher median values for the FSNs without modification (classical methods, **Rt** and **Rb**). Even though there isn't much difference in the patterns of the different FSNs, there are differences in the scales depending on the number of studies per meta-analysis ($n = 15$, $n = 30$, and $n = 60$). As expected, more studies under meta-analysis imply a higher FSN.

The following results set the scenario in which all unities of the simulation have 60 initial studies, where it is expected more stability of the meta-analytic results.

According to the expected, Table 3 reveals that with larger effect sizes, there is an increase in the number of studies that are needed to 'nullify' it. For the true null effect

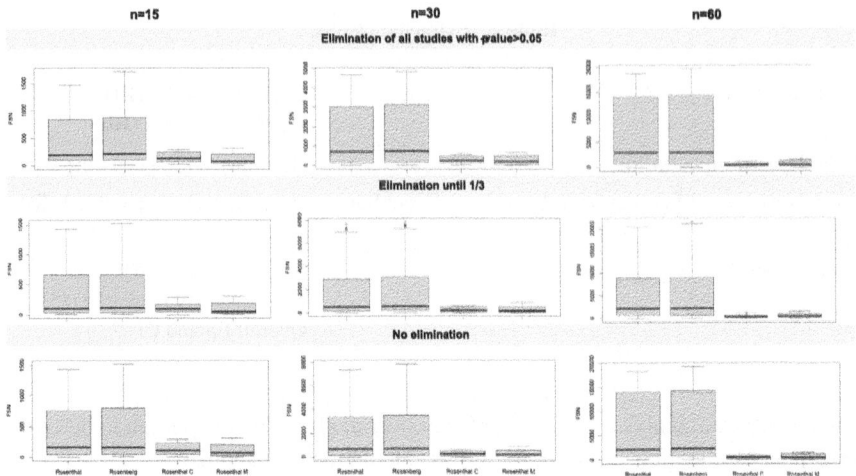

Fig. 2. Distribution of the four different FSNs considering the number of included studies in each meta-analysis ($n = 15$, $n = 30$, and $n = 60$) and different selective pressures (deleting all studies with p-values >0.05, deleting up to 1/3 of studies with p-values >0.05 and no deletion of studies).

sizes (ES = 0), the **Rt**, **Rtc** and **Rb** generate values that are higher than the modified FSNs under analysis (**Rtm**), which is one limitation of classic procedures.

Regarding the scenario where all studies with p-values >0.05 are deleted, only nine meta-analyses presented p-values <0.05 and included an average of nine studies per meta-analysis. The scenario without the elimination of studies represents a control scenario. Therefore, it is natural that when the effect is null, the combined effect of the meta-analyses tends to be null, and when the overall effect is not significant the calculation of FSNs is not suitable to be applied. However, for $n = 15$ (low true meta-analysis samples sizes) the control scenario reveals for ES = 0, 37 meta-analyses with positive results and p-values <0.05 with FSNs given by **Rt** = 4, **Rb** = 12, **Rtc** = 25 and **Rtm** = 3, showing better results the classic and the modified Rosenthal FSNs. A low FSN suggests that minimal effort is required to nullify the effect, implying that the overall significance is weak or not robust.

Because of the elimination of huge simulation unities in these two previous scenarios, we suggest exploring the results of simulation studies with a selective pressure through studies with non-positive effect size and p-values >0.05 up to 33.3%.

To discuss the bias of the FSNs under analysis, meta-analyses with 60 studies and selective pressure up to 33.3% were considered. Table 4 describes the square root of the mean squared error for each FSN and the percentage of times each FSN was equal or higher than the number of deleted studies, regarding the different effect sizes. The classic FSNs (**Rt** and **Rb**) present higher error values than the other FSNs under analysis (**Rtc** and **Rtm**). As expected, the larger the effect sizes, the greater the error.

For ES = 0, all the FSNs under analysis reveal a high percentage of results (more than 80%) where the FSN is higher than the number of studies that were eliminated (maximum selective pressure of 33.3% on studies with p-values < 0.05).

Table 3. Description of the median number of studies eliminated, the median of the FSNs, and the number of meta-analyses with positive results and p-value <0.05 with different selective pressures for simulation scenarios with 60 initial studies.

n = 60						
Elimination of **all** studies without positive results and without p-values < 0.05	Medians					
	No. of deleted studies	**Rt**	**Rb**	**Rtc**	**Rtm**	No. of meta-analyses with positive results and p-values < 0.05
ES = 0	51	8	45	120	4	9
ES = 0.1	47	581	575	200	160	301
ES = 0.2	35	2915	2974	440	476	400
ES = 0.5	4	14930	15447	1060	1297	400
Elimination of studies without positive results and without p-values < 0.05 until 1/3	Medians					
	No. of deleted studies	**Rt**	**Rb**	**Rtc**	**Rtm**	No. of meta-analyses with positive results and p-values < 0.05
ES = 0	18	268	305	98	92	244
ES = 0.1	17	710	733	117	187	400
ES = 0.2	13	2126	2188	373	390	400
ES = 0.5	1,5	15726	16230	1062	1338	400
No deletion of studies	Medians					
	No. of deleted studies	**Rt**	**Rb**	**Rtc**	**Rtm**	No. of meta-analyses with positive results and p-values < 0.05
ES = 0	-	.	.	.	-	0
ES = 0.1	0	599	641	100	163	400
ES = 0.2	0	2054	2214	360	380	400
ES = 0.5	0	15144	15682	1060	1308	400

Table 5 describes the obtained results regarding the possible establishment of cut-off rules (rule of thumb) in FSN to evaluate the robustness of the significance of the overall meta-analytic effect detected. In these results we kept the scenario with 60 studies and selective pressure up to 33.3%. Firstly, we present the results for the rule proposed by Rosenthal [10]. When ES = 0, we observe that the classical FSNs (Rt and Rb) point to over 50% of meta-analyses with robustness in rejecting the null effect, whereas ideally, all studies with ES = 0 should have FSN values of 5k + 10 or lower. The 5k + 10 cutoff rule was expected to work well for the Rosenthal´s FSN (Rt) because it was created for this procedure. We observe that it is unsuitable in the null effect scenario, but it seems

Table 4. The square root of the mean squared error for each FSN regarding the different effect sizes and the percentage of times each FSN was equal or superior to the number of deleted studies (n = 60).

Square root of the mean squared error				
	Rt	Rb	Rtc	Rtm
ES = 0	462	556	165	116
ES = 0.1	2551	2627	255	356
ES = 0.2	2658	2771	363	425
ES = 0.5	15600	16098	1009	1325
FSN > = No. of deleted studies				
ES = 0	86%	96%	82%	82%
ES = 0.1	100%	100%	77%	100%
ES = 0.2	100%	100%	100%	100%
ES = 0.5	100%	100%	100%	100%

adequate for the modified positive effect sizes. Additionally, for the modified Rosenthal's FSN, in a global way, the 5k + 10 cutoff works well.

Table 5. Evaluation of two decision rules for the FSNs (n = 60 and selective pressure up to 33.3%).

Rosenthal's FSN evaluation/decision rule	FSN > 5k + 10			
	Rt	Rb	Rtc	Rtm
ES = 0	66%	70%	34%	0%
ES = 0.1	100%	100%	26%	25%
ES = 0.2	100%	100%	91%	100%
ES = 0.5	100%	100%	100%	100%

It is observed that **Rt**, **Rb** and **Rtm** procedures exhibit an increasing trend as the standard deviation between studies (and heterogeneity) increases (see for example Fig. 3 the results for **Rtm**).

4 Discussion and Conclusions

This study conducted a detailed simulation-based comparison of four FSN estimators—Rosenthal's original estimator (**Rt**), Rosenberg's estimator (**Rb**), a counting-based variant (**Rtc**), and a modified version of Rosenthal's estimator incorporating the Iyengar & Greenhouse correction (**Rtm**). By systematically removing studies with non-significant

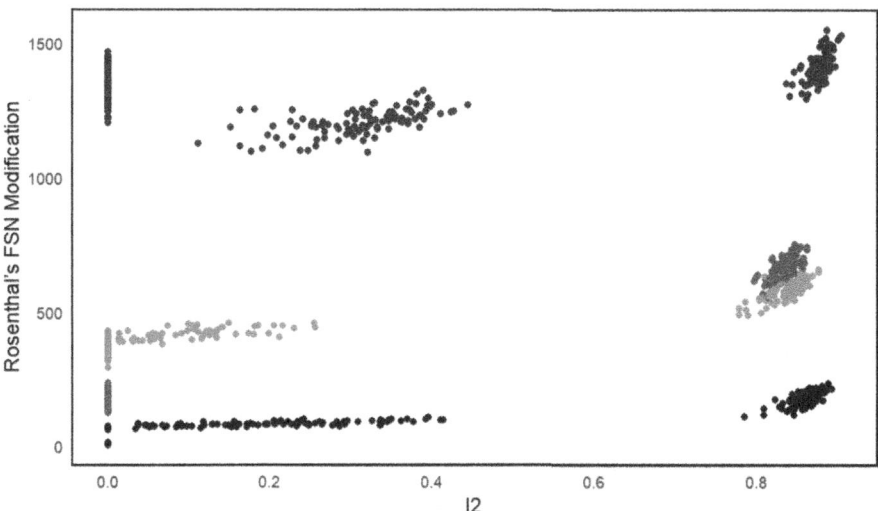

Fig. 3. Scatter plot Rosenthal's FSN Modification (**Rtm**) vs I^2 heterogeneity measure, with different sizes represented by different colors (n = 60 and selective pressure up to 33.3%).

results (p > 0.05), we explored how selective reporting and effect size strength influence FSN estimates.

Our findings suggest that **Rtm** consistently offers more reliable and conservative estimates under varying conditions. Specifically, it produces lower FSNs in the presence of true null effects, reflecting higher sensitivity to the absence of a real effect and reduced risk of false robustness. When compared with classical estimators, **Rtm** showed smaller errors across different effect size magnitudes and levels of selective pressure.

In conclusion, these results highlight that **Rtm** should be preferred when there is concern about publication bias or small effect sizes. In particular, researchers should interpret low FSNs (especially under **Rtm**) as indicators of fragility in the evidence and consider them alongside other bias-detection tools. The overestimation observed with **Rt** in null scenarios underscores the risk of relying solely on classical thresholds such as Rosenthal's "5k + 10" rule, which may give a false sense of confidence.

This work provides a practical guide for meta-analysts choosing between FSN estimators and evaluating the robustness of their results. Future research could extend these findings by integrating FSN estimation into more complex bias-adjustment frameworks or by validating them on empirical datasets with known levels of publication bias. Another promising direction is the development of FSN approaches that adapt to heterogeneity or use Bayesian priors to better model uncertainty in missing studies.

To sum up, while all FSNs offer insight into meta-analytic robustness, the **Rtm** estimator appears better suited to detecting fragility and mitigating bias in realistic scenarios.

Acknowledgments. This work is partially supported by Portuguese funds through CIDMA, The Center for Research and Development in Mathematics and Applications of University of Aveiro, and the Portuguese Foundation for Science and Technology (FCT – Fundação para a Ciência e a Tecnologia), within project UIDB/04106/2020 (https://doi.org/10.54499/UIDB/04106/2020), project UIDP/04106/2020 (Thematic Line BIOMATH) (https://doi.org/10.54499/UIDP/04106/2020), project PALOP/BD/155077/2024 and under the projects UID/00006/2025 and UIDB/00006/2020. https://doi.org/10.54499/UIDB/00006/2020.

Disclosure of Interests. The authors have no competing interests to declare that are relevant to the content of this article.

References

1. Literature Review: Systematic literature reviews. https://libguides.csu.edu.au/review/Systematic. Accessed 28 April 2025
2. Cochrane Handbook for Systematic Reviews of Interventions version 6.4 (updated August 2023). https://training.cochrane.org/handbook. Accessed 28 Apr 2025
3. Haidich, A.: Meta-analysis in medical research. Hippocratic **14**(Suppl 1), 29–37 (2010)
4. Drucker, A.: Research techniques made simple: assessing risk of bias in systematic reviews. J. Investig. Dermatol. **136**(11), e109–e114 (2016)
5. DeVito, N.: Catalogue of bias: publication bias. BMJ Evidence-Based Med. **24**(2), 53–54 (2019)
6. Mlinarić, A.: Dealing with the positive publication bias: why you should really publish your negative results. Biochem. Med. (Zagreb) **27**(3), 030201 (2017)
7. Ropovik, I.: Neglect of publication bias compromises meta-analyses of educational research. PLoS ONE **16**(6), e0252415 (2021)
8. Dalton, J.: Publication bias: the elephant in the review. Anesth. Analg. **123**(4), 812–813 (2016)
9. A brief history of the Fail-Safe Number in Applied Research. https://arxiv.org/abs/1010.2326. Accessed 28 Apr 2025
10. Rosenthal, R.: The "file drawer problem" and tolerance for null results. Psychol. Bull. **86**(3), 638–641 (1979)
11. Iyengar, S.: Selection models and the file drawer problem. Stat. Sci. 109–117 (1988)
12. Rosenberg, M.: The file-drawer problem revisited: a general weighted method for calculating fail-safe numbers in meta-analysis. Evolution **59**(2), 464–468 (2005)

Investigating Student Retention in an Economics Degree Programme

Francesca Pierri[1]([✉])[iD] and Chrys Caroni[2][iD]

[1] Department of Economics, University of Perugia, Perugia, Italy
`francesca.pierri@unipg.it`
[2] Department of Mathematics, National Technical University of Athens, Athens, Greece
`ccar@math.ntua.gr`

Abstract. For financial and reputational reasons, every university and degree course is committed to the goal of increasing the number of enrollments and improving indicators of students' success, including decreasing the time taken by students to obtain their degree and reducing the incidence of dropping out. High rates of dropping out from university courses and excessive time to graduation are matters of great practical importance, with substantial financial and social costs. Student retention or dropout depends on a combination of various factors, the influence of which is mediated by the student's ability to integrate into the academic system. The identification of those factors which may affect the outcome and upon which the academic system can act, is an object of extensive study and research.

In order to examine this topic, we collected data at the University of Perugia at the time of initial registration for three bachelor degrees in Economics. The 2015 cohort of students was tracked up to 2025, a period substantially exceeding the nominal duration of their degree courses, allowing the determination of each student's current status at the time of data extraction.

Applying binary and multinomial logistic regression, survival analysis and competing risks (graduation and dropout) analysis, we explore which factors influence the students' performance and highlight pros and cons of the applied statistical methodologies in this context.

Keywords: university dropout · student retention · logistic regression · survival analysis · competing risks

1 Introduction

One of the primary challenges faced by universities in the last decade is to increase the number of students enrolled annually and the expansion of the provision of university training through the opening of new courses has surely encouraged this growth. Concurrently, universities are busy enhancing their support to reduce the extent of the phenomenon of dropout, and improve and accelerate

O. Gervasi et al. (Eds.): ICCSA 2025 Workshops, LNCS 15887, pp. 377–392, 2026.
https://doi.org/10.1007/978-3-031-97589-9_26

academic study pathways, thus assisting young people in understanding their aptitudes, capabilities, and desires through guidance programmes that could help students to choose the University path that suits them best. These aims have both social and economic aspects; in Italy, the funds that a University receives from the Ministry of University and Research for ordinary operations (FFO) depend on the number of students regularly enrolled with a period of stay within a bachelor's degree no longer than four years (the nominal length of the degree programme being three years). Simultaneously, the annual enrolment fee paid by students rises with the length of their stay. Regional subsidies, such as those for canteen access or grants, decrease, leading to increased household spending. Recent reviews [1,3] state that student retention depends on a mixture of individual and external factors, which are not always controllable and have determinants not known a priori. Consequently, our study focuses attention on personal characteristics, rather than on others where there is an impossibility of intervention during the academic course of the students: sociodemographic background or external conditions. In this study, we focus attention on students' characteristics, educational background and performance, instead of on behavioural and relational aspects such as integration into academic and social life.

For this purpose, we used data provided by the students at the time of registration and collected in the University's official database. A cohort of students enrolled in 2015 in the three bachelor degrees in Economics taught by the University of Perugia was followed up to 2025. As a first step, in the present paper we aim to use these data to contribute to the identification of the strongest predictors of the risk of dropping out. In a subsequent analysis, additional data on the annual credits obtained and the academic performance of the students will be taken into account. This section is followed by a brief description of the methodology applied and then the Application section, data description and results illustration are provided. Finally, the Conclusion highlights the main findings, differences between the methodologies applied and future research directions.

2   Methodology

An event probability may be explored in a variety of ways, applying different statistical methodologies that are well known in risk analysis. The response variable may be treated as binary or multinomial, depending on the number of possible outcomes that represent objects of study (two or more); moreover we may or may not take into account the time of the occurrence of the outcome event (or occurrences if more than one), and whether these events are in competition with each other.

Here, we applied binary logistic regression to investigate the probability of academic success (that is, graduation) and a multinomial logistic regression to consider different causes of dropping out. Next, a classical survival analysis was applied considering as censored all the observations without a closure date at the time of data extraction (that is, students whose university career was still incomplete) and a competing risk model to analyse the survival curve for each different event, considering others as competitors. The development of models was preceded by descriptive analysis. SAS® software was used, specifically the procedures LOGISTIC [27] and PHREG [26] for logistic regression and survival analysis, respectively. A brief reminder of logistic and survival models is provided in the following Section.

In addition, a high performance procedure, HPSPLIT [25, 28], often employed for tasks such as customer segmentation [11], risk assessment [15, 21] and predictive modelling [7, 10, 14, 19, 30], was applied. This procedure builds tree-based statistical models for classification and regression for either continuous or categorical variables. In our context, the decision tree method was applied mainly for the advantage it offers in terms of interpretability and visualisation. During the decision tree building process, the Gini index and entropy method are used to assess candidate splits for each node. Moreover, a smaller subtree is obtained, starting from the full tree, applying a cost-complexity pruning.

2.1 Logistic Models

The logistic model, widely applied in various field such as medicine [4], social sciences [20], economics and finance [17], and machine learning [31], is a statistical method that models the probability of a binary outcome based on one or more predictor variables. Let Y be the Bernoulli random variable taking value 1 when the event occurs (award of the university degree) and 0 otherwise (academic course not completed or interrupted). Let $\mathbf{x}' = (x_1, x_2, ..., x_p)$ be a covariate vector representing risk factors thought to be related to the event under study. The logistic model is expressed by

$$P(Y = 1|\mathbf{x}) = \frac{e^{\alpha + \beta' \mathbf{x}}}{1 + e^{\alpha + \beta' \mathbf{x}}} \tag{1}$$

where α is the intercept, and $\beta' = (\beta_1, \beta_2, \ldots, \beta_p)$ is a vector of unknown coefficients whose value, if positive, indicates an increase in the likelihood of the event as the value of the corresponding covariate increases, or a decrease, if negative. Results may also be evaluated in terms of the odds ratio (OR), where $\mathrm{OR} = e^\beta$, which is the change in the odds of the outcome occurring for a one-unit increase in the value of the predictor variable: when an OR is greater than 1 the event is more likely to happen and the opposite when it is less than 1, while when it is equal to 0 there is no effect.

A multinomial logistic regression model is applied when there are more than two possible outcomes

$$P(Y = j|\mathbf{x}) = \frac{e^{\alpha_j + \beta_{1j} x_1 + \beta_{2j} x_2 + \ldots + \beta_{pj} x_p}}{1 + \sum_{k=1}^{J-1} e^{\alpha_k + \beta_{1k} x_1 + \beta_{2k} x_2 + \ldots + \beta_{pk} x_p}} \tag{2}$$

$P(Y = j|\mathbf{x})$ expresses the probability of the outcome j given the predictors $\mathbf{x}$; $\alpha_j, \beta_{1j}, \ldots, \beta_{pj}$ are the coefficients for the predictors for outcome j, with J indicating the number of categories.

In our case the categorical dependent variable is of nominal type: one category is chosen as the reference, and the model estimates the odds of the other categories relative to this reference.

Maximum likelihood estimation was used to estimate the parameters of the logistic regression models, carried out by the LOGISTIC procedure [27] using either the Fisher scoring algorithm or the Newton-Raphson algorithm.

To identify the optimal model, stepwise selection was implemented after evaluating multicollinearity among variables. The significance of the individual predictors was assessed through the Wald test: a *p-value* < 0.25 was fixed for each parameter to enter into the model and a *p-value* < 0.05 to stay in. Therefore the final model shows only the predictors that were statistically significant at the fixed *p-value* < 0.05. The Hosmer and Lemeshow Goodness-of-Fit test [13] was used to assess how well the logistic regression model fits the data.

2.2   Survival Models

Survival models are widely used in risk analysis to analyze the expected duration of time until one or more events occur [6], such as onset of a disease [18] or death in biological organisms [2], failure in mechanical systems [24] or bankruptcy in firms [22,32]. This type of analysis is also known as time-to-event analysis or event history analysis. After setting start and end dates for an observational period, the exit date and corresponding cause are recorded, while subjects still alive (that is, without an event) at the end of observation are considered to have right-censored event times.

Let T be the random time until the event and $\boldsymbol{\beta}$ the vector of coefficients denoting the effects of the vector of covariates $\boldsymbol{x}$ upon T. The values of these covariates for each student are measured at time 0 and are time independent. The survival function

$$S(t|\mathbf{x}) = P(T > t|\mathbf{x}), \tag{3}$$

expresses the probability that a subject will survive until at least time t. This function can conveniently be estimated non-parametrically using the Kaplan-Meier estimator and the equality of survival curves that have been obtained for disjoint subgroups of the data can be tested by the logrank test. The cumulative incidence function that gives the probability of the event under study up to time t, is

$$F(t|\mathbf{x}) = P(T \leq t|\mathbf{x}). \tag{4}$$

An important role is played by the hazard function $h(t)$ that expresses the instantaneous event rate at time t among subjects that have survived that long:

$$h(t) = \lim_{\delta t \to 0} \frac{P[t < T \leq t + \delta t|T > t]}{\delta t} = \frac{f(t)}{S(t)}. \tag{5}$$

In the popular semi-parametric proportional hazards model (Cox regression [8]), the covariates act multiplicatively on an unspecified baseline hazard rate $h_0(t)$ through the factor $e^{\boldsymbol{\beta}'\mathbf{x}}$:

$$h(t|\mathbf{x}) = h_0(t) \exp\{\boldsymbol{\beta}'\mathbf{x}\} \tag{6}$$

The effect of covariate x_i is expressed by the hazard ratio e^{β_i}: an increase of one unit in the value x_i (while keeping the values of other covariates constant) multiplies, from (6), the hazard by this amount.

Competing risk survival models are used when individuals in a study can experience multiple types of events, and the occurrence of one event prevents the occurrence of others. Two different approaches exist in this field: the cause-specific hazard model and the subdistributional hazard model or Fine & Gray model [9,12,23]; in the present context we consider the latter, which focuses on the probability that the event of interest occurs over time, accounting for the fact that other competing events might take place.

The subdistribution hazard function estimates the risk of failure from cause k,

$$h_k^s(t) = \lim_{\delta t \to 0} \frac{P[t < T \leq t + \delta t \bigcap D = k | T > t \bigcup (T \leq t \cap D \neq k)]}{\delta t}, \quad (7)$$

and expresses the instantaneous rate of failure at time t among students that have not yet experienced an event of type k.

3 Application

3.1 Data

The University of Perugia provided data on the 2015 cohort of students who entered three bachelor's degree programmes in Economics: Business Administration in the provinces of Perugia (programme code L021) and Terni (programme code L025) (two different districts of the Umbria Region) and Business for Tourism (programme code L026). This cohort was followed from first registration in 2015 until January 2025. Table 1 shows the distribution of these 515 students by course and gender. For each student we have an anonymous numerical identification code, information about gender, region and district of residence, type of secondary school attended, diploma obtained and the related mark. Moreover, we know the student's current status: that is, graduated (status = 1); officially dropped out from studies, which is often done in order to switch to another degree course (status = 2); deleted, if at least eight years have passed since registration and no examinations have been taken in the last three years or if three years have elapsed since the last payment of tuition fees without passing any examination (status = 3); or active, if at least one examination has been taken even if with negative result (status = 0). The dates of change of status are known. States 1, 2 and 3 each marks the end of the student's career in this university, so they represent competing risks in the terminology of survival analysis. Students in state 0 have not yet reached an endpoint, so they have right-censored durations of studies.

In Table 2, which shows the distribution of students' status in 2025 by course, we see that 54.6% of the students obtained their degree within 10 years, while as many as 37% of the initial entrants had ceased to be students on these courses for various reasons, and 8.2% had not yet reached a conclusion.

Table 1. Distribution of students by degree course and gender

Degree Code	Female		Male		Total	
	N	%	N	%	N	%
L021	150	67.6	236	80.5	386	75.0
L025	43	19.4	40	13.7	83	16.1
L026	29	13.1	17	5.8	46	8.9
Total	222	43.1	293	56.9	515	100

Table 2. Distribution of students' current status by course

Degree Code	Sex	Status				
		0	1	2	3	Total
L021						
	F	8	95	23	24	150
	M	16	120	60	40	236
L025						
	F	8	20	8	7	43
	M	7	24	6	3	40
L026						
	F	1	17	5	6	29
	M	2	5	3	8	17
Total	N	42	281	101	88	515
	%	8.2	54.6	20.2	17.1	100

Table 3. Distribution of type of school attended by gender.

School		Female	Male	Total
Classical	N	45	24	69
	%	20.27	8.19	13.40
Scientific	N	45	113	158
	%	20.27	38.57	30.68
Mixed*	N	21	1	22
	%	9.46	0.34	4.27
Professional	N	20	21	41
	%	9.01	7.17	7.96
Technical	N	86	122	208
	%	38.74	41.64	40.39
Outside Italy	N	5	12	17
	%	2.25	4.1	3.30
Total	N	222	293	515

*Includes elements of classical and scientific

Looking at the students' background (Table 3), the higher percentage held a technical (40.4%) or scientific (30.7%) certificate (or secondary school diploma) with significant differences by gender (χ^2 test of association =54.22 with 5° of freedom, $p < 0.0001$, Cramer's V = 0.32); relatively fewer female than male students had attended a scientific secondary school, while relatively more had attended schools of classical or mixed type.

The mean graduation mark was 80.4. Examination of Q-Q plots indicated that marks were not normally distributed, hence Wilcoxon tests rather than t-tests were used to compare marks between groups of students. A significant difference ($p < 0.001$) was found between females (82.9) and males (78.1). There were no significant differences in this respect between the three bachelor's degree programmes.

Table 4. Effects of covariates in Binary Logistic Regression: Parameter Estimate, Standard Error (SE), Wald χ^2 and its probability, Odds Ratio (OR) and Wald 95% Confidence Interval (CI)

	Estimate	SE	Wald χ^2	Pr>χ^2	OR	95% CI
Intercept	-3.816	0.665	32.950	<.0001		
School type*						
Mixed	-1.350	0.488	7.667	0.006	0.259	0.100 - 0.674
Classical	-0.216	0.311	0.482	0.488	0.806	0.438 - 1.482
Professional	-1.956	0.412	22.550	<.0001	0.141	0.063 - 0.317
Outside Italy	1.771	0.976	3.293	0.070	5.876	0.868 - 39.795
Technical	-0.835	0.234	12.746	<.0001	0.434	0.274 - 0.686
School Grad.mark	0.060	0.009	46.379	<.0001	1.061	1.043 - 1.080

Reference category: *Scientific
Hosmer and Lemeshow Goodness-of-Fit Test $p = 0.26$

3.2   Results

Logistic Regressions. The binary logistic regression model obtained after a stepwise selection procedure (Table 4) identified the school graduation mark and the type of high school attended as significant predictors (Wald test, $p<0.05$) of academic success among those factors that had been recorded at the date of enrolment (sex, graduation mark, high school attendance and residence).

More specifically, while there were no significant differences between students who attended high schools with scientific and classical orientations, these were much more likely to be successful than students who had attended technical (Odds Ratio = 0.434, 95% Confidence Interval 0.24–0.686), professional (OR = 0.141 CI = 0.063–0.317) or other secondary schools (OR = 0.259 CI = 0.100–0.674). Moreover, the higher the graduation mark, the higher was the probability of avoiding drop-out (OR = 1.061 CI = 1.043–1.080).

For further analysis of data and results, justified on the basis of other research [21] the high performance procedure HPSPLIT that creates the decision tree

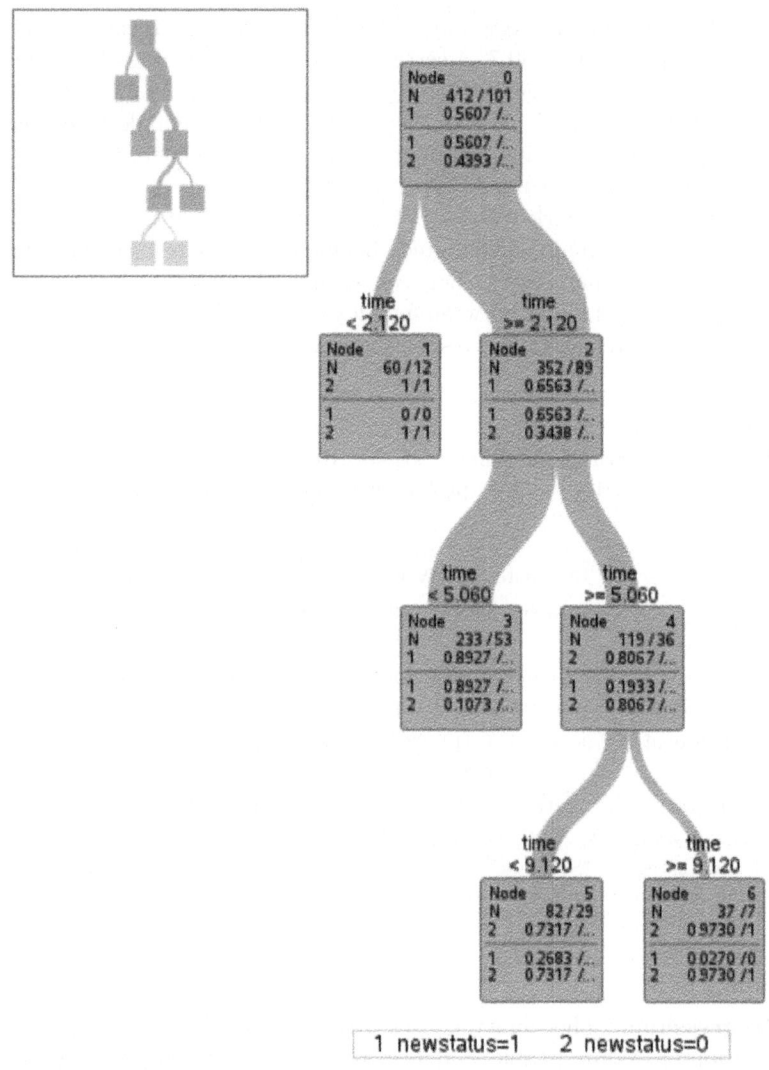

Fig. 1. HPSPLIT output: newstatus = 1 represents the students who graduated, new-status = 0 is the group with interrupted studies.

model was applied. The length of stay within the degree programme was included among the other covariates in this analysis. As seen in Fig. 1, the first branching is evident at time ≤ 2.120, a time shorter than the duration of any course, in fact, here are allocated all subjects belonging to group 0, while a high percentage of graduated students are assigned to node number 3 when time is less than 5.06. Upon investigation, the group in node number 2 was found to include students who had formally abandoned their studies (status 2), probably in order to

Table 5. Effects of statistically significant covariates ($p<0.05$ for Wald χ^2) in Multinomial Logistic Regression: Odds Ratio (OR) and Wald Confidence Interval (CI)

	status = 0		status = 2		status = 3	
	OR	95% CI	OR	95% CI	OR	95% CI
School type*						
Mixed	0.802	0.091–7.09	4.164	1.298–13.362	8.211	2.338–28.842
Classical	0.702	0.214–2.303	1.411	0.658–3.026	1.582	0.622–4.022
Professional	0.780	0.088–6.932	8.083	2.943–22.202	18.107	6.123–53.553
Outside Italy	0.916	0.071–11.737	0.135	0.013–1.419	0.046	0.004–0.569
Technical	1.549	0.718–3.342	2.126	1.184–3.816	3.484	1.727–7.027
Degree course**						
L025	3.047	1.459–6.364	0.715	0.363–1.408	0.676	0.306–1.494
L026	1.137	0.297–4.355	0.492	0.187–1.298	1.092	0.462–2.582
School Grad. Mark	0.968	0.941–0.996	0.946	0.926–0.967	0.917	0.893–0.942

Reference categories: status = 1, *Scientific, ** L021
Hosmer and Lemeshow Goodness-of-Fit Test $p = 0.86$

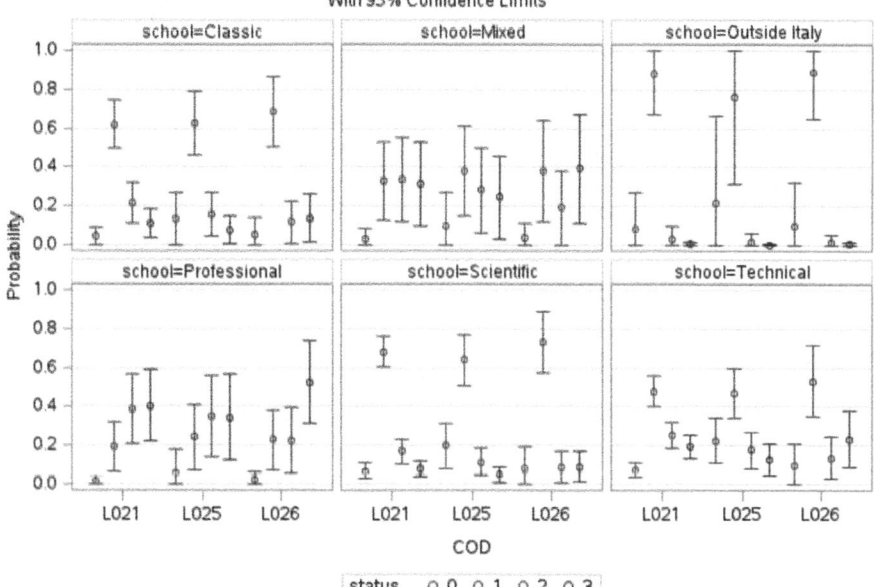

Fit computed at Grad_mark=76.3

Fig. 2. Multinomial Logistic Regression predicted probabilities: Degree course, and school attended.

switch to another degree programme. Therefore, multinomial logistic modelling was applied, considering the four different ten-year outcomes and using the group of students who successfully completed their studies as the reference. The most significant factors, highlighted after a stepwise selection procedure, and having a Wald χ^2 with $p<0.05$, were the degree course, the school graduation mark and the type of high school attended. (For greater clarity, Table 5 presents the odds ratios and their corresponding confidence intervals for the covariates selected in the stepwise model. The relation between the odds ratio and the parameter estimate is explained in the methodology section). Students enrolled in the L025 course were more likely to extend their academic career beyond eight years (status $= 0$) in comparison to students enrolled in the L021 course: OR $= 3.047$ with 95% Confidence Interval 1.459–6.363. On the other hand, these two courses did not differ regarding the other statuses, because the odds ratio includes the number 1. Moreover, (taking the scientific high schools as reference category) a technical or professional secondary school background made it more likely that students would not complete their studies (status $= 2$), or would drop out (status $= 3$). For these two statuses, the respective odds are quite high but with wide confidence intervals.

The odds ratios below one for the three different causes of failure indicate the importance of the school graduation mark: as it increases, the probability of dropping out in any way decreases.

Observing Fig. 2 we notice that for a school graduation mark equal to 76.3, the highest probability of success (status $= 1$) is for students who attended a classical or scientific secondary school or a school outside Italy.

Furthermore, the contribution of the students' graduation mark is clearly shown in the graph obtained as an output from the HPSPLIT procedure applied to assess variable importance in the multinomial model (Fig. 3): the first split is into two branches for graduation marks less than or greater than 76, and subsequently the distinction by type of secondary school attended is evident.

Survival Analysis. The Kaplan-Meier non-parametric estimates of the survival functions by school of attendance (Fig. 4) and degree course (Fig. 5) show that students coming from a scientific or classical school, or enrolled in course L021, have significantly lower probability of remaining within the university for more than three years than students from other schools or from other courses, respectively; that is they have a shorter academic career with a better chance of success within the normal course duration. Similar analyses did not show significant differences by gender or region (Logrank test $p > 0.05$).

The classical survival analysis (Cox regression), after stepwise selection, returned a model with results that are in line with those obtained in binary logistic regression: the significant predictors on the basis of the Wald test were school and graduation mark. In order to test the validity of the proportional hazards assumption for these two predictors, their interaction with time was added to the model [29]. This inclusion turned out to be significant (Wald $\chi^2, p < 0.001$). It appeared that both predictors' influence decreased over time, in particular

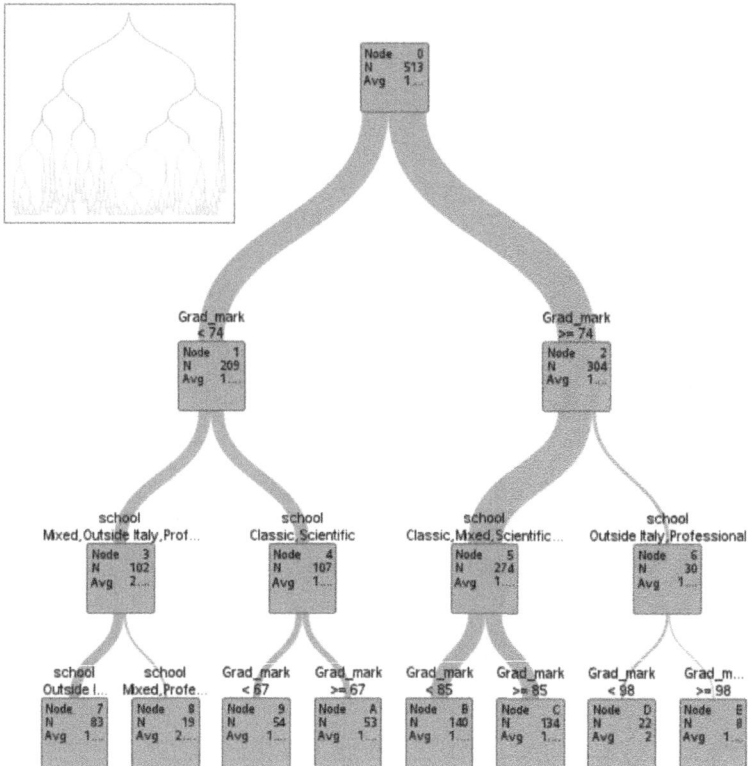

Fig. 3. HPSPLIT tree output: Assessing variable importance.

the graduation mark coefficient has a value equal to 0.223 with a hazard ratio equal to 1.25 meaning that each unit increase in graduation mark increases the hazard by 25%, while the interaction with time, having a negative coefficient value (-0.159) with a hazard ratio less than one shows that the effect of the mark decreases over time.

The Fine and Gray subdistributional hazard model was applied to verify if there were differences by status. In this analysis we considered as censored the students still active at the time of data extraction (status = 0) and we ran three different survival models, one for each status, considering the other two as competing.

The proportional hazard assumption was found to be violated both for the school and graduation mark predictors, but only for events 2 and 3. Therefore interactions with time were included and after this different models were obtained for each event.

For status 1 the graduation mark and the high school attended were again the most significant factors. A hazard ratio greater than one with confidence interval not containing the number 1, fosters belonging to the group. Therefore,

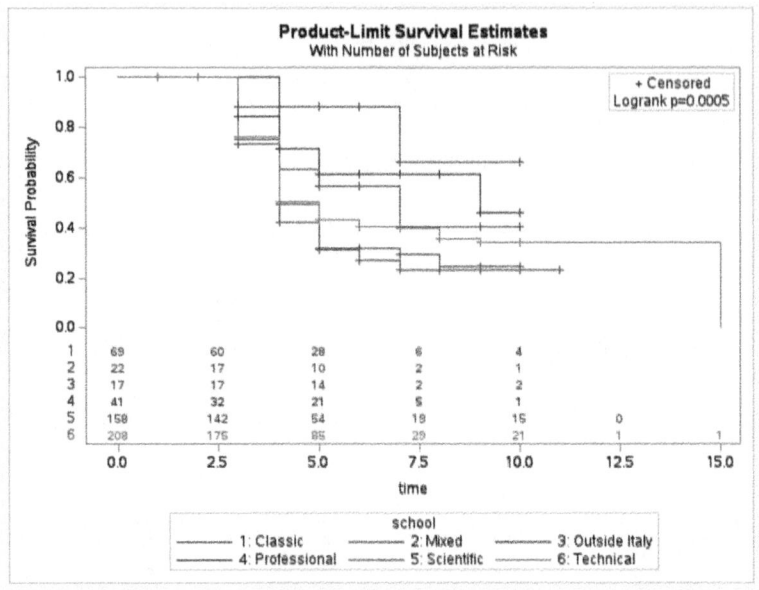

Fig. 4. Kaplan-Meier estimate of the survival curves by type of school attended: here, "survival" means that the student is still active, that is, has not yet graduated.

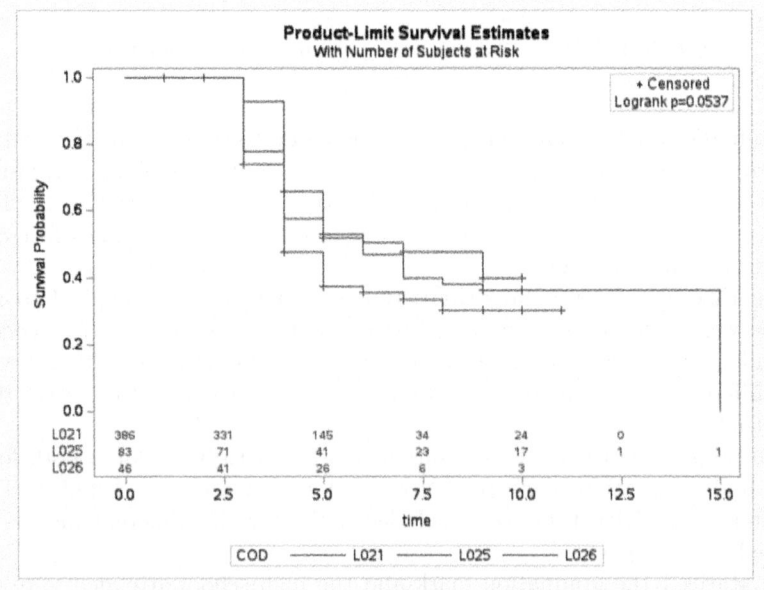

Fig. 5. Kaplan-Meier estimates of the survival curves by university course.

Table 6. Effect of covariates in Fine & Gray subdistributional hazard regression model: Hazard Ratio (HR) and Confidence Interval (CI)

	status = 1		status = 2		status = 3	
	HR	95% CI	HR	95% CI	HR	95% CI
School*						
Mixed	0.441	0.246–0.794				
Classical	0.928	0.676–1.273				
Professional	0.300	0.173–0.521				
Outside Italy	1.486	0.407–5.427				
Technical	0.649	0.514–0.820				
Degree Course**						
L025					0.453	0.225–0.912
L026					1.370	0.838–2.239
Sex***						
Female			0.668	0.496–0.901		
School Grad.Mark	1.039	1.029–1.049	1.037	1.028–1.046	0.940	0.930–0.950
Time-by-Mark interaction			0.956	0.949–0.963	1.028	1.023–1.034

Reference categories: *Scientific, **L021, ***Male

a unit increase in graduation mark and a science-based school background both increase the probability of successful graduation (status = 1), while attending a technical, professional or mixed school tends to increase the probability of failing to complete the course.

For status 2 the school and the degree course attended were no longer significant, but gender was included in the model besides graduation mark and its interaction with time. The negative coefficient for being female reduced the subdistribution hazard, and the hazard ratio equal to 0.668 implies that, at any given time, females have a 33% lower cumulative incidence of the event compared to males, assuming other variables are constant. Moreover the effect of graduation mark on the subdistribution hazard changes over time, and is modelled as: $\beta(t) = 0.03637 - 0.04507 \times \log(\text{time})$.

A possible interpretation is that high-performing students are initially at greater risk (e.g., changing study programmes), but over time they stabilise or succeed, reducing risk.

For status 3 a significant predictor, besides graduation mark and its interaction with time, was the degree course attended. Students in group L025 had a 55% lower cumulative incidence of this event compared to those in the L021 category (HR = 0.453), suggesting a strong significant difference ($p = 0.027$) in risk between the L025 and L021 courses. In addition, the negative coefficient (-0.06218) of the graduation mark suggests that better school performance is associated with a reduced risk: for each unit increase in graduation mark, the subdistribution hazard decreases by about 6% (HR = 0.940) and this result is highly significant (p < 0.0001). Moreover, the positive interaction term for time-varying effect (0.02783) indicates that the effect of graduation mark increases slightly over time, that is for each unit increase in graduation mark, the hazard ratio (HR = 1.028) increases by 2.8% over time. This suggests that the protective effect of graduation mark becomes somewhat stronger over time.

4   Conclusion

Failure to complete a course of university study is an important problem world-wide, representing a major waste of resources. It can be an issue even in Schools with highly competitive entry [5]. In this study we began an investigation of the problem of students' dropping out from three different degree courses in Economics of the University of Perugia, having a regional base (85.8%) and a success rate only just over 50%. A first analysis split the students into two groups: graduates and non-graduates. It identified graduation mark and type of secondary school attended as factors predictive of a positive outcome. Then, more deeply, as in other studies [16], we considered the different causes of dropping out, both applying high performance procedures which allow the identification of the most important factors, and implementing classical quantitative methods such as multinomial logistic regression and competing risk models. Even though the analyses lead to conceptually similar results, identifying the same important factors, various different facets have been distinguished.

In multinomial logistic regression (Table 5) we used as reference category the students who graduated, highlighting differences among various types of dropout. Conversely, in survival analysis one of the dropout causes (status = 0) naturally represents censored data. Therefore, the competing risk models (Table 6) focused attention separately on the probabilities of events 1, 2 or 3 considering the other two events in turn as competing. Results are therefore not directly comparable but of certain interest from an interpretative point of view. On the basis of the results obtained, the type of secondary school attended and graduation mark achieved seem to be the two factors that mainly influence the probability of academic success or dropout. Furthermore, the methodological differences between logistic regression and survival analysis allow us to detect how the passage of time influences the effect of some significant predictors in different directions for different causes of exit. The competing risk analysis, in addition, includes the gender variable, suggesting that females are less prone to change course (status = 2) compared to males.

However, this study will be improved in the near future by using data on annual student credits. It will then be possible to identify if there are any further points of attention, apart from those relating to the basic preparation acquired by students attending different types of secondary schools. The need to delve deeper into the topic will also lead to consideration of the cohorts of enrolment years after 2015.

References

1. Aina, C., Baici, E., Casalone, G., Pastore, F.: The determinants of university dropout: a review of the socio-economic literature. Socio-Econ. Plann. Sci. **79**, 101102 (2022). https://www.sciencedirect.com/science/article/pii/S003801212100094X

2. Anderson, J.J.: A vitality-based stochastic model for organism survival. In: Individual-Based Models and Approaches in Ecology, pp. 256–277. Chapman and Hall/CRC (2018)

3. Apumayta, R.Q., Cayllahua, J.C., Pari, A.C., Choque, V.I., Valverde, J.C.C., Atay-poma, D.H.: University dropout: a systematic review of the main determinant factors (2020–2024). F1000Research **13**, 942 (2024)

4. Boateng, E.Y., Abaye, D.A., et al.: A review of the logistic regression model with emphasis on medical research. J. Data Anal. Inf. Process. **7**(04), 190 (2019)

5. Caroni, C.: Graduation and attrition of engineering students in Greece. Eur. J. Eng. Educ. **36**(1), 63–74 (2011). https://doi.org/10.1080/03043797.2010.539676

6. Caroni, C.: Regression models for lifetime data: an overview. Stats **5**(4), 1294–1304 (2022). https://doi.org/10.3390/stats5040078

7. Cho, S.K., Mattke, S., Gordon, H., Sheridan, M., Ennis, W.: Development of a model to predict healing of chronic wounds within 12 weeks. Adv. Wound Care **9**(9), 516–524 (2020)

8. Cox, D.R.: Regression models and life-tables. J. Roy. Stat. Soc. Ser. B (Methodol.) **34**(2), 187–202 (1972)

9. Fine, J.P., Gray, R.J.: A proportional hazards model for the subdistribution of a competing risk. J. Am. Stat. Assoc. **94**(446), 496–509 (1999)

10. Fox, H., Topp, S.M., Lindsay, D., Callander, E.: A cascade of interventions: a classification tree analysis of the determinants of primary cesareans in Australian public hospitals. Birth **48**(2), 209–220 (2021)

11. Gupta, D., Gupta, D.: Telecommunication case study. In: Applied Analytics through Case Studies Using SAS and R: Implementing Predictive Models and Machine Learning Techniques, pp. 161–220 (2018)

12. Heisey, D.M., Patterson, B.R.: A review of methods to estimate cause-specific mortality in presence of competing risks. J. Wildl. Manag. **70**(6), 1544–1555 (2006)

13. Hosmer, D.W., Lemeshow, S.: Goodness of fit tests for the multiple logistic regression model. Commun. Stat. Theory Methods **9**(10), 1043–1069 (1980)

14. Huschka, T., et al.: 119 investigating factors influencing diagnostic safety in emergency department patients using decision trees. Ann. Emerg. Med. **82**(4), S52 (2023)

15. Jaffe, D., et al.: Chi-square automatic interaction detection (CHAID) analysis: understanding and informing treatment choice of second-line metastatic urothelial cancer therapy. Value Health **21**, S213–S214 (2018)

16. Kehm, B.M., Larsen, M.R., Sommersel, H.B.: Student dropout from universities in Europe: a review of empirical literature. Hung. Educ. Res. J. **9**(2), 147–164 (2019)

17. Menard, S.W.: Logistic Regression: From Introductory to Advanced Concepts and Applications. Sage (2010)

18. Ohno-Machado, L.: Modeling medical prognosis: survival analysis techniques. J. Biomed. Inform. **34**(6), 428–439 (2001)

19. Oyebanjo, M.O., Coker, O.M., Osaiyuwu, O.H.: Predicting the body weight of indigenous goat breeds from morphological measurements using the classification and regression tree (CART) data mining algorithm. Biotechnol. Anim. Husbandry **39**(1), 33–49 (2023)

20. Pho, K.H., McAleer, M.: Specification and estimation of a logistic function, with applications in the sciences and social sciences. Adv. Decis. Sci. **2**, 1–30 (2021)

21. Pierri, F.: Variable selection in binary logistic regression for modelling bankruptcy risk. In: Kitsos, C.P., Oliveira, T.A., Pierri, F., Restaino, M. (eds.) Statistical Modelling and Risk Analysis, pp. 143–155. Springer International Publishing, Cham (2023). https://doi.org/10.1007/978-3-031-39864-3_12

22. Pierri, F., Caroni, C.: Bankruptcy prediction by survival models based on current and lagged values of time-varying financial data. Commun. Stat. Case Stud. Data Anal. Appl. **3**(3–4), 62–70 (2017)

23. Putter, H., Schumacher, M., van Houwelingen, H.C.: On the relation between the cause-specific hazard and the subdistribution rate for competing risks data: the Fine-Gray model revisited. Biom. J. **62**(3), 790–807 (2020)

24. Rasheed, M.: Analyzing applications and properties of the exponential continuous distribution in reliability and survival analysis. J. Positive Sci. **4**(5), 71–79 (2023)

25. Rodriguez, R.N.: Statistical model building for large, complex data: five new directions in SAS/STAT ® software. In: Proceedings of the SAS Global Forum Conference, Las Vegas, NV, USA, pp. 18–21 (2016)

26. SAS: SAS/STAT® 9.2 user's guide. https://support.sas.com/documentation/cdl/en/statug/63033/HTML/default/viewer.htm#phreg_toc.htm. Accessed 16 Mar 2025

27. SAS: SAS/STAT® 9.22 user's guide. https://support.sas.com/documentation/cdl/en/statug/63347/HTML/default/viewer.htm#statug_logistic_sect004.htm. Accessed 16 Mar 2025

28. SAS: SAS/STAT® 9.22 user's guide. https://support.sas.com/documentation/onlinedoc/stat/141/hpsplit.pdf. Accessed 16 Mar 2025

29. Therneau, T., Crowson, C., Atkinson, E.: Using time dependent covariates and time dependent coefficients in the Cox model (2024). https://cran.r-project.org/web/packages/survival/vignettes/timedep.pdf

30. Venkatasubbu, P., Ganesh, M.: Used cars price prediction using supervised learning techniques. Int. J. Eng. Adv. Technol. (IJEAT) **9**(1S3), 216–223 (2019)

31. Wang, P., Zheng, X., Li, J., Zhu, B.: Prediction of epidemic trends in COVID-19 with logistic model and machine learning technics. Chaos, Solitons Fractals **139**, 110058 (2020)

32. Zelenkov, Y.: Bankruptcy prediction using survival analysis technique. In: 2020 IEEE 22nd Conference on business informatics (CBI), vol. 2, pp. 141–149. IEEE (2020)

Time-Dependent and Non-linear Predictor Effects in Survival Analyses: A Case Study Comparing Alternative Models for Cancer Mortality

Michal Abrahamowicz[1]([✉]) [iD], Marie-Eve Beauchamp[2] [iD], Richard J. Cook[3] [iD], Malka Gorfine[4], Jason Agulnik[5], Bruno Gagnon[6], and Steve Ferreira Guerra[1] [iD]

[1] McGill University, Montreal, QC H3A 1G1, Canada
michal.abrahamowicz@mcgill.ca
[2] Research Institute of the McGill University Health Centre, Montreal, QC H4A 3S5, Canada
[3] University of Waterloo, Waterloo, ON N2L 3G1, Canada
[4] Tel Aviv University, 6997801 Tel Aviv, Israel
[5] McGill University, Montreal, QC H3T 1E2, Canada
[6] Université Laval, Québec, QC G1J 1Z4, Canada

Abstract. Regression analysis with multivariable survival data requires specification of a model describing the relationship between predictors and some function of the event time distribution. Popular choices include proportional hazards (PH), accelerated failure time (AFT), and additive hazards (AH) models. Each model imposes an *a priori* assumption that, respectively, hazard ratios, relative time scales, or hazard differences, associated with a given change in a predictor value, are constant during the entire follow-up period. However, the effects of *some* of the predictors of interest may not be consistent with the underlying modeling assumption, which requires extending the model to include time-dependent effects. In addition, for each continuous covariate a suitable functional form of its relationship with the outcome has to be determined. Several flexible methods for addressing these modeling challenges were proposed in the literature but there is little evidence regarding head-to-head comparisons of flexible extensions of PH vs. AFT vs. AH models in real-world analyses. We first present a brief overview of selected flexible methods available to estimate time-dependent effects and, for continuous variables, non-linear effects. We also identify the software that allows the implementation of such computationally intensive flexible models. The practical importance of these challenges is illustrated using a case study of prognostic factors associated with cancer mortality.

Keywords: Biostatistics · Survival Analysis · Splines · Prognostic Studies

1 Introduction

The ultimate goal of statistical research is to develop validated methods to allow accurate analyses of real-world data. One of the most common goals of real-world analyses is to explore associations of different risk and prognostic factors, treatments, lifestyle

O. Gervasi et al. (Eds.): ICCSA 2025 Workshops, LNCS 15887, pp. 393–410, 2026.
https://doi.org/10.1007/978-3-031-97589-9_27

characteristics and environmental or occupational exposures with relevant outcomes. If the outcome is a binary (presence/absence) or a continuous variable, then its associations with multiple covariates can be directly modeled. In contrast, if the outcome is defined as a time to a specific event, such as death or cancer diagnosis, the analyses are complicated by the fact that for some study participants no outcome may be observed until the end of the study. This results in right-censored observations, and requires more specialized analytical methods, being developed by statisticians working in the field of survival analysis or time-to-event analysis. One common challenge in this field is that the outcome, for individual i, is bivariate, i.e. includes (a) a continuous value of total follow-up time T_i, and (b) a binary indicator of status at time T_i, with $\Delta_i = 1$ indicating the event and $\Delta_i = 0$ a censored observation [1]. Thus, while using regression modeling to estimate and test the associations of interest, the dependent variable has to be represented as some function of the event times rather than the directly observed individual (bivariate) outcome. Accordingly, in statistical literature, several alternative models were proposed for regression analyses of right-censored time-to-event outcomes, each of which postulates a different mathematical relationship between the predictors and some function of event times.

In real-world applications of survival analysis, by far the most popular regression model is the proportional hazards (PH) model, typically estimated using the maximum partial likelihood estimation procedure developed by Sir David Cox [2], in the original publication that has close to 64,000 citations on Google Scholar. The PH model estimates the effects of predictors on the hazard, i.e. the instantaneous risk, and the popularity of the Cox model is largely related to the fact that it avoids the need to specify the parametric form of the hazard function [2]. However, more recently the Cox model has been criticized for so-called built-in selection bias [3], i.e. systematic bias toward a null effect induced by the presence of an unmeasured or unaccounted for risk factor or "frailty" [4]. An alternative regression model for survival analysis is the additive hazards (AH) model proposed by Aalen [5, 6]. In the AH model, the predictors are also acting on the hazard function but, in contrast to the PH model, their effects are assumed to be additive, i.e. are quantified using hazard differences [5], rather than multiplicative hazard ratios (HRs). Finally, more recently, there is an increased interest in the accelerated failure time (AFT) model, which assumes that predictors affect directly the event time and, thus, their effects are estimated using multiplicative event time ratios [7]. In their classic forms, each of the three models imposes a strong assumption that, respectively, hazard ratios [2], hazard differences [8] or event time ratios [7] associated with a given change in the predictor are constant across the entire follow-up period. Yet, interestingly, only if the underlying hazard function is constant, corresponding to the simple exponential model, the AFT, AH and PH models are compatible with each other [7]. In all other situations, if the data are truly generated e.g. by the AH model, then the assumptions underlying the AFT and PH models are violated, and *vice versa*. However, even if the different models may be more suitable for different datasets, in a vast majority of real-world survival analyses, the PH, AFT or AH model is selected *a priori,* without presenting any clinical and/or statistical evidence supporting such choices. Indeed, the head-to-head comparisons of any two of the three regression models for survival analysis are very limited [9], and we are not aware of any empirical study that compared all three models for the same dataset.

A related issue is that if the assumptions underlying a given *a priori* selected model are violated, then the resulting estimates are biased and lead to incorrect interpretation of the way predictors are associated with the outcome. For example, if the Cox model is selected even if the PH assumption is violated, the resulting estimates will incorrectly suggest that a given change in the predictor value is associated with a constant HR, while in reality the true HR varies across the follow-up period [10]. In fact, in his original AH publications, Aalen has proposed a flexible formulation of the AH model that allows for hazard differences to vary during follow-up [5]. In a similar spirit, in the 1990's several authors have proposed various flexible extensions of the PH model, each of which uses some spline modeling to estimate time-dependent (TD) hazard ratios (see, e.g., a brief review in [10]). Finally, recently, two different extensions of the AFT model have been proposed to allow flexible modeling of TD predictor effects [11, 12]. Yet, again, except for a comparison of selected models for TD effects in the PH framework, there is a paucity of empirical head-to-head comparisons of TD extensions of PH vs. AH vs. AFT models. Furthermore, additional modeling assumptions are required regarding the functional form of the, possibly non-linear, dose-response function expressing how the outcome (e.g., log hazard in the PH framework) is associated with a continuous predictor. In the PH framework, we have demonstrated that the non-linear (NL) and TD effects of the same continuous predictor have to be assessed jointly to avoid biased estimates and incorrect conclusions [13]. We have then developed and validated flexible extensions of the PH model [14] and, more recently, AFT model [12] that allow for joint estimation of TD and NL effects of multiple predictors on the hazard, and likelihood ratio tests (LRTs) of their statistical significance. However, no comparison of TD/NL estimates between PH vs. AFT models, applied to the same empirical or simulated dataset(s), has been reported in the literature to date. Furthermore, to the best of our knowledge, no publications have reported NL estimates in the AH modeling framework, and the fundamental AH papers do not discuss explicitly flexible modeling of the functional forms for continuous covariates, either under constant additive effects [8] or under time-dependent effects [5].

To fill the aforementioned knowledge gaps, the current study carries out empirical head-to-head comparisons of PH, AH and AFT models and their flexible extensions with TD and/or NL effects of predictors on the hazard. The various models are employed in a real-world prognostic study of predictors of all-cause mortality in a non-small cell lung cancer. In Sect. 2, we describe the models being compared, including their flexible TD/NL extensions. Then, Sect. 3 describes how these models are employed to assess the effects of different biomarkers for mortality in non-small cell lung cancer. A brief discussion concludes the paper.

2 Alternative Regression Models for Survival Analyses

In this section, we present the alternative regression models for multivariable survival analyses. For each of the three models – PH, AFT and AH models – we first define its classic version, in which the effect of each covariate is estimated using a single parameter and thus is constrained to be constant-over-time and, for each continuous predictor, a linear dose-response relationship is assumed. Next, we introduce the flexible extensions of each of the three models that allow the modeling of both (i) time-dependent (TD) effects of either binary or continuous covariates, and (ii) possibly non-linear (NL) effects of continuous covariates.

2.1 Proportional Hazards Model and Its Flexible Extensions

The classic proportional hazards (PH) model assumes that predictors have multiplicative constant-over-time effects on the hazard. The model is typically written as [2]:

$$\lambda(t|\mathbf{X}) = \lambda_0(t)\exp(\mathbf{X}^T\boldsymbol{\beta}) \tag{1}$$

where $\lambda_0(t)$ is the baseline hazard, corresponding to a hypothetical reference population with all predictor values equal to 0 ($\mathbf{X} = 0$), $\mathbf{X} = (X_1, \ldots, X_p)$ is a vector of p, possibly time-dependent, predictors, and $\boldsymbol{\beta} = (\beta_1, \ldots, \beta_p)$ the vector of regression coefficients, representing the log hazard ratios (HRs). In the classic PH model (1), the adjusted HRs for all predictors are constrained to be constant over time and the continuous predictors are assumed to have linear relationships with the log hazard.

The regression parameters ($\boldsymbol{\beta}$) of the PH model (1) are commonly obtained using maximum partial likelihood estimation proposed by Cox [2], in which the baseline hazard is a nuisance parameter. However, it is possible to get the full maximum likelihood estimation (MLE) using, for example, the approach developed and validated in our earlier study [15]. More details are presented below, in the context of the flexible extension of the PH model.

In the 1990's different flexible extensions of the PH model were proposed, most involving spline modeling of either TD or NL effects of predictors (see, e.g., a brief review in [10]). However, we have demonstrated that the NL and TD effects of the same continuous predictor must be assessed jointly, i.e. adjusted for each other, to avoid biased estimates and incorrect conclusions [13]. Therefore, we proposed the following flexible extension of the PH model, which incorporates both the TD effects and, for continuous predictors, the NL effects on the log hazard [13]:

$$\lambda(t|\mathbf{X}) = \lambda_0(t)\exp\big[\boldsymbol{\beta}(t)\mathbf{g}(\mathbf{X})\big] \tag{2}$$

where the TD effect is represented by $\boldsymbol{\beta}(t)$ which models the change over time in the log(HR) for the effect of $\mathbf{X}$, and $\mathbf{g}(\mathbf{X})$ represents the NL effect of $\mathbf{X}$ which models how the log(HR) changes with increasing value of $\mathbf{X}$. In the flexible model (2), $\boldsymbol{\beta}(t)$ and $\mathbf{g}(\mathbf{X})$ can be modeled using (unpenalized) polynomial regression B-splines [13].

Direct estimation of model (2) will be impossible due to an identifiability problem that occurs because the $\boldsymbol{\beta}(t)$ and $\mathbf{g}(\mathbf{X})$ functions for the same continuous predictor X are multiplied by each other [13]. To avoid such problems, we have proposed to use the iterative alternating conditional estimation (ACE) [14] that we have validated in extensive simulations [16]. The ACE algorithm alternates between two steps, each involving conditional maximization of the partial likelihood for either $\boldsymbol{\beta}(t)$ or $\mathbf{g}(\mathbf{X})$, while holding the parameters of the other function fixed at their current values. This repeated updating process allows ACE to circumvent nonidentifiability constraints.

Because the constant-in-time β parameter and the linear function are both special cases of the polynomial B-spline, the classic PH model (1) is nested within the flexible model (2) [13]. Thus, statistical significance of, respectively, the TD and NL effects can be tested using model-based likelihood ratio tests (LRTs) [13].

2.2   Accelerated Failure Time Model and Its Flexible Extension

Another important class of survival models is provided by the accelerated failure time (AFT) class of models [7, 17]. In its classic form, the AFT model can be written as:

$$\log(T) = -\mathbf{X}^T\boldsymbol{\delta} + W \tag{3}$$

where T denotes the event time, $\mathbf{X}$ is again the vector of covariates, and $\boldsymbol{\delta} = (\delta_1, \ldots, \delta_p)$ is the corresponding vector of regression coefficients. W is an error term assumed to follow some distribution (e.g., Gaussian, logistic, or extreme value) which determines the distribution of T [7]. In contrast to the PH and AH models, where the covariates are assumed to modify the hazard function, either multiplicatively or additively, the AFT parametrization in (3) implies that changes in the predictor value are associated with an additive change in the logarithm of the survival time, implying a multiplicative change in the expected event time. In particular, a one-unit increase in a given continuous predictor X_j is associated with increasing the log survival time by the corresponding regression coefficient, δ_j in Eq. (3) [7]. Thus, the AFT model regression parameters $\boldsymbol{\delta}$ directly quantify the impact of covariates on the time scale, extending or shrinking the expected survival time by $\exp(\boldsymbol{\delta})$, which can be intuitively appealing to end-users and clinicians. On the other hand, specifying the error distribution can be challenging in practice, and its misspecification may lead to biased results, as demonstrated in simulations [18, 19]. To avoid this limitation, recently Pang et al. [18] have proposed a more flexible AFT model that replaces parametric assumptions about the event time distribution by cubic spline modeling of the baseline hazard and demonstrated its advantages in simulations.

An alternative way to present the AFT model, mathematically equivalent to the classic formulation in (3), describes the predictor effects on the hazard function [7]:

$$\lambda(t|\mathbf{X}) = \exp\left(\mathbf{X}^T\boldsymbol{\delta}\right)\lambda_0\left(\exp\left(\mathbf{X}^T\boldsymbol{\delta}\right) \cdot t\right) \tag{4}$$

where $\lambda_0(\cdot)$ is the baseline hazard, corresponding to a hypothetical reference population with all predictors equal to 0 ($\mathbf{X} = 0$). Notice that the regression parameter vector $\boldsymbol{\delta}$ in (4) has exactly the same interpretation as in (3). Model (4) reveals that in the AFT framework, predictors $\mathbf{X}$ affect the hazard in two different ways. Firstly, there is a "vertical" shift: at a given time t the baseline hazard is multiplied by $\mathbf{X}^T\boldsymbol{\delta}$. Secondly, there is a "horizontal" shift where the time t in $\lambda(t)$ is multiplied by the same constant $\mathbf{X}^T\boldsymbol{\delta}$.

Both AFT models (3) and (4) constrain the estimated predictor effects to be constant-over-time and linear. Although, already in 1984, Cox and Oakes [7] outline the general approach for incorporating TD predictor effects in the AFT setting, practical implementations and real-world applications emerged only recently. Crowther, Royston, and Clements [11] introduced a flexible AFT framework, which allows estimating TD acceleration factors. However, they do not discuss the estimation of NL effects of continuous predictors on the logarithm of the event time [11]. To the best of our knowledge, the first extension of the AFT model that incorporates both TD and NL effects was proposed by Pang *et al.* [12]. These authors developed a flexible hazard-based AFT model that extends model (4) to include joint spline-based full maximum likelihood estimation of (i) the baseline hazard, (ii) TD covariate effects on the hazard, and (iii) nonlinear (NL) relationships for continuous predictors. Their flexible AFT model is written as [12]:

$$\lambda(t|\mathbf{X}) = \exp\left(\mathbf{g}(\mathbf{X})^T \delta(t)\right) \lambda_0 \left(\exp\left(\mathbf{g}(\mathbf{X})^T \delta(t)\right) \cdot t\right) \tag{5}$$

where $\delta(t)$ models the change over time in the log acceleration factor, and $\mathbf{g}(\mathbf{X})$ represents the NL effects of $\mathbf{X}$ that estimate its associations with the log event time. To avoid aforementioned identifiability problems, Pang *et al.* [12] adapted the ACE algorithm outlined in Sect. 2.1 above. Statistical significance of the NL and TD predictor effects is assessed using model-based LRTs.

2.3   Additive Hazards Model and Its Flexible Extensions

Another alternative to the proportional hazards (PH) formulation (1) is the additive hazards (AH) model [20, 21]. In contrast to the PH model (1), where covariates act multiplicatively on the baseline hazard, the AH model assumes that changing the predictor value is associated with adding or subtracting a constant to/from the baseline hazard function. Formally, the AH model is written as:

$$\lambda(t|\mathbf{X}) = \lambda_0(t) + \mathbf{X}^T \boldsymbol{\alpha} \tag{6}$$

where $\lambda_0(\cdot)$ is the baseline hazard, defined as in Eqs. (1) and (4), and $\boldsymbol{\alpha} = (\alpha_1, \ldots, \alpha_p)$ are the regression coefficients. Here, each α_j represents the difference in the hazard associated with a one-unit increase in the jth covariate, holding other covariates fixed. Various estimation procedures were proposed for AH models [6, 21, 22]. The interpretation of coefficients in AH models may be considered more intuitive in settings where absolute differences in hazard rates are of direct interest. However, the estimation has to ensure that the resulting hazards, associated with all covariate vectors present in a given analysis, are always strictly positive.

In the classic AH model (6), the estimated hazard differences are assumed to be constant-over-time and linear for continuous predictors. Although various forms of AH models have been proposed and used [6, 8], the original publications by Aalen already included an extension of the AH model that incorporated non-parametric estimation of time-dependent effects of predictors [5, 6]. Specifically, the Aalen's AH model is written as:

$$\lambda(t|\mathbf{X}) = \lambda_0(t) + \mathbf{X}^T \boldsymbol{\alpha}(t) \tag{7}$$

where each $\alpha_j(t)$ is allowed to vary flexibly over time. Notice that in Aalen's AH model (7), the estimation and interpretation of TD effects focus on the cumulative functions:

$$A_j(t) = \int_0^t \alpha_j(s) \mathrm{d}s. \tag{8}$$

This allows for easy estimation of $A(t)$ through least squares [5, 6], although MLE is also possible [22]. At any particular time t, one can interpret the estimate of the cumulative function $\widehat{A}_j(t)$ in (8) as the accumulated effect of a one-unit increase in X_j on the hazard up to time t. The corresponding estimates $\widehat{\alpha}_j(t)$ of the TD effect of X_j on the current hazard at time t can be obtained by taking the derivative of $\widehat{A}_j(t)$ with respect to t. TD effects in Aalen's model (7) can be tested via two alternative null hypotheses, either $H_{01} : \alpha_j(t) = 0$ or $H_{02} : \alpha_j(t) = c$, for a given constant c (see [23] for details).

Aalen's non-parametric AH model (7) has been further extended by McKeague & Sasieni [8] to allow for some predictors to have TD effects and others constant-in-time effects. Their semi-parametric AH model is written as [8]:

$$\lambda(t|\mathbf{X}) = \lambda_0(t) + \mathbf{X}^T \boldsymbol{\alpha}(t) + \mathbf{Z}^T \boldsymbol{\eta} \tag{9}$$

where the $\boldsymbol{\eta}$ components represent fixed-in-time coefficients for predictors $\mathbf{Z}$.

Neither Aalen [5, 6] nor McKeague and Sasieni [8] discuss how the respective AH models can be extended to include the estimation of NL effects of continuous predictors on the hazard. Indeed, to the best of our knowledge, there is no publicly available software that allows such modeling. To address this gap, below we propose a pragmatic approach for flexible modeling of additive NL effects of continuous predictors on the hazard in the AH framework, and indicate how statistical significance of departures from the linear effects can be tested. Our approach involves two steps for each predictor. The first step focuses on the estimation of the NL effect of a continuous predictor X_j. To this end, in the multivariable AH model that adjusts for other variables as constant-in-time covariates, we include two separate terms related to X_j. The first term represents the untransformed X_j and models its linear association with the hazard. The second term represents the departure from linearity, modeled using unpenalized cubic B-splines, with 1 interior knot at the median of the sample distribution of X_j. To avoid identifiability problems, one of the spline coefficients has to be constrained to 0 [13], this implies a 4-degree-of-freedom (df) function. Next, the spline coefficients, estimated at the first step, are used to calculate, for each study participant i, a new variable representing the spline-transformed value of the predictor, $BS[X_{i,j}]$. Then, in the second step, to test the statistical significance of the NL effect of X_j, we refit the multivariable model by including both (i) the untransformed value of X_j and (ii) the resulting spline-transformed value $BS[X_j]$. Finally, to test whether X_j has a statistically significant NL effect, when adjusting for its linear effect, we simply test whether the coefficient for $BS[X_j]$ is significantly different from 0.

2.4 Software

The classic PH model was estimated with the coxph function in the survival R package [24]. The latest version of the R scripts to estimate the flexible extension of the PH model [14] is available at https://github.com/mebeauchamp/CoxFlex. R scripts for implementing the AFT model with splined-based estimation of the baseline hazard [18] can be found at https://github.com/MenglanPang/Spline-based-AFT-Model. R scripts for the flexible extension of the AFT model including TD/NL effects [12] are available at https://github.com/MenglanPang/Flexible-AFT-Model. Aalen's AH model (7) and

McKeague and Sasieni's model (9) can be fit using the `aalen` function of the timereg R package. The new extension of the AH model that allows B-spline modeling of NL effects (Sect. 2.3) can be implemented using our R code shown in Appendix.

3   Case Study of Prognostic Factors for Mortality in Lung Cancer

3.1   Data Source

In this section, to provide head-to-head comparisons between PH, AH and AFT models, and their flexible extensions, we present a case study of all-cause mortality in non-small cell lung cancer (NSCLC). Lung cancer is one of the most commonly diagnosed cancers globally, and remains the leading cause of cancer-related deaths, with about 1.8 million fatalities worldwide [25]. NSCLC represents 85% of all lung cancer cases, making it the most prevalent subtype [26]. Unfortunately, half of NSCLC cases are diagnosed at the most advanced stage 4, which is associated with a short median survival [27]. However, recent advancements in molecular testing, targeted therapies, and immunotherapy have significantly improved survival in NSCLC [28].

To unravel complex associations of different clinical and demographic variables with mortality in NSCLC, we rely on clinical data collected for a cohort of patients, newly diagnosed with NSCLC, who were treated at the Jewish General Hospital Pulmonary Oncology Clinic in Montreal, QC, Canada, from 9 April 2002 to 18 September 2008 [29]. Their follow-up was continued until 15 March 2009. A total of 269 patients had complete data on all relevant variables and were included in our analyses.

Specifically, we focus on the values, measured at cancer diagnosis, of several plasma biomarkers, which our team has previously demonstrated to improve prognostication of NSCLC outcomes [30]. Albumin, a marker of nutritional status, plays a role in DNA replication and cell proliferation, with low levels linked to poor responses to anticancer therapies [31]. C-reactive protein (CRP) plays a crucial role in the acute phase response, and its production is increased in response to inflammation under the influence of pro-inflammatory cytokines, involved in cancer development [32]. High pre-treatment levels of lactate dehydrogenase (LDH) are associated with a poor prognosis since cancer cells shift from oxidative phosphorylation to aerobic-anaerobic glycolysis, converting pyruvate to lactate [33]. Because high neutrophil-to-lymphocyte ratio is a robust marker of poor overall survival in various tumors, including NSCLC [34], we evaluated the effects of both its components: the absolute neutrophil count (ANC) and the lymphocyte levels. Finally, we assess the impact of cancer stage (high vs. lower), chemotherapy treatment, current smoking, and patient's sex and age.

3.2 Methods of Analysis

Multivariable Modeling of Mortality in NSCLC. All analyses used time-to-event methods for right-censored survival outcomes. Time 0 was defined as the date of NSCLC diagnosis. The event of interest was death of any cause. Study participants who did not have the event until the administrative end of the study on 15 March 2009 were censored at that time. There were no loses to follow-up. All analyses relied on multivariable models that always included the same set of predictors, selected *a priori* based on clinical considerations. Predictors included four binary variables: patient's sex, smoking status at diagnosis (yes vs. no), chemotherapy type (double-agent vs. single-agent), and cancer stage at diagnosis (IIIB + pleural effusion/IV vs. IIIA/IIIB). The six continuous variables, all assessed at the time of NSCLC diagnosis, included the patient's age and values of five biomarkers, briefly described in Sect. 3.1 above: CRP, albumin, LDH, ANC, and lymphocyte levels. Because of very positively skewed distributions, both CRP and LDH values were log-transformed (with base 2), consistently with the way they are typically analyzed [29]. To avoid numerically unstable estimates, all continuous variables were converted to z-scores, with mean 0 and standard deviation of 1.

We first estimated the classic versions of the multivariable PH, AH and AFT models, in which all predictor effects are constrained to remain constant across the entire follow-up time, and all continuous predictors were assumed to have linear dose-response relationships. For full maximum likelihood estimation of the AFT model, the baseline hazard was estimated using a quadratic regression B-spline [18]. Next, we estimated flexible extensions of each of the three models. To decide which of the possible TD and/or NL effects of the predictors result in statistically significant improvement of the model's fit to data and, thus, should be included in a given flexible final model, we relied on a forward selection algorithm described in the next subsection. Finally, we compared the results of flexible extensions of the PH, AH and AFT models. These comparisons focused mostly on two issues. First, we assessed if the final conclusions regarding whether particular predictors had TD and/or NL effects varied depending on whether the analyses relied on PH vs. AH vs. AFT models. Secondly, we compared graphically the corresponding TD and/or NL estimates across the three types of regression models.

Selection of TD and/or NL Effects in the Final Flexible Multivariable Models. The selection algorithm described in this subsection were independently employed for each of the flexible extensions of PH, AFT and AH models.

Earlier real-world analyses and simulation studies [12, 14] indicate that statistical significance of TD or NL effects of a given continuous predictor X_j may vary considerably depending on whether the model includes both: (i) respectively, the NL or TD of the same predictor, and/or (ii) TD and NL effects of other predictors. Therefore, it is important to use a systematic algorithm to build the final multivariable model by selecting those TD and/or NL effects of specific variables that improve the prediction of the outcome. For large datasets with a limited number of predictors, backward elimination may be recommended for this purpose [14]. However, backward elimination requires fitting, at the first step, the full flexible model with TD effects of all predictors and NL effects of all continuous predictors. Given that our dataset includes four binary and six continuous predictors, this would require a model with about 74 df (10*5 df for TD effects + 6*4 df for NL effects). With only 211 deaths, this would definitely violate the minimum requirement of 5 events for each df in the estimated model, resulting in very unstable estimates and inaccurate statistical inference.

To avoid these problems, our analyses relied on forward selection of TD and/or NL effects, which does *not* involve fitting the full flexible model. Forward selection involves starting with a simple model with no TD or NL effects, and gradually building up the model by adding TD and/or NL effects of a single predictor at each step. At the first step, in separate models, we tested the TD and/or (for continuous variable) NL effects of a single variable, while adjusting for constant-over-time and linear effects of the nine other predictors. For binary variables, this involved simply testing statistical significance of their TD effects, at $\alpha = 0.05$. In contrast, for each continuous variable, we had to decide what combination of potential TD and/or NL functions represents best its adjusted effect. Yet, previous simulations indicated that the p-value for the NL effect of X_j may change considerably if the TD effect of X_j is adjusted for, and *vice versa* [13, 14]. Thus, for a continuous variable X_j, we first fit three alternative flexible models with combinations of presence/absence of TD and/or NL effects, while adjusting for constant-over-time linear effects of the nine other predictors. Then, if both TD and NL effects of X_j were significant at $\alpha = 0.05$, while adjusted for each other, X_j was assigned the lower of the two corresponding p-values, and both effects were candidates for the final model. If neither effect was significant when adjusted for each other, but one or both yielded a p-value < 0.05 in separate models that included only one of the two effects, the effect with a lower p-value was considered as a candidate for selection. If neither TD nor NL effect of X_j was significant in any of the three flexible models, these effects were *not* considered as candidates for selection at this step of the forward procedure. After all models for all variables were run, we compared the p-values for all effects considered as candidates for selection (according to the above rules) at the first step of forward selection, and included into the final multivariable model the TD and/or NL effects of a single predictor, corresponding to the lowest of the relevant p-values. At the second and subsequent steps of forward selection, the same models were fit for each variable without any TD/NL effects yet included in the final model, adjusting for all TD and NL effects of other predictors, selected at the earlier steps, as well as for the linear constant-in-time effects of other variables. The selection process stopped when all of the remaining TD and NL effects were statistically non-significant (p-value > 0.05).

3.3 Results: Comparison of the Alternative Estimates of Predictor Effects

During a median follow-up of 8.6 months, 211 (78.4%) patients died. Table 1 summarizes the results of multivariable analyses based on classic PH, AFT and AH models, in which all estimated effects were *a priori* constrained to be constant-over-time and linear, corresponding to, respectively, models (1), (4) and (6) in Sect. 2. (An asterisk indicates estimates statistically significant at $\alpha = 0.05$). Results are quite consistent across the three different models. All three models indicate statistically significant: (i) increases in mortality for patients with higher cancer stage and for smokers, and (ii) decreases for those who received double chemotherapy. For sex, whereas point estimates seem to vary from decreased (PH and AH models) to increased (AFT model) hazard for women, in all three models the effects are non-significant, so these apparent discrepancies reflect mostly sampling errors. For continuous variables, all three models reveal statistically significantly higher mortality associated with higher values of $\log_2$ CRP, $\log_2$ LDH and ANC, and with lower lymphocyte counts, and a lack of a significant association with age (Table 1). The only, minor, discrepancy between the three models is that while higher albumin is always associated with lower mortality, this relationship is statistically significant only in the AFT model (Table 1).

Table 1. Estimates and confidence intervals (CIs) for classic constant/linear effects of PH, AFT and AH models.

	PH model, Hazard ratio (CI)	AFT model, Time ratios (CI)	AH model, Hazard differences (CI)
Stage (higher vs. lower)	1.87 (1.31, 2.67)*	1.67 (1.04, 2.34)*	9.56e-04 (3.07e-04, 1.60e-03)*
Smoking (ever vs. never)	2.01 (1.29, 3.12)*	1.75 (1.23, 2.59)*	1.11e-03 (1.11e-04, 1.81e-03)*
Chemotherapy (double-vs. single-agent)	0.62 (0.43, 0.89)*	0.69 (0.57, 0.95)*	−1.21e-03 (−2.21e-03, -2.12e-04)*
Sex (female vs. male)	0.99 (0.74, 1.33)	1.02 (0.90, 1.11)	−1.23e-04 (−8.46e-04, 6.00e-04)
$\log_2$ CRP	1.30 (1.10, 1.53)*	1.23 (1.00, 1.55)*	6.15e-04 (2.27e-04, 1.00e-03)*
Albumin	0.93 (0.78, 1.10)	0.94 (0.89, 0.96)*	−2.35e-04 (−6.25e-04, 1.55e-04)
$\log_2$ LDH	1.64 (1.43, 1.88)*	1.45 (1.16, 1.78)*	1.51e-03 (8.75e-04, 2.15e-03)*
ANC	1.32 (1.13, 1.54)*	1.21 (1.04, 1.46)*	7.52e-04 (1.66e-04, 1.34e-03)*
Lymphocytes	0.84 (0.72, 0.98)*	0.87 (0.76, 0.96)*	−2.76e-04 (−5.46e-04, -5.52e-06)*
Age	1.02 (0.89, 1.18)	1.03 (-0.00, 0.00)	4.37e-05 (−2.50e-04, 3.38e-04)

* Indicates a statistically significant effect with two-tailed tests with $\alpha = 0.05$.

Table 2 compares the results of the flexible extensions of the PH, AFT and AH models, built using the forward selection of TD and/or NL effects described in Sect. 3.3. Specifically, in Table 2 a symbol "NL", "TD" or "TD + NL" indicates if the final flexible multivariable model (identified in the heading of the corresponding column) included, respectively, the non-linear, time-dependent or both effects for the predictor in the corresponding row. (See Figs. 1 and 2 for graphs of the corresponding estimated TD/NL effects.) For predictors for which neither the TD nor the NL effect was selected, Table 2 shows the point estimate of the adjusted parametric effect, corresponding to a constant hazard ratio, time ratio or hazard difference, respectively. Generally, these parametric estimates in Table 2 are very similar to the corresponding estimates in Table 1, indicating that for these variables adjusting for TD and/or NL effects of other predictors has not materially affected the results. For all binary variables, regardless of the model, no TD effects were identified (top 4 variables of Table 2), providing consistent evidence that their effects are constant across the follow-up. In contrast, for each of the six continuous variables, at least in one of the three models the TD and/or NL effect(s) were selected (Table 2). Furthermore, except for the TD effect of albumin that was significant in all three models, for the other predictors different effects were selected in different models. Generally, the results of AFT and AH analyses were similar regarding the TD effects, selected in both models for several predictors, but NL effects were not selected at all in AFT models (Table 2). Interestingly, in the AH framework for four predictors both the TD and NL effects were statistically significant.

Table 2. Estimates from the final flexible extensions of PH, AFT and AH models.

	PH model, Hazard ratio	AFT model, Time ratio	AH model, Hazard difference
Stage (higher vs. lower)	1.85	1.69	1.19e-03
Smoking (ever vs. never)	2.21	1.72	1.38e-03
Chemotherapy (double- vs. single-agent)	0.59	0.69	-1.24e-03
Sex (female vs. male)	1.04	1.06	1.23e-04
$\log_2$ CRP	TD + NL	TD	6.25e-04
Albumin	TD	TD	TD + NL
$\log_2$ LDH	1.62	TD	TD + NL
ANC	1.28	TD	TD + NL
Lymphocytes	0.83	TD	-2.51e-04
Age	1.00	1.04	TD + NL

TD/NL indicates that this effect was selected.

Figure 1 shows the TD estimates that were selected into respective final flexible models as shown in Table 2. For each predictor, the TD curve shows how the strength of its either NL or linear relationship with the hazard varies with increasing follow-up time, depending on whether the NL effect of the same predictor was selected or not in the same model (see Table 2). For flexible AH analyses, to produce the TD plots, representing $\hat{\alpha}_j(t)$ in Eqs. (7) and (9), we first performed a piece-wise linear regression of $\hat{A}_j(t)$ against time using the segmented function of the eponymous R package. Then, in Fig. 1, the slope of these linear segments was plotted to approximate $\hat{\alpha}_j(t)$. Thus, the resulting TD estimates are unsmooth but still illustrate how the strength of the effect varies over follow-up. The decreasing curve in Fig. 1b shows that the linear effect of $\log_2$ CRP in the AFT model becomes gradually weaker as time since NSCLC diagnosis increases but at any time higher CRP is associated with higher mortality, because the values are always > 0. Figure 1a shows that the NL effect of $\log_2$ CRP in the flexible

PH model (shown in Fig. 2a) also decreases over time. Thus, both models indicate that higher CRP at diagnosis is a strong predictor of early mortality, in the next 6 months, but not for later mortality. In contrast, Fig. 1f shows an *increasing* curve for TD effect of $\log_2$ LDH in the flexible AFT model, indicating that higher LDH at diagnosis is an important predictor of later mortality, after the first year of follow-up.

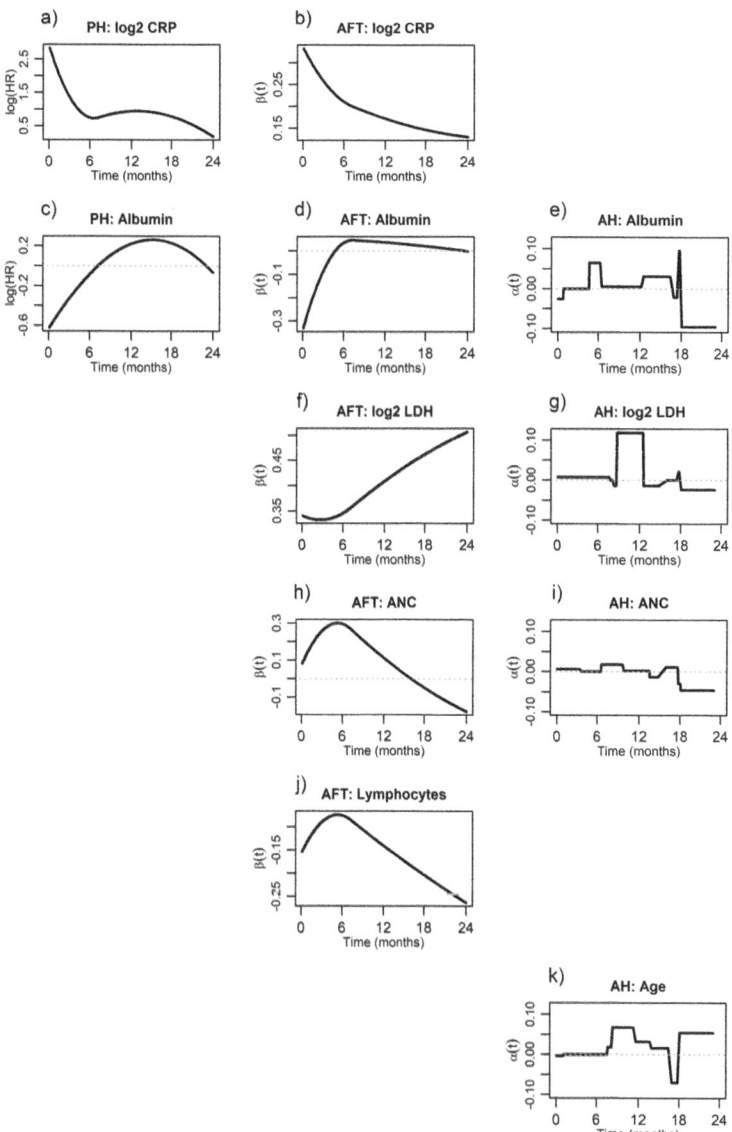

Fig. 1. Time-dependent (TD) estimates in the final PH, AFT, and AH models.

Figure 2 shows the estimated dose-response curves for those predictors whose NL effects were selected in the flexible extensions of the PH or AH models (as indicated by "NL" in the respective cell of Table 2). Figure 2a suggests a complex, possibly non-monotone effect of $\log_2$ CRP, normalized to z-scores, in the flexible extension of the PH model. However, the non-linearity is limited to both tails of the $\log_2$ CRP distribution, where there are only a few observations, whereas the relationship is close to linear for the middle range of values that do not deviate by more than one standard deviation (SD) from the mean. In flexible AH analyses, the NL effect of age indicates that mortality increases strongly as age increases from 3 to 2 SDs below the mean but not beyond (Fig. 2e), and if albumin at diagnosis is at least 2 SDs below the mean (Fig. 2b).

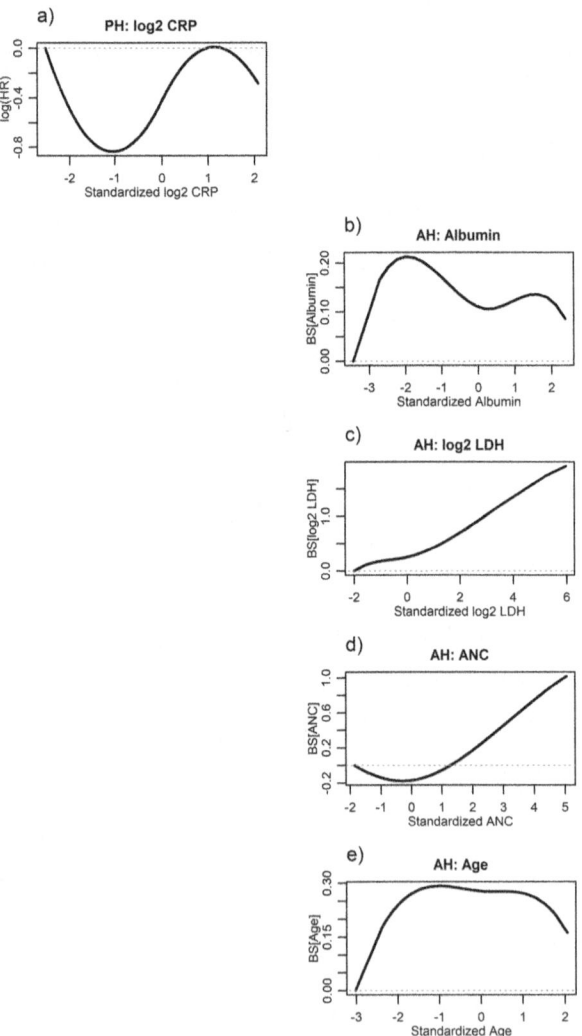

Fig. 2. Non-linear (NL) estimates in the final flexible extensions of PH and AH models

4 Discussion

Recent parallel advances in statistical methodology and in computational resources allow us nowadays to estimate complex, flexible multivariable models for survival analyses. In this paper, we outline the range of alternative models that can be estimated in real-world analyses. Then, using a case study of predictors of mortality in advanced lung cancer, we provide empirical evidence of both (a) the practical importance of accounting for time-dependent and/or non-linear effects, and (b) the possible dependence of the final estimates and conclusions on whether the analyses rely on proportional hazards (PH), accelerated failure time (AFT) or additive hazards (AH) models. However, because (i) PH model is estimated using partial MLE while AFT model requires full MLE, and (ii) publicly available software for AH does not produce the model's deviance, it is difficult to assess which model fits best in a given real-world study. Future research should develop common estimation frameworks for all three models and use extensive simulations to compare their performance across a range of plausible scenarios.

Acknowledgments. Funding by the Canadian Institutes of Health Research (grant PJT-180634).

Disclosure of Interests.   The authors have no competing interests to declare. Michal Abrahamowicz is a Distinguished James McGill Professor at McGill University.

Appendix

As described in Sect. 2.2, this R code demonstrates how to test for non-linear (NL) effects in an additive hazards (AH) model using the `aalen` function from the timereg package. It first fits for a covariate X_j both a linear term and a cubic B-spline $BS[X_j]$ (omitting one basis to avoid collinearity), to create a "deviation" from linearity. The corresponding p-value for that spline-based variable, $BS[X_j]$, indicates whether there is a significant NL effect, which in this example below ($p = 0.00018$) confirms a NL effect of "age". A similar approach can be used for time-dependent effects by omitting the `const` function in the model. Note that this simple code uses a model with a single predictor, whereas the analyses in Sect. 3 used multivariable models.

```
## EXAMPLE CODE TO CONSTRUCT BS[] TO TEST FOR NL EFFECT OF AGE ##

library(survival)
library(splines)
library(timereg)
data(sTRACE)

AH.bs_AGE <- aalen(Surv(time, status==9) ~
                    const(bs(age, degree=3,
                         knots=c(median(age)))[,1:3]) +
                    const(age), data=sTRACE)
sTRACE$NL.AGE <- as.vector(bs(sTRACE$age, degree=3,
                         knots=c(median(sTRACE$age)))[,1:3] %*%
                    coef(AH.bs_AGE)[1:3,1])

set.seed(12305202)
AH.bs_AGE_test <- aalen(Surv(time, status==9) ~ const(NL.AGE) +
                    const(age), data=sTRACE)
AH.bs_AGE_test
```

References

1. Andersen, P.K., et al.: Analysis of time-to-event for observational studies: guidance to the use of intensity models. Stat. Med. **40**(1), 185–211 (2021)
2. Cox, D.R.: Regression models and life tables (with discussion). J. Roy. Stat. Soc. [Ser. B] **34**(2), 187–220 (1972)
3. Hernán, M.A.: The hazards of hazard ratios. Epidemiology **21**(1), 13–15 (2010)
4. Gail, M.H., Wiesand, S., Piantadosi, S.: Biased estimates of treatment effect in randomized experiments with nonlinear regressions and omitted covariates. Biometrika **71**(3), 431–444 (1984)
5. Aalen, O.O.: A linear regression model for the analysis of life times. Stat. Med. **8**(8), 907–925 (1989)
6. Aalen, O.O.: A model for nonparametric regression analysis of counting processes. In: Proceedings, Sixth International Conference: Mathematical Statistics and Probability Theory; Wisła (Poland): Springer New York, NY (1980)
7. Cox, D.R., Oakes, D.: Analysis of Survival Data. Chapman and Hall/CRC, New York (1984)
8. McKeague, I.W., Sasieni, P.D.: A partly parametric additive risk model. Biometrika **81**(3), 501–514 (1994)
9. Etezadi-Amoli, J., Ciampi, A.: Extended hazard regression for censored survival data with covariates: a spline approximation for the baseline hazard function. Biometrics **43**, 181–192 (1987)
10. Abrahamowicz, M., MacKenzie, T., Esdaile, J.M.: Time-dependent hazard ratio: modeling and hypothesis testing with application in lupus nephritis. J. Am. Stat. Assoc. **91**(436), 1432–1439 (1996)
11. Crowther, M.J., Royston, P., Clements, M.: A flexible parametric accelerated failure time model and the extension to time-dependent acceleration factors. Biostatistics (2022)
12. Pang, M., Platt, R.W., Schuster, T., Abrahamowicz, M.: Flexible extension of the accelerated failure time model to account for nonlinear and time-dependent effects of covariates on the hazard. Stat. Methods Med. Res. **30**(11), 2526–2542 (2021)

13. Abrahamowicz, M., MacKenzie, T.: Joint estimation of time-dependent and non-linear effects of continuous covariates on survival. Stat. Med. **26**(2), 392–408 (2007)
14. Wynant, W., Abrahamowicz, M.: Impact of the model-building strategy on inference about nonlinear and time-dependent covariate effects in survival analysis. Stat. Med. **33**(19), 3318–3337 (2014)
15. Wynant, W., Abrahamowicz, M.: Flexible estimation of survival curves conditional on non-linear and time-dependent predictor effects. Stat. Med. **35**(4), 553–565 (2016)
16. Wynant, W., Abrahamowicz, M.: Validation of the alternating conditional estimation algorithm for estimation of flexible extensions of Cox's proportional hazards model with non-linear constraints on the parameters. Biom. J. **58**, 1445–1464 (2016)
17. Wei, L.J.: The accelerated failure time model: a useful alternative to the cox regression model in survival analysis. Stat. Med. **11**(14–15), 1871–1879 (1992)
18. Pang, M., Platt, R.W., Schuster, T., Abrahamowicz, M.: Spline-based accelerated failure time model. Stat. Med. **40**(2), 481–497 (2021)
19. Komárek, A., Lesaffre, E., Hilton, J.F.: Accelerated failure time model for arbitrarily censored data with smoothed error distribution. J. Comput. Graph. Stat. **14**, 726–745 (2005)
20. Cox, D.R.: Analysis of Survival Data. Chapman and Hall/CRC (2018)
21. Lin, D.Y., Ying, Z.: Semiparametric analysis of the additive risk model. Biometrika **81**(1), 61–71 (1994)
22. Lu, C., Goeman, J., Putter, H.: Maximum likelihood estimation in the additive hazards model. Biometrics **79**(3), 1646–1656 (2023)
23. Martinussen, T., Scheike, T.: Dynamic Regression Models for Survival Data. Springer, New York (2006)
24. Therneau, T.M.: A Package for Survival Analysis in R. R package, version 3.8–3 (2024). https://CRAN.R-project.org/package=survival
25. Sung, H., et al.: Global cancer statistics 2020: GLOBOCAN estimates of incidence and mortality worldwide for 36 cancers in 185 countries. CA: Cancer J. Clin. **71**(3), 209–249 (2021)
26. Govindan, R., Page, N., Morgensztern, D., Read, W., Tierney, R., Vlahiotis, A., et al.: Changing epidemiology of small-cell lung cancer in the united states over the last 30 years: analysis of the surveillance, epidemiologic, and end results database. J. Clin. Oncol. **24**(28), 4539–4544 (2006)
27. Wao, H., Mhaskar, R., Kumar, A., Miladinovic, B., Djulbegovic, B.: Survival of patients with non-small cell lung cancer without treatment: a systematic review and meta-analysis. Syst. Rev. **2**(1), 10 (2013)
28. Goring, S., Varol, N., Waser, N., Popoff, E., Lozano-Ortega, G., Lee, A., et al.: Correlations between objective response rate and survival-based endpoints in first-line advanced non-small cell lung cancer: a systematic review and meta-analysis. Lung Cancer **170**, 122–132 (2022)
29. Gagnon, B., Abrahamowicz, M., Xiao, Y., Beauchamp, M.E., MacDonald, N., Kasymjanova, G., et al.: Flexible modeling improves assessment of prognostic value of C-reactive protein in advanced non-small cell lung cancer. Br. J. Cancer **102**(7), 1113–1122 (2010)
30. Gagnon, B., Agulnik, J.S., Gioulbasanis, I., Kasymjanova, G., Morris, D., MacDonald, N.: Montreal prognostic score: estimating survival of patients with non-small cell lung cancer using clinical biomarkers. Br. J. Cancer **109**(8), 2066–2071 (2013)
31. Chandra, R.K.: Nutrition and immunology: from the clinic to cellular biology and back again. Proc. Nutr. Soc. **58**(3), 681–683 (1999)
32. Balkwill, F., Mantovani, A.: Inflammation and cancer: back to Virchow? Lancet **357**(9255), 539–545 (2001)

33. Semenza, G.L.: Oxygen sensing, homeostasis, and disease. N. Engl. J. Med. **365**(6), 537–547 (2011)
34. Guthrie, G.J.K., Charles, K.A., Roxburgh, C.S.D., Horgan, P.G., McMillan, D.C., Clarke, S.J.: The systemic inflammation-based neutrophil–lymphocyte ratio: experience in patients with cancer. Crit. Rev. Oncol. Hematol. **88**(1), 218–230 (2013)

Factors Influencing Trust in Human-Robot Interaction: A Case Study

Letícia Cocato[1], Wolfram Erlhagen[1], Estela Bicho[2], Paulo Vicente[2], and Flora Ferreira[1,2(✉)]

[1] Centre of Mathematics, University of Minho, Guimarães, Portugal
fjferreira@math.uminho.pt
[2] Algoritmi Center, University of Minho, Guimarães, Portugal

Abstract. The goal of this article is to investigate factors that influence trust in Human-Robot Interaction (HRI), focusing on communication variables and social behaviors that might shape the users' perception of robots. The research was conducted within the I-CATER project, which explores social robots in work environments. A questionnaire combining the Godspeed Questionnaire Series (GQS) and the Big Five Inventory-10 (BFI-10) was created to assess trust perceptions in different scenarios featuring different communication settings in error situations, initiatives to start a task, and varying facial expressions. Data analysis with the Friedman and Wilcoxon tests revealed that justifications and apologies improve perceptions of likeability and intelligence, while dynamic facial expressions increase perceptions of anthropomorphism, likeability, and animacy. Although age, occupation in the technology field, and ownership of robotic equipment at home did not significantly correlate with trust dimensions, weak gender correlations indicated that male participants tended to rate trust-related dimensions lower. The study contributes to the understanding of how robot communication and social behaviors influence trust in HRI.

Keywords: Trust in Human-Robot Interaction · Godspeed Questionnaire Series · Nonparametric Analysis · Correlation Analysis

1 Introduction

The evolution of robotics has transformed the relationship between humans and robots, promoting a shift in perception that positions robots as active partners in both daily life and work environments. As human-robot teams increasingly emerge across diverse settings [1,19], the success of these collaborations hinges on a fundamental element: trust. Trust, defined as the acceptance of vulnerability associated with relying on others [15,19,20], is a dynamic construct that can fluctuate over time, particularly in response to trust violations, such as errors made by robots [7,8].

Researchers have explored numerous strategies to mitigate the negative impacts of these violations, including trust repair strategies such as apologies,

O. Gervasi et al. (Eds.): ICCSA 2025 Workshops, LNCS 15887, pp. 411–424, 2026.
https://doi.org/10.1007/978-3-031-97589-9_28

denials, explanations, and promises [11]. At the core of this exploration is the realization that trust is deeply influenced by users' perceptions of robots as trustworthy agents capable of fulfilling their roles effectively [4]. This multidimensional nature of trust encompasses factors such as reliability, robustness, familiarity, comprehensibility, and the ability to explain intentions—all critical for fostering positive human-robot interactions (HRI) [3,12].

The robustness of a robot significantly influences its perceived status, impacting whether it is viewed as a lifelike entity or merely a machine [3]. Research by Fu et al. (2023) [9] highlights the critical role of emotional expressiveness in human-robot collaboration, demonstrating that a robot's happy facial expressions and appropriate gaze direction markedly enhance perceived intelligence and teamwork effectiveness. Their findings revealed that collaboration improved notably when the robot initially displayed a cheerful expression, and participants rated the robot as more intelligent when it showcased positive emotions at the conclusion of the interaction. These results underscore the importance of anthropomorphic design and the ability to convey emotions in fostering trust in robotic systems.

Robots must employ effective verbal and non-verbal communication systems, that improve comprehensibility and influence users' impressions of likeability, intelligence, and animacy. Intelligence, whether cognitive or emotional, is vital in this communication process, as it affects how information is conveyed and interpreted, fundamentally shaping interactions [16]. Furthermore, likeability and warmth-based trust have been shown to positively impact users' intentions to utilize robots in the future [4].

Moreover, there is evidence suggesting that personality significantly influences perceptions and interactions with robots [13]. The Big Five personality model, which encompasses dimensions such as extraversion, agreeableness, conscientiousness, neuroticism, and openness, serves as a valuable framework for understanding individual differences in user interactions with robotic systems [17]. Emerging evidence indicates that user personality traits and attitudes correlate with various social outcomes in human-robot interaction (HRI). For example, Elson et al. (2020) [6] found that individuals with high openness personality traits are more likely to trust humanoid robots. Additionally, extraversion has been shown to affect user impressions of robots, further illustrating the importance of personality in shaping HRI dynamics [13].

Given these dynamics, further studies are needed to explore user perceptions and trust in HRI. This research aims to collect data to explore how sociodemographic characteristics, previous experiences with robots, and personality traits correlate with trust. It will investigate how robot communication following mistakes affects perceived intelligence and likeability, assess the impact of the robot's initiative on its animacy, likeability, and perceived intelligence, and analyze how facial expressions influence factors such as anthropomorphism, animacy, and likeability. Through these insights, we seek to further understand the interplay between user characteristics and robot behaviors to foster trust and effective collaboration in human-robot partnerships.

The remainder of this paper is organized as follows: In the Sect. 2, we present the guiding hypotheses and the experimental framework, including the video scenarios of the HRI and the overall questionnaire. The Data Collection and Analysis section outlines the processes involved in data acquisition and the subsequent analytical techniques used. In the Results section, we present the findings of our study. Finally, the Conclusion section summarizes the key insights, highlights the study's contributions to the field, and suggests directions for future research.

2   Research Hypotheses and Experimental Design

This study employed a structured video-based methodology to evaluate trust-related factors in HRI. These videos were a key component of a comprehensive questionnaire designed to assess factors influencing trust in HRI. The questionnaire incorporated the Godspeed Questionnaire Series (GQS) [2] to measure dimensions related to trust, complemented by the Big Five Inventory-10 (BFI-10) [14] to assess participants' personality traits. The GQS focuses on five sections: Anthropomorphism, Animacy, Likeability, Perceived Intelligence, and Perceived Safety. In this study, we evaluated the first four, excluding Perceived Safety, as participants' assessments were based solely on video observations, which do not provide sufficient context to meaningfully evaluate safety-related perceptions. Regarding the BFI-10, since personality is not the main focus of this study and to minimize the length of the questionnaire for participants, we opted for the 10-item version. Both questionnaires (GQS and BFI-10) utilize a Likert scale to assess participants' responses, allowing for the measurement of perceptions and attitudes in a nuanced manner.

Sawyer, a robot featured in prior studies by Cunha et al. (2020) [5] and Wojtak et al. (2021) [18], was selected for its established role in HRI research (Fig. 1).

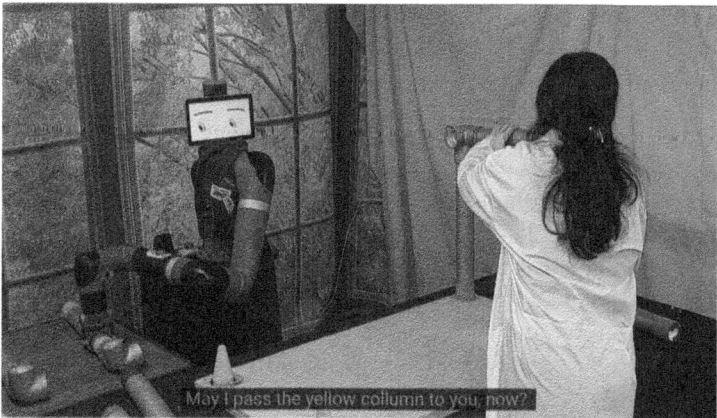

Fig. 1. Image from one of the produced videos for the study.

The objective of the first set of videos was to assess how Sawyer's communication strategies impact trust, specifically examining participants' perceptions in various scenarios. In each scenario, Sawyer's task was to pass a yellow column, but he made an error by dropping it prematurely. Each of the three videos illustrated a different response from Sawyer following the mistake:

Scenario 1.1: The robot apologizes for the committed error without offering an explanation for it.
Scenario 1.2: The robot offers a justification for the error and then apologizes.
Scenario 1.3: The robot justifies the error but does not apologize.

After each video, participants evaluated Sawyer's intelligence and likeability. This set of scenarios aimed to test the following research hypotheses (RH), inspired by Cameron et al. (2021) [4]:

RH1 Apologizing increases participants' perceptions of the robot's likeability.
RH2 Explaining the error improves participants' perceptions of the robot's intelligence.
RH3 Apologizing without providing an explanation leads to lower perceived intelligence compared to scenarios that include an explanation.

The second set of videos explored how Sawyer's initiative influences trust. In each scenario, Sawyer attempts to pass a yellow column, with varying levels of initiative:

Scenario 2.1: The robot begins the task without any prior communication.
Scenario 2.2: Before starting the task, the robot asks for permission to proceed and, after receiving approval, executes the task.
Scenario 2.3: The robot clearly communicates its intentions before executing the task.
Scenario 2.4: The robot only initiates the task after receiving an explicit request.

Participants' perceptions of Sawyer's animacy, likeability, and intelligence were assessed after each video. Hypotheses tested in this set include:

RH4 Lack of communication decreases participants' perceptions of the robot's animacy, likeability, and intelligence.
RH5 Requesting permission before acting increases participants' perceptions of the robot's animacy, likeability, and intelligence.
RH6 Clearly communicating the robot's intentions before executing the task increases participants' perceptions of robot's animacy.
RH7 The robot interacting with the user before taking action increases participants' perceptions of robot's intelligence and likeability.

The three last video scenarios presented Sawyer's facial expressions under different conditions, following each with questions on anthropomorphism, animacy, likeability, and intelligence:

Scenario 3.1: The tablet that simulates the robot's face is turned off, displaying a black screen, with no facial expression.

Scenario 3.2: The robot's face is displayed on the tablet but with no eye movement, keeping the facial expression static.

Scenario 3.3: The robot's face, displayed on the tablet, includes eye movement, making the facial expression more dynamic and realistic.

The objective here is to evaluate how the robot's facial expressions affect trust, considering the formulated hypotheses:

RH8 The lack of facial expression reduces participants' perceptions of the robot's anthropomorphism, animacy, and likeability.

RH9 Even without eye movement, displaying a face on the tablet increases participants' perceptions of the robot's anthropomorphism, animacy, and likeability compared to when no facial expression is visible.

RH10 Eye movement increases participants' perceptions of the robot's anthropomorphism, animacy, and likeability.

3 Data Collection and Analysis

Data was collected via Google Forms between April and June 2024, with the questionnaire offered in both English and Portuguese versions. To recruit participants, institutional emails were sent to faculty members, students, and staff, and the questionnaire was also promoted through social media. Printed QR codes were distributed to enable quick and direct access to the questionnaire via mobile devices.

After the data collection period, the first step in data analysis involved cleaning and preprocessing the dataset. All Portuguese responses were translated into English to ensure consistency in data analysis. The dataset was imported into R software for further analysis. Variables were appropriately formatted for analysis, and participants were asked to indicate the exact time they completed the questionnaire. To ensure thoughtful engagement, only participants who spent at least 15 min completing the questionnaire were included in the analysis—reflecting the minimum time needed to view all videos and respond adequately. Additionally, demographic factors such as age, gender, and occupation were collected.

In the preliminary analysis, descriptive analysis was conducted, and the quality and reliability of the questionnaire were assessed using Cronbach's Alpha test, ensuring that the measurement scales were valid and consistent. Point-biserial correlation coefficient and Kendall's tau coefficient were calculated to assess the strength and direction of relationships. The point-biserial correlation was used to analyze the relationships between binary variables and the scores for each GQS dimension obtained in each scenario. Meanwhile, Kendall's tau was employed to examine the relationships between age and the scores for each GQS dimension in each scenario. Radar charts were then employed to visually compare GQS dimension scores across scenarios, providing an intuitive overview of perception trends. Non-parametric statistical tests were applied for further analyses, specifically Wilcoxon tests utilized to identify specific group differences. A significance threshold of $p < 0.05$ was adopted for all inferential statistical analyses.

4   Results

4.1   Participant Demographics

Among the 114 participants who completed the questionnaire, 26 responses were excluded from the analysis—one due to the participant being under 18 years old and 25 because they finished the questionnaire in less than 15 min. Table 1 presents descriptive statistics detailing the demographic characteristics of the study participants, including age, gender, main occupation, technology field affiliation, and possession of robotic equipment at home.

Table 1. Descriptive statistics presenting the number of cases (n) and the percentage (%) for each category of the analyzed variables.

Variables	n	%
Age Group		
18 to 24 years	23	26.14
25 to 34 years	16	18.18
35 years or older	49	55.68
Gender		
Female	44	50
Male	44	50
Other	0	0
Main Occupation		
Student	29	32.95
Employed (full-time or part-time)	45	51.14
Other	14	15.91
Technology Field		
Yes	37	42.05
No	51	57.95
Robotic Equipment at Home		
Yes	33	37.5
No	55	62.5

The sample is balanced by gender, with 50% identifying as female and 50% as male. The age distribution shows that 55% are 35 years or older, 18% are between 25 and 34 years old, and 26% are 18 to 24 years old. In terms of occupation, participants are predominantly employed, whether full- or part-time (51%), or are students (33%), while 16% indicated other occupations. Regarding affiliation with the technology field, 42% are part of this sector. Lastly, approximately 63% of the participants do not have robotic equipment at home.

4.2   Reliability of Questionnaires

The value obtained for α for the GodSpeed Questionnaire was 0.98, indicating an excellent internal consistency of the data. In contrast, the BFI questionnaire resulted in a low Cronbach's alpha of 0.192, suggesting that individuals in the sample may have diverse or differing responses. This variation could arise from different interpretations of the questionnaire items or inherent differences in personality traits. This diversity can lead to inconsistencies in the data, making it challenging to reliably assess the targeted associations. Consequently, we have excluded the results of the BFI questionnaire from further analysis.

4.3   Correlation Analysis

Age, being in the technology field and possession of robotic equipment at home did not show significant correlations with GQS (Table 2). However, some positively weak but statistically significant correlations ($p < 0.05$) were identified for gender, indicating that male individuals tended to rate intelligence, likeability, and animacy lower in some scenarios.

4.4   Influence of Error Responses on Perceptions

In the first scenario, which examines the robot's response to errors, Scenario 1.2—where the robot provides a justification for its error followed by an apology—achieved the highest scores in both perceived intelligence and likeability. This contrasts with Scenario 1.1, where the robot offers only an apology and is rated higher for likeability, and Scenario 1.3, in which the robot solely justifies its error and is perceived as demonstrating greater intelligence. Median values are also presented in Table 3, along with the results of the Wilcoxon test, which indicate significant differences between the scenarios. These findings are illustrated in Fig. 2, which compares perceived intelligence and likeability across the different scenarios based on aggregated Likert scale scores.

4.5   Influence of Verbal Interaction on Perceptions

In the second set of scenarios, those that involved verbal interaction consistently achieved the highest scores. Notably, Scenarios 2.2 and 2.4, which both featured human-robot communication, demonstrated elevated scores across animacy, perceived intelligence, and likeability. Scenario 2.3, where the robot communicates its intentions prior to taking action, maintained a similar pattern of high scores, ranking particularly high in animacy, followed by perceived intelligence and likeability. Conversely, Scenario 2.1—which did not involve prior communication—recorded the lowest scores, emphasizing the critical role of communication in shaping perceptions of animacy, intelligence, and likeability. These differences are supported by the results of the Wilcoxon rank sum tests presented in Table 4. The p-values indicate statistically significant differences ($p < 0.05$) in all assessed dimensions (animacy, intelligence, and likeability) when comparing Scenario 2.1

Table 2. Correlation coefficients: Kendalls' tau for Age and Point-Biserial correlation coefficients for Gender, Technology field, and Robotic equipment, relating to Anthropomorphism, Animacy, and Likeability in different scenarios (SC).

	Age	Gender	Technology field	Robotic equipment at home
SC 1.1 - Likeability	−0.01	0.10	−.007	0.01
SC 1.1 - Intelligence	−0.11	0.11	−0.06	.008
SC 1.2 - Likeability	−0.04	**0.22**	−0.05	0.11
SC 1.2 - Intelligence	0.00	**0.25**	−0.11	0.03
SC 1.3 - Likeability	0.13	0.04	0.02	0.13
SC 1.3 - Intelligence	0.00	**0.20**	−0.08	0.02
SC 2.1 - Animacy	.007	0.17	−0.02	−0.12
SC 2.1 - Intelligence	−0.10	0.16	−0.03	0.15
SC 2.1 - Likeability	−0.10	0.02	−0.07	0.02
SC 2.2 - Animacy	0.02	**0.26**	−0.04	−0.16
SC 2.2 - Intelligence	−.001	0.17	−0.04	0.01
SC 2.2 - Likeability	−0.03	0.16	−0.02	0.01
SC 2.3 - Animacy	−0.03	0.17	0.06	−0.13
SC 2.3 - Intelligence	−0.01	**0.22**	−0.07	−0.05
SC 2.3 - Likeability	−0.04	0.12	−0.11	−0.05
SC 2.4 - Animacy	0.04	0.07	0.02	−0.02
SC 2.4 - Intelligence	0.01	0.06	−0.06	0.01
SC 2.4 - Likeability	−.002	−.005	0.02	0.10
SC 3.1 - Anthropomorphism	−0.07	0.05	0.10	−0.06
SC 3.1 - Animacy	−0.16	0.05	0.16	−0.12
SC 3.1 - Likeability	−0.02	−0.17	−0.04	0.07
SC 3.2 - Anthropomorphism	−0.07	0.09	0.07	−0.05
SC 3.2 - Animacy	−0.16	0.12	0.13	−0.07
SC 3.2 - Likeability	−0.14	0.08	−0.04	0.04
SC 3.3 - Anthropomorphism	−0.13	0.07	0.12	−0.10
SC 3.3 - Animacy	−0.18	0.13	0.18	−0.16
SC 3.3 - Likeability	−0.16	0.12	0.06	−0.06

Significant p-values are indicated in bold.

Table 3. Median scores and Wilcoxon test results for GQS dimensions across scenarios (SC) 1.

GQS dimension	Median			SC 1.1 vs 1.2	SC 1.2 vs 1.3	SC 1.1 vs 1.3
	SC 1.1	SC 1.2	SC 1.3			
Likeability	18.0	20.0	15.0	p<.001, W=277[a]	p<.001, W=116.5[b]	p<.001, W=640[c]
Intelligence	16.0	20.0	17.0	p<.001, W=213.5[a]	p<.001, W=213.5[b]	p=.022, W=1016[d]

[a] H1: SC 1.1 < SC 1.2, [b] H1: SC 1.3 < SC 1.2, [c] H1: SC 1.3 < SC 1.1, [d] H1: SC 1.1 < SC 1.3.

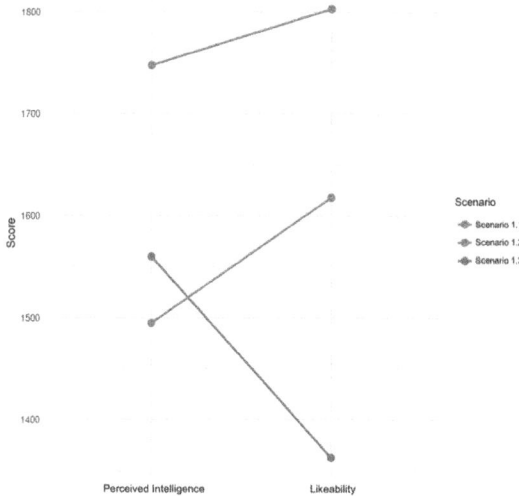

Fig. 2. Comparison of Perceived Intelligence and Likeability characteristics in Scenario 1. The graph is based on the sum of the Likert scale scores for each component of the scenario.

against other scenarios. Specifically, Scenarios 2.2 and 2.3 displayed significantly higher scores compared to Scenario 2.1, confirming that verbal interaction positively influences a robot's perceived characteristics. These results are further depicted in Fig. 3, which illustrates a comparison of these characteristics across the different scenarios based on the aggregate Likert scale scores.

4.6   Influence of Facial Expressions on Perceptions

In analyzing the third scenario, the condition where the tablet was off (Scenario 3.1) recorded the lowest scores across anthropomorphism, animacy, and likeabil-

Table 4. Median scores and Wilcoxon test results for GQS dimensions across scenarios (SC) 2.

GQS dimension	Median				SC 2.1 vs 2.2	SC 2.1 vs 2.3	SC 2.1 vs 2.4	SC 2.2 vs 2.3	SC 2.2 vs 2.4	SC 2.3 vs 2.4
	SC 2.1	SC 2.2	SC 2.3	SC 2.4						
Animacy	14	21	20	21	p<.001, W=31[a]	p<.001, W=159[b]	p<.001, W=197[c]	p=.020, W=892[d]	p<.001, W=1367[e]	p=.033 W=1077.5[f]
Intelligence	16	20	19	20.5	p<.001, W=120[a]	p<.001, W=400[b]	p<.001, W=381[c]	p<.001, W=452.5[d]	p<.001, W=683[b]	p<.001 W=613[f]
Likeability	15	20	18	20	p<.001, W=73.5[a]	p<.001, W=288[b]	p<.001, W=110.5[c]	p<.001, W=392[d]	p=.115, W=700.5[e]	p<.001 W=321.5[f]

[a] H1: SC 2.1 < SC 2.2, [b] H1: SC 2.1 < SC 2.3, [c] H1: SC 2.1 < SC 2.4,
[d] H1: SC 2.3 < SC 2.2, [e] H1: SC 2.2 < SC 2.4, [f] H1: SC 2.3 < SC 2.4.

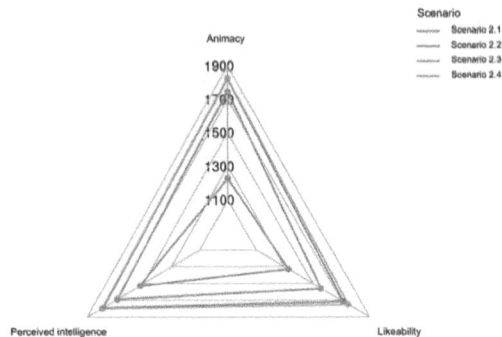

Fig. 3. Comparison of Animacy, Perceived Intelligence, and Likeability characteristics in Scenario 2. The graph is based on the sum of the Likert scale scores for each component of the scenario.

Table 5. Median scores and Wilcoxon test results for GQS dimensions across scenarios (SC) 3.

GQS dimension	Median			SC 3.1 vs 3.2	SC 3.1 vs 3.3	SC 3.1 vs 3.3
	SC 3.1	SC 3.2	SC 3.3			
Anthropomorphism	8	11	15	$p < .001$, $W = 227.5^a$	$p < .001$, $W = 46.5^b$	$p < .001$, $W = 158.5^c$
Animacy	9	11	16	$p < .001$, $W = 388^a$	$p < .001$, $W = 62^b$	$p < .001$, $W = 66.5^c$
Likeability	13	15	18.5	$p < .001$, $W = 199.5^a$	$p < .001$, $W = 68^b$	$p < .001$, $W = 53^c$

[a] H1: SC 3.1 < SC 3.2, [b] H1: SC 3.1 < SC 3.3,
[c] H1: SC 3.2 < SC 3.3

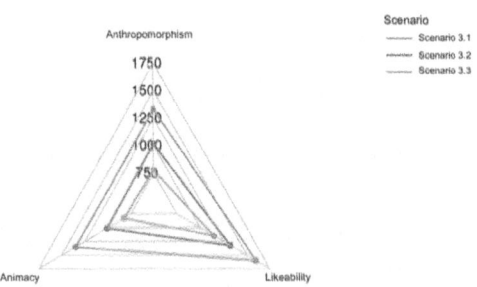

Fig. 4. Comparison of Anthropomorphism, Animacy, and Likeability characteristics in Scenario 3. The graph is based on the sum of the Likert scale scores for each component of the scenario.

ity. In contrast, Scenario 3.3, which incorporated dynamic facial expressions, excelled in all these dimensions, with likeability being particularly prominent.

The results of the Wilcoxon rank sum tests indicate statistically significant differences ($p < 0.001$) in each of the measured characteristics when comparing Scenario 3.1 to Scenarios 3.2 and 3.3, highlighting its notably reduced perceptions across anthropomorphism, animacy, and likeability (Table 5).

Scenario 3.2, featuring static facial expressions, achieved similar scores for anthropomorphism and animacy, yet still fell short compared to Scenario 3.3, which demonstrated significant advantages in these dimensions as well ($p < 0.001$). These findings underscore the importance of integrating interpersonal dynamics, such as facial expressiveness, alongside functional aspects in designing socially interactive technologies.

The findings are visually represented in Fig. 4, which provides a comparison of anthropomorphism, animacy, and likeability characteristics across the different scenarios, utilizing the sum of the Likert scale scores.

5 Conclusions

This study examined the factors influencing trust in human-robot interactions (HRI), focusing on the robot as a social actor expected to meet social norms and behave appropriately within its environment. Trust was defined as the ability to perform tasks effectively, with key dimensions including familiarity, comprehensibility, and robustness, underscoring the importance of communication and perceived intelligence.

The descriptive analysis revealed a well-balanced participant demographic in terms of gender, age, and occupation. While age, being in the technology field, and ownership of robotic equipment at home did not show significant correlations with trust dimensions, weak correlations with gender emerged, with males tending to rate some trust-related dimensions slightly lower. While suggestive, these findings do not indicate a strong or consistent influence of gender on trust. These results are consistent with previous research indicating that females reported higher levels of trust and perceived trustworthiness in an autonomous security robot compared to males [10]. However, the weak nature of the correlation indicates that other factors may also significantly shape trust perceptions. Thus, while gender may contribute to a nuanced understanding of trust, these findings should be interpreted with caution, and further research is essential to explore the complexity of these relationships more comprehensively.

1. **Error responses:** The scenario in which the robot explained its error and subsequently apologized received the highest ratings for likeability and perceived intelligence. This supports **RH1**, demonstrating that apologies improve the perceived likeability of the robot. Providing a justification for an error followed by an apology further improves perceived likeability, while a simple apology is rated higher than only justifying the error. However, justification improves perceptions of intelligence, confirming **RH2**. The lack of explanations correlates with lower perceived intelligence assessments, aligning with **RH3**.

2. **Verbal interactions:** The highest ratings for animacy, likeability, and perceived intelligence occurred when the robot sought permission before proceeding with tasks and executed tasks only upon user request. This scenario validates **RH4**, indicating that lack of communication can diminish user trust in the robot. Actively engaging with users prior to action, as noted in this scenario, supports **RH5** and suggests that the robot is viewed as having greater animacy, likeability, and intelligent when it interacts with users beforehand. Moreover, establishing communication improves the perceived intelligence and likeability, supporting **RH7**.

3. **Facial expressions:** The use of dynamic facial expressions on the robot resulted in higher ratings for anthropomorphism, animacy, and likeability. This outcome validates **RH8**, as the absence of facial expressions reduces perceptions of anthropomorphism, animacy, and likeability. It was also observed that displaying a face on the tablet, even without eye movement, improves perceptions of anthropomorphism, corresponding with **RH9**. Specifically, eye movement positively influences the perceptions of anthropomorphism, animacy and likeability, thus confirming **RH10**.

This study contributes to the understanding of trust in human-robot interactions; however, it has limitations that must be acknowledged. While the sample size was balanced, it may not fully represent diverse demographics, which could limit the generalizability of the findings. Furthermore, the scenarios tested were limited in scope, and reliance on self-reported measures may introduce bias in trust assessments. Future research should build on this study by utilizing larger and more diverse samples to enhance the validity of the findings. Given the low reliability (Cronbach's alpha value of 0.192) observed with the Big Five Inventory (BFI) questionnaire, which restricted our ability to assess personality traits, future studies should consider alternative measurement tools to more accurately capture this dimension. Additionally, exploring a wider range of interactive contexts and incorporating longitudinal designs could provide deeper insights into how trust develops over time in human-robot interactions.

Acknowledgment. This work has been supported by FCT within the Project I-CATER: Intelligent robotic Coworker Assistant for industrial Tasks with an Ergonomics Rationale, reference PTDC/EEI-ROB/3488/2021, and the project UID/00013: Centre of Mathematics of the University of Minho (CMAT/UM).

References

1. Barfield, J.K.: Self-disclosure of personal information, robot appearance, and robot trustworthiness. In: 2021 30th IEEE International Conference on Robot & Human Interactive Communication (RO-MAN), pp. 67–72. IEEE (2021)
2. Bartneck, C., et al.: Godspeed questionnaire series: translations and usage. In: International Handbook of Behavioral Health Assessment (2023)

3. Bishop, L., van Maris, A., Dogramadzi, S., Zook, N.: Social robots: The influence of human and robot characteristics on acceptance. Paladyn, J. Behav. Robot. **10**(1), 346–358 (2019)
4. Cameron, D., et al.: The effect of social-cognitive recovery strategies on likability, capability and trust in social robots. Comput. Hum. Behav. **114**, 106561 (2021)
5. Cunha, A., et al.: Towards collaborative robots as intelligent co-workers in human-robot joint tasks: what to do and who does it? In: ISR 2020; 52th International Symposium on Robotics, pp. 1–8. VDE (2020)
6. Elson, J.S., Derrick, D.C., Ligon, G.: Trusting a humanoid robot: exploring personality and trusting effects in a human-robot partnership. In: HICSS, pp. 1–10 (2020)
7. Esterwood, C., Robert, L.P.: Do you still trust me? Human-robot trust repair strategies. In: 2021 30th IEEE International Conference on Robot & Human Interactive Communication (RO-MAN), pp. 183–188. IEEE (2021)
8. Esterwood, C., Robert, L.P.: Having the right attitude: how attitude impacts trust repair in human—Robot interaction. In: 2022 17th ACM/IEEE International Conference on Human-Robot Interaction (HRI), pp. 332–341. IEEE (2022)
9. Fu, D., Abawi, F., Wermter, S.: The robot in the room: influence of robot facial expressions and gaze on human-human-robot collaboration. In: 2023 32nd IEEE International Conference on Robot and Human Interactive Communication (RO-MAN), pp. 85–91. IEEE (2023)
10. Gallimore, D., Lyons, J.B., Vo, T., Mahoney, S., Wynne, K.T.: Trusting robocop: gender-based effects on trust of an autonomous robot. Front. Psychol. **10**, 482 (2019)
11. Gillespie, N., Lockey, S., Hornsey, M., Okimoto, T.: Trust repair: a multilevel framework. In: Understanding Trust in Organizations, pp. 143–176. Routledge (2021)
12. Jian, J.Y., Bisantz, A.M., Drury, C.G.: Foundations for an empirically determined scale of trust in automated systems. Int. J. Cogn. Ergon. **4**(1), 53–71 (2000)
13. Kabacińska, K., Dosso, J.A., Vu, K., Prescott, T.J., Robillard, J.M.: Influence of user personality traits and attitudes on interactions with social robots: systematic review. Collabra: Psychol. **11**(1) (2025)
14. Rammstedt, B., John, O.P.: Measuring personality in one minute or less: a 10-item short version of the big five inventory in English and German. J. Res. Pers. **41**(1), 203–212 (2007)
15. Rossi, A., Dautenhahn, K., Koay, K.L., Walters, M.L.: How social robots influence people's trust in critical situations. In: 2020 29th IEEE International Conference on Robot and Human Interactive Communication (RO-MAN), pp. 1020–1025. IEEE (2020)
16. Urakami, J., Sutthithatip, S.: Building a collaborative relationship between human and robot through verbal and non-verbal interaction. In: Companion of the 2021 ACM/IEEE International Conference on Human-Robot Interaction, pp. 257–261 (2021)
17. Vinciarelli, A., Mohammadi, G.: A survey of personality computing. IEEE Trans. Affect. Comput. **5**(3), 273–291 (2014)
18. Wojtak, W., Ferreira, F., Vicente, P., Louro, L., Bicho, E., Erlhagen, W.: A neural integrator model for planning and value-based decision making of a robotics assistant. Neural Comput. Appl. **33**(8), 3737–3756 (2021)

19. Xu, J., Howard, A.: Would you take advice from a robot? Developing a framework for inferring human-robot trust in time-sensitive scenarios. In: 2020 29th IEEE International Conference on Robot and Human Interactive Communication (RO-MAN), pp. 814–820. IEEE (2020)
20. You, S., Robert, L.: Trusting robots in teams: examining the impacts of trusting robots on team performance and satisfaction. In: You, S., Robert, L.P. (eds.) Trusting robots in teams: Examining the impacts of trusting robots on team performance and satisfaction, proceedings of the 52th Hawaii international conference on system sciences, pp. 8–11 (2018)

Author Index

A

Abrahamowicz, Michal 393
Afreixo, Vera 300, 365
Agulnik, Jason 393
Alba, Riccardo 53
Al-Noor, Nadia Hashim 332
Amaral, André Renato Sales 163
Angelelli, Mario 300

B

Beauchamp, Marie-Eve 393
Bicho, Estela 411
Biščević, Helena 237
Bogdanov, Alexander 103

C

Cabral, Jorge 300
Cação, Isabel 195
Cannatella, Daniele 67
Caprio, Enrico 53
Caroni, Chrys 377
Cerreta, Maria 67
Chamberlain, Daniel Edward 53
Chiroma, Haruna 27
Cocato, Letícia 411
Cochis, Francesca 53
Conte, Dajana 133, 208
Cook, Richard J. 393
Cristina Braga, Ana 269, 314
Cunha, Ângelo 347

D

D'Ambrosio, Raffaele 225, 237
De Toni, Andrea 53
Dell'Ovo, Marta 53
Di Donato, Simone 225
Dik, Aleksandr 103
Dik, Gennady 103
Dimas, Isabel Dórdio 287

E

Elhabchi, Imane 16
Elobaid, Rafida M. 332
Erlhagen, Wolfram 411

F

Falcão, M. Irene 195
Falcão, Maria Irene 150
Felgueiras, Miguel 365
Ferreira Guerra, Steve 393
Ferreira, Flora 411

G

Gagnon, Bruno 393
Gatto, Rachele Vanessa 16, 40
Gonçalves, A. Manuela 347
Gorfine, Malka 393
Grieco, Benedetta 67

I

Irene Falcão, Maria 181
Iscaro, Samira 208

K

Khvatov, Valery 103
Kiyamov, Jasur 103
Korkhov, Vladimir 115

L

Lemos, Daniela 314
Leone, Mattia Federico 84
Lhaden, Karma 287

M

Macedo, Francisco 300
Macedo, Pedro 300
Miranda, Fernando 150, 181
Murano, Ivan 84

O. Gervasi et al. (Eds.): ICCSA 2025 Workshops, LNCS 15887, pp. 425–426, 2026.
https://doi.org/10.1007/978-3-031-97589-9

N
Nogueira, Rosete   269, 314
Nolè, Rafaele   40

O
Obaiys, Suzan J.   332
Oliveira, Márcia   269

P
Pagano, Giovanni   133
Pappalardi, Vincenza   40
Paternoster, Beatrice   208
Pierri, Francesca   377
Piliero, Angelica   16
Poli, Giuliano   84

Q
Quinteros, Jean Paul   3

R
R. Malonek, Helmuth   195
Regaiolo, Irene   53
Rocha, Filipa   365
Rocha, Vanusa   365

Ronchi, Silvia   53

S
Sacco, Sabrina   67
Savkov, Egor   103
Scapini, Valeria   3
Scorza, Francesco   16, 40
Serôdio, Rogério   249
Severino, Ricardo   150, 181
Shchegolev, Aleksandr   103
Slepenkov, Gleb   115
Somma, Maria   84

T
Tomaz, Graça   195

V
Vicente, Paulo   411
Vitória, José   249

Z
Zampirolli, Karyne Alves   163
Zapata-Román, Gabriela   3

The manufacturer's authorised representative in the EU is Springer
Nature Customer Service Centre GmbH, Europaplatz 3, 69115 Heidelberg,
Germany. If you have any concerns regarding our products, please
contact ProductSafety@springernature.com

Printed and bound by CPI Group (UK) Ltd, Croydon, CR0 4YY
24/04/2026
02096367-0019